CODIFICATION, MACAULAY AND THE INDIAN PENAL CODE

INTERNATIONAL AND COMPARATIVE CRIMINAL JUSTICE

Series Editors:

Mark Findlay, *Institute of Criminology, University of Sydney, Australia*
Ralph Henham, *Nottingham Law School, Nottingham Trent University, UK*

This series explores the new and rapidly developing field of international and comparative criminal justice and engages with its most important emerging themes and debates. It focuses on three interrelated aspects of scholarship which go to the root of understanding the nature and significance of international criminal justice in the broader context of globalization and global governance. These include: the theoretical and methodological problems posed by the development of international and comparative criminal justice; comparative contextual analysis; the reciprocal relationship between comparative and international criminal justice and contributions which endeavour to build understandings of global justice on foundations of comparative contextual analysis.

Other titles in the series:

Exploring the Boundaries of International Criminal Justice
Edited by Ralph Henham and Mark Findlay
ISBN 978 0 7546 4979 3

The International Criminal Court and National Courts
A Contentious Relationship
Nidal Nabil Jurdi
ISBN 978 1 4094 0916 8

The Limits of Criminal Law
A Comparative Analysis of Approaches to Legal Theorizing
Carl Constantin Lauterwein
ISBN 978 0 7546 7946 2

Domestic Deployment of the Armed Forces
Military Powers, Law and Human Rights
Michael Head and Scott Mann
ISBN 978 0 7546 7346 0

Democracy in the Courts
Lay Participation in European Criminal Justice Systems
Marijke Malsch
ISBN 978 0 7546 7405 4

Codification, Macaulay and the Indian Penal Code

The Legacies and Modern Challenges of Criminal Law Reform

Edited by

WING-CHEONG CHAN
National University of Singapore

BARRY WRIGHT
Carleton University, Canada

STANLEY YEO
National University of Singapore

Routledge
Taylor & Francis Group
LONDON AND NEW YORK

First published 2011 by Ashgate publishing

Published 2016 by Routledge
2 Park Square, Milton Park, Abingdon, Oxfordshire OX14 4RN
711 Third Avenue, New York, NY 10017, USA

First issued in paperback 2016

Routledge is an imprint of the Taylor & Francis Group, an informa business

British Library Cataloguing in Publication Data
Codification, Macaulay and the Indian Penal Code : the
legacies and modern challenges of criminal law reform. --
(International and comparative criminal justice)
1. India. Indian Penal Code--History. 2. Criminal law--
Codification--History. 3. Macaulay, Thomas Babington
Macaulay, Baron, 1800-1859.
I. Series II. Chan, Wing Cheong. III. Wright, Barry, 1957-
IV. Yeo, Stanley Meng Heong.
345-dc22

Library of Congress Cataloging-in-Publication Data
Codification, Macaulay and the Indian Penal Code : the legacies and modern challenges of criminal law reform / by Wing-Cheong Chan, Barry Wright and Stanley Yeo.
p. cm. -- (International and comparative criminal justice)
Includes bibliographical references and index.
ISBN 978-1-4094-2442-0 (hardback) -- ISBN 978-1-4094-2443-7 (ebook)
1. Macaulay, Thomas Babington Macaulay, Baron, 1800-1859. 2. India. Indian Penal Code--History. 3. Criminal law--Codificiation--History. I. Chan, Wing Cheong. II. Wright, Barry, 1957- III. Yeo, Stanley Meng Heong.
K5015.4.C63 2011
345--dc22

2011003505

ISBN 13: 978-1-138-25589-0 (pbk)
ISBN 13: 978-1-4094-2442-0 (hbk)

Contents

Preface

The Indian Penal Code 1860 (IPC), which was largely the work of Thomas Babington Macaulay, was the first codification of criminal law in the British Empire and is the longest serving criminal code in the common law world. It was informed by the ideas of utilitarian reformers, notably Jeremy Bentham, who advocated a wide range of reforms to English criminal law and its administration in the early nineteenth century. Macaulay embraced Bentham's 'science of legislation' and his aspiration for 'universal jurisprudence' after Macaulay developed a close association with James Mill during the passage of the India Charter Act 1833. Although the IPC was followed in the nineteenth century by the draft Jamaica and English codes, and codes implemented in Canada (1892), New Zealand (1893) and Queensland (1899), Macaulay's effort, drafted in 1837, came closest to Bentham's ambitious conception of comprehensive codification – one that was designed to displace the common law entirely and characterised by the principles of lucidity and accessibility of provisions, and consistency of expression and application.

Following its enactment, the IPC was adopted in other British colonies in South Asia. In the twentieth century, and particularly since national independence, the IPC and its offshoots have diverged to a degree by way of local legislative amendments and inconsistent judicial development of doctrines influenced by the decisions in other common law jurisdictions.

To mark the 150th anniversary of this significant achievement in criminal law reform, a three-day symposium was organised by the editors of this book and held from 9 to 11 June 2010 at the National University of Singapore. The relevance of the IPC to Singapore is that it was introduced into that country by the nineteenth century British colonial administrators. The Code remains as that nation's principal criminal law statute.

For the symposium, 16 experts were assigned topics to work on and were instructed to produce papers with the 'Key Issues' below in mind. They were also provided with Barry Wright's essay 'Macaulay's Indian Penal Code: Historical Context and Originating Principles' (Chapter 2 in this volume) and were asked to reflect on it when writing their papers. The experts comprised six academic law staff of the National University of Singapore and ten specially invited international researchers from Australia, Canada, England, India and Malaysia.

KEY ISSUES

The IPC was intended by Macaulay and his fellow Code framers to be regularly revised by legislative amendment whenever gaps or ambiguities were found. Unfortunately, this did not occur, with the result that the courts have largely had to undertake this task, sometimes with unsatisfactory outcomes. This was in part due to the failure of the courts to recognise or follow the drafting philosophy that underpins the IPC. Many courts have instead been influenced by English common law developments or have followed the decisions of other jurisdictions in an inconsistent fashion. Legislative amendments have tended to be *ad hoc* and reactive, responding to local circumstances and pressing policy challenges rather than involving systematic attempts to combine local needs with attention to Macaulay's general codifying principles.

How might the IPC look today if the original Code framers, maintaining their basic principles and philosophical stance, undertook a major revision? In addressing that question, let us imagine that they would examine the 150 years of judicial interpretations of the IPC and would study recent common law and criminal code developments from other comparable jurisdictions such as Australia, Canada and England. No doubt they would be prepared to move away from their original philosophical stance if there were sufficiently strong public policy reasons (evinced, for example, by the wide acceptance of a particular criminal law principle by the current criminal laws of major jurisdictions). But we can suppose that any such departures would likely be minimised and that new provisions would be crafted with the same care and rigour as those drafted originally, and made compatible with the rest of the modernised code.

At the same time we recognise that the philosophical stance and basic principles of the original IPC framers are the product of a particular time, culture and policy context. The originating aspiration of 'universal' and 'scientific' legislation warrants some scholarly scepticism. Nonetheless, the attributes of comprehensiveness, accessibility and consistency remain as progressive aims for law reform in the twenty-first century.

ABOUT THIS BOOK

We wish to emphasise that this is no mere collection of conference papers on related themes. The book comprises a selection of the symposium papers, carefully revised after the symposium, focusing on the challenges of comprehensive law reform. The papers were edited before the symposium and the event was actively used as an opportunity to further integrate the contributions, refine common themes and develop appropriate cross-references. The result is a book that stands as a coherent scholarly examination of the IPC and its legacy, one that promises to hold wide international appeal.

The chapters of this book have been classified into four parts. Part I sketches general themes, issues and the historical context which form the backdrop for the rest of the book. In line with the idea of 'revitalising' the IPC by having a modern and workable set of general principles of criminal responsibility, Part II comprises chapters dealing with principles of culpability (offence elements and extensions of liability), while Part III contains chapters on principles of exculpation (defences). In Part IV the discussion goes beyond the IPC to consider recent efforts at criminal law codification in Australia and England, and reflects on the challenges to such codification and criminal law reform in general.

The content of this book is therefore unique, comprising not only a description of the general principles found in the IPC but also a consideration of modern views and developments on those principles and related doctrinal issues, along with proposals for reforming the IPC in the light of those views and developments, and within the spirit of Macaulay's original draft Code. While the matters examined in this book are directly applicable to South Asian jurisdictions, they are also directly relevant to criminal law reform debates in the wider common law world (for example, Australia, Canada, England and New Zealand). Efforts at codifying criminal law are ongoing, as is the law reform of its general principles.

All told, we believe that this book will serve as a helpful and reliable source of authority for legal academics, judges, legal practitioners and criminal law reformers. Additionally, it promises to have wider scholarly appeal, being of interest to legal theorists, historians and policy specialists. In particular, we trust that this book will reveal the genius of Macaulay as a law reformer and remove altogether the stain on his legacy occasioned by the following unfair criticism from some quarters:

> [H]is code is … wholly worthless … [with] scarcely a definition that will stand the examination of a lawyer or layman for an instant, and scarcely a description or provision through which a coach and horses may not be driven. All hope of Macaulay as a lawyer, and also as a philosopher was over as soon as his code was seen.[1]

We wish to acknowledge the generous financing of the symposium by the Singapore Ministry of Education's Academic Research Fund Tier 1 (WBS No R-241-000-059-112) and Connie Yew, Wendy Wee, Lim Yu Hui and Jonathan Kao who helped to make the symposium a success. We would also like to thank Pam Bertram for her excellent editing of this book.

Wing-Cheong Chan
Barry Wright
Stanley Yeo

1 May 2011

1 Obituary, *Law Times*, 7 January 1860, p. 184.

List of Abbreviations of Law Reports Cited

The country of origin of the report is England unless otherwise stated.

A & E	Adolphus and Ellis' Reports
A Crim R	Australian Criminal Reports (Australia)
AC	Law Reports, Appeal Cases
AIR All	All India Reporter, Allahabad (India)
AIR Bom	All India Reporter, Bombay (India)
AIR Cal	All India Reporter, Calcutta (India)
AIR Lah	All India Reporter, Lahore (India)
AIR MP	All India Reporter, Madhya Pradesh (India)
AIR Nag	All India Reporter, Nagpur (India)
AIR Ori	All India Reporter, Orissa (India)
AIR Pat	All India Reporter, Patna (India)
AIR PC	All India Reporter, Privy Council (India)
AIR Rang	All India Reporter, Rangoon (India)
AIR SC	All India Reporter, Supreme Court (India)
All ER Rep	All England Reports Reprint
All ER	All England Reports
B & C	Barnewall and Cresswell's King's Bench Reports
BHC (CrC)	Bombay High Court Reports (Criminal Cases) (India)
BLR	Bombay Law Reporter (India)
Bom CR	Bombay Criminal Cases (India)
C & P	Carrington and Payne's Nisi Prius Reports
Car & K	Carrington and Kirwan's Nisi Prius Reports
CCC	Canadian Criminal Cases (Canada)
CCC (2d)	Canadian Criminal Cases (Second Series) (Canada)
CCC (3d)	Canadian Criminal Cases (Third Series) (Canada)
Cl & F	Clark and Finnelly's House of Lords Reports
CLR	Commonwealth Law Reports (Australia)
Co Rep	Coke's King's Bench Reports
Cox CC	Cox's Criminal Cases
CR (3rd)	Criminal Reports (Third Series) (Canada)
CR (4th)	Criminal Reports (Fourth Series) (Canada)
CR (6th)	Criminal Reports (Sixth Series) (Canada)
Cr App R	Criminal Appeal Reports
Cri LJ	Criminal Law Journal (India)
Crim LR	Criminal Law Review
D & B	Dearsly and Bell's Crown Cases Reserved
Dears	Dearsly's Crown Cases Reserved
Den	Denison's Crown Cases Reserved

E & B	Ellis and Blackburn's Queen's Bench Reports
East	East's Term Reports, King's Bench
EHRR	European Human Rights Reports
El & El	Ellis and Ellis' Queen's Bench Reports
ER	English Reports
EWCA Crim	England and Wales Court of Appeal (Criminal Division)
EWHC Admin	England and Wales High Court (Administrative Division)
F & F	Foster and Finlason's Nisi Prius Reports
F.2d	Federal Reporter (Second Series) (USA)
Fam	Law Reports, Family Division
FCA	Federal Court of Australia (Australia)
HCA	High Court of Australia (Australia)
ILR All	Indian Law Reports, Allahabad (India)
ILR Bom	Indian Law Reports, Bombay (India)
ILR Cal	Indian Law Reports, Calcutta (India)
ILR Mad	Indian Law Reports, Madras (India)
IR	Irish Reports (Ireland)
JC	Justiciary Cases (Scotland)
JP	Justice of the Peace
KB	Law Reports, King's Bench
L & C	Leigh and Cave's Crown Cases Reserved
Leach	Leach's Cases in Crown Law
Lewin	Lewin's Crown Cases on the Northern Circuit
LR CCR	Law Reports, Crown Cases Reserved
LR HL	Law Reports, House of Lords
LR QB	Law Reports, Queen's Bench
LSCA	Lesotho Court of Appeal (Lesotho)
LTR	Law Times Reports
M & W	Meeson and Welsby's Exchequer Reports
Man R (2d)	Manitoba Reports (Second Series) (Canada)
MHC	Madras High Court Reports (India)
MLJ	Malayan Law Journal (Malaysia and Singapore)
Moore (KB)	Moore's King's Bench Reports
NI	Northern Ireland Law Reports (Northern Ireland)
NLR	New Law Reports (Ceylon)
NSWCCA	New South Wales Court of Criminal Appeal (Australia)
NSWLR	New South Wales Law Reports (Australia)
NSWSC	New South Wales Supreme Court (Australia)
NZLR	New Zealand Law Reports (New Zealand)
OR (3d)	Ontario Reports (Third Series) (Canada)
PLD	All Pakistan Legal Decisions (Pakistan)
Plowden	Plowden's Reports
QB	Law Reports, Queen's Bench
QBD	Law Reports, Queen's Bench Division
QCA	Queensland Court of Appeal (Australia)
QR	Queensland Reports (Australia)
Raj.L.W.	Rajasthan Law Weekly (India)

RTR	Road Traffic Reports
SA	South African Law Reports (South Africa)
SASR	South Australian State Reports (Australia)
SCC	Supreme Court Cases (India)
SCC	Supreme Court of Canada (Canada)
SCR	Supreme Court Reports (Canada)
SE.2d	Southeastern Reporter (Second Series) (USA)
SGCA	Singapore Court of Appeal (Singapore)
SGDC	Singapore District Court (Singapore)
SGHC	Singapore High Court (Singapore)
SGMC	Singapore Magistrate's Court (Singapore)
SLR(R)	Singapore Law Reports (Reissue) (Singapore)
SLT	Scots Law Times (Scotland)
SR (NSW)	New South Wales State Reports (Australia)
St Tri	Howell's State Trials
Tas R	Tasmanian Reports (Australia)
UKHL	United Kingdom House of Lords
UNTS	United Nations Treaty Series (United Nations)
US	United States Supreme Court Reports (USA)
VR	Victorian Reports (Australia)
WASCA	Western Australia Supreme Court (Australia)
WLR	Weekly Law Reports
WWR	Western Weekly Reports (Canada)

List of Contributors

Kumaralingam Amirthalingam, Professor, Faculty of Law, National University of Singapore.

Wing-Cheong Chan, Associate Professor and Amaladass Fellow, Faculty of Law, National University of Singapore.

Cheah Wui Ling, Assistant Professor, Faculty of Law, National University of Singapore.

Chris Clarkson, Professor, School of Law, University of Leicester.

Gerry Ferguson, Distinguished Professor, Faculty of Law, University of Victoria.

Mark Findlay, Professor, Faculty of Law, Singapore Management University; Professor, School of Law, University of Leeds; Professor, School of Law, University of Sydney.

Matthew Goode, Special Counsel, Attorney-General's Department, South Australia; Adjunct Associate Professor of Law, University of Adelaide.

Michael Hor, Professor, Faculty of Law, National University of Singapore.

Ian Leader-Elliot, Emeritus Fellow, School of Law, University of Adelaide; Adjunct Professor, School of Law, University of South Australia.

Neil Morgan, Inspector of Custodial Services, Western Australia; Professor, Faculty of Law, University of Western Australia.

Bob Sullivan, Professor, Faculty of Law, University College London.

Barry Wright, Professor, Departments of Law and History, Carleton University.

Stanley Yeo, Professor, Faculty of Law, National University of Singapore; Adjunct Professor, School of Law, University of Sydney.

PART I
Background and Overview

The opening chapter of this work sets out some of the major themes and issues raised in the chapters that follow. In 'Revitalising Macaulay's Indian Penal Code', Stanley Yeo and Barry Wright make the case for saying that, while the Indian Penal Code (IPC) has served India and several other jurisdictions for 150 years, it has become antiquated in some respects and encumbered with random judicial modification and legislative amendment. These developments run contrary to the originating legislative principles, regarded by Thomas Macaulay, the principal drafter of the Code, as the hallmarks of a good criminal code. These principles remain relevant and sound ones today. A General Part is required to restore precise, comprehensible and accessible criminal provisions and to advance future legislative reform. The chapter concludes by outlining a strategy for implementation and a call for legislatures to fully support this much-needed exercise.

Chapter 2 takes the reader back to the time when the IPC was drafted in order to deepen our understanding of the influences and thinking behind the Code. In 'Macaulay's Indian Penal Code: Historical Context and Originating Principles', Barry Wright examines the significant impact of nineteenth-century English criminal law reform debates, the policy context and the main features of what became the first British jurisdiction criminal code. It represented a revolutionary Benthamite break in the conception, form and presentation of the criminal law, and although most of the substantive doctrines derived from existing English laws, they reflected liberal and utilitarian rationalising sensibilities. The chapter concludes by contending that while the Code was imposed as a means to make the law, and by extension British rule, more effective and legitimate, Macaulay's achievement of comprehensive, lucid and consistent provisions remains a progressive example of legislative reform.

Chapter 1

Revitalising Macaulay's Indian Penal Code[1]

Stanley Yeo and Barry Wright

The year 2010 marked the 150th anniversary of the Indian Penal Code 1860 (IPC), making it the longest serving criminal code in the common law world. Soon after its inception, the IPC received high praise for its clear articulation and thinking concerning criminal responsibility. For example, the English jurist and codifier James Fitzjames Stephen was led to proclaim that:

> The Indian Penal Code is to the English criminal law what a manufactured article ready for use is to the materials out of which it is made. It is to the French Penal Code and, I may add, to the north German Code of 1871, what a finished picture is to a sketch. It is far simpler, and much better expressed, than Livingston's Code for Louisiana; and its practical success has been complete.[2]

Stephen's lavish praise was entirely warranted given the overly complex, confusing and cumbersome state that English criminal law was in at the time. It was also warranted because Thomas Macaulay, the principal framer of the IPC, had done a superb job of drawing on leading ideas from early nineteenth-century English criminal law reform debates, notably Jeremy Bentham's advocacy of codification. He also drew from existing rationalisations of criminal law such as Robert Peel's English consolidations, the 1810 French Penal Code by Jean-Etienne-Marie Portalis and the 1826 draft Code of Louisiana by Edward Livingston.

However, Stephen's observations were made over 125 years ago and even the best codes are bound to lose many of their attributes if they remain unaltered or details are randomly modified over such an extended period of time. To use Stephen's metaphor, as a manufactured article, the IPC has not even been serviced, let alone remodelled, since leaving the codifier's desk. As a result, the IPC struggles to remain the principal repository of the foundational principles of criminal responsibility in India and other jurisdictions like Malaysia, Nigeria, Pakistan, Singapore, Sri Lanka and the Sudan which have adopted it, having had hardly any influence on the development of subsequent penal legislation. A proper recognition of the IPC as the primary penal legislation would require all other penal legislation to make the Code a pivotal source of reference. Additionally, the IPC has left many unintended problems of interpretation for the courts which have had the unenviable task of finding ways, not always successful, of applying the nineteenth-century attitudes and approaches embodied in the Code to social and moral situations in the twentieth and twenty-first centuries.

In this introductory chapter, we propose that the best solution to this unfortunate state of affairs is to enact a General Part which will significantly revitalise the IPC and restore many of its original technical attributes. A realistic strategy for drafting and enacting such a Part is suggested, and we

1 Parts of this chapter have previously appeared in an article by S. Yeo, 'Revitalising the Penal Code with a General Part' (2004) *Singapore Journal of Legal Studies* 1.

2 Cited in G.O. Trevelyan, *The Life and Letters of Lord Macaulay* (London: Longmans, Green & Co., 1923) 303.

make the claim that the collection of essays comprising this book constitutes a strong springboard to launch it.

Such law reform is not only relevant to IPC jurisdictions. The issues and debates raised resonate directly with criminal law reform issues in the wider common law world, as reflected in the contributions of our authors from Australia, Canada and England. While we recognise the formidable challenges in all jurisdictions of making principled codifying reform a legislative priority, especially given the contemporary political and policy climate around the management of crime,[3] farsightedness and nothing less than commitment to the values of the rule of law suggest that it is imperative. We make a specific call upon legislators to commit themselves to a model IPC for the twenty-first century and hope that such a model will also inspire renewed efforts for principled codifying reform in non-IPC jurisdictions. We begin our case for such reform by illustrating how far removed the Code is in its present-day functioning from what its principal creator, Macaulay, envisioned.

A GOOD CODE NO LONGER

According to Macaulay, a good code should have the qualities of precision and comprehensibility, and should reflect legislative rather than judicial law-making, with associated features of comprehensiveness and accessibility. The first three characteristics are encapsulated in the following passage of Macaulay's letter to Lord Auckland, the Governor General of India in Council, which accompanied his draft Penal Code:

> There are two things which a legislator should always have in view while he is framing laws: the one is that they should be as far as possible precise; the other that they should be easily understood … That a law, and especially a penal law, should be drawn in words which convey no meaning to the people who are to obey it, is an evil. On the other hand, a loosely worded law is no law, and to whatever extent a legislature uses vague expressions, to that extent it abdicates its functions, and resigns the power of making law to the Courts of Justice.[4]

We recognise here that the philosophical stance and basic principles of the original IPC are the product of a particular time, culture and policy context. The Benthamite aspirations of 'scientific legislation' and 'universal jurisprudence', a primary influence on Macaulay, also warrant some scholarly scepticism. Although some concepts underlying the IPC are problematic or have become obsolete, Macaulay's general principles of precision, comprehensibility and active legislative law-making have nonetheless stood the test of time and remain as progressive general aims for law reform in the twenty-first century.

Regarding the need for precision, while most of the provisions of Macaulay's Code have this quality, there are some which are ambiguous. The enacted version added complexities and

3 As Chapter 15 in this volume (M. Findlay, 'Principled Criminal Law Reform: Could Macaulay Survive the Age of Governing through Crime?') highlights.

4 T.B. Macaulay, J.M. Macleod, G.W. Anderson and F. Millett, *A Penal Code Prepared by the Indian Law Commissioners* (London: Pelham Richardson, 1838) (reprinted by the Lawbook Exchange, Ltd, 2002) v. See also the statement of the Full Bench of the Ceylon Supreme Court in *Kachcheri Mudaliyar v. Mohomadu* (1920) 21 NLR 369, at 373, that the policy of the Penal Code was that '[t]he criminal law should be defined and should be in such form as to be capable of administration in all parts of the Island by both principal and subsidiary courts and, further, that it should be in such a form that the population of the country should clearly understand their obligations'.

ambiguities. Many more gaps and inconsistencies in the Code provisions have shown up in the course of time since enactment which have, like the ambiguous provisions, required the attention of the courts. Numerous examples will be given in this book.

As for comprehensibility, the IPC may have been understood by the ordinary people of Macaulay's time who were familiar with the words used and could relate well to the many factual illustrations which he used to help explain the law. But ever since its inception, there have been parts of the Code which have necessitated clarification by the courts on account of their incomprehensibility. Furthermore, while much of the Code remains understandable to the present-day citizen, there are many words or concepts which are likely to cause puzzlement.[5]

In relation to the need for a code to be the product of active legislative engagement, the underlying premise is that:

> [S]ince the criminal law is arguably the most direct expression of the relationship between a State and its citizens, it is right as a matter of constitutional principle that the relationship should be clearly stated in a criminal code the terms of which have been deliberated upon by a democratically elected legislature.[6]

While modern codification may be premised on democratic legislative ideals, it must be acknowledged that attributing democratic claims to Macaulay's emphasis on legislative activism is problematic. As Wright notes in the next chapter, the original drafting and enactment of the IPC reflect the processes of an appointed legislative council and a larger context of British imperial politics, policy concerns about promoting effective and legitimate authority, and continuing gulfs between colonisers and the colonised. Concerns about the nature of legislative politics continue in the twentieth and twenty-first centuries. However, if we set these important political questions to one side (and acknowledge their relevance and importance for a broader understanding of the IPC) and proceed with a 'positivist' assumption about duly constituted, democratic legislative authority, hard questions remain regarding the exercise of legislative and judicial powers. The *ad hoc* nature of legislative amendment, instead of systematic legislative review as contemplated by Macaulay, is illustrated in the next section of this chapter and addressed in our discussion of principled codifying reform. Judicial activism is also a primary concern. The fact that so many parts of the IPC have been subjected to judicial interpretation and elaboration runs counter to Macaulay's insistence that the Code should be the creation of 'the legislature, by those who make the law, and who must know more certainly than any judge can know what the law is which they mean to make'.[7]

There are then the final features of a good code in Macaulay's eyes, related to the above qualities, namely that it must be comprehensive and accessible. Macaulay envisaged that all the penal laws which the legislature enacted from time to time would be framed in such a manner as to fit into the Code. It should contain the entirety of the criminal law and its applicability in effect in a jurisdiction, encompassing all punitive sanctions administered by the state following conviction for offences against the person, property, state and public interests, as well as less tangible harms. Macaulay also proposed that each member of the population should be furnished with a copy of

5 For example, 'wantonly' (s. 153); 'maliciously' (s. 219); 'malignantly' (s. 270); 'common intention' (s. 34); 'unsoundness of mind' (s. 84); 'sufficient in the ordinary course of nature' (s. 300); and 'cruel or unusual manner' (exception 4 to s. 300) to name but a few.

6 Law Commission for England and Wales, *Criminal Law: A Criminal Code for England and Wales* (vol. 1) (Law Com. No. 177) (London: HMSO, 1989) para. [2.2].

7 Macaulay, Macleod, Anderson and Millett, above n. 4, at v, referring to the legislative quality of the illustrations appearing in the proposed Code.

the Code in their own native language.[8] Such goals may not be feasible today in the light of the huge amount of penal legislation and related regulatory dimensions, although they may be reached in another way, to be explored later in this chapter. For now, it may be said that the law, even if we were concerned with just that covered by the IPC, is inaccessible to the layperson. Most certainly, a person has more ready access to a copy of the Code than ever before, thanks to the electronic age. But that is not the point here. Rather, it is that the Code is no longer the sole repository of the law which it purports to cover but has to be read together with a very large body of case law. As evidence of this, a quick browse through an Indian criminal law commentary will reveal that it is heavily devoted, no less than its counterparts from common law jurisdictions such as Australia, Canada and England, to the discussion of case law.[9]

To Macaulay's list of qualities of a good code may be added another related quality of contemporary relevance or modernity. Values, ways of thinking about criminal responsibility and policies inevitably change according to time and place, and it is incumbent upon legislative authority to keep abreast with these changes, assisted by specialist law reform commissions, in order to actively update the Code and maintain its effectiveness. It would be an immense surprise if the many pronouncements concerning criminal responsibility in a criminal code enacted for the nineteenth-century British subjects in India accurately reflected the values and views of Indian citizens in the twenty-first century.

In short, the IPC as we know it today fails to satisfy any of the attributes which Macaulay regarded as essential for a good code, and presents the danger of perpetuating the moral judgments, values and policies of a bygone era. The following observation succinctly describes this unfortunate state of affairs:

> [T]he common law Codes [of which the Indian Penal Code was one] ... are in origin nineteenth century codes, albeit much amended. The knowledge and understanding of the principles of substantive law have, through the work of judges and jurists, greatly increased since then. Moreover, while all of these codes are available for assessment by specialist lawyers, they are less readily to hand for the profession as a whole and still less to the general public ...[10]

EXPLAINING THE UNSATISFACTORY STATE OF THE IPC

Little blame can be laid directly on Macaulay for the current dismal state of the IPC. He was the first to acknowledge that his creation was not perfect and that there were bound to be deficiencies in its interpretation and application which would require fixing. In line with his insistence that the Code should be the work of the legislature and not of the courts, Macaulay proposed putting in place a revision mechanism. It was that, whenever an appellate court reversed a lower court decision on a point of law not previously determined or whenever two judges of a higher court disagreed on the interpretation of a provision of the Code, the matter should be automatically referred to the legislature which should decide the point and, if necessary, amend the Code.[11] Regrettably, this

8 *Ibid.*, at viii.

9 See, for example, the 4,900-plus page H.S. Gour, *The Penal Law of India* (11th edn, Allahabad: Law Publishers (India) Pvt. Ltd., 2000); and the 2,900-plus pages in R. Ratanlal and K.T. Dhirajlal, *Ratanlal and Dhirajlal's The Indian Penal Code* (32nd edn, New Delhi: LexisNexis Butterworths Wadhwa Nagpur, 2010).

10 Law Commission for England and Wales, *Codification of the Criminal Law: A Report to the Law Commission* (Law Com. No. 143) (London: HMSO, 1985) para. [13].

11 A. Gledhill, *The Penal Codes of Northern Nigeria and the Sudan* (London: Sweet & Maxwell, 1963) 19.

mechanism was not adopted in India or in any of the other jurisdictions which have adopted the Code, leaving any ambiguities in the Code to be rectified by the legislature as it saw fit, or else to be dealt with by the courts as best they could.

In India itself, the IPC was considerably amended during enactment and the immediate years following. Many changes were retrograde, and the 1883 Ilbert Bill controversy noted in the next chapter highlights the persistence of procedural discrimination that ran counter to Macaulay's aim of equal legal status. The IPC encountered several subsequent and discrete phases of criminal justice policy which have been explored in detail by B.B. Pande.[12] A new phase opened in the wake of the Indian Jails Committee Report, 1919–20, which introduced the rehabilitative ideal in punishment. Another was introduced with independence, 1949–50, resulting from a new federal court structure, more diversity in the interpretation of provisions and the proliferation of new criminal offences outside the IPC. The new Constitution, which entrenched rights and introduced the possibility of judicial review of rights violations, began to have an impact by the 1960s, particularly in relation to due process matters, and this introduced a progressive phase of constitutionalism. This now seems to be increasingly eclipsed by a reversion to repressive control, with a proliferation of special measures to combat terrorism, extremism and sectarianism. All these phases have tended to result in the proliferation of penal laws outside the IPC, and its provisions have remained neglected. The few legislative revisions have been *ad hoc* in nature and most changes are the result of judicial interpretation, drawing unevenly, sometimes inappropriately and certainly contrary to Macaulay's intent, from precedents in other common law jurisdictions. There have been some exceptions to the general pattern of inattention to the IPC. Constitutionalism has led to some notable striking down or judicial modification of elements of some offences, such as the decriminalisation of homosexuality in relation to s. 377.[13] The Penal Code Reform Seminar of the Indian Law Institute resulted in the publication in 1962 of critical essays on legislative and judicial developments, and a revised collection of those essays was published in 2005.[14] While such initiatives have informed IPC amendment bills (1972 and 1978), the bills lapsed on the dissolution of Parliament.

This narrative of neglect and uneven amendment is a familiar one across IPC jurisdictions. Legislatures have rarely taken the initiative to rectify defects in the Code which have come to the attention of the courts and commentators.[15] Sadly, in quite a few of the instances when a legislature has done so, the results have been far from satisfactory, adding further confusion or complexity to the law. A likely explanation is that the drafters of the legislative amendments have paid scant regard to the relationship between their amendment on the one hand and existing provisions in the Code and their philosophical underpinnings on the other. By way of specific example, after the IPC was promulgated, the legislature felt the need to create criminal liability for causing 'the

12 B.B. Pande, 'Context, Method and Contents of the Indian Penal Code Reforms', a paper presented at the symposium *A Model Indian Penal Code Adhering to the Philosophy of Macaulay*, Singapore, 9–11 June 2010.

13 See *Naz Foundation v. Government of NCT* 2010 Cri LJ 94. A number of constitutional challenges in the 1970s and 1980s were directed at provisions such the mandatory death penalty in the IPC, s. 303.

14 Indian Law Institute, *Essays on the Indian Penal Code* (New Delhi: Indian Law Institute, 1962); K.N.C. Pillai and S. Aquil (eds), *Essays on the Indian Penal Code* (New Delhi: Indian Law Institute, 2005).

15 It was in anticipation of just such legislative inertia that Macaulay saw the need for a revision mechanism to be implemented. See also the Law Commission for England and Wales, above n. 6, at paras. [3.43]–[3.51]; and Chapters 13 and 14 of this volume (M. Goode, 'An Evaluation of Judicial Interpretations of the Australian Model Criminal Code' and C. Clarkson, 'Recent Law Reform and Codification of the General Principles of Criminal Law in England and Wales: A Tale of Woe' respectively).

death of any person by doing a rash act not amounting to culpable homicide'.[16] However, the new provision did not define what 'rash' meant, leaving it to the courts to define.[17] In this regard, the legislature may be criticised for effectively handing over its democratically ordained law-making powers to the judiciary. Additionally, if the courts are correct in defining rashness as constituting knowledge that one's act might cause death,[18] how does this differ from the mental state for the offence of culpable homicide of knowledge that one's conduct is likely to cause death?[19] The qualities of precision and comprehensibility of a good code would have been met if the legislature had made the effort to define its newly introduced concept of rashness in the light of very similar ones appearing in the Code.

Another example is the Singaporean legislature's decision in 1935 to replace its Penal Code provisions on intoxication with a new ones loosely based on the English common law at the time.[20] The revision included a provision[21] which spelt out certain conditions enabling an intoxicated accused person to be dealt with in the same way as one who successfully pleaded the defence of unsoundness of mind under s. 84 of the IPC. To achieve the qualities of precision, comprehensibility and accessibility, the obvious course the drafters of the new provision should have taken was to adopt, as far as possible, the terminology of the defence of unsoundness of mind. Instead, they introduced new terms which have plagued the courts and commentators ever since. Is the term 'insane' used in the new provision identical to 'unsoundness of mind' under s. 84? Is there a distinction between 'did not know that such act or omission was wrong or did not know what he was doing' under the new provision and the 'incapable of knowing the nature of the act, or that he is doing what is either wrong or contrary to law' clause under s. 84? Different answers given by the courts have added to the confusion, rendering the law imprecise, incomprehensible and inaccessible to lawyers and laypeople alike – the characteristics of a bad code.

Since the legislature has not been at all forthcoming in initiating ongoing review and revision of the IPC, the task has fallen upon the courts. Judges often refuse to do it, saying that it is the work of the legislature. When judges do it, they often perform poorly and are criticised for doing so. But the fault does not really lie with the judges since, in many instances, they are required to handle cases where 'criminality has taken new forms which are difficult to cope with under old structures and under a philosophy which binds judges to a strict and literal reading of prohibition'.[22]

Furthermore, the judges are left entirely in the dark concerning the correct approach to take to resolve an ambiguity, gap or inconsistency in the IPC. There appear to be at least three approaches open to them. The first, and by far the most popular, has been for the courts to rely on the English

---

16 IPC, s. 304A reads: 'Whoever causes the death of any person by doing any rash or negligent act not amounting to culpable homicide, shall be punished with imprisonment of either description for a term which may extend to two years, or with fine, or with both.'

17 See Chapter 3 of this volume (N. Morgan, 'The Fault Elements of Offences') at 62, 68, and 77–8.

18 *Re Nidamarti Nagabhushanam* (1872) 7 MHC 119. See further Morgan, *ibid.*

19 IPC, s. 299, the relevant part of which reads: 'Whoever causes death by doing an act … with the knowledge that he is likely by such act to cause death, commits the offence of culpable homicide.'

20 By the insertion of new ss. 85 and 86 to the Singaporean Penal Code which were influenced by the House of Lords' decision in *DPP v. Beard* [1920] AC 479.

21 Section 85(2) read with Singaporean Penal Code, s. 86(1). See further Chapter 11 of this volume (G. Ferguson, 'Intoxication') at 261–3.

22 Law Reform Commission of Canada, *Criminal Law: Towards a Codification of Canadian Criminal Law, Study Paper* (Ottawa: Law Reform Commission of Canada, 1976) 18, describing the experience of Canadian judges in interpreting the Canadian Criminal Code which was first enacted in 1892. See also Law Reform Commission of Canada, *Our Criminal Law* (Ottawa: Law Reform Commission of Canada, 1976).

common law. But is it permissible to assume that the English common law is the primary source of law for the purposes of interpreting the Code? Macaulay expressly denied this when he claimed that his Code was 'not a digest of any existing system, and that no existing system [had] furnished [him] even with a ground work'.[23] And if the primary source of the IPC was, indeed, the English common law, should it not be the law as it then stood[24] in Macaulay's time rather than the contemporary English law? Neither answer to this question is satisfactory. If it were in the affirmative, it would be a retrograde step since the nineteenth-century English common law was in a state of shambles. While a negative answer might be better, it results in the invocation of laws which have been judicially formulated under a legal system whose approach to criminal responsibility is, in many major respects, very different from that of India.[25]

Consequently, some judges have opted for the second approach, which is to refuse to apply the English common law, insisting that the answer to any problem is to be found in the wording of the IPC alone.[26] But this stance is also unsatisfactory where an ambiguity in a Code provision was the very reason why the matter came before the courts. Admirable as this judicial stance might be in insisting on the maintenance of a democratically made code, justice is not served because experience shows that the particular ambiguity will continue unresolved on account of legislative inattention.

There is a third approach which has been suggested by some commentators but which, to date, has rarely been taken up by the courts. It is that the judges should consider the criminal laws of Commonwealth jurisdictions other than England, such as Australia and Canada.[27] These jurisdictions have a stronger claim to relevance for India and other IPC jurisdictions than the English common law because they have experience with the working of criminal codes. These jurisdictions also provide examples that are perceived to be less freighted with colonialist baggage, and of criminal law reforms that accord directly with common challenges of nation-building in plural and multicultural societies. This approach is arguably the best one available but requires a fair degree of judicial creativity since it involves the solving of 'novel problems … through the discovery and extension of principles that are basic to the [Indian Penal] Code'.[28] Criminal justice would certainly be advanced by such a method of judicial law-making, but at a price. The need for the courts to 'discover and extend' the basic principles of the criminal law contained in the IPC will further compound the problems of imprecision, incomprehensibility, inaccessibility and judicial rather than legislative law-making besetting the Code.

In sum, the current impoverished nature of the IPC cannot be rectified by the courts simply because their involvement is antithetical to the formulation of a good code. This is not to say that judges will inevitably perform poorly at interpreting code provisions. What is being said is that

23 Macaulay, Macleod, Anderson and Millett, above n. 4, at iii.

24 The Australian High Court in *Brennan v. The King* (1936) 55 CLR 253, at 263, thought so in relation to the Griffith Code of 1899. However, the court held that, since the Griffith Code was intended to displace the common law, that law was therefore inapplicable.

25 Consider, for instance, that England continues to have trial by jury while India does not, and that the English legal system imposes the burden of disproving a defence on the prosecution whereas, in India, the burden lies with the defence to prove a defence.

26 For example, see *Gopal Naidu v. King-Emperor* (1922) ILR 46 Mad 605; *Emperor v. Joti Prasad Gupta* (1931) ILR 53 All 642.

27 See M. Sornarajah, 'The Interpretation of the Penal Codes' [1991] 3 *Malayan Law Journal* cxxix; W. Chan, 'The Present and Future of Provocation as a Defence to Murder in Singapore' (2001) *Singapore Journal of Legal Studies* 453.

28 Sornarajah, *ibid.*, at cxxxiv.

a good code will not require the judges to perform this task. Of course, this is only an ideal since no code can ever be entirely without blemish. The point is that, whenever judges discover some ambiguity or inconsistency in the Code, the legislature should be required to promptly rectify the defect. Once the decision is taken that a nation's criminal laws should be governed by a code, the die is cast that it is for the legislature and not the courts to promote and maintain the qualities of a good code. While the legislatures of nations possessing the IPC have been remiss in discharging this duty, it is never too late to do so. We turn now to consider how this can be done.

FIXING THE IPC WITH A GENERAL PART

The revision of a nineteenth-century legal instrument such as the IPC can be conducted in two ways. The first is a tidying-up exercise which deals with ambiguities, gaps and inconsistencies in the Code and modernises the language used. While this may be a worthwhile exercise, it does not examine the foundational structure and conceptual underpinnings of the IPC in any meaningful way.[29] Such an examination is well overdue. It is worth emphasising that the IPC is 150 years old and much may have changed by way of thinking about criminal responsibility since Macaulay's time. This is not to dismiss the possibility that legislatures may find that many of the general principles of criminal responsibility contained in the Code continue to closely reflect the contemporary views and values of our society, but the Legislature will not know this unless and until it undertakes the above-mentioned examination.

The second way of revising an antiquated code is to re-examine the general principles of criminal responsibility contained in the Code with a view to evaluating whether they correspond with contemporary thinking on the subject matter. This assumes, of course, that those general principles are readily to be found in the Code. The ensuing chapters in this book will show that several of these principles are either non-existent or unclear. We suggest that the best method of conducting this exercise is to produce a General Part for the Code. The reason why it is so described is because this Part will contain the foundational principles of criminal responsibility which are generally applicable to all offences, including those found outside the Code.

The creation of a General Part has been a tried and tested method for successfully[30] generating sound modern criminal code proposals for Commonwealth jurisdictions such as Australia, Canada and England. The Part normally comprises: (i) the physical (or conduct) elements of a crime; (ii) the fault (or mental elements) of a crime; (iii) the general defences; and (iv) ancillary (or abetment and vicarious) liability and the inchoate crimes of attempt and conspiracy. Parts II and III of this book on 'Principles of Culpability' and 'Principles of Exculpation', respectively, examine many of these dimensions of liability and exceptions in detail, describing and critiquing

29 M.R. Goode, 'Constructing Criminal Law Reform and the Model Criminal Code' (2002) 26 *Criminal Law Journal* 152, at 165, commenting on such an exercise by a 1992 Queensland Criminal Code Review Committee on the Griffith Code. See further Chapter 13 of this volume, above n. 15.

30 By 'success', we mean that the new criminal codes have received the substantial support of all parties involved in the exercise, including judges, legal practitioners, legal academics and other interested bodies. That the English and revised Canadian codes have not been enacted is not a meaningful measure of anticipated failure as effective and workable pieces of legislation. Rather, this is due to a lack of political will and the low legislative priority given to these projects on the part of governments. See Chapter 14 of this volume, above n. 15, on the situation in England and Wales; and for an excellent description of the political inertia which has operated in Canada and elsewhere, see G. Ferguson, 'From Jeremy Bentham to Anne McLellan: Lessons on Criminal Law Codification' in D. Stuart, R. Delisle and A. Manson (eds), *Towards a Clear and Just Criminal Law: A Criminal Reports Forum* (Toronto: Carswell, 1999) 192.

existing approaches, drawing upon leading doctrinal developments in the common law world and proposing provisions in accordance with the most progressive aspects of Macaulay's originating principles.

Introducing a General Part does not necessarily mean a complete revision and rewriting of the IPC. By undertaking the exercise of producing the General Part, the legislature is made to come to terms with and resolve the problems which have led to the current impoverished state of the Code. The exercise will allow whatever that may be found to be sound or desirable in the Code to be retained. Indeed, as the chapters in this book will show, there are many provisions in Macaulay's original draft Code of 1837 and in the IPC which are conceptually sound and in good working order.

Having a General Part has the further benefit of reinstating the IPC as the main repository of the substantive criminal law. Once the General Part is enacted, it will be possible to begin the gradual revision of all other existing penal legislation to accord with the general principles and rules of interpretation found in the General Part. By the same token, future penal legislation should be drafted with the General Part fully in mind. In this way, the quality of accessibility of a good code will be achieved insofar as the general principles of criminal responsibility to which every offence is subject will be contained in the one volume. The following pertinent observations were made by an English law reform body when describing the advantages of having a General Part in a criminal code:

> The law would immediately become more accessible; all users would have an agreed text as a common starting-point and the scope for dispute about its terms and application should be reduced. The source of the general principles of criminal liability would be found in little more than fifty sections of an Act of Parliament instead of many statutes, thousands of cases and the extensive commentaries on them to be found in the textbooks.[31]

Part IV of this book, 'Challenges of Codification and Criminal Law Reform', examines recent codifying failures and successes, while Barry Wright's chapter in Part I examines the larger historical context of this reform in the common law world and the debates which animated Macaulay. Bentham's advocacy ensured a prominent place for codification in nineteenth-century English criminal law reform debates, and it appeared to be on the legislative agenda from the time of Henry Brougham's appointment of the Criminal Law Commissioners in 1833. Their work ended inconclusively with their mid-century reports, but Stephen's draft English Code of 1878 came close to success when it was referred to a Royal Commission and presented in modified form as a bill at Westminster in 1880. It died with the fall of the government, although the draft English Code lived on as the primary influence, combined with local consolidations, in the Canadian and New Zealand Codes of 1892 and 1893 respectively. Chris Clarkson's chapter examines the unfortunate fate of the modern codification project in England and Wales in the form of the 1985 and 1989 Law Commission reports, which proceeded from a focus on the General Part. A similar fate of legislative neglect has met the Law Reform Commission of Canada's efforts, which had culminated in the recommendation of the addition of a General Part to the Canadian Criminal Code.[32]

31 Law Commission for England and Wales, above n. 6, at para. [2.6]. The number of sections mentioned here is that found in the draft criminal code proposed by the Criminal Code team.

32 Law Reform Commission of Canada, *Report on Recodifying Criminal Law* (Ottawa: Law Reform Commission of Canada, 1986). See also Ferguson, above n. 30.

If further evidence were needed that the production of a General Part is the best way to revitalise the IPC and to ensure that it reflects modern notions concerning criminal responsibility, it is to be found by studying the recent rather more successful efforts at re-codification in Australia.[33]

For those unfamiliar with Australia, the criminal law there is, generally speaking, not a Commonwealth matter (that is, it is not under primary federal jurisdiction as in Canada) but is vested in the various States and Territories of Australia. This decentralisation is similar to the situation in the US, where Herbert Wechsler's Model Penal Code was developed to inspire great consistency and serve as an exemplar for modernisation.[34] In Australia, two systems of criminal law exist, the first being the common law jurisdictions such as New South Wales, South Australia and Victoria which are based on the English common law and supplemented by statute. The second comprises codified criminal law jurisdictions such as Queensland and Western Australia. These code jurisdictions are mostly based on Samuel Griffith's 1899 Queensland Code, which was rather more comprehensive than the Canadian and New Zealand Codes but has languished, like the IPC, from legislative neglect.[35]

In the early 1990s, a movement to formulate a model criminal code in Australia began in earnest, with the backing of the Attorneys-General of all the States and Territories. The primary aim of this exercise was to rationalise the growing number of federal criminal laws, eradicate inconsistency and reduce significantly the huge diversity of criminal laws found amongst the various jurisdictions. A Model Criminal Code Officers Committee was established in 1991 with representatives from the Attorney-General's Departments of all the States and Territories, and published its first report at the end of 1992. This report spelt out the general principles of criminal responsibility which were to form the General Part of the Committee's model code.[36] To date, this General Part has been adopted by the Commonwealth (that is, Federal) Parliament and the Australian Capital Territory.[37] Although a federal code is now in place, the impact of the model code on jurisdictions other than the Australian Capital Territory remains inconclusive. Matthew Goode, a leading contributor to the deliberations of the committee, has this to say:

> The Committee decided very early in its life that the very first project in a codification exercise must be the foundational general principles of the criminal law. Hence, the Committee began with a Discussion Paper and Final Report on the general principles. That decision turned out to be absolutely correct. The general principles guided the deliberations of the Committee in its work on the specific offences to be included in the Code in ways which were fundamental to the structure

33 See Chapter 13 of this volume, above n. 15. Australia serves as the best example of a relatively successful and recent codifying reform endeavour.

34 Experiences with the older US codes are beyond the scope of this study; they appear to have had limited influence on the jurisdictions examined here. Livingston's Louisiana Code was not implemented and the most notable later nineteenth-century codes were developed by David Dudley Fields. On the development of the US Model Penal Code, see S.H. Kadish, 'The Model Penal Code's Historical Antecedents' (1987–8) 19 *Rutgers Law Journal* 521.

35 See B. Wright, 'Criminal Law Codification and Imperial Projects: The Self-Governing Jurisdiction Codes of the 1890's' (2008) 12 *Legal History* 19.

36 Criminal Law Officers Committee of the Standing Committee of Attorneys-General, *Model Criminal Code, Report, Chapters 1 and 2, General Principles of Criminal Responsibility* (1992) (available online at http://www.scag.gov.au/lawlink/SCAG/ll_scag.nsf/vwFiles/MCLOC_MCC_Chapter_1_and_2_Report.pdf/$file/MCLOC_MCC_Chapter_1_and_2_Report.pdf, last accessed 7 February 2011).

37 See the Criminal Code Act 1995 (Cth); Criminal Code Act 2002 (ACT).

> and drafting of the recommended provisions of the Code. The most important of these provisions were those which dealt with [the] fault elements of offences.[38]

The reference in the last sentence to the fault elements of offences is of particular significance to our discussion. It illustrates how the production of a General Part requires the legislators to decide between adopting the position found in a nineteenth-century code or the recent common law pronouncements on the matter. Put simply, the choice is between the code stance of objective criminal responsibility, which was thought at the time to be the common law position, and of subjective criminal responsibility formulated by the courts in recent years. By way of illustration, in the Australian code jurisdictions, a person charged with rape may escape liability only if he reasonably believed that the complainant was consenting, whereas in the common law jurisdictions, the prosecution will have to prove that the accused knew or was recklessly indifferent to the lack of consent of the complainant. For the purposes of the present discussion, there is no need to decide which is the better position. The point is that, without undertaking the production of a General Part, it is unlikely that our legislators will consider issues of such fundamental importance as this. Rather, they are much more likely to be content, and without due deliberation, to leave the objective criminal responsibility found in the IPC for the offence of rape unchanged.[39]

In closing, the nineteenth-century criminal codes we have been studying cannot be dismissed out of hand merely because they did not have a General Part. The absence of such a Part does not mean that the codes are devoid of the general principles of criminal responsibility. Their drafters clearly realised the need to express these principles, but used a different technique to do so. In their view, these principles should be embedded in the specific offence and defence provisions rather than consigned to a separate part of the code. Thus, Stephen has written that 'the only means of arriving at a full comprehension of the expression *mens rea* is by detailed examination of the definition of particular crimes'.[40] Unfortunately, based on the experiences of the jurisdictions having codes of this nature, this technique has not been successful in making the law precise, comprehensible and accessible. The fact that modern law reformers who have been asked to re-codify their criminal codes have all recommended a General Part speaks for itself.

COMMENCING WORK ON A GENERAL PART FOR THE IPC

As a result of the above concerns and views, a project with a symposium at its centre was planned by the editors of this volume. The primary objective of the symposium was to argue for a modern set of general principles of criminal law that would be consistent with the spirit of Macaulay's original draft, and which could be incorporated into an updated version of the IPC. Secondary objectives of the symposium included considerations of legal history and comparative analyses to help mould the law – these would form valuable sources of information for law reformers, scholars and legal practitioners. A year before the symposium, a select number of criminal law specialists were each assigned a general principle to research and write on, and their papers would be scrutinised at the symposium. The specialists were instructed to tailor their papers on the basis of the following inquiry:

38 Goode, above n. 29, at 157.

39 IPC, s. 375. See C.M.V. Clarkson, 'Rape: Emasculation of the Penal Code' (1988) 1 MLJ cxiii and Chapter 5 of this volume (K. Amirthalingam, 'Mistake and Strict Liability').

40 J.F. Stephen, *A History of the Criminal Law of England* (vol. 2) (London: Macmillan and Co., 1883) 95.

> How might the IPC look today if the original Code framers, maintaining their philosophical stance, undertook a major revision? In addressing that question, let us imagine that they would examine the 150 years of judicial interpretations of the IPC, and study recent common law and criminal code developments from other comparable jurisdictions such as Australia, Canada and England. No doubt they would be prepared to move away from their original philosophical stance if there were sufficiently strong public policy reasons (evinced, for example, by the wide acceptance of a particular criminal law principle by the current criminal laws of major jurisdictions). But we can suppose that any such departures would be to the minimum extent necessary, and should be compatible with the rest of the modernised Code.[41]

This volume is the result of the symposium, which was held in June 2010 and was hosted by the National University of Singapore. The symposium was actively used as an opportunity to integrate the papers, refine common themes and develop appropriate cross-references. From the outset, it was realised that it would be expecting too much of the specialists to agree on the form and substance of each and every one of the general principles. However, at the symposium it transpired that broad agreement was reached on many principles. Where there was strong disagreement, the specialists have acknowledged in their chapters the opposing views and sought to defend their preferred position. Accordingly, this volume stands as a coherent scholarly examination of the IPC and its legacy, one that promises to hold wide international appeal. The volume also contains a final Part comprising three chapters which, while not dealing directly with the IPC, engage with important themes which carry this project to the next stage. They include the political reality of implementing the proposed General Part and its handling by the courts should implementation be achieved.

AN IMPLEMENTATION STRATEGY

As the last three chapters of this volume amply demonstrate, arguing in favour of a General Part for the IPC is one thing; getting it implemented is quite a different matter. A major obstacle to implementation is that the need for a General Part lacks sufficiently high visibility to demand public and professional debate and attention. As far as the public is concerned, their seeming disinterest may be explained by the fact that the IPC has for so long been incomprehensible and inaccessible to the layperson that the law has become virtually the sole domain of lawyers. As for professionals, particularly legislators and lawyers, their inattention may be explained by the absence of any mechanism for singling out this issue for special attention by the government.

A proactive stance must therefore be initially taken by those who are convinced of the importance of revitalising the IPC. We would like to suggest that the best team to spearhead this effort is a government-sponsored law reform body[42] working in close collaboration with criminal law academics. That such a team can readily meet the challenge of drafting a General Part for the IPC is, to our minds, beyond doubt. But their efforts will be in vain if the project does not have the support of the government from the very start.[43]

In 1980, the English Law Commission welcomed the proposal of the Criminal Law Sub-Committee of the Public Teachers of Law that a team should be drawn from its members to

41 Instructions to specialist contributors from the editors of this volume, dated 15 April 2009.

42 For other suggestions, see Chapters 13 and 14 of this volume, above n. 15.

43 See Chapters 13 and 14 of this volume, *ibid.*

consider and make proposals to the Commission in relation to a criminal code.[44] The Code Team's terms of reference included:

> To formulate, in a manner appropriate to [a criminal code] –
> (a) the general principles which should govern liability under it;
> (b) a standard terminology to be used in it; [and]
> (c) the rules which should govern its interpretation.[45]

An IPC re-codification team could also be given these terms of reference and instructed to draft a General Part. Additionally, the team should be instructed to select specific offences for drafting in the light of the general principles proposed.[46] The English codification exercise found this essential to test the adequacy of the principles in the General Part,[47] as did the Australian codification exercise.

Once completed, the General Part and selected offences drafted by the IPC re-codification team should be disseminated widely to the public, the legal profession and people or groups with day-to-day practical experience in the workings of the criminal law. The English initiative of establishing 'scrutiny groups' of lawyers to examine particular parts of the draft in detail and to report back to the re-codification team could also be emulated.[48] Representatives of the judiciary should likewise be asked to undertake such an exercise. Indeed, the involvement and support of the judiciary is vital to the success of the IPC re-codification project.[49] All of this makes sense when we appreciate that it will be the judges and legal practitioners who would, if the draft became law, be its main users.

Only after changes have been made to the draft General Part, in the light of this extensive process of consultation and review, will it be ready for tabling in Parliament. More revisions may need to be made on account of the ensuing legislative debate before it is finally enacted. Once enacted, the process of amending all penal legislation so as to accord with the General Part can begin.

So much for the mechanics of seeing to the drafting of a sound and workable General Part of the IPC. We strongly suspect, though, that however strong the case may be made for the introduction of a General Part and however perfect its drafting, the project will flounder and eventually fail if certain other practical concerns are not allayed from the beginning. One of these is the human tendency to be comfortable with what we know, whether or not it serves us or others well. Legal practitioners and judges may object to re-codification on the ground that they have learnt the law once and should not be required to learn it again. We do not think that our lawyers and judges would be so unwilling or unable to relearn the criminal law, especially when they are told that the law will be made more precise and comprehensible. There is no doubting that re-codification will

44 Law Commission for England and Wales, above n. 6, at para. [1.8]. England, of course, is a common law criminal jurisdiction so that the project was one of codification rather than re-codification of the criminal law. However, the aims of both codification and re-codification are identical, as the Law Commission report indicates: see paras. [2.1]–[2.11].

45 *Ibid.*, at para. [1.9].

46 One or two offences against the person and against property will suffice, for instance, culpable homicide and theft. See Chapter 3 of this volume as an example of the use of the homicide provisions in the IPC to test the proposed definitions of fault elements.

47 Law Commission for England and Wales, above n. 6, at para. [1.13].

48 *Ibid.*

49 The history of codification of the criminal law in other jurisdictions has shown that resistance from the judiciary can be a major obstacle to enactment: see, for example, the Law Commission for England and Wales, above n. 10, at paras. [3] and [5].

involve 'some painful short-term consequences'[50] for users of the Code, but such an experience will not be new to them, given the often rapid and radical changes to legislation occurring in other fields of the law such as in respect of taxation, company law and securities regulation.

Another practical concern is whether re-codification of the IPC will be costly in economic terms. Apart from the initial miniscule outlay of reprinting the Code, re-codification will actually substantially reduce the economic costs of meting out criminal justice. Making the criminal law precise and comprehensible will minimise the number of appeals in order to 'discover' the general principles of the criminal law or their application to a set of circumstances.[51] When there is litigation, judges would be better guided by the Code when confronted with a new problem. In the words of the Canadian Law Reform Commission re-codifying the criminal law:

> Instead of finding the justification for a principle in a long chain of precedents, of doubtful import in some instances, the judge could refer to codified statements and draw conclusions from them by using basically the same methods and reasoning he uses at present.[52]

Indeed, we daresay that the positive economic impact will be felt throughout all stages of the criminal justice system, from the appellate courts to the operational decisions of law enforcement agents.

Still on the matter of costs, the enactment of a precise and comprehensible General Part for the IPC will result in incalculable savings derived from people becoming more law-abiding. It has thus been contended that '[m]aking the law more accessible brings it down to the level of the ordinary citizen, and helps prevent crime through education'.[53]

CONCLUSION

The IPC, when first implemented, was well ahead of its time, thanks largely to the legislative genius of Macaulay. But like all good things which are not regularly maintained and improved, the Code has become a pale shadow of its former self. Ambiguities, gaps and inconsistencies found in its provisions have been left to the courts to handle. When undertaking this task, the judges have often found themselves constrained by the wording or principles of the IPC. Furthermore, the judges have not been given any guidance from the Code as to which source of law they should draw upon to resolve a problem of interpretation. The result has been the growth of a huge body of case law on the Code, including numerous conflicting judicial rulings affecting the whole range of general principles of criminal responsibility. Consequently, for many decades now, the IPC has lost its once-admirable qualities of being a precise, comprehensible, democratically made and accessible legal instrument.

What is required for so huge a problem is major remedial surgery rather than a band-aid revision exercise. The introduction of a General Part is needed to revitalise the IPC and to return it to its former self. We are confident that the intellectual capacity and talent to undertake this task can readily be found. A dedicated law reform body working together with leading criminal law

---

50 The Law Commission for England and Wales was keenly aware of such resistance to change from the legal practitioners: see above n. 6, at para. [2.24].

51 See M. Goode, 'Codification of the Australian Criminal Law' (1992) 16 *Criminal Law Journal* 5, at 13.

52 Law Reform Commission of Canada, *Criminal Law: Towards a Codification of Canadian Criminal Law*, above n. 22, at 24.

53 *Ibid.*, at 23.

academics can fulfil this role. Macaulay's remarkable accomplishments as both a law reformer and a scholar – his clear, rational and pragmatic approach – continue to provide a guiding inspiration for such an exercise.

Indeed, the chapters in Parts II and III of this volume provide a good starting foundation for such a project, canvassing, with Macaulay's originating principles firmly in mind, leading developments in general principles of liability and defences. The chapters in Part IV provide a comparative picture of the promise and perils of such reform. While the challenges of developing a model IPC for the twenty-first century are faced most directly in a number of South Asian jurisdictions, the issues examined here are also directly relevant to the wider common law world, notably Australia, Canada, England and New Zealand, where codification of criminal law and law reform of its general principles remain subjects of debate. The fate of codification and the major revision of existing codes in those jurisdictions is a worthy subject of further study. When doing so, inspiration can be taken from reform of the IPC, which holds out the promise to be as influential in the larger common law world in the twenty-first century as Macaulay's original version was in the nineteenth century.

For IPC jurisdictions, the major challenge is to convince governments that a modern IPC project is an important public policy worth undertaking for the betterment of our societies. This proposed re-codification exercise would ideally lead to the enactment of a new IPC, produced locally and reflecting more accurately our identity as a nation of Indians, Malaysians, Nigerians, Pakistanis, Sri Lankans, Singaporeans or Sudanese as the case may be, and our common values as a people living in the twenty-first century.[54] Macaulay would have applauded the effort.

54 Adapting a statement of the Law Reform Commission of Canada, above n. 32, at 3.

Chapter 2

Macaulay's Indian Penal Code: Historical Context and Originating Principles

Barry Wright

INTRODUCTION

Criminal law codification was never realised in England, despite its central place in nineteenth-century law reform debates there. Codes were developed in other British jurisdictions and the first of these, and the one most directly influenced by the ideas of Jeremy Bentham, was Thomas Babington Macaulay's Indian Penal Code (IPC). Bentham coined the term codification, a sweeping legislative reform based on his critique of the common law and his ambitious 'science of legislation'. All existing laws were to be replaced by comprehensive provisions set out in a rational, consistent and accessible form amenable to efficient administration and minimal judicial discretion. Such a code, anchored in the principles of utility, would not only enhance the rule of law, but held out promise of a 'universal jurisprudence', applicable to places as diverse as England and Bengal as Bentham put it, later predicting that he would be the 'dead legislative of British India'.[1] In the year following his death in 1832, imperial authority in India was reconstituted under fellow utilitarian James Mill's direction and Macaulay was appointed legal representative to the Governor General of India's new Legislative Council. Macaulay's productive sojourn in India was highlighted by the drafting of the IPC, a concise, lucid and comprehensive code that aimed to minimise discretion, differences in legal status and concessions to local circumstances. K.J.M. Smith observes that the IPC and its antecedents are an important episode in the development of criminal jurisprudence and nineteenth-century intellectual history.[2] It is also an important episode for those British-codified jurisdictions that were directly or indirectly influenced by the IPC.

*

The Charter Act 1833 reorganised British government in India by creating a unified legislative body in the form of an appointed Legislative Council headed by the Governor General, which centralised and co-ordinated civil and military authority and East Indian Company commercial interests.[3] A law commission was created under Macaulay's direction shortly after his arrival as

1 See J. Bentham, 'On the Influence of Time and Place in Matters of Legislation' (1782) in J. Bowring (ed.), *The Works of Jeremy Bentham* (vol. 1) (Edinburgh: W. Tait, 1843), 169–94. Bentham's prescient comment about India appears in vol. X and at the end of his life he consulted closely with James Mill and drafted long letters to Governor General Bentinck. See also below n. 3 and n. 7.

2 K.J.M. Smith, 'Macaulay's Indian Penal Code: An Illustration of the Accidental Function of Time, Place and Personalities in Law Making' in W.M. Gordon and T.D. Fergus (eds), *Legal History in the Making: Proceedings of the Ninth British Legal History Conference, Glasgow, 1989* (London: Hambledon Press, 1991), 145.

3 James Mill, author of the influential *History of British India* (London: Baldwin, Cradock and Joy, 1817) was an active influence on East India House, promoting utilitarian policies to replace orientalist deference to local customs: see Eric Stokes, *The English Utilitarians and India* (Oxford: Clarendon Press, 1959), xii.

the Council's legal representative. Undeterred by the complexities of India, Macaulay pursued an ambitious agenda to modernise laws and the colonial governance of civil society. As Eric Stokes puts it:

> The physical and mental distance separating East and West was to be annihilated by the discoveries of science, by commercial intercourse, and by transplanting the genius of English laws and English education. It was the attitude of English liberalism in its clear, untroubled dawn, and its most representative figure in both England and in India was Macaulay.[4]

By 1836 law reforms ended prior restraint of the press as well as the special privileges accorded to expatriate British residents in civil cases. Macaulay's education reforms widened accessibility and modernised the curriculum. The IPC, completed in 1837, was the culmination of these progressive initiatives. This first code of criminal law in the British Empire, largely authored by Macaulay, is arguably his most influential and lasting achievement.[5]

Macaulay faced less formidable legal professional resistance in India than reformers in England and was in a strong position to act as a utilitarian 'enlightened despotic' legislator. Yet he was no mere *factotum* or translator of Bentham's theories, nor could it be predicted that he was to become perhaps the most successful utilitarian legislator of his generation. Macaulay came from a Clapham sect background, was never part of the British circle of Bentham and Mill disciples, and identified with an older Whig tradition.[6] Before becoming an MP he practised briefly as a barrister, but was best known for contributions to the *Edinburgh* and *Westminister Reviews* that emphasised the importance of liberties, the dangers of arbitrary power and the virtues of gradualism as they were manifested in British experience. Radical legislative reform did not sit well with these libertarian ideas and, indeed, Macaulay's publications expressed suspicion of Bentham and Mill's ideas of enlightened legislative despotism and their reductionist view of human behaviour and public policy.[7] Their theories neglected historical experience and failed to sufficiently value the

---

4 Stokes, *ibid.*, at xiii–xiv.

5 Stokes describes the IPC as Macaulay's most enduring legacy (above n. 3, at 226) and the importance of the project to Macaulay is highlighted in John Clive, *Macaulay: The Shaping of the Historian* (Cambridge, MA: Harvard University Press, 1987). The original IPC draft appears, along with the Report of the Indian Law Commissioners of 14 October 1837, in T.B. Macaulay, J.M. Macleod, G.W. Anderson and F. Millett, *A Penal Code Prepared by the Indian Law Commissioners* (London: Pelham Richardson, 1838) (reprinted by the Lawbook Exchange, Ltd, 2002). See also T.B. Macaulay, *The Complete Works of Lord Macaulay* (vol. XI) (Albany edition) (London: Longmans, Green & Co., 1898), 3–198. For Macaulay's correspondence, see T. Pinney (ed.), *The Selected Letters of Thomas Babington Macaulay* (vol. 3) (Cambridge: Cambridge University Press, 1982) January 1834–August 1841. Although the Law Commissioners as a group were responsible for drafting the code, as fellow commissioner John Macleod testified in 1848, 'I may state a fact already generally known when I say that Mr. Macaulay is justly entitled to be called the author of the Indian Penal Code': J.M. Macleod, *Notes on the Report of the Indian Law Commissioners on the Indian Penal Code* (London: W. Clowes, 1848) vi; see also Clive, *ibid.*, at 443.

6 See Smith, above n. 2, at 147; Stokes, above n. 3, at 191–5. His father Zachary was a prominent abolitionist; Smith notes that James Stephen of the Colonial Office, father of James Fitzjames and Leslie Stephen, and whose own father was a colleague of Zachary, was offered the post as the Council's law member. Mill's influence was probably decisive.

7 As Stokes, *ibid.*, puts it (at 176–7), 'Legislation is a science, a task for the ablest philosophic mind, a subject for dispassionate study and expert knowledge, not the sport of political passion or of popular and ignorant prejudice. Bentham found himself more at home with enlightened despots than turbulent political assemblies'. Yet Bentham also stated, 'Reform the world by example, you act generously and wisely; reform

late seventeenth-century constitutional compromises and more recent parliamentary reforms that secured British liberties, Parliament's supremacy (forever banishing the prospect of a return to Tudor and Stuart excesses that the Restoration reactionaries had threatened) and Britain's trading prosperity. These themes were later elaborated in his *History of England from the Accession of James II* which celebrated the British constitution, the benefits of which were to be eventually transmitted throughout the Empire on the foundation of trade and enlightened government – the 'Whig theory of history' famously critiqued by Herbert Butterfield in 1931.[8]

Macaulay distinguished himself as erudite contributor to the debates around the 1832 Reform Act and the final legislative steps in the long abolitionist campaign against slavery throughout the British Empire (1834). More surprisingly, he became a prime mover of the 1833 Charter Act bill drafted by James Mill, with whom he became acquainted in 1832 as Secretary of the government's Board of Control, charged with supervising the East India Company and Indian public affairs. Macaulay's embrace of utilitarianism appears to date from this time. Stokes suggests that Macaulay's ambivalence about utilitarian political and moral theories did not extend to Bentham's legal theory.[9] John Clive suggests that Macaulay participated in the politics of utilitarian absolutism as a means to an end, to put into effect developments that would lead to eventual freedom and independence, and that the colony should benefit from impartial and enlightened imposed reforms until that time.[10] Macaulay himself declared in parliamentary debate on the Charter Act:

> I believe that no country ever stood so much in need of a code of laws as India, and I believe also that there never was a country in which the want might be so easily supplied … A code is almost the only blessing – perhaps it is the only blessing which absolute governments are better fitted to confer on a nation than popular governments.[11]

Such were the contradictions of nineteenth-century British liberalism. They were more easily overlooked in an overseas setting where the executive powers of colonial government gave Macaulay wide latitude to experiment with a dramatic reconstituting of legal authority in what was deemed, under utilitarian premises and imperial policy, to be for the general public good. As we shall see, the metropole's political classes were also increasingly concerned about the legitimacy of British colonial rule, its conformity to constitutional claims and the legal bases for the exercise of British power. In this respect it is telling that the delayed enactment of the IPC was sparked by the crisis of the Indian Mutiny. The IPC became a legislative priority because restoring the semblance of legality,

---

the world by force, you might as well reform the moon, and the design is fit only for lunatics' (Bowring, above n. 1, vol. 4, at 416). Jennifer Pitts challenges the assumption that Bentham shared James Mill's view of empire. Despite his 'dead legislative of India' reference, other writings called for self-rule and expressed scepticism of European imperial ventures. She attributes the view of utilitarianism as imperialist to Stokes and Elie Helevy's influential portrayal of Bentham as a deeply authoritarian thinker: see J. Pitts, 'Legislator of the World? A Rereading of Bentham on Colonies' (2003) 31 *Political Theory* 200.

8 See for example, T.B. Macaulay, 'Utilitarian Logic and Politics'; 'Bentham's Defence of Mill' and 'Utilitarian Theory of Government' written in the late 1820s; H. Butterfield, *The Whig Interpretation of History* (London: G. Bell and Sons, 1931).

9 Stokes, above n. 3, at 191–2: 'He rejected the Utilitarian idea of the general renovation of society by means of an abstract universal theory … Instead he adhered to expediency and pragmatism, which he dignified with the authority of Bacon's inductive method … Macaulay accepted Bentham's jurisprudence but not the general political theory…'.

10 Clive, above n. 5, at 467–73. See also Pinney, above n. 5, 'Introduction', at vii–xi; 112–15.

11 House of Commons, *Parliamentary Debates* (3rd series) (10 July 1833) vol. 19, at cols. 531 and 533.

in a manner that aimed to enhance the rule of law and minimise the future need to resort to arbitrary emergency measures or military intervention, became a political priority. The IPC was designed to make imperial authority more effective and legitimate. And there were to be retreats regarding Macaulay's aim of equal legal status. Little was done to confront the substantive inequalities or the larger gulfs between the colonisers and the colonised. Macaulay and his utilitarian colleagues were nonetheless remarkably optimistic in the 1830s and, in boldly intervening into what seemed to be the intractable complexities of India, they expressed the hope that the IPC would be emulated elsewhere in the British Empire.[12]

*

This historical study examines the originating premises and principles underlying the IPC and the drafting process 1835–7, and surveys the events that eventually resulted in its enactment in 1860. It also examines selected provisions but it does not track the numerous and significant changes to the 1837 draft in the enacted version, or its adoption in other British colonies of South Asia.[13] It does, however, attempt to place the drafting of the IPC in broader law reform, policy and political contexts. These illuminate the significance of the IPC as the groundbreaking and most Benthamite criminal code in the common law world, but also as a similarly important initiative in the modernisation of colonial governance.

The basic objectives and principles of the IPC can be briefly summarised. The Code was to replace a patchwork of Muslim and Hindu laws overlaid with a mixture of transplanted English laws and East Indian Company regulations to ensure, as much as possible, a singular standard of justice. Macaulay rejected the idea of mere consolidation and sought a code that would apply to the entire Indian Empire (although local conditions, in particular the autonomy of the Princely States, would entail compromises to universality). He noted how the criminal law had been the focus of reformers since Beccaria and the policy preoccupation of politicians ranging from Peel to Brougham; given the continuing chaotic state of English criminal law, notwithstanding the ongoing work of Henry Brougham's Criminal Law Commissioners, he expressed hope that the IPC would inspire the stalled codification project in England itself.[14] He succinctly described the core objectives of his project in his 4 June 1835 Minute to Council, paraphrased as follows:

- It should be more than a mere digest of existing laws, cover all contingencies and 'nothing that is not in the Code ought to be law'.

12 See an early expression of this ambition in a letter to James Mill, 24 August 1835, reproduced in Pinney, above n. 5, at 146–51.

13 K.J.M. Smith's succinct overview is difficult to emulate, let alone improve upon. Essential background studies include Clive and Stokes. Older scholarly assessments begin with J.S. Mill (1838) XXXI *Westminster Review* 395 and James Fitzjames Stephen's close study is notable – see J.F. Stephen, *A History of the Criminal Law of England* (vol. III) (London: Macmillan and Co., 1883), 283. See also S.G. Vesey-Fitzgerald, 'Bentham and the Indian Codes' in G.W. Keeton and G. Schwarzenberger (eds), *Jeremy Bentham and the Law: A Symposium* (London: Stevens, 1948) 222; and M.C. Setalvad, *The Common Law in India* (London: Stevens, 1960). Modern assessments that examine the IPC from the perspective of rights, cultural heterogeneity and colonial rule debates include V. Dhagamwar, *Law, Power and Justice: The Protection of Personal Rights in the Indian Penal Code* (New Delhi: Sage Publications, 1992); R. Singha, '"No Needless Pains or Unintended Pleasures": Penal "Reform" in the Colony, 1825–45' (1995) 11 *Studies in History* 29 and *A Despotism of Law: Crime and Justice in Early Colonial India* (Delhi: Oxford University Press, 1998); and E. Kolsky, 'Codification and the Rule of Colonial Difference: Criminal Procedure in India' (2005) 23 *Law and History Review* 631.

14 Macaulay to Mill, 24 August 1835 in Clive, above n. 5, at 436–8.

- It should suppress crime with the least infliction of suffering and allow for the ascertaining of the truth at the smallest possible cost of time and money.
- Its language should be clear, unequivocal and concise. Every criminal act should be separately defined, its language followed precisely in indictment and conduct found to fall clearly within the definition.
- Uniformity was to be the chief end and special definitions, procedures or other exceptions to account for different races or sects should not be included without clear and strong reasons.[15]

Macaulay had these principles in mind as early as his parliamentary speech on the Charter Act when he declared '[u]niformity where you can have it; diversity where you must have it; but in all cases certainty'.[16] They were a concrete and practical version of Bentham's legislative aspirations.

Early commentators who did not dismiss Macaulay's achievement nonetheless tended to minimise the dramatic break from existing laws and downplay Bentham's influence. As Fitzjames Stephen put it:

> The Indian Penal Code may be described as the criminal law of England freed from all technicalities and superfluities, systematically arranged and modified in some few particulars (they are surprisingly few) to suit the circumstances of British India.[17]

This bias was corrected by Stokes, and even Stephen acknowledged elsewhere that '[t]o compare the Indian penal code with English criminal law was like comparing *Cosmos* with *Chaos*'.[18] Yet, as we shall see, Bentham's precise impact remains difficult to determine.

There is little doubt that the IPC was influenced by the leading utilitarian ideas expressed in the early nineteenth-century English law reform debates. Although utilitarian hopes that the IPC would inspire stalled efforts in England itself were to be disappointed, it was followed by Robert Wright's draft Jamaica Code and codes in Canada (1892), New Zealand (1893) and Queensland (1899). While there were a number of retrograde changes in the enacted IPC, and Stephen as a later Indian law commissioner helped to further modify it, the IPC proved to come closest of all the nineteenth-century British jurisdiction codes to a practical expression of Bentham's codifying ideals. Stephen's 1878 draft English Code, the basis for the failed 1880 bill which proved England's best chance at codification and the main external influence on the Canadian and New Zealand Codes, strayed far from Bentham's ideals.

Macaulay's objective of according formal equal legal status to all subjects under modernised laws represented a huge advance and, while it was compromised by the continuation of procedural discrimination after enactment, Macaulay's originating principles of comprehensiveness, consistency and accessibility are durable, have in many respects stood the test of time and remain progressive law reform aims in the twenty-first century. If there were systematic amendment and elaboration according to these principles of existing IPC provisions, or other modern attempts to codify or recodify for that matter, we would certainly see considerable improvement in our criminal laws.

However, in reflecting on the 150th anniversary of the IPC and the prospects for similar criminal law reform in the twenty-first century, it must be acknowledged that the task of updating the IPC is

---

15 See Macaulay's Minute 4 June 1835 in Macaulay, *The Complete Works of Lord Macaulay*, *ibid.*

16 Macaulay, above n. 5 (10 July 1833).

17 Stephen, above n. 13, at 300.

18 Social Science Association, 'Mr. Fitzjames Stephen on Codification' (1872–3) 54 *Law Times* 44, at 45, quoted in A. Phang, 'Of Codes and Ideology: Some Notes on the Origins of the Major Criminal Enactments of Singapore' (1989) 31 *Malaya Law Review* 46, at 55.

a difficult one and the aim of 'perfecting' it in accordance with original principles, while admirable, is perhaps impossible. Hard questions must be asked about any claim of 'orthodoxy' in relation to Macaulay, or Bentham for that matter. Bentham's legislative ideals that inspired Macaulay proved elusive, despite Macaulay's ideal opportunity to pursue them.

As he elaborated his legislative science, Bentham struggled with the tension between inductive and deductive logics, and the challenge of crafting specific provisions that accounted for particulars from abstract principles of utility. It is a reflection of Macaulay's remarkable energies that while taking on the bulk of the work on the IPC, he wrote a biography of Bacon, representative of the British pragmatist tradition that has more affinity with case-by-case incremental development of general principles, characteristic of the common law, than the principled abstraction of Plato or the Cartesian identification of first principles and derived implications characteristic of the Roman-civilian legal tradition. Macaulay may have been inspired in this regard by Peel, who quoted liberally from Bacon to undercut opposition to his criminal law consolidation bills at Westminster. Like Bentham, Macaulay did not resolve the tensions between the universal and the situational. Aspiring to craft universal laws, Macaulay was obliged to take time and place into account, as even Bentham acknowledged was necessary. Macaulay sought to shift law-making from the courts to the legislature and limit judges to simple application of the law, but even Bentham realised that the discretionary powers of judges could not be eliminated. That the IPC fell short of the ideals of scientific legislation and universal jurisprudence is of little surprise to modern legal realists and legislative sceptics. It is recognised that legislation is coloured by local and particular influences when adopted and applied in varying settings. Novel situations, developments and new issues cannot be fully anticipated. Experience shows that the systematic updating required for comprehensive codes is seldom a legislative priority, and amendment is usually achieved through *ad hoc* reactive legislation or by the bench. And we know that judges tend to overlay legislation with constructions and engage in inconsistent statutory interpretation. To the claim that Stephen's code did not represent true codification, it could be argued that recognition of the limits of legislation means there is still a place for flexible common law and the more explicit and open judicial obligations associated with it.[19]

Nor, of course, did Macaulay's reform occur in a vacuum. Careful historical enquiry obliges us to consider the context in which the IPC was produced and implemented. It was the product of a particular time, place, cultural and intellectual context, and was an expression of British imperial policy. Macaulay's premises were informed by the limits of his experience, outlook and the intellectual milieu of British liberalism and European Enlightenment rationalism that also influenced Mill and Bentham. Nor was the IPC a disinterested initiative, despite liberal and utilitarian legislative conceits. It was crafted and implemented within a political and policy context of a modernising British state concerned about effective colonial governance and challenges to its sovereignty. It involved more than legislating efficient rational legal responses to crime. It was also a quasi-constitutional projection of British rule that aimed to better regulate relations between the colonisers and the colonised. While the promotion of the rule of law and the reduction of archaic forms of discretionary authority and status differences represent an advance, the aim of making the law more effective and legitimate in culturally diverse frontier settings was also about sovereignty. Macaulay's vague aim of a free India at a distant point in the future was in contradiction with

19 See generally Smith, n. 2 above, and K.J.M. Smith, *James Fitzjames Stephen: Portrait of a Victorian Rationalist* (Cambridge: Cambridge University Press, 1988) on the influences of the British pragmatist tradition and Peel's consolidations on codification. For vivid examples of judicial law-making with the IPC, see M. Sornarajah, 'The Interpretation of the Penal Codes' [1991] 3 *Malayan Law Journal* cxxix.

the adoption of the IPC by authoritarian legislative decree, the denial of indigenous factors and demands for common obligations of citizenship as defined by an external power while colonial difference persisted. These reflect the limits of assimilative liberal ideals and tensions between sovereignty and liberal rationalities.[20]

That the IPC fell somewhat short of comprehensive scientific legislation and a universal jurisprudence (or 'an attempt to legislate for the world' as William Twining and others have put it) is not surprising given the limits of law reform and the imperial context.[21] We must nonetheless be wary of teleological assessment and oversimplification, and it is reductionism to dismiss the IPC as essentially an exercise in power. It stands as an important practical manifestation of nineteenth-century debates about criminal law reform, articulating Bentham's ideas in a practical working form. Macaulay did a remarkable job of balancing these ideas with situational pragmatism and, unlike Bentham, drafted a code that worked, was widely adopted elsewhere and proved to be an enduring form of criminal law that arguably surpasses successor codifications. We now turn to a detailed consideration of these matters, following a deductive rather than an inductive path, from the context to the particulars of the IPC.

HISTORICAL CONSIDERATIONS: THE POLITICAL, POLICY AND LEGAL CONTEXTS

The recent resurgence of historical interest in comparative colonial histories and global networks reflects a shift away from positive and negative generalisations about empire. The latter critical approaches dominated scholarship over the past few decades as many historians turned to previously-neglected local experiences, social and cultural histories from below, specific national narratives and the recovery of subordinated and diverse voices. Very recently, however, there has been cautious retreat from micro-histories and post-colonial paradigms premised on nationalist teleologies. This does not represent a displacement of history from 'below' by history from 'above', the restoration of whiggish imperial narratives that celebrate empire or a reversion to attempts to discern universal truths from comparative history.[22] It recognises particular local circumstances as well as broader networks and developments, including legal matters which were not simply the product of directives from London, but were informed by local struggles and ideas circulating between geographically distant places, facilitated by the inter-colonial migration of political and legal personnel.[23] The IPC is a particularly good example of the wide reach of British legal networks. Our understanding of it can be deepened by comparative histories and reflection about the role of criminal law reform in matters of state development and colonial government.

---

20 Kolsky, above n. 13, at 636–8.

21 W. Twining, 'Imagining Bentham' (1998) 51 *Current Legal Problems* 1, at 22.

22 See, for example, C.A. Bayly, *The Birth of the Modern World, 1780–1914: Global Connections and Comparisons* (London: Blackwell Publishers, 2004); *Imperial Meridian: The British Empire and the World, 1780–1830* (London: Longman, 1989); 'Colonial Rule and the "Informational Order" in South Asia' in N. Crook (ed.), *The Transmission of Knowledge in South Asia: Essays on Education, Religious, History and Politics* (New Delhi: Oxford University Press, 1996); and 'Returning the British to South Asian History: The Limits of Colonial Hegemony' (1994) 17(2) *South Asia* 1. See also P. Duara, *Rescuing History from the Nation* (Chicago: University of Chicago Press, 1995).

23 See, for example, B. Kercher, *An Unruly Child: A History of Law in Australia* (Sydney: Allen & Unwin, 1995); H. Foster, B.L. Berger and A.R. Buck (eds), *The Grand Experiment: Law and Legal Culture in British Settler Societies* (Vancouver: University of British Columbia Press, 2008); J. McLaren, *Dewigged, Bothered and Bewildered: British Colonial Judges on Trial, 1800–1900* (forthcoming, 2011).

Many of the basic political and administrative challenges arising throughout the British Empire in the second quarter of the nineteenth century were latent in the Second Empire that emerged in the wake of the American Revolution. These reflected unresolved tensions between the rule of law and liberties on the one hand and the requirements of sovereignty and state power on the other.[24] C.A. Bayly surveys liberal and utilitarian-inspired administrative reforms which were designed to meet unresolved issues about the constitutional and legal status of colonies, intensified by renewed colonial crises and repressive responses that contradicted formal claims about enlightened British government, constitutionalism and legality (as well as the persisting problem of financing the Empire):

> Viewed in the longer term, though, the 1830s and 1840s still seem to represent a watershed in the style of government both in the colonies and Britain, though it would be naïve to see this simply as a watershed between the *ancien régime* and liberalism. The decline of what some Canadians called 'Pitt's system' and what with justice could also be called 'the Wellesley system' was a long process marked by savage breaks such as the Canadian rebellion of 1837, the Great Famine in Ireland or the Indian Mutiny of 1857.[25]

The largely European settler colonies, beginning with the Canadas, enjoyed increasing responsible and self-government. India became the main laboratory for many of the other innovations in imperial administration.

Bayly also notes that recent scholarship on the rise of the modern state tends to neglect the associated colonial narratives and observes that the emergence of a more unified and effective system, inspired by utilitarianism, through departments such as the Colonial Office, mirrored reforms and were often more marked than domestic initiatives in the metropole.[26] His research focuses on South Asia and utilitarian-inspired informational orders that included surveys, assessments and mapping that helped to regularise revenue collection and facilitated trade with transformative epistemological and conceptual dimensions that helped to promote wider allegiance, compliant identity and public order:

> [B]y the late nineteenth century, most regimes throughout the world were attempting to control closely defined territories by means of uniform administrative, legal, and educational structures … They attempted to abolish the rights ... of special categories of subjects who claimed superior status, or alternatively were condemned to inferior status, under law or government.[27]

Our central concern, of course, is the place of criminal law codification in such colonial modernisation. Elizabeth Kolsky has drawn attention to the significance of criminal law reform and the relevance of codification in India to contemporary debates in England, but notes:

---

24 See J.G.A. Pocock, *The Discovery of Islands: Essays in British History* (Cambridge: Cambridge University Press, 2005), 114–63. Pocock highlights the influence of the late seventeenth-century constitutional compromises, which were celebrated by Macaulay, and the political theories of Hobbes and Locke.

25 Bayly, *Imperial Meridian*, above n. 22, at 237–8.

26 See Bayly, 'Returning the British to South Asian History', above n. 22.

27 Bayly, *The Birth of the Modern World, 1780–1914*, above n. 22, at 247–8.

> Despite these connections, there is a dearth of scholarship on the history of codification and empire and even fewer 'intertwined' histories that place codification in European metropoles and colonial locales in a unitary field of analysis.[28]

Kolsky calls for more scholarship on the legal and political contexts that made codification such a key element of Macaulay's vision of colonial governance,[29] adding that:

> Given that codified laws are extremely vital and potent examples of the lasting power of colonial institutions – most of them remain on the books in South Asia today – the history of codification in colonial India holds critical contemporary relevance.[30]

Indeed, the IPC can be understood as a key reform connected to the modernisation of British colonial rule and a manifestation of concerns about the effectiveness and legitimacy of that rule.

These concerns also reflect the important role of crisis in the nineteenth-century narratives of politics, policy and law reform. Nasser Hussain's examination of the relationship between law and political exigencies of emergency highlights the importance of the experience of nineteenth-century colonial rule in India:

> Indeed, the history of the British colonial state in India, from the very beginning, was shaped by these persistent questions of power and legitimacy ... The ideological justification for the British presence in India drew heavily on a much-vaunted tradition of ancient British liberty and lawfulness ... Government by rules became the basis for the conceptualization of the 'moral legitimacy' of British colonial rule.[31]

Discretionary authority and custom was seen to characterise early colonial and non-European forms of sovereignty, and Hussain quotes Fitzjames Stephen on the importance of promoting the rule of law through colonial law reform:

> The establishment of a system of law which regulates the most important parts of the daily life of the people, constitutes in itself a moral conquest more striking, more durable, and far more solid, than the physical conquest which renders it possible.[32]

R.W. Kostal's study of the Jamaica rebellion and Governor Eyre's controversial response also illustrates how arbitrary responses to colonial public order crises revealed the tensions between sovereignty and the rule of law and, in particular, how they prompted intense debate about the legitimacy of imperial rule amongst the Victorian political classes in London.[33] The Jamaica controversy led the British government to initiate Wright's codification project. As we shall see, while drafted well before the 1857 Indian Mutiny, the IPC was only implemented in its wake. This

---

28 Kolsky, above n. 13, at 632.

29 *Ibid.*, at 635.

30 *Ibid.*, at 638.

31 N. Hussain, *The Jurisprudence of Emergency: Colonialism and the Rule of Law* (Ann Arbor: University of Michigan Press, 2003) 3–4.

32 Hussain, *ibid.*, at 4, quoting from J.F. Stephen's *Minute on the Administration of Justice in British India.*

33 R.W. Kostal, *A Jurisprudence of Power: Victorian Empire and the Rule of Law* (Oxford: Oxford University Press, 2005).

public order crisis helped to make codification a legislative priority, a recurring theme around the drafting or enactment of other nineteenth-century British jurisdiction codes.

Recent historical scholarship on imperial networks helps to illuminate the policy and political contexts of the IPC. Codification was not only a utilitarian-inspired mapping and re-ordering of the criminal law that sought to make it widely known and its administration predictable. It was also meant to displace more arbitrary forms of discretionary authority with a more credible rule of law-based authority and the routine administration of justice. It aimed to enhance the effectiveness of the rule of law in diverse frontier settings and engender greater compliance to British rule and public order, matters that were pressing those colonies where crisis lent urgency to such ambitious legislative projects. The IPC was the first British criminal code, but it was by no means an isolated response. Reformers operated within a global network, and while the codification project failed in England itself, it is to the domestic English criminal law reform debates that we must turn in order to understand the particular legal context of Macaulay's project.

Criminal law codification was a prominent theme in nineteenth-century English law reform debates and its domestic failure marks a curious exception to the general relationship between codes and modern forms of authority. Andrew Amos (the first Chair of English Law at University College London, one of Brougham's original English Law Commissioners and successor to Macaulay as legal representative on India's Legislative Council) ascribed this failure to 'codiphobia', a chauvinistic tendency to see codification as alien to the English legal tradition, which was pronounced amongst leading elements of the bar and bench determined to preserve the common law. Lindsay Farmer deconstructs the conceptual gulf between common law traditionalists, who saw criminal law as primarily about the protection of private interests and an adjunct to private law, and the utilitarian reformers, who saw it as public law governing relations between the state and citizens and an expression of sovereignty that must be explicitly and clearly articulated.[34] He notes that from the broader perspective of political and social theory, notably Max Weber's concept of 'formal legal rationality', the failure of codification illustrates the 'peculiarities of the English' and the common law exception that persisted in the face of the typical legal forms of modernity.[35] As Farmer observes, and Michael Lobban and K.J.M. Smith also suggest, the dismissal of codification as alien to the English legal tradition (its proponents portrayed as foreigners or philosophical radical interlopers unversed in the common law) neglects its prominence in nineteenth-century English criminal law reform debates.[36] It is also myopic, failing to account for codes enacted in other British common law jurisdictions.

Bentham developed the term 'codification' to describe his ambitious legislative agenda and radical break from the common law tradition. William Blackstone's *Commentaries*, an Enlightenment-inspired attempt to lend rational order to the common law,[37] were described as 'a

34 L. Farmer, 'Reconstructing the English Codification Debate: The Criminal Law Commissioners, 1833–45' (2000) 18 *Law and History Review* 397, 400.

35 See Farmer, *ibid.* See also, for example, C. Varga (J. Payne trans.), *Codification as a Socio-Historical Phenomena* (Budapest: Akademici Kiado, 1991) and H.J. Berman and C.J. Reid, 'Max Weber as Legal Historian' in S. Turner (ed.), *The Cambridge Companion to Weber* (New York: Cambridge University Press, 2000) 32. The common law exception is attributed in part to the late seventeenth-century British constitutional compromises which constrained repressive powers, removing one of the incentives behind the modern European criminal codes.

36 Farmer, above n. 34; M. Lobban, *The Common Law and English Jurisprudence, 1760–1850* (Oxford: Clarendon Press, 1991); K.J.M. Smith, *Lawyers, Legislators and Theorists: Developments in English Criminal Jurisprudence, 1800–1957* (Oxford: Clarendon Press, 1998).

37 W. Blackstone, *Commentaries on the Laws of England* (Oxford: Clarendon Press, 1765–9).

work of light in comparison with the darkness which previously covered the whole face of the Law'[38] but, despite the advance in the technical arrangement of English law, Bentham dismissed his former teacher's work as 'an elegant palliative to the inherently chronic confusion of the common law'.[39] The common law was beyond the reach of rational reform, its arcane nature and needless complexities the invariable result of random cases and self-serving judges. Bentham's ambitious *pannomion*, composed of civil, penal and constitutional codes, aimed for nothing less than the comprehensive regulation of all social relationships and sovereign power, with the legislator occupying a position analogous to the 'gaze' of his *panopticon*.[40]

The criminal code occupied much of Bentham's attention because it involved matters of vital public policy, liberties and individual happiness, and was the area of law in the most urgent need of reform. It was the most commonplace reflection of the exercise of state power and involved the deliberate infliction of harm. Such important matters could not be entrusted to the courts but were properly a matter for Parliament and systematic legislative action. Bentham's 'science of legislation', as set out in his *An Introduction to the Principles of Morals and Legislation*,[41] called for legislative reformulation informed by the rational principles of utility and the objective of deterrence. His exhaustive taxonomy of criminal harms, prohibitions and penalties took the rationalising spirit of the Enlightenment much further than Blackstone. The entirety of the criminal law was to be mapped out and categorised, all offences, forms of liability and defences were to be set out so that there would be no *terra incognitae*, and the law was to be expressed so clearly that an average person would understand it and the average judge would be unable to claim not to.

While codification remained central to Bentham's thinking, he never completed a working code (despite offers to draft for various countries) and he came to recognise the complex practical challenges.[42] He remained estranged from the dominant figures of the legal profession who saw the common law as the essence of the English legal culture and their identity.[43] The sweeping institutional changes to the administration of English criminal law that gained momentum in the 1820s and the decades that followed (the introduction of the new police, the 'professionalisation' of the criminal trial and the emergence of the penitentiary as the primary site of punishment)

---

38 J. Bentham, 'View of a Complete Code of Laws' in Bowring, above n. 1, vol. 3, 163. In addition to numerous references to codification in the Bowring edition of his *Works*, see J. Bentham, *A Comment on the Commentaries and a Fragment on Government* (J.H. Burns and H.L.A. Hart, eds) (London: Athlone Press, 1977) and *An Introduction to the Principles of Morals and Legislation* (J.H. Burns and H.L.A. Hart, eds) (London: Athlone Press, 1970).

39 Quoted in Smith, above n. 36, at 11. See Smith's discussion at 9–12 for a succinct summary of debates around the reform of substantive criminal law doctrine; see also R. Cross, 'Blackstone v. Bentham' (1976) 92 *Law Quarterly Review* 516; S.F.C. Milsom, 'The Nature of Blackstone's Achievement' (1981) 1 *Oxford Journal of Legal Studies* 1; D. Kennedy, 'The Structure of Blackstone's Commentaries' (1978–9) 28 *Buffalo Law Review* 205; H.L.A. Hart, *Essays on Bentham: Studies in Jurisprudence and Political Theory* (Oxford: Clarendon Press, 1982) Chapter 1 ('The Demystification of Law').

40 Smith, *ibid.*, at 20, 28–9; Farmer, above n. 34, at 423.

41 Above n. 38.

42 While the *pannomion* aspired to be a deductive code, Bentham himself struggled with the tensions in the inevitability of inductive reasoning and juridical application of the law – see Lobban, above n. 36, at 120–55. Codification is a prominent theme in Bentham's published work (see above n. 38) and outlines and unfinished drafts are scattered though his unpublished work from c. 1780–1826. He offered to draft codes for officials in America (twice approaching President Madison and writing to most state governors), France and Russia.

43 There were few lawyers in Bentham's circle of disciples, although he received an honorary call at Lincoln's Inn in 1817, where Macaulay was soon to become a member.

were influenced by a number of factors.[44] Institutional and administrative transformations were not matched by changes to the criminal law, although there was much debate about the need to rationalise the criminal law. Yet, as Vesey-Fitzgerald observed:

> ... arid and remote from reality though much of his much more abstract thinking is, it would be a grave mistake to underestimate its importance ... it was Bentham's particular merit that he taught lawyers – at any rate lawyers of the high quality who framed the Indian Codes – to think always of the law as a symmetrical and logical whole and of the law not merely as it is but as it ought to be; to dissect every idea; to base themselves always on first principles and to ask of every rule, 'what useful purpose does this serve?' He also inculcated a simplicity of language which he himself sometimes failed to maintain.[45]

Colonial settings experienced the most dramatic reforms to the criminal law and it was Macaulay who came closest to implementing Bentham's codifying ideas in practice.

Before turning to colonial codification successes, it should be noted that the domestic project was a near-success. There was some consensus on the need to rationalise English criminal law, with proposals ranging from cautious 'consolidations' (reducing existing criminal law legislation from numerous statutes to one) to more ambitious 'digests' (attempts to present the law, including common law, in an organised fashion), to 'codes' that aimed for a more systematic reorganisation that abrogated common law elements but fell short of the Benthamite conception of full elimination of the common law and reform according to exclusively utilitarian premises. Robert Peel's consolidation acts of 1827–32 repealed or modernised hundreds of obsolete statutes and scaled back the death penalty from over 200 to a dozen offences. Brougham, appointed Lord Chancellor after the fall of Wellington's government, launched a criminal law commission in 1833 mandated to produce a single digest of criminal statutes, and one of common law, and to consider combining both. But Lord Chief Justice Ellenborough's implacable defence of judicial powers had already set the tone for conservative elements of the English bar and bench, and the common law cause was reinforced by the emergence of law as an academic discipline and procedural reforms.[46] The criminal law commissioners became increasingly divided and eight commission reports culminated in a combined digest presented to an unreceptive government in 1845, followed by more reports and failed bills. Judicial opposition frustrated attempts to restart the project after the early 1850s and Charles Greaves's 1861 consolidation merely updated Peel's reforms.[47]

Smith notes the close connections between the mid-nineteenth-century English reformers and the successors to Macaulay in India, beginning with Amos, who was uncomfortable with Macaulay's draft. Positivist legal theorists in general, anxious to play a role in emerging legal

---

44 Bentham's influence on English reforms is much debated – see, for example, S.E. Finer, 'The Transmission of Benthamite Ideas, 1826–1839' in G. Sutherland (ed.), *Studies in the Growth of Nineteenth-Century Government* (London: Routledge & Kegan Paul Ltd, 1972); H. Beynon, 'Mighty Bentham' (1981) 2 *Journal of Legal History* 62. For an overview of the institutional transformations, see R. McGowen, 'The Image of Justice and Reform of the Criminal Law in Early Nineteenth-Century England' (1983) 32 *Buffalo Law Review* 89.

45 Vesey-Fitzgerald, above n. 13, at 231–2.

46 See Smith, above n. 36, at 361, 364. James Mackintosh's 1819 Committee, which paved the way for Peel's consolidations, avoided the judges, but they were routinely consulted on subsequent criminal law reforms (Smith, above n. 36, at 56–63).

47 See Smith, *ibid.*, at 136–8; Farmer, above n. 34, at 404–5; M. Lobban, 'How Benthamatic was the Criminal Law Commission?' (2000) 18 *Law and History Review* 427.

scholarship, moderated Bentham's ideas and sought to render them less threatening to the legal profession. Twining observes:

> The story of the displacement of Bentham by Austin as the Father of English Jurisprudence has often been sketched, but the puzzle remains: Why this extraordinary misjudgement ... none makes the case for treating Austin as being a thinker of comparable stature in respect of originality, penetration, breadth, or even readability. The most that can be said for him was that he took analysis of fundamental legal conceptions a bit further, he was more sympathetic to the common law than Bentham, and his simplemindeness was more congenial to practitioners ... and the first generation of scholar-teachers of law ...[48]

James Fitzjames Stephen made a rather more constructive contribution and authored the final nineteenth-century attempt to codify English criminal law which, like the IPC, proved influential in other jurisdictions. As we have seen, Stephen praised Macaulay's efforts, although he was much more sympathetic to the common law than Bentham and Macaulay. A conservative utilitarian, he favoured pragmatism to conceptual abstraction and accepted judicial discretion as useful and inevitable.[49] His 1878 draft English Code set out indictable offences but left defences to the common law, and the minimal general part did not attempt to define liability. Stephen's Code went to a commission and was converted into a bill the following year, but the government fell just after its introduction in 1880. Stephen's middle course satisfied neither the progressive codifiers nor the defenders of the common law, Lord Chief Justice Cockburn declaring disingenuously that the proposal was inconsistent with the idea of codification and that no code was better than a half-baked one.[50]

The defeat of Stephen's Code ended the best prospects for codification in England (the discouraging recent experience in England and Wales is fully described by Chris Clarkson in Chapter 14 of this volume), but the prospects were better in other British jurisdictions. The utilitarian reformers were relatively influential in the Colonial Office and its related departments, there were fewer professional and judicial obstacles overseas, and local crises made such big projects more of a legislative priority. In the British jurisdictions that enjoyed increasing responsible government and self-government, codification was also attractive as a measure that would help to modernise authority and make the rule of law more effective in new settings. Stephen's code became the main reference for the first wave of these latter 'self-governing' jurisdiction codifications, beginning with Canada in 1892.[51]

---

48 W. Twining, 'Reading Bentham' (The Maccabean Lecture in Jurisprudence 1989) 75 *Proceedings of the British Academy* 97 at 138.

49 See Stephen, above n. 13, at 347–52, where he summarises his approach following a careful review of the IPC and Cockburn's critique of the Draft English Code. See also Smith, *James Fitzjames Stephen: Portrait of a Victorian Rationalist*, above n. 19.

50 Smith, above n. 36, at 143–50. As Smith also notes (at 81–2), there were Home Office and Lord Chancellor's office reservations, the profession was contending with new procedures introduced by the Judicature Acts and there was little appetite for reforms on the scale of a criminal code.

51 For a succinct survey, see M.L. Friedland, 'Codification in the Commonwealth: Earlier Efforts' (1990) 2 *Criminal Law Forum* 145. For further exploration of the themes introduced in this section in the context of the Canadian, New Zealand and Queensland Criminal Codes, see B. Wright, 'Criminal Law Codification and Imperial Projects: The Self-Governing Jurisdiction Codes of the 1890's' (2008) 12 *Legal History* 19.

Mill's Charter Act and Macaulay's embrace of 'enlightened despotism' marked the growing influence of utilitarianism on imperial policy, although it was far from a policy coup.[52] When Macaulay began work on the IPC, he boasted that he was cooking up something that would make 'old Bentham' jump from his grave.[53] However, resident Europeans in India resisted the idea of having the same legal status as local indigenous populations, and conflicting colonial politics and policies nearly derailed the project. As for the IPC's immediate influence elsewhere, despite Macaulay's hopes, echoed by figures such as John Stuart Mill, the first code in the British Empire was dismissed by much of the English profession as suitable only for backward overseas colonies where the prevailing attitude was that 'it was necessary to keep things simple for the native population and magistrates of limited ability'.[54] The Colonial Office attempted to promote the IPC as a means to make English law more effective in other foreign settings and curb abuses of justice and over-reliance on costly military responses,[55] and it was adopted in Ceylon, the Straits Settlements and some African colonies.[56] The 1865 Jamaican uprising and the controversy concerning the legality of Governor Eyre's repressive response, noted earlier, prompted the Colonial Office to commission Wright to revise and update the IPC for that colony.[57] The Jamaica Code was introduced in 1877, but was not enacted. It was adopted elsewhere in the West Indies, and displaced the IPC as an influence until a new Colonial Office model code was produced in 1925.[58] Wright's efforts on the Jamaica Code were criticised by Stephen as he began work on his own code project for the Lord Chancellor's office.[59]

There are similarities as well as differences between the 'imposed imperial' codes and those of the self-governing jurisdictions of Canada, New Zealand and Queensland which essentially combined local consolidations with Stephen's draft English Code. The similarities related to local challenges and colonial legacies that lent momentum to codification. If English criminal law, especially pre-consolidation, was complex, the criminal law in established British colonial settings was even more so. Before the IPC, the applicable criminal laws in India included Muslim (Bengal, Madras and other parts of the north, east and south) and Hindu laws (Bombay), overlaid with East India Company regulations. European residents were governed by received English laws and the 1773 Regulating Act (13 Geo. III c. 63) established a Supreme Court in Calcutta and confirmed that English criminal law in effect in 1726 was binding on all Calcutta residents and European

52 Utilitarian policy did not entirely displace orientalism, which enjoyed a resurgence in the late nineteenth century, and policy integrity was compromised by military and commercial pressures – see, for example, Stokes, above n. 3; and R. Cross, 'The Making of English Criminal Law: (5) Macaulay' [1978] *Criminal Law Review* 519.

53 Macaulay to Ellis, 3 June 1835: see Pinney, above n. 5, at 146.

54 G. Parker, 'The Origins of the Canadian Criminal Code' in D.H. Flaherty (ed.), *Essays in the History of Canadian Law* (vol. 1) (Toronto: University of Toronto Press, 1981) 251.

55 See references to the IPC in Colonial Office circulars: for example, 'Some Considerations Preliminary to the Preparation of a Penal Code for the Crown Colonies' and Sir Henry Taylor's Benthamite treatise, 'Subjects Affecting Colonies Generally, Confidential Print', 20 May 1870, National Archives (UK) (formerly PRO) CO 885/3/19. Taylor's treatise was later appended (August 1877) to R.S. Wright's draft of the Jamaica Code: see M.L. Friedland, 'R.S. Wright's Model Criminal Code: A Forgotten Chapter in the History of the Criminal Law' (1981) 1 *Oxford Journal of Legal Studies* 307.

56 See Phang, above n. 18 from p. 57 onwards for the legislative history in Malaysia and Singapore.

57 See Friedland, above n. 55. Wright's update of Macaulay included definitions of liability, but he proposed not using examples as found in the IPC.

58 After a false start on a replacement for Wright by J.F. Stephen's son Henry, Samuel Griffith's 1899 Queensland Code was widely used as a model and it was a primary influence on Albert Ehrhardt's 1925 effort: see R.S. O'Regan, 'Sir Samuel Griffith's Criminal Code' (1991) 7 *Australian Bar Review* 141.

59 Smith, above n. 36, at 151–2.

residents throughout India. This received English law was amended in 1828 when 9 Geo. IV c. 74 introduced some of Peel's consolidations.[60] The Charter Act 1833 set the scene for a uniform system applicable to all inhabitants throughout India, but the complexities remained until the IPC's enactment. While the emerging self-governing jurisdictions were largely populated by British settlers and there tended to be little or no treaty recognition of indigenous laws, the applicable criminal laws were also complex. English criminal law was formally received at different dates and the received laws were subsequently amended by diverse local legislation. The situation was further complicated by the emergence of new colonies out of the territories of older ones (such as Upper Canada from Quebec, New Brunswick from Nova Scotia, and Victoria and Queensland from New South Wales) and by the opposite process of colonial union, such as that of Upper and Lower Canada in 1840. The latter prefaced the larger challenge faced by the Dominion of Canada in 1867 which, unlike the Commonwealth of Australia in 1901, assumed jurisdiction over criminal law and faced the immense task of reconciling the diverse criminal laws of the British North American colonies, each with different reception dates and subsequent local amendments.[61]

Local consolidations had simplified the accumulated layers of law in the self-governing jurisdictions and codification seemed a logical and compelling next step. Unlike England, it was a reform which tended to have wide professional support. The local bar and bench were relatively distant from the culture of the common law. Formidable practical challenges were faced accessing the sources of law, and the idea of a complete, succinct and portable *compendium* of law was appealing.[62] Local receptiveness to codification was also enhanced by colonial experience with executive influence over local government and the administration of justice. Abuses of colonial executive powers and partisan uses of the law to fend off challenges and maintain the authority of local elites conflicted with expectations of the British constitution and legality. These experiences informed local struggles for criminal law reform as well as responsible government.[63] Post-colonial receptiveness to codification was therefore enhanced by the perceived need to simplify the law and make it more accessible, and greater professional receptivity, as well as a recognition that it could serve as a constraint on state power. Codification was associated with self-government, greater autonomy and Smith observes that codification had symbolic national unity connotations in many nineteenth-century codifying jurisdictions.[64] Such experiences and aspirations generated

60 Stephen, above n. 13, at 290–94. See also Setalvad, above n. 13, at 118–22.

61 The informal reception of English law, determinations of the reasonable applicability of English law according to local circumstances and the legal status of residents depended on imperial instructions and colonial executive discretion (see, e.g., *Calvin's Case* (1608) 7 Co Rep 1a, 77 ER 377). English law came into fuller formal effect with the development of representative legislative institutions and colonial courts, with those English laws then in effect usually serving as the foundation of that jurisdiction's law. Local legislatures and courts were empowered to amend these laws as conditions required, subject to imperial supervision. The situation was more complex where there were treaties or where elements of pre-existing legal systems were kept.

62 Local judges, unlike those on the English bench, were among the strongest proponents of codification. Professional attitudes were shaped in significant part by the difficulties of access to relevant statutes and legal texts. Institutional holdings were limited. See D.H. Brown, *The Genesis of the Canadian Criminal Code of 1892* (Toronto: University of Toronto Press, 1989) 42, 71.

63 Judicial independence was compromised by colonial judges holding office according to royal pleasure rather than good behaviour as determined by Parliament, as well as by frequent reliance on *extra-judicial* opinions and the practice of appointing chief justices to colonial executive and legislative councils. Colonial Crown law officers relied heavily on controversial prosecutorial prerogatives, and trial by jury was typically compromised or non-existent.

64 Smith, above n. 36, at 83–4.

constitutional momentum lacking in England itself where, as Farmer notes, debate focused on the effectiveness of the criminal law rather than how a code might regulate state power.[65]

At the same time, these jurisdictions were not receptive to Colonial Office encouragement of codes written by British imperial administrators that involved little local input. Such colonialist baggage did not burden Stephen's draft English Code and his modest and pragmatic approach was loose enough in conception to be easily combined with local consolidations. Local developments could be accommodated rather than rejected in favour of a purer Benthamite conception. Stephen was embraced by the drafters of the Canadian, New Zealand and Queensland Codes as their primary external reference.[66] While they represented a distinct trajectory of codification from the imposed imperial efforts of Macaulay and Wright, they were informed by the same English law reform debates. The reduction of discretionary authority and enhancing the effectiveness of the rule of law in culturally diverse frontier settings were important common aims. Crisis also appears to have lent urgency to the large, time-consuming self-governing legislative projects, as it did in the case of the IPC's enactment and the drafting of the Jamaica Code.[67]

THE DRAFTING AND IMPLEMENTATION OF THE IPC

Macaulay arrived in India in the summer of 1834 as legal representative on the Legislative Council and President of the Committee of Public Instruction. The appointment of a specialised law commission to examine a uniform system of law was envisaged by s. 53 of the Charter Act 1833 and James Mill's December 1834 despatch on its implementation. Acting Governor General Metcalfe and his legislative council, guided by Macaulay, created a law commission in May 1835. The council authorised the IPC in principle the following month, and it was at this time that Macaulay wrote: 'I have immense reforms in hand ... such as would make old Bentham jump in his grave'[68] (or, to be more accurate, Bentham's *auto-ikon* would cackle from its perch at University College London). Macaulay's commission presented an initial draft of the IPC to Governor General Auckland in May 1837 and a complete version to his council in October 1837.

Macaulay moved quickly on a range of other law reforms before this. He led the council's passage of the Press Act 1835, which ended prior restraint of the press and censorship by licensing, and Act XI, 1836 (sometimes called the 'Black Act'), which abrogated the special privileges of British residents on matters of civil jurisdiction and appeals, provoking decades of European

---

65 Farmer, above n. 34, at 423–4.

66 Most of Stephen's legislative renderings of the common law were adopted, but in most cases of legislated provisions, local consolidations were favoured over his renderings of English versions. Conceptually, Stephen's narrow approach to codification and retention of the common law for liability and defences characterise the original Canadian and New Zealand Codes, and while most of Griffith's external references are to Stephen, his comprehensive approach, inspired by Zanardelli's 1889 Italian Code, resembled the IPC: see Wright, above n. 51.

67 Canada's Code was spurred on by the 1885 North West Rebellion and that of New Zealand by a government contending with growing resistance to Maori land confiscations and indefinite detentions in 1883. The New Zealand draft preceded Canada, but legislative difficulties delayed enactment to 1893, a year after Canada. Queensland's Code was prefaced by a general strike, the emergence of the Labour Party and perceived threats to local politics, as well as the federation project in which Samuel Griffith had played an important role: see Wright, *ibid.*

68 Macaulay to Thomas Flower Ellis, 3 June 1835: see Pinney, above n. 5, at 146. See also Clive, above n. 5, at 429–30.

resistance to procedural reforms that culminated in the Ilbert Bill controversy of 1883.[69] These advances were accompanied by Macaulay's decisive interventions into education, but the IPC was by far his biggest project.

Macaulay's law commission colleagues (whom he regarded as an uneven group that included Charles Hay Cameron, successor to Macaulay and Amos as legal member of the council, John Macleod, who worked tirelessly to keep the IPC draft alive, G.W. Anderson and Frederick Millet as Secretary) were informed that their broad objective was comprehensive codification not only of criminal law, but also of criminal procedure and civil rights and civil procedure as envisaged by Mill and Bentham. Their immediate mandate, however, was criminal law reform as authorised by Metcalfe's council, where Macaulay noted that the subject had been the primary focus of reformers since Beccaria, the subject of extensive scholarly scrutiny and commentary, and the focus of statesmen from Peel to Brougham. Reforms in the sphere of criminal jurisdiction had commercial import and were necessary for the promotion of trade. Macaulay informed his commissioners that the council anticipated something more than a mere consolidation or digest. A code was envisaged and Macaulay expressed his originating principles, noted earlier. The code should cover all contingencies and be informed by the simple aims of suppressing crime with the least infliction of suffering and ascertaining truth at the smallest possible cost of time and money. Terminology and language should aim to be clear, unequivocal and concise, with every criminal act separately defined, the terms followed for all indictments with the accused's actions falling within them, and there were to be no special exceptions (for example, for races or sects) without clear and strong reasons.[70] These instructions were formally approved by the council on 15 June 1835 and formed the commission's terms of reference.

Dissent had been expressed in council on the grounds that the Charter Act 1833 had merely envisaged a commission to enquire into and report on the state of existing laws, not devise a code. Opposition to Macaulay's project grew, particularly on the part of English residents and the bar in Calcutta, sparked by the Black Act. Difficulties were created in London over the Press Act by John Cam Hobhouse, President of the Board of Control, who advised Melbourne on Metcalfe's replacement, Auckland.[71] Macaulay was increasingly vilified in the press and avoided by the British community in Calcutta, but his ambitious project proceeded according to the council's original instructions. Macaulay wrote that the project 'is indeed one of the finest employments of the intellect' and expressed optimism that it would be completed by the commission in a few months. He wrote to James Mill expressing hope that the project would inspire the stalled codification project in England itself.[72] In early 1836 Macaulay reassured Hobhouse that progress was being made and that he had won the support for the project from two of the three judges of the Calcutta Supreme Court.[73]

Macaulay was overly sanguine. The other commissioners then fell sick, becoming inactive through the summer and autumn of 1836, and the entire burden of drafting fell to Macaulay. He wrote numerous chapters alone and revised all other parts already completed with his fellow

---

69 Clive, *ibid.*, 323. See below at n. 89; see also Kolsky, above n. 13, for resistance to equal legal status, from the Black Act to the Ilbert Bill controversy in 1883.

70 See Minute 4 June 1835, above n. 15; Clive, *ibid.*, at 436–7; Stokes, above n. 3, at 220–22; Smith, above n. 2, at 149–50.

71 See Clive, *ibid.*, at 323.

72 Macaulay to Ellis, 25 August 1835: see Pinney, above n. 5, at 152–3; Macaulay to James Mill, 24 August 1835: see Pinney, *ibid.*, at 146–51.

73 Clive, above n. 5, at 439.

commissioners. Responding to critics who suggested he was delaying, he observed in a Minute to Governor General Auckland at the beginning of 1837:

> ... when I remember the slow progress of law reforms at home and when I consider that our Code decides hundreds of questions ... every one of which if stirred in England would give occasion to voluminous controversy and to many animated debates, I must acknowledge that I am inclined to fear that we have been guilty rather of precipitation than of delay.[74]

The law commission submitted a complete draft to Auckland on 2 May and the final printed draft, in a slightly revised form, was submitted along with the commissioners' final report on 14 October.[75] The report emphasised that the code was more than a digest of existing laws, that the provisions aimed to be comprehensive (but acknowledged that there could be omissions), containing the whole of the law with precise definitions, enacting clauses and punishments. The provisions were accompanied by illustrations to fully convey their meaning as well as explanatory notes.

Macaulay confided that his code might appear ill-done in places when looked at by itself, but it was a huge advance on existing criminal laws, including Peel's recent consolidating and amending legislation, and was superior to the Portalis and Livingston codes.[76] He was anxious to return to England and had little to do with the expatriate community. He wrote a letter of resignation to Hobhouse in April 1837, who in turn told Auckland that while Macaulay's achievements were impressive, his successor should be less difficult and more capable of conciliation.[77] The IPC became something of a political football for legal theorists and policy-makers as it encountered what Smith calls 'the great dead weight power of governmental and administrative inertia'.[78]

Auckland wrote to Hobhouse in the summer of 1838, detailing objections from the bar and bench in Madras and missionaries, who drafted a memorial against provisions prohibiting interference with religious freedom.[79] Auckland delayed the wider circulation of the IPC to judicial and administrative branches until late 1839 and Macaulay's successor Amos, preoccupied with maintaining his influence in council, neglected the law commission.[80] Macaulay returned home to a senior appointment as Secretary of State for War and Colonies, but he was on the margins of the new Whig political elite and was regarded as too eccentric for future political prominence.[81] His interests turned to literature and history, reignited by his work on Bacon in India.[82]

---

74 Quoted in Clive, *ibid.*, at 440.

75 See *ibid.*

76 Macaulay to Ellis, 8 March 1837: see Pinney, above n. 5, at 210–12. See n. 93 below on the French and draft Louisiana Codes.

77 Macaulay to Hobhouse, 17 April 1837: Pinney, *ibid.*, at 213–14; Macaulay to Governor General in Council, 1 May 1837: see Pinney, *ibid.*, at 214; Clive, above n. 5, at 462.

78 Smith, above n. 2, at 160.

79 Clive, above n. 5, at 463.

80 Dhagamwar, above n. 13, 77–85. Sornarajah, above n. 19, cxxxii at note 24. Amos was one of Brougham's English Law Commissioners and this may have contributed to his ambivalence.

81 This prestigious appointment, passed from Lords Glenelg and Normanby, came with an onerous file on the aftermath of the Canadian rebellions, which had entailed a commitment of British troops that was only exceeded in the next quarter-century by the Indian Mutiny, numerous legal complications and Lord Durham's famous report on colonial responsible and self-government. James Stephen was appointed Permanent Under-Secretary in 1836 (after serving since 1814 as legal counsel for the Colonial Office).

82 See Clive, above n. 5, at 467.

John Stuart Mill praised the IPC in the *Westminster Review*, echoing Macaulay's hope, as Kolsky puts it, 'that modernity in the colony would "re-act" upon the metropole',[83] and downplayed criticisms which came mostly from those aggrieved about the ending of special privileges but, as we have seen, it was also roundly dismissed by the conservative English legal profession. The *Law Times* obituary for Macaulay (7 January 1860), quoted in the preface of this volume,[84] revealed the depth of professional hostility to such ambitious codes.

Amos had submitted the IPC for detailed comments to all the Supreme Court judges in Bombay, Madras and Calcutta and other experts. These were collected by the commissioners, notably Macleod. Ellenborough, Auckland's successor in 1842 (recalled in 1844), also had little interest in reform, held the council's law representative and the law commission in lower regard, and was preoccupied with the Afghan wars and battling Company directors. His successor, Hardinge, revived the IPC project by requesting a report from the commissioners.[85] Charles Hay Cameron (Amos's successor) and commissioner Daniel Elliot eventually issued lengthy reports (First Report, 1846; Second Report, 1847) that summarised criticisms and recommended enactment. Macleod, in consultation with Macaulay, published *Notes on the Report of the Indian Law Commissioners on the Indian Penal Code* in London in 1848.[86] Dalhousie replaced Hardinge as Governor General and Cameron as law councillor by an old acquaintance of Macaulay's, Drinkwater Bethune, who nearly became the IPC's nemesis.

The status of the IPC remained in limbo until 1851 when it was again proposed that the Black Act's civil procedural changes (later consolidated in the Civil Procedure Act 1859) be extended to criminal cases and Dalhousie realised that this could not proceed until a new uniform criminal code was enacted. Macleod testified at length in favour of the IPC the following year to a House of Lords Select Committee on India.[87] In the meantime, Bethune made wide-ranging criticisms of the IPC in Dalhousie's Legislative Council, in particular objecting to Macaulay's illustrations and language, unknown to English lawyers, where essential terms with settled meaning in English law were set aside in favour of innovations that reflected 'a mere love of singularity which ought not to be indulged'.[88] Bethune drafted his own code as a substitute, and Dalhousie sent it to London requesting a choice be made between it and Macaulay's IPC. Sir Charles Wood, President of the Board of Control, had no preference and a Parliamentary Commission was charged with making a definitive recommendation. The IPC was endorsed and Bethune's capable successor, Sir Barnes Peacock, spent the following six years on detailed revisions and shepherding it through the Council. Work on the bill gained momentum and urgency in the wake of the Indian Mutiny in 1857–8 and revisions were finalised by the Legislative Council in 1858. The IPC was enacted as Act XLV in October 1860, under Canning as the first Viceroy of India, to come into force on 1 January 1862.[89]

83 Kolsky, above n. 13, at 633.

84 At ix.

85 See Dhagamwar, above n. 13, at 75–91 for a succinct and more complete account of relations between the Governors General, the law members of council and the law commissioners.

86 Clive, above n. 5, at 464.

87 Select Committee of the House of Lords on Operation of the Act for the Better Government of Her Majesty's Indian Territories, Parliamentary Papers XXX (1852–3), Macleod testimony 2 December 1852.

88 Clive, above n. 5, at 464.

89 See Stephen, above n. 13, at 299–300 for a concise description of the political and legislative forces around implementation; see also Smith, above n. 49, at 126–31, Stokes, above n. 3, at 262; and Dhagamwar, above n. 13, from 91 onwards. The enacted IPC was delayed by criminal procedure legislation (Act XXV, 1861 amended by Act X, 1872), retrograde steps that compromised Macaulay's premises of equal legal status. European residents were not to be subject to legal processes before Indian judges and magistrates. The IPC

The IPC project was delayed by governmental and legislative inertia, resistance by European residents to having the same legal status as indigenous populations and the loss of reforming momentum in the metropole, as professional resistance to ambitious legislative projects that threatened the common law solidified and positivist legal scholars distanced themselves from Bentham's legacy. The project was kept alive most notably by John Macleod, who stoutly defended and steered it through the complex vicissitudes of Indian public affairs until events of 1857–8 focused the political and legislative mind.[90] The Mutiny restored the IPC as a legislative priority, as Stephen recognised:

> Then came the Mutiny which in its essence was the breakdown of the old system ... The effect of the Mutiny on the Statute Book was unmistakeable ... The credit of passing the Penal Code into law, and of giving to every part of it the improvements which practical skill and technical knowledge could bestow is due to Sir Barnes Peacock, who held Macaulay's place during the most anxious years through which the Indian Empire has passed.[91]

The Governor General was mocked as 'clemency Canning' for restraint after the Cawnpore massacre of English civilians, but both the revolt and its suppression were bloody indeed. Resorts to martial law (Guyana or Demerara, 1824; Quebec, 1838; and Ceylon, 1848) and to the courts martial of civilians (Ireland, 1798–1800; and the Canadas, 1838–9) had become increasing controversial for the English political classes, who saw the legitimacy of British rule, founded on claims of constitutionalism and the rule of law, undermined by such repressive responses. Enactment helped to address these concerns and, it was hoped, would minimise the need to resort to such expedients to restore public order and uphold British rule.

OUTLINE OF THE IPC: ASSESSMENT OF PROVISIONS AND INNOVATIONS

Macaulay's IPC draft is divided into three parts. The provisions define offences succinctly and precisely, with consistent liability standards and maximum punishments. They are accompanied by *Examples* that illustrate the application of the provisions to hypothetical cases, serving as authoritative precedents set by legislators rather than judges. Finally, explanatory *Notes*, referred to when the IPC was revised by Peacock but dropped from the enacted Code, succinctly criticise existing English laws and discuss the influences and conceptual features of key provisions.

The commission's 1837 report emphasised that the Code was not based on any existing laws: '[T]he system of penal law which we propose is not a digest of any existing system; and ... no existing system had furnished us even with a groundwork.'[92] The provisions were to replace all existing criminal laws and were to apply to all persons under British administration. Macaulay was consistently emphatic about his primary debt to Bentham and the explanatory *Notes* reflect sustained criticism of existing English laws from this perspective with only occasional reference

---

was further supplemented by Fitzjames Stephen's Evidence Act 1872, whose predecessor Henry Maine, law member from 1862 to 1869, expressed reservations about the Benthamite hue of the legislation, observing that 'nobody cares about criminal law except theorists and habitual criminals' (quoted in Smith, *ibid.*, at 127). Courtney Ilbert's attempt to curb the procedural discrimination and return to Macaulay's aim of uniform jurisdiction helped spark the 'white mutiny' of 1883: see Kolsky, above n. 13, at 673–82.

90 Clive, above n. 5, at 463.

91 Quoted in Setalvad, above n. 13, at 124.

92 Letter from the Indian Law Commissioners 2 May 1837, quoted in Stokes, above n. 3, at 227.

to Peel's consolidations and the Portalis and Livingston Codes.[93] Macaulay had no reverence for the common law or associated professional loyalties, observing as he started the IPC: 'I ought however to tell you that the more progress I make as a legislator the more intense my contempt for the mere technical study of law becomes.'[94] But, as we noted previously, Bentham never drafted a code, despite the centrality of codification to his reform agenda. He acknowledged that the constraints of language were such that concise codes would need to be accompanied by a detailed explanation of the importance of provisions. He also recognised the tension between inductive and deductive logics, and admitted that the articulation of general principles and the application of rules in myriad real situations would invariably involve some judicial discretion.[95] Macaulay and his commissioners were obliged to confront these practical challenges directly and, in doing so, they made pragmatic compromises between Bentham's legislative prescriptions and substantive doctrines derived from familiar English laws.

The focus in much of the existing scholarship on the IPC is about characterisation, whether it was a true reflection of Bentham's aspirations for comprehensive, scientific legislation and a universal jurisprudence or simply updated English law adjusted to the circumstances of India. Bentham's influence tends to be downplayed in the older commentary and there is some sloppy dismissal of the IPC as the work of a non-lawyer, a confusion of Macaulay's views as a historian and law reformer, and a failure to distinguish between Macaulay's draft Code and the enacted IPC. Some of this is influenced by the nineteenth-century climate of professional reaction against Bentham's scathing attack on the common law and positivist theorists distancing themselves from Bentham's legacy. The more careful older assessments, by commentators such as Whitley-Stokes, Rankin, Vesey-Fitzgerald and Setalvad, tend to endorse Fitzjames Stephen's characterisation of the IPC as 'the criminal law of England free from all technicalities and superfluities, systematically arranged and modified ... to suit the circumstances of British India'. As Setalvad puts it:

> It appears that Macaulay and his colleagues, striving all the time to keep away from the established systems of criminal law, and particularly the English system, so that they might arrive at a result truly suited to India's needs, travelled unconsciously but inevitably along the track of principles in which they had been trained and to which they were accustomed.[96]

---

93 Stokes, *ibid.*, at 226. The 1810 French *Code Penal* derived from the revolutionary 1791 codification, much modified primarily by Jean-Etienne-Marie Portalis. Although described as a 'utilitarian' code, there was only minor reference to Bentham during the legislative processes: see M. Morin, 'Portalis v. Bentham? The Objectives Pursued by the Codification of the Civil and Criminal Law in France, England, and Canada' (Ottawa: Law Commission of Canada, 2000) at 139–217 (available online at http://hdl.handle.net/1866/1468, last accessed 7 February 2011). Edward Livingston, influenced by Bentham and the French Codes, completed a draft Code for Louisiana in 1826. Before Herbert Wechsler and the US Model Penal Code, influential nineteenth-century US criminal law codifications came from David Dudley Fields, beginning in 1849, with the 1881 New York State Code being the most prominent: see S.H. Kadish, 'Codifiers of the Criminal Law: Wechsler's Predecessors' (1978) 78 *Columbia Law Review* 1098; 'The Model Penal Code's Historical Antecedents' (1987–8) 19 *Rutgers Law Journal* 521.

94 Macaulay to Ellis, 25 August 1835: see Pinney, above n. 5, at 152.

95 See Lobban, above n. 36, at 120–55; G.J. Postema, *Bentham and the Common Law Tradition* (Oxford: Clarendon Press, 1986) 421–39.

96 Setalvad, above n. 13, at 127–8.

Stephen's characterisation can be seen as generally accurate when it comes to the substantive doctrines, but it does require qualification since it neglects other important aspects of the IPC and the tendency of mid- and late Victorian law reformers to downplay Bentham's influence.

Stokes's magisterial study of British utilitarianism in India rejects the characterisation of the IPC as a rationalised *compendium* of English law. He carefully examines the connections between Macaulay and Bentham and highlights the central importance of Bentham's influence:

> ... it is quite false to Macaulay's viewpoint to suggest ... that his Code was merely an attempt to apply a reformed English law to Indian conditions. The emphatic disclaimer which the Law Commissioners made on the completion of the draft code must be taken as genuine ... Macaulay's aim was a code that was not derivative from the laws of any creed or country but sprang from the universal science of jurisprudence ... That outlook, which was Bentham's, is to be seen in Macaulay's insistence on the vital interconnexion of the Penal Code with the prospective codes of procedure and substantive civil law, and in his emphasis on the Penal Code as but one portion of the great pannomium.[97]

Stokes adds that '[d]espite modification [the IPC] retained the cast Macaulay had given it. That cast was Bentham's, a code of law drawn not from existing practice or from foreign law systems, but created *ex nihilo* by the disinterested philosophical intelligence ...'.[98] He concedes that the influence of English law cannot be entirely neglected: '[U]ndoubtedly the Penal Code is in substance English law ... but this in no way diminishes the importance and directness of Bentham's influence and the distinctiveness with which it invests Macaulay's code.'[99] Stokes concludes that '[i]t would be idle to draw far-fetched parallels of the details of the Penal Code with the ideas expressed in Bentham's writings ... the debt to Bentham is rather to be sought in the design and informing spirit of the Code'.[100]

Indeed, Macaulay's discernable debt to Bentham is mostly general rather than specific in nature, in conception more than detail. The IPC marks a radical conceptual departure from existing English law in approaching reforming legislation as a taxonomic exercise. The law is expressed and presented in dramatically new ways. Yet the substantive provisions mostly resemble English laws, reworked and simplified with a more general rationalising and modernising sensibility. For the most part, the doctrines are not reinvented but derive from the laws Macaulay and his commissioners were familiar with. Smith sums things up by saying that 'essentially, Macaulay brought to law-making an attitude which could be aptly described as a fusion of utilitarian clarity and rigour with Burkean pragmatism'.[101]

Innovations in Legal Form

The IPC's form (organisation of provisions, presentation and language) was a dramatic departure from existing English law and represented an advance in legislative drafting unmatched by the English Criminal Law Commissioners' proposals or those of Wright. As Stephen recognised:

97 Stokes, above n. 3, at 226–7.
98 Stokes, *ibid.*, at 224–5.
99 Stokes, *ibid.*, at 226–7.
100 Stokes, *ibid.*, at 225.
101 Smith, above n. 2, at 153.

> The Penal Code was the first specimen of an entirely new and original method of legislative expression ... In the first place the leading idea to be laid down is stated in the most explicit and pointed form which can be devised. Then such expressions in it as are not regarded as sufficiently explicit are made the subject of definite explanations. This is followed by equally definite exceptions, to which, if necessary, explanations are added, and in order to set the whole in the clearest light the matter thus stated explained and qualified is illustrated by a number of concrete cases.[102]

Among Bentham's important contributions to legal theory was the extension of the logic of classification in the natural sciences to his legislative science, an exercise in taxonomy that went much further than Blackstone and aimed for an accurate, systematic and exhaustive classification of criminal harms and attendant prohibitions and penalties. Macaulay's practical execution of Bentham's approach resulted in a comprehensive typology and categorisation of the criminal law.[103]

To this was added the concise and direct nature of legal expression and presentation. The IPC is characterised by simplicity, clarity and lack of technicality within a rationally organised and self-contained legislative whole. Stokes notes that this was strongly influenced by Bentham's principles of 'nomography'.[104] Smith adds that technical terms with long pedigrees were banished in favour of ordinary language. Uniform meaning of words and expressions was carefully maintained and accessibility was combined with precision.[105] The objectives of accessibility and precision in language were not always compatible, and the law commissioners in their 14 October 1837 report admitted that they 'repeatedly found [themselves] under the necessity of sacrificing neatness and perspicuity to precision'. Macaulay acknowledged the limitations of language and in his attempts to minimise vagueness he accepted that some imperfections of language could not be overcome. Uncertainties were inevitable and must be subject to common sense, and he avoided a defect he saw in Livingston's Louisiana draft Code of elaborate technical distinctions that would confuse practical import. He also devised provisions that would prevent judges from inventing distinctions.[106]

Perspicuity and precision in expression were sustained and reinforced by Macaulay's innovations in the presentation and organisation of the law which followed Bentham's suggestions closely, beginning with explicit definition of terms, the consistent use of those terms to the exclusion of any other, the use of categorical enactive clauses, the division of classes of offences into chapters and the numbering of paragraphs with the allocation of a separate paragraph to each distinct idea or proposition.[107] The IPC opens with a statement of jurisdiction and operation, followed by a chapter called General Explanations which sets out terminological definitions and general doctrines, a chapter on punishments and a chapter on general exceptions (exemptions from liability and defences, or what Bentham called 'grounds of justification and exemption'). The preliminary part

---

102 Stephen, above n. 13, at 302–3.

103 Such an approach was attempted in other areas of legal doctrine later in the nineteenth century, but none were as wide-ranging and influential in practice. See, for example, B. Sherman and L. Bently, *The Making of Modern Intellectual Property Law: The British Experience* (Cambridge: Cambridge University Press, 1999).

104 Stokes, above n. 3, at 230. Section 2 of Chapter I on General Explanations states that 'Every expression which is explained in any part of this code is used in every part of this code in conformity with the explanation', which is characteristic of Macaulay's lucid and minimalist yet comprehensive approach. The elegant simplicity of s. 40 (Chapter II on punishments) is another example.

105 Smith, above n. 2, at 154 and 157.

106 Clive, above n. 5, at 445.

107 Stokes, above n. 3, at 230–31.

concludes with a chapter on accessories, abetment and concealment of offences.[108] The chapter headings that followed broadly conformed to Bentham's *An Introduction to the Principles of Morals and Legislation* in classification and nomenclature. Offences were broadly classified according to the public and private interests affected, and were set out in four classes: offences against the public, person, property and condition/reputation. This 'natural' division replaced the technical and complex common law denominations and arrangements that made highly esoteric distinctions between tort, misdemeanour, felony and treason. As Stokes notes, Bentham had classified offences in a dual manner: first, according to the entity affected (self, private, semi-private or public) and, secondly, according to their effect (person, property, reputation or condition). The first created the primary divisions and then each class was divided according to the second, but Bentham never grappled with the practical difficulties of drafting a code according to this scheme. Macaulay avoided the potential complexities caused by a rigid adherence to this scheme by adopting a simpler and looser ordering, influenced by the 1810 French Code by Portalis. Thus, the IPC begins with public offences rather than those that affect individual rights as Bentham had suggested.[109]

Macaulay's illustrative *Examples*, or precedents in effect devised by legislators rather than judges, were designed to exhibit the entire meaning and range of application of a provision, and aimed to minimise judicial discretion and law creation. Often regarded as one of Macaulay's innovations, it was inspired by Bentham who had explicitly contemplated the device.[110] Livingston's Lousiana draft Code also used illustrative examples, but the technique was rejected by the English Law Commissioners (the Fourth Report, 1839), who argued that provisions should be expressed to render illustration unnecessary, and by Wright in his Jamaica draft Code.[111]

Clive emphasises how the experience of drafting the IPC honed Macaulay's expressive skills as a writer and historian, drawing parallels between the challenges faced by the legislator and historian of capturing both the particular and the general. The examples were a byproduct of Macaulay's method of subjecting his draft definitional general statements to hypothetical exceptions. If doubts or uncertainties were raised, the definition was revised to accommodate the exceptions. This sharpened the language, logical distinctions and perspicuity, clarifying difficult concepts and making them more concise and comprehensible. The illustrative examples were then generated out of his thinking about exceptions.[112]

The explanatory *Notes* offer remarkably concise and incisive critiques of existing laws as well as explanations and rationales for key provisions. They reflect Macaulay's historical sensibilities and his skill with theoretical and technical synthesis, and warrant recognition as one of the most interesting examples of the nineteenth-century criminal law treatise form.[113] The separate appearance of the rationales for the laws was a departure from Bentham's legislative method

108 Setalvad, above n. 13, at 156–60.

109 Stokes, above n. 3, at 227–8. These include offences against the state, army, navy and public tranquillity, as well as abuses of public powers by officials and offences against public justice, revenue, coin, weight and measures, public health and safety, and quasi-public offences concerning religion and caste, commercial interests and the press. Offences relating to private interests include those affecting the human body, property, documents, the illegal pursuit of legal rights, breach of contracts and service, and offences relating to marriage, defamation, criminal intimidation and insult.

110 Stokes, *ibid.*, at 230.

111 This was one of Stephen's criticisms of the Wright Code: see Smith, above n. 2, at 155.

112 Clive, above n. 5, at 461–2.

113 See Wright, 'Renovate or Rebuild?: Treatises, Digests, and Criminal Law Codification' in M. Dubber and A. Fernandez (eds), *The Treatise in Legal History* (forthcoming, 2011).

(Livingston, following Bentham, had attempted to weave rationales into provisions, with unwieldy results) and Stokes explains:

> The difficulties which [Macaulay] felt in 1835 over attaching reasons to the laws prevented him from using Bentham's device ... of interweaving a rationale into the statement of laws. Macaulay contented himself with appending a series of Notes, which explain the grounds for the various provisions ... As usual Bentham's pursuit of the 'exhaustive method' led him into excessive elaboration, but in its simplest form he divided the wording of a law into main text, expository matter, and rationale. This was the principle followed by Macaulay, except that he detached the rationale completely.[114]

The *Notes* also reveal the significant place of existing laws as Macaulay's starting point. This represented a departure from Bentham's injunction, following on from his critique of Blackstone, to reformulate the criminal law entirely anew.

Innovations in Substantive Law

Most of the substantive doctrines were not reinventions, although much is rationalised and modernised and the innovations reflect progressive advances. Indeed, many of the original provisions remain more advanced than current English criminal laws or those in Stephen Code-influenced jurisdictions. These are well summarised by Smith,[115] and the other chapters of this volume provide a more detailed examination of the provisions concerned most directly with liability and exemptions, and track the changes made to them in enactment and in the years since. My survey here simply illustrates the main themes and tenor of Macaulay's reforms. While the principles of liability are not defined in a general part, there is consistent attention to fault requirements, standards and terms. The arcane English laws of murder and theft are thoroughly reconstituted, and other provisions reflect a concern about the abuse of state powers, the exploitation of vulnerable groups, endangering acts and intangible harms. These reforms, along with the rationalisation of punishment, reflect broader liberal and libertarian values in addition to utilitarianism.

The fault required for particular crimes in the IPC is never left to the common law (unlike the Stephen-influenced codes) but is explicitly set out in the definition of each offence and accompanying exceptions. Matters of culpability in the IPC are examined at length in Part II of this volume, but a number of earlier commentators observe that one of the striking features of the IPC is, as Vesey-Fitzgerald puts it, '[t]he care with which the Indian Penal Code ... distinguishes between various mental states which may be ingredients in crime'.[116] Macaulay favoured subjective intent as the liability standard, lesser standards of 'rashness' and 'negligence' were limited (mostly to endangering offences where public duties were specified) and he opposed liability for omissions. Smith highlights the modern nature of Macaulay's subjectivist approach and aptly sums up:

> The key to subtle gradations and appropriate labelling of criminal culpability is clarity in the terminology of fault. These linguistic building blocks of liability received scrupulous and detailed

114 Stokes, above n. 3, at 229–30.

115 See Smith, above n. 2, at 158 onwards.

116 Vesey-Fitzgerald, above n. 13, at 232. See also Stokes, above n. 3, at 112; and Setalvad, above n. 13, at 137. Vesey-Fitzgerald identifies this as one of the more discernable influences of Bentham.

> attention ... This served Macaulay's objective of ensuring that fixed degrees of culpability could be accurately and reliably included in individual offence definitions and not subject to the infinite vagaries of applying indistinct common law notions.[117]

Defences are also handled consistently and are discussed further in Macaulay's *Note B* accompanying the draft Code (the innovations here and developments since Macaulay's time are examined further in the chapters in Part III of this volume).[118]

That said, some inconsistent liability terms and common law-influenced defences were introduced in the enacted version and the principles of liability are not defined. As Neil Morgan notes in Chapter 3 in this volume, the 'general explanations' and 'general exceptions' chapters in the preliminary parts of the IPC cannot be considered a 'General Part' in that they contain no definition of the basic principles of liability spelling out the mental elements of intent or the subjective and objective elements of criminal rashness and negligence. There are also unexamined implications in relation to the physical elements of the offence, as noted by Bob Sullivan in Chapter 4 of this volume. The lack of definition has resulted in uncertainty in the departures from subjectivism and the application of objective standards. The IPC is nonetheless a huge advance over existing and even current English law.

Macaulay's IPC rejects the English doctrines of constructive liability and attempts to infer mental states from the act, including the arcane notion of malice aforethought. Macaulay distinguished heinous offences caused by misadventure. Inchoate crimes of 'abetment', conspiracy and attempts are examined in detail in Chapter 6 of this volume by Wing-Cheong Chan, while issues of vicarious liability and 'crimes of confederacy' are covered in Chapter 7 by Michael Hor. Unlike Livingston, omissions were not generally punishable since, as Macaulay put it, the Code was not designed to serve motives for doing good. At the same time there is groundbreaking attention to intangible harms and threat-related provisions (criminal intimidation, insults and annoyances) where actual injury does not result.[119] A number of endangering offences were created, which are applicable even if no harm results. As Stephen observed:

> The subject of public nuisances is very fully provided for in sections 268–289, which provide punishment for a great number of offences which in England would not be punishable at all, and would not in some cases afford ground even for a civil action ... Many of the sections referred to punish negligent acts dangerous to human life whether death or bodily harm is caused or not. This is highly characteristic of the Code. Its authors have throughout been much impressed with the theory that neither the motive nor the result, but the intention of an act ought to be the measure of its criminality.[120]

Homicide is typically a focus of criminal law commentary and these provisions open the chapter on 'Offences Affecting the Human Body'. Macaulay radically reconstituted the existing English law

---

117 Smith, above n. 2, at 158.

118 See Macaulay, Macleod, Anderson and Millett, above n. 5. Exemptions are also discussed at length in Setalvad, above n. 13, at 142–55. See also Sornarajah, above n. 19, at cxxxv–cxxxvii on provocation and automatism; and S. Yeo, 'The Application of Common Law Defences to the Penal Code in Singapore and Malaysia' in A.J. Harding (ed.), *The Common Law in Singapore and Malaysia* (Singapore: Butterworths, 1985).

119 Stephen, above n. 13, at 320–21.

120 *Ibid.*, at 310. See also Macaulay, Macleod, Anderson and Millett, above n. 5, Note M (On Offences Against the Body); Smith, above n. 2, at 159–60.

here and his theft provisions also differed dramatically from the highly technical English larceny offences.[121] Referring to the original provisions in Macaulay's draft Code, Smith observes that they 'were an impressive model of progressive thinking and clear formulation quite outclassing the English Commissioner's contemporary efforts'.[122] Macaulay put forward a strictly subjectivist definition of the mental elements of 'voluntary culpable homicide' expressed in terms of 'intention of causing or the knowledge that he is likely to cause death', which is consistent with Bentham (although Bentham sought to avoid the term 'voluntary', which he saw as leading to possible confusion between intention and motive). Voluntary culpable homicide was to be considered murder unless the act came under specified exceptions: committed in response to grave and sudden provocation, in excess of the right of private defence or discharge of public duty, or where the victim gives and is capable of giving consent. Accidental death caused by negligence was not considered culpable homicide. There was no general manslaughter offence, although such harms could fall under other provisions.

Bethune attempted revisions to Macaulay's draft Code that reflected the complex state of English law, but this retrograde step was avoided by the Select Committee headed by Peacock. The murder and culpable homicide provisions were nonetheless significantly revised in the enacted version. Stephen criticised them as the weakest part of the IPC, and other forms of intention-based fault for murder contained objective elements, on the premise that a purely subjective definition was unacceptable on policy grounds.[123]

There are of course many other important areas of doctrinal innovation. A number of provisions radically clarified and advanced complex and arcane areas of criminal law, further illustrating the nature of Macaulay's reforming approach. Stephen singles out for extended commentary Macaulay's reforms to libel as a clear example of his style and the tenor of his law reforms.[124] Following Bentham's lead, Macaulay expanded the term 'defamation' to cover libels and slander as well. His provision simply states:

> Whoever, by words either spoken or intended to be read, or by signs, or by visible representations, attempts to cause any imputation concerning any person to be believed in any quarter, knowing that the belief thereof would harm the reputation of that person in that quarter, is said, except in the cases [hereinafter mentioned], to defame that person.[125]

---

121 Macaulay, Macleod, Anderson and Millett, *ibid.* Some of the highly technical aspects of the English laws of larceny were compensated for by offences related to breach of trust and misappropriations. Stephen, above n. 13, at 318, noted that 'the elaborate discussions and many technicalities connected with the subject which have disfigured the law of England have not been transplanted into India'. See also Vesey-Fitzgerald, above n. 13, at 229; and Setalvad, above n. 13, at 134–5.

122 Smith, above n. 2, at 159.

123 Stephen, above n. 13, at 313, stated 'The definitions of culpable homicide and murder are, I think, the weakest part of the Code' and added that that he contributed to the work of the Legislative Council in amending the provisions to expand liability for death caused by negligence. The effect of creating four branches of culpable homicide considered to be murder was to create an offence of culpable homicide not amounting to murder (in effect involuntary manslaughter). Yeo argues that '[they] are a significant improvement on Macaulay's original provisions. The improvement lies primarily in the schematic gradations of degrees of culpability … from the highest level of fault for murder to the lowest level of fault for culpable homicide not amounting to murder'. See S. Yeo, *Fault in Homicide* (Annandale: Federation Press, 1997) 98–101.

124 Stephen, above n. 13, at 301–3, 318–20.

125 Macaulay's draft Code, cl. 469.

Stephen uses this clause to illustrate Macaulay's mode of legislative expression, setting out the leading idea in the most explicit and pointed form that can be devised (and those expressions that are not sufficiently explicit are subject to further explanation), followed by exceptions (accompanied by explanations if necessary), and in order to set the whole in the clearest possible light, the matter is illustrated by cases. The result, as Stephen describes it, is 'that it is practically impossible to misunderstand the Penal Code', adding that in over 20 years of use and countless decisions, no ambiguity has been discovered.[126] In the case of defamation, there are four further explanations (imputations on deceased persons, companies or groups, irony and the limits of the word imputation itself) and several exceptions set out where imputations are lawful. Unlike English law until Lord Campbell's Libel Act 1843, and unlike the French and Louisiana Codes, truth is a defence. Macaulay gives the examples of a person who warns the mercantile community against a notorious client or advises families not to admit into intimacy a known seducer of innocence.[127] Macaulay's provisions also clearly owed a debt to Bentham's discussion of offences against condition and reputation. As Stephen observes, on the one hand, the defamation provisions go further than English laws in protecting character as much as person and reputation, but '[o]n the other they are singularly liberal, permitting every kind of discussion considered to be advantageous to the public complete liberty from all restraint whatsoever'.[128] He adds that '[t]he doctrine that libel is an offence because it tends to breaches of the peace had no influence at all upon the provisions of the Indian Penal Code'.[129] This, together with Macaulay's exceptions for imputations that are true and such that their publication is for the public good, opinions concerning the conduct of public servants, imputations on the conduct of any person concerning public questions, true reports of legal proceedings and criticisms made in good faith, have the effect of eliminating the common law of seditious libel.[130]

Indeed, the political offences generally warrant attention and reflect Macaulay's libertarian sensibilities about oppressive state powers and his view of the implications of the late seventeenth-century constitutional advances as a significant check on the powers of the state. The offence of treason, regarded as the most serious crime in English criminal law and applicable elsewhere in much of the British Empire, is limited and narrowly defined. Instead of the three major heads ('compassing' the sovereign's death, 'adhering' to the sovereign's enemies and 'levying' war/insurrection), treason is confined to levying war, following the lead of the US where the Constitution limited it in this manner as a singular and special federal offence.

Unfortunately, Macaulay's reforms to the classic provisions on political offences were amended when Stephen was on council to include the equivalent of the 1848 UK Treason Felony Act, which created liability for conspiracy to wage insurrection, assisting enemies at war and planning the sovereign's death (including the advocacy of republicanism), thus expanding the reach of treason, albeit in a lesser form punishable by life imprisonment. Further revisions were added in 1870 to deal with words, publications and conspiracies contrived to cause breaches of the peace, a

126 Stephen, above n. 13, at 303.

127 Macaulay, Macleod, Anderson and Millett, above n. 5, at 133, Note R (On the Chapter of Defamation).

128 Stephen, above n. 13, at 318.

129 Stephen, *ibid.*, at 319.

130 As noted earlier, Macaulay ended censorship with the Press Act. For a discussion of the press and the new informational order, see Bayly, 'Colonial Rule and the "Informational Order" in South Asia', above n. 22, at 302–6.

retreat on Macaulay's abolition of seditious libel.[131] There have been wider-ranging changes to political offences in most IPC jurisdictions in more recent years. Macaulay's sensibilities would undoubtedly be offended by special national security-related emergency powers to combat communist insurgency or terrorism since the Second World War.

Macaulay's provisions on riot and unlawful assembly were robust, as were those concerning false evidence and the spreading of false news. The experience of the Indian Mutiny underscored the importance of such provisions.

Offences relating to abuse of office were groundbreaking (for example, illegal gratification and unlawful exercise of authority) while existing laws relating to contempt or resistance to the lawful authority of officials were developed. Persons who gave bribes in compliance with demands from public servants were not to be considered guilty of inciting public servants to receive bribes (in English law the giver of bribes was seen as more deserving of punishment than the receiver, whereas Macaulay's perception of India was that justice was impossible without bribes and therefore an appropriate exception should be made).[132] Stephen attributes the elaborate provisions here to the particular circumstances where 'the official body in India occupies a position and is charged with functions of far greater importance than those which belong to any corresponding body of officials in the world'.[133] It is also the case that some of these provisions involved parliamentary privilege in British jurisdictions that had elected legislatures.[134]

It appears that Macaulay's libertarian Whig outlook influenced his approach to many of the public order offences. Yet another form of liberalism, derived from Macaulay's Clapham sect background, appears to have informed his approach to religion, to the exploitation of indentured labour, women and children, and to punishment. The Benthamite aspiration of universal jurisprudence was also compromised in various ways. Yet, as Leslie Stephen noted, Macaulay tested the limits of Bentham's tacit assumption that there is an average person and differences in personal behaviour and national character could be transcended.[135] Macaulay's approach was a marked departure from the policies of 'orientalism' and the provisions were anything but parochial, proving to be readily transferable to other settings. But pragmatism also entailed some concessions to the realities of India's cultural diversity.

---

131 Stephen, above n. 13, at 308. Stephen sets out the traditional perspective of presumed deference to authority and the Lockean contractual notion of allegiance in his discussion of political offences, above n. 13, vol. 2, at 299. He maintained the traditional categories of high treason and the treason felony conspiracy extensions in his draft English Code and, as a judge, adopted an expansive approach in the Fenian dynamiters cases. While expressing doubts as to the continued existence of the offence of seditious libel, he included the offence in his Draft Code: see D.H. Brown and B. Wright, 'Codification, Public Order, and the Security Provisions of the Canadian Criminal Code, 1892' in B. Wright and S. Binnie (eds), *Canadian State Trials Volume 3: Political Trials and Security Measures, 1840–1914* (Toronto: University of Toronto Press, 2009).

132 Similar examples given by Macaulay relate to intentional deceit, which he described as usual business practice: see Clive, above n. 5, at 455.

133 Stephen, above n. 13, at 308.

134 Such powers extended to public servants. The jurisdiction was jealously guarded from judicial intrusion and reflected Parliament's ancient and residual function as a court. It not only protected the freedom of speech of members but included legislative sanctions for contempt which were extended to public servants under ministerial responsibility. Although Canada's experiences of protecting these privileges were associated with struggles for responsible government, the Queensland Code codified similar offences to those in the IPC (Chief Justice Griffith claiming inspiration from David Dudley Field's New York Code): see B. Wright, 'Self-Governing Codifications of English Criminal Law and Empire: The Queensland and Canadian Examples' (2007) 26 *University of Queensland Law Journal* 39 at 62.

135 L. Stephen, *The English Utilitarians* (vol. 1) (London: Duckworth, 1900), 299.

Macaulay's replacement of the arcane common law of blasphemy recognised cultural plurality and anticipated modern measures against cultural denigration. He noted that '[t]here is perhaps no country in which the Government has so much to apprehend from religious excitement among the people' and in framing the pertinent provisions, his objective was to allow all fair latitude for religious freedom while preventing the proselytisers from exploiting religious tolerance to intentionally insult what others held sacred.[136] The reform sparked Evangelical condemnation of Macaulay (he was called 'churchwarden of the idol', criticism that had ironically been directed originally at the orientalists). Fitzjames Stephen also expressed disapproval, remarking that offences forbidding insults of existing creeds 'appear to me to carry the principle of tolerating and protecting all religions whatever to a length which cannot be justified' and '[i]t is characteristic of English people to consider their modern liberalism as not only true but self-evident, and certain to be popular at all places and in all times. In fact, it is a very modern growth, and extends over a small part of the world'.[137] Conversely, Dhagamwar's modern criticism suggests that Macaulay did not go far enough to accommodate cultural difference:

> The utilitarian and liberal influence on him was at least partly responsible for his belief that human beings were essentially the same all the world over. This belief in the existence of rational human nature ... might have been considerably modified if he had become acquainted with the people for whom he was to draft laws. Such contact would have immediately made him aware of the irrational, cumulative social forces which mould the attitudes of the people at least as much as do the 'rational' common elements. But apart from his servants and a few uneducated ex-rajahs, pathetic in their dependence on their British masters, and childish in the extreme, Macaulay seems to have met no Indians.[138]

Macaulay's liberal premises and utilitarian aspirations meant minimising account for local conditions apart from the most obvious requirements of time and place. Whether he went too far to accommodate local cultural diversity or not far enough is a complex question which in itself is influenced by the different perspectives of time and place. While the provision has been replaced in some IPC jurisdictions, there is little doubt that it represented a huge advance on the existing common law, one that reflected toleration while addressing intangible harms in a manner that minimised contested moral and ethical criteria.

The IPC provisions on exploitation, rape and sexual offences have attracted recent criticism that tends not to reflect on the fact that Macaulay drafted them over a century and a half ago or to compare them with prevailing laws elsewhere at the time. Stephen stated that these provisions were 'most elaborate, and form a singular contrast to the meagreness of the law of England on these subjects'.[139] However, Dhagamwar contends that Macaulay's approach fails to adequately address the issues raised by these matters because the reform was externally imposed and reflected a lack of sensitivity to local conditions.[140]

Macaulay's comments in *Note B* make it clear that there was to be no exemption from liability for offences committed against indentured labourers. He included an offence applicable to persons

---

136 Macaulay, Macleod, Anderson and Millett, above n. 5, at 102, Note J (On the Chapter of Offences Relating to Religion and Caste).

137 Stephen, above n. 13, at 312–13.

138 Dhagamwar, above n. 13, at 71.

139 Stephen, above n. 13, at 317. The reason for the more elaborate provisions is obvious, according to Stephen, *ibid.*, 'the offences in question were common in India and almost unknown in England'.

140 Dhagamwar, above n. 13, at 73.

who illegally export labourers by sea. On the basis of the 1834 imperial anti-slavery legislation which he had worked on, he thought that there was no need for clauses that made an explicit declaration against slavery or the sale of human beings. He was concerned about persistent vestiges of slavery but even his modest provisions concerning indentured labour and assumptions about the enforcement of the imperial act caused a great deal of unease amongst senior officials of the East India Company. They argued that residual practices of slavery in India were mild, that interference would incite landowners to rebel and that the trade of indentured labourers to elsewhere in the Empire would be compromised. The matter became a preoccupation in subsequent reviews of the IPC, leading to heated debates in council and pressure from the Court of Directors. In the end, limited provisions were included in the enacted IPC, including prohibitions on the import, export, removal, buying, selling, hiring or otherwise disposal of persons as slaves; compelling a person to labour against his will; and provisions concerning children and sexual exploitation.[141]

Macaulay's *Note M* suggested that the provisions on wrongful restraint and wrongful confinement were adequate to deal with kidnapping and abduction. Restraint and confinement without violence or harm were minor offences, becoming serious only where kidnapping was committed with grievous bodily harm or for the purposes of reducing persons to slavery, rape or unnatural lust. The Select Committee revised the provisions out of concern that they did not go far enough to deal with the particular problems of exploitation of women and children in India, including separate offences relating to kidnapping and abduction. The Committee also made the punishment more severe where the restraint or confinement was for the purposes of kidnapping (which was distinguished as violating the rights of the guardian) or abduction and aimed to more directly curb practices such as the sale of children by their parents and attempts to compel marriage and sexual intercourse.[142]

The IPC provisions contain mixed advances for women. Departures from existing English law included the recognition of the right of women to own and independently manage property. Nor did marriage result in wives being considered one person with their husbands. Macaulay's private defence was clearly applicable to cases of domestic violence (although this combined defence of self and property also attempted to promote Western values, as noted in Chapter 8 of this volume by Cheah Wui Ling). Macaulay explains the provisions related to marriage in *Note Q* in the context of the variable customs in India concerning polygamy and adultery. Bigamy is heavily punished as a form of fraud and exploitation but the commissioners were divided about the effectiveness of criminalising adultery, which in some places was tolerated, in others was a cause for divorce and in yet others was punished by stoning. It was not a crime in English law and Macaulay preferred to leave moral and ethical questions that did not involve clear harms out of the Code. However, adultery became an offence, available only for the husband to prosecute, in the enacted version of the IPC. Stephen explains this departure as a concession to indigenous needs, noting that European residents chose to ignore it, instead pursuing divorce proceedings.[143] Yet customs on these matters varied and Macaulay's *Notes* emphasise the policy aim of deterring husbands from taking the law into their own hands. Like a number of other British jurisdictions that criminalised abortion for the first time in the early nineteenth century, the causing of a miscarriage is made an offence.

The rape provision reflects utilitarian simplicity but also persistent Victorian attitudes. It simply states that rape is sexual intercourse when it is against a woman's will, or is without consent when

141 Dhagamwar, *ibid.*, at 118–22.

142 Dhagamwar, *ibid.*, at 108–11. In jurisdictions such as Malaysia, provisions related to the sexual exploitation of children have been elaborated yet further in recent years.

143 Stephen, above n. 13, at 318.

she is insensible or consent is obtained under threat or fraud (fear of death or of hurt, or obtained under the mistaken impression that the accused is her husband). The provision is silent on the question of whether the accused has to know the victim has not consented, a curious omission in light of Macaulay's emphasis on subjective liability. However, relative to the English laws of the period, the provision was an advance. Despite the silence on the question of knowledge of consent in rape, Macaulay's otherwise careful consideration of consent in other provisions were informed, as Stanley Yeo describes it, by individualistic liberalism where individual autonomy is placed ahead of competing interests.[144] As a result, as Yeo contends:

> ... the Penal Code offers women much greater protection against rape than the laws of many other Commonwealth jurisdictions. This is because, upon the prosecution proving a woman's lack of consent to sexual intercourse, the legal burden rests with the accused to prove on a balance of probabilities that he reasonably believed that she had consented to having sexual intercourse with him.[145]

Sexual intercourse, with or without consent, when the victim is under nine years of age is rape, but sexual intercourse by a man with his wife is not. Subsequent reviews suggesting that consent by fear of hurt be replaced by fear of grievous harm, in line with the recommendations of the English law commissioners, and that concubines also be taken into account were fortunately rejected. A recommendation to raise the age of consent to 10 years of age was accepted.

The provisions on rape are followed by 'unnatural' offences involving others or animals for the purpose of gratifying unnatural lust. Macaulay calls them an 'odious class of offences', adding that:

> We are unwilling to insert, either in the text or in the notes, any thing which could give rise to public discussion on this revolting subject; as we are decidedly of the opinion that the injury which would be done to the morals of the community by such discussion would far more than compensate for any benefits which might be derived from legislative measures framed with greater precision.[146]

There was subsequent debate over whether to retain the provisions on the basis that the offences were common and rarely reported, but they were retained with little change. Dhagamwar notes the contrast with the approach taken with abduction and rape:

> On the other hand, where sodomy, homosexuality or any other unnatural sexual practices were under consideration, mutual consent was no protection and the age of the parties was irrelevant. It seems that Macaulay and his successors were less concerned with the degree of harm or injury resulting from [the] practice than with their own detestation of it, for it could hardly be said that the utilitarian theory of law required severe punishment of an unnatural sexual practice indulged by two individuals by their mutual consent.[147]

---

144 S. Yeo, 'Constructing Consent under the Penal Code' in D. Neo, H.W. Tang and M. Hor (eds), *Lives in the Law* (Singapore: National University of Singapore Faculty of Law and Academy Publishing, 2007).

145 Yeo, *ibid.*, at 179.

146 Macaulay, Macleod, Anderson and Millett, above n. 5, at 117, Note M (On Offences Against the Body).

147 Dhagamwar, above n. 13, at 118.

The double standards are obvious, and in line with the modern decriminalisation of homosexual relations, the provision has been recently challenged with success in India.[148] This decision represents undoubted progress. Where the contemporary critique and assessment of the provision falls short is in the failure to address the prevailing criminal laws in Macaulay's time. To fault him without comparing the provision to those laws is teleological presentism. Indeed, John Stuart Mill's ideas about restricting criminal interventions to tangible harms were still being developed and debates around these matters remained contentious well into the twentieth century, as highlighted by the Wolfenden Report and the Hart-Devlin debate.

Macaulay's approach to these offences represented modest progress but certainly did not transcend time and place. There are indeed contradictions and divergences from the liberal focus on the prevention of harm and limits on the repressive interventions of the state, and a number of provisions reflected dominant cultural and moral standards and public interests that were perceived as essential. These exceptions compromised the integrity of utilitarian principles in the IPC and qualify characterisation of the IPC as a progressive code. The resulting inconsistencies in the original draft were compounded in the revisions leading up to enactment. Subsequent administration of the provisions only reinforced cultural and class perceptions of appropriate identity and roles, biases involving social status and reputation, and concerns about local practices and resistance.[149] However, historians are concerned with assessment relative to the prevailing state of criminal law and legal practices of the time, and not with the standards of toleration and pluralism of the late twentieth or early twenty-first century. In these terms Macaulay's relative constancy in adhering to the utilitarian principles of legislation, his relative detachment from established attitudes and the relatively advanced nature of the reforms represent real progress. In matters of form the IPC represented a revolutionary break, in substantive laws, a more modest, progressive reform of existing English doctrines. These features reflect the elusiveness of Bentham's science of legislation and universal jurisprudence, the real or practical constraints faced by Macaulay, and the limits of his experience and outlook.

Macaulay's approach to punishment is yet another reflection of the progressive qualities of the IPC. Discussed at length in *Note A,* it expresses both the influence of Bentham and Macaulay's Clapham sect values that denounced capital and corporal punishment as well as slavery. Peel's English consolidations marked a dramatic shift away from the pre-modern approach to punishment, as capital offences were reduced from over 200 to a dozen, paving the way for the penitentiary and the demise of the discretionary conditional pardon and transportation. Macaulay's reform was even more dramatic, specifying the death penalty for only two offences, treason and murder, both of which were more narrowly and carefully defined, as we have seen. Corporal punishments such as flogging and the pillory were abolished outright. Other punishments, mostly prison terms or fines set out as maximum penalties, were to be simple, economical and commensurate with the gravity of the offence. Most non-IPC British jurisdictions did not develop such reforms until the twentieth century. Macaulay would not have liked inflexible mandatory penalties, the expansion of capital punishment and the reintroduction of corporal penalties seen in current IPC jurisdictions.

Bentham, like Beccaria before him, stressed that deterrence is the only rational justification for punishment and that the culpability of the offender is of central importance. Bentham demonstrated that certainty of punishment, with penalties rationally proportionate to the gravity of the offence, achieves the objective of deterrence much more effectively than the severity of the punishment.

148 *Naz Foundation v. Government of NCT* 2010 Cri LJ 94. In Malaysia, on the other hand, the provision has been elaborated upon with the introduction of corporal punishments.

149 Dhagamwar, above n. 13, at 112–16.

The utilitarians did not accept retribution or rehabilitation as primary aims or justifications for punishment. However, Stokes, the legal member of council in the late 1870s, criticised Macaulay for not considering retribution and gratification of natural public feeling, and Fitzjames Stephen agreed that punishment should entail an element of public denunciation.[150]

Bentham's 'felicific calculus' of punishment, which sought to determine the precise *quantum* of efficacious punishment in order to maximise the deterrent effect, was not followed in the IPC. Instead, the IPC set out a maximum punishment for each offence, in most cases in the form of imprisonment or fines (Chapter II sets out a hierarchy of punishments from death, transportation, imprisonment and banishment from East India Company territories to property forfeitures and fines, but prison terms could be substituted in the relatively few cases where transportation and banishment were specified). Macaulay also called for flexibility in sentencing according to the circumstances of the offender. Inflexibility and minimum sentences were also to be avoided to discourage judicial manipulation of the fault requirement in difficult cases. Inspired by Bentham's idea of the *panopticon*, Macaulay recommended that prison discipline entail the use of solitary confinement and hard labour, unpleasant stays during which inmates were to face no gratuitous cruelties but were otherwise to be deprived of every indulgence not necessary to health.[151] He acknowledged that such heavy reliance on imprisonment for those convicted of serious offences would require extensive prison reform and construction to accompany the implementation of the IPC.[152]

CONCLUSION

As we have seen, Macaulay had been critical of the political theories of Bentham and Mill, expressing a libertarian Whig suspicion of utilitarian 'enlightened despotism'. Yet he embraced utilitarian legal theory to become the most successful utilitarian legislator of his generation. The IPC was a progressive and liberal code, certainly for the standards of the time and even compared to, in many respects and with relatively few exceptions, current criminal law in common law jurisdictions. It represented a revolutionary break in the form of the criminal law and made significant advances in substantive doctrines and for the rule of law more generally. But the IPC was concerned with more than the rational management of crime. Implemented literally as 'enlightened despotism', it was connected to the legal and political legitimacy of British rule. The aim of reducing discretionary authority and status differences and of enhancing of the rule of law was not simply about rights. It was about sovereignty and reconstituting the relations between the state and subject with the aim

150 Smith, above n. 2, at 160. Whitley Stokes, law member of the council from the late 1870s, was particularly critical of Macaulay's views of punishment. See also Smith, *James Fitzjames Stephen: Portrait of a Victorian Rationalist*, above n. 19.

151 Macaulay, Macleod, Anderson and Millett, above n. 5, at 70, Note A (On the Chapter of Punishments); see also Stokes, above n. 3, at 218.

152 The law commissioners, in consultation with the judges of in the Calcutta Supreme Court, issued a preliminary recommendation in 1838 that penitentiaries be built centrally in six to eight districts for convicts sentenced to a year or more, but the proposal went no further with Auckland: see Clive, above n. 5, at 447–50. In Note A, *ibid.*, at 71, Macaulay also called for a special exemption from long terms of imprisonment to be created for convicted European residents, specifying banishment instead. He justifying this on the basis that prison discipline in such a miserable climate would be cruel and that the presence of such individuals in a degraded state with the general inmate population would erode esteem for the English national character; see also Stokes, *ibid.*, at 231–2.

of engendering greater conformity to the law, enhancing public order and making British authority more pervasive, effective and legitimate.

To dismiss the IPC as entirely or simply an instrument of British imperial rule is, however, unscholarly reductionism. It is to neglect its virtues as a body of law reform with attributes that continue to impress. Of all the nineteenth-century codes, the IPC comes closest to a working realisation of Bentham's conception of criminal law codification and represents a giant advance on the then-existing consolidations and quasi-codified digests. It was a rationalisation of criminal law that went much further than Stephen's later draft, which retained common law elements and greatly influenced the later self-governing jurisdiction codes. Macaulay, like Bentham, aimed to have legislators fully exploit the modern public policy potential of the law and strictly limit judicial powers in the application of law. His code was designed to displace all existing criminal laws with provisions formulated according to consistent principles, informed by the utilitarian notion that crime should be suppressed by the least infliction of suffering, that the law should be clear and widely known, and that its administration should be as economical as possible. The law was presented systematically and each offence was defined precisely and clearly to maximise certainty, with accompanying elements of liability and exceptions explicitly spelt out. It was to be applied as uniformly as possible with illustrations that aimed to anticipate the entire range of possibilities in order to minimise judicial discretion. Special definitions, procedures and exceptions were avoided. As Smith puts it, '[w]ithout any direct effort on his part, Bentham achieved his most tangible codifying success in the form of the Indian Penal Code'.[153]

That said, while the IPC dramatically reduced the archaic, arcane and discretionary elements of English criminal law, it was not quite the revolutionary scientific legislation and universal jurisprudence envisaged by Bentham. As even Stokes concedes, Macaulay fell short of Bentham's ideal.[154] Numerous exceptions compromised the utilitarian aspirations. Macaulay faced the practical challenge of producing a working code and, despite his eloquence, recognised the limits of language and of his examples. He confronted perhaps irreconcilable tensions between principles and pragmatism, rules and discretion, and means and ends, tensions that became more obvious as the IPC moved from conception and drafting and on to enactment and implementation. The accumulated divergences became increasingly difficult to reconcile with the originating principles. Fitzjames Stephen, who along with Henry Maine played a key role in implementing the IPC, expressed immense admiration for Macaulay's aims while recognising that laws could not be entirely framed on abstract principles as if they were mathematical theories detached from the places and people they affected.[155] Macaulay could not reconcile the abstract universal and the situational. Neither could Bentham, at least had he faced the practical challenge of drafting a real code. The administrative realities of applying the law generated further complications, and unanticipated new conditions and disputes emerged. Codes, no matter how universal in design, adopted and applied in varying settings, will be coloured by local and particular influences, overlaid

153 Smith, above n. 2, at 164.

154 Stokes, above n. 3, at 225.

155 Smith, above n. 19, at 128. Although he was not inclined to go as far as Macaulay in embracing Benthamite legal ideas, Fitzjames Stephen was similarly impatient with arcane technicalities and agreed that dithering over legal *minutiae* was best met by strenuous and frequent legislative revision: see Smith, *ibid.*, at 130.

with judicial constructions by way of inconsistent statutory interpretation.[156] Comprehensive codes require comprehensive updating, something that is seldom a legislative priority.[157]

As we have seen, while the doctrines of the IPC resembled English law, the form, language and presentation of the provisions were distinctive and here Bentham's influence is the most obvious. Clear, concise and comprehensive provisions were accompanied by illustrations of application, a legislative *aide memoire* that attempted to anticipate all possibilities and minimise judicial discretion. Macaulay's accompanying *Notes* provided trenchant critiques of existing laws and explanations of his reforms. The substantive doctrines were less of a radical Benthamite break but were advanced for their time and many remain so even by present-day standards. Here, the starting point was English law filtered through a utilitarian sensibility in a more general way and inflected with liberalism reflecting Macaulay's libertarian Whig inclinations and Clapham sect background. The careful attention and consistent approach to liability, reforms to political offences, provisions that anticipate the modern state and a plural civil society, and the rationalisation of punishment all stand out as substantive advances.

The IPC is not simply an isolated artefact of legal theory manifested in practical law. The modern literary scholar John Clive illuminates some of the complexities left unconsidered in the older assessments. They include how Macaulay's work reflects a privileged outlook, a particular culture and perceptions of Indian life as seen by British rulers. At the same time, Macaulay was in favour of progress, equality before the law and extending liberal political freedoms, and he demonstrated some awareness of the inherent paternalism of moving towards these objectives by way of despotic government.[158] The dualism in Clive's assessment of Macaulay is also evident in the examination of the IPC in this chapter. Despite its many virtues as a body of law reform, the IPC was bound up with the imperatives of British sovereignty and rule. These factors inevitably coloured the utilitarian project of modern universal reforming legislation.

Attention to context in this study has attempted to situate the production of the IPC, the intellectual currents of the period that influenced it and the policies that it was a part of. Our discussion shows that it was the product of law reform debates flowing from the broader influences of the European Enlightenment, British utilitarianism and debates about public policy and English law reform in the nineteenth century. The drafting and implementation of the IPC involved many of the *dramatis personae* connected to those debates. These debates also influenced reforms in other British jurisdictions and later codifications. The promotion of the IPC by the Colonial Office and its adoption in other British jurisdictions reflect the important place of codification in the reform of colonial governance within global networks. We also observe how the ideals of constitutionalism and legality, which dominated Victorian political discourse and led to reform calls to renew the legitimacy of British sovereignty and its 'imperial burden', also formed an important background to such law reform projects. The contradictions between formal legal and constitutional claims and the exercise of imperial power became apparent in response to colonial crises involving the suspension of civil authority and military intervention. The enactment of the IPC, delayed until after the 1857–8 Indian Mutiny, helped to disguise the contradictions and restored the moral legitimacy of British rule for the English governing classes at least. Imperial anxieties soon resurfaced with the 1865 Jamaica uprising and the Governor Eyre controversy, prompting heated debate as well as division amongst our *dramatis personae,* notably John Stuart Mill and Fitzjames

156 As Sornarajah, above n. 19, puts it at cxxxiv: 'There is a measure of judicial creativity that is necessary [even] in the interpretation of comprehensive codes.'

157 See Chapter 13 of this volume (M. Goode, 'An Evaluation of Judicial Interpretations of the Australian Model Criminal Code').

158 Clive, above n. 5, at 472–3, 451–2.

Stephen.[159] Wright's Jamaica Code and the British self-governing jurisdiction codifications of the 1890s followed a similar pattern. Public order crises helped to make these codes a political and legislative priority.

Situated, then, within this broader imperial political and policy context, the IPC cannot be divorced from fundamental aims of making British colonial rule more modern, effective and legitimate. The IPC was implemented in the liberal spirit of reducing archaic forms of discretionary authority and differences in status in order to make the rule of law more effective in culturally diverse frontier settings. This was certainly an advance, but one concerned about sovereignty as well as rights, and was an important qualification in the imperial context to the historian E.P. Thompson's observation that the rule of law is an unqualified good. Equal rights and status did not eliminate the practical differences or gulfs between the coloniser and the colonised. The reforms also demanded more comprehensive obligations and greater compliance.

At the same time, the IPC must also be assessed according to the standards of the time, and to comprehend the IPC entirely in functional terms as a modern expression of power is teleological and ahistorical. The IPC clearly represented progress from what then existed in India, England and throughout the British Empire. The fuller implementation of the rule of law by way of a clear and consistent expression of legal powers and the minimising of discretionary authority and status differences were significant advances. These represented material checks on the powers of the state and, in particular, the state's repressive institutions, measures and practices in civil society. The aspirations of disinterested reform based on a universal jurisprudence were, in significant part, the conceit of privilege and power, the product of confidence of the British Enlightenment intellectuals and early Victorian empire-builders, unhindered by the burden of complexities that preoccupied twentieth-century intellectuals, law reformers and public policy specialists. Despite this, one cannot but help admire the ambitious law reform endeavours of Macaulay, this early 'eminent Victorian'.

159 See Kostal, above n. 33.

PART II
Principles of Culpability

This Part comprises a set of chapters dealing with general principles which render a person criminally liable.

In Chapter 3, 'The Fault Elements of Offences', Neil Morgan describes the hallmarks of Macaulay's draft Code, namely simplicity of language and drafting, a largely subjective approach to criminal responsibility, and symmetry between the fault elements and physical elements of offences. However, the draft Code provided little guidance on the meaning of the four primary fault elements of intention, knowledge, rashness and negligence. The Indian Penal Code (IPC), as enacted, retained most of Macaulay's draft but its definitions of culpable homicide and murder generated complexity and uncertainty. In the modern era, there has also been a good deal of confusion over 'strict liability' offences. Overall, however, it is contended that the IPC has stood the test of time rather well and requires renovation, not reconstruction. The chapter reviews the options for strict liability and calls for the inclusion of statutory definitions of the major fault elements. Drawing on Macaulay's core values, it suggests some possible definitions which are then tested in the context of the homicide offences.

In Chapter 4, Bob Sullivan discusses 'The Conduct Element of Offences', noting that neither Macaulay's draft Code nor the IPC contains general provisions which deal comprehensively with this element. This is in line with Macaulay's aspiration to draft offences which contain in the offence specification all the elements to be proved without reference to further provisions. Despite the general merits of this approach, Sullivan shows that it does not always provide sufficient guidance for courts when resolving uncertainties that may arise in particular cases concerning whether the conduct element is proved. With this in mind, some provisions relating to the conduct element of offences which will apply generally to all IPC offences are proposed. Additionally, a general provision offering guidance on causation is put forward. Finally, consideration is given to the question of whether the IPC should be more sparing or more demanding in the matter of liability based on omissions. The current position on omissions in the IPC, which is faithful to Macaulay's views on the subject of liability based on omission, is confirmed.

In Chapter 5, 'Mistake and Strict Liability', Kumaralingam Amirthalingam analyses the mistake defence in the IPC, suggesting that the defence may have been a historical accident and that its application, as it has been understood and applied, is problematic. He then considers strict liability cases and discusses the application of the IPC mistake defence to that regime. Finally, the chapter considers whether mistake of law should be a defence, before proposing a reformulated defence of mistake.

The provisions relating to abetment, criminal conspiracy and attempt under Macaulay's draft Code and the present IPC are examined by Wing-Cheong Chan in Chapter 6. The contention is made that the modern additions made to Macaulay's draft Code have needlessly altered the simplicity and coherence in his proposals, which were meant to depart from the prevailing uncertainties of the common law at the time. While some minor improvements to Macaulay's provisions are needed, Chan argues for a return to be made to the fundamental ideas implicit in his Code.

The last chapter of this part, Chapter 7, is entitled 'Vicarious Responsibility'. In it, Michael Hor wrestles with the question of the extent to which members of a criminal enterprise ought to be responsible for collateral crimes committed by a member of the enterprise, but which are not within the scope of what was jointly intended. This troublesome matter has plagued jurisdictions around the world, from the United States and Canada to the United Kingdom, Israel, Australia and the International Criminal Tribunals of Yugoslavia and Cambodia. The IPC jurisdictions have not been exempt. Hor explains how the apparently simple and straightforward provision in Macaulay's draft Code was set aside in favour of two possible sources of group liability and that this has caused endless problems in Singapore in particular. Hor then attempts to clarify what the problems are and to suggest a draft provision that might deal satisfactorily with most of them.

Chapter 3
The Fault Elements of Offences

Neil Morgan

INTRODUCTION

In examining the fault elements in the Indian Penal Code (IPC), it is important to reflect on the core values underpinning Macaulay's draft Code. They include:[1] *comprehensibility* (easily understood); *accessibility* (the law is contained in a code, not buried in case law); *precision* and *certainty* (the language and expression are not loose or vague); and *democracy* (the criminal law is primarily the responsibility of a democratically elected legislature, not of judges, and the Code should therefore be as *comprehensive* as possible).[2]

Reflecting these values, Macaulay intended a radical departure from common law traditions, which he criticised and regarded as inappropriate and unworkable in India. Certainly, when read as a whole and properly understood, the IPC has an attractive simplicity and symmetry. As the eminent jurist James Stephen put it: 'To compare the Indian penal code with English criminal law was like comparing Cosmos with Chaos.'[3]

Unfortunately, the cosmos has become obscured by two rather dark clouds. The first is that the homicide provisions, the usual starting point in any study of the criminal law, are 'probably the most tricky in the IPC and are so technical as frequently to lead to confusion'.[4] Importantly, the homicide provisions as enacted were very different from Macaulay's original draft and, in many important respects, are out of line with the general structure of the IPC.[5]

The second cloud is that there has been excessive and confusing reference (at least in Malaysia and Singapore, which have adopted the IPC) to the common law doctrine of *mens rea*, often at the expense of the structure of the Code itself. Using *mens rea* merely as a shorthand label for the fault element of an offence would probably not be a major issue, although Macaulay, who rejected pretentiousness and unnecessary Latin, would turn in his grave. The real problem is that the maxim *actus non facit reum nisi mens sit rea* has been used to interpret the law, especially in the context of new offences outside the IPC where no fault element has been specified. As a result, there has been copious reference to common law cases on the question of whether a fault element should be 'read in' or whether the offence is to be construed as one of 'strict' or

1 See Chapter 2 of this volume (B. Wright, 'Macaulay's Indian Penal Code: Historical Context and Originating Principles'); S. Yeo, N. Morgan and W. Chan, *Criminal Law in Malaysia and Singapore* (Singapore: LexisNexis, 2007) paras. [1.33]–[1.35].

2 One interesting example of this is that Macaulay proposed that there should be a reform process whereby issues of uncertainty before the courts would be referred to the legislature for attention. See further Chapter 1 of this volume (S. Yeo and B. Wright, 'Revitalising Macaulay's Indian Penal Code') at 6–7.

3 Quoted by A. Phang, 'Of Codes and Ideology: Some Notes on the Origins of the Major Criminal Enactments of Singapore' (1989) 31 *Malaya Law Review* 46, at 55. For the influences on the development of Macaulay's guiding principles and the break from existing English law, see Chapter 2 of this volume, above n. 1.

4 *Tham Kai Yau v. PP* [1977] 1 MLJ 174, at 176, *per* Raja Azlan Shah F.J.

5 See below at 66–8.

'absolute' liability.[6] There are three major problems with this uncritical use of the common law. First, it is at odds with the basic principles of codification to consider 'reading in' elements that are not specified. Secondly, the IPC aimed to be comprehensive and fault is ascribed through defences as well as through specified fault elements. The natural structure of the Code is that if no fault element is specified, culpability should be addressed through the defences, and mistake will play a particular role in this.[7] Thirdly, the IPC provides that these defences apply throughout the criminal law, and not just the Code itself, unless they are expressly excluded.[8]

I suggest that when these two distractions are set to one side, the fault elements in the IPC have largely stood the test of time and should generally be retained. The four main fault elements in Macaulay's draft and in the enacted versions of the Code are intention, knowledge, rashness and negligence. There are also a number of other more specific fault elements, notably in relation to the property offences. However, the precise meanings of the various fault terms and the relationship between them are sometimes unclear. For this reason, I submit that statutory definitions should be included in an early chapter of the IPC and suggest some possible definitions. The task of defining and explaining the fault elements is greatly assisted by the use of illustrations, another valuable technique in Macaulay's draft.

It is abstract and artificial to examine fault elements without also examining how specific offences should be defined. For example, if it is decided that the fault element for murder should be 'intention', this does not resolve the question of whether it should be necessary to prove an intention to kill or whether an intention to do grievous hurt should suffice. The final section of this chapter therefore maps out the issues that will arise when reforming the homicide provisions of the IPC in light of the suggested fault elements.[9] It is recognised that there are risks in focusing on homicide and the other offences against the person because these are, in numerical terms, just a small component of the modern criminal law. However, greater clarity in defining these offences should provide the foundation of legal principles and language on which other offences can be built.

It is also artificial to consider the substantive law in isolation from other fundamental questions relating to proof and punishment. For example, the scope that is ascribed to the offence of murder may depend in part on whether it attracts a mandatory penalty, especially if that is the death penalty. And questions of fault can hinge just as much on the defences as they do on any fault elements that are specified in the definition of an offence. Indeed, there are times when

6 See generally Yeo, Morgan and Chan, above n. 1, Chapter 7 and the other extensive literature cited there. K.N.C. Pillai and S. Aquil (eds), *Essays on the Indian Penal Code* (New Delhi: Indian Law Institute, 2005) provides a striking example of the reliance on English common law. The essay entitled 'The Guilty Mind' begins with the words: 'In the entire field of criminal law there is no more important doctrine than that of *mens rea*. The fundamental principle of English criminal jurisprudence, to use a maxim which has been familiar to lawyers following the common law for several centuries is "*actus non facit reum nisi mens sit rea*."' The essay then discusses leading English cases on strict liability and makes copious reference to English cases on intention and recklessness.

7 See below at 70–1 and Chapter 5 of this volume (K. Amirthalingam, 'Mistake and Strict Liability').

8 IPC, s. 40 states that the General Exceptions in the Penal Code apply not only to offences under the Code but also to offences 'under any other law for the time being in force'.

9 The Australian Commonwealth Criminal Code, as a recent example of comprehensive codification, is a useful reference point. This Code identifies three aspects to the physical elements of offences, namely 'conduct', 'circumstances' and 'results'. For the sake of simplicity, this chapter treats the fault elements as primarily about results. Attention can be given to conduct and circumstances after there has been some resolution of questions relating to (i) any new principles relating to the voluntariness of conduct and (ii) the best terminology for fault elements in the context of results.

the defences essentially do all the work in ascribing fault under the IPC. In many legal systems, the majority of the defences only place an evidential burden on the accused, so that it is for the prosecution to disprove the defence beyond a reasonable doubt. However, under the IPC and its associated Evidence Act, the accused must prove all defences on the balance of probabilities. The fundamental importance of this is explored again later in this chapter.[10]

FAULT ELEMENTS UNDER MACAULAY'S DRAFT CODE: SIMPLICITY, SUBJECTIVITY AND SYMMETRY

Macaulay's *Notes* and draft Code offer surprisingly little guidance on the primary fault elements. There are few definitions in the early, definitional chapters of Macaulay's draft, and the offence definitions themselves treat the fault elements as largely self-explanatory and non-controversial. This part of the chapter therefore examines the structure of the Code and some of the substantive provisions in order to understand the way Macaulay approached the fault elements. Three features stand out: simplicity, subjectivity and symmetry.

Fault Elements in Chapter I of the Draft Code

Chapter I of the draft Code is headed 'General Explanations'. Only two of the clauses in this chapter deal with fault elements. Clause 26 states: 'A person is said to cause an effect "voluntarily" when he ... intended to cause it, or ... knew [he was] likely to cause it.'[11] This definition played a limited role because in many instances, when the word 'voluntary' and its variants were used, there was specific reference to intention or knowledge. For example, Macaulay's draft Code defined 'voluntary culpable homicide' by reference to the person intending to kill another or knowing that death was likely.[12] However, there were a number of places where the word 'voluntarily' was used without further elaboration, so that recourse to cl. 26 was necessary.[13]

The other fault term that was defined in Chapter I was 'fraudulently': 'Whoever does anything with the intention of causing wrongful gain to one party by means of wrongful loss or risk of wrongful loss to another party is said to do that thing fraudulently.'[14] It is beyond the scope of this chapter to analyse some of the highly technical issues that arise with respect to the fault elements for the property offences, but three points may be made. First, 'fraudulently' was defined by reference to an *intention* to cause wrongful loss or gain – in other words, nothing less than 'intention' will suffice.[15] However, there was no definition of intention itself. Secondly, the Code as enacted retained the definition but labelled this state of mind 'dishonestly' rather than 'fraudulently'. Thirdly, this definition has generally stood the test of time rather well.[16]

10 See below at 71–2.

11 This definition is in line with the definition that was often given to the word 'wilfully' in some other codes: see Yeo, Morgan and Chan, above n. 1, at para. [4.25].

12 Macaulay's draft Code, cl. 294. Similarly, the offences of voluntarily causing hurt or grievous hurt were specifically defined by reference to intention or knowledge that the result was likely: cls. 316 and 317.

13 See n. 74 below for examples under the enacted IPC.

14 Macaulay's draft Code, cl. 16. The phrases 'wrongful gain' and 'wrongful loss' were defined in cl. 15.

15 See below at 80.

16 See Yeo, Morgan and Chan, above n. 1, Chapters 13–15.

Fault Elements in Offence Definitions

As with Chapter I of Macaulay's draft Code, there is also very little discussion of fault elements in either the definitions of the various offences or the accompanying *Notes*. The 'Offences Affecting the Human Body' (Chapter XVIII) illustrate this particularly well. Four main fault terms are used in this context, namely intention to cause a result, knowledge that a result is likely, rashness and negligence. The offence of 'voluntarily causing hurt' required proof that the accused intended to cause hurt or knew that hurt was likely,[17] while 'voluntary culpable homicide' required proof that the accused intended to cause death or knew that death was likely.[18] Interestingly, the illustrations to these sections all assume that the person had the requisite intention or knowledge and focus mainly on issues relating to causation and omissions. Similarly, *Note M* (On Offences Against the Body) discusses omissions and causation and then moves on to provocation, consent and defence without any discussion of the fault elements.

Given Macaulay's view that a code should be comprehensible, accessible, precise and comprehensive, it is not easy to explain this silence. Two potential explanations come to mind. First, Macaulay and his colleagues probably considered that the terms they had used had been defined with sufficient certainty or were self-explanatory. For example, they did not leave the word 'knowledge' to stand alone; generally, the question was whether the accused knew an outcome to be *likely*. And some words that were inherently uncertain, such as 'fraudulently', were given a detailed definition. The word 'intention' was not defined but was probably regarded as a well-understood term that was capable of being applied sensibly by a judge or jury.

Secondly, it could be argued that there was little need to agonise over the precise boundaries of words such as 'intention' because the offence definitions generally coupled intention and knowledge together, so that knowledge was the threshold for liability. Thus, in cases of voluntarily causing hurt it did not particularly matter whether the accused intended hurt or just knew hurt to be likely. The two lower level fault elements, rashness and negligence, were also coupled together in offence definitions, so that the precise boundaries between these terms would rarely be at issue.

These explanations do have some force but are far from satisfactory. First, words such as 'rashness' are not self-explanatory and were not defined. Secondly, on occasion, 'intention' stands alone and therefore determines the threshold of liability (one example, already noted, is the definition of 'fraudulently'). Thirdly, a number of other non-defined and ambiguous fault terms such as 'malignantly' and 'wantonly' sometimes creep into the offence definitions.[19] This is particularly surprising given Macaulay's care with language. Finally, even if the basic concept of negligence – falling below objectively acceptable standards – is well understood, other issues arise, such as the degree of negligence that is required for criminal responsibility.[20] The draft Code therefore left a number of areas of uncertainty.

---

17 Macaulay's draft Code, cl. 316.

18 *Ibid.*, cl. 294.

19 See, for example, the offence of malignantly *and* wantonly provoking a riot in Macaulay's draft Code, cl. 136, which was modified to become malignantly *or* wantonly provoking a riot in the enacted IPC (s. 153).

20 Macaulay's failure to address this issue is perhaps less surprising. Barry Wright, commenting on an earlier draft of this chapter, noted that debates about the distinction between civil and criminal standards of negligence seem to be essentially a twentieth-century phenomenon.

Subjectivity

Macaulay's draft Code embodies a strong subjective focus.[21] One very important example of this is the rejection of the common law felony-murder rule which was transported into a number of other nineteenth-century criminal codes. For reasons of utility and justice, Macaulay adamantly rejected such an approach:

> To punish as a murderer every man who, while committing a heinous offence, causes death by pure misadventure, is a course which evidently adds nothing to the security of human life ... For example, hundreds of persons in some great cities are in the habit of picking pockets. They know that they are guilty of a great offence ... Unhappily one of these hundred attempts to take the purse of a gentleman who has a loaded pistol in his pocket. The thief touches the trigger, the pistol goes off, the gentleman is shot dead. To treat the case of this pick-pocket differently from that of the numerous pick-pockets who steal under exactly the same circumstances, with exactly the same intentions, with no less risk of causing death ... appears to us an unreasonable course.[22]

The emphasis on subjectivity can also be seen in the way in which the offences are defined. The vast majority require proof of intention or knowledge. Rashness (which is also essentially subjective) and negligence (which is objective) play a far more limited role. For example, the draft Code provided offences of causing death or grievous hurt by rashness or negligence,[23] but the offences against the person that involved lower levels of harm (hurt and assault) were limited to intention or knowledge. Furthermore, where offences based on rashness or negligence were provided, they carried much lower penalties.[24]

The provisions relating to 'receiving stolen property' provide another good example of subjectivity. In Macaulay's draft the prosecution needed to prove not only that the accused was 'fraudulent' (defined by reference to intention) but also that he or she actually *knew* the property in question had been stolen.[25]

Symmetry: Aligning the Physical and Fault Elements

One of the most striking features of Macaulay's draft Code is the careful alignment of the physical element with the fault element. The provisions relating to the non-fatal offences against the person provide the clearest illustration of this symmetry. 'Grievous hurt' is an aggravated form of 'hurt' and a person can only be convicted of 'voluntarily causing grievous hurt' if he or she intended to cause grievous hurt or knew that grievous hurt was likely. Thus, if the accused

---

21 See also Chapter 2 of this volume, above n. 1, at 43; K.J.M. Smith, 'Macaulay's Indian Penal Code: An Illustration of the Accidental Function of Time, Place and Personalities in Law Making' in W.M. Gordon and T.D. Fergus (eds), *Legal History in the Making: Proceedings of the Ninth British Legal History Conference, Glasgow, 1989* (London: Hambledon Press, 1991) 145.

22 T.B. Macaulay, J.M. McLeod, G.W. Anderson and F. Millett, *A Penal Code Prepared by the Indian Law Commissioners* (London: Pelham Richardson, 1838) (reprinted by the Lawbook Exchange, Ltd, 2002) Note M (On Offences Against the Body) 111–12.

23 Macaulay's draft Code, cls. 304 and 327.

24 For example, the maximum penalty for causing death by rashness or negligence was only two years' imprisonment.

25 Macaulay's draft Code, cl. 390.

caused grievous hurt but only intended to cause hurt and did not know that grievous hurt was likely, the offence would only be one of 'voluntarily causing hurt'.[26] Alternatively, if the accused intended to apply force but did not intend to cause hurt and did not know that hurt was likely, the offence would be one of assault and not 'voluntarily causing hurt', even if hurt actually resulted.[27]

This alignment of the fault element and the physical element reflected a commitment to subjectivity as well as a desire for logic and symmetry; accused persons should not be held responsible for consequences which were not within their contemplation at the time of the offence. Macaulay's approach stands in marked contrast to the offence of assault occasioning bodily harm found in many other jurisdictions. The fault element for assault is usually an intention to apply force or subjective recklessness as to whether force will result,[28] and the offence of assault occasioning bodily harm generally only requires proof that there was an assault and that bodily harm resulted from it. In other words, there is no need to prove that the accused contemplated bodily harm.[29]

The desire for alignment and symmetry also fed into Macaulay's provisions with respect to 'voluntary culpable homicide' and 'causing death by rashness or negligence'. The offence of voluntary culpable homicide required proof that the accused intended to cause death or knew that death was likely.[30] Thus, an intention to cause grievous hurt or knowledge that grievous hurt was likely would not suffice. In a similar vein, causing death by rashness or negligence[31] required proof that there was a 'want of due regard for *human life*'. Merely showing a lack of due regard for 'the *safety* of *others*' would not suffice for a homicide offence, though it was sufficient for the offence of causing grievous hurt by negligence.[32]

FAULT ELEMENTS UNDER THE IPC

The IPC retains Macaulay's basic structure and generally works around the same primary fault elements of intention, knowledge that something is likely, rashness and negligence. Like the draft Code, the IPC does not adopt the felony-murder rule. Generally speaking, it also embodies an alignment between the physical element and the fault element. The best examples of this are the offences of voluntarily causing hurt or grievous hurt, which remain as originally drafted.

However, the provisions relating to culpable homicide and murder are very different from those of the draft Code. They depart radically from the alignment principle and the revised provisions have implications for the interpretation of fault elements throughout the IPC. Predictably, given the lack of definitions, the scope of the terms 'rashness' and 'negligence' and their inter-relationship has also given rise to considerable difficulty.

Before outlining the main issues with respect to the culpable homicide and murder provisions and the issues surrounding rashness and negligence, it is necessary to note a number of other changes made in the IPC to the draft Code with respect to the fault elements.

---

26 *Ibid.*, cl. 317.

27 *Ibid.*, cls. 316 and 340.

28 *R v. Venna* [1976] QB 421. See further at 77.

29 *R v. Savage; R v. Parmenter* [1992] AC 699; for a comparison with the Penal Code, see Yeo, Morgan and Chan, above n. 1, paras. [11.15] and [11.31].

30 Macaulay's draft Code, cl. 294.

31 *Ibid.*, cl. 304.

32 *Ibid.*, cl. 327 provided for an offence of causing grievous hurt where the act or omission was 'so rash or negligent as to indicate a want of due regard for the safety of others'.

Injection of New Fault Elements

The IPC, as enacted, contains a number of fault elements that were not in the draft Code, particularly in the context of property offences. First, as noted earlier, the word 'dishonestly' replaced 'fraudulently' in Chapter I. However, the word 'fraudulently' was retained and given a new, and singularly unhelpful, meaning: 'A person is said to do a thing fraudulently if he does that thing with intent to defraud but not otherwise.'[33] This phrase has added a layer of complexity to the provisions relating to cheating that is still unresolved today.[34] A second change, and one which has again caused difficulty, was the addition of a new clause containing the word 'wilfully' into the definition of criminal breach of trust.[35] The word 'wilfully' has no single natural meaning (though at common law it is often used in the same way as 'voluntarily' under the Code) but, contrary to Macaulay's precepts, was simply not defined. The word 'corruptly' was also introduced – again without a definition – in the context of the offences against public justice.[36]

The fourth example, arising from amendments to the offence of receiving stolen property, is more comprehensible. It is also instructive of the fact that the IPC became somewhat less subjective than Macaulay's draft Code. In Macaulay's draft, receiving stolen property required proof that the accused knew the property to be stolen. This would have involved a purely subjective inquiry and proof of actual knowledge on the part of the accused.[37] As enacted, the IPC includes an additional fault element, namely that the accused had 'reason to believe' that the property was stolen.[38] Consistent with the principles of codification, 'reason to believe' is given a statutory definition: 'A person is said to have "reason to believe" a thing if he has sufficient cause to believe that thing but not otherwise.'[39] The result of these amendments was to lower the threshold of liability and to make it more objective.[40]

In summary, the IPC as enacted contains at least five fault elements that were not in Macaulay's draft Code. The four new terms were 'dishonestly' (used in lieu of the word 'fraudulently'), 'wilfully', 'reason to believe' and 'corruptly'. There was also a new definition of 'fraudulently'. These changes primarily affected the scope of the property offences. The offences against the person used the same basic fault elements as Macaulay (intention, knowledge, rashness and negligence). However, changes to the definitions of homicide offences impacted on the interpretation of these fault terms throughout the IPC.

---

33 IPC, s. 25.

34 See *King-Emperor v. Tha By Aw* (1907) 4 BLR 315; *Queen-Empress v. Abbas Ali* (1897) ILR 25 Cal 512; *Seet Soon Guan v. PP* [1955] MLJ 223; and the discussion in Yeo, Morgan and Chan, above n. 1, at paras. [14.77]–[14.80].

35 Yeo, Morgan and Chan, *ibid.*, at paras. [14.45]–[14.52].

36 For example, IPC, ss. 196, 198 and 200.

37 Macaulay's draft Code, cls. 390 and 391.

38 IPC, ss. 411–414.

39 *Ibid.*, s. 26.

40 See Yeo, Morgan and Chan, above n. 1, at paras. [15.8]–[15.10] for a discussion of subjectivity and objectivity in this context. See also below at 80.

Culpable Homicide and Murder

The provisions relating to culpable homicide and murder in the IPC differ radically from Macaulay's original draft and these changes have implications for the whole of the IPC. The ensuing discussion does not purport to provide a detailed critique of what has become (quite contrary to Macaulay's precepts) an over-subtle, labyrinthine and controversial area of law.[41] Rather, the aims are to identify the way in which the changed wording reflected some fundamental differences of approach and the Code-wide impact of the revised wording.

Macaulay's draft Code was very simple. Clauses 294–9 provided the following model:

- Murder was a 'subset' of the generic offence of voluntary culpable homicide (a very different structure from the common law model of murder and manslaughter).
- Voluntary culpable homicide was committed where the accused intended to kill or knew that death was likely.
- Voluntary culpable homicide was murder unless it was committed under the terms of one of three special exceptions, namely provocation, consent or excessive private defence.

This model was not without its difficulties.[42] On the one hand, the fault element appears quite restrictive in the sense that it required the accused to have contemplated *death*. This preserved Macaulay's symmetry but it also meant that other highly culpable states of mind, such as an intention to do grievous hurt, were not covered. For example, a torturer may intend to do quite unspeakable things to victims but may have no intention of killing them and may never have contemplated that they would die (indeed, the purpose of the torturer's calculated cruelty may be to keep them alive to endure further suffering). The torturer may also be more blameworthy than the person who forms an intention to kill on the spur of the moment. On the other hand, it could be argued that knowledge that death is 'likely' sets the threshold too low for the most serious offence known to the criminal law and that a higher level of fault should be required.

The IPC as enacted reflected these concerns. For present purposes, the key changes were as follows:

- Murder is still a subset of culpable homicide. However, 'culpable homicide not amounting to murder' can be committed on the basis of a lower degree of fault and not just on the basis of the special exceptions.[43]
- The three fault elements for culpable homicide are:
  - intention to kill;
  - intention to cause 'such bodily injury as is likely to cause death'; and
  - knowledge that death is likely.
- The five fault elements for murder are:
  - intention to kill (s. 300, first limb);
  - intending 'such bodily injury as the offender knows to be likely' to cause death (s. 300, second limb);
  - intending to cause a bodily injury 'and the bodily injury intended to be inflicted is sufficient in

41 It is puzzling that despite trenchant criticism by the courts and writers, the legislative provisions have remained unchanged for so long.

42 S. Yeo, *Fault in Homicide* (Annandale: Federation Press, 1997) 98–101.

43 Two other special exceptions were also added, namely sudden fight and exceeding the powers of a public servant.

the ordinary course of nature to cause death' (s. 300, third limb);
- knowledge that the act is 'so imminently dangerous that it must in all probability cause death' (s. 300, fourth limb); and
- knowledge that the act is 'so imminently dangerous that it must in all probability cause such bodily injury as is likely to cause death' (s. 300, fourth limb).

These changes were out of line with Macaulay's values and they have had a dramatic effect. Five main points may be made. First, in terms of *comprehensibility* and *accessibility*, the sheer complexity of the terminology (somewhat simplified above) has been a source of continual angst. Secondly, in terms of *certainty* and *democracy*, a good deal depends on judicial interpretation and not on the clarity of legislative expression.[44] Thirdly, Macaulay's *symmetry* has been abandoned: people can be convicted of murder or of culpable homicide not amounting to murder if they intended a bodily injury but had no contemplation of death (or even of grievous hurt).

Fourthly, in line with comments already made about some of the other changes, the enacted provisions are *more objective.* For example, the second limb of s. 299 does not require proof that the accused knew that death was likely – the questions are: (i) whether the person intended a bodily injury; and (ii) whether that injury was objectively likely to cause death.[45] The third limb of s. 300 is also objective in the sense that there is no need to prove that the accused knew that the injuries were sufficient in the ordinary course of nature to cause death.[46] However, the exact meaning of this limb has generated some very complex debates around the question of whether it must be proved that the accused intended to cause the particular injuries that resulted in death or whether it is sufficient to prove an intention to cause some type of injury.[47] The second part of the fourth limb of s. 300 also creates some difficult questions in terms of the balance between subjectivity and objectivity.[48]

Finally, the wording of the fourth limb of s. 300 has implications for the interpretation of intention throughout the Code. Many systems of criminal law now regard knowledge that something must 'in all probability' result (or words to similar effect) as equivalent to intention.[49] However, given that s. 300 expressly distinguishes intention (s. 300, first limb) from knowledge that a result must in all probability occur (s. 300, fourth limb), that does not appear possible under the IPC.

---

44 This has proved especially true of the third limb of s. 300; see also below, n. 47 and at 82–3.

45 See the discussion in Yeo, Morgan and Chan, above n. 1, at para. [9.58].

46 *Ibid.*, at para. [9.59]. For a different and more detailed perspective, see V.V. Ramraj, 'Murder without an Intention to Kill' [2000] *Singapore Journal of Legal Studies* 560.

47 The more important cases include: *Virsa Singh v. State of Punjab* AIR 1958 SC 465; *Jai Prakash v. Delhi Administration* (1991) 2 SCC 32; *Ike Mohamed Yasin bin Hussin v. PP* [1974–6] SLR(R) 596; *PP v. Visuvanathan* [1977–8] SLR(R) 27; and *PP v. Lim Poh Lye* [2005] 4 SLR(R) 582. Singapore appears to have generated the most complex case law and the liveliest academic debates: see M. Sornarajah, 'The Definition of Murder under the Penal Code' [1994] *Singapore Journal of Legal Studies* 1; Ramraj, *ibid.*; S. Yeo, 'Fault for Homicide in Singapore' in J. Horder (ed.), *Homicide Law in Comparative Perspective* (Oxford: Hart Publishing, 2007); S. Yeo, 'Academic Contributions and Judicial Interpretations of Section 300(c) Murder', *Singapore Law Gazette* (April 2004) 21; A. Tan, 'Revisiting Section 300(c) Murder in Singapore' (2005) 17 *Singapore Academy of Law Journal* 693; W. Chan, 'What's Wrong with Section 300(c) Murder?' [2005] *Singapore Journal of Legal Studies* 462; Yeo, Morgan and Chan, above n. 1, at paras. [9.65]–[9.80].

48 Yeo, Morgan and Chan, *ibid.*, at paras. [9.46]–[9.49].

49 See below at 74–7.

Rashness and Negligence

The IPC retained the concepts of rashness and negligence from Macaulay's draft with some subtle but significant changes. The main features and changes are as follows:

- As in Macaulay's draft Code, rashness and negligence are bracketed together in the offence definitions.
- The enacted IPC extended liability for negligence into more areas than Macaulay's draft. In particular, the offence of voluntarily causing hurt by rashness or negligence was introduced.[50]
- As in Macaulay's draft, much lower penalties applied to cases of rashness and negligence than to cases of intention or knowledge. For example, causing death by rashness or negligence carried a maximum of two years' imprisonment compared with a maximum of life imprisonment for most forms of culpable homicide not amounting to murder.
- Macaulay's draft did not define either rashness or negligence. However, it did state that in cases involving death, it was necessary to prove a 'want of due regard for human life', whereas a more general 'want of due regard for the safety of others' was sufficient for the offence of causing grievous hurt by rashness or negligence. The equivalent provisions in the enacted Code simply refer to a 'rash or negligent act not amounting to culpable homicide'.[51] Case law has therefore needed to provide definitions of rashness and negligence and to try and explain the degree of fault required.
- The cases on rashness and negligence have not been consistent in their definitions and interpretations. However, the better view, and the one supported by most of the leading cases, is that rashness is subjective and involves proof that the accused knew there was a risk of harm. Negligence, on the other hand, is objective; it essentially involves the accused falling beneath the standards that would be expected of a reasonable person in such circumstances.
- In some cases a fully objective approach to negligence has been adopted whereby the test is purely that of a hypothetical 'reasonable person'. In others this test appears to be slightly qualified in that the courts ask whether the accused would themselves have recognised the risk if they had turned their minds to the question.[52]
- Singapore has recently amended its Penal Code to provide for higher penalties in cases of rashness as opposed to negligence.[53] This means that the boundaries between rashness and negligence need to be firmed up and made consistent.
- There has been considerable confusion over the standard of negligence that must be proved. The courts in Malaysia and Singapore have now rejected the 'gross negligence' standard that applies in the common law. At least in Singapore, the courts have also rejected the idea of some type of 'intermediate' standard falling between civil negligence and gross negligence. Instead, they apply the same standard as the civil law. In Singapore (and probably in Malaysia), the only differences between civil negligence and criminal negligence lie in the standard of proof and in the fact that the

50 Macaulay's draft Code limited offences based on rashness and negligence to cases where death or grievous hurt resulted; see above at 64.

51 The sections dealing with hurt, grievous hurt and endangerment (IPC, ss. 336–338) still refer to conduct that is so rash or negligent as to endanger human life or the personal safety of others.

52 See below at 78–9. See generally Yeo, Morgan and Chan, above n. 1, at paras. [4.47]–[4.28], [4.32]–[4.36] and [10.15]–[10.40].

53 For example, causing death by rashness now attracts a maximum of five years' imprisonment whereas causing death by negligence still attracts a maximum of two years.

criminal law is said to involve a stricter causation test.[54]

This brief summary shows that there has been a good deal of confusion over the boundaries of rashness and, particularly, of negligence. In reforming the IPC, it will be appropriate to add definitions of rashness and negligence; to differentiate the two terms more clearly (something that will be increasingly important if, as in Singapore, the penalties are to differ); and to clarify issues such as the standard of negligence.

MODERN DISCOURSES AND MODERN PROVISIONS

Most of the books on the IPC adopt the approach of discussing the Code section by section. However, as we have seen, the fault elements are not defined in a single part of the Code but often emerge only in the offence definitions. As a result, the discussion of fault elements in the classic Indian texts is generally quite dispersed and there is often no single overall analysis of terms such as intention, knowledge, rashness and negligence.[55] A good deal of the discussion in academic articles on the IPC has focused on specific areas, such as the interpretation of the third limb of s. 300[56] and the vexed question of strict liability.[57] These discussions are extremely valuable but, as law reform endeavours in other jurisdictions have illustrated, any process of modernising the Code will require a thematic focus on fault provisions across the board.

The following discussion and the draft proposals draw on the scholarly literature and on reforms in other jurisdictions but also endeavour to keep faith with Macaulay's overriding values and to reflect the adage that 'if it ain't broke, why fix it?'.

Basic Principles and Values

There is a very real risk that in seeking to 'modernise' and 'improve' the IPC, we may lose some of its attractive simplicity. We may be tempted to over-define terms that are workable and have a common-sense meaning or to inject too many subtleties and variants. However, the preceding discussion has shown that there is room for greater clarity around a number of key concepts. It is therefore recommended that the 'General Explanations' at the start of the IPC (currently Chapter II) should be expanded and amended to include: (i) some general principles relating to fault

54 *Lim Poh Eng v. PP* [1999] 1 SLR(R) 428; *Ng Keng Yong v. PP* [2004] 4 SLR(R) 89; *S Balakrishnan v. PP* [2005] 4 SLR(R) 249.

55 Some of the books in Malaysia and Singapore have adopted a more thematic analysis of the fault elements: see K.L. Koh, C.M.V. Clarkson and N.A. Morgan, *Criminal Law in Singapore and Malaysia: Text and Materials* (Singapore: Malayan Law Journal, 1989) Chapter 3; Yeo, Morgan and Chan, above n. 1, Chapter 4.

56 See above n. 47.

57 See B. McKillop, 'Strict Liability Offences in Singapore and Malaysia' (1967) 9 *Malaya Law Review* 118; M. Sornarajah, 'Defences to Strict Liability Offences in Singapore and Malaysia' (1985) 27 *Malaya Law Review* 1; C.M.V. Clarkson, 'Rape: Emasculation of the Penal Code' [1988] 1 *Malayan Law Journal* cxiii; M. Hor, 'Strict Liability in Criminal Law: A Re-Examination' [1996] *Singapore Journal of Legal Studies* 312; W. Chan, 'Requirement of Fault in Strict Liability' (1999) 11 *Singapore Academy of Law Journal* 98; M. Hor, 'Managing *Mens Rea* in Singapore' (2006) 18 *Singapore Academy of Law Journal* 314, 358–68.

elements; and (ii) workable definitions of key fault elements.[58] As part of this process, obsolete or otiose fault terms should be deleted from the Code.

Although it is easy to pick fault with some parts of the Code, notably the homicide provisions, it is also important to remember that most of the Code has stood the test of time remarkably well. Its main fault elements probably generate fewer problems than common law concepts such as recklessness, and the Code terminology is familiar to its users. The following proposals therefore use existing Code terminology as far as possible.

Offences Where No Fault Element is Specified

'Absolute' and 'Strict' Liability

Since Macaulay's time, criminal laws have expanded rapidly to cover aspects of human endeavour that could never have been in his contemplation. These include modern industrial and commercial activities, road traffic, communications, international travel, drug control and other areas of essential regulation. Not infrequently, legislation which is enacted in such areas does not specify a fault element that must be proved by the prosecution. Even within the IPC itself, there are some very serious offences – notably rape – for which no fault element is specified.

In such cases, difficult questions arise as to what level of culpability is involved in the offence. At common law, application of the maxim *actus non facit reum nisi mens sit rea* leads to a presumption that the prosecution must prove subjective *mens rea* (often 'knowledge') even if the legislation is silent. However, this presumption may be rebutted in some circumstances, especially if the infraction is not considered 'truly criminal' in nature and if it relates to a matter of public health or safety where a conviction will promote greater compliance.[59]

It is often said that in cases where the presumption of *mens rea* is rebutted, the offence is one of 'strict liability'. However, different jurisdictions use the term 'strict liability' in different ways. In English law, strict liability generally means that there is no fault element and no scope to negate liability through a defence such as mistake (though some other defences such as necessity may apply). However, in Australian law, the term 'strict liability' refers to cases where a defence of honest and reasonable mistake is available, even if there is no fault element as such; the term 'absolute' liability is then used in cases where no such defence is available.[60] The Australian usage is adopted here.

IPC Structure and Non-Code Offences

Amirthalingam has questioned whether Macaulay really intended to provide a general defence of mistake of fact.[61] However, from early on, the courts have interpreted s. 79 as constituting such a defence. Section 79 is one of the 'General Exceptions' in Chapter IV and s. 40(2) provides that the Chapter IV exceptions apply to 'a thing punishable under this Code or under any other law for the time being in force'. It follows, logically, that there should be no offences of absolute

---

58 See further Chapter 1 of this volume, above n. 2.

59 See *Gammon (Hong Kong) Ltd v. Attorney General of Hong Kong* [1985] AC 1.

60 That terminology is now well recognised in Singapore and to some extent is also recognised in Malaysia; see Yeo, Morgan and Chan, above n. 1, at para. [7.6].

61 See Chapter 5 of this volume, above n. 7.

liability in IPC jurisdictions unless the legislature has made clear its intention to remove the mistake of fact defence.

It is therefore most unfortunate that courts in IPC jurisdictions have sometimes ignored this basic structure and resorted to common law doctrines, and it is interesting to compare the approach of the 'Griffith Code' courts in Queensland and Western Australia. The Griffith Code shares much of the same basic structure as the IPC and the courts have adhered far more rigorously to that structure. Griffith Code courts rarely use the term *mens rea* (even as shorthand for the fault element), eschew reference to strict liability and do not read in fault elements that are not inherent in the wording of the statute.[62]

Defences, Offence Elements and Onus of Proof

The defence of mistake plays a pivotal role in ascribing blame under the IPC. By way of example, rape is defined, in essence, as sexual intercourse with a woman without her consent.[63] The prosecution must therefore prove, beyond a reasonable doubt, that the accused man: (i) had sexual intercourse with the woman; and (ii) that the intercourse was not consensual. However, even if these offence elements are proved, the accused may argue that he believed the woman had consented to sexual intercourse. Legal systems have two main options in dealing with such an argument. The natural reading of the IPC is that the man's claim should be tested through the defence of mistake of fact: in other words, did he believe, 'in good faith'[64] that she was consenting?[65] The common law, on the other hand, has approached the problem by asking whether the accused 'intended' to penetrate the woman without her consent or was 'reckless' as to whether she consented.

There are two major differences between these approaches which must be understood in considering options for reform. First, the common law is subjective: if the accused believed that the woman was consenting, he is not guilty, even if his belief was unreasonable.[66] Under the defence of mistake approach, however, the court must consider not only whether he made a mistake as to consent but also whether that mistake was made 'in good faith' – essentially an inquiry into reasonableness.

An even more fundamental difference relates to the onus of proof. The common law requires the prosecution to prove beyond reasonable doubt that the accused did not genuinely believe the woman was consenting. However, under the Evidence Act that complements the IPC, general exceptions must be proved by the accused on the balance of probabilities.[67] In the rape example, the accused must therefore establish on the balance of probabilities that: (i) he made a genuine mistake about consent; and (ii) his mistake was made 'in good faith'.

---

62 An excellent and short example, which also illustrates the onus of proof issues raised below, is *R. v. Hutchinson* [2003] WASCA 323 (Supreme Court of Western Australia).

63 IPC, s. 375.

64 IPC, s. 52. 'Good faith' essentially involves asking whether the accused exercised due care and attention in the circumstances, taking account of that person's capacity and experience: see *State of Orissa v. Ram Bahadur Thapa* 1960 Cri LJ 1349; *Chirangi v. State* AIR 1952 Nag 282; *Tan Khee Wee Iris v. PP* [1995] 1 SLR(R) 723; *PP v. Mohd Amin bin Mohd Razali* [2002] 5 MLJ 406.

65 This is now clearly accepted as the correct approach; see *PP v. Teo Eng Chan* [1987] SLR(R) 567 and the discussion in Yeo, Morgan and Chan, above n. 1, at paras. [12.87]–[12.91].

66 *DPP v. Morgan* [1976] AC 182.

67 The Indian Evidence Act 1872 (Act 1 of 1872), s. 105. See also the Malaysian Evidence Act 1950 (Act 56), s. 105 and the Singaporean Evidence Act (Cap. 97, 1997 Rev. Ed.), s. 107.

In terms of the substantive law, the Queensland and Western Australian Criminal Codes adopt a similar structure to the IPC in that mistakes as to consent are considered through the defence of mistake rather than through a positive fault element. The defence of mistake also involves an objective as well as a subjective inquiry. However, the onus of proof rules are radically different in that the accused need only satisfy an evidential onus. In other words, he must adduce sufficient evidence of a reasonable mistake for the issue to be considered by the court (a much lower hurdle than proving a matter on the balance of probabilities). If he satisfies this evidential onus, he will be acquitted unless the prosecution can prove beyond reasonable doubt that either: (i) he did not really believe the person was consenting; or (ii) his belief in consent was unreasonable.

Reform Options

It is necessary as part of the reform process to consider how to deal with cases where no fault element has been set. The common law 'presumption of *mens rea*' approach is certainly not viable. It does not accord with the principles underpinning codification (including accessibility, certainty, precision and comprehensiveness) or with the basic structure of the IPC.

In light of the preceding discussion, this leaves three options: (i) continue to rely on the defences with the current onus of proof rules; (ii) continue to rely on the defences but alter the onus of proof rules in line with the Griffith Code; or (iii) select a 'default' term that will apply in cases where the legislation is silent.

The Australian Commonwealth Criminal Code uses option (iii) and the default term is generally recklessness.[68] Translated into IPC language, one option would therefore be to set a default term of 'rashness'. This would change the law substantially in that the prosecution would have to prove the default term beyond reasonable doubt. This would, for example, bring the law relating to rape more into line with the common law.

The first option is far simpler in the sense that it reflects the current law, but it should be chosen only after careful debate. All criminal law systems have some defences (typically insanity) which must be proved on the balance of probabilities by the defence. And where policy arguments specifically justify this, they may provide that in some circumstances a different rule applies to standard defences such as mistake.[69] However, it can be argued that the IPC's *general rule* that an accused must prove a defence places too great a burden on the accused and is difficult to reconcile with the presumption of innocence. This issue obviously has implications not only for cases where no fault term is set but also for the defences in general.

It is therefore recommended that, in parallel with the process of reforming the IPC, there should be a review of the provisions of the associated Evidence Act with respect to the appropriate onus of proof for the defences. This review should consider: (i) the circumstances in which the prosecution should be required to disprove a validly raised defence beyond reasonable doubt; and (ii) the circumstances in which the accused should be required prove a defence on the balance of probabilities.

---

68 Section 5.6(2). For a general discussion of this Code, see Chapter 13 of this volume (M. Goode, 'An Evaluation of Judicial Interpretations of the Australian Model Criminal Code').

69 For example, in cases involving sexual offences against children, the Western Australian and Queensland Criminal Codes require an accused who raises a defence of mistake of age to prove, on the balance of probabilities, that he honestly and reasonably believed the child was at least 16 years of age. See *Hutchinson*, above n. 62.

Motive and Desire

Fault elements such as intention and knowledge are different from concepts such as desire and motive. Desire and motive involve a consideration of a person's feelings or of their reasons for acting in a particular way. Intention, knowledge and other fault terms are more 'neutral'. As a matter of evidence, it is obvious that motive and desire may be relevant to considering whether the person had the requisite intention,[70] but they must not be equated with intention. For example, people who board an aeroplane in Mumbai bound for London intend to go to London even if they loathe the place and would much prefer to stay where they are.[71] And a person who destroys property in order to prevent a fire spreading intends to destroy that property even though he or she has a laudable motive for doing so. Generally, motive is only relevant in the context of a defence (in this example, the defence of necessity). If it is to be relevant to the elements of an offence, this should be specified.[72]

These principles are well recognised and largely uncontroversial. However, by way of completeness, it would be appropriate to consider including in the IPC a provision along the following lines:

> (1) Unless otherwise expressly declared, the motive by which a person is induced to do or omit to do an act is immaterial to criminal responsibility;[73]
>
> (2) A person may intend something even if he or she would prefer a different outcome.
>
> *Illustration*
>
> A is the mother of a nine-year-old son, V. V is terminally ill and will die soon. A smothers V with a pillow and V dies from suffocation. A has killed V. A intended to kill V even though her motive was to relieve his suffering and she would have preferred that he could live.

Voluntarily

Section 39 of the IPC uses 'voluntarily' as an umbrella term to embrace two fault elements, namely intention and knowledge that a result is likely. In many cases where the word 'voluntarily' is used, such as the offences of voluntarily causing hurt and grievous hurt, reference to s. 39 is unnecessary because the offence definitions specifically restate these fault elements. However, in some cases, the word 'voluntarily' stands alone, so recourse to s. 39 is required.[74] In effect,

70 For a recent example, see *Mohamed Ali bin Johari v. PP* [2008] 4 SLR(R) 1058.

71 This example is based on one given by Lord Bridge of Harwich in *R v. Moloney* [1985] AC 905.

72 There may be some situations where motive is seen as necessary in determining blame over and above the defences. For example, a man may spank a child for legitimate reasons of discipline or for illegitimate sexual satisfaction. The English case of *R v. Court* [1989] AC 28 took the view that it was only by looking at the accused's motive that it could be decided whether this was an indecent assault. The same issue may not arise under the Code's roughly equivalent offence of 'outraging modesty' under s. 354: see Yeo, Morgan and Chan, above n. 1, at paras. [12.72]–[12.76]. But the basic point remains: if motive is to be relevant, it should be expressly stated to be relevant.

73 This draws on Criminal Code (WA), s. 23, which states: 'Unless otherwise expressly declared, the motive by which a person is induced to do or omit to do an act, or to form an intention, is immaterial so far as regards criminal responsibility.' This provision has largely stood the test of time.

74 The more important sections in the IPC include ss. 107 and 112 (abetment); ss. 118 and 120 (concealing offences); ss. 128 and 186 (offences relating to public servants); ss. 277 and 278 (pollution); s. 339 (wrongful restraint); and s. 377 ('unnatural' offences).

therefore, the word 'voluntarily' either provides a convenient label for an offence or a shorthand term for two separate fault elements.

'Voluntarily' is a potentially confusing word which is more commonly used with reference to a person's conduct than with reference to the results of that conduct.[75] In principle, it is also preferable to avoid umbrella terms and for each section that creates an offence to specifically state the required fault element(s). It is therefore recommended that the definition of 'voluntarily' under s. 39 should be repealed[76] and that there should be specific provisions to embed the principle that acts or omissions must be 'voluntary'.[77]

Intention

At the risk of over-simplification, it can be said that, after some tortured debates, Australian and English common law generally attribute a threefold meaning to intention. A person will be held to intend something if: (i) it was their direct aim or purpose; (ii) they knew that it was absolutely certain to occur as a result of pursuing that direct aim/purpose; or (iii) they knew that the consequence was 'virtually certain' to occur (or a formulation to similar effect). For example, in one leading Australian case, it was said that: 'If a person does something that is virtually certain to result in another event occurring and knows that that event is certain or virtually certain to occur, for legal purposes at least he or she intends it to occur.'[78] The Australian Commonwealth Criminal Code adopts a different formulation but the effect is similar: 'A person has intention with respect to a result if he or she means to bring it about or is aware that it will occur in the ordinary course of events.'[79]

Under the terms of Macaulay's draft Code, it would have been possible to give intention the same scope as these formulations because knowledge that something is 'virtually certain' to occur involves a much higher degree of fault than knowledge that something is 'likely'. However, the amendments to culpable homicide and murder in the enacted Code mean that intention probably only embraces points (i) and (ii) above, namely a person's direct aim or knowledge of an absolute certainty. This is because s. 300 very specifically distinguishes between an intention to kill (s. 300, first limb) and knowledge that an act is 'so imminently dangerous that it must in all probability cause death' (s. 300, fourth limb) – a formulation that is extremely close to point (iii) above.[80] Given the principle that words in a statute should bear the same meaning

---

75 See also Chapter 4 of this volume (B. Sullivan, 'The Conduct Elements of Offences') at 101.

76 If s. 39 is repealed, it will be necessary to work through the offences where the word 'voluntarily' currently stands alone and to decide on the appropriate fault element. Repealing s. 39 would not necessarily prevent the continued use of the labels 'voluntarily causing hurt' and 'voluntarily causing grievous hurt', labels that are familiar and well understood by IPC practitioners.

77 This can be done through a 'positive' statement about voluntariness, as suggested by Gerry Ferguson in Chapter 10 of this volume ('Insanity') at 254–5. It can also be achieved through a 'negative' definition which outlines situations where an act or omission will not be voluntary, as suggested by Sullivan in Chapter 4 of this volume, above n. 75, at 99–101.

78 *R v. Peters* (1998) 192 CLR 493, *per* McHugh J. The judge was clearly drawing on English cases such as *R v. Nedrick* [1986] 3 All ER 1 (itself the culmination of a series of earlier cases such as *R v. Moloney* [1985] AC 905 and *R v. Hancock* [1986] AC 455). For a more recent English exposition, see *R v. Woollin* [1999] AC 82.

79 Criminal Code (Cth), s. 5.2(3).

80 See above at 66–8.

throughout that statute (unless otherwise provided), this means that intention throughout the Code must carry a narrower meaning than other modern formulations suggest.

There are two main options in terms of providing a statutory definition of intention. On the one hand, it can be argued that the strict use of the English language dictates the adoption of the 'narrow' interpretation currently embodied in s. 300. If I am taking a shot at goal in a game of football, my intention is to score a goal. Scoring a goal – nothing more and nothing else – is my only intention. This is so even if, as a result of my ineptitude or the difficulty of the shot, I know that I will in all probability miss the target. One option is therefore to define intention in this 'narrow', linguistically precise sense.

On the other hand, it can be argued that it is better to work within the Code's more usual fourfold typology (intention, knowledge that something is likely, rashness and negligence). If this approach is taken, it would be appropriate to give intention a meaning that broadly accords with currently accepted usage in Australian and English law. In other words, knowledge that death 'must in all probability result' would still form part of the fault element for murder but would be embraced by the 'intention to kill'.

Since a number of other areas of law, including the law of attempts[81] and the definition of dishonesty, are also defined by reference to intention, a broader definition of intention will have some impact on these areas. However, that does not appear to be problematic or unworkable. Even as the law under the IPC stands now, knowing that something must in all probability result in death is so close to intending death (both morally and linguistically) that it provides evidence from which a court 'may find it easy to infer' that the person intended that result.[82]

On balance, and recognising that the proposal does some injustice to strict English language usage, the second approach is therefore recommended. As shown later, this will bring some benefits in terms of simplifying, clarifying and modernising the Code, and especially the homicide provisions.[83] This approach will also bring the Code definition of intention more into line with current Australian and English legal usage.

In terms of drafting, there are a number of options. However, it is recommended that the existing Code language – knowing that something will in all probability occur – should probably be retained. This language is at least as precise and workable as options such as 'foresight of a virtual certainty' or being 'aware that something will occur in the ordinary course of events.' It has the added benefit of being familiar to Code practitioners. The following definition of 'intention' is therefore suggested:

> A person intends something if he or she:
> (a) means to bring it about;
> (b) knows that it is absolutely certain to occur; or
> (c) knows that it will in all probability occur.[84]
>
> *Illustrations*
>
> (a) A sets fire to a house. A knows that V is in the house and lights the fire with the purpose of killing V. V dies. A intends to kill V.

---

81 See further Chapter 6 of this volume (W. Chan, 'Abetment, Criminal Conspiracy and Attempt').

82 On dishonesty, see below at 79–80.

83 See below at 81–4.

84 Of the other options, the writer prefers the phrase 'knows that it is virtually certain to occur' to the phrase 'knows that it will occur in the ordinary course of events.' The former is simpler and clearer, and also offers better symmetry with the rest of the drafting. On the use of 'knowledge', see the next section of this chapter.

(b) A decides to kill V by shooting V through a glass window. A knows that the window will be broken if he or she shoots at V. A intends to kill V. A also intends to break the window.

(c) A sets fire to a house. A knows that V is in the house. A says that his or her purpose was not to kill V but only to frighten V. A is very sorry when V dies in the fire.[85] If A knows that what he or she is doing will in all probability cause death, A intends to kill, even if he or she does not desire or aim to kill.

Knowledge

It can be argued that, strictly speaking, knowledge is an 'absolute' term that should only be used in relation to facts. For example, I either know that Singapore's international passenger airport is called Changi or I do not know this. Knowledge may sometimes be used in a similarly absolute way in the criminal law. However, an 'absolutist' view of knowledge presents some difficulties. The most serious crimes are result crimes and it would be extremely rare to be able to say that you know with absolute certainty that something will happen. Even if I intend to kill you by shooting you from point-blank range, I cannot be 'absolutely certain' that you will die as you may, unknown to me, be wearing a bulletproof vest.

Therefore, like intention, knowledge tends to be used in a less absolute way. However, the extent to which it is broadened varies between jurisdictions. The IPC has always used 'knowledge that something is likely' as the threshold for most of its more serious crimes. The Australian Commonwealth Criminal Code does not extend knowledge this far: 'a person has knowledge of a circumstance or result if he or she is aware that it exists or will exist in the ordinary course of events'.[86]

There is obviously room to debate the linguistic merits of the proposition that you can *know* something to be *likely*. Arguably, it is more accurate to ask whether the person *believes* or *realises* that something is likely. However, it is submitted that common sense and workability must sometimes take priority over linguistic nicety.[87] There is no indication that judges and jury members have been unable to understand or apply the 'knowledge of likelihood' test, and it is such a familiar part of the IPC that it may be pointless and even detrimental to alter the language. Most importantly, knowledge that a result is likely provides an appropriate threshold of liability for the more serious offences, with offences based on rashness and negligence attracting a lower level of liability.

There is room to debate whether the word 'likely' should be given a further statutory definition or whether an alternative word such as 'probable' should be used. However, it is submitted that the word 'likely' is capable of sensible application and that attempts to further explain such terms will add complexity but no practical value.

---

85 This illustration draws in part on the illustration to s. 39 (the definition of 'voluntarily'). This illustration also tends to affirm the view expressed in the text that intention currently carries a narrow meaning in the Code:

> A sets fire, at night, to an inhabited house in a large town, for the purpose of facilitating a robbery, and thus causes the death of a person. Here A may not have intended to cause death and may even be sorry that death has been caused by this act; yet, if he or she knew that he was likely to cause death, he or she has caused death voluntarily.

86 Criminal Code (Cth), s. 5.3.

87 Chapter 9 of this volume (S. Yeo, 'Duress and Necessity'), at 229, also emphasises the need to reconcile principle with pragmatism. See also Chapter 2 of this volume, above n. 1, at 41, 43 and 53.

In terms of the relationship with other fault elements, knowledge that something is likely can sensibly be differentiated from knowledge that something 'must in all probability' result (which, under the earlier proposals, will be embraced by intention). It can also be readily differentiated from lower levels of risk recognition that may be encompassed by the concept of 'rashness'. Taking these considerations into account, the following definition of knowledge is suggested:

> A person knows something is likely if he or she realises or believes that it is likely to happen.
> *Illustration*
> A throws a small stone in the direction of V's head. If A knows that this will in all probability cause hurt to V, A intends to cause hurt to V. If A realises that V is likely to suffer hurt, A has knowledge that hurt to V is likely. If A realises that there is some degree of risk in throwing the stone but believes that the risk of hitting or hurting V is quite low, A does not know that hurt is likely (but may be found to have been 'rash').

Rashness

As we have seen, the IPC does not currently define rashness and the courts have not always been consistent in their definitions. However, it is generally agreed that rashness involves proof that the accused did recognise that there was a risk of the prohibited harm occurring – in other words, it involves 'advertent' risk taking.[88]

Viewed in this way, rashness is essentially the same as what has commonly been called 'subjective recklessness'.[89] However, a number of cases on recklessness, especially under road traffic legislation, have taken the view that recklessness should also embrace some forms of inadvertent risk-taking. In particular, the Malaysian courts have followed some English case law in holding that people who fail to give attention to serious and obvious risks that they have created should be regarded as reckless.[90]

In developing a definition of rashness, it will be necessary to consider whether there should be any extension beyond advertent risk-taking. However, it is submitted that it is preferable to limit cases of rashness to advertent risk-taking and to leave cases of inadvertent risk-taking to negligence. The question of whether there is any need to use recklessness in legislation outside of the IPC and, if so, whether it should be extended to the failure to give attention to an obvious risk is a matter for separate debate.

The previous section recommended that the IPC should continue to use 'knowledge that something is likely' as the threshold for the more serious offences. Consequently, it will be

88 In the leading case of *In re Nidamarti Nagabhushanam* (1872) 7 MHC 119, *per* Holloway J. at 120, it was said that 'culpable rashness is acting with the consciousness that the mischievous and illegal consequences may follow, but with the hope that they will not, and often with the belief that the actor has taken sufficient precaution to prevent their happening. The imputability arises from acting despite the consciousness'.

89 The subjective approach to recklessness was exemplified by cases such as *R v. Cunningham* [1957] 2 QB 396 and *R v. Stephenson* [1979] 1 QB 695. See generally C.M.V. Clarkson and H.M. Keating, *Criminal Law: Text and Materials* (5th edn, London: Sweet & Maxwell, 2003) 144–72.

90 *PP v. Zulkifli bin Omar* [1998] 6 MLJ 65, adopting the views of the English House of Lords in *R v. Reid* [1992] 3 All ER 673, *R v. Caldwell* [1982] AC 341 and *R v. Lawrence* [1982] AC 510. See generally N. Morgan and S. Yeo, 'Defining the Fault Elements of Driving Offences' (2007) 19 *Singapore Academy of Law Journal* 205. More recently, English law has reverted to a subjective interpretation of recklessness: *R v. G* [2004] 1 AC 1034.

necessary, in defining rashness, to embed a lower level of risk recognition. Drawing on IPC experience and, to some extent, the wording of the Australian Commonwealth Criminal Code, the following drafting is recommended:

> A person behaves rashly if:
> (a) he or she is aware that the prohibited harm may result[91] from his or her acts or omissions; and
> (b) having regard to the circumstances known to him or her it is unjustifiable to take that risk.

Negligence

It is accepted that negligence is objective in the sense that the person can be liable even if he or she did not recognise any risk that the prohibited harm would occur. However, two main issues require clarification in any statutory definition.

First, it will be necessary to decide whether the test of negligence is wholly objective or embodies some reference to the capacity of the accused. A wholly objective test would ask whether a completely objective, hypothetical reasonable person would have recognised the risks of what he or she was doing. An alternative view is that the test should be whether the particular accused, given his or her intellectual capacity and experience, should have recognised the risk.

Secondly, the definition should clarify the standard of negligence that is required. The current position, at least in Singapore, is that the criminal law and civil law standards are the same. The main justifications for this are said to be the difficulty of establishing different standards, the fact that the penalties for negligence-based offences are relatively low, the fact that the criminal law imposes a higher standard of proof and the view that the causation tests are stricter in the criminal law than the civil law.[92] However, it can also be argued that it is possible to have different standards of negligence (as shown, for example, in road traffic legislation) and that there should be a sharper delineation of criminal liability from civil liability.

The arguments on all of these issues have been debated for many years and have no easy resolution. The following proposal is therefore somewhat tentative. However, in the spirit of Macaulay, with his preference for subjectivity, it embodies the view that in assessing negligence, some account should be taken of the position of the capacity and experience of the particular accused. It also builds in a test of criminal negligence that is higher than the civil standard:

---

91 The word 'may' is taken from *In re Nidamarti Nagabhushanam,* above n. 87. The Australian Criminal Code (Cth), s. 5.4, uses the test of whether a person is aware of a '*substantial* risk' that the result will occur. However, this begs the question of what 'substantial' means. Sullivan in Chapter 4 of this volume (above n. 75, at 92) observes that 'substantial' is a 'term of art' in the context of causation and means 'more than minimal'. Goode in Chapter 13 of this volume (above n. 68, at 317–18), notes that 'substantial risk' has been interpreted in the context of recklessness to mean 'real or of substance'. Terms of art should have no place in a code. And to define 'substantial' as 'more than minimal' simply does not accord with normal usage. When I eat a plate of food in a restaurant I am happy to be served a 'substantial' portion, but a portion that is merely 'more than minimal' will leave me feeling angry, disappointed and hungry. If a perceived risk is so insubstantial that it should not attract criminal liability, the case can be ruled out by a sensible application of paragraph (b) on the basis that taking such a risk was justifiable.

92 *Lim Poh Eng v. PP*, above n. 54; *Ng Keng Yong v. PP*, above n. 54; *S Balakrishnan v. PP*, above n. 54. See Yeo, Morgan and Chan, above n. 1, at paras. [4.33] and [10.32]–[10.37].

A person is negligent if his or her conduct:

(a) falls well short of the standard of care that a reasonable person with the same capacity and experience as the accused would exercise in the same circumstances; and

(b) is so far below such standards that it merits criminal punishment.[93]

Although, under these proposals, rashness will be defined subjectively to set it apart from objective negligence, it must be recognised that negligence can involve some very high levels of culpability. For example, the sustained failure to provide food to a young child in one's care may be more deserving of greater censure than a momentary lapse of judgment resulting in subjective risk-taking. And failing to take account of a very obvious and very high risk may sometimes be more blameworthy than consciously choosing to run a low-level risk. For these reasons – and recognising that this may be somewhat at odds with Macaulay's subjectivity – some cases involving negligence may well be deserving of a higher penalty than some cases of rashness.

Other Fault Terms

Once the meanings of the four primary Code terms – intention, knowledge, rashness and negligence – have been determined, it will be necessary to consider whether the other fault elements should be retained, repealed or amended. As we have seen, they include 'dishonestly', 'reason to believe', 'fraudulently', 'wilfully', 'wantonly', 'malignantly' and 'corruptly'. By far the most significant and widely used of these other terms are 'dishonestly' and 'reason to believe'.

It is beyond the scope of this chapter to analyse all these terms, as that is an exercise that will need to be undertaken as part of further reviews of specific offence definitions. However, some key points will be made.

Dishonestly

'Dishonestly' is defined by reference to intention and it is well established that taking a risk of causing wrongful gain or wrongful loss, or being grossly negligent, will not constitute dishonesty. It must be proved that the accused *intended* such loss or gain.[94] This imposes important limitations on the scope of the property offences. It has also been stated in some recent cases on criminal breach of trust that the law must be flexible enough to recognise the commercial reality that entrepreneurial activities and investment decisions will very often involve some degree of risk.[95]

The definition of intention proposed above would mean that dishonesty would be established if it could be proved that the accused knew that wrongful gain or wrongful loss would in all probability result, even this was not their direct aim. However, this should not offend the principle that legitimate entrepreneurial activities commonly involve some level of risk. First, dishonesty requires proof of an intention to cause *wrongful* gain or loss, not just an intent to cause loss or gain. Wrongful gain is 'gain by *unlawful means* of property to which the person gaining is *not legally entitled*' and wrongful loss is 'loss *by unlawful means* of property to which the person

93 The draft proposal is, in effect, a somewhat simplified version of the formulation in the Australian Commonwealth Criminal Code.

94 See Yeo, Morgan and Chan, above n. 1, at paras. [14.41]–[14.44] and the cases discussed there.

95 See, for example, *Cheam Tat Pang v. PP* [1996] 1 SLR(R) 161.

losing it is legally entitled'.[96] The italicised words embody a number of protections for legitimate activities. Secondly, if it is proved that the accused knew that wrongful loss or gain 'would in all probability result', that person was exhibiting a high degree of fault and should not escape liability solely on the basis that his or her direct aim was not to cause wrongful gain or loss.

In summary, and subject to the findings of a full review of property offences, the definition of dishonesty has stood the test of time and can be retained.

Reason to Believe

Macaulay did not use the term 'reason to believe', but it was introduced in s. 26 of the IPC. To establish 'reason to believe', it must be proved that the accused had 'sufficient cause to believe'. Macaulay had adopted a more subjective approach to the offences in question (such as receiving stolen property) and had specified that actual knowledge was required. The injection of 'reason to believe' was designed to make the Code somewhat less subjective. However, the phrase does have both subjective and objective components: 'the court must assume the *position* of the actual individual involved (that is, including his knowledge and experience), but must *reason* (that is, infer from the facts known to such an individual) from that position like an objective reasonable man'.[97]

Unless it is decided to revert to a wholly subjective approach, requiring actual knowledge, the IPC definition of 'reason to believe', as explained in the case law, appears sufficiently clear and workable as to require no amendment.

Other IPC Fault Terms

After the four principal fault terms – intention, knowledge, rashness and negligence – have been defined, it will be necessary to address the mishmash of other fault terms such as 'wilfully', 'fraudulently', 'corruptly', 'wantonly' and 'malignantly', which are scattered throughout the Code.

Where such terms have a clear and defined role (such as 'dishonestly' and 'reason to believe'), attention should be given to their most appropriate definition. Other terms, such as 'wilfully', 'fraudulently', 'corruptly', 'wantonly' and 'malignantly',[98] will need to be examined to determine whether: (i) they are otiose and can be deleted; (ii) they are capable of being replaced by other defined terms; or (iii) they serve a clear purpose and are capable of workable definition.

Other Legislation

This chapter concerns the Penal Code, but it is obvious that there is a great deal of other criminal legislation. For example, road traffic legislation in Malaysia and Singapore has caused a great deal of difficulty because many of the offences that are specified therein (such as 'causing death by dangerous driving' and 'reckless driving') overlap with but use different terms from the

---

96 IPC, s. 23.

97 *Koh Hak Boon v. PP* [1993] 2 SLR(R) 733, at para. [13], *per* Yong Pung How C.J. (emphasis in the original).

98 Recent analyses have pointed to the difficulty of understanding the role of words such as wilfully (in the context of criminal breach of trust) and fraudulently (in the context of cheating): see Yeo, Morgan and Chan, above n. 1, at paras. [14.45]–[14.52] and [14.77]–[14.80].

Penal Code ('negligence' and 'rashness').[99] Given the pivotal role of the Penal Code in setting the parameters and principles of the criminal law as a whole, other legislation should, as far as possible, adopt the Code terminology. If this is not possible for some reason, the terms that are used should be defined.

It is therefore recommended that after the fault terms contained in the IPC have been revised, other legislation should be examined and, where possible, brought into line with that Code.[100] Where alternative fault terms are chosen, they should be defined in the legislation in question.

PROPOSED FAULT ELEMENTS IN THE CONTEXT OF HOMICIDE

The following discussion does not attempt a full analysis of how the homicide laws might be reformed. It aims simply to test, in the context of an area of law that has caused enormous difficulty, the workability of the fault elements that have been proposed above.

Basic Structure

The current structure, involving murder, culpable homicide not amounting to murder, causing death by rashness and causing death by negligence is workable and should be retained. In particular, murder should remain as a subset of culpable homicide rather than being separately defined. However, causing death by rashness should be uncoupled from causing death by negligence so that the IPC will contain four levels of homicide offence: murder; culpable homicide not amounting to murder; causing death by rashness; and causing death by negligence.

Fault Element for Murder

The following proposals are based on the view that the fault element for murder, as the most serious offence in the criminal calendar, should be subjective. This will bring murder into line with Macaulay's original thinking, with the major non-fatal offences against the person in the IPC and with the common law.

The first fault element for murder should be an 'intention to kill', with intention bearing the meaning set out earlier. As we have seen, Macaulay favoured a strict alignment between the physical element and the fault element, and one option would be to revert to that alignment and provide that an intention to kill and nothing less will suffice for murder. This position certainly has some force, especially when murder carries a mandatory death penalty, as it does in Malaysia and Singapore.[101] On the other hand, as shown by the earlier example of the torturer, there are also good policy arguments for extending the fault element for murder to cases where the accused intended very serious injury. The most obvious option would be to say that murder can also be based on an intention to do grievous hurt.

---

99 Morgan and Yeo, above n. 90. A search of the words 'reckless' and 'recklessly' in Indian legislation online at http://www.commonlii.org suggests that Indian law has largely eschewed the term. It appeared in the 1939 Motor Vehicles Act but the relevant provisions appear to have been repealed by the 1988 Motor Vehicles Act. It is only sporadically used elsewhere.

100 See further Chapter 1 of this volume, above n. 2, at 15.

101 My view is that the death penalty, if it is retained, should not be mandatory and that the courts should be afforded a choice between the death penalty and life imprisonment, as they are in India.

However, before any concrete proposals can be developed with respect to murder, it will be essential to re-examine the definition of grievous hurt. The current definition, which is based on a number of specific forms of injury, is antiquated, somewhat anomalous and lacks clarity.[102] Discussion of any changes to this definition should take account of the fact that it may be used not only to designate offences of grievous hurt but also in the context of the fault element for murder.

The common law has failed dismally to define 'grievous bodily harm'[103] and will be of no assistance in developing the IPC. However, recent Western Australian experience is instructive. Under the Western Australian Criminal Code, 'grievous bodily harm' means, in essence, either: (i) an injury 'of such a nature as to endanger, or be likely to endanger … life' (which is termed a *life-threatening* injury below); or (ii) an injury that causes or is likely to cause *permanent injury to health*. Following a review by the Western Australian Law Reform Commission,[104] the homicide laws were amended in 2008 to provide that only an intention to kill or an intention to cause *life-threatening* injury will suffice for murder.[105] An intention to cause a permanent injury to health is not sufficient. This importance of this is that it shows that it is possible to use only the most serious forms of grievous hurt in defining the fault element for murder.

As a precondition to reforming the law of homicide, it is therefore necessary to reform the definition of grievous hurt and to decide which types of grievous hurt are so serious that they should be incorporated into the definition of murder. Subject to such reforms,[106] it is tentatively proposed that the fault element for murder should be an intention to cause death or grievous hurt. Given the definition of 'intention' that was set out earlier, this means that the prosecution would need to prove that the accused: (i) meant to kill; (ii) meant to do grievous hurt; (iii) knew that death was absolutely certain to occur; (iv) knew that grievous hurt was absolutely certain to occur; (v) knew that death would in all probability occur; or (vi) knew that grievous hurt would in all probability occur.

In terms of comparing the suggested provisions with the existing IPC provisions, this clearly covers the first limb of s. 300 (intention to kill). The second limb of s. 300 (an intention to cause such bodily injury as the offender knows to be likely to cause death) will be covered by an intention to do grievous hurt. The first part of the fourth limb of s. 300 (knowledge that death must in all probability result) will be covered by an intention to kill. There seem to be very few, if any, cases where the badly worded second part of the fourth limb of s. 300 is ever invoked and it can safely be repealed.

This means that the main change under the above proposal would relate to the third limb of s. 300. This limb has proved highly controversial and after 150 years its scope is still not entirely clear. It involves a more objective inquiry than the proposal set out above but is also limited

102 Under IPC, s. 320, it includes 'emasculation', permanent privation of sight or hearing (partial or full); bone fractures and dislocations; permanent disfigurement of the face or head; and 'any hurt which endangers life, or which causes the sufferer to be, during the space of 20 days, in severe bodily pain, or unable to follow his ordinary pursuits'. For analysis of these provisions, see Yeo, Morgan and Chan, above n. 1, at paras. [11.33]–[11.42].

103 It seems essentially to mean any form of 'really serious' bodily harm: see *DPP v. Smith* [1961] AC 290; *R v. Janjua* [1999] 1 Cr App R 91.

104 Law Reform Commission of Western Australia, *Review of the Law of Homicide: Final Report* (Perth: Law Commission of Western Australia, 1997).

105 Criminal Code (WA), s. 279.

106 The proposal to include an intention to do grievous hurt does assume that the threshold of grievous hurt is not set too low.

by the fact that the intended injury must be 'sufficient in the ordinary course of nature to cause death'.

A subjective inquiry into whether the accused intended grievous hurt (which will include knowledge that grievous hurt will in all probability result) should lead to appropriate outcomes in cases that are currently addressed through the third limb of s. 300. For example, in the controversial Privy Council case, on appeal from Singapore, of *Ike Mohamed Yasin bin Hussin v. PP*,[107] the accused had thrown the victim, a slightly built 58-year-old woman, to the ground. He had then raped her and, in the course of the struggle, had forcibly sat on her chest. The case descended into some highly technical discussion as to whether the type of injuries that he intended were sufficient in the ordinary course of nature to kill (and not just to injure) the victim. It would have been far more straightforward – and on these particular facts no less likely to have resulted in a murder conviction[108] – to have asked the subjective question of whether he intended to cause grievous hurt.

Fault Element for Culpable Homicide Not Amounting to Murder

Currently, the fault elements for culpable homicide under the IPC are: (i) an intention to kill; (ii) an intention to cause a bodily injury that is objectively likely to cause death; and (iii) knowledge that death was likely.

In line with the suggestions with respect to murder, it is tentatively suggested that the fault element for culpable homicide not amounting to murder should be amended to cover: (i) an intention to kill; (ii) an intention to do grievous hurt; (iii) knowledge that death was likely; and (iv) knowledge that grievous hurt was likely.

Fault Element for Causing Death by Rashness

The suggested definition of rashness refers to the accused realising that there is a risk that the 'prohibited harm' may occur. In defining the offence of causing death by rashness, it is also necessary to take account of the fact that culpable homicide may embrace knowledge of grievous hurt as well as knowledge of death.

It is therefore suggested that the fault element for the offence of causing death by rashness is satisfied if: (a) the accused was aware that death or grievous hurt may result; and (b) having regard to the circumstances known to the accused, it was unjustifiable to take that risk.

Fault Element for Causing Death by Negligence

The fault element for causing death by negligence should be very straightforward. The test would be whether the person's conduct: (a) fell well short of the standard of care that a reasonable person with the same capacity and experience as the accused would exercise in the same circumstances;

107 Above n. 47.

108 A conviction for murder was overturned by the Privy Council and replaced with a conviction under s. 304A. Surprisingly, the Privy Council gave virtually no consideration to the question of whether it might have been an offence of culpable homicide not amounting to murder under s. 299.

and (b) was so far below such standards that it merits criminal punishment. Although conceptual clarity suggests that the offences of causing death by rashness and causing death by negligence should be separated, the legislature will also need to consider, in setting maximum penalties, that some cases involving negligence may be very serious and may be deserving of a higher penalty than some cases of rashness.

CONCLUSION

In this chapter I have argued that, properly understood, the IPC has generally stood the test of time and should be renovated not reconstructed. In terms of its format, the use of explanations and illustrations is a particularly valuable technique that should be adopted more widely in legislation. In terms of its conceptual underpinnings, the generally subjective starting point to defining offences is a positive feature. Furthermore, the four primary fault elements (intention, knowledge, rashness and negligence) are workable and should be retained. However, in my view, it is time to permanently erase the maxim *mens non facit reum nisi mens sit rea* from the lexicon in IPC jurisdictions, as has largely happened in those Australian jurisdictions that adopted the Griffith Code:[109] it is unnecessary, misleading and out of line with the structure of the IPC.

I have also argued that it is important to provide statutory definitions of the primary fault terms and that these definitions belong in Chapter I of the Code. However, given the fact that the current interpretation of the fault elements is integrally tied to the complex wording of the offence of murder, there must be a contemporaneous review of culpable homicide and murder (and, as part of that review, a review of the meaning of 'grievous hurt'). Once the definitions of the four primary fault terms have been determined, attention can be given to the question of the retention, repeal or reform of the other fault terms. Of these, the definitions of 'dishonesty' and 'reason to believe' appear workable, but words such as 'wantonly', 'malignantly', 'fraudulently', 'corruptly' and 'wilfully' are obscure and may be capable of being replaced by other terms or simply removed as otiose.

The process of reform should start from the presumption that the physical element and the fault element of offences should be aligned unless – as has been suggested is the case with murder and culpable homicide not amounting to murder – there are good policy reasons to the contrary. In addition, given the critical role of the defences in ascribing fault in the criminal law, it has been argued that there should be a full review of the question of the onus of proof for the defences.

The longevity of the IPC is, of course, a tribute to Macaulay. And it is appropriate to reflect on two points. First, longevity and brevity seem to be related: the draft Code was only 67 pages long and attracted the following eulogy from Stephen:

> Pocket editions of these Codes are published, which may be carried about as easily as a pocket Bible; and I doubt whether, even in Scotland, you would find many people who know their Bibles as Indian civilians know their Codes.[110]

109 Primarily the States of Western Australia and Queensland.

110 As quoted by G.O. Trevelyan, *The Life and Letters of Lord Macaulay* (Teddington: Echo Library, 2006) 254.

Stephen was definitely exaggerating the piety of the Scots and was probably waxing too lyrically about Indians' devotion to the law, but the point is well made. In addition – and this point may well be directly related to the previous point – Macaulay was neither a vastly experienced criminal lawyer nor a devoted criminal law theorist.[111] His skills were to work incisively, consistently and logically from first principles and to use relatively simple, accessible language. The biggest challenge for modern-day scholars and reformers is to live up to these achievements.

111 See Chapter 12 of this volume (I. Leader-Elliott, 'Provocation') at 285.

Chapter 4
The Conduct Element of Offences

Bob Sullivan

It might seem on first reflection obvious that all forms of criminal offence should require proof of some form of conduct or some kind of external point of reference aside from and additional to the mere presence of the defendant (D). It is notoriously the case that some crimes require nothing more than a conduct element, requiring nothing by way of a mental (or fault) element.[1] But criminal liability without proof of any act, omission or link with some external state of affairs seems conceptually incoherent. As Antony Duff has persuasively argued, logically prior to any finding of criminal liability must be some finding of responsibility on the part of D for something done or omitted to be done or for some state of affairs that could have been avoided by means available to D.[2] A finding of responsibility need not entail a subsequent finding of criminal liability. For instance, D may be responsible for a harm on the basis that his or her conduct caused the harm, but further conditions beyond mere causation may be set down by the legislature or legal doctrine as necessary for criminal liability regarding the harm.[3] But if an initial finding of responsibility for something that is designated a criminal wrong cannot be made, then there is no grounding for any subsequent imposition of criminal liability. However, some jurisdictions have imposed criminal liability despite the lack of any grounds for finding D responsible in relation to the matter for which he or she is found criminally liable.[4] It should be one of the aims of any modern penal code to ensure that criminal liability cannot ensue in the absence of grounds of responsibility. Whether fulfilment of this aim entails that all crimes must have a conduct element in any real or palpable sense is a matter that should be discussed in any revision of the Indian Penal Code (IPC).

There is currently no provision in the IPC that enshrines the principle of no liability without responsibility.[5] Furthermore, there are other central matters germane to the conduct element of criminal offences that are not addressed. Our first task must be to examine the nature and extent of

1 The IPC does not contain strict liability offences but this form of liability seems well entrenched by way of other statutes: see Chapters 3 and 5 of this volume (N. Morgan, 'The Fault Elements of Offences' and K. Amirthalingam, 'Mistake and Strict Liability', respectively); and S. Yeo, N. Morgan, and W. Chan, *Criminal Law in Malaysia and Singapore* (Singapore: LexisNexis, 2007) Chapter 7.

2 R.A. Duff, *Answering for Crime: Responsibility and Liability in the Criminal Law* (Oxford: Hart Publishing, 2007) Chapters 1–3 and 5. See also G.R. Sullivan, 'Conduct and Proof of Conduct: Two Fundamental Conditions for the Imposition of Criminal Liability' in K.H. Kaikobad and M. Bohlander (eds), *International Law and Power: Perspectives on Legal Order and Justice* (Leiden: Martinus Nijhoff Publishers, 2009) 235, at 237–48.

3 In addition to causation, a legislature might require proof of some form of culpability. The responsibility condition can be satisfied by proof of an act, omission or state of affairs, but responsibility need not entail liability. Responsibility is a necessary but not invariably a sufficient condition for criminal liability.

4 See n. 26 below and at 94 and 98–9.

5 Macaulay's drafting technique was to specify the liability conditions for any given offence in the particular offence-creating provision. The liability conditions of IPC offences respect a requirement of responsibility as a prerequisite of criminal liability. However, a general provision in the matter of a responsibility requirement might be useful in any revision of the IPC if it were stated to be applicable to

the provision made in Macaulay's draft Code and in the enacted IPC with respect to the conduct element of offences. Then we will be in a position to identify what matters should be addressed in any revision of the IPC.

THE CONDUCT ELEMENT UNDER MACAULAY'S DRAFT CODE

There is very little said in the draft Code on the conduct element of crimes.[6] That of itself is unsurprising given that Macaulay's scheme did not include a comprehensive section dealing with what we would now call the General Part of the criminal law. But there are some provisions legislating in general terms for these matters to be found in the following clauses:

> Clause 4. Wherever the causing of a certain effect by an act or by an omission is an offence it is to be understood that the causing of the effect partly by an act and partly by an omission is the same offence.
> Clause 25. The word 'act' denotes as well a series of acts as a single act: the word 'omission' denotes as well a series of omissions as a single omission.
> Clause 26. A person is said to cause an effect 'voluntarily,' when he causes it by means whereby he intended to cause it, or by means which, at the time of employing those means, he knew to be likely to cause it.

First, some brief comment on each of these clauses as they stand before offering more general reflections. Clause 4, dealing with situations where D causes an effect by a mix of acts and omissions, must be taken as a provision 'for the avoidance of any doubt'. The illustration following the clause clearly makes this point: 'A voluntarily causes Z's death partly by illegally omitting to give Z food and partly by beating Z. A has committed voluntary culpable homicide.' Given that A was legally obliged to feed Z and compounded his illegal and injurious omission by beating Z, it is hard to see how, even in the absence of cl. 4, a fact-finder could fail to find that A caused Z's death. Indeed, the clause is rather distracting because a cautious reader might fear that he or she has rather missed the point of it. But further reflection does not bring to the surface any further revelation, at least for this reader. From that perspective, there seems to be no imperative to include such a provision in any reformulation of the IPC.

In denoting that 'act' may include a series of acts and likewise for 'omission', cl. 25 will offer useful guidance where the conduct element of the offence is conveyed in such phrases as 'if D by any act' or 'if D by any act or illegal omission', etc. Of course, the conduct element of many offences is specified in language receptive to accommodating a course of conduct in addition to discrete acts or omissions, as is the case for locutions such as 'causing', 'allowing', 'permitting', etc. For offences employing such terms, the interpretive guidance of cl. 25 is not required.

---

offences created outside the framework of the IPC. Chapter 3 of this volume (above n. 1) raises a similar point about the need for further definition of liability in a General Part; see also n. 6 below.

6 Yeo, Morgan and Chan, above n. 1, at para. [3.32] state:

> The [IPC] would be considerably improved by having provisions of general application which spell out the physical elements of a crime. Presently, all the Code has is a provision stating that the word 'act' includes an illegal omission, another provision which defines an illegal omission, and a third which stipulates that the words 'act' and 'omission' [include] a series of acts and a series of omissions.

The comment is equally in point for the draft Code.

The nature and ambit of cl. 26 is at first not easy to discern. It prescribes when an effect is considered to be caused 'voluntarily'. D will cause an effect voluntarily if he or she intends to cause the effect or foresees that the effect will be caused. One might be tempted to assume that in Macaulay's draft Code, for a factual cause of an effect to amount to a legal/imputable cause of an effect, D must intend or foresee the effect. Yet a perusal of his draft soon disabuses us of that assumption. For instance, in the case of the offence of causing death by a rash or negligent act, there is a reference simply to causing death.[7] By contrast, D will not be liable for the offence of voluntarily causing V hurt unless he or she intended or foresaw that he or she would cause hurt to V.[8] Therefore the best analysis seems to be that the draft Code employs a basic, unarticulated notion of cause but for some offences imports a culpability requirement of intention or knowledge on the part of D that he or she will cause the specified result by stipulating a meaning for 'voluntarily' in terms of an intention or knowledge as to the effects of one's conduct. Once this is grasped, this does not give rise to any confusion, at least when working within the terms of reference of the draft Code. However, two questions need to be addressed. First, can a modern criminal code do without a provision dealing at least in part with the legal meaning of the concept of causation? Secondly, for a modern criminal code, is the term 'voluntarily' the best term to use to import *mens rea* elements into offences? The first question is prompted by the sheer extent of the appellate case law and academic literature centred on questions of causation.[9] If guidance is possible for a concept that gives rise to such disputation in the matter of its application, then guidance should be given. The second question reflects a concern with usage. In the modern criminal law the terms 'voluntary' or 'voluntarily' are typically used to denote the freedom to act or refrain from acting. Arguably, matters of intention and knowledge should be addressed in their own right and not at one step removed by way of a restictive stipulation of what counts as voluntary. This reservation will have a particular point if any revision of the IPC were to include a general provision on the physical element of offences which stipulates in what circumstances conduct is to be regarded as involuntary.

Despite the conspicuous merits of the Macaulay draft taken in its entirety, one must conclude that the clauses dealing with the conduct element of crimes leave much unsaid. To what extent do the provisions of the IPC provide more guidance?

THE CONDUCT ELEMENT UNDER THE IPC

The IPC contains the following sections relating to the conduct element of offences:

> Section 32. In every part of this Code, except where a contrary intention appears from the context, words which refer to acts done extend also to illegal omissions.
> Section 33. The word 'act' denotes as well a series of acts as a single act; the word 'omission' denotes as well a series of omissions as well as a single omission.

---

7 Macaulay's draft Code, cl. 304.

8 *Ibid.*, cl. 316.

9 One may note an important recent publication on causation in the criminal law: M.S. Moore, *Causation and Responsibility: An Essay in Law, Morals and Metaphysics* (Oxford: Oxford University Press, 2009). As Moore's monograph demonstrates so well, there are many intractable issues relating to causation which frequently divide appellate courts.

> Section 36. Wherever the causing of a certain effect, or an attempt to cause that effect, by an act or omission, is an offence, it is to be understood that the causing of that effect partly by an act and partly by an omission is the same offence.
> Section 39. A person is said to cause an effect 'voluntarily' when he causes it by means whereby he intended to cause it, or by means which, at the time of employing those means, he knew or had reason to believe to be likely, to cause it.
> Section 43. The word 'illegal' is applicable to everything that is an offence, or which is prohibited by law, or which furnishes ground for a civil action; and a person is said to be 'legally bound to do' whatever it is illegal in him to omit.

A mere glance at these sections of the Code informs us that the gestation period between Macaulay's draft and the enactment of the IPC did not lead to any substantial revision or extension of the treatment of the conduct element of crimes. All that we need do is briefly note the changes between the draft Code and the IPC. Sections 32 and 43 of the IPC are new and important. 'Illegal' omissions are taken to be tantamount to acts for offences where a conduct element is expressed in terms of an act. Famously, Macaulay rejected any general moral equivalence between effects made to happen by way of positive acts and effects allowed to happen by way of failures to intervene. For him, any failure to intervene, however easy the intervention and however dire the consequences of non-intervention, was a matter merely for social disapproval rather for penal sanction.[10] Of course, this judgment by Macaulay related to circumstances where D was under no legal obligation to act and the IPC too refrains from imposing any general duties to intervene to secure the health and safety of others, although it should be noted that the IPC contains a number of offences obliging D to take positive steps in particular circumstances to prevent harmful events.[11]

Section 32 of the IPC makes illegal omissions tantamount to acts. This assimilation of illegal omissions to acts carries over only if the act in question produces an effect: the implication of s. 32 is that when it is criminal to cause an effect by a positive act, it is equally criminal to allow the same effect to arise by illegally failing to prevent the realisation of the effect. Note that s. 43 gives the widest possible meaning as to what constitutes an illegal omission, including failures to do things falling within purely private contractual arrangements ('which furnishes ground for a civil action'). Clearly, in any revision of the IPC, consideration should be given to whether s. 43 may on occasion cast the net of criminalisation too widely. From another direction of travel, consideration should also be given to the question of whether a duty to intervene should sometimes arise without the trigger of a pre-existing legal obligation. Should a modern criminal code impose a general duty of 'easy rescue' in addition to more specific duties of intervention in dangerous situations of regular occurrence?

Sections 33 and 36 are carried over from cls. 4 and 24 of the draft Code and require no additional comment, save to mention that s. 36, unlike cl. 4, carries over the informing principle to attempts as

---

10 T.B. Macaulay, J.M. Macleod, G.W. Anderson and F. Millet, *A Penal Code Prepared by the Indian Law Commissioners* (London: Pelham Richardson, 1838) (reprinted by the Lawbook Exchange, Ltd, 2002) 105, Note M (On Offences Against the Body):

> It is, indeed, most highly desirable that men should not merely abstain from doing harm to their neighbours, but should render active service to their neighbours. In general, however, the penal law must content itself with keeping men from doing positive harm, and must leave to public opinion, and to the teachers of morality and religion, the office of furnishing men with motives for doing positive good.

11 For example IPC, s. 119 makes it an offence for a public servant to conceal a design on the part of others to commit an offence it is his duty to prevent.

well as to completed crimes. Section 39, like cl. 26 in the draft, perpetuates the idea of 'voluntary' causation. There is however an important difference: whereas cl. 26 is in subjective terms, s. 39 extends voluntary causation to include effects that D 'had reason to believe to be likely' and caused by his or her conduct. If s. 39 were read as covering causation in general, D would only be said to cause those effects that he or she intended, foresaw or had reason to foresee would be caused by his or her conduct. Broader accounts of causation such as 'take your victim as you find him' would not apply. But, as already discussed, the better view is that the term 'voluntary causation' is in effect a term used to denote the culpability for particular offences[12] rather than a provision of general import relating to causation.[13] Questions already posed in relation to the draft Code remain outstanding: should there be a general provision dealing with causation? Should the culpability for offences always be addressed directly rather than by stipulating a meaning for 'voluntary' causation?

THE CONDUCT ELEMENT IN A MODERN CRIMINAL CODE: AN INVENTORY OF ISSUES

What is most striking about the IPC in terms of the conduct/physical element of offences are the absences when compared to more recent criminal codes. To be sure, the current provisions raise some matters that any revision exercise must consider. There is a clear-cut position on the criminalisation of omissions, a position that may survive any critical examination. Such an examination must consider whether the current stance on omissions in the IPC is in some respects over-inclusive and in other respects under-inclusive.

As the better view of s. 39 of the IPC is that it is a provision dealing with culpability rather than causation, thought must be given to what guidance a revised IPC should provide when a factual cause of an event is a candidate for a finding that it is a legal, imputable cause of the event. In light of the frequent disputes causal issues give rise to, guidance should be offered if it is possible to give effective guidance.[14] One essential matter in any review of legal causation is to resolve ways of dividing the multiplicity of those necessary conditions essential for the realisation of any given event into conditions which are candidate causes and those conditions which can be eliminated from the scope of any forensic causal inquiry.

One favoured device for reducing the number of those conditions which may be considered candidate causes is to apply a test of reasonable foreseeability. D should not be held responsible for any effect arising from his or her acts or omissions unless, from the perspective of a reasonable person in the same circumstances as D, the effect seemed likely to arise given the conduct of D. There are some strong arguments of principle for limiting the ambit of imputable cause in that fashion[15] rather than adopting the default position for England and Wales, namely that D will be found causally responsible for any effect flowing from any conduct of D's that makes a direct[16]

12 See n. 9 above at 89.

13 For instance, IPC, s. 299 defines the offence of culpable homicide where it suffices in terms of the *actus reus* for D merely to cause V's death, whereas the offence of voluntarily causing grievous bodily harm in IPC, s. 322 requires D to intend or foresee that grievous bodily harm will be caused to V.

14 The Indian Law Commissioners did consider whether to provide guidance on causal questions but considered that the sheer variety of circumstances which might give rise to causal issues militated against the framing of any general principles: see above n. 10.

15 As advocated in Yeo, Morgan and Chan, above n. 1, Chapter 5.

16 A quality of directness is not a defining condition of what counts as an imputable cause. The term is employed here simply to earmark the straightforward cases where the causal inquiry is not complicated by other human interventions occurring after D's intervention or by any unusual natural event.

and substantial[17] contribution to the effect, however unlikely *ex ante* that this would be the case.[18] Any new version of the IPC must make an explicit choice as to what will be the basis for causal attributions in the core case of D's conduct directly causing an effect. Provision should also be made for significant non-core cases, most notably the case where D does something which is arguably a necessary cause of the ultimate harm suffered by V which is then followed by conduct on the part of V, a third party or a natural event which, taken in isolation, is a sufficient cause of the ultimate harm suffered by V. Disputes about the resolution of such cases have recently arisen in England and Wales, particularly in cases where D illegally supplied a controlled drug to V which V went on to take with fatal consequences.[19]

But before those questions are addressed, a very basic question should at least be posed: why causation at all? This may seem a fanciful question. A criminal code that does not contain offences where causing harm is the focus may seem no more than an ivory tower fantasy. And perhaps it is. But there is a strong tradition in moral philosophy, indelibly associated with Kant, that questions the significance of the causing of effects to moral judgments and any punishment associated with those judgments.[20] In the briefest of terms, the argument goes that we can only justly be held responsible for the thoughts in our heads and those movements of our body (or failures to move our body) that are induced by such thoughts. Everything else is physics, something beyond the domain of moral judgments.[21] And there are some real-world examples of dispensing with causation when redrafting criminal offences. In England and Wales, prior to the Fraud Act 2006,[22] there was a confusing patchwork of different fraud offences, but they had in common the causing of effects by

17 The term 'substantial' is a term of art in English criminal law, meaning a contribution that is more than minimal: *R. v. Hennigan* [1971] 3 All ER 133; *R. v. Cato* [1976] 1 All ER 260.

18 For example, there was a causal finding against D for the death of V in the much-discussed case of *R. v. Blaue* [1975] 3 All ER 446, where V, on religious grounds, refused a life-saving blood transfusion following her stabbing by D. Arguably, such a finding would not have been made on a reasonable foresight standard as the wound was not life threatening *per se* and neither D nor a reasonable person would have been on notice that V belonged to a minority religious sect that prohibited accepting another person's blood.

19 For over a decade, separate panels of the English Court of Appeal differed on whether a finding could be made that D had caused the death of V on the basis of the supply of a controlled drug which V voluntarily took with knowledge of the kind of drug it was. The matter has now been resolved by the House of Lords in *R. v. Kennedy (No. 2)* [2008] AC 269 in favour of D. The appellate committee, in a unanimous judgment, strongly asserted a principle that where the last and supervening causal factor in the realisation of harm is contributed by a voluntary actor, the causal narrative begins and ends with that actor. The facts of *Kennedy* indicate how forceful the assertion of this voluntary actor principle was: V was a heroin addict expressing to D a strong need for the drug, a need that D attended to immediately by preparing the syringe that V used to take the drug. It is clear from the judgment that even where V's voluntary conduct of the type at issue is a likely and foreseeable result of D's earlier conduct, D's conduct nonetheless drops away as a candidate cause. Where the supervening intervention is by way of performance of a public duty, D's earlier conduct will remain in play as a candidate cause if the intervention was foreseeable – *Pagett* (1983) 76 Cr App R 279 – and where the intervention consists of medical treatment or a natural event, it seems that D's earlier conduct remains in play as a candidate cause unless the treatment or event takes a quite exceptional form: *Cheshire* [1991] 3 All ER 670; *Environment Agency v. Empress Car Co. (Abertillery) Ltd.* [1999] 2 AC 22.

20 I. Kant, *The Metaphysics of Morals* (translated and edited by M. Gregor) (Cambridge: Cambridge University Press, 1996).

21 For a recent and extensive defence of the view that results are irrelevant to findings of culpability, see L. Alexander and K.K. Ferzan, *Crime and Culpability: A Theory of Criminal Law* (Cambridge: Cambridge University Press, 2009) Chapters 5–7.

22 Chapter 35.

fraudulent conduct. Among the reductions and simplifications accomplished by the Fraud Act 2006 is dispensing with causal issues in terms of events that have occurred. So, to give one example, instead of an offence of obtaining property by deception, there is now an offence of making a false pretence with intent to obtain property. What matters for liability for this new offence is the making of the false pretence with the intent to obtain property. Whether property is obtained is irrelevant.[23]

As a technical matter, it would be perfectly possible to roll out the model of the Fraud Act 2006 across the rest of the substantive criminal law. And if this model is to be rejected, we need reasons that go beyond declining the effort that would be involved and the reiteration of ideas that are only habits of mind. We need to think afresh why it is important for a modern criminal code to contain some key offences based on the causation of effects; why it is important sometimes to conjoin harm and culpability rather than rest content merely with proof of culpability.[24] And if these are good reasons, they should inform what conception of causation a revised IPC should adopt.

The most significant aspect missing from the current IPC in the matter of the conduct element is anything on the form and structure of these elements. Most offences of course will have as their basic conduct component some form of act or series of acts on the part of D. A modern code should have something to say about differentiating mere bodily movements on the part of D – reflexes, fits, falls, etc. – from bodily movements that are a product of the exercise of D's agency and are thus to be counted as his or her acts. It should be a fundamental principle that bodily movements not attributable to D's agency are, without more, an insufficient basis for criminal liability even of the strict variety. Admittedly, some social protection issues may arise if this conception of an act is insisted upon, but there are better ways of dealing with these concerns[25] than convictions imposed despite the absence of voluntary conduct.

Conduct in its most basic sense is controlled bodily movement. But conduct will derive its social meaning from the attendant circumstances. Consideration must be given to whether a revised IPC should formally separate out conduct elements from circumstance elements in the specifications of offences. This is not merely a matter of clarifying what exactly must be proved in terms of the external elements of the offence. It may well be appropriate to have different forms of mental element with respect to conduct elements on the one hand and circumstance elements on the other. If guidance on causation is to feature in any reiteration of the IPC, a tripartite division of what are sometimes called 'result' crimes into conduct elements, circumstance elements and consequence elements may well be in order. Again, this may assist clarity and help in the calibration of the mental element.

A modern criminal code must include some liability based on omission although, as alluded to already, the proper extent of liability based on omission is contentious. Also included in the code must be forms of regulation based on D's association with particular kinds of objects or on D's implication in particular happenings, such as sales carried out on his or her behalf or on the failure of his or her children to attend school. In mind here are offences of possession, offences of vicarious liability and offences based on status. Such offences, though essential to ensure effective social regulation, can take us to the very edges and beyond of anything that can be plausibly called a crime requiring proof of a conduct or physical element. But whatever the

23 This is not to say that causal issues are wholly irrelevant for this offence. To impose liability, one must still have in mind victims who are the target audience for the false representation and who D intends to induce *by the false representation* to pass money or property to D.

24 Some too will reject treating harm and culpability as two separate components in an appraisal of D's conduct. Some theorists, notably Antony Duff, consider that the causing of harm impinges on the level and extent of D's culpability: see R.A. Duff, *Criminal Attempts* (Oxford: Clarendon Press, 1996) Chapter 4.

25 See further n. 33 below at 96.

social necessity for these offences, they must satisfy what may be called the 'no criminal liability without responsibility' constraint. As touched upon already, criminal liability must rest on some prior finding of responsibility. Almost invariably, the responsibility of D must be based on some voluntary conduct on his or her part. But occasionally a responsibility judgment can justly be made even in the absence of voluntary conduct on the part of D at the point of commission of the offence. It is very important to specify with great precision the conditions for justly imposing a responsibility which may lead to liability despite the absence of voluntary conduct at the time of the offence. As some notorious English cases demonstrate,[26] when dealing with offences of this kind it is quite possible to reach verdicts that can be justly castigated as the 'acme of strict injustice'.[27]

We can now resolve those matters to be examined in any reform of the IPC regarding the conduct/physical element of crimes. First, we will look at the form and structure of these elements, with a particular emphasis on the restraining principle that any criminal liability imposed on D must presuppose some form of responsibility that D has incurred. Then we will turn to how the IPC should legislate for causation, including the question of whether a code should include crimes which specify results that D's conduct must cause. Finally, we will turn to the appropriate scope of criminal liability based on omissions.

THE FORM AND STRUCTURE OF THE CONDUCT/PHYSICAL ELEMENT OF OFFENCES: MEETING THE RESPONSIBILITY CONSTRAINT

The core of the substantive criminal law will always centre on an act or series of acts done by D in specified circumstances. For what are referred to as 'conduct' crimes, it suffices that the act is done and that the circumstances specified as elements of the offence exist: it is not necessary to prove that the act causes any particular effect. What are referred to as 'result' crimes do require proof that the act caused a particular effect.[28] We will defer for the moment whether it is necessary for a modern criminal code to enact result crimes in addition to conduct crimes. But a criminal code that does not have as its central concern the proscription of active conduct is currently unthinkable. For crimes with a positive act requirement, what we have termed the responsibility constraint is most easily met. Yet there will be cases at the margins where dispute or uncertainty may arise.

26 Perhaps the most notorious is *R. v. Larsonneur* (1933) 24 Cr App R 74, where D was found guilty of an immigration offence even though her presence in the United Kingdom was, at the material time, entirely a product of *force majeure*. One may also note the consistently intransigent line taken in cases of parental criminal responsibility for their truanting children. Parents have been consistently found liable in circumstances where not even the most conscientious parent could have ensured the attendance of his or her child at school. For recent examples, see *Barnfather v. Islington Education Authority* [2003] 1 WLR 2318; and *New Forest Local Education Authority v E* [2007] EWHC 2584 (Admin). See further n. 38 below at 98–9.

27 The description of Jerome Hall for the decision in *Larsonneur*: J. Hall, *General Principles of Criminal Law* (2nd edn, Indianapolis: Bobbs-Merrill) 329.

28 One may note a recent rejection by Moore of any meaningful distinction between conduct crimes and result crimes: Moore, above n. 9, at 15–19. One example he takes is the crime of burglary, often cited as a pure conduct crime. His point is that the event at the core of this crime – an entry as a trespasser into a building – is a causal effect of a voluntary bodily movement. It may be allowed, following Moore, that the conduct crime/result crime distinction is not analytically tight, yet the distinction may still be used as useful labels for, on the one hand, crimes where a bodily movement in particular circumstances of itself fulfils the *actus reus* requirement and, on the other hand, crimes where some physical event (a wound, a death) must occur as a consequence of the bodily movement if the *actus reus* requirement is to be fulfilled. It is in the latter kind of case that the litigated causal issues arise.

Acts and Responsibility

Acts on the part of D must be distinguished from mere movements of his or her body in time and space. If D falls from a balcony rail above a throng of dancing people and his or her body crashes into V, one of the dancers below, it would be a misdescription of the event to say that he or she injured V by his or her *act* of falling from the balcony. It would make perfect sense to say that he or she injured V by an act had he or she jumped from the balcony. But a fall is not a jump – it is something that happens to D, not something that he or she does. Normally we will not be responsible for things that happen to us because things like falls, reflex movements, a sudden sneeze, an epileptic fit and so on are typically things we cannot prevent. But in the case from which the balcony example is drawn, D was drunk.[29] His drunken condition explained his dangerous act of climbing onto the balcony rail and very probably had a part to play in the losing of his balance. Yet these observations do not transmute the fall into an act; his agency was not engaged with the fall itself.[30] However, what the incident does demonstrate is that persons may be responsible (and blameworthy) for the things that happen to them as well as for the things that they do. When legislating for the conduct requirement for crimes typically perpetrated by positive acts, thought must be given to the treatment of harmful and harm-threatening movements of D's body which cannot be accommodated within the conception of an act defined in terms of voluntary, willed movement. It may well be that criminal liability can be in order with respect to movements that were beyond D's control in the instant moment but that are movements that would not have occurred had D at an earlier point in time been more prudent.[31] But when legislating for the blameworthy, we must avoid exposing to criminal liability persons who are not responsible and hence not blameworthy for their loss of control.

One class of blameless persons who should be specifically mentioned are persons afflicted with internal conditions that may result in episodes of loss of control. The case list will be familiar to students of criminal law: it includes persons with diabetes, epilepsy, arteriosclerosis and sleep disorders. Some of the persons within those descriptions may lose control of their movements in ways dangerous to others and in ways that might recur. English criminal law has given absolute priority to public safety concerns in such cases and has done so by treating such persons as legally insane.[32] Unsurprisingly, many defendants will plead guilty to the offence charged rather than put themselves at the disposal of the court under the rubric of insanity. Two brief comments will be

29 *R. v. Brady* [2006] EWCA Crim 2413.

30 In *Brady*, *ibid.*, the English Court of Appeal considered that a fall could not be considered a malicious act for the purposes of a charge of malicious wounding. Even though D was drunk, the fall was to be considered an accident. As such, it did not attract the principle that if D, despite a lack of consciousness caused by the voluntary taking of drink or drugs, is capable of moving his or her body, the presence of *actus reus* and *mens rea* will be presumed if the crime is one of basic intent. The court considered that a conviction for the offence might have been possible had the prosecution based its case on D's climbing onto the balcony rail.

31 That is why in the draft legislative proposals offered below, provision is made for circumstances where it may be considered appropriate to treat mere movements as acts rather than a provision that an act must always take the form of a voluntary bodily movement.

32 The leading case is *R. v. Sullivan* [1984] AC 156, where the House of Lords confirmed a line of authority that any internal disorder which affects the faculties of memory, reason and understanding, on however temporary a basis, is to be regarded as a 'disease of the mind' within the meaning of that expression in the M'Naghten Rules. In accordance with that view, D's epilepsy which gave rise to his fit was a condition falling within the Rules. Similar findings have been made regarding automatous conditions arising from diabetes, arteriosclerosis and sleep disorders.

made. First, the public safety concerns that drive this process can be much exaggerated.[33] Secondly, if it should be the case that coercive procedures over a particular person following his or her involuntary conduct are in the public interest, they should be done by way of mental health law processes and not through the criminal law.[34] Accordingly, no special provision for public safety concerns is made in the proposals relating to defining the conduct element of crimes.[35] There are, however, proposals relating to the cases where an act requirement may be considered satisfied despite involuntariness at the time of the commission of the offence. For that reason there is no all-embracing provision to the effect that voluntary conduct is required in all cases as a predicate of criminal liability.

Omissions and Responsibility

For our present discussion, we make the safe assumption that in any reformulation of the IPC, certain omissions will attract criminal liability. We postpone for the moment the important question

---

33 An instructive study demonstrates that persons afflicted with conditions such as epilepsy and diabetes rarely cause harm to others in circumstances associated with the symptoms of their conditions and, should they do so, they are even more rarely involved in repeat incidents: P. Fenwick, *Automatism, Medicine and the Law* (Cambridge: Cambridge University Press, Psychological Research Monograph No. 17, 1990).

34 Two conditions currently inappropriately characterised as forms of insanity do however give rise to public safety concerns, namely sleep disorders and states of disassociation arising from post-traumatic stress disorder (PTSD). These conditions can give rise to recurrent and dangerous episodes of automatism, causing harm to others. On recurrent sleep disorders, see I. Ebrahim, W. Wilson, R. Marks, K. Peacock and P. Fenwick, 'Violence, Sleepwalking and the Criminal Law: (1) The Medical Aspects' [2005] *Criminal Law Review* 601. The status of PTSD as an excususing condition has not been considered at appellate level in England and Wales and rarely in Commonwealth courts. Categorisation is not easy as the expression is used to cover a number of conditions, not all of which would amount to states of automatism. The condition is prevalent in service personnel who have been exposed to combat. A study conducted for the National Association of Probation Officers (England) concluded that one-half of the 8,500 combat veterans in English prisons were suffering from PTSD or depression: *The Guardian*, 15 April 2010. It is better that the coercive measures that may be desirable for sleep disorder and PTSD cases should be resolved by way of diversionary mental health law procedures where there is evidence that such factors were in play at the time of the harmful incidents. If such evidence should arise for the first time in the course of a criminal trial, acquittals should ensue in the absence of proof of voluntary conduct, but the court should be granted a jurisdiction to enforce attendance at a Mental Health Review Tribunal hearing if public safety concerns so require. No such mechanisms are in place in England and Wales.

35 In Chapter 10 of this volume (G. Ferguson, 'Insanity'), there is a proposal (at 254–5) for a new provision to be added to the IPC, s. 83A, which provides for a defence of mental impairment, a defence which if successful will leave the defendant at the disposal of the court if public protection measures are in point. This defence will be the only mode of acquittal for persons whose involuntary conduct is attributable to such conditions as epilepsy and diabetes. The appropriate disposal of cases involving involuntary conduct arising from such causes has yet to be a major issue for courts in Malaysia and Singapore. As of 2007, it seems there were only two reported cases involving automatism in Malaysia and none in Singapore: Yeo, Morgan and Chan, above n. 1, at para. [26.4]. The learned authors recommend that the IPC should be amended to make explicit provision for automatism, but that in the meantime incidents of dangerous automatism arising from internal conditions which may recur should be regarded as cases where D is raising unsoundness of mind within the terms of IPC, s. 84: paras. [26.21]–[26.33]. It seems that they would regard automatism arising from conditions such as epilepsy and diabetes as cases of unsound mind (which at least avoids the term insanity), as did the Malaysian High Court in *PP v Kenneth Fook Mun Lee (No. 1)* [2002] 2 MLJ 563.

of how far the net of omissions liability should be cast. Our concern for now is to ascertain when we can justly be held responsible for an omission in the narrow sense of determining whether the conduct that we omitted to perform was something that we could have done had we been minded to do it. That would seem to be the minimum required to satisfy the 'no liability without responsibility' condition.

To some extent we cannot keep entirely separate the question of our responsibility for a failure to do something and issues about the scope of those things we should be made to do. In the main, the IPC tethers the scope of omissions to the ambit of what we have called result crimes. Typically, one will only be criminally liable on the basis of an omission if it causes a result which it would be criminal to cause knowingly by way of a positive act. Liability is further qualified by the stipulation that the omission must be illegal. While this is a widely drawn condition, at least it ensures that there is a pre-existing duty to act and that punitive sanctions for a failure to perform the duty are limited to circumstances where the failure results in the realisation of a specific harm. Importantly, this will ensure that D will be sensitised to the existence of his or her relevant duty and the need to perform that duty in order to avoid the harm.

The same degree of fair notice will not be guaranteed in cases of 'pure' omission, situations where D will be held liable merely for the failure to do his or her duty. It is these cases of liability based on the bare failure to act that we will deal with in the course of making proposals for the structure of the conduct element. We will deal with omissions and their relationship to given results in the section on causation. On first principles, D's responsibility and any ensuing liability for a failure to act requires adequate notice to D of the duty to act. Furthermore, the duty should be a duty that he or she was capable of performing. Indeed, there is a case for requiring subjective awareness on the part of D of the duty in question, departing from the orthodoxy that ignorance of the law is no excuse.[36] In cases where adequate notice of a legal duty to act was provided, it may seem fair to put a persuasive burden on D to establish his or her lack of knowledge. Where the duty is cast on members of the public in their capacity as members of the public, limiting conditions of this kind should be insisted upon.

The insistence that in the case of duties imposed on the general public, D should not be liable unless capable of performing the duty is particularly important. A zealous government may, say, cast a duty on all members of the public to pick up any litter they see in the street. If D is an elderly lady afflicted with arthritis who cannot stoop down to pick up some item of litter, it would be preposterous to punish her failure to remove the offending item. Arguably, a stricter test might be in point for persons who have voluntarily undertaken special responsibilities or who are within the jurisdiction but are non-citizens, and subject to specific regulations. For example, suppose D joins the government litter service aware that a statute makes criminal any knowing failure on the part of a government litter worker to pick up litter. Because of a football injury which he did not reveal to his employers, D cannot bend down more than a few times each day. Arguably, he should be found liable for any failure to pick up litter.

Liability for omissions in what we have called the pure sense may take criminal liability beyond any realistic sense of a conduct element requirement. Consider D, who is taking a four-week holiday in a foreign country. At the point of entry there are multilingual signs stating in the clearest of terms that all persons present on a visitor's visa must report in person to the office for

---

36 The Privy Council advice in *Lim Chin Aik v. R.* [1963] AC 160 (Singapore) could be cited in support of such an approach, though it would have to be conceded that the *mens rea* requirement of actual knowledge of the ordinance that required D to report his continuing presence within the jurisdiction (which was read into a seemingly strict liability offence) was by way of response to an unpublished ordinance.

aliens on a weekly basis during their stay. These signs pass D by in the excitement of her arrival and she is driven from the airport to a remote spot far from any branch of the office for aliens. If, on her second visit to the airport for her return flight, she is arrested for the crime of failure to report her presence, she cannot complain within the terms we have set as necessary requirements for any finding of responsibility with respect to omissions arising from special responsibilities or from non-citizen status. She had adequate notice and in the light of that notice could have arranged her stay so as to comply with the duty to report. But there is no conduct associated with her crime in any robust sense. Nor has her crime any other external manifestation. She was just on holiday, blithely unaware that she was doing anything wrong. There is just an absence for which she is responsible within the terms set.[37] But liability of this sort should be a matter of last resort, reserved for matters of vital importance and where no other mode of regulation would suffice. To repeat, where the duty is imposed on persons outside of any employment, official capacity or non-citizen status, there is a strong case for requiring proof that D was aware of the existence of the duty or, at the very least, for allowing D to prove her lack of awareness of the duty.

Status Offences and Responsibility

On the face of it, status offences present the greatest challenge to meeting the responsibility condition.[38] It is all too easy for courts to ignore fundamental conditions pertaining to the intelligible imposition of criminal liability and to read all too literally the legislative prescription for liability. Perhaps the most notorious example from English criminal jurisprudence is the case of *R. v. Larsonneur*,[39] a prosecution for the offence of being an alien, present in the UK, after leave to land had been refused. It suffices for present purposes to say that D's presence in the UK after refusal of leave to land was entirely involuntary, a product of *force majeure.* That did not prevent conviction: according to the Lord Chief Justice of the day, 'the circumstances of her entry [into the UK after refusal of leave] were entirely immaterial'.[40] Unfortunately, the case is not a relic from some earlier, less tutored era. From many examples of the same literalist approach, one might single out the frequently prosecuted offence of being a parent of a child of compulsory school age who is failing to attend school regularly.[41] A well-established and contemporary body of authority establishes beyond doubt that even a parent who is blameless in the most basic sense for his or her child's failure of attendance – the circumstances leading to non-attendance may be completely

---

37 The same pattern of liability without conduct can be found in cases of liability based on mere possession of contraband. Consistently in anglophone jurisdictions, an owner/occupier of domestic or business premises will be taken to be in possession of any article stored on the premises if a reasonable person in the shoes of D would have been aware of the presence of the item or an item of the same type. From the case law, there are many examples of persons (parents of drug-taking teenage children, persons allowing a friend to use their lock-up garage, etc.) who are found guilty of possessory offences simply on account of living their lives in a trusting or naïve manner.

38 For a searching analysis and critique of criminal liability cast in this fashion, see P.R. Glazebrook, 'Situational Liability' in P.R. Glazebrook (ed.) *Reshaping the Criminal Law* (London: Stevens and Sons, 1978).

39 Above n. 26.

40 *Ibid.* at 75.

41 Education Act 1996 (Chapter 56) (UK), s. 444(1) provides: 'If a child of compulsory school age who is a registered pupil at school fails to attend regularly at the school, his parent is guilty of an offence.'

beyond the control of the most competent and conscientious parent – will be guilty of the offence on the basis of the child's lack of regular attendance, however it may arise.[42]

There is nothing inevitable about these implacable verdicts. Status offences, although inherently problematic in terms of any robust conception of a conduct/physical element requirement, are an inevitable part of modern state regulation. But the acquisition of the status must be something within the control of D. To punish D for a state of affairs impossible for him or her to avoid by any reasonable steps he or she might take is not merely unjust, it is incoherent.[43] Things which are blamelessly beyond our control are things beyond our personal field of responsibility.[44] To repeat again, a minimum condition of liability is a finding of responsibility. It is vitally important to respect this condition in the case of status offences.[45]

Formulating a Conduct Element Provision for a Revised IPC

The IPC should contain a comprehensive, general provision for the conduct/physical element of offences. Conventionally, the basic predicate for criminal liability can take one of three forms: (i) an act or series of acts; (ii) an omission; or (iii) some form of association with a state of affairs. We will follow that convention here. Wherever existing provisions of the IPC are in point, they will be used, but supplementation is required:

1.(1) D is not guilty of an offence unless his or her liability is based on:
   (a) an act;
   (b) an omission to perform an act;
   (c) an association with some external state of affairs.

---

42 For a sustained critique of these cases, see J. Horder, 'Whose Values Should Determine When Liability is Strict?' in A.P. Simester (ed.), *Appraising Strict Liability* (Oxford: Oxford University Press 2005); see also G.R. Sullivan, 'Parents and their Truanting Children: An English Lesson in Liability without Responsibility' (2010) 12(2) *Otago Law Review* 285.

43 For an attempt to unpack the conceptual incoherence (in addition to the injustice) of status liability imposed without respecting the minimum conditions for responsibility, see Sullivan, above n. 2.

44 Perhaps the most striking recent example of liability without responsibility for the truanting offence is *New Forest Local Education Authority v E*, above n. 26, where not even threats of death and serious bodily harm from D's 15-year-old drug-dealing son deflected liability for the offence. The Divisional Court accepted that D, a single parent, had made her best efforts to ensure her son's attendance at school but, confirming long-standing authority, ruled that the offence looked solely to the truanting conduct of the child and that liability for the parent followed irrespective of the standard of parenting and any other exonerating factor.

45 The implacable approach of English courts to situational liability does not appear to be replicated in Malaysia and Singapore: Yeo, Morgan and Chan, above n. 1, at para. [3.17]. Reference is made there to the Singaporean Common Gaming Houses Act (Cap 49, 1985 Rev. Ed.), s. 8(3), which creates an offence of being an occupier of a public place used for unlawful gaming. The learned authors note that on the face of it no act or omission is required for liability. They conclude, however, that 'such a crime has an implicit conduct component since it in effect incriminates D for the act of taking on the role of occupant of the premises, or of failing to remove himself or herself from that position upon becoming aware of the unlawful business operation'. Provided sufficient time and opportunity were allowed to the occupier to terminate gaming activity he or she had not instigated, the offence as interpreted by the authors would meet the no liability without responsibility condition. It would seem to be a good idea to place within a revised IPC a general provision to ensure that offences of situational liability are interpreted in this manner.

(2) The word 'act' denotes as well a series of acts as a single act; the word 'omission' denotes as well a series of omissions as a single omission.

2. (1) Subject to subsection 2(2), the following are not acts:
   (a) any bodily movement during unconsciousness or sleep;
   (b) any bodily movement that is a reflex or convulsion;
   (c) any bodily movement that otherwise is not a product of any effort or determination on the part of D, either conscious or habitual.

(2) Any bodily movement which is not an act under the terms of 2(1) is nonetheless to be regarded as an act if:
   (a) the movement occurs when D is voluntarily intoxicated; or
   (b) the movement is attributable to an earlier act of D and that earlier act was done with the fault element for the offence charged.

3 (1) Subject to 3(2), liability for an offence may not be based on an omission to do an act unaccompanied by any acts unless:
   (a) a duty to act and a penalty for failure to do the act is imposed by law; and
   (b) D was aware of the existence of the duty before or at the time of his or her omission; and
   (c) D was physically capable of performing the act.

(2) Where a duty to act and a penalty for failure to do the act is imposed by law on D as an incident of any office, employment, interest in property, or on the basis of non-citizen status, liability may ensue for a failure to perform the act if a diligent person placed in the same circumstances as D would have done the act in question.

4. Liability for an offence may not be based on an association with a state of affairs unless D was aware that he or she would become associated with the state of affairs specified in the offence charged and in the manner required by the offence and he or she failed to take any reasonable steps that would have avoided his or her association with the state of affairs.

Explanation 1 – Clause 1 ensures that criminal liability is confined to circumstances where the prosecution must prove some act or omission on the part of D or an association with some external state of affairs.

Explanation 2 – Clause 2 ensures that when the prosecution's case contains allegations of an act or a series of acts on the part of D, those allegations will not be proved unless it is proved that D's acts were the product of his or her deliberation and will. However, proof of an act or a series of acts will be presumed if a lack of deliberation and will is attributable to D's state of voluntary intoxication or where his lack of deliberation and will on the part of D is explained by any earlier act done with the fault element for the offence with which he or she is charged.

Explanation 3 – Clause 3 ensures that where a duty to act and associated penalty is imposed on D in his or her capacity as a member of the public, criminal liability cannot be based on a failure to do the act unless it is proved that D was physically capable of performing the act and that he or she was aware of the legal obligation to do the act before or at the time of his or her omission to do the act. Where however a duty is imposed on D in some special capacity (office-holder, employee, holder of a proprietary interest, non-citizen) criminal liability can be imposed on the basis of his or her failure to do the act if a diligent person possessed of the same special capacity and in the same circumstances as D would have done the act in question.

Explanation 4 – Clause 4 ensures that D will not be held criminally liable on the basis of some status description applicable to him or her (for example, being a parent of a child of compulsory school age, not in regular attendance at school) unless he or she was aware that the status would apply and such a state of affairs could be avoided by the taking of reasonable steps.

Illustrations

(a) D suffers an epileptic fit and during the fit inadvertently strikes V with D's fist. There is no punishable act perpetrated by D.

(b) D suffers an epileptic fit and during the fit inadvertently strikes V with D's fist. D had gone to a disco hoping that the strobe lights would induce a fit and cause D to lash out. There is a punishable act perpetrated by D.

(c) D voluntarily becomes very intoxicated and in that condition inadvertently strikes V with D's fist. There is a punishable act perpetrated by D.

(d) A statute is passed obliging all members of the public to pick up any item of litter found in a public place. D is unaware of the litter law and fails to pick up litter that D sees. There is no punishable omission on the part of D.

(e) As in (d) above, save that D is aware of the litter law. D is unable to pick up litter that D sees because of a back injury. There is no punishable omission on the part of D.

(f) A statute makes it an offence without more to be a parent of a child of compulsory school age who is not attending school regularly. D is aware that D's son is frequently truanting from school. At this time D was in prison and had no means of access to him. D is not guilty of the school attendance offence.

(g) As in (f) above, save that D was at home and made no attempt to ensure the attendance of D's son at school. D is guilty of the school attendance offence.

Causation

Section 39 of the IPC is the only section in the Code that could arguably be read as dealing with causation.[46] If it were to be read in that way, if any effect is to be considered to be caused by the conduct of D, it would have to be intended or foreseen by D or be reasonably foreseeable. But, as already discussed, the better view of s. 39 seems to be that the section is only concerned with those offences which require some effect to be 'voluntarily' caused. There are other provisions which simply require effects to be caused.[47] In substance, s. 39 seems not to be directly concerned with causation at all. It offers no guidance on questions of causation as such and essentially imports a culpability requirement of intention, foresight or negligence for crimes which require an effect to be caused voluntarily. The passage of time since the enactment of the IPC has not brought about any general convergence on the controversial causal issues. Guidance on some key causal matters could be usefully provided in any revision of the Code. If we are to start from the beginning, we must first address a basic question: why causation at all? It would be perfectly possible to draft a criminal code where causation in the sense of bringing about physical effects going beyond bodily movements carried out in specified circumstances was dispensed with. We have already provided the example of the English Fraud Act 2006 where the point of entry for proscribing fraudulent conduct has changed to acts whereby D is liable as soon as he or she tries to make fraudulent gains rather than waiting until he or she has succeeded in making a fraudulent gain. Recently, the

---

46 It may be useful to repeat here the wording of this provision: 'A person is said to cause an effect "voluntarily," when he causes it by means whereby he intended to cause it, or by means which, at the time of employing those means, he knew or had reason to believe to be likely, to cause it'.

See Chapter 3 of this volume, above n. 1, at 74, where this section is considered as a provision dealing with fault.

47 For example, the conduct element for culpable homicide contrary to IPC, s. 299 is expressed as follows: 'Whosoever causes death by the doing of an act ...'

US criminal law theorists Larry Alexander and Kimberly Kessler Ferzan have presented strong arguments of principle for the view that the causation of results arising from a particular episode of conduct does not bear on the culpability of that conduct.[48] If, for instance, D were to shoot at V from point-blank range with the intention of killing V, D stands in the same moral case whether V lives or dies, at least according to Alexander and Ferzan and many other theorists besides.[49] Moreover, Alexander and Ferzan give practical expression to their position by drafting a criminal code that formulates criminal offences which avoid liability elements set in terms of the causation of results.[50] For present purposes we will assume that the reasoning supportive of this 'results don't matter to morality' thesis is sound. Also, we should be mindful that simplicity and economy of means are great virtues in a criminal code. If a code can completely or largely dispense with causal questions, much court time and effort could be saved.

However, in a real-world redrafting exercise, one may have the greatest doubts concerning the public acceptability of a criminal code taking a radically, non-causal turn. Results matter enormously in terms of psychological/emotional reactions to harmful events. Surgeons, say, might carry out a difficult yet warranted procedure with great care and skill, yet thereby cause the patient's death. Close relatives of the deceased would not be comforted if the surgeons confined their remarks after the event to their own blamelessness: '[I] did my considerable best; these things happen.' Mere causal agency of itself imposes social duties to express regret and offer condolence.[51] Where the causal agency is additionally accompanied by a blameworthy state of mind, the damaging results of the conduct will intensify the anger and resentment of those adversely affected and will play a potent part in the negative public perception of the person responsible for the bad outcome. There are no signs whatever that these very human reactions to harm-causing events are on the wane. They are in no sense discreditable feelings and they must be given institutional recognition in a criminal code, particularly for cases of death and serious injury.[52]

Accordingly, careful thought must be given to capturing those connections between D's conduct and any harm to the person or other legally protected interests of V which can be considered causal connections. In forensic contexts, the search is not for *the* cause of an event but merely for some input from D that can be considered a cause of the event. The most straightforward situations will take the form of unmediated events, as when D, say, starts a fire or fires a gun, and the effects of such interventions can be examined *ex post* without any complications caused by subsequent supervening acts. If we can be sure that the legally relevant upshot – the damaged building or the wound suffered by V – would not have occurred at all, or would have occurred in some materially different way, we can draw the causal connection between D's intervention and the event. Should we qualify this conclusion with the proviso that the causal connection must be foreseeable? If so,

48 Above n. 21.

49 For fuller discussion and references, see A.P. Simester and G.R. Sullivan, *Criminal Law: Theory and Doctrine* (3rd edn, Oxford: Hart Publishing, 2007) at 189–91, 320–22.

50 Above n. 21, Chapter 8.

51 Some theorists go further and insist that causation of a harmful effect of itself is sufficient to warrant a legal duty to make reparation and may even justify criminal liability. See, for example, T. Honoré, *Responsibility and Fault* (Oxford: Hart Publishing, 1999) Chapter 2. See also J. Gardner, *Offences and Defences* (Oxford: Oxford University Press, 2007) Chapter 9.

52 Arguably, feelings of anger and resentment have been given too much leeway recently in the UK: for instance, in less than a decade, the maximum sentence for causing death by dangerous driving has gone from 5 years to 14 years. The Court of Appeal recently revised upwards the custodial sentences for what is known informally as 'one punch' manslaughter, citing the increase in custodial sentences for causing death by dangerous driving as a major reason for doing so: *Times Online*, 19 December 2009.

not all things directly caused in fact may be held to be imputably caused in law. The foreseeability proviso when applied to direct cases of the kind under discussion is something that constrains causal findings that otherwise would be made.[53] It is more straightforward in cases of direct causation to limit liability by reference to the mental element for the crime. Furthermore, for result crimes of strict liability, such a straightforward approach goes with the grain of these offences.[54] In the class of events to be considered directly caused by D would be included cases where he or she is under a legal duty to act and where performing his or her duty would have prevented the effect he or she is deemed to have caused.[55]

Matters become more complicated where, after D's intervention, an act or an event occurs which is the immediate and sufficient cause of the result D is alleged to have caused. For such cases, D's causal responsibility for the effect can only be sustained if the supervening event was something that D foresaw arising from his or her earlier intervention or, failing foresight on his or her part, was something that was reasonably foreseeable. But what if the event that was foreseen was something done voluntarily by a mentally competent, sufficiently informed actor? Take a case where D induces P to kill V by paying P in advance to do so. It may be entirely foreseeable that D's payment to P will result in V's death at the hands of P. Obviously, P is a causal agent in the matter of V's death. But is the same true of D? For the theorists John Gardner[56] and Michael Moore,[57] the answer is affirmative: they would assert a causal connection between D's payment and V's death. By contrast, Herbert Hart and Tony Honoré,[58] Glanville Williams[59] and a unanimous House of Lords[60] say otherwise. For them, in the eyes of the law, the exclusive causal agent is P.

In terms of the social meaning of causation, it is considered that Gardner and Moore have the better of the argument. To be sure, when speaking of causal influences on voluntary human conduct, we cannot attain the same certitude as when we, say, examine the impact of an explosion on the destruction of a building. But there are a host of non-coerced, undeceptive interchanges between D and P which would be difficult to explain and discuss in normal English usage unless a causal dependency between D's intervention and P's subsequent conduct is assumed. Because of this, the question arises of whether we should give full effect to an account of causation unconstrained by the dogma that a supervening act on the part of a voluntary, informed actor makes for a breach with any causal part played by previous actors and events. The position taken here is that we should drop the dogma and adopt a more expansive account of legal causation. One important side-effect of this would be to confine the class of accomplices to persons whose acts of encouragement, assistance and other forms of inducements were of a non-causal nature. This may be perceived

---

53 Such a constraint is strongly favoured in Yeo, Morgan and Chan, above n. 1, Chapter 5, where it is clearly demonstrated that the foreseeability restraint is a dominant trend in the causation jurisprudence of Malaysia, Singapore and India.

54 Honoré, above n. 51, for one would approve of this approach as he considers that D has what he calls 'outcome responsibility' for any event he directly causes. Obviously, such a way of thinking will not appeal to persons indisposed to strict liability.

55 Such an inclusion would be hotly disputed by Moore, who considers it logically impossible for an omission, a nullity, to cause anything: above n. 9 at 51–68. But even he allows that D may be assigned responsibility for an outcome if there is assurance that D had the means to prevent the outcome, although he considers that form of responsibility less morally freighted than positive causal agency.

56 J. Gardner, 'Complicity and Causality' (2007) 1 *Criminal Law and Philosophy* 127.

57 Above n. 9, Chapter 12.

58 H.L.A. Hart and T. Honoré, *Causation in the Law* (2nd edn, Oxford: Clarendon Press, 1985) 326–40.

59 G. Williams, '*Finis* for *Novus Actus*?' (1989) 48 *Cambridge Law Journal* 391.

60 *Kennedy (No. 2)*, above n. 19.

as an advantage, but other commentators may be wary of undermining the current structure of complicity by such an expansion of causal doctrine.[61] Persons of that inclination would opt for something different from the clause offered below.

A proposed provision for causation

1 .(1) Subject to subsection 1(2), D causes a result which is an element of an offence when:
   (a) D does an act which makes a more than negligible contribution to its occurrence; or
   (b) D omits to do an act which would prevent its occurrence and D's omission to do an act is an illegal omission.
2. D does not cause a result where, after D does such an act or makes such an omission, an act or an event occurs:
   (a) which is the immediate and sufficient cause of the result;
   (b) which D did not foresee; and
   (c) which could not in the circumstances reasonably have been foreseen arising from D's earlier act or omission.
3. An illegal omission is any omission prohibited by law or which furnishes ground for a civil action.

Explanation – The standard case of causation is where D directly makes a more than negligible contribution to a result which is an element of an offence. Where such a contribution can be proved, a finding of causation can be made even if the result was unforeseeable in the circumstances. A more than negligible contribution to a result can be made by way of illegal omission as well as by positive act, provided it can be proved that the result would not have occurred had D performed the duty to act imposed by law. Normally D will not be found to have made a more than negligible contribution to a result where after D's act or illegal omission, an act or event occurs which is the immediate and sufficient cause of the result. But D's earlier act or omission may yet be regarded as a cause of the result if the subsequent act or event could have reasonably been foreseen to follow from D's act or omission. Where a subsequent act is reasonably foreseeable in the manner indicated, it is immaterial that the subsequent actor acted voluntarily.

Illustrations

(a) D and P jointly attack V with knives and V dies from the attack. V probably would have died from the major wound inflicted by P, although the lesser wound inflicted by D made the major wound more difficult to treat. D and P have caused V's death.

(b) D stabs V. A blood transfusion that would have saved V's life was offered to V but refused on account of her religious beliefs. D has caused V's death.

(c) D, a doctor, refuses to visit his terminally-ill patient V despite any medical or any other justification for the refusal. Had D made the visit V would still have died from his incurable condition but some weeks later than his actual time of death. D has caused V's death.

(d) D punches V heavily in the face and runs away. Some 20 minutes later, V is fatally stabbed by P, a mentally disordered person who has just escaped from prison. In his confused and dazed condition, V did not notice the approach of P. D has not caused V's death.

---

61 For a strong defence for a law of complicity based on the dogma that voluntary conduct is uncaused conduct, see S.H. Kadish, 'Complicity, Cause and Blame: A Study in the Interpretation of Doctrine' (1985) 73 *California Law Review* 323.

(e) D punches V in the face on the seashore, causing V concussion. D runs away. V is drowned by the incoming sea. D has caused the death of V.
(f) P shoots and kills V because he was paid to do so by D. Both P and D have caused V's death.

THE SCOPE OF OMISSIONS LIABILITY

The conditions that must be met for liability for omissions in terms of ensuring that D can cogently be held responsible and if need be liable for D's failure to act have already been discussed. A distinction was drawn between two types of omission, namely what was called the 'pure' omission, where liability is imposed without more for a failure to act, and those omissions where the gist of the offence is allowing an effect to occur. The focus now moves to what the content of omissions liability should be or, in other words, a consideration of what failures to act are appropriately penalised in a modern liberal democracy.

First, let us consider those omissions where liability is triggered by allowing things to happen, things which would not have happened had D performed his or her duty to act. In a sense, under the IPC the content of the duty for what may be termed result crimes is defined: if it is an offence to cause a particular result positively, it is the same offence to allow the result to happen by way of an illegal omission.[62] There can be no objection to this, provided the assimilation of acts to illegal omissions is fair and so is the assimilation of allowing to cause. Essentially, a conscientious legislator should be satisfied that the circumstances whereby a duty to act arises systemically track situations where a failure to act to prevent harm is as morally culpable as causing that harm by a positive act. The circumstances that trigger a duty to act to prevent harm to legally protected interests under the IPC are broad[63] but are largely in line with other common law jurisdictions. In addition to duties explicitly imposed on citizens by general law, the illegal omission necessary for a results-based offence may consist of any private law obligation imposing a duty to act.

Undoubtedly, this basis for omissions liability will embrace situations of great moral turpitude. D1 and D2 may decide to kill their infant V by poisoning. Failing to find a suitable poison, they decide instead to starve V to death. It would be casuistic to seek any moral distinction between these two ways of killing V.[64] But we soon encounter less clear-cut assimilations between the respective act and its counterpart omission. Take D, a trained carer, who has contractually arranged with the infirm V to bath, shop and cook for him. By her gross failure to follow even the most basic principles of food hygiene, she causes V fatal food poisoning. If homicide based on negligence is acceptable, then this would be a straightforward instance of this form of liability. But what if D had suddenly resigned her post with V without serving out her three-month period of notice because of a better offer elsewhere? She might know that V is too proud and independent to seek help elsewhere and that he will likely die from lack of sustenance. But should what is essentially a failure to see out a contractual arrangement be a basis for a homicide conviction?[65]

Even greater reservations may be raised about circumstances where a voluntary assumption of a legal duty of care is the basis of an omissions-based liability for a homicide or other serious

62 IPC, s. 32.

63 IPC, s. 43 provides: The word 'illegal' is applicable to everything that is an offence or which is prohibited by law, or which furnishes ground for a civil action; and a person is said to be 'legally bound to do' whatever it is illegal in him to omit.

64 But see Moore, n. 9, Chapter 12.

65 Under the IPC, the combined effects of ss. 32 and 43 would appear to allow a conviction for a negligence-based homicide offence.

offence. The well-known English case of *R. v. Stone and Dobinson*[66] is salutary in this regard. D and his partner agreed to house V, his partner's adult anorexic sister, although there was no legal obligation to do so. This act of charity, combined with D's very ineffectual attempts to persuade V to eat and to find medical help for her, were found to constitute the assumption by D of a legal duty of care. So ineffectual was his assistance that it was found to be a grossly negligent breach of the duty of care and hence a sufficient basis for a conviction for manslaughter. A reading of the case may well leave the impression that D was punished for his inadequacy (he was borderline learning disabled) rather than any lack of concern, let alone indifference, towards V. In addition, the case illustrates a tendency to overlook causal issues in cases of omission. Anorexia is of course a very intractable eating disorder; whether even the best of attention would have saved V was an issue unexplored at trial and on appeal in *Stone and Dobinson*.

The formulation for an illegal omission in the IPC is of long standing and doubtless well integrated into the working practices and expectations of prosecutors and criminal lawyers generally. No proposal for any change will be made here, although if a proposal were to be made, it would have been to narrow the base of liability.

We turn now to the case of pure omission, liability based on the bare failure to act. The functioning of modern states is dependent on active duties based on general civic responsibilities and also specific duties pertaining to particular roles and functions, often of an official or specialised nature. The extent and nature of these duties will vary according to the state of economic development of the jurisdiction in question and its political and cultural conditions. What matters for duties of this kind is that what we have called the responsibility condition should be met, a matter already addressed above.

A matter for the consideration of all modern states is to what extent it should place what may be termed horizontal duties on its citizens to help each other. By and large, jurisdictions in the common law tradition forbear from imposing duties to assist others even where the stakes for the imperilled person are high and the steps available to others to render effective assistance are easy and without risk. In brief, in a typical common law jurisdiction there is no duty of easy rescue. It has been forcefully argued, most notably by Andrew Ashworth,[67] that this should change and that there are strong moral and cultural arguments in favour of a duty to render assistance in circumstances where a good citizen would come to the aid of a person in danger. Before we give consideration to this matter, one limiting condition will be put in place. If the IPC were to be changed to accommodate a duty of easy rescue, a failure to make such a rescue would be an illegal omission. As such, a failure to carry out an easy rescue could be used as a predicate for further, more serious offences such as homicide offences. The discussion below assumes any offence based on a failure to give assistance will be cordoned off from other illegal omissions to ensure that the criminal liability arising from a failure to rescue will be confined to the specific failure to rescue offence.

Should the IPC be changed to legislate for such an offence? The moral argument in favour of a failure to give assistance offence is that the indifference and lack of concern instantiated by a failure to make easy rescue warrants retributive punishment. That claim will not be examined here. All that will be said is that the reasons explaining any instance of non-assistance are varied. They may range from callous indifference to social and culturally-based inhibitions which may deter even persons of good will. Moreover, there is no entailment relationship between moral wrongs,

66 [1977] QB 354.

67 A. Ashworth, 'The Scope of Criminal Liability for Omissions' (1989) 105 *Law Quarterly Review* 424.

even egregious moral wrongs, and criminal offences. The better focus is not on the punishment of wrongs *per se* but on whether the civic condition will be improved if particular wrongs are subject to criminal sanctions.

Ashworth lays particular stress on civic values. In multicultural societies where, outside the circle of family and friends, contact with others is typically of a commercial or service-based kind, social commitments based on group solidarity and feelings of belonging are hard to achieve. But, so the argument goes, we can all face perils which are equally threatening, whatever our ethnicity and culture. We can confidently reach out to each other when such perils arise. The state can foster this limited but important form of social solidarity by imposing a duty of easy rescue.

We cannot here even scratch the surface of a question which raises important issues in political social and moral theory.[68] However, it will be asserted that recourse to the criminal law should always be a matter of last resort and that ways of improving society not based on condemnation and punishment should be considered first.[69] Before passing a law which punishes failures to make easy rescue, a conscientious legislator might ask the following questions: in my country, are there systemic and widespread failures to make easy rescues and significant harms arising from such failures? Would a duty to make easy rescues diminish the incidence of such harms? Is there strong public support for a change in the law? Can the new law be fairly and consistently enforced? As the answers to these questions for countries with IPC-derived criminal codes are unknown, at least to this commentator, no proposal for a failure of assistance offence is made.

As no proposals with respect to any aspect of omissions liability have been made, no legislative clauses are put forward for examination.

---

68 M. Ignatieff, *The Needs of Strangers* (London: Chatto & Windus, 1984) provides a good point of entry into these issues.

69 This principle of restraint has been lost sight of for at least a decade in the UK, where there has been a plethora of criminal justice legislation including over 3,000 new criminal offences: see Simester and Sullivan, above n. 49, Chapter 16; and Chapter 14 of this volume (C. Clarkson, 'Recent Law Reform and Codification of the General Principles of Criminal Law in England and Wales: A Tale of Woe').

Chapter 5
Mistake and Strict Liability

Kumaralingam Amirthalingam

INTRODUCTION

This chapter considers the law of mistake and examines the extent to which the Indian Penal Code (IPC) measures up in this area. Macaulay's draft of the IPC was completed in 1837 and the IPC itself was enacted in 1860 after further revision by the Indian Law Commission. This period coincided with a critical period in criminal law when major shifts were taking place,[1] resulting in a landscape of criminal law at the turn of the twentieth century that was significantly different from that in the early to mid-nineteenth century, particularly with respect to criminal fault. Significantly, the latter part of the nineteenth century saw the advent of 'strict liability' in the context of regulatory offences, heralding a whole new jurisprudence of criminal law.[2] Arguably, therefore, any doctrine of mistake introduced in the 1860s was likely to be out of touch with the realities of criminal law theory in the twentieth century.

There is very little on the law of mistake that can be derived from Macaulay's work or from the IPC itself. Yet mistake is a central concept to a system that determines criminal liability largely on the basis of an individual's mental state. A mistaken belief may in many cases negate the fault element required or otherwise provide a basis for exculpation. Even in statutes that do not specify a fault element such that the prosecution need not prove *mens rea* in the conventional sense, an accused's mistaken belief may serve to excuse him or her from criminal liability.

There are, broadly speaking, three significant issues relating to mistake: first, whether the burden of proof should be on the prosecution or the accused;[3] secondly, whether, and to what extent, a mistake needs to satisfy an objective standard of reasonableness for it to have exculpatory effect; and, thirdly, whether mistake of law should ever be recognised as an excuse.[4] Where the

1 See generally, L. Farmer, *Criminal Law, Tradition and Legal Order: Crime and the Genius of Scots Law, 1747 to the Present* (Cambridge: Cambridge University Press, 1997); J. Hostettler, *The Politics of Criminal Law Reform in the Nineteenth Century* (Chichester: Barry Rose Law Publishers Ltd, 1992); A.W. Norrie, *Crime, Reason and History: A Critical Introduction to Criminal Law* (London: Weidenfeld & Nicolson, 1993). See also Chapter 2 of this volume (B. Wright, 'Macaulay's Indian Penal Code: Historical Context and Originating Principles') at 25–34.

2 See generally C. Howard, *Strict Responsibility* (London: Sweet & Maxwell, 1963). The preferred use of the term 'strict liability' is in the Australian/Canadian sense, that is, in the case of an offence which does not specify any fault element (or *mens rea*), the prosecution only has to prove the physical elements of the offence, but the accused may negate criminal liability by showing that the offence was committed due to a mistake of fact or despite acting with due diligence; see below under the heading 'Strict Liability'.

3 See further Chapter 3 of this volume (N. Morgan, 'The Fault Elements of Offences') at 71–2.

4 Mistake of law is generally not recognised as a defence in the common law world, although it has limited application in some jurisdictions. See, for example, G. Artz, 'Ignorance or Mistake of Law' (1976) 24 *American Journal of Comparative Law* 646; and U. Neumann, 'Mistake of Law' (1996) 30 *Israel Law Review* 207. Under Article 32(2) of the Rome Statute of the International Criminal Court, 2187 UNTS 90, mistake of law also has limited exculpatory effect in international criminal law: see K.J. Heller, 'Mistake of Legal

mistake relates to a subjective fault element, an honest mistake – even if unreasonable in the circumstances – should deny criminal liability.[5] The burden of proving the offence, and therefore overcoming any hurdles presented by the accused's mistake, lies with the prosecution.

Where the fault element is based on objective standards – and also in cases of strict liability – only a reasonable mistake should assist the accused. The IPC, however, appears to treat all cases of mistake as defence matters, as the two provisions dealing with mistake, namely ss. 76 and 79, are located within Chapter IV, which deals with general exceptions to criminal liability. This has resulted in many cases wrongly applying the 'defence' of mistake when the issue simply was whether or not the accused had acted with the relevant *mens rea*.[6]

This chapter is divided into three sections. The first section deals with the law of mistake under the IPC. It makes a preliminary argument that the IPC, as originally drafted, did not set out a general defence of mistake. However, acknowledging that the conventional view holds otherwise, namely that the IPC does contain the defence of mistake, this section goes on to suggest that the defence of mistake in the IPC rests on theoretically shaky ground. The next section considers the development of strict liability offences and the judicial responses to it in the leading common law jurisdictions, which relied in part on mistake to avoid punishing morally innocent defendants. The third section briefly deals with mistake of law and considers the extent to which this type of mistake may be relevant under the IPC.

MISTAKE IN THE INDIAN PENAL CODE

A Mistaken Defence of Mistake?

This chapter begins with a provocative, and perhaps mischievous, question. Did the IPC actually include a defence of mistake when it was originally drafted or did the defence of mistake enter it by accident? Macaulay's extensive notes on the IPC do not contain even a passing mention of the defence of mistake,[7] which is generally assumed to be found in ss. 76 and 79. The precursors to ss. 76 and 79 in the original draft Code by Macaulay – cls. 62 and 63 – do not explicitly refer to mistake:

> 62. Nothing is an offence which is done by a person who is or in good faith believes himself to be commanded by law to do it.
>
> *Illustrations*
>
> (a) A, a soldier, fires on a mob, by the order of his superior Officer, in conformity with the commands of the law. A has committed no offence.

Element, the Common Law, and Article 32 of the Rome Statute' (2008) 6 *Journal of International Criminal Justice* 419.

5 *DPP v. Morgan* [1976] AC 182.

6 An example of this kind of erroneous reasoning is the case of *Chirangi v. State of Nagpur* AIR 1952 Nagpur 282. See also A.T.H. Smith, 'Error and Mistake of Law in Anglo-American Criminal Law' (1985) 14 *Anglo-American Law Review* 3, at 21. The term *mens rea* is used in this chapter to refer to the subjective culpable mental state of an offence.

7 See Macaulay's notes on the general defences in T.B. Macaulay, J.M. Macleod, G.W. Anderson and F. Millett, *A Penal Code Prepared by the Indian Law Commissioners* (London: Pelham Richardson, 1838) (reprinted by the Lawbook Exchange, Ltd, 2002) Note B (On the Chapter of General Exceptions). This lack of explanation was criticised by the Indian Law Commissioners: *Special Report on the Indian Penal Code: First Report* (1846) (reprinted in the British Parliamentary Papers 1847–8, vol. XXVIII) para. [116].

(b) A, an officer of a Court of Justice, being ordered by that Court to arrest Y, and being led into a belief that Z is Y, arrests Z, believing in good faith that in arresting Z he is obeying an order which he is commanded by law to obey. Here A may, under certain circumstances, be liable to a civil action, but he has committed no offence.

63. Nothing is an offence which is done by a person in the exercise, to the best of his judgment exerted in good faith, of any power given to him by law.

Illustrations

A sees Z commit what appears to A to be a murder. A in the exercise, to the best of his judgment exerted in good faith, of the power which the law gives to all persons of apprehending murderers in the fact, seizes Z, in order to bring Z before the proper authorities. A has committed no offence.

The explicit reference to mistake is inserted later when the IPC was enacted by way of these additional provisions:

76. Nothing is an offence which is done by a person who is, *or who by reason of a mistake of fact and not by reason of a mistake of law in good faith believes himself to be*, bound by law to do it.

79. Nothing is an offence which is done by any person who is justified by law, *or who by reason of a mistake of fact and not by reason of a mistake of law in good faith, believes himself to be justified by law*, in doing it.

(Emphasis added)

It is argued that, properly construed, the exceptions in ss. 76 and 79 are not general mistake defences, but are much narrower defences: they only apply when the accused was either bound or justified by law to act, or where the accused believed in good faith that he or she was so bound or justified. The language in Macaulay's draft Code is clearer: the accused must be *commanded* or *specifically empowered* by law. There are several reasons why ss. 76 and 79 should not be read as laying down a general defence of mistake. The text itself makes this plain. For example, in s. 79, the main clause is 'Nothing is an offence which is done by any person who is justified by law, ...'. The sub-clause merely extends the defence to those who believe in good faith that they are justified by law.

The illustrations to ss. 76 and 79 do not suggest a general defence of mistake; rather, they are confined to situations where an accused was acting under a particular legal authority or duty.[8] The statutory context lends further support to this argument. Sections 76, 77, 78 and 79, being the first four sections in Chapter IV of the IPC, all deal with situations where an accused was acting under some particular form of legal authority or duty – actual or perceived – in a bid to enforce or advance the law.[9] The First Report on the draft Code is instructive regarding the scope of ss. 76 and 79:

> Sir R Comyn objects, that 'to permit a person who has committed an injury to set up his private intentions as defence of excuse, and to allege that he did the injury from virtuous motives, or from a wrongful impression of the law or the fact, would frequently produce a defect in justice, and allow offenders to escape'. We do not find that it is permitted to any person to set up his private intentions, or to allege virtuous motives, simply as a defence or excuse under a criminal

8 See, for example, *State of West Bengal v. Shew Mangal Singh* AIR 1981 SC 1917 for an illustration of this application of s. 76.

9 IPC, s. 76 (act of person when bound by law); s. 77 (act of judge when acting judicially); s. 78 (act pursuant to judgment or order of court); s. 79 (act of person when justified by law).

> charge ... But no such thing is allowed by the two clauses above mentioned, in which good faith is recognised to a certain extent as a ground of defence. *Under both there must be a bona fide intention to advance the law ...*[10]

As a matter of general principle, there is no requirement for an accused to have an 'intention to advance the law' when pleading mistake as a defence. There was a further objection that ss. 62 and 63 potentially allowed an accused to rely on mistake of law as a defence, which would have been contrary to the *ignorantia juris non excusat* maxim. Recognising this possibility, the Commission advised as follows:

> To make it perfectly clear, we would suggest that the following proviso be subjoined to the clause : – 'Provided that this exception shall not extend to any person who, by reason of a misconception at law, and not by reason of a misconception of fact, believes himself to be commanded by law to do any thing'.[11]

As a result of this, the present clause with respect to mistake was almost certainly inserted into ss. 76 and 79 for the sole purpose of clarifying that ignorance or mistake of law could not be used by an accused to assert that he or she believed that he or she was bound or justified by law. However, the wording enacted in the IPC is arguably open to a broader interpretation and in practice this has happened: the explicit reference to mistake, intended merely as a qualification, has supplanted the actual defences enacted in ss. 76 and 79. Courts, proceeding on the assumption that s. 79 was intended to be a general mistake defence, have interpreted 'justified by law' to be the equivalent of anything not prohibited by law.[12]

There is a significant difference between what is justified by law and what is not prohibited by law. Where conduct has to be justified by law, it presupposes that the conduct itself is initially wrongful and therefore needs legal justification.[13] The classic example would be killing another in private defence. Killing another is a wrong, but where it is done in private defence, it is justified by law. Similarly, from the civil law of negligence, it is *prima facie* negligent to take foreseeable risks, but in some cases where a risk is taken to avoid a greater risk, the initial conduct is justified.[14] As such, conduct that is not *prohibited* by law need not be *justified* by law.

The judicial interpretation of 'justified by law' also makes no sense in the context of the main limb of s. 79: 'Nothing is an offence which is done by any person who is justified by law ...' Under the current interpretation, this limb simply says that nothing is an offence which is done by a person who does anything not prohibited by law; this is not particularly helpful legislation. Further, if the current interpretation is correct, that is, s. 79 is a general mistake defence and anything that is not prohibited by law is justified, then s. 76 becomes irrelevant as it is subsumed within s. 79.[15] This

10 Indian Law Commissioners, above n. 7, at para. [114] (emphasis added).

11 *Ibid.*, at para. [116].

12 *Abdullah v. R.* [1954] MLJ 195.

13 *Raj Kapoor v. Laxman* AIR 1980 SC 605, at para. [9], *per* Krishna Iyer J.: 'The position that emerges is this. Jurisprudentially viewed, an act may be an offence, definitionally speaking but; [*sic*] a forbidden act may not spell inevitable [guilt,] the law itself declares that in certain special circumstances it is not to be regarded as an offence ... Section 79 makes an offence a non-offence. When? Only when the offending act is actually justified by law or is *bona fide* believed by mistake of fact to be so justified'.

14 See, for example, *Watt v. Hertfordshire County Council* [1954] 1 WLR 835.

15 Clearly, if you believe you were bound by law to act, you must believe that you were justified in law to act.

kind of superfluous drafting and internal inconsistency would have been anathema to Macaulay, for whom clarity and simplicity were fundamental principles which underpinned the drafting of the Code.[16]

Finally, the argument advanced here is supported by the general philosophy of Macaulay and the political context of the time the Code was drafted. The IPC, while ahead of its time in terms of its liberal and progressive nature, also served an instrumental purpose of facilitating the British rule of India and promoting law and order.[17] Sections 76 and 79 were critical both in terms of protecting those who were charged with enforcing the law in India and in terms of encouraging individuals to be proactive in enforcing the law.[18] For the above reasons, it is suggested that s. 79 is not a defence of mistake, but a narrower defence of 'justified by law'. The insertion of mistake into the defence by way of a subordinate clause was categorically to exclude any reliance on ignorance of law as a basis of arguing the defence.

It is commonplace to see s. 79 referred to as a mistake defence[19] rather than as a 'justified by law' defence, even though the illustration focuses on the latter.[20] With respect, this is a misguided view, but it now has such currency that it does represent the law across all IPC jurisdictions. Interestingly, the erroneous interpretation also rendered the IPC capable of coping with the demands of modern regulatory offences.

The Law Commission of India produced a draft Indian Penal Code (Amendment) Bill (1978), which recommended abolishing s. 79 and replacing s. 76 with two new provisions:

> Act done by a person bound or justified by law
> 40. Nothing is an offence which is done by a person bound by law to do it or is justified by law in doing it.

---

16 See Wright, Chapter 2 of this volume, above n. 1, at 23.

17 In Macaulay's speech to the House of Commons Select Committee in 1831 on codification of the criminal law in India, he is reported to have said:

> It may be that the public mind of India may expand under our system till it has outgrown that system; that by good government we may educate our subjects into a capacity for better government, that having become instructed in European knowledge, they may, in some future age, demand European institutions ... To have found a great people sunk in the lowest depths of slavery and superstition, to have so ruled them as to have made them desirous and capable of all the privileges of citizens, would indeed be a title to glory all our own ... There is an empire exempt from all natural causes of decay. Those triumphs are the pacific triumphs of reason over barbarism; that empire is the imperishable empire of our arts and our morals, our literature and our laws.

Hansard, July 10, 1833, vol. 19, col. 536. Cited in Hostettler, above n. 1, at 169. See also Chapters 2 and 8 of this volume (Wright, above n. 1; and Cheah Wui Ling, 'Private Defence', respectively).

18 See also above n 8. In each of the instances, the particular provision is aimed at protecting an individual who is acting under a legal obligation, to protect a legal interest or to enforce the law.

19 See, for example, B.M. Gandhi, *Indian Penal Code* (Lucknow: Eastern Book Company, 1996) 10; K.D. Gaur, *A Textbook on The Indian Penal Code* (New Delhi: Oxford & IBH Publishing Co Pvt Ltd, 1992) 93, 99; S. Yeo, N. Morgan and W. Chan, *Criminal Law in Malaysia and Singapore* (Singapore: LexisNexis, 2007) para. [17.2].

20 The illustration to s. 79 states: 'A sees Z commit what appears to A to be a murder. A in the exercise, to the best of his judgment exerted in good faith, of the power which the law gives to all persons of apprehending murderers in the act, seizes Z, in order to bring Z before the proper authorities. A has committed no offence, though it may turn out that Z was acting in self-defence'.

> Act done by a person by mistake of fact believing himself bound or justified by law
> 41. Nothing is an offence which is done by a person who, by reason of a mistake of fact and not by reason of a mistake of law, in good faith believes himself bound by law to do it or justified by law in doing it.

The intention may have been to extract a general mistake defence, but by linking the mistake to a belief that the person was bound or justified by law, the proposed s. 41 is simply a subsidiary of the proposed s. 40.

Analysing s. 79

Having argued that, in theory at least, the IPC does not contain a defence of mistake, it is recognised that in practice s. 79 has been applied as such. It will be contended here that the application of s. 79 remains unsatisfactory. Theoretically, mistake is a concept that operates in two distinctive ways. First, the mistake may operate to deny responsibility for the alleged criminal conduct itself. Typically, this would be where the mistake serves to negate an offence element, often with respect to the relevant mental state, for example, intention or knowledge. To give an illustration of this, a person who intends to shoot a deer but mistakenly shoots a man cannot fairly be held to have committed murder since the person did not intend to injure, let alone kill, another human being.

Secondly, the mistake may operate not to negate an offence element, but rather to deny moral blameworthiness. Thus, while the accused may fairly be held to be the author of the conduct, it would be unfair to hold him or her criminally liable for the conduct. Broadly, this can arise in one of two forms. The mistake may serve to support a formal defence, for example, private defence or necessity. Thus, if a person deliberately kills another, mistakenly believing on reasonable grounds that it was necessary to do so to save life, that person may not be morally blameworthy. Alternatively, in the absence of any fault element to be negated or positive defence to be advanced, a mistake may nevertheless render an accused morally innocent and undeserving of criminal censure. The strict liability jurisprudence provides the clearest operation of this type of mistake.

These two ways by which mistake operates are fundamentally different: in the first instance, the accused is essentially saying 'I did not do the deed', while in the second instance, the accused is saying 'I did the deed, but I did nothing wrong'. In the first way, the mistake does not operate as a formal defence; it is simply a part of the totality of the evidence that the prosecution has to deal with in proving the offence. The question of whether the mistake was reasonable in the circumstances, or whether the accused deserved the benefit of the mistake, should not arise.[21] The burden is on the prosecution to prove all the elements of the crime and, insofar as the accused's mistake may be relevant, the prosecution simply has to deal with it. In the second way, the offence elements have all been established and the mistake operates as a defence: this invites an objective evaluation of the mistake and may fairly place the burden of proof on the accused.

The conflation of the two distinct ways in which mistake operates is partly responsible for the unsatisfactory state of the law. Courts have often improperly applied s. 79 to cases where the accused had acted under a mistaken belief. Returning to the first way, the real question, using the deer-homicide example, is whether the accused intended to kill or seriously harm a human being. The fact is that the accused intended to kill a deer. It is the accused's intention – not the accused's mistake –

---

21 Cf. G.P. Fletcher, *Rethinking Criminal Law* (Boston: Little, Brown and Co, 1978) 690.

that is the critical issue. Insofar as murder is a crime of intention,[22] an accused who intended to kill a deer does not have the necessary fault for murder. By focusing on the accused's mistake, rather than on the prosecution's burden of proving the elements of the crime, courts have relieved the prosecution of the burden of proving *mens rea* in every case where the accused made a mistake.[23]

At common law, it is generally accepted that an honestly held mistake of fact may negate *mens rea*.[24] From a historical perspective – even though in theory this may be wrong – one can explain why a mistake has to be reasonable before it can negate *mens rea*. Indeed, there is common law authority for this. For example, in the Privy Council case of *Bank of New South Wales v. Piper*,[25] it was stated that 'the absence of *mens rea* really consists in an honest and reasonable belief entertained by the accused of the existence of facts which, if true, would make the act charged against him innocent'.[26] Thus, in the mid-nineteenth century when the IPC was drafted, there was conceivably no inconsistency in applying objective standards to negate *mens rea*.[27]

This objective approach to mistake was also supported by the now discredited rule that a person is presumed to intend the natural and probable consequence of his or her conduct.[28] For practical purposes, it was difficult to prove what a person had subjectively intended, and courts relied on the presumption that a person intended the natural consequences of his or her actions. This resulted in *mens rea* being assessed objectively by juries: what was a 'natural' consequence was determined by asking what a reasonable or ordinary person would have foreseen to be the natural consequence.[29]

The requirement of 'good faith' in s. 79 adds another layer of complexity to the law of mistake in the IPC. 'Good faith' is defined in s. 52 of the IPC as follows: 'Nothing is said to be done or believed in "good faith" which is done or believed without due care or attention.' The General Clauses Act 1897 (GCA) in India, on the other hand, defines the term differently: 'A thing shall be deemed to be done in good faith where it is in fact done honestly, whether it is done negligently or not.' This definition of 'good faith' in the GCA applies to all laws other than the IPC. The two definitions of 'good faith' appear contradictory, with the GCA equating good faith with honesty and the IPC equating good faith with due care and attention. The distinction is significant, as one is based on a subjective test while the other is objective. The Indian Law Commission, in its draft Indian Penal Code (Amendment) Bill 1978, sought to reconcile the two definitions by proposing this replacement to s. 52:

> Good faith
> 12. A thing is said to be done or believed in 'good faith' if it is done or believed honestly and with due care and attention.

---

22 Leaving aside for the moment the various mental elements for murder under IPC, s. 300 and in various common law jurisdictions.

23 The damage is twofold. First, s. 79 reverses the burden of proof and, secondly, it turns a subjective fault crime into an objective one.

24 *DPP v. Morgan*, above n. 5; *The Queen v. Brown* (1975) 10 SASR 139; *R. v. McEwan* [1979] 2 NSWLR 926.

25 [1897] AC 383.

26 *Ibid.*, at 389–90, *per* Sir Richard Couch.

27 See J.W.C Turner, *Kenny's Outlines of Criminal Law* (16th edn, Cambridge: Cambridge University Press, 1952) 20.

28 *DPP v. Smith* [1961] AC 290. This presumption has been abolished by legislation in England and rejected by courts in Australia, India and Singapore.

29 J.W.C. Turner, *Russell on Crime* (vol. 1) (12th edn, London: Sweet & Maxwell, 1964) 33.

This proposal does not make any material difference because the requirements of honesty and due care are conjunctive rather than disjunctive; even if the accused had an honest belief, that belief would only be effective if the accused had exercised due care and attention. Ultimately, the inquiry remains an objective one. Nevertheless, an examination of the Indian cases suggests that courts have applied the good faith test in a highly subjective manner, bringing it closer to the GCA definition than the IPC definition. The focus of the court's inquiry is not so much on the reasonableness of the belief as on the genuineness of the belief. The standard of due care and attention is so highly tailored to the particular circumstances as to lose its objective base.[30]

In the oft-cited case of *Bonda Kui v. Emperor*,[31] the accused had killed another woman, mistakenly believing her to be an evil spirit. The court, in acquitting her, accepted her testimony as to her state of mind, holding that it was 'difficult to come to any other conclusion than that the appellant is telling the truth when she says that she did not take the deceased to be a human being at all'.[32] The good faith test was thus used as a means of testing the genuineness of the accused's belief. Again, as another court put it in *State of Orissa v. Ram Bahadur Thapa*,[33] '[i]n view of the clear evidence ... to the effect that the respondent thought that he was attacking ghosts, he would be entitled to the benefit of [s. 79], unless from the facts and circumstances established in the case it can be reasonably held that he did not act in good faith'.[34] The court accepted that the accused had acted in good faith even though it acknowledged that all the accused had to do was to flash the torch he held in his hand to realise that the moving figures were in fact people and not ghosts.[35]

As argued earlier, there is no need for recourse to s. 79 when it comes to *mens rea* offences.[36] However, if s. 79 is to be used for such offences, the good faith test should be assessed on the basis of the genuineness rather than the reasonableness of the mistake. Where s. 79 is used with respect to affirmative defences and strict liability offences, an objective test is appropriate. However, the standard should be one that fairly takes into account the defendant's particular circumstances. The Singaporean courts have required the accused to meet an inordinately high standard of care in order to discharge the good faith requirement. The high watermark is *Tan Khee Wan Iris v. PP*, where the court said:

> The mistake may be a natural one to make and it may be one which reasonable persons often make. Nevertheless, the defence is not made out unless it is shown on a balance of probabilities that the appellant exercised due care and attention.[37]

The facts in the above case suggest that the standard is set at an unrealistic level and ignores the particular circumstances in which the accused was operating. The accused was charged under the

30 See, for example, *State of Orissa v. Ram Bahadur Thapa* AIR 1960 Ori 161 and references therein to *Emperor v. Abdeol Wadood Ahmed* ILR 31 Bom 293; *Bhawoo Jiwaji v. Mulfi Dayal* ILR 12 Bom 377; and *Po Mye v. The King* AIR 1940 Rang 129.

31 AIR 1943 Pat 64.

32 *Ibid.*, at para. [4].

33 Above n. 30.

34 *Ibid.*, at para. [7].

35 *Ibid.*, at para. [9]. See also *Waryam Singh v. Emperor* AIR 1926 Lah 554 for a similar approach to good faith.

36 If the mistake negates an offence element, the prosecution fails without the defendant having to raise any defence under Chapter IV.

37 [1995] 1 SLR(R) 723, at para. [19].

then Public Entertainments Act[38] with providing public entertainment without a valid licence. The licence had been issued until 31 December 1993 and the accused had held the performance in the early hours of 1 January 1994. There was an ambiguity on the face of the licence; although it stated the validity as until 31 December, it also included the approved programme which was stated to run for 12 hours from 6 pm on 31 December to 6 am on 1 January. The court accepted that the licensing officer and the prosecution had made the same mistake as the accused, but nevertheless held that s. 79 was not applicable because the accused had not met the required standard of due care and attention.

It should be noted that *Iris Tan* was a strict liability case, which might have justified a higher standard of care and diligence, but even on that basis, the interpretation of good faith in *Iris Tan* seems inappropriate. Separately, *Iris Tan* raises an interesting question as to whether s. 79 should be applied to strict liability offences. It should be recalled that the strict liability regime is a development that postdates the IPC and an argument can be made that it should be governed by its own special rules, which the common law courts have developed.[39]

STRICT LIABILITY

To avoid confusion, it should be clarified at the outset that strict liability means different things in different jurisdictions. In England, it refers to liability without fault, which is traditionally interpreted as liability without the need to prove *mens rea*. In Australia and Canada, courts have developed a midway category between offences which require proof of *mens rea* and those which do not.[40] This middle category, which generally allows for a defence of reasonable mistake of fact (as in Australia) or due diligence (as in Canada), is called strict liability. Offences where proof of *mens rea* is not required and which do not permit the above-mentioned defences are called absolute liability. The preferred use of the term 'strict liability' is in the Australian/Canadian sense and will be applied here.

Although strict liability offences are generally described as offences not requiring proof of *mens rea*, the concept of strict liability is more nuanced, as pointed out by various academic commentators.[41] Some academics in IPC jurisdictions have argued that whatever the position is in the common law, the position under the IPC is clear. If a statute creates an offence without the need to prove *mens rea*, courts should respect that. The argument is that all such offences would still be governed by Chapter IV of the IPC and the accused would still be entitled to rely on the general exceptions, which include mistake.[42] This, however, has not been the case, with the courts importing some of the common law jurisprudence on strict liability.[43]

---

38 Cap. 257, 1985 Rev. Ed.

39 See, generally, M. Sornarajah, 'Defences to Strict Liability Offences in Singapore and Malaysia' (1985) 27 *Malaya Law Review* 1. As will be elaborated below, different common law courts have developed different solutions.

40 See *He Kaw Teh v. The Queen* (1985) 157 CLR 523; and *The Queen v. City of Sault Ste. Marie* [1978] 2 SCR 1299. See further Morgan, Chapter 3 of this volume, above n. 3, at 70.

41 D.N. Husak, 'Varieties of Strict Liability' (1995) 8 *Canadian Journal of Law and Jurisprudence* 189; S.P. Green, 'Six Senses of Strict Liability' in A.P. Simester (ed.), *Appraising Strict Liability* (Oxford: Oxford University Press, 2005); P. Cane, *Responsibility in Law and Morality* (Oxford: Hart Publishing, 2002) 82–3.

42 See, for example, W. Chan, 'Requirement of Fault in Strict Liability' (1999) 11 *Singapore Academy of Law Journal* 98; G.L. Peiris, *General Principles of Criminal Liability in Ceylon: A Comparative Analysis* (2nd edn, Colombo: Lake House Investments Ltd, 1980) 60–61.

43 See, for example, *PP v. Teo Kwang Kiang* [1992] 2 SLR(R) 560; *Chng Wei Meng v. PP* [2002] 2 SLR(R) 566.

The earliest form of strict liability in English law was vicarious liability, as seen in *R. v. Marsh*,[44] where Littledale J. stated: 'A master in some cases is answerable criminally for the act of his servant, when the act is done by the servant for the benefit of the master in the course of his employment.'[45] The first reported case of direct strict liability in criminal law may well be the 1846 decision of *R. v. Woodrow*,[46] involving a prosecution based on the Tobacco Act 1842 (UK).[47] Courts in the mid-nineteenth century were reluctant to convict without proof of *mens rea*,[48] but as the criminal law became less harsh in terms of punishments and as legislative drafting improved, courts gradually became more willing to give effect to statutes imposing strict liability.[49]

Many of the strict liability offences in the nineteenth century focused on public health and welfare, and were based on three important UK Acts: the Sale of Food and Drugs Act 1875, the Public Health Act 1875 and the Liquor Licensing Act 1872. The Sale of Food and Drugs Act 1875, while imposing strict liability for selling adulterated food products, also provided for a due diligence defence whereby a defendant could avoid liability by proving that the food was purchased for sale under a warranty that it was not adulterated.[50] The Liquor Licensing Act 1872 resulted in the historic decision of *Sherras v. De Rutzen*,[51] where Day J. held that the omission of a *mens rea* word did not mean proof of *mens rea* was irrelevant, but merely that the burden of proof lay with the defendant.[52] While the courts remained uncomfortable with the idea of strict liability, there was a growing acceptance that these offences were not truly criminal and therefore did not stigmatise the accused. Consequently, a relaxation of the *mens rea* requirement was acceptable.[53]

However, the same could not be said for certain other strict liability offences, for example, felony murder, sexual assault of a minor and bigamy. *R. v. Prince*[54] was one of the most important decisions dealing with strict liability in the context of a crime *mala in se*. The defendant was charged with unlawfully taking an unmarried girl, under the age of 16 years, out of the possession and against the will of her father. His conviction was upheld despite his plea that he honestly and reasonably believed the girl to be over 16 years of age. The majority justified the conviction in the absence of proof of *mens rea* on the ground that the defendant's conduct was morally blameworthy. Bramwell B. stated: 'The act forbidden is wrong in itself, if without lawful cause. I do not say illegal, but wrong.'[55] Blameworthiness in *Prince* was apparently attributed on the ground that the

---

44 (1824) 2 B & C 717, 107 ER 550.

45 *Ibid.*, at 723. See also *Mullins v. Collins* (1874) 9 LR QB 292; and *Brown v. Foot* (1892) 66 LTR 649.

46 (1846) 15 M & W 404, 153 ER 907.

47 Some have argued that *Woodrow* was not truly a criminal case as much as a tax case, with a fine replacing an existing tax. See R.G. Singer, 'The Resurgence of *Mens Rea*: III – The Rise and Fall of Strict Criminal Liability (1988–9) 30 *Boston College Law Review* 337, at 341–3.

48 See, for example, *Hearne v. Garton and Stone* (1859) 2 El & El 66, 121 ER 26; and *R v. Sleep* (1861) 8 Cox CC 472.

49 See C. Manchester, 'The Origins of Strict Criminal Liability' (1977) 6 *Anglo-American Law Review* 277 at 282.

50 See *Pain v. Boughtwood* (1890) 24 QBD 353, where the court emphasised the existence of this defence in recognising that the statute did not require proof of *mens rea*.

51 [1895] 1 QB 918.

52 *Ibid.*, at 921.

53 See *Provincial Motor Cab Company, Ltd. v. Dunning* [1909] 2 KB 599 at 602–3, *per* Lord Alverstone C.J.: 'A breach of [a public welfare] regulation is not to be regarded as a criminal offence in the full sense of the word … The doctrine that there must be a criminal intent does not apply to criminal offences of that particular class which arise only from the breach of a statutory regulation'.

54 (1874–80) All ER Rep 881.

55 *Ibid.*, at 884.

defendant knew he was taking the girl without her father's consent. Strictly speaking, there was an absence of *mens rea* with respect to a critical element of the offence, namely the girl's age, but the court took a broad view of what constituted moral blameworthiness. Brett J., although dissenting, agreed with the majority's approach on this point and stated that '[t]his and similar decisions go rather to show what is *mens rea* than to show whether there can or cannot be a conviction for crimes proper without *mens rea*'.[56]

Judicial Responses to Strict Liability

Strict liability remains a contentious issue, both for theoretical and normative reasons.[57] Reluctant to convict such individuals, English courts at the turn of the twentieth century held that an honest and reasonable belief in circumstances which, if they existed, would make the defendant's conduct innocent should be a defence.[58] Courts have also insisted on a presumption of *mens rea* where the statute had no express *mens rea* requirement.[59] Through this mechanism, the common law courts have tended to restrict the use of strict liability in the growing regime of statutory offences.

The Australian courts adopted the English approach to strict liability offences by allowing an accused to raise a defence of honest and reasonable mistake of fact. The classic Australian authority is *Proudman v. Dayman*,[60] where Dixon J. stated:

> As a general rule an honest and reasonable belief in a state of facts which, if they existed, would make the defendant's act innocent affords an excuse for doing what would otherwise be an offence.[61]

This honest and reasonable mistake of fact defence appears to exclude ignorance of fact, since the defence requires 'a reasonable *belief* in the existence of circumstances'. There have been differences of opinion within academic and judicial circles on whether the *Proudman* defence excludes ignorance of fact, but the more recent and dominant view appears to be that it is excluded.[62] One argument in favour of the inclusive view is that the focus should be on the blameworthiness of the accused rather than the nature of the error. As one judge put it: 'In either case there may or may not be blameworthiness. A man may be unreasonable in arriving at a mistaken conclusion; he may not be unreasonable in not thinking about the matter at all.'[63] Nevertheless, a recent Federal Court of Australia decision has re-affirmed that mere ignorance of fact will not be sufficient to invoke the *Proudman* defence.[64]

---

56 *Ibid.*, at 892.

57 See the collection of essays in Simester, above n. 41.

58 *R. v. Tolson* (1889) 23 QBD 168; *Bank of New South Wales v. Piper*, above n. 25; *Sherras v De Rutzen*, above n. 51.

59 *Sweet v. Parsley* [1970] AC 132; *Gammon (Hong Kong) Ltd v. AG of Hong Kong* [1985] AC 1.

60 (1941) 67 CLR 536.

61 *Ibid.* at 540.

62 *Mei Ying Su v. Australian Fisheries Management Authority (No. 2)* [2008] FCA 1485; *Clough v. Rosevear* (1997) 94 A Crim R 274; *Griffin v. Marsh* (1994) 34 NSWLR 104; *State Rail Authority of NSW v. Hunter Water Board* (1992) 65 A Crim R 101.

63 *Kain and Shelton Pty. Ltd. v. McDonald* (1971) 1 SASR 39 at 45.

64 *Mei Ying Su v Australian Fisheries Management Authority (No. 2)*, above n. 62.

Canadian courts developed a different response to strict liability offences, beginning with the landmark case of *The Queen v. City of Sault Ste. Marie*,[65] which involved a prosecution for environmental pollution.[66] The Supreme Court of Canada relied on the Australian development of the honest and reasonable mistake defence for strict liability crimes, and extended that defence to include due diligence. Rather than restrict the defence to a reasonable belief in particular circumstances, the defence was based on the exercise of due diligence, or an absence of negligence. The catalyst for this decision was the Canadian Law Reform Commission's report on strict liability, which recommended negligence as a fault element for crimes without *mens rea*.[67] Later Canadian developments have also been influenced by the Canadian Charter of Rights and Freedoms, particularly s. 7 of the Charter.[68]

The recognition of due diligence as a defence was a significant development.[69] Although Dickson J. referred to the honest and reasonable mistake defence in *Proudman v. Dayman*, he viewed due diligence as a much broader defence, of which honest and reasonable mistake of fact was simply one aspect.[70] This was significant, as it did not restrict the defence to a positive state of mind. Whether the accused turned his or her mind to a particular issue was not as important as whether the accused was deserving of blame. It therefore avoided the confusion between an absence of belief and *mens rea*. As a consequence of the Canadian Charter of Rights, Canadian courts have been provided a constitutional basis for requiring absence of due diligence as a minimum fault element for any offence which carried a sentence of imprisonment or even a threat of imprisonment (as an alternative to non-payment of a penalty).[71]

The US, in addition to drawing on constitutional arguments,[72] recognised a reasonable care defence. For example, in *US v. US District Court for the Central District of California, Los Angeles (Kantor's case)*,[73] a child pornography case, it was held by the Ninth Circuit that although knowledge of the child's age did not have to be proved by the prosecution, it was open to the accused to prove that they had acted in good faith and had no reason to believe that the child was below the legal age. Although the principal reason for recognising the reasonable care defence in *Kantor* was to protect First Amendment rights, the court also recognised the injustice in punishing the morally innocent.[74] This trend of moving away from no fault liability and embracing a moral

65 Above n. 40.

66 Ontario Water Resources Commission Act R.S.O. 1970 (c 332), s. 32(1).

67 Law Reform Commission of Canada, *Report: Our Criminal Law* (Ottawa: Law Reform Commission of Canada, 1976) 22–3; Law Reform Commission of Canada, *Criminal Law – Meaning of Guilty – Strict Liability* (Working Paper No. 2) (Ottawa: Law Reform Commission of Canada, 1974).

68 Canadian Charter of Rights and Freedoms, s. 7, provides that: 'Everyone has the right to life, liberty and security of the person and the right not to be deprived thereof except in accordance with the principles of fundamental justice.'

69 See A. Tuck-Jackson, 'The Defence of Due Diligence and the Presumption of Innocence' (1990–91) 33 *Criminal Law Quarterly* 11.

70 Above n. 40, at 1315.

71 *Reference re Section 94(2) of the Motor Vehicle Act (BC)* [1985] 2 SCR 486. See also J. Keefe, 'The Due Diligence Defence: A Wholesale Review' (1992–3) 35 *Criminal Law Quarterly* 480; *R v. Wholesale Travel Group Inc* [1991] 3 SCR 154; and *Canada v. Pharmaceutical Society (NS)* (1993) 15 CR (4th) 1.

72 See A.C. Michaels, 'Imposing Constitutional Limits on Strict Liability: Lessons from the American Experience' in Simester, above n. 41.

73 858 F.2d 534 (9th Cir. 1988).

74 *Ibid.*, at 542–3.

blameworthiness approach has been described by various American writers in terms of the courts recognising 'mandatory culpability',[75] 'constitutional innocence'[76] and 'good faith defences'.[77]

What is of interest is that in all of these jurisdictions there was recognition that, while there could be criminal liability without proof of *mens rea*, there should not be criminal liability where the accused was morally innocent. Moral innocence was something that could be established objectively. The underlying question was whether or not the defendant could fairly be blamed for his or her conduct. Unlike the earlier English cases which linked the absence of *mens rea* with reasonable mistake, the modern jurisprudence delinks the two. Even as far back as *Proudman v. Dayman*,[78] Dixon C.J. expressed it thus:

> There may be no longer any presumption that *mens rea*, in the sense of a specific state of mind, whether of motive, intention, knowledge or advertence, is an ingredient in an offence created by a modern statute; but to concede that the weakening of the older understanding of the rule of interpretation has left us with no *prima facie* presumption that some mental element is implied in the definition of any new statutory offence does not mean that the rule that honest and reasonable mistake is *prima facie* admissible as an exculpation has lost its application also.[79]

Does s. 79 provide an adequate solution to strict liability offences in the IPC jurisdictions? It should be recalled that s. 79 was not enacted to deal with strict liability, but rather was intended to negate criminal fault in the form of *mens rea*. As Sornarajah puts it, '[strict liability] offences came onto the scene long after the Penal Code was drafted and are based on theoretical foundations which cannot be accommodated within the Code'.[80] While this argument is theoretically correct, s. 79, as interpreted by the courts, can be applied to strict liability offences. Under s. 79, a defendant believing in good faith – that is, after exercising due care or diligence – that he or she was not doing anything prohibited by law in carrying out the act that constituted the strict liability offence, can fairly be said to be morally innocent.

CRIMINAL CULPABILITY, MORAL INNOCENCE AND MISTAKE OF LAW[81]

This section briefly deals with the question of whether ignorance or mistake of law should be relevant to a defendant's criminal liability.[82] In some cases, it may fairly be said that a person who has committed an offence as a result of a reasonable mistake of law is morally innocent and not deserving of criminal sanction. Ultimately, criminal liability should be a judgment about wrongdoing and moral blameworthiness. However, our current approach to criminal fault –

---

75 J.S. Wiley Jr., 'Not Guilty by Reason of Blamelessness' (1999) 85 *Virginia Law Review* 1021.

76 A.C. Michaels, 'Constitutional Innocence' (1998–9) 112 *Harvard Law Review* 829.

77 L.L. Levenson, 'Good Faith Defenses: Reshaping Strict Liability Crimes' (1992–3) 78 *Cornell Law Review* 401.

78 Above n. 60.

79 *Ibid.*, at 540–41.

80 Sornarajah, above n. 39, at 28.

81 Part of this section is reproduced or adapted from an earlier work: K. Amirthalingam, 'Ignorance of Law, Criminal Culpability and Moral Innocence' [2002] *Singapore Journal of Legal Studies* 302.

82 The author's views on this issue have been expressed at length elsewhere: see K. Amirthalingam, 'Mistake of Law: A Criminal Offence or a Reasonable Defence?' (1994) 18 *Criminal Law Journal* 271; K. Amirthalingam, 'Mens Rea and Mistake of Law in Criminal Cases: A Lesson from South Africa' (1995) 18 *University of New South Wales Law Journal* 428; Amirthalingam, *ibid.*

typically based on the orthodox doctrine of *mens rea* – is problematic when it comes to mistake of law.

The doctrine of *mens rea* was designed to ensure agency responsibility and moral blameworthiness. A person could be held guilty only if he or she acted with a culpable mental state. Unfortunately, the ignorance of law rule has cut the heart out of this doctrine. If a person does not know that the conduct is prohibited, in some cases it cannot fairly be said that the person ought to be held criminally culpable and punished. Explaining this in the context of insanity, Alan Brudner says:

> Thus to be liable to punishment as a criminal, one must both intend the product of one's act and *know that one's act is outlawed* by the standard of intersubjective reason. This, I submit, is what *mens rea* in the full sense means. In the normal case, however, the full content of *mens rea* is not explicitly at issue, for there is a presumption (which is simply a truism) that rational agents know the wrongfulness of unjustified homicide, coercion, takings, and so on. Thus the only part of *mens rea* normally in question is the intentionality of the deed, not of the wrong: we ask, for example, whether the accused intended to kill the victim, taking for granted that he knew killing another person is wrong. When, however, the presumption of rationality is removed, the full meaning of *mens rea* is engaged. The insane accused will be exonerated either if he did not understand what he was doing or if he could not know that what he was doing was wrong.[83]

Thus, with respect to non-insane persons, the critical indicator of criminal culpability, namely knowledge of the lawfulness of the conduct, is presumed. The presumption of knowledge of the law is fictitious and is no longer held.[84] A doctrine of criminal fault that ignores a defendant's ignorance or mistake of law risks punishing the morally blameless. George Fletcher, in his influential work on criminal law, has argued that a person is not morally blameworthy if he or she does not have a fair opportunity to avoid the act of wrongdoing.[85] A person who is reasonably mistaken or ignorant of the law is, according to him, not morally blameworthy, or conversely should be treated as morally innocent. As the Supreme Court of Canada put it, '[*m*]*ens rea* … refers to the guilty mind, the wrongful intention of the accused. Its function in criminal law is to prevent the conviction of the *morally innocent* – those *who do not understand* or intend the consequences of their acts'.[86]

C.S. Kenny, the eminent criminal lawyer at the turn of the twentieth century, once stated: 'In all ordinary crimes the psychological element which is thus indispensable may be fairly accurately summed up as consisting simply in "intending to do what you know to be illegal".'[87] According to Kenny, *mens rea* meant voluntarily doing what you *knew to be illegal*. Yet, in a footnote at the end of the above sentence, Kenny qualified his statement by saying 'what you know to belong to a class

---

83 A. Brudner, *The Unity of the Common Law: Studies in Hegelian Jurisprudence* (Berkeley: University of California Press, 1995) at 238 (emphasis added).

84 See *Nathan Brothers v. Tong Nam Contractors Ltd.* [1959] MLJ 240, at 241, referring to *Evans v. Bartlam* [1937] AC 473. See also J. Austin, *Lectures on Jurisprudence* (R. Campbell, ed.) (5th edn, London: J. Murray, 1885, reprinted 1972) (vol. 1) 481–2, where he stated: 'That any system is so knowable, or that any system has even been so knowable, is so notoriously and ridiculously false that I shall not occupy your time with proof of the contrary.'

85 Fletcher, above n. 21, at 510.

86 *R. v. Théroux* [1993] 2 SCR 5, at 17, *per* McLachlin J. (emphasis added).

87 C.S. Kenny, *Outlines of Criminal Law* (4th edn, Cambridge: Cambridge University Press, 1909) 39.

of conduct that is (whether you know it or not) forbidden by law',[88] This dispenses with the very psychological element that he claimed was indispensable.

The ignorance of law rule is well established in common law jurisdictions as well as in IPC jurisdictions which have all been former colonies of the motherland of the common law. The rule is not as entrenched in the civilian jurisdictions, with several countries recognising a defence of reasonable or unavoidable mistake of law.[89] South Africa has gone a step further and recognised a complete defence of mistake of law.[90]

Blackstone is generally referred to as an authoritative source for the ignorance of law rule, although his attribution of the rule's origin to Roman law has been questioned[91] and his common law authority appears to be a minority judgment in a civil case.[92] The rule has survived and has been staunchly defended over the centuries. Blackstone originally defended it on the presumption of knowledge of the law – a presumption that is no longer held.[93] Austin defended the rule on grounds of pragmatism. As he put it, if ignorance of law were permitted as a defence, the courts 'would be involved in questions which it were scarcely possible to solve, and which would render the administration of justice next to impracticable'.[94] This is not a persuasive defence of an unjust rule and Holmes in fact rejected Austin's rationale for the rule, arguing that '[i] f justice requires the fact to be ascertained, the difficulty of doing so is no ground for refusing to try'.[95] Holmes justified the rule on purely utilitarian grounds, namely that to permit the rule would encourage ignorance, and public policy demanded that the individual be sacrificed for the general good.[96]

Contemporary scholars are less sanguine about the ignorance of law rule. While not rejecting the rule, their support for it is more qualified. Fletcher, relying heavily on German criminal law, where unavoidable mistake of law is recognised as a defence,[97] supports a reasonable ignorance or mistake of law defence. He argues that a person who has not had a fair opportunity to avoid the act of wrongdoing should not be considered morally blameworthy.[98] In some instances, a person who, despite all reasonable efforts, was ignorant or mistaken as to the law cannot be said to have had a fair opportunity to avoid breaking the law and is therefore deserving of an excuse. Andrew Ashworth has defended the rule on the basis of an individual's duty to know the law as a responsible citizen. Mere ignorance of law would be a breach of this duty and the accused should not be permitted to plead such ignorance as a defence. However, an accused who had taken

88 *Ibid.*, at 39, n. 5.

89 For example, Germany (Penal Code of 1871, s. 17); France (Criminal Code of 1992, Art. 122–3); Austria (Criminal Code, s. 9).

90 *S v. De Blom* 1977 (3) SA 513 (A).

91 V. Bolgar, 'The Present Function of the Maxim *Ignorantia Iuris Neminem Excusat* – A Comparative Study' (1966–7) 52 *Iowa Law Review* 626, 630–31; L. Hall and S.J. Seligman, 'Mistake of Law and Mens Rea' (1940–41) 8 *University of Chicago Law Review* 641, 646 contend: 'Blackstone was in error in ascribing the origin of the [*ignorantia*] rule to the Roman law.'

92 *Brett v Rigden* (1568) 1 Plowden 340, 75 ER 516.

93 W. Blackstone, *Commentaries on the Laws of England* (vol. 4) (Oxford: Clarendon Press, 1765–9) 27.

94 Austin, above n. 84, at 483.

95 O.W. Holmes, *The Common Law* (Boston: Little, Brown and Co., 1881, 42nd reprint, 1948) 48.

96 *Ibid.*

97 Fletcher, above n. 21.

98 *Ibid.*, at 510.

reasonable measures to comply with the law and was nevertheless reasonably ignorant or mistaken should be allowed a defence.[99]

Courts are cognisant of the inherent unfairness of the rule and have recognised several exceptions to it. Some of the broad categories of exceptions include the following:

- the mistake gives rise to a claim of right;
- the mistake is relevant to a definitional element of the offence;
- the mistake creates an estoppel argument; and
- it is impossible to know the law creating the offence.[100]

The fourth category listed above is one which has been recognised in both Malaysia and Singapore. *Lim Chin Aik v. R.*,[101] an important decision in this context, concerned the prosecution of an individual for contravening a ban on his entering and remaining in Singapore. The Privy Council held that the defendant was not guilty because he could not possibly have known of the ban, which was directed at an individual and was not required to be gazetted. In effect, the court recognised an exception to the ignorance of law rule. However, it was an extremely narrow exception as it applied only when it was impossible for the defendant to have known of the law; it did not apply in cases where the appellant was ignorant *simpliciter*, or even reasonably ignorant. Courts in Malaysia and Singapore have expressly held the line on this by refusing to extend the *Lim Chin Aik* exception to include reasonable ignorance.[102]

However, one case that deserves special mention is *Koo Cheh Yew v. PP*.[103] This case concerned the prosecution of two defendants for contravening s. 135(1)(a) of the Malaysian Customs Act 1967. The provision reads as follows:

> 135(1) Whosoever –
> is concerned is concerned in importing or exporting any uncustomed goods or any prohibited goods contrary to such prohibition whether such uncustomed goods or any prohibited be shipped, unshipped, delivered or not ...
> 135(2) In any prosecution under this section of s. 139 any dutiable, uncustomed or prohibited goods shall be deemed to be dutiable, uncustomed or prohibited goods, as the case may be, to the knowledge of the defendant, unless the contrary be proved by such defendant.

The two defendants had imported pianos from South Africa, something which was prohibited under the Act. The defendants argued that they were ignorant of the particular prohibition. They were convicted at trial and had the conviction reversed on appeal to the High Court. The High Court judge, Arulanandam J., referring to English and Australian decisions,[104] held that the provision should be read to include a *mens rea* element. Further, Arulanandam J. held that when

99 A. Ashworth, *Principles of Criminal Law* (6th edn, Oxford: Clarendon Press, 2009) 220–1.

100 For a detailed discussion, see Amirthalingam, above n. 81, at 311–27.

101 [1963] AC 160.

102 *PP v. Koo Cheh Yew* [1980] 2 MLJ 235; *PP v. Yuen Wai Loon* [2009] SGDC 117. See also the Indian Supreme Court decision of *State of Maharashtra v. Hans George* AIR 1965 SC 722, which referred to *Lim Chin Aik*.

103 [1978] 1 MLJ 141.

104 *Frailey v. Charlton* [1920] 1 KB 147; *Sweet v. Parsley*, above n. 59; *Proudman v. Dayman*, above n. 60; *R. v. Turnbull* (1944) SR (NSW) 108.

rigid adherence to the ignorance of law rule would result in the conviction of a morally innocent person, the court should take that into account in determining its verdict.

The prosecution appealed against the decision, identifying three questions of public interest.[105] Arulanandam J. added a fourth question, which was a bold challenge to the ignorance of law rule and cut to the heart of the matter:

> In a proceeding against the accused under s. 135(1)(a) of the Customs Act, 1967, of being concerned in importing prohibited goods contrary to a prohibition, *if all the circumstances of the case point to an innocent mind of the accused*, is the court entitled to take cognisance of this fact before giving verdict?[106]

The Federal Court of Malaysia heard the appeal and held by majority that the ignorance of law rule should not be required to yield to any potential risk of convicting a morally innocent person. A bright line was drawn on the authority of *Lim Chin Aik* – the only exception was where it was impossible for an individual to know the existence of the law. In his dissenting judgment, Suffian L.P. took the view that as s. 135(2) presumed knowledge of prohibition unless the contrary could be proved by the defendant, it remained open to the defendants to deny such knowledge, including on the basis of ignorance of the law concerning the prohibition.

From the point of view of codification, the approach of the courts cannot be faulted, as s. 79 clearly excludes mistake of law from the defence. Yet, courts in the IPC jurisdictions have not been as disciplined with respect to strict liability; they have imported the common law presumption of *mens rea* instead of applying the IPC provisions strictly. The majority in the Federal Court in *Koo Cheh Yew*, while rejecting Arulanandam J.'s approach in the High Court to mistake of law, endorsed his approach to strict liability in preference to that of the trial judge, H.S. Ong J. Ong J. had adopted a literal approach, holding that if the statute did not specify a *mens rea* requirement, then no such requirement should be read in. The principal reason for importing a *mens rea* requirement when the statute is silent is the concern that morally innocent individuals risk being convicted. As Arulanandam J. put it, strict liability 'could lead to the conviction and punishment of persons who are in the particular circumstances of a case totally blameless'.[107] It is suggested that the same sentiments apply equally to mistake of law.

CONCLUSION

It has been argued in this chapter that s. 79 was not enacted as a general mistake defence although it has evolved into one. There are theoretical problems with the application of s. 79 to *mens rea* offences and strict liability offences. Applying s. 79 to *mens rea* offences is conceptually unsound as

---

105 The three questions identified by the public prosecutor were:

(a) In a prosecution against the accused under s. 135(1)(a) of the Customs Act, 1967, of being concerned in importing prohibited goods contrary to a prohibition, does a denial by the accused of knowledge of the relevant prohibition order entitle him to an acquittal?

(b) Is not the denial of knowledge under s. 135(2) of the Customs Act, 1967, limited only to denial of knowledge as to the facts and not as to the law concerning prohibited goods?

(c) Is it not sufficient for the prosecution to prove that the goods imported were of the description mentioned in the prohibition order in order to show that such importation was contrary to the prohibition?

106 *PP v. Koo Cheh Yew*, above n. 102, at 237 (emphasis added).

107 Above n. 103, at 144.

it wrongly reverses the burden of proof and applies objective standards to negate subjective mental states. During the period in which the IPC was drafted, the strict liability regime of regulatory offences was still in its infancy, and it was unlikely that Macaulay or the Indian Law Commission had considered the impact of much wider reliance on strict liability. Clearly, there is need for reform in this area to clarify how mistakes should be dealt with under the IPC.

Any reform of the IPC should identify clearly, whether by way of provision or illustration, when a purely subjective mistake is relevant, when only reasonable mistake will suffice, when mistake of law may be relevant and how strict liability offences should be resolved. Where the mistake goes towards negating an offence element, the normative quality of the mistake is not at issue. It is simply a factual question. Did the accused act under a mistaken belief such that, had the facts been as the accused had believed them to be, he or she would not have satisfied one of the offence elements? The burden is on the prosecution to prove the offence elements, taking into account the accused's mistake, failing which the accused would not be guilty.

Where the mistake is with respect to an excusatory or justificatory factor, or operates in the context of strict liability, the mistake has a normative quality. An objective test is justified in such cases because the accused is essentially making the argument that he or she believed that in so acting, he or she was either justified or excused. Although the particular circumstances of the accused should be taken into account, the standards of the 'reasonable person' or 'ordinary person' can fairly be called upon. Whether the mistake is one of fact or law should not be the focus of the inquiry. Instead, the focus should be on whether, as a result of the mistake, the accused honestly and reasonably believed that he or she was not acting wrongfully; in other words, does the mistake show that the accused was morally innocent?[108]

To account for the above propositions, a reformulated defence of mistake under the IPC could read as follows, replacing the current ss. 76 and 79:

Act done under a mistaken belief

Nothing is an offence which is done by a person who, honestly and reasonably, mistakenly believes that what he is doing is not prohibited by law.

Provided that:

1. This exception shall not apply where the belief is based simply on ignorance of the particular law on which the charge is based, unless the circumstances were such that it was impossible for the defendant to know the law;
2. This exception shall apply in all other cases where the belief is based on ignorance of law, as long as the circumstances of the case point to the moral innocence of the accused.

Explanation 1 – This section only applies once the prosecution has proved all the necessary elements constituting the offence with which the person is charged.

Explanation 2 – A judge should take the particular circumstances of the case into account in determining whether an accused's mistaken belief is reasonable.

Illustrations

(a) A, while working in the fields late at night, intentionally shoots and kills B, mistakenly believing that B is a wild animal. This section does not apply. A is not guilty of murder because there is no evidence that A possesses any of the relevant mental states for murder.[109]

---

108 See, for example, *PP v. Koo Cheh Yew*, above n. 102, at 237, *per* Arulanandam J.: '... if all the circumstances of the case point to an innocent mind of the accused, is the court entitled to take cognisance of this fact before giving verdict?'

109 This illustration is modified from the facts of *Chirangi v. State of Nagpur*, above n. 6.

(b) A, a soldier on patrol duty, exercises his right of private defence and intentionally kills B, a young child whom A, honestly and reasonably, mistakenly believes is an enemy soldier about to shoot at A. A is not guilty of murder.[110]

(c) A is charged with an offence of importing poppy seeds contrary to a law prohibiting the importation of prohibited goods. A, honestly and reasonably, mistakenly believed that the said poppy seeds had been cleared for importation by the authorities. A is not guilty of the charged offence.

(d) A is charged with an offence of importing poppy seeds contrary to a law prohibiting the importation of prohibited goods. A, honestly and reasonably, mistakenly believed that it was not an offence to import poppy seeds. A is guilty of the offence.

(e) A is charged with a public order offence for permitting table top dancing at a public venue. A, relying on erroneous official advice and a court decision that was subsequently overturned, honestly and reasonably, mistakenly believes that table top dancing was not a prohibited act under the law. A is not guilty of the offence.[111]

The proposed reformulation preserves the distinction between offence and defence elements, and ensures that the prosecution bears the burden of proving all the offence elements. Mistake is left to operate purely as a defence where the burden of proof may justifiably be placed on the defendant. Further, the proposed reformulation clarifies that the defendant must show that his or her mistake was reasonable in the circumstances for the mistake to have exculpatory effect. What is reasonable in the circumstances will be a matter for courts to decide, taking into account all the facts of the case. Finally, the proposed defence allows a defendant to rely on ignorance or mistake of law under limited conditions. It does not allow simple ignorance of law as a defence, as this would be contrary to the duties of citizenship and responsible behaviour, which require people to make an effort to know the law. However, in some cases where the defendant's ignorance or mistake of law demonstrates the moral innocence of the defendant, it would be fair to allow the defendant to rely on such ignorance or mistake as a defence. The five illustrations, drawn from actual cases, help explain how the defence would operate in the various scenarios described.

---

110 This illustration is modified from the facts of *GFL Ewin v. PP* [1949] MLJ 279.

111 This illustration is modified from the facts of *R. v. Campbell* [1973] 2 WWR 246.

Chapter 6
Abetment, Criminal Conspiracy and Attempt

Wing-Cheong Chan

INTRODUCTION

All criminal justice systems recognise that there are certain circumstances when it is permissible to criminalise preliminary[1] acts which are steps towards an ultimate goal that is criminal. The rationale is that these steps will eventually lead to the desired offence, and law enforcement agencies must be able to intervene early enough to apprehend the offender(s) before the offence is committed. Reliance on preliminary offences is needed because it may not always be possible for the law to render these early steps as criminal offences in themselves. Macaulay was keenly aware of this issue, as can be seen in his comments to cls. 308 and 309 of his draft Code, which criminalises attempted murder and attempted voluntary culpable homicide respectively:

> [Clauses 308 and 309] appear to us absolutely necessary to the completeness of the Code. We have provided, under the head of bodily hurt, for cases in which hurt is inflicted in an attempt to murder;[2] under the head of assault, for assaults committed in attempting to murder;[3] under the head of criminal trespass, for some criminal trespasses committed in order to murder.[4] But there will still remain many atrocious and deliberate attempts to murder which are not trespasses, which are not assaults, and which cause no hurt. A, for example, digs a pit in his garden, and conceals the mouth of it, intending that Z may fall in, and perish there. Here, A has committed no trespass, for the ground is his own; and no assault, for he has applied no force to Z. He may not have caused bodily hurt, for Z may have received a timely caution or may not have gone near the pit. But A's crime is evidently one which ought to be punished as severely as if he had laid hands on Z with the intention of cutting his throat.[5]

There are obvious limits to this approach to criminalisation since making liability very broad could come too close to punishing a person for his or her evil thoughts alone. One such limit is that there must be some demonstrable risk of causing harm manifested by the would-be offender. Thus, with respect to attempts to commit an offence, a formula found in the criminal law of many jurisdictions is that the accused must have committed an act that was 'more than merely

---

1 The term 'preliminary' is used here instead of 'inchoate' because it is a misnomer to describe the offences of abetment, criminal conspiracy and attempt as inchoate since they are complete in themselves. An attempt to commit murder, for example, is complete in itself. It is only the 'murder' that is inchoate.

2 Clause 320.

3 Clause 343.

4 Clause 428.

5 T.B. Macaulay, J.M. Macleod, G.W. Anderson and F. Millett, *A Penal Code Prepared by the Indian Law Commissioners* (London: Pelham Richardson, 1838) (reprinted by the Lawbook Exchange, Ltd, 2002) Note M (On Offences Against the Body).

preparatory to the commission of the offence'[6] or have taken 'a substantial step in a course of conduct planned to culminate [in the offence]'.[7] With respect to conspiracies, which are the most far-reaching of the preliminary offences, there must have been a 'meeting of minds' or an agreement between two or more persons which heighten the risk of causing harm.

An indication of Macaulay's desire to avoid what may be seen as a thought crime is his approach to the classic political offences: he gave a narrow definition of treason and eliminated seditious libel in his draft Code. Treason was limited to waging war against the government only,[8] despite the prevailing English law at the time, which included anyone who 'compasses' or 'imagines' the sovereign's death within the scope of treason.[9]

This chapter will review the law regarding the criminalisation of the preliminary offences of abetment, criminal conspiracy and attempt under the Indian Penal Code (IPC).[10] It will be argued that while the IPC's provisions on these offences have largely worked well, several amendments are needed to remove inconsistencies in the Code and to fulfil Macaulay's emphasis on subjective culpability with respect to the fault element of offences.[11] However, as will be noted from the ensuing discussion, culpability in Macaulay's draft Code was not premised on subjective notions alone.[12]

The offences of abetment, criminal conspiracy and attempt will be considered separately. A historical background is provided for each by reference to Macaulay's draft Code, followed by an analysis of the departures made by the IPC from that Code. The issue of whether a person can be held liable for any of these offences if, unknown to him or her, the acts cannot possibly lead to the substantive offence being committed is then examined. The chapter concludes by drawing all these ideas together in a proposal to reformulate the present IPC so as to bring it more into line with what was intended by Macaulay and, it will be argued, to express the scope of liability for preliminary crimes in clear and acceptable terms.

---

6 For example, Criminal Attempts Act 1981 (Chapter 47) (UK), s. 1(1); Criminal Code (Cth), s. 11.1; Criminal Code (WA), s. 4; Criminal Code (Canada), s. 24.

7 US Model Penal Code, s. 5.01(1).

8 Macaulay's draft Code, cl. 109. See Chapter 2 of this volume (B. Wright, 'Macaulay's Indian Penal Code: Historical Context and Originating Principles') at 46–7 for discussion of these political offences.

9 Treason Act (1351) 25 Edw. 3, st. 5, c. 2 and its successive Acts. Constructive forms of treason were added to the Malaysian and Singaporean Penal Codes by way of ss. 121A and 121B by the colonial legislature in 1872 via the Penal Code Amendment Ordinance 3 of 1872. It is likely that accused persons charged with these offences in Malaysia and Singapore would not be punished for their thoughts alone, since some 'overt act' to accompany the treasonable intention had long been required in English law; see *R. v. Thistlewood* (1820) 33 St Tr 681.

10 For further information, see S. Yeo, N. Morgan and W. Chan, *Criminal Law in Malaysia and Singapore* (Singapore: LexisNexis, 2007) Chapters 34 and 36.

11 See Chapter 3 of this volume (N. Morgan, 'The Fault Elements of Offences').

12 A subjectivist approach would attribute blame to the would-be offender based on his or her intention to commit the substantive offence. It would not matter if the offence were prevented because of luck or chance, which are matters beyond the person's control. Similarly, it would not matter if the offence was in fact impossible to achieve. On the other hand, objectivists would require a showing that the acts could have caused demonstrable harm before they can be criminalised. See also R.A. Duff, *Criminal Attempts* (Oxford: Clarendon Press, 1996), in his description of 'objectivist' and 'subjectivist' conceptions of criminal liability.

ABETMENT

The Law under the Draft Code

An unnecessarily complicated scheme existed at common law at the time of Macaulay's draft Code in distinguishing between principals in the first degree (the actual perpetrator of the crime), principals in the second degree (persons who rendered aid and were present at the offence) and accessories before the fact. The distinctions depended on whether the accused had incited a felony or a misdemeanour and if the suggested offence was committed or not.[13] The view at the time of the draft Code was that principals in the second degree were so different from accessories before the fact that the indictments were not interchangeable.[14] Furthermore, for some inexplicable reason, one could also not be liable for being an accessory before the fact to manslaughter.[15] The common law scheme was replaced by Macaulay in his draft Code with the simple concept of abetment, which was stated to be of two kinds, namely previous abetment and subsequent abetment.[16] Previous abetment, the subject of this chapter, is the equivalent of accessories before the fact at common law, whereas subsequent abetment is the equivalent of accessories after the fact at common law.

The draft Code provided for four types of previous abetment:

> A person is said previously to abet the doing of a thing who,
> *First*, Instigates any person to do that thing; or
> *Secondly*, Engages in any conspiracy for the doing of that thing; or,
> *Thirdly*, Aids by any act or by any illegal omission the doing of that thing; or
> *Fourthly*, Conceals by any act or by any illegal omission the existence of a design to do that thing, intending or knowing it to be likely that he may, by such concealment, facilitate the doing of that thing.
> *Explanation*. A person may previously abet the doing of a thing in any one of the four ways hereinbefore mentioned, though the thing abetted be not done.[17]

The scope of liability for abettors under the draft Code was, in general, not meant to depart from the prevailing English law. A similarly broad reach was given in the draft Code to cover all persons who had in some way lent countenance to the commission of an offence, as the common law did.[18] It was pointed out by the Indian Law Commissioners in their first report on the draft Code that '[t]he effect [of the abetment provisions] is the same as by the English Law, but without the forced construction by which the English Law is strained for the purpose'.[19]

---

13 J.F. Stephen, *A History of the Criminal Law of England* (vol. 2) (London: Macmillan and Co., 1883) 230 onwards; Law Commission of India, *Indian Penal Code* (42nd Report) (New Delhi: Government of India, 1971) para. [5.1].

14 *R. v. Gordon* (1789) 1 Leach 515, 168 ER 359.

15 *Bibithe's Case* (1597) 4 Co Rep 43b, 76 ER 991; *Goose's Case* (1597) Moore (KB) 461, 72 ER 695. Cf. *R. v. Gaylor* (1857) D & B 288, 169 ER 1011; and *R. v. Smith* (1847) 2 Cox CC 233.

16 Clause 85. It should be pointed out that an abetment is an offence only if the act abetted is itself an offence punishable under the IPC or other criminal laws: see n. 58 below. The abetment of a civil wrong is not an offence.

17 Clause 86.

18 J.W.C. Turner, *Russell on Crime* (11th edn, London: Stevens and Sons, 1958) 160.

19 Indian Law Commissioners, *Report on the Indian Penal Code* (1846) (reprinted in Parliamentary Papers 1847–8, vol. XXVIII) para. [182]. For the current developments in English law, see Chapter 14 of this

The Law under the IPC

The present formulation for abetment is expressed in s. 107 of the IPC as follows:

> A person abets the doing of a thing, who –
> *First.* Instigates any person to do that thing; or
> *Secondly.* Engages with one or more other person or persons in any conspiracy for the doing of that thing, if an act or illegal omission takes place in pursuance of that conspiracy, and in order to the doing of that thing; or
> *Thirdly.* Intentionally aids, by any act or illegal omission, the doing of that thing.
> *Explanation 1.* A person who, by wilful misrepresentation, or by wilful concealment of a material fact which he is bound to disclose, voluntarily causes or procures, or attempts to cause or procure, a thing to be done, is said to instigate the doing of that thing.
> *Illustration*
> A, a public officer is authorised by a warrant from a Court of Justice to apprehend Z. B, knowing that fact and also that C is not Z, thereby intentionally causes A to apprehend C. Here B abets by instigation the apprehension of C.
> *Explanation 2.* Whoever, either prior to or at the time of the commission of an act, does anything in order to facilitate the commission of that act, and thereby, facilitates the commission thereof, is said to aid the doing of that act.

One can immediately see that while the first clause of the draft Code has stayed the same in the IPC, the second and third clauses have changed somewhat, while the fourth clause of the draft Code has not been enacted.

Changes Made to the Draft Code by the IPC

The Physical Element for Abetment

It would appear that no change had been made by not enacting the fourth clause in the draft Code since this merely amplifies that 'aiding' may be by way of concealment as well if it facilitates the commission of the offence. The same idea is now found in explanation 2 to s. 107 of the IPC.

The second clause in the draft Code, that of abetment by conspiracy, now has the added requirement that 'an act or illegal omission takes place in pursuance of that conspiracy' in the IPC. In the scheme envisaged by Macaulay, a person who abets an offence by engaging in a conspiracy to commit that offence is, if the offence is committed in pursuance of that conspiracy, punished with the punishment provided for that offence.[20] However, if the offence is not committed, the person is punished (up to one-quarter of the longest term provided for that offence or fined) only if any act or illegal omission takes place in pursuance of that conspiracy.[21] Presumably, Macaulay did not think a person should be punished for engaging in a conspiracy *per se* if it did not result

---

volume (C. Clarkson, 'Recent Law Reform and Codification of the General Principles of Criminal Law in England and Wales: A Tale of Woe') at 353–9.

20 Clause 95. Hence, a person may be considered an abettor even if the offence is completed. This causes an overlap with the concept of vicarious liability whereby parties to a completed offence may be held jointly liable: see n. 57 below.

21 Clause 96.

in an offence being committed and no act or illegal omission had taken place in pursuance of the conspiracy. Therefore, culpability of the accused is not premised on a purely subjective mental state since some harm must result or the agreement to commit an offence must at least be manifested through an act or illegal omission.

The IPC provision on abetment by conspiracy now requires an act or illegal omission to take place in pursuance of that conspiracy in *all* cases.[22] This is clearer. If the offence is committed in pursuance of the conspiracy, the fact of the commission of the offence would be more than sufficient to satisfy the requirement of an act or illegal omission in pursuance of the conspiracy. If the offence is not committed, the present IPC requires proof of an act or illegal omission in pursuance of the conspiracy to be shown, just like the draft Code.

The Fault Element for Abetment

It can be seen that abetment by aiding expressly stipulates that the fault element has to be of acting 'intentionally'.[23] This may indeed be what Macaulay had in mind, since it was stated in cl. 97 of his draft Code that:

> Whoever previously abets any offence by doing any act, or omitting what he is legally bound to do, with the *intention* of aiding the commission of that offence, shall, if that offence is committed, be punished with the punishment provided for that offence.[24]

On the other hand, the fourth type of abetment in the draft Code suggests that the aiding may be done intentionally *or with knowledge* that the act or illegal omission will aid the commission of the offence. There is also an illustration to cl. 87 of the draft Code which shows that the mental state of 'belief' is concerned more with knowledge than with intention:

> A aids B to take a horse out of Z's possession. Here if B took the horse fraudulently B is guilty of theft. But if A aided B, believing that B had a right to take the horse, A is not said to have abetted the theft committed by B, though he has abetted the taking of the horse.

Subsequent provisions in the draft Code also make it clear that an abettor may be punished on the basis of what he or she *knew* to be likely to be committed, even if a different offence is eventually committed.[25]

Since the IPC only expressly provides for the fault element for abetment by aiding, this might suggest that the other forms of abetment (instigation and conspiracy) may be committed with other types of fault, such as acting rashly or negligently.[26] In the interest of clarity, it is submitted

---

22 If the offence is committed as a consequence of the abetment, the abettor is punished with the same punishment provided for the offence (IPC, s. 109). If the offence is not committed as a consequence of the abetment, the punishment depends on whether the offence abetted is one which is punishable with death or imprisonment for life, whether hurt was caused and whether the person abetted was a public servant whose duty is to prevent the commission of the offence (IPC, ss. 115 and 116).

23 See Chapter 3 of this volume, above n. 11, at 74–6, for a discussion on the meaning of 'intention'.

24 Macaulay's draft Code, cl. 97 (emphasis added). The illustrations thereunder are omitted.

25 *Ibid.*, cls. 98 and 99. It is noted in passing that this position may be contrasted with the English case of *R. v. Saunders and Archer* (1575) 2 Plowden 473, 75 ER 706.

26 In a Singaporean case, *PP v. Hendricks Glen Conleth* [2003] 1 SLR(R) 426, it has even been suggested that in cases of abetment by aiding, liability can be imposed on the basis of negligence despite the

that a provision should be added to the IPC stipulating that the fault element for abetment can be either intention or knowledge of the offence abetted. In favour of recognising knowledge, a person who gives his or her support to another, but does not know that the act supported is a criminal act, cannot realistically be said to have abetted that offence. This also accords with the other instances in the IPC where the fault element of the abettor is satisfied by proof of an intention or knowledge that the offence will be committed.[27]

However, mere knowledge of some offence being committed is not enough. While knowledge of the abetted offence is required, it should not be necessary for the abettor to know all the details pertaining to that offence or the exact manner in which that offence was going to be committed.[28] In the Singaporean case of *Nomura Taiji v. PP*, the following was said to be the fault element required for abetment by conspiracy:

> [A]lthough there must be knowledge of a common design, it is not necessary that all the co-conspirators should be equally informed as to the details. However, they must at least be aware of the general purpose of the plot and that plot must be unlawful.[29]

What if the principal offence abetted is one which does not require proof of fault, such as a 'public welfare offence'? Is a fault element nevertheless required for the abetment? Contradictory signals have been given by the Indian cases. In *State of Maharashtra v. Abdul Aziz*,[30] the Bombay High Court held that since the main offence and its abetment were provided for in the same section of the Imports and Exports (Control) Act 1947,[31] both offences should be treated the same way, that is, no fault element is required for the abetment. Subsequently, in *Kartar Singh v. State of Punjab*,[32] although the Supreme Court of India agreed with the Bombay High Court's ruling, it held that acts of abetment under s. 2 of the Terrorist and Disruptive Activities (Prevention) Act 1987[33] nevertheless required knowledge or reason to believe that the persons were engaged in terrorist and disruptive activities.

In the interests of limiting the scope of liability of preliminary offences to those who are the most culpable (bearing in mind that no real harm has been caused in such cases), it is proposed that the fault element for abetment should, at a minimum, require proof of knowledge of the offence to be committed even where the main offence itself does not require this.[34]

---

explicit requirement of 'intentional' aiding. The IPC was adopted practically in its entirety by Singapore's colonial administrators. Both codes are still very similar in many respects despite amendments made to them over the years.

27 See, for example, IPC, s. 113.

28 The Law Commission of India made the same recommendation, above n. 13, at para. [5.3]. This is consistent with the common law approach in *R. v. Bainbridge* [1960] 1 QB 129 and is reflected in some criminal law codifications such as Criminal Code (Cth), s. 11.2(3)(a): 'the offender's conduct would aid, abet, counsel or procure the commission of any offence ... *of the type* [that was] committed' (emphasis added).

29 [1998] 1 SLR(R) 259, at para. [110].

30 AIR 1962 Bom 243.

31 Act XVIII of 1947.

32 (1994) 3 SCC 569.

33 Act No. 28 of 1987.

34 England has adopted this approach for the new offences of encouraging or assisting crime in the Serious Crime Act 2007 (Chapter 27), ss. 44–46. Cf. Chapter 4 of this volume, above n. 19, at 353–9, which criticises this approach in the context of English law.

CRIMINAL CONSPIRACY

The Law under the Draft Code

The offence of criminal conspiracy was originally developed by the Court of Star Chamber and was extended in the eighteenth century.[35] Its definition at common law as comprising an 'agreement of two or more to do an unlawful act, or to do a lawful act by unlawful means'[36] has been said to be so wide[37] that it would cover agreements to do any act which the court disliked even on moral grounds.[38] The definition has been criticised as being 'clumsy' if what was intended to be conveyed is that an agreement to do anything unlawful is covered, regardless of whether the thing agreed upon is in itself the ultimate object or only a means to an end which may or may not be unlawful.[39] The offence of criminal conspiracy has also been criticised for being unduly wide, since no physical act for the purposes of effecting the aim of the criminal conspiracy is needed. All that is required is the mutual consent to a common purpose. On the other hand, the approach taken by Macaulay's draft Code considered conspiracy only as a form of abetment.[40] To be liable for abetment by conspiracy under the draft Code, the offence either had to be committed or, if it is not committed, an act or illegal omission must take place in pursuance of that conspiracy. Forms of 'agreement' are punished only in certain specific contexts in the draft Code, such as belonging to a gang of 'thugs'[41] (cl. 310) and assembling for the purposes of committing 'dacoity'[42] (cl. 381).

---

35 The earliest meaning given to conspiracy was limited to a combination to carry on legal proceedings in a vexatious or improper way: Stephen, above n. 13, at 228; Sayre, 'Criminal Conspiracy' (1921–2) 35 *Harvard Law Review* 393, 396.

36 *Mulcahy v. R.* (1868) LR 3 HL 306, 317, *per* Wilkes J. Older references to this expression can be found, for example, in *R. v. Seward* (1834) 1 A & E 706, 713, 110 ER 1377, 1380, *per* Lord Denman C.J.

37 Or 'capable of almost indefinite extension': Stephen, above n. 13, at 229.

38 Turner, above n. 18, at 214.

39 Turner, *ibid.*, at 215, note 54, opined: 'the unlawful means must be expressed in acts; it would be better to [say] "to do an unlawful act, whether as the ultimate end, or as a means to an end which may itself be lawful"'.

40 Curiously, and inexplicably, Macaulay's draft Code refers to 'criminal conspiracy' in an illustration to the meaning of 'to fabricate false evidence' (cl. 189) when such an offence was not provided for: 'A, with the intention of causing Z to be convicted of a criminal conspiracy, writes a letter in imitation of Z's handwriting, purporting to be addressed to an accomplice in such criminal conspiracy, and puts the letter in a place which he knows that the officers of the Police are likely to search. A has fabricated false evidence'.

This illustration is found in the IPC, s 192. The reference to 'criminal conspiracy' would only have made sense after 1913 upon the amendment of the IPC enacting this offence.

Clause 365 of Macaulay's draft Code also imposes a higher punishment for theft committed within a building used as a human dwelling or for the custody of property, etc., in pursuance of a conspiracy between persons residing or employed within the building, etc., and those who do not. This clause was not enacted in the IPC.

41 A 'thug' is defined as a person who gains a livelihood by inveigling and murdering travellers in order to take their property (Macaulay's draft Code, cl. 310, which largely followed the earlier Indian Act No. XXX of 1836).

42 'Dacoity' is defined as six or more persons conjointly committing or attempting to commit robbery (Macaulay's draft Code, cl. 376). The IPC has lowered the required number for dacoity to five (s. 391) as well as having far more provisions relating to dacoity, including making preparation to commit dacoity and belonging to a gang of dacoits or thieves (ss. 399–401).

The Law under the IPC

The IPC departed from Macaulay's stance in criminalising conspiracies as a form of abetment only. The first departure, albeit a limited one, came about by an amendment made to the IPC in 1870[43] which criminalised conspiracies to wage war against the Queen or the Government of India.[44] It was also specifically provided in the explanation therein that '[t]o constitute a conspiracy under this section, it is not necessary that any act or illegal omission shall take place in pursuance thereof'.

The second departure, in 1913,[45] was a major one which introduced the concept of 'criminal conspiracy' by enacting s. 120A of the IPC. The purpose of this provision was said to be to 'assimilate the provisions of the IPC to those of the English law'.[46] Section 120A provides:

> When two or more persons agree to do, or cause to be done –
> (1) an illegal act, or
> (2) an act which is not illegal by illegal means,
> such agreement is designated a criminal conspiracy:
> Provided that no agreement except an agreement to commit an offence shall amount to a criminal conspiracy unless some act besides the agreement is done by one or more parties to such agreement in pursuance thereof.
> *Explanation.* It is immaterial whether the illegal act is the ultimate object of such agreement, or is merely incidental to that object.

Changes Made to the Draft Code by the IPC

The Physical Element for Criminal Conspiracy

The IPC formulation closely follows the common law definition of criminal conspiracy outlined above[47] and which has been adopted by some criminal codes.[48] Section 120A of the IPC covers: (i) an agreement to commit an offence; (ii) an agreement to commit an illegal but not criminal act; and (iii) an agreement to commit a legal act by illegal means. An overt act is required where the object of the criminal conspiracy is the commission of acts not amounting to an offence. The Indian Law Commission in its review of the IPC in 1971 was critical of this formulation:

> This distinction between (ii) [an agreement to commit an illegal but not criminal act] and (iii) [an agreement to commit a legal act by illegal means] is obscure and may be without any real

---

43 Indian Penal Code (Amendment) Act 1870 (Act XXVII of 1870). See Stephen, above n. 13, at vol. 3, 308.

44 IPC, s. 121A.

45 Criminal Law (Amendment) Act 1913 (Act VIII of 1913).

46 See Statement of Objects and Reasons of the Amendment Act, *ibid.* A new s. 120B, a punishment provision, was also added at the same time to the IPC.

47 The word 'illegal' in the IPC is defined in s. 43 (as that which is an offence, is prohibited by law or furnishes ground for a civil action) and would cover the situations envisaged as 'unlawful' under the common law.

48 For example, Criminal Code (Qld), s. 543.

difference: achievement of any object by illegal means must involve the doing of something illegal, i.e. the committing of an illegal act.[49]

Under s. 120A, an agreement to commit a tort or a breach of contract, if accompanied with an act done in pursuance of the agreement, is punishable as well. It is difficult to see why non-criminal conduct by an individual should suddenly become more dangerous and worthy of criminalisation if someone agrees with him or her. The Indian Law Commission in 1971 opined that it was 'strongly of the view that there is neither theoretical jurisdiction nor practical need for punishing agreements to commit petty offences or non-criminal illegal acts'.[50] In line with this, the Commission recommended that the offence of criminal conspiracy should be limited to agreements to commit offences which are punishable with at least imprisonment for a term of two years or upwards.[51]

It is also noteworthy that, as a preliminary offence, conspiracies already widen the net to tackle incipient criminal behaviour and should not be further stretched to include 'a dubious area of non-criminality'.[52] The reach of the offence of criminal conspiracy is already wider than the offence of attempt since there is no proximity requirement.[53] This means that two persons can be guilty of the crime of criminal conspiracy even if they would not have been guilty of an attempt had they been acting on their own.

Furthermore, the common law's preference for a wide scope for liability for criminal conspiracies may be explicable on the basis that there is a need to cover the various forms of fraudulent behaviour through the offence of conspiracy to defraud.[54] This argument, however, is not convincing with respect to the IPC, as this aspect is already covered by the wide-ranging offence of cheating[55] in the Code.

Perhaps the most significant criticism against having the offence of criminal conspiracy in the IPC is that it results in all acts of abetment by conspiracy under s. 107 also coming within criminal conspiracy. Consequently, the Law Commission of India recommended in 1971 that, with the enactment of s. 120A, abetment by conspiracy in s. 107 should be deleted.[56] It is however

49 Law Commission of India, above n. 13, at para. [5.30].

50 *Ibid.*, at para. [5.37].

51 *Ibid.* Amending the IPC in the way proposed will be in line with developments which have taken place in other jurisdictions having a codified system of criminal law such as New Zealand, Victoria and Western Australia, which have narrowed the offence of conspiracy exclusively to an agreement to commit an offence.

52 Law Commission for England and Wales, *Inchoate Offences: Conspiracy, Attempt and Incitement* (Consultation Paper No. 50) (London: HMSO, 1973) para. [12]. The recommendation that the law of conspiracy should not be extended beyond conspiracies to commit crimes was adopted in a subsequent report, *Report on Conspiracy and Criminal Law Reform* (Law Com. No. 76) (London: HMSO, 1976) 6–8, 123. The main proposals of the latter report were enacted by the Criminal Law Act 1977 (Chapter 45), which placed conspiracies on a statutory footing, but the common law offences of conspiracy to corrupt public morals and conspiracies to outrage public decency were unfortunately allowed to continue.

53 See below under the heading 'The Physical Element for Attempt'.

54 See, for example, Crimes Act (Vic), s. 321F(2). The Law Commission for England and Wales has recommended the abolition of conspiracy to defraud: *Fraud* (Law Com. No. 276) (London: The Stationery Office, 2002).

55 IPC, ss. 415, 417.

56 Law Commission of India, above n. 13, para. [5.2]. But a differently constituted Law Commission subsequently disagreed: Law Commission of India, *Indian Penal Code* (156th Report) (New Delhi: Government of India, 1997) para. [4.08].

submitted that a better solution would be to return to the original provision in the draft Code where the only general offence relating to conspiracies is that of abetment by conspiracy.[57] Hence, it is the offence of criminal conspiracy that should be removed from the IPC. This change will mean that agreements to commit acts which are non-criminal in nature will no longer be punishable, since the offence of abetment only applies to abetment of an 'offence' only.[58] This is preferable to the current law under s. 120A of the IPC with its extremely wide scope of criminal liability.

The Fault Element for Criminal Conspiracy

The Singaporean case of *Kannan s/o Kunjiraman v. PP*,[59] which considered the fault element for criminal conspiracy under s. 120A of the IPC, followed the Supreme Court of Canada decision in *R. v. O'Brien*[60] that there must be an intention to agree and also an intention to carry out the common object of the agreement. Should the fault element be widened so that it can be satisfied by lesser states of mind such as knowledge, recklessness or negligence? One view is that if the complete crime may be committed by any of these lesser forms of fault or even without proof of fault, then so should the preliminary offence of criminal conspiracy. The opposing view is that since there is so little required in terms of the physical element for criminal conspiracy, the fault element of intent and nothing less on the part of the conspirators should be required. This view has the support of the Law Commission for England and Wales:

> We think that the law should require full intention and knowledge before a conspiracy can be established. What the prosecution ought to have to prove is that the defendant agreed with another person that a course of conduct should be pursued which would result, if completed, in the commission of a criminal offence, and further that they both knew any facts which they would need to know to make them aware that the agreed course of conduct would result in the commission of the offence.[61]

---

57 The offences of abetment and criminal conspiracy overlap with the concept of vicarious liability through which a member of the group can be held liable for the offence committed by one of his or her compatriots (see Chapter 7 of this volume: M. Hor, 'Vicarious Liability'). If the offence is committed, the person who conspires or abets the offence will be subject to the same penalty as the person who actually commits it (IPC, ss. 109, 120B(1)); this is the same result as a person who is held jointly liable for the offence committed by his or her colleague (IPC, ss. 34, 149). One way to tidy up the law is to have abetment and criminal conspiracy deal with situations where the intended offence is not committed, leaving the vicarious liability provisions to deal with situations where it is committed. However, a case can be made for retaining the present scheme, in that they portray different degrees of involvement in the criminal endeavour even if the intended offence is committed. The vicarious liability provisions are appropriate only if the offender has gone beyond the stage of assisting in the crime as an abettor or conspirator such that he or she has become an accomplice. Although the penalties may be the same, there is a difference in the labels used. However, I recognise that the conceptual difference is hard to put into practice and, judging from Singapore's record on the interpretation of s. 34 (see Chapter 7 of this volume, *ibid.*), the scope of liability under it can be wider than under the offence of abetment and criminal conspiracy.

58 IPC, ss. 109, 115, 116. 'Offence' is defined in IPC, s. 40 as 'a thing punishable under [the] Code, or under any special or local law'.

59 [1995] 3 SLR(R) 294.

60 (1954) 110 CCC 1.

61 Law Commission for England and Wales, *Report on Conspiracy and Criminal Law Reform*, above n. 52, at 17. See also the House of Lords case of *R. v. Saik* [2007] 1 AC 18, where it was held that statutory conspiracy under the Criminal Law Act 1977 (Chapter 45), s. 1(2) required proof of knowledge on the part

In agreement, it is proposed that intention should be required for conspiracy under the IPC. However, as contended earlier,[62] the better course would be for the offence of criminal conspiracy to be abolished altogether and for such conduct to be regulated by the offence of abetment by conspiracy under the IPC.

ATTEMPT

The Law under the Draft Code

The development of the doctrine of attempt at common law was associated, in part, with public order concerns related to activities such as duelling.[63] Seconds and other auxiliaries to the duel who took part in preliminary steps were regarded as having committed the distinct offence of an attempt to commit duelling itself. The modern law on attempt began to take form from the early nineteenth century following the English case of *R. v. Higgins*.[64]

The draft Code did not contain any general provision criminalising attempts to commit an offence, but there are numerous provisions in the draft Code which criminalised specific attempted offences.[65] The provisions on attempted murder and attempted voluntary culpable homicide in particular are noteworthy because they are comprehensive in covering the situations in which such attempts are criminalised. They read as follows:

> Clause 308. Whoever does any act, or omits what he is legally bound to do, with such intention or knowledge and under such circumstances that if he by that act or omission caused death he would be guilty of murder, and carries that act or omission to such a length as at the time of carrying it to that length he contemplates as sufficient to cause death, shall be punished with transportation for life, or with rigorous imprisonment for a term which may extend to life, and must not be less than seven years, and shall also be liable to fine.
>
> *Illustrations*
>
> (a) A, intending to murder Z by means of a spring gun, purchases such a gun. A has not yet committed the offence defined in this Clause. A sets the gun loaded in Z's path, and leaves it there. A has committed the offence defined in this Clause.
>
> (b) A, intending to murder Z by poison, purchases poison, and mixes the same with food which remains in A's keeping. A has not yet committed the offence defined in this Clause. A places

---

of the conspirators that a circumstance element will be present even where the substantive offence did not require proof of such a fault element. The Law Commission for England and Wales has now recommended otherwise: see *Conspiracy and Attempts* (Law Com. No. 318) (London: The Stationery Office, 2009) paras [2.137] and [2.146].

62 See above at 138.

63 J. Hall, *General Principles of Criminal Law* (2nd edn, Indianapolis: Bobbs-Merrill, 1960) 558–74; W.S. Holdsworth, *A History of English Law* (vol. 5) (3rd edn, London: Methuen and Co Ltd, 1945) 201.

64 (1801) 2 East 5, 102 ER 269.

65 See, for example, Macaulay's draft Code, cl. 109 (attempting to wage war against the government), cl. 138 (attempting to obtain gratification), cl. 340 (attempting to use force to commit an offence), cl. 378 (attempting to commit robbery) and cl. 397 (attempting to cheat by personation). It has been suggested that the absence of a general provision on attempts was because the concept was not firmly entrenched until *R. v. Eagleton* (1855) Dears 515, 169 ER 826, which was after the draft Code was submitted to the Governor General of India in Council in 1837: see K.L. Koh, C.M.V. Clarkson and N.A. Morgan, *Criminal Law in Singapore and Malaysia* (Singapore: Malayan Law Journal Pte Ltd, 1989) 252.

the food on Z's table, or delivers it to Z's servants to place it on Z's table. A has committed the offence defined in this Clause.

Clause 309. Whoever does any act, or omits what he is legally bound to do, with such intention or knowledge and under such circumstances that if he, by that act or omission, caused death he would be guilty of voluntary culpable homicide, and carries that act or omission to such a length as at the time of carrying it to that length he contemplates as sufficient to cause death, shall be punished with imprisonment of either description for a term which may extend to three years, or fine, or both.

Illustrations

(a) A, on grave and sudden provocation, fires a pistol at Z, under such circumstances that if he thereby caused death he would be guilty of manslaughter. A has committed the offence defined in this Clause.

(b) A lights a pile prepared for Suttee, under such circumstances that if he thereby caused death he would be guilty of voluntary culpable homicide by consent. A has committed the offence defined in this Clause.

(c) A pursues a thief, and fires at him, under such circumstances that if he killed the thief he would commit voluntary culpable homicide in defence. A has committed the offence defined in this Clause.

The Law under the IPC

When the IPC was finally enacted, a general provision was added in the form of s. 511. However, the provisions on attempted murder and attempted culpable homicide (which closely follow the draft Code) were not deleted but amended and enacted alongside this general provision. These overlapping provisions have created theoretical and practical difficulties which need to be sorted out. They read as follows:

Section 307. Whoever does any act with such intention or knowledge, and under such circumstances that, if he by that act caused death, he would be guilty of murder, shall be punished with imprisonment of either description for a term which may extend to ten years, and shall also be liable to fine, and if hurt is caused to any person by such act, the offender shall be liable either to imprisonment for life, or to such punishment as is hereinbefore mentioned.

Illustrations

(a) A shoots at Z with intention to kill him, under such circumstances that, if death ensued, A would be guilty of murder. A is liable to punishment under this section.

(b) A with the intention of causing the death of a child of tender years exposes it in a desert place. A has committed the offence defined by this section, though the death of the child does not ensue.

(c) A, intending to murder Z, buys a gun and loads it. A has not yet committed the offence. A fires the gun at Z. He has committed the offence defined in this section, and if by such firing he wounds Z, he is liable to punishment provided by the latter part of the first paragraph of this section.

(d) A, intending to murder Z, by poison, purchases poison and mixes the same with food which remains in A's keeping; A has not yet committed the offence defined in this section. A places the food on Z's table or delivers it to Z's servant to place it on Z's table. A has committed the offence defined in this section.

Section 308. Whoever does any act with such intention or knowledge and under such circumstances that, if he by that act caused death, he would be guilty of culpable homicide not amounting to murder, shall be punished with imprisonment of either description for a term which may extend to three years, or with fine, or with both; and, if hurt is caused to any person by such act, shall be punished with imprisonment of either description for a term which may extend to seven years, or with fine, or with both.
Illustration
A, on grave and sudden provocation, fires a pistol at Z, under such circumstances that if he thereby caused death he would be guilty of culpable homicide not amounting to murder. A has committed the offence defined in this section.

Section 511. Whoever attempts to commit an offence punishable by this Code with imprisonment for life or imprisonment, or to cause such an offence to be committed, and in such attempt does any act towards the commission of the offence, shall, where no express provision is made by this Code for the punishment of such attempt, be punished with imprisonment of any description provided for the offence, for a term which may extend to one-half of the imprisonment for life or, as the case may be, one-half of the longest term of imprisonment provided for that offence, or with such fine as is provided for the offence, or with both.
Illustrations
(a) A makes an attempt to steal some jewels by breaking open a box, and finds after so opening the box, that there is no jewel in it. He has done an act towards the commission of theft, and therefore is guilty under this section.
(b) A makes an attempt to pick the pocket of Z by thrusting his hand into Z's pocket. A fails in the attempt in consequence of Z's having nothing in his pocket. A is guilty under this section.

The general attempt provision in s. 511 covers all offences punishable under the IPC except for those punishable with death or with a fine only. The offence of murder is punishable with either death or imprisonment for life,[66] and the offence of culpable homicide not amounting to murder is punishable with imprisonment for life or imprisonment with or without hard labour.[67]

Does the general attempt provision in s. 511 cover cases of attempted murder and attempted culpable homicide as well, or must resort be made to ss. 307 and 308 only in such cases?[68] If s. 511 covers cases of attempted murder and attempted culpable homicide as well, problems may arise as the physical and fault elements required under s. 511 are potentially different from ss. 307 and 308. For example, the fault element for s. 308 can be satisfied by the accused doing an act with either the intention to kill the victim or knowledge that it is likely to do so. Section 511 is silent on this. Furthermore, in terms of the physical element, the wording of s. 308 suggests that the accused must come quite close to causing the death of the victim ('does any act ... under such circumstances that, if he by that act caused death ...'), whereas the literal words of s. 511 suggest the opposite ('does

66 IPC, s. 302.

67 *Ibid.*, s. 304.

68 For examples of cases which have held that s. 511 does not apply to attempt to commit murder, see *Queen-Empress v. Niddha* (1892) ILR 14 All 38; and *Vasudeo Balwant Gogte v. Emperor* (1932) 34 BLR 571. For examples of cases holding otherwise, see *Cassidy* (1867) 4 BHC (CrC) 17; and *Jiwan Das* 1904 Cri LJ 1078.

any act towards the commission of the offence'). The physical and fault elements for attempts generally under s. 511 are examined in the next section of this chapter.

There do not appear to be any strong reasons why the physical and fault elements for attempted murder and attempted culpable homicide should be decided on different criteria from attempts to commit other offences. One argument for retaining the different attempt provisions is that ss. 307 and 308 are exceedingly narrow in requiring that the attempt must be one which the accused would have 'by that act caused death'. Injustice can arise if resort must be made to ss. 307 and 308 alone in all cases of attempted murder and attempted culpable homicide. Take, for example, a case which does not fall within s. 307 because the accused's act was not sufficient to cause death, despite having an intention to cause death. Arguably, such an accused should be liable for attempting to kill, utilising s. 511, instead of merely being an offence of causing hurt or grievous hurt.[69] Describing what the accused tried to do as causing hurt or grievous hurt does not accurately reflect what he or she wanted to do, and the punishment levels for causing hurt and grievous hurt are lower in comparison with that for attempted murder.[70]

It is suggested that a better solution would be to extend the scope of attempted murder and attempted culpable homicide if it is felt that the conduct is deserving of harsher penalties in the first place. Some decisions of the Indian Supreme Court, for example, have apparently gone beyond the restrictive wording of s. 307 in holding that it is not necessary for bodily injury capable of causing death to be inflicted before a conviction under the section can be justified.[71] However, this does not solve the problem of potentially different criteria being applied for the physical and fault elements for the attempted offences under ss. 307 and 308 on the one hand, and under s. 511 on the other. The better solution is to allow s. 511 to regulate all attempted offences, including cases of attempted murder and attempted culpable homicide.

Changes Made to the Draft Code by the IPC

The Physical Element for Attempt

There must be a sufficient physical element to justify the imposition of criminal liability for attempts to commit an offence. Exactly when that element is satisfied has troubled many jurists and commentators. One oft-quoted starting point in English law is the following statement by Parke B. in *R. v. Eagleton*:

> The mere intention to commit a misdemeanour is not criminal. Some act is required, and we do not think that all acts towards committing a misdemeanour are indictable. Acts remotely leading towards the commission of the offence are not to be considered as attempts to commit it, but acts immediately connected with it are ...[72]

69 See J.D. Mayne, *Mayne's Criminal Law of India* (4th edn, Madras: Higginbothams, 1914) 533.

70 The imprisonment term for causing hurt is a maximum of one year (s. 323). For causing grievous hurt it is a maximum of seven years (s. 325), whereas for attempted murder it is a maximum of ten years or life imprisonment if hurt is caused (s. 307).

71 *State of Maharashtra v. Balram Bama Patil* AIR 1983 SC 305; *Sagayam v. State of Karnataka* (2000) 4 SCC 454.

72 Above n. 65, at 835.

Parke B. followed up this statement by saying that '[i]t was the last act, depending on himself ... and therefore it ought to be considered as an attempt'.[73] This 'last act' test has been criticised as being too narrow. For example, a person who was on the verge of shooting or stabbing his or her victim, but is stopped just in time by a passer-by before he or she could pull the trigger or stab the victim, and also in cases of slow poisoning, will not be guilty of attempted murder.

At the other extreme, there have been English judicial statements which place the time when the offence of attempt is committed at a much earlier point. For example, Lord Denman C.J. in *R. v. Chapman* said that 'any step taken with a view to the commission of a misdemeanour is a misdemeanour',[74] and Coleridge J. in *Dugdale v. R.* said that 'the first step towards the committing of the misdemeanour'[75] would be enough.[76]

The wording of s. 511 of the IPC clearly rejects the 'last act' test and Indian cases have consistently done the same.[77] On the other hand, a literal reading of the provision may lead one to think that the 'first step' test[78] is to be applied since it is provided that 'whoever ... does any act toward the commission of the offence ... shall be punished'.[79] The 'first step' approach has been generally rejected by the Indian courts[80] and it may be objected to on the basis that it does not accord with justice. As the Law Commission for England and Wales has said:

> [T]his approach would not be generally acceptable as it would be feared that it would lay such stress upon the proof of intention as establishing the commission of an attempt, rather than on proof of activities, that it may lead to a miscarriage of justice.[81]

---

73 *Ibid.*

74 (1849) 1 Den 432, at 439, 169 ER 314, at 317.

75 (1853) 1 E & B 435, at 439, 118 ER 499, at 500.

76 There are also supposed definitions which do not give any guidance at all on when the physical element is satisfied: see, for example, J.F. Stephen, *A Digest of the Criminal Law* (7th edn, London: Sweet & Maxwell, 1926) (first published in 1877) Art. 67:

> An attempt to commit a crime is an act done with intent to commit that crime, and forming part of a series of acts, which would constitute its actual commission if it were not interrupted.
> The point at which such a series of acts begins cannot be defined; but depends upon the circumstances of each particular case ...

77 See, for example, *Abhayanand Mishra v. State of Bihar* AIR 1961 SC 1698; *Sudhir Kumar Mukherjee v. State of West Bengal* AIR 1973 SC 2655; and *State of Maharashtra v. Mohammad Yakub* AIR 1980 SC 1111.

78 Some jurisdictions may, however, adopt this approach: see, for example, Criminal Code (Qld), s. 4(1):

> When a person, intending to commit an offence, begins to put the person's intention into execution by means adapted to its fulfilment, and manifests the person's intention by some overt act, but does not fulfil the person's intention to such an extent as to commit the offence, the person is said to attempt to commit the offence.

79 The phrase can also be found in IPC, s. 309, which criminalises attempted suicide: 'Whoever attempts to commit suicide, and does any act towards the commission of such offence ...'.

80 *The Queen v. Peterson* (1876) ILR 1 All 316; *R. v. Padala Venkatasami* (1881) ILR 3 Mad 4; *King-Emperor v. Srinivasan* (1902) ILR 25 Mad 726; *Hari Mohapatra v. State of Orissa* 1996 Cri LJ 2952.

81 Law Commission for England and Wales, *Inchoate Offences: Conspiracy, Attempt and Incitement* (Consultation Paper No. 50), above n. 52, at para. [69]. The Law Commission for England and Wales later proposed a new offence of 'criminal preparation' – *Conspiracy and Attempts* (Consultation Paper No. 183) (London: The Stationery Office, 2007) – but this was abandoned owing to a lack of support for the proposal (Law Commission for England and Wales, *Conspiracy and Attempts*, above n. 61).

The rejection of the 'first step' test is reinforced by the fact that since the IPC has specific provisions to cater to acts of preparation, the role for attempt must be to regulate conduct which is more than preparatory in nature.[82] Examples of provisions in the IPC which regulate acts of preparation are s. 122 (preparation to wage war against the Government of India), s. 126 (preparation to commit depredations on the territories of a friendly country) and s. 399 (preparation to commit dacoity).[83]

On the other hand, cases which have considered liability for attempted murder by firearms have pointed to the illustrations accompanying s. 307 to find that a person cannot be held liable for attempted murder unless he or she had fired the weapon and missed. Loading the firearm and pointing it at the victim will not be sufficient.[84] In other words, it is the 'last act test' that is adopted for attempted murder by firearms under the IPC. It is submitted that it cannot be right for different rules of attempt to be applied for different acts. The rationale proposed for adopting a different rule for attempted murder by firearms, that 'the nature of the offence was such that no more than one act was necessary for the commission of the offence',[85] is unconvincing.

In the face of such uncertainty, better guidance should be given on when the physical element for attempt is satisfied. The basic premise is that the acts must have progressed to a stage that the offender is sufficiently close to the commission of the offence as to present a 'vivid danger'[86] and a 'clear threat of harm'.[87] How can this be best expressed?

Looking first to Macaulay's draft Code, cl. 308 provides that the offender must carry 'that act or omission to such a length as at the time of carrying it to that length he contemplates [it] as sufficient'. Unfortunately, this formulation uncomfortably juxtaposes the physical and fault elements of attempt with one another. Proximity to the achievement of the intended offence, as an objective fact, should not depend on whether the offender subjectively believes himself or herself to be sufficiently close to achieving the intended offence.[88]

---

82 Acts of preparation may however amount to abetment: for example, a person who asks a shopkeeper to supply him with poison to feed to his wife has not attempted to commit murder yet, but may be guilty of abetting the shopkeeper to commit murder. Minor offences may also be thought of as specific instances of penalising acts of preparation: for example, the offence of using criminal force to outrage the modesty of a woman (IPC, s. 354) is a necessary precursor to the offence of rape (IPC, s. 376). An offender can be convicted of the former even if rape or attempted rape cannot be proven.

83 The offence of dacoity (see above n. 42) was considered so serious that other preliminary stages of dacoity were also criminalised. A person may not be guilty of dacoity or making preparations to commit dacoity yet be guilty of assembling for the purpose of dacoity: *Ramesh Chandra Banerji v. Emperor* (1913) ILR 41 Cal 350.

84 *Om Prakash v. State of Punjab* AIR 1961 SC 1782. Compare this with the English case of *R. v. Jones* [1990] 1 WLR 1057, where such acts were found to be sufficient for attempted murder.

85 *Abhayanand Mishra v. State of Bihar*, above n. 77, at para. [35].

86 Law Commission for England and Wales, *Conspiracy and Attempts* (Consultation Paper No. 183), above n. 81, at para. [12.16].

87 *Ibid.*, at para. [15.6].

88 Proximity, not in terms of physical proximity to the intended offence but proximity of the intention of the would-be offender to the intended offence, was also proposed by Chinnapa Reddy J. in *State of Maharashtra v. Mohammad Yakub*, above n. 77, where he said:

> In order to constitute 'an attempt' first there must be an intention to commit a particular offence, second, some act must have been done which would necessarily have to be done towards the commission of the offence and, third, such act must be proximate to the intended result. *The measure of proximity is not in relation to time and action but in relation to intention* … [T]he act must reveal, with reasonable certainty, in conjunction with other facts and circumstances and not necessarily in isolation, an intention, as distinguished from a mere desire or object, to commit

The Singaporean courts have adopted the test of whether the offender has 'embarked on the crime proper' from English common law.[89] Although this test purports to be 'midway between "a series of acts" and "crossing the Rubicon"',[90] its application in England has led to unsatisfactory and inconsistent outcomes. On the one hand, offenders who are dangerously close to committing the offence have been held not liable for an attempt apparently on the basis that there must be at least a confrontation with the victim or property before it can be said that the offender had embarked on the crime proper.[91] For example, in *R. v. Geddes*,[92] the accused who trespassed on school premises and was waiting in a boy's lavatory equipped with a knife, rope and masking tape with a view to abducting a boy when one entered the lavatory was held not liable for attempted false imprisonment since he had not 'actually tried' to commit the offence. In contrast, there have been convictions for attempted rape even though it could not realistically be said that the accused had 'embarked on the crime' of rape.[93] The formulation of 'embark on the crime proper' also does not fit in well with the concept of impossible offences (dealt with below) where the crime simply cannot materialise in the circumstances.

Cases from India on attempted rape illustrate the uncertainty and injustice of the law in discerning if the accused's acts are sufficiently proximate to the intended offence to rank as an attempt. In *Harischandra Narayan Khadape v. State of Maharashtra*,[94] the accused extinguished a lamp in the kitchen, stripped off his clothes below the waist, embraced the victim and tried to take off her clothes. These were considered to be only acts of preparation which did not amount to an attempt to commit rape. To the same effect is the case of *State of Madhya Pradesh v. Babulal*,[95] where the accused caught hold of the victim, assaulted her with a stick and caused her to fall down. He then snatched away her clothes and made her naked. This was also held not to be a case of attempted rape as the accused 'did not expose or attempted to expose his private part' to the victim. In *Jai Chand v. The State*,[96] the accused caught hold of the victim, forcibly laid her down on the bed, broke the string of her pyjamas, tore her underwear and gave her a bite on her left cheek. The victim pushed him away and escaped to another part of the building. These acts were held to be merely preparatory in nature and did not qualify as attempted rape. In each of these cases,

---

> the particular offence, though the act by itself may be merely suggestive or indicative of such intention, but that it must be indicative or suggestive of the intention. (Emphasis added)

It is submitted that it is wrong to adopt this approach to proximity because it conflates the physical and fault elements of the offence as well as being at variance with the requirement that the act be 'towards the commission of the offence'. See also B.B. Pande, 'An Attempt on "Attempt"' (1984) 2 *Supreme Court Cases* 42 (Journal).

89 *Chua Kian Kok v. PP* [1999] 1 SLR(R) 826, following the English case of *R. v. Gullefer* [1990] 3 All ER 882. See also *R. v. Osborne* (1919) 84 JP 63, which asked whether the accused was 'on the job'.

90 *Chua Kian Kok v. PP*, *ibid*. 'A series of acts' is treated as a first act test in that a criminal attempt is constituted as soon as any act is done in furtherance of the criminal intention, and 'crossing the Rubicon' is treated as a last act test in that the offender must have done all within his or her power to commit the crime before it is treated as a criminal attempt. Both of these interpretations can be disputed.

91 See C.M.V. Clarkson, 'Attempt: The Conduct Requirement' (2009) 29 *Oxford Journal Legal Studies* 25.

92 [1996] Crim LR 894.

93 See the cases of *Patnaik*, *Dagnall* and *Attorney-General's Reference (No. 1 of 1992)* referred to in Clarkson, above n. 91, at 28.

94 1983(1) Bom CR 296.

95 AIR 1960 MP 155.

96 1996 Cri LJ 2039.

the accused persons were convicted instead of the alternative offence of using criminal force on a woman with intent to outrage her modesty under s. 354 of the IPC.

By contrast, in *Sulekhan Singh v. State*,[97] the accused was held liable for attempted rape when he caught hold of the victim, tore off her clothes and threw her on the ground. And in *Nathu Ram v. State of Haryana*,[98] the accused and another co-accused were found in a state of undress, with the victim unconscious and her clothes undone. They were held liable for attempted rape. It is not clear at all that the accused in these two cases were somehow more proximate to the offence of rape, had 'embarked on the crime proper' or were more morally reprehensible than those who were held not liable for attempted rape in the cases mentioned above.

The formulation found in the US Model Penal Code[99] affords a better approach, which is simply that the offender is found to satisfy the physical element for attempt if he or she does an act which is 'a substantial step towards the commission of the offence'. Section 511 could be amended to include this test, with illustrations provided of situations which can or cannot meet it. The substantial step test is better than the proximity-based tests in that it requires a court to consider how much the accused has already done, rather than debatable speculation about how much more needs to be done in order to commit the offence. In the attempted rape cases described above, the accused's acts of taking hold of the victim, undoing her clothes and so on can be said to be a substantial step towards the commission of rape in most cases. Under this test, it would not matter if the accused had not exposed himself or was foiled by the victim's shouts or struggles.

That said, the substantial step test has been criticised as being too imprecise so as to permit a possible unjustifiable extension of the criminal law.[100] This criticism could be allayed by adding a provision which states that an act shall not be regarded as a substantial step in the commission of an offence unless it is strongly corroborative of the actor's criminal purpose.[101] To avoid having different tests for the physical element of attempts under ss. 307 and 308 of the IPC and under s. 511, it is proposed that ss. 307 and 308 should be deleted. The revised s. 511 will then have to be relied on for what conduct will or will not amount to attempted murder or attempted culpable homicide not amounting to murder.

The Fault Element for Attempt

It should be noted that s. 511 of the IPC does not express any specific fault element. However, cases from India and other IPC jurisdictions like Malaysia and Singapore have imposed a requirement that the offender have the 'intention' to commit the offence.[102] In common with the other preliminary

97 1999 Cri LJ 3798.

98 1994 Cri LJ 1095.

99 Above n. 7.

100 Law Commission for England and Wales, *Attempt, and Impossibility in Relation to Attempt, Conspiracy and Incitement* (Law Com No. 102) (London: HMSO, 1980) 18–19.

101 See US Model Penal Code, s. 5.01(2). Support for the substantial step test may be found in G. Williams, 'Wrong Turnings in the Law of Attempt' [1991] *Criminal Law Review* 416 as well as in international criminal law: see the Rome Statute of the International Criminal Court (UN Doc. 2187 UNTS 90), Art. 25.3(f), which states that '... a person shall be criminally responsible and liable for punishment for a crime ... if that person ... attempts to commit such a crime by taking action that commences its execution by means of a substantial step ...'.

102 *Abhayanand Mishra v. State of Bihar*, above n. 77; *Mohd Ali Jaafar v. PP* [1998] 4 MLJ 210; *Chua Kian Kok v. PP*, above n. 89.

offences of abetment and criminal conspiracy, it may be asked why this should be so, particularly where the complete offence may be committed with a lesser fault element. The answer given by the Singapore High Court in *Chua Kian Kok v. PP*[103] is that since no real harm has been inflicted in the attempt, the most culpable mental state, namely intention, is required before the law can justify interfering with the freedom of individuals to do as they please.

On the other hand, the failure to extend the fault element in attempts to whatever that is deemed sufficient for the complete offence seems illogical.[104] A person may be convicted of voluntarily causing hurt if he or she had the intention to cause hurt or the knowledge that he or she was thereby likely to cause hurt.[105] If the hurt did not materialise because of sheer fortune (or misfortune from the perspective of the would-be offender), he or she is only liable for the attempted offence if he or she had the intention to cause hurt but failed. It would seem unfair for the required fault element to change based on circumstances over which the would-be offender had no control. Moreover, a person who succeeds in committing an offence may very well have lesser culpability than a person who tries but fails, and yet the former will suffer a more severe penalty. For example, A, who causes hurt to B knowing that hurt is likely, will be liable for up to one year's imprisonment,[106] but C, who intentionally tries to cause hurt to B but fails, will only be liable for attempted causing of hurt and half of A's penalty.

A compromise solution is now adopted in English law, which is that there must be an intention with respect to the penalised consequences, but the mental element with respect to the circumstances need merely mirror the mental element required for the complete crime, such as recklessness.[107] While this may be attractive, it is submitted that a better solution is to adopt the fault element in the original scheme envisaged by Macaulay which is now also found in the presently enacted provisions of the IPC on attempted murder and attempted culpable homicide.[108] These provisions require the mental element for attempt to be either intention or, at a minimum, knowledge that the intended offence is likely to be committed. This serves to limit the scope of liability to those who are most culpable and takes into account the lack of real harm caused. In the case of those offences which do not have a fault element or which may be committed negligently, a person may only be convicted of attempting those offences if he or she had acted intentionally or knowingly. It is therefore proposed that s. 511 of the IPC be amended to clearly state this as the required fault element for attempt.

103 Above n. 89.

104 G. Williams, *Criminal Law* (2nd edn, London: Stevens and Sons, 1961) 619. See also H.L.A. Hart, *Punishment and Responsibility* (New York: Oxford University Press, 1968) 126–7; and J.C. Smith, 'Two Problems in Criminal Attempts Re-examined I' [1962] *Criminal Law Review* 135.

105 IPC, s. 321.

106 The penalty for voluntarily causing hurt is imprisonment (with or without hard labour) for up to one year, a fine of up to 1,000 rupees, or both: IPC, s. 323.

107 The Singaporean case of *Chua Kian Kok v. PP*, above n. 89, considered the English cases of *R. v. Khan* [1990] 2 All ER 783 and *Attorney-General's Reference (No. 3 of 1992)* [1994] 2 All ER 121, but was of the opinion that they misconstrued the applicable statute (Criminal Attempts Act 1981 (UK) (Chapter 47), s. 1(1)).

108 Some Indian cases have, however, required a showing that the offender 'intended' to commit murder despite the clear wording in IPC, s 307. See, for example, *Om Prakash v. State of Punjab*, above n. 84.

IMPOSSIBILITY

Abetment to Commit Acts which are Impossible

The development at common law as to whether preliminary offences such as conspiracy and attempt can be independently committed regardless of whether the ultimate object of these offences can be committed has been complex and uncertain.[109] In the face of such uncertainty, it was not surprising that Macaulay's draft Code made a break with the common law in holding that there is no necessity for the offence abetted to be actually committed before the abettor is held liable. In the explanation to cl. 86, it was provided that '[a] person may previously abet the doing of a thing ... though the thing abetted be not done'. The IPC also adopts this stance.[110]

Curiously, however, the Indian case law appears to have made an exception in the case of abetment by aiding such that the charge cannot be sustained if the principal offender is acquitted.[111] The basis for this exception is said to flow from the word 'aid' as well as explanation 2 to s. 107 of the IPC, which seems to imply the actual commission of the offence aided. That explanation reads:

> Whoever, either prior to or at the time of commission of any act, does anything in order to facilitate the commission of that act, and thereby *facilitates the commission thereof*, is said to aid the doing of that act. (Emphasis added)

However, this position is probably more due to the influence of English common law than the provisions of the IPC. At common law, it is necessary to prove that the principal offence had been committed before a person may be convicted of aiding and abetting it, even though it is not necessary for the principal offender to be brought to justice or for the identity of the principal offender to be known.[112]

---

109 The difficulty may be attributed to the fact that these offences emerged out of the law of principal and accessory, and these offences were not recognised as distinct offences until the end of the eighteenth century: Turner, above n. 18, at 184. There was also at that time a common law doctrine that 'no accessory can be convicted or suffer any punishment where the principal is not attained or hath the benefit of his clergy' (*Syer's Case* (1561) 4 Co Rep 43b, 76 ER 990) such that there was doubt over whether a person who instigated another to commit a felony would be guilty of a crime if the felony was not committed (Turner, *ibid.*; see also *R. v. Fitzmaurice* [1983] 1 All ER 189). On the other hand, there was no difficulty at common law to finding that the crime of incitement was committed even if the person incited refused to accede to the suggestion or failed in his or her attempt to commit the incited offence: *R. v. Higgins*, above n. 64; *R. v. Gregory* (1867) LR 1 CCR 77; *R. v. de Kromme* (1892) 17 Cox CC 492. Turner, *ibid.*, 209, noted: 'But even where a crime is not in fact committed, those who have unsuccessfully solicited or incited another to commit it are, at common law, guilty of an indictable misdemeanor ...'.

110 This principle can now be found in the IPC, explanation 2 to s. 108: 'To constitute the offence of abetment, it is not necessary that the act abetted should be committed, or that the effect requisite to constitute the offence should be caused.' See also the illustrations thereunder. If the act abetted is committed, punishment for abetment would be greater than if it was not committed.

111 *Faguna Kanta Nath v. State of Assam* AIR 1959 SC 673; *Jamuna Singh v. State of Bihar* AIR 1967 SC 553. The distinction is also followed in Malaysia by *Periasamy s/o Sinnapan v. PP* [1996] 2 MLJ 557 and initially in Singapore by *Ong Ah Yeo Yenna v. PP* [1993] 1 SLR(R) 349 until it was corrected by *Chua Kian Kok v. PP*, above n. 89.

112 For example, in the English case of *Thorton v. Mitchell* [1940] 1 All ER 339, the driver of a bus relied on the signals of the conductor as he reversed the bus. The conductor gave the driver the signal to reverse and two pedestrians were knocked down. The driver was charged with driving without due care

By way of criticism, it is extremely odd for one form of abetment in the IPC to be treated differently from the other forms. The basis of the abetment offences in the IPC is different from the concept of derivative liability for accessories at common law.[113] Explanation 3 to s. 108 of the IPC also points out that it is not necessary that the person abetted should be legally capable of committing that offence.[114] Therefore, a case may be made for holding a person liable for abetting another to commit an offence even if the offence was not committed, notwithstanding the type of abetment which took place. Consequently, the person will also be liable even if the offence was in fact impossible to carry out, provided that the failure was due to facts not known to him or her. This will accord with what is discussed below for criminal conspiracies and attempts.

Criminal Conspiracies to Commit Acts which are Impossible

Under the English common law, a person may or may not be liable for an agreement to commit an offence which is impossible to achieve; liability will depend on the substance of the agreement. In *DPP v. Nock*,[115] two persons intended to manufacture cocaine by using ingredients which they mistakenly thought could produce the drug. The House of Lords held that it was not an unlawful conspiracy if it was factually impossible to produce cocaine by the specific process contemplated in the agreement. It would be a different case, however, if the agreement had been to manufacture cocaine generally if and when they could find suitable raw materials, in which case the failure to use the right ingredients would only be a temporary setback. This approach has not been followed in Scotland[116] and has been overturned by statute in England[117] and Victoria.[118]

Since the IPC does not deal with this issue, it has been left to the courts, which have taken an approach similar to *Nock*. In the Bombay High Court case of *Emperor v. Hiremath*,[119] two persons agreed to kill their intended victim by means of witchcraft. It was held that they would be guilty of a criminal conspiracy if the agreement was to commit murder, even if the means agreed upon were not likely to prove effective. On the other hand, if it was merely to do an act which is not illegal, in the hope and belief that the act may result in the death of some person, it will not amount to a criminal conspiracy. On the facts before it, the court found that the agreement was to cause the death of the victim, with the means to be tried first being a form of witchcraft. They were therefore liable for criminal conspiracy to commit murder.

---

and attention and the conductor for aiding and abetting the offence. The court case against the driver was dismissed and it was held that the conductor could not be liable for aiding and abetting an offence which had not been committed.

113 Limited departures from the general concept have evolved at common law: see, for example: *R. v. Bourne* (1952) 36 Cr App R 125; *R. v. Cogan and Leak* (1975) 61 Cr App R 217; and *R. v. Millward* [1994] Crim LR 527.

114 Hence, a person who abets a child or a person unsound in mind will nevertheless be guilty of the offence of abetment even if the person abetted does not bear criminal liability.

115 [1978] AC 979.

116 *Maxwell v. HM Advocate* [1980] SLT 241.

117 Criminal Attempts Act 1981 (UK) (Chapter 47), s. 5(1).

118 Crimes Act (Vic), s 321(3).

119 AIR 1940 Bom 365. For a discussion of *Hiremath* and *Nock*, see S. Yeo, 'Clarifying Impossible Attempts and Criminal Conspiracies' (2007) 19 *Singapore Academy of Law Journal* 1.

The approach in *Nock* and *Hiremath* has been criticised for being too uncertain and based on how the agreement is formulated linguistically.[120] However, if the role of the criminal law is thought of as being based on liability for dangerous situations which a person brings about, conspirators should only be liable for acts which are impossible to achieve if the reason for the impossibility is due to circumstances beyond their control. Should the impossibility be due to factors within their control (such as using an inadequate weapon or drug), then there is not, in fact, a dangerous situation for the law to regulate. In the context of attempts, the Indian case of *Asgarali Prahania v. Emperor* explained that:

> ... if one who believes in witchcraft, puts a spell on another, or burns him in effigy, or curses him, with the intention of causing him hurt, and believing that his actions will have that result, he cannot, in my opinion, be convicted of an attempt to cause hurt. Because what he does is ... an act towards the commission of something which, cannot, according to human experience, result in hurt to another, within the meaning of the Penal Code. His failure to cause hurt is due to his own act or omission, that is to say, his act was intrinsically useless, or defective, or inappropriate for the purpose he had in mind, owing to the undeveloped state of his intelligence, or to ignorance of modern science. His failure was due, broadly speaking, to his own volition.
>
> Similarly, if a man with intent to hurt another by administering poison, prepares and administers some harmless substance, believing it to be poisonous, he cannot, in my opinion, be convicted of an attempt to do so.[121]

Under this approach, criminal liability will follow only if the failure is due to intervention by a third party, such as being apprehended by the police or switching a glass laced with poison meant for the victim with a glass of water without the would-be murderer's knowledge. Persons who, pursuant to a conspiracy, choose a totally ineffective means to achieve their intended goal in the mistaken belief that it will be effective should not be held liable.[122] Accused persons who conspire to perform acts which any right-minded person will regard as harmless in the misguided belief that they will serve their intended aim are most likely in need of psychological help than punishment through the criminal law.

Attempts to Commit Acts which are Impossible

It was at one time thought that there was no crime in attempting to do that which was physically impossible to complete. Examples of this include shooting at a figure which the would-be offender mistakenly thinks is his or her victim with intention to kill, but the figure turns out to be a block of wood; putting sugar into a cup of tea believing it to be arsenic; or opening an empty box with the intent to steal its contents. The reason for this is the sentiment that it would be unduly harsh to punish a harmless act solely on the basis of the intention of the doer to do harm. Hence, in the

120 Koh, Clarkson and Morgan, above n. 65, at 301.

121 *Asgarali Pradhania v. Emperor* (1933) ILR 61 Cal 54, *per* Lort-Williams J.

122 Cf. Duff's proposal, above n. 12, that a person should not be liable for conduct which 'failed to engage with the world as an attempt to commit that offence'. Conduct is said to fail to engage with the world if it is not directed towards a victim or object of a kind whose existence is required for commission of the offence, or if it would be obvious to any reasonable person that it could not result in the commission of the offence.

English case of *R. v. Collins*,[123] it was held that a conviction for attempting to steal from a pocket must be quashed because the question of whether the pocket was empty was not left to the jury. A change of view subsequently came about in *R. v. Brown*[124] and was affirmed by *R. v. Ring*.[125] In each case, there was a mistake of fact on the part of the would-be offender which should be irrelevant to his or her culpability. If the prosecution can successfully prove the would-be offender made a mistake, for example, by shooting at a figure he or she supposed to be alive, the intention to commit murder can nevertheless be shown.

The sole exception to liability for impossible attempts is where a person does something which is in fact not a crime under the law. For example, a person who imports sugar into the country wrongly believing that it is a crime to do so cannot be held liable for attempting to evade a non-existent prohibition on sugar imports.[126]

The approach of the IPC clearly imposes liability for acts even if they are not capable of ultimately resulting in the intended offence. The two illustrations to s. 511 of the IPC on attempts clearly depart from the prevailing English law at the time, as exemplified in *Collins*.They read:

> (a) A makes an attempt to steal some jewels by breaking open a box, and finds after so opening the box, that there is no jewel in it. He has done an act towards the commission of theft, and therefore is guilty under this section.
>
> (b) A makes an attempt to pick the pocket of Z by thrusting his hand into Z's pocket. A fails in the attempt in consequence of Z's having nothing in his pocket. A is guilty under this section.

Unfortunately, these illustrations only refer to instances of *factual* impossibility, which may lead to doubts over whether the same principle can be applied to *legal* impossibility.[127] Factual impossibility occurs where the result that is intended by the would-be offender cannot be achieved because of an extraneous factual or physical circumstance. An example is trying to pick an empty pocket, as instanced in illustration (b) to s. 511 of the IPC. Legal impossibility arises where even if the would-be offender achieves what he or she sets out to do, it would not result in the crime he or she believed would be committed. Examples of this type of impossibility include trying to 'steal' his or her own umbrella thinking it belongs to another, or trying to 'kill' a victim who is already dead. The House of Lords in *Haughton v. Smith*[128] also drew dubious distinctions based on types of impossibility. The matter was finally settled in England by the enactment of the Criminal

---

123 (1864) L & C 471, 9 Cox CC 497. See also the earlier case of *R. v. M'Pherson* (1857) D & B 197, 7 Cox CC 281; and *R. v. Taylor* (1859) 1 F & F 511, at 512, 175 ER 831, at 832, *per* Pollock C.B., where he opined: 'The act must be one … committed by the prisoner under such circumstances that he has the power of carrying his intention into execution.'

124 (1890) 24 QBD 357.

125 (1892) 17 Cox CC 491.

126 *Chua Kian Kok v. PP*, above n. 89. This situation is different from 'legal impossibility' since what the accused thinks he or she is doing does not amount to an offence known to that jurisdiction, whereas in the case of legal impossibility, what the accused thinks he or she is doing does.

127 K.L. Koh, 'Trends in Singapore Criminal Law' in *Review of Judicial and Legal Reforms in Singapore* (Singapore: Butterworths Asia, 1996) 318, at 354.

128 [1975] AC 476.

Attempts Act 1981, which rejected distinctions based on types of impossibility.[129] Other criminal law codifications have similarly come to the same conclusion.[130]

However, in line with what was proposed above with respect to impossible conspiracies, it is similarly proposed that a difference in culpability should be recognised for attempt, which is not based on the *type* of impossibility but on the *reasons* for failure. Only a person who fails to achieve his or her criminal objective because of circumstances unknown to him or her, or due to facts outside of his or her control, deserves punishment. An illustration of this proposal comes from the Indian case of *Asgarali Pradhania* and the Federation of Malaya case of *Munah binte Ali v. PP*.[131] In the former case, it was held that the accused could not be convicted of an attempt to cause a miscarriage since the substances given to the woman to procure the miscarriage were not shown to be capable of doing so. The failure was not due to a factor independent of the accused. On the other hand, the accused in the latter case was properly convicted of an attempt to cause a miscarriage by inserting an instrument into the woman with the intention to cause her to miscarry. The defence argument that the woman was not pregnant at the time only showed that the failure was due to a factor independent of the accused. In short, accused persons who try to commit offences by inept means should not be dealt with through the law of attempts,[132] but those who are thwarted by events outside of their control should be. This view is also supported by illustrations (b), (c) and (d) to s. 307 of the IPC.[133]

PROPOSALS FOR REFORM OF THE IPC

Despite what had been said at the beginning of this chapter about difficulties of rendering preliminary acts as offences in themselves, present-day legislators have found ways to criminalise certain kinds of dangerous behaviour at a very early stage. For example, the mere possession of housebreaking implements can be made an offence[134] without the police having to wait for the act of housebreaking to be about to take place before stepping in. New offences created in response to acts of terrorism have also increasingly shifted the balance of criminalisation towards acts of preparation.[135] It may be argued that the importance of preliminary offences has decreased with these developments. However, the fact remains that the bulk of the criminal law still relies heavily

129 This was confirmed in *R. v. Shivpuri* [1986] 2 All ER 334.

130 For example, Criminal Code (Qld), s. 4; Criminal Code (Tas), s. 2(2); Criminal Code (WA), s. 4; and Criminal Code (Canada), s. 24(1). But see the New Zealand case of *The Queen v. Donnelly* [1970] NZLR 980, which qualified the provision in the Crimes Act (NZ), s. 72 by distinguishing factual impossibility (liable) from legal impossibility (not liable).

131 [1958] MLJ 159.

132 Convictions for lesser offences are of course proper if the physical and fault elements of the lesser offences are satisfied.

133 Illustrations (c) and (d) appear as illustrations (a) and (b) to cl. 308 in Macaulay's draft Code (see above at 139–40).

134 With respect to Singapore, see Miscellaneous Offences (Public Order and Nuisance) Act (Chapter 184, 1997 Rev. Ed.), s. 22.

135 For example, Terrorism Act 2006 (Chapter 11) (UK), s. 5(1) makes it an offence to engage in any conduct in preparation for giving effect to an intention to commit acts of terrorism or assist another to commit such acts; Criminal Code (Cth), s. 101.6(1) makes it an offence to do any act in preparation for, or planning, a terrorist act; and Criminal Code (Canada), s. 83.19(1) criminalises anyone who knowingly facilitates a terrorist activity. Far-reaching preventive detention orders may also be made by the Executive in Malaysia and Singapore against suspected terrorists and those involved in organised crime: see Yeo, Morgan and Chan, above n. 10, at paras. [2.52]–[2.60].

on the devices of abetment, criminal conspiracy and attempt to extend its reach. Hence, it is still important to have a clear framework for criminal liability in these areas.

The various proposals made in this chapter can be readily incorporated into the IPC by making the following amendments.

Fault Element for Abetment

The following new provisions should be added to the IPC:

> A person abets an offence only if he or she has the intention or knowledge that the offence abetted will be committed.
>
> A person abets an offence notwithstanding absence of knowledge as to which offence will be committed so long as he or she intends or knows to be likely that one or more of a number of offences will be committed as a consequence of the abetment.

These provisions clarify that the fault element for abetment is either intention or knowledge; however, the accused does not need to know all the details relating to the offence.

The third limb of s. 107 of the IPC (abetment by aiding) should also be amended by deleting the word 'intentionally'. The requisite fault element for all types of abetment will now be found in the proposed new provisions. No other changes are needed to the other limbs relating to abetment by instigation and abetment by conspiracy.

Abetment to Commit Acts which are Impossible

The following provision should be added to the IPC:

> A person abets an offence notwithstanding the existence of any facts or circumstances which, unknown to him or her or outside his or her control, render the commission of the offence impossible.

This means that an accused will be liable for abetting an offence even if it fails to materialise due to an external factor. However, if the failure is due to inadequate means, such as giving a substance to be used as a poison when it is in fact harmless, liability will not follow.

Abolishing the Offence of Criminal Conspiracy

The offence of criminal conspiracy should be abolished by deleting s. 120A of the IPC. Agreements to commit offences in general will therefore be considered as a form of abetment only. Consequential amendments to the IPC where a conspiracy is referred to, such as s. 121A and illustration (c) to s. 192, need to be made to indicate that it is a reference to abetment by conspiracy.

Abolishing Attempt to Commit Murder and Culpable Homicide under ss. 307 and 308 of the IPC

Sections 307 and 308 of the IPC should be deleted. Cases of attempted murder and attempted culpable homicide will therefore need to be dealt with under the general provision of s. 511. With this change, the punishment provision in the revised s. 511 will also need to be amended to cater for imprisonment for a certain number of years in cases of attempted murder, since it is not possible to fix the imprisonment term to one-half of the term of imprisonment for the offence where it is the death penalty.[136]

Attempt to Commit Offences

Section 511 of the IPC should be replaced with the following provision:

> A person attempts to commit an offence only if he or she:
> (a) acts with such intention or knowledge as required for the offence; and
> (b) takes a substantial step in a course of conduct towards the commission of the offence.
> *Explanation* – Conduct shall not be held to constitute a substantial step towards the commission of the offence unless it is strongly corroborative of the person's criminal purpose.
>
> A person attempts to commit an offence notwithstanding the existence of any facts or circumstances which, unknown to him or her or outside his or her control, render the commission of the offence impossible.

These provisions clearly describe the fault element (intention or knowledge) and physical element (a substantial step towards the commission of the offence) required for liability for an attempted offence. As with abetment to commit acts which are impossible, an accused is also not liable for attempting to commit acts which are impossible if the impossibility is due to his or her inept means.

All told, it can be said with confidence that the enactment of the above-proposed amendments will go a long way towards clarifying and simplifying the current state of the law on preliminary offences in the IPC.

136 Life imprisonment is treated as being equivalent to imprisonment for 20 years (IPC, s. 40), so it is possible to apply s. 511 in such cases.

Chapter 7
Vicarious Liability

Michael Hor

CRIMES OF CONFEDERACY

It is the kind of story one would come across in detective novels or police dramas on television. This is a venerable version which is found in Macaulay's famous draft of the Indian Penal Code (IPC):

> B, with arms, breaks into an inhabited house at midnight, for the purpose of robbery. A watches at the door. B being resisted by Z, one of the inmates, murders Z. Here, if A considered murder as likely to be committed by B in the attempt to rob the house, or in the robbing of the house, or in consequences of the robbing of the house, A is liable to the punishment provided for murder.[1]

Thus with elegant simplicity did the creator of the IPC settle a question which vexes criminal courts the world over to this day – the matter of the precise ambit of liability of members of a criminal enterprise for what is done outside the explicit or implicit agreement of the parties. It has acquired different terminology in different jurisdictional contexts – 'common intention' for the IPC, 'common purpose' in the common law and more recently 'joint criminal enterprise' (JCE) in international criminal law[2] – but the core issue is the same. Should the criminal law make it easier to convict a member of a JCE for an offence which another committed in the course of carrying out the enterprise, usually murder, and, if so, how much easier?

The purists amongst us might well ask what is wrong with the usual principles of ascription of criminal liability. JCE or no, the person who commits murder is liable for murder. The confederates in the robbery are to be judged individually. If murder was part of the joint enterprise, then they are liable for murder as well.[3] If they had abetted the murder in any way – in the words of the IPC, either by instigation, conspiracy or intentional aiding – they stand responsible for abetment of murder.[4] In short, if murder was not part of the criminal plan, the confederates are not liable for murder unless it can be established that they have themselves individually fulfilled the requirements of murder –

---

1 Macaulay's draft Code, cl. 98, illustration (a).

2 These terms are used interchangeably in this discussion, unless the context makes it otherwise clear.

3 Ironically, this fundamental principle of individual assessment of culpability is found in IPC, s. 35, the much-neglected step-sister of the much-discussed s. 34, a section which has caused much grief:

> Whenever an act, which is criminal only by reason of its being done with a criminal knowledge or intention, is done by several persons, each of such persons who joins in the act with such knowledge or intention, is liable for the act in the same manner as if the act were done by him alone with that knowledge or intention.

This is a variation of Macaulay's original version in cl. 3 of his draft Code.

4 IPC, s. 107 identifies the three forms of abetment. IPC, s. 109 prescribes that the abettor is subject to the same punishment as the primary offender if the act abetted is committed in consequence of the abetment. See Chapter 6 of this volume (W. Chan, 'Abetment, Criminal Conspiracy and Attempt').

that is, the particular confederate must have caused death with either the intention to cause death or the knowledge that death was likely, to use Macaulay's original formulation.[5] Nor are they liable for abetment of murder unless the requirements of a conspiracy, instigation or intentional aiding are met.

The most problematic person is the confederate who neither planned to kill nor abetted the murder, but who either foresaw or perhaps ought to have foreseen that a member of the criminal enterprise might commit murder.[6] The normal principles of liability would make him guilty of robbery, or one of the aggravated forms thereof. With respect to the unintended killing, he cannot be responsible because he did not cause or abet death. There is much to be said for adhering strictly to this scheme of things. He is already guilty of robbery and is to be sentenced for it. If he had, or ought to have had, any inkling of death, that can be taken into account in sentencing. Why the compulsion to make him responsible for the murder as well?

I must confess that I remain unconvinced that the result reached by the usual principles of criminal liability are somehow deficient and that something must be done to fix the troublesome confederate with murder as well. One line of argument appears to proceed along quasi-moral considerations. It tends to appeal to ideas like 'taking the risk' and 'package deals',[7] but that merely describes the result and does little to provide the basis on which liability for murder is said to be founded. The position is simply that the normal principles of liability already lay down the requisite moral preconditions for liability for murder or the abetment thereof. 'Package deals' tell us nothing about why the deals are packaged in that way and no other, or why they ought to be packaged at all. 'Taking the risk'[8] elevates that state of mind to the level of causing death with the intention of causing death or the knowledge that death was likely – a meteoric promotion by any measure. The crux of the matter is whether the large 'retributive' shortfall in establishing either murder or the abetment thereof is somehow made up by the confederate being part of a criminal enterprise with respect to the robbery.

Much is made of the danger of group crimes escalating into violence and death, but why is it that the usual response of the criminal law is thought to be retributively insufficient? The members of the group are punished for the group crime and the person who escalates it with violence is punished accordingly.

The second line of argument also capitalises on the phenomenon of group crimes being more insidious than individual crimes – members fortify and encourage one another in the criminal

5 Macaulay's draft Code, cls. 294 and 295.

6 Joint enterprise liability potentially includes all crimes, primary and collateral, but two kinds of situations – the robbery-murder and the assault-murder – are, from experience, virtually the only combinations which are prosecuted. An apology (in the Greek sense) is perhaps in order for the unfashionable use of the masculine pronoun 'he' and cognate expressions to better reflect the preponderant male share of criminality.

7 The Singapore Court of Appeal in *Lee Chez Kee v. PP* [2008] 3 SLR(R) 447, at para. [250], seemed to have been impressed by the 'clarity and logic' of an attempt to justify joint enterprise liability in terms of these metaphors. The entire edifice seems to have rested on this puzzling assertion by A.P. Simester, 'The Mental Element in Complicity' (2006) 122 *Law Quarterly Review* 578, at 599: 'Yet her commitment to the common purpose implies an acceptance of the choices and actions that are taken by P [the actual doer] in the course of realising that purpose.' Just why there is such an implied acceptance is not clear. This kind of 'logic' is not capable of generating any meaningful limits to the doctrine. Because this 'implied acceptance' is essentially a fiction, we do not know if it should extend to foreseeable, probable or even just any consequences, nor do we know what would amount to a radical departure (as opposed to other less fundamental kinds).

8 Another example of the way 'taking the risk' justifications are used when all else fails is in strict liability – there is strict liability because the person who causes the injury or damage without the required fault element is still criminally liable because he 'takes the risk' by indulging in that kind of activity.

enterprise, which then has the potential to escalate into violence and death. There is an especial need, it is said, to deter such activity. Again, it is not easy to understand why, for deterrent as for retributive purposes, the usual principles of liability are insufficient. If group crimes are, as a matter of policy, considered to be very dangerous, the criminal law should reflect that in increased penalties for group crimes and perhaps especially those with a propensity to develop into violence. Why is there thought to be a need to make all members of a gang of robbers guilty of murder which they did not intend, abet or cause? One could of course continue to pile deterrence upon deterrence, but where is the evidence that the usual rules of criminal liability have been insufficiently deterrent?

While I see no persuasive logic that the problematic confederate should somehow be made responsible for a killing which he did not himself commit or abet, the urge has been strong to have the criminal law 'do something' extraordinary to fix him with murder. It is not easy to pin down precisely what motivates the feeling or desire to hold the confederate constructively, or vicariously, liable for the murder that he himself did not commit. Perhaps it is a certain sense that one who has embarked on a crime no longer deserves to be treated 'normally' and thus ought to 'take the risk' (to some extent, at least) for the consequences which flow from the criminal enterprise. Someone in the course of executing a criminal purpose is somehow disentitled from the usual calculations of *mens rea* and *actus reus*. This dynamic is seen most clearly in the historic doctrine of felony-murder. When someone kills in the course of committing a felony, it is murder regardless of any *mens rea* with respect to the killing. Rationalist reformers were eventually able to exorcise this demon – in particular, Macaulay expressly and emphatically rejected the doctrine for the IPC.[9]

The other emotion that may be driving the desire to punish the confederate for the murder that he himself did not commit or abet is perhaps a primal instinct about guilt by association. Which one of us has not been guilty of judging others by the company they keep? In more savage times, entire families were punished for crimes which someone associated with these social entities committed.[10] The urge is strongest when there is felt to be a crime situation 'getting out of control'. Witness the strange gang robbery or 'dacoity' provisions of the IPC, one of which is the offence of 'belonging to a gang of persons associated for the purpose or habitually committing gang robbery'.[11] Notice

9 Macaulay explained his revulsion towards the felony-murder rule in terms which would apply to joint enterprise liability for murder in his *Notes* to the Indian Penal Code: T.B. Macaulay, J.M. Macleod, G.W. Anderson and F. Millett, *A Penal Code Prepared by the Indian Law Commissioners* (London: Pelham Richardson, 1838) (reprinted by the Lawbook Exchange, Ltd, 2002). His summation, at 111, Note M (On Offences Against the Body), is this: 'To punish as a murderer every man who, while committing a heinous offence, causes death by pure misadventure, is a course which evidently adds nothing to the security of human life.'

One could have imagined a lesser Macaulay propounding the view that the intended felony and the unintended death is but a package deal, and that the felon must take the risk that things might go out of control and someone might die.

10 M.A. LeFande, *Aspects of Legalist Philosophy and the Law in Ancient China* (2000) (available online at http://www.commonwealthprotection.org/AncientChinaLaw.pdf, last accessed 15 February 2011), who quotes this passage from J.J.L. Duyvendak, *The Book of the Lord Shang* (London: Arthur Probsthain, 1928; reprinted 1963): 'Therefore, do I say that if there are severe penalties that extend to the whole family, people will not dare to try (how far they can go), and [as] they dare not try, no punishments will be necessary.' Typically, the ancient Chinese choose to emphasise the utilitarian benefits of guilt by association.

11 Witness the obsession over 'gang robbery' (or 'dacoity' in the IPC) which the IPC spreads over five sections: ss. 395, 396, 399, 400 and 402. IPC, ss. 400 and 401 contain the two remarkable associational crimes: that of belonging to a gang of habitual gang robbers and of a wandering gang of (non-gang) robbers or thieves. L.A. Benton, *Law and Colonial Cultures: Legal Regimes in World History 1400–1900* (New York: Cambridge University Press, 2001),says at 150:

also that relic of the post-war Malayan emergency offence of 'consorting' or being 'found in the company' of persons unlawfully carrying firearms – offences still in the books.[12] A more recent example is the peculiar provision in the Singaporean Misuse of Drugs Act which makes members of a group liable for possession by any one of them if there was 'knowledge and consent', whatever that may mean precisely.[13]

These examples sound exotic, prosecutions are at best very rare and most people probably do not even know they exist. But JCE liability is alive and well, as if all our more primitive instincts and urges had been channelled into it.

The rational response is to reject JCE liability altogether. The confederate who did not kill is guilty of murder only if the criminal enterprise explicitly or implicitly encompassed murder, or if he could be said to have abetted murder in some other way by the normal rules of abetment. But the law has not been allowed to be rational. The desire to found liability for murder with something less than that has proven to be too strong. Once the road towards constructive murder is taken, we are at once cast upon a sea of uncertainty – how much less than the requirements of abetment of the collateral crime, how much more than the requirements of a joint enterprise to commit the primary crime? Extremely difficult questions of line-drawing arise: is it a matter of pure causation or one of foreseeability, is it actual or reasonable foreseeability, is it foreseeability of a possibility or a probability, is it foreseeability of only the *actus reus* or of *mens rea* as well, is it foreseeability of death or merely injury, to what extent should what was foreseeable match with what actually happened – the victim, the weapon, the motive of the killer? Because we are no longer working with logic, there is no right answer – only a choice between one which promotes our emotional urges or one which limits them. This is not only the probable but also the unavoidable consequence of our initial decision to allow the normal requirements of murder, or whatever the collateral crime may be, to be watered down.

DIAL M FOR MACAULAY

Even Macaulay, utilitarian rationalist that he was, did not think that the IPC could do without a form of liability for JCE. But the provision which he came up with was revolutionary for a time when the common law was, it appears, not even sure whether foreseeability of any kind was necessary to trigger liability for offences of others outside of the JCE. Francis Sayre, writing as late as 1930, said: 'Whether or not the crime committed is a "proximate consequence" of the crime ordered or procured is often an exceedingly nice question.'[14]

The British used the term dacoity to describe a range of forms of rural violence, including famine looting and gang raids, and even the more extreme forms that became more common in the mid-nineteenth century when whole villages were held and plundered.

Macaulay himself described dacoity as 'that atrocious crime' for which 'punishment of exemplary severity' had to be provided: Macauly, Macleod, Anderson and Millett, above n. 9, at 121, Note N (On the Chapter of Offences Against Property).

12 Now Arms Offences Act (Chapter 14, 2008, Rev. Ed.) (Singapore), s. 7, a direct descendent of the original Malayan Emergency Regulations 1948, reg. 5: *Lee Yoon Choy v. PP* [1948] MLJ 167. See the very rare prosecution in *PP v. Ong Boon Jun* [2008] SGDC 65.

13 Misuse of Drugs Act (Chapter 185, 2008, Rev. Ed.) (Singapore), s. 18(4), taken from, surprisingly, the Canadian Criminal Code, s. 4(3), where the concept of 'joint possession' operates as a general doctrine – in Singapore it is peculiar to the Misuse of Drugs Act.

14 F.B. Sayre, 'Criminal Responsibility for the Acts of Another' (1929–30) 43 *Harvard Law Review* 689, at 705. Sayre traces the origins of the principle operating up to the nineteenth century (at least) in a 1578

The nicety of the question, no doubt, was made much nicer by the absence of a clear enough understanding of what the conditions of liability were. Yet Macaulay had, just shy of a century earlier in 1836, crafted a formulation of great clarity for the IPC. It bears reproduction:

> Wherever … in the commission of an offence, or in the consequence of the commission of an offence, a different offence is committed, then whoever by instigation, conspiracy, or aid, was a previous abettor of the first mentioned offence shall be liable to the punishment for the last mentioned offence, *if the last mentioned offence were such as the said abettor knew to be likely to be committed* … in the commission of the first mentioned offence, or in consequence of the commission of the first mentioned offence
> *Illustrations*
> (a) …
> (b) A instigates B to resist a distress. B in consequence, resists that distress. In offering the resistance B voluntarily causes grievous hurt to the officer executing the distress. As B has committed both the offence of resisting legal process and the offence of voluntarily causing grievous hurt, B is liable to cumulative punishment for these offences; and *if A knew B was likely voluntarily to cause grievous hurt* in resisting the distress, A will also be liable to cumulative punishment.[15]

We should be clear that even this provision deviates from the strict requirements of the normal criminal law – for A has neither committed murder, nor has he abetted murder, but he is liable for murder because he abetted robbery knowing that murder was a likely consequence thereof. We also notice, nonetheless, the care with which Macaulay took to confine its operation within narrow and clearly defined limits. It is almost as if Macaulay realised the sacrifice to principle that was being made and the great potential that such a doctrine could go out of hand. We will probably never know why he did not simply discard it, as he did for felony-murder – but, having decided to provide for it, he gave it about as narrow a compass as he thought he could get away with. There must be actual knowledge or forseeability; it is foreseeability of a likelihood and not a mere possibility; it is the entire offence, *actus reus* and *mens rea*, that must be foreseen. The 'constructive' jump, although still significant, is not as large it may first seem. A abets robbery knowing that it is likely to result in the murder of the victim, albeit by another member of his gang. He did not kill the victim, nor did he intend the victim to be killed, but he chose to take part in the robbery and thus helped bring about a situation which he knew would be likely to result in the murder of the victim. Macaulay defined murder in the same original draft of the IPC as causing death with the intention of causing death or the knowledge that death was likely.[16] Close enough to be tolerable, some would think – the *mens rea* (knowledge of likelihood of death) at least is identical. It does not solve all the problems which will necessarily attend the choice of preserving or introducing constructive criminal liability – for example, there is still the need to decide whether

note by Plowden, quoted in *ibid.*, at 698, n. 37, which appeared to be based on 'natural' consequences – that is, liability on the basis of mere causation.

15 Macaulay's draft Code, cl. 98 (emphasis added). For illustration (a), see above at 155.

16 This is the result of Macaulay's draft Code's definition of murder as voluntarily causing death (cls. 294 and 295) and of 'voluntarily' as having either an intention to cause death or the knowledge that death was likely to be caused (cl. 26). Those who came after him took the word 'voluntary' out of the definition of murder (IPC, s. 300) and altered the definition of 'voluntarily' to also include the apparently objective state of having 'reason to believe' (IPC, s. 39). Both changes have caused untold mischief – but that is another story. See Chapter 3 of this volume (N. Morgan, 'The Fault Elements of Offences').

or not a particular deviation from what was foreseen is to be considered as material or merely technical. But perhaps of all the formulations that are on the table, this is the least evil of them all.

PEACOCK'S PERPLEXING PROVISIONS

Regrettably, Macaulay's simple and sensible scheme never saw the light of day.[17] Another committee of rather more cautious and traditional legal specialists, headed by Sir Barnes Peacock, Chief Justice of the Calcutta High Court, worked Macaulay's draft over.[18] We may never know for certain why the committee did not simply preserve Macaulay's carefully crafted provision. What was in fact done continues to this day to confound IPC jurisdictions which have had to live with the committee's handiwork ever since. Essentially Peacock and company did two things. First, they drew a distinction between the liability of the abettor for a different 'act' being done and for a different 'effect' being caused. The two distinct regimes in the IPC should now be set out:

> Section 111. When an act is abetted and *a different act is done*, the abettor is liable for the act done, in the same manner, and to the same extent, as if he had directly abetted it.
> Provided the act done was a *probable consequence* of the abetment, and was committed under the influence of the instigation, or with the aid or in pursuance of the conspiracy which constituted the abetment
> ...
> Section 113. When an act is abetted with the intention on the part of the abettor of causing a particular effect, and an act for which the abettor is liable in consequence of the abetment causes *a different effect* from that intended by the abettor, the abettor is liable for the effect caused, in the same manner, and to the same extent, as if he had abetted the act with the intention of causing that effect, provided he *knew that the act abetted was likely to cause that effect.*[19]

What is immediately apparent is the different criterion of liability for a 'different act' being done (exemplified by the robbery-murder scenario) and for a 'different effect' being caused (exemplified by the assault-murder situation). Different-act liability is to be on the basis of 'probable consequences' – the plain meaning being that which is objectively foreseeable as being likely to

17 Nor did the long interval between 1838, when Macaulay produced the draft Code, and 1860, when the IPC was enacted, allow the legal establishment to catch up with him. J.F. Stephen, quoted in G.O. Trevelyan, *The Life and Letters of Lord Macaulay* (London: Longmans, 1876), perceptively noted that 'Lord Macaulay's great work was far too daring and original to be accepted at once', or perhaps, in the context at hand, at all.

18 J.F. Stephen, *A History of the Criminal Law of England* (vol. 2) (London: Macmillan and Co, 1883) 299, said that Peacock and his team conducted a 'minutely careful and elaborate revision' of Macaulay's draft – minute and elaborate, yes, but whether there was enough care is something which is highly contestable. Surprisingly, it was Macaulay, who had limited experience as a practising lawyer, whose instincts have stood the test of time, and not those of the lawyers of his time. The ludicrous judgment of the legal fraternity on Macaulay's draft is perhaps expressed in an obituary in the *Law Times*, 7 January 1860, 184:

> All hope of Macaulay as a lawyer ... was over as soon as his code was seen. These remarks may appear severe, but they are not wholly out of place or beyond the mark. His penal code ... was found, when published, to be wholly unpractical and impracticable; it might be admired at a distance, but it could not be obeyed; it would not work.

19 Emphasis added.

happen.[20] However, different-effect liability is to be governed by a different rule – that which the abettor actually knew to be likely to happen.

I doubt very much if anyone will ever be able to come up with a sensible reason why an abettor's liability for something he did not intend should be different just because a different act as opposed to a different effect happens.[21] So what really did Peacock have in mind? I do not believe a fully satisfactory account is possible. My guess is that this practical man saw immediately that Macaulay's conceptually pure draft did not comport with what was then the common law – which Sayre demonstrated as having a 'probable consequences' formulation. If conformity with the prevailing common law was what was intended, then it would have been simple enough to effect a suitable amendment to Macaulay's draft by replacing knowledge of likelihood with probable consequences – which was apparently what another Chief Justice, Sir Samuel Griffith, of Queensland and then Australia, did when he drafted his influential criminal code.[22] It is tempting to try to speculate why this far simpler and more logical route was not taken. Perhaps there was dissention within the ranks and an expedient but illogical course was taken, as is not uncommon in political compromises. That which King Solomon threatened – to divide the proverbial baby into two – did in fact come to pass.[23]

Messrs Peacock and others did one other thing – and this was to plague generations of jurists and academics around the world. They inserted s. 34 into the IPC:

> When a criminal act is done by several persons, [in furtherance of the common intention of all,] each of such persons is liable for that act in the same manner as if the act were done by him alone.[24]

There is much evidence that this provision, both before and after the addition of that fateful phrase 'in furtherance of the common intention of all', was never meant to have anything to do with

---

20 A very early commentary on the IPC contains this terse comment on s. 111: 'It is not, it seems, necessary that the abettor should know it to be a probable consequence': W. Morgan and A.C. McPherson, *The Indian Penal Code with Notes* (Calcutta: G.C. Hay and Co, 1861) 91. After the authors discuss s. 113, they simply conclude that 'the illustrations shew clearly the distinct operation of this section and section 111': *ibid.*, at 92.

21 The Peacock variation is the only instance where this dichotomy is employed.

22 Griffiths put it this way, in cl. 10 of his draft, enacted as Criminal Code Act of 1899 (Queensland), s. 8:

> When two or more persons form a common intention to prosecute an unlawful purpose in conjunction with one another, and in prosecution of such purpose an offence is committed of such nature that its commission was a probable consequence of the prosecution of such purpose, each of them is deemed to be have committed the offence.

Presumably, Griffiths too could make neither head nor tail out of Peacock's compromise. See the collection of historical documents available online at http://ozcase.library.qut.edu.au/qhlc/criminal_code.jsp (last accessed 17 February 2011).

23 One is also tempted to see a very similar dynamic driving the infamous alternative definition of murder under the third limb of IPC, s. 300 – probably another Peacock compromise. Macaulay's definition was profound, but too pure – requiring either an intention to cause death or knowledge that it was likely. English common law was still romancing with felony-murder. So Peacock abolished felony-murder in general, but preserved a specific form of it in the third limb of IPC, s. 300 – where the 'felony' is intentionally causing hurt, any hurt.

24 Macaulay's draft did not have any provision resembling this and, of course, never employed the term 'common intention'.

liability for offences committed beyond the common intention of the parties.[25] After replacing Macaulay's provision with the logically and practically incoherent double standard in ss. 111 and 113, it is barely conceivable that these legal specialists would now muddy the waters even further by including another provision to cover very similar ground, but without any clarity as to what the basis of liability should be. Perhaps then the subsequent inclusion of the phrase 'in furtherance of the common intention of all' reflected a legislative wish that s. 34 ought to embark on the business of constructing crimes not within the common intention of all? Unfortunately for this theory, the evidence is quite the opposite;[26] the inclusion was apparently to make it clear that liability covered only to the extent of the common intention and no further, and not to extend liability beyond what was commonly intended in order to cover criminal acts which were nonetheless committed 'in furtherance' of the common intention. How indeed can something be in furtherance of the common (criminal) intention, but not part of it?

Be that as it may, 'some things that should not have been forgotten were lost'[27] and somewhere along the way someone imagined more than a linguistic connection between 'common intention' in s. 34 and 'common purpose' in the common law.[28] There were, and remains, jurisdictional differences in attitude towards s. 34. In India and Malaysia, there appears to be conflicting *dicta* about whether s. 34 encompasses liability for crimes not commonly intended.[29] But in both these jurisdictions, although the point never seems to have been properly argued, there is much evidence that the courts there do not normally regard s. 34 as a means to extend liability to crimes not commonly intended.[30] In Singapore, however, s. 34 and the 'doctrine of common intention' proved irresistibly attractive to prosecutors, who began to use it for constructive purposes, practically to the exclusion of ss. 111 and 113.

Peacock's decision to replace Macaulay's single regime to rule them all with two towers of shaky construction was inexcusable, but perhaps the requisitioning of s. 34 and its 'common

25 See Gillian Douglas, 'Joint Liability in the Penal Code' (1983) 25 *Malaya Law Review* 259. Essentially, IPC, s. 35 seems to say that in the context of a JCE, a confederate is liable for collateral crimes only if he possesses the 'knowledge and intention' necessary for the commission of the collateral crime. The Singapore Court of Appeal disagreed with this reading of s. 34 in *Lee Chez Kee*, above n. 7. Given that the court also decided that s. 34 throws the net of liability no further than s. 113 (as we shall see), it is probably not worth our while looking into the correctness of this holding. This is mildly regrettable in that should a future court decide to decouple s. 34 and s. 113, the need to decide what s. 34 means arises again.

26 See my own 'Common Intention and the Enterprise of Constructing Criminal Liability' [1999] *Singapore Journal of Legal Studies* 494, at 514. The phrase was apparently meant to embody an early Indian decision which held that liability went only so far as what the confederate consented or assented to.

27 P. Boyens, P. Jackson and F. Walsh, *The Lord of the Rings: The Fellowship of the Ring* (transcript), available online at http://www.council-of-elrond.com/fotrse.html (last accessed 17 February 2011).

28 Griffith's association, in the Queensland Code discussed above, between 'common intention' and probable consequences is perhaps an early example of this.

29 See the Singapore Court of Appeal's almost despairing analysis of the Indian (which did not offer 'much assistance') and Malaysian cases (which did not yield a 'convincing account') in *Lee Chez Kee v. PP*, above n. 7, at paras. [182]–[187]. Malaysia and Singapore have adopted the IPC almost in its entirety.

30 The *dicta* is legion, but for a recent example, the Malaysian Federal Court decision in *Krishna Rao a/l Gurumurthi v. PP* [2009] 3 MLJ 643, at para. [62], declared:

> For a charge premised on common intention to succeed it is essential for the prosecution to establish by evidence, direct or circumstantial, that there was *a plan or meeting of mind of all the accused persons to commit the offence for which they are charged* with the aid of s 34 … (Emphasis added)

The Indian Supreme Court pronounced to much the same effect in *Komal v. State of Madhya Pradesh* AIR 2009 SC 1958, at para. [7].

intention' for a third source of liability was not entirely or even substantially the fault of either Peacock or the movers of the subsequent amendment. It is to the uncertain fortunes of 'common intention' as an unfortunate basis of constructive liability that we now turn.

SINGAPORE SWING

In the ensuing discussion, all references to the 'Penal Code' are to the Singapore Code, although it should be noted that its provisions on the present subject at hand are identical in numbering and wording to those found in the IPC. If the reported decisions of the Singapore courts are anything to go by, no one seemed to have been aware of the possibility of constructive liability for JCEs until about half a century after the advent of the Penal Code in Singapore. When the matter did arise for consideration in 1936, it was not in the context of s. 111 or 113, but of common intention under s. 34. The Court of Criminal Appeal of the Straits Settlements, in a classic robbery-murder situation in *R. v. Vincent Banka*,[31] ruled decisively in favour of an early Burmese decision that liability for murder was made out only where the common intention was not only to rob, but to kill if necessary. The prevailing English common law doctrine of 'common design' was understandably pressed upon the court, but it was rejected because 'decisions in England have gone further than decisions in India or in this Colony, under the more restricted provisions of s. 34 of the Penal Code, could possibly go'. It was more than a little curious that s. 111 was never raised or even mentioned by the prosecutor or the court, for one might have thought that the doctrine of 'probable consequences' therein clearly embraced the English common law doctrine of common design. This exclusive focus on 'common intention' in the context of JCE liability was to set the tone for judicial and legal discourse in 'the Colony' and then 'the Republic' of Singapore.

When the same court, a few months later in *R. v. Chhui Yi*,[32] attempted to 'clarify' the requirements of common intention liability, it said that the earlier decision 'does not, of course, mean that, in the case of murder, there need have been a common intention actually to kill; but there must have been a common intention to do any of the acts which are described in sections 299 and 300 of the Penal Code and the doing of which, if death in fact results, amounts to murder'. We reap what we sow for ignoring s. 113, which did seem to capture a situation where the common intention is only to wound (and not to kill) – the illustration is very clear in that even where the JCE is to cause grievous hurt, the confederate is not liable for murder unless he 'knew that the grievous hurt abetted was likely to cause death'. Why should 'common intention', in an identical situation, require any less? That said, the reported decisions do not reveal any clear instance of the court finding a confederate liable for murder where there was no knowledge of the likelihood of death.

There matters rested for another 36 years. Then in 1972 the sensational murder trial of *Wong Mimi v. PP*,[33] eventually to be the first woman in Singapore to suffer execution, produced a decision which plagues Singapore jurisprudence to this day. Although it appeared to have been accepted by all the trial and appellate judges that Mimi and her husband possessed nothing less than a common intention to kill, the Court of Appeal uttered these fateful words:

31 [1936] MLJ 53. Singapore was then part of the legal entity called the Straits Settlements which was disbanded after the Second World War.

32 [1936] MLJ 142. The three-judge bench had only one judge in common – Whitley C.J., then J., in *Vincent Banka*, *ibid.*

33 [1971–3] SLR(R) 412.

> The intention … of the actual doer … must be distinguished from the common intention of the doer and his confederates. It may be identical … or it may not. Where it is not identical … it must be nevertheless consistent with the carrying out of the common intention …[34]

It is not an easy decision to understand at almost any level one would care to look. The court had clearly accepted the confession of the confederate that he had partaken in a plan to kill the victim, so the issue of constructing liability for murder did not arise. It remains a mystery why the court felt that it should pronounce on situations where there was no common intention to kill. That said, the court then adopted the language of 'consistency' as a basis for constructive liability for murder. The problem with this is of course that where there is neither an explicit nor implicit common intention to kill, should silence be treated as being consistent or inconsistent with the JCE? Apart from possessing the *mens rea* necessary to make the confederate part of the JCE, the 'consistency' rule tells us nothing about what extra bit of *mens rea* he must possess in order to be guilty of the murder which he did not himself commit. Clearly, according to the court in *Wong Mimi* at least, it need not be an intention to kill. But what is indeed required by 'consistency' spans an entire spectrum of *mens rea* less reprehensible than an intention to kill. Is it knowledge or negligence; and must those states of mind be with respect to death, serious injury or just any injury; or could it be a form of strict liability in which, as a subsequent court proposed, liability for murder is based solely on whether or not the actual murderer thought that he was killing in order to carry out the JCE? Astonishingly, until very recently, the Singapore courts consistently avoided explaining what *Wong Mimi* meant, choosing instead to say that the law was clear and then to apply whatever unspoken standard the court in that particular case was operating on.[35]

Curiously, *Wong Mimi* neither cited nor discussed *Vincent Banka, Chhui Yi* or the common law. Instead it drew inspiration from two Indian Privy Council decisions, both of which had nothing to do with a situation where a confederate of the actual murderer did not possess an intention to kill if necessary. One concerned an odd situation where two persons independently possessed an intention to kill the same victim, each not realising the intent of the other, with the Privy Council holding that there was in the event no 'common' intention.[36] The other involved the liability of a confederate playing the role of a look-out in an armed robbery where the JCE clearly encompassed the eventuality of death.[37] It does appear that the Singapore court had created the 'consistency' criterion out of thin air.

The court did however offer a tantalising 'illustration':

> Thus if A and B form a common intention to cause injury to C with a knife and A holds C while B stabs C deliberately in the region of the heart and the stab wound is sufficient in the ordinary course of nature to cause death, B is clearly guilty of murder. Applying s 34 it is also clear that B's act in stabbing C is in furtherance of the common intention to cause injury to C with a knife because B's act is clearly consistent with the carrying out of that common intention and as their 'criminal act', *ie* that unity of criminal behaviour, resulted in the criminal offence of murder punishable under s 302, A is also guilty of murder.[38]

---

34 *Ibid.*, at para. [25].

35 I discussed this in detail in 'Common Intention and the Enterprise of Constructing Criminal Liability', above n. 26, at 497–501.

36 *Mahbub Shah v. Emperor* AIR 1945 PC 118.

37 *Barendra Kumar Ghosh v. Emperor* AIR 1925 PC 1.

38 Above n. 33, at para. [25].

The astute reader will notice that the factual scenario the court gave is identical to the illustration to s. 113. That provision is very clear in that even if the common intention was to cause grievous (and not just any) hurt, the confederate is not liable for murder unless he actually believes that death will be a likely result. It is, in my view, inconceivable that had the court been sufficiently aware of s. 113 and its illustration, it would still have interpreted s. 34 in the way it did: why forsake a clear and explicit standard in favour of one which is neither?

Wong Mimi was to spark off a golden age of 'common intention' prosecutions in Singapore. Just why the prosecution did not go for a charge under ss. 111 and 113 remains a mystery. Perhaps those in the prosecutorial service were simply unaware of these two provisions, just as the court in *Wong Mimi* appeared to have been. Perhaps also those who were aware of those provisions consciously chose to use s. 34 in the hope that common intention might spread the net of liability for murder wider than the abetment provisions would. Thus, for, coincidentally, another 36 years, a curious curial dance was performed with prosecutors pressing common intention upon the courts, and the courts almost always refusing to make it clear what 'consistency' meant – and on the one occasion where a courageous judge did tackle the question head-on, the court opted for strict liability[39] – it did not matter what the confederate thought or should have thought beyond joining the criminal enterprise – common intention liability is imputed to him if the actual doer thought that he killed in order to carry out the joint enterprise.

The Singapore Court of Appeal eventually took the bull by the horns in 2008 in a decision of magisterial sweep in *Lee Chez Kee*.[40] It was a breathtaking piece of housekeeping and in one courageous stroke achieved two significant things: first, it unified the criterion of liability in all the major provisions of the Code prescribing JCE liability – s. 34's common intention, s. 111's probable consequences, s. 113's knowledge of likelihood and even s. 149's common object; and, secondly, it declared that for all these provisions, the touchstone of liability was actual knowledge, or foreseeability, of the offence which was not within the compass of the JCE.

The decision was as correct as it was bold. Two of the four provisions – ss. 113 and 149 – explicitly require actual knowledge of the likelihood of the collateral offence occurring. Section 111 apparently has an objective foreseeability criterion, while s. 34 yields no obvious standard. The choice of actual knowledge over an objective standard is enlightened and very much in line with the philosophy that if we must depart from the usual norms of criminal responsibility, let us do it as parsimoniously as possible. The boldness of it all is demonstrated in the court's willingness to override the plain, and perhaps only possible, meaning of s. 111. 'Probable consequences' cannot by the usual tools of statutory interpretation mean actual knowledge, especially when Peacock took pains to say exactly that in s. 113. Nor does that phrase mean actual knowledge in the jurisdictions which employ it – notably, the Griffith-inspired criminal codes of Australia and elsewhere. The court was, to its credit, not phased. Although the court did not so express it, the refusal to give 'probable consequences' its only semantically legitimate meaning is perhaps best justified by the argument from constitutional equality[41] – the s. 111/s. 113 bifurcation simply has no rational basis

39 *PP v. Too Yin Sheong* [1998] SGHC 286. Maddeningly, the judgment on appeal totally ignored this obviously novel and provocative idea: [1998] 3 SLR(R) 994.

40 Above n. 7. There has been rich academic interest: S. Yeo, 'Common Intention in the Indian Penal Code: Insights From Singapore' (2008) 50 *Journal of the Indian Law Institute* 640; K. Amirthalingam, 'Clarifying Common Intention and Interpreting Section 34: Should There Be a Threshold of Blameworthiness for the Death Penalty' [2008] *Singapore Journal of Legal Studies* 435; N.Y. Khng and S. Chen, 'Recent Developments in Common Intention: *Lee Chez Kee v PP*' [2009] 21 *Singapore Academy of Law Journal* 557.

41 Constitution of the Republic of Singapore, Art. 12, which guarantees 'equal protection of the law'. In line with constitutional regimes the world over, different treatment must at least have a rational basis:

or nexus, and the 'discrimination' must be erased. So s. 111 has to be 'read up' to actual knowledge to correct the imbalance. The decision was also courageous in its decisive interpretation of s. 34's 'furtherance' and *Wong Mimi's* 'consistency' to require actual knowledge of the likelihood of the collateral offence occurring. There were a host of other more liability-expansive alternatives to choose from.

Further afield, in the subjective versus objective foreseeability war that is being waged around the world, the tide has perhaps turned, although the battle is not yet won. Objective foreseeability is still very much the standard in the Griffith Codes of Australia, but the High Court of Australia has declared that the rival subjective foreseeability is the standard for the Australian common law.[42] In Canada, an explicit objective foreseeability standard for JCE liability was held to be unconstitutional and had to be read up to require subjective foreseeabilty, but only where the collateral offence is murder.[43] In the US, the *Pinkerton v. US*[44] doctrine in federal criminal law still goes by the standard of what can be 'reasonably foreseen as a necessary or natural consequence of the unlawful agreement', although the influential Model Penal Code and most states reject any sort of JCE liability altogether.[45] The English common law has moved decidedly in favour of subjective foreseeability.[46] Significantly, the emerging international criminal concept of JCE liability seems to have adopted the criterion of actual foreseeability.[47] The Singapore court's choice of subjective foresight does appear to put Singapore on the winning side of the battle.

Indeed, we seem to have come full circle. If s. 113 is to be the governing standard for all situations of liability for JCEs, then more than a century of tampering with Macaulay's original draft provision by both the legislature and the courts is to be reversed. The result is that Macaulay's original formulation of JCE liability is now the only one to be used, whether there is common intention or not, whether it is a different act or a different effect. And that is as it should be.

Ong Ah Chuan v. PP [1981] AC 648.

42 *McAuliffe v. R.* [1995] HCA 37. The High Court described the evolution of the doctrine from being an objective to a subjective one. The surreal result is that the same court has to apply the subjective test for common law jurisdictions and the objective test when hearing appeals from the Griffith Code jurisdictions.

43 *R. v. Sit* [1991] 3 SCR 124. Canadian Criminal Code, s. 21(2), provides:

> Where two or more persons form an intention in common to carry out an unlawful purpose and to assist each other therein and any one of them, in carrying out the common purpose, commits an offence, each of them who knew or ought to have known that the commission of the offence would be a probable consequence of carrying out the common purpose is a party to that offence.

The result of Supreme Court jurisprudence is that where the collateral crime is murder, and attempted murder, the test of subject foresight (of probable consequences) applies, but for all other collateral crimes, objective foreseeability is sufficient.

44 328 US 640 (1946).

45 For an interesting account in the context of murder, see M.A. Pauley, 'The *Pinkerton* Doctrine and Murder' (2005–6) 4 *Pierce Law Review* 1, which surprisingly argues in favour of *Pinkerton*'s objective foreseeability standard even for murder. The author himself admits that academic commentary is 'overwhelmingly negative'.

46 *R. v. Powell; R. v. English* (1999) 1 AC 1.

47 *Prosecutor v. Tadić*, Appeals Chamber Decision, 15 July 1999, IT-94-1-A, 99:

> It should be noted that more than negligence is required. What is required is a state of mind in which a person, although he did not intend to bring about a certain result, was aware that the actions of the group were most likely to lead to that result but nevertheless willingly took that risk.

This version of joint enterprise liability was, perhaps controversially, held to be no less than customary international law.

UNFINISHED BUSINESS

Or at least that is what one hopes the *Lee Chez Kee* decision has done for Singapore. Because of the court's focus on the question of whether JCE liability is to be based on intention, actual or objective foreseeability or otherwise, it did not seem to have addressed explicitly what is to be done with the other elements which are necessary for liability. It is to these potential problems that we now turn.

'In Furtherance of' versus 'In the Course of'

It is now clear that actual foresight of the collateral crime is the key – but is it the only one? Does anything remain of the apparent need for the collateral crime to have been 'in furtherance of' the crime commonly intended, or does it suffice if the collateral crime was committed 'in the course of' the JCE? A simple example is this: two persons combine to hold up a store – the plan being to get the money and then to escape as quickly as possible. One of the them knows that the other bears a grudge against the storekeeper and foresees that, given an opportunity, the person bearing the grudge might, or is likely to, try to kill the storekeeper, even if resistance is not offered. That is not in the plan, and indeed any attempt by the other person to kill the storekeeper would be inconsistent with the common intention to rob and get away quickly. Just as that which was done by one of them in furtherance of the joint enterprise need not have been foreseen, that which was foreseen need not necessarily be in furtherance of the JCE. This was perhaps the kind of problem that Lord Mustill sensed in *Powell and English* when he considered the example of a situation 'where S foresees that P may go too far; sincerely wishes that he will not, and makes this plain to P; and yet goes ahead, either because he hopes for the best, or because P is an overbearing character, or for some other reason'.[48] The House of Lords seems to have been of the view that although the collateral crime was contrary to the common criminal purpose, that did not prevent the confederate from being liable because there was 'foresight of the crime as *a possible incident* of the common unlawful purpose'.

We do not know what the Singapore Court of Appeal would have said if this issue had been raised squarely before it. There is language that might indicate that it would have decided differently – the collateral crime must not only be foreseen, but must also have been foreseen as something done in furtherance of the common criminal intention:

> [T]he secondary offender must subjectively know that one in his party *may likely commit* the criminal act constituting the collateral offence in furtherance of the common intention of carrying out the primary offence.[49]

So our grudge murderer and Lord Mustill's overbearing murderer who went 'too far' could not have been foreseen to have killed 'in furtherance of' the common criminal enterprise. On the other hand, there is also evidence that the court was moved by 'the universal truth and principles that stand independent from the static hard law which is etched onto our statutory material'.[50]

---

48 Above n. 46, at 11.

49 Above n. 7, at para. [236] (emphasis in the original).

50 Ibid., at para. [250]. As the discussion hopes to demonstrate, there is anything but a universal understanding of joint enterprise liability – witness the clumsy and unconvincing attempts by the International Criminal Tribunal for the former Yugoslavia to create such a supposedly universal concept for the purposes of what it apparently thinks is customary international law: Tadić, above n. 47; Prosecutor v. Karadžić, Appeals

We do not know if this 'universality' extended only so far as the objective versus subjective foresight issue or if it was meant to go further than that. There is also some indication that the drafters of the Penal Code[51] did not envisage liability to go as far as the modern common law of England. Section 34 requires, of course, the collateral crime to have been done 'in furtherance of the common intention'. More tellingly, s. 111 demands not only that the collateral crime be a 'probable consequence' but also that it was 'committed under the influence of the instigation, or with the aid or in pursuance of the conspiracy'. The three illustrations to s. 111 seem to bear out the proposition that mere foreseeability is not enough. The positive illustrations (a) and (c) are both situations where the collateral crime furthered the JCE – so there is liability if they were foreseen. The negative illustration (b) is this:

> *A* instigates *B* to burn *Z*'s house. *B* sets fire to the house, and at the same time commits theft of property there. *A*, though guilty of abetting the burning of the house, is not guilty of abetting the theft; for the theft was a distinct act, and not a probable consequence of the burning.

Notice that if the yardstick had been a 'free-standing' foreseeability criterion, then A would still be liable for the collateral theft if it could have been foreseen. But the illustration is categorical in that there is to be no liability here, foreseeable or not – the collateral theft was simply a 'distinct act', meaning, I would suggest, something which did not or was not intended to further the common criminal enterprise. If even more evidence were needed, we could turn to the doctrine of 'common object' in s. 149, which stipulates that members of an unlawful assembly are liable only for collateral acts 'such as the members of that assembly knew to be likely to be committed *in prosecution of* that [common criminal] object'.

If my analysis is correct, then the Singapore Court of Appeal's unified theory of joint enterprise criminal liability in the Penal Code is not the same as that which seems to now govern the English common law. The common law would appear to have no requirement that the collateral crime be committed in order to further the common criminal enterprise, but the Penal Code would.

Is the Code or the prevailing common law superior? This is perhaps the most difficult question of all. At the end of the day, it all depends on how expansive we want our constructive liability to be. There is no longer a question of principle here, for we are already on unprincipled ground. Once we embark on the slippery slope of constructive criminality, there is no principled point at which we can say 'thus far and no further'. We could follow the logic of the general principles of criminal liability and say that if we must make an exception, then let it be as small as possible and tied very closely to the joint enterprise,[52] or we could follow the logic of the exception and say that if the collateral crime is foreseen, then it should not matter if it was done in order to further the joint enterprise or for some other extraneous reason.[53]

Chamber Decision, 25 June 2009, IT-95-5/18-AR72.4. The same ugly question is now pending before the Extraordinary Chambers in the Courts of Cambodia (ECCC): see Ieng Sary's appeal filed on 18 January 2010 and the various subsequent replies and responses, available on the ECCC website: http://www.eccc.gov.kh/english/default.aspx (last accessed 17 February 2011).

51 It is interesting that Macaulay's draft Code, cl. 98, would have opted for Lord Mustill's position with its express inclusion of the phrase 'in consequence of'. Peacock's version is discussed in the text.

52 As apparently Macaulay and, to a lesser extent, Peacock did.

53 As apparently the House of Lords currently thinks.

Probability versus Possibility

Unfortunately, our problems have only just begun. The confederate must have actually foreseen something, but with what conviction must he have believed that the collateral crime will or might happen? Bloody battles are being fought in *fora* as varied as the High Court of Australia and the International Criminal Tribunal for Yugoslavia (ICTY) over whether it ought to be foresight of a possibility, albeit a significant or 'real' one, or whether it has to be the higher standard of foresight of a probability, or whether it ought to be the even stricter requirement of foresight of a near-certainty. The difference between these alternatives is probably best illustrated by the different standards of proof in the law of evidence. Foresight of a real possibility is like entertaining a reasonable doubt, while belief of a probability is like the civil burden of belief that something is more likely than not to have happened. Belief to a near-certainty is like the criminal standard of belief beyond a reasonable doubt.

The lowest standard of foresight of a real possibility appears to be the governing standard in the English and Australian common law, and apparently in the ICTY.[54] Once again, because of the Singapore Court of Appeal's concentration on the issue of subjective versus objective foresight, it did not clearly state a position with respect to the degree of conviction the confederate must have. On the one hand, the court seemed to quote with approval the common law formulations of foresight of a real possibility such as 'might kill' or 'might commit murder'.[55] But again we do not know if the common law was approved of only in the context of the subjective versus objective foresight issue or more generally. On the other hand, the court also appeals to the Penal Code provisions which are clearly partial to the alternative formulation of foresight of a probability or likelihood of the collateral offence taking place. Section 111 speaks of 'probable consequences' and both ss. 113 and 149 of the collateral offence being 'likely' to happen.[56] This is the kind of formulation which was rejected, most recently in the ICTY, in favour of the lower standard of 'possible' consequence. The Singapore Court of Appeal in the end seems to settle for something like a hybrid of the two: 'the secondary offender must subjectively know that one in his party *may likely* commit the criminal act constituting the collateral offence'.[57] 'May' comes from the common law and 'likely' from the Code. To be fair, the court was not addressing this particular matter and, when it does, it is likely that the Penal Code's option for foresight of a probability or likelihood will be recognised. The highest possible standard – that of foresight to a near-certainty – is the suggestion of Justice Michael Kirkby, who had, until his recent retirement, been leading a remarkable one-person crusade in the High Court of Australia to curb the common purpose doctrine.[58]

Like the previous issue, it is again impossible to say as a matter of principle who is right and who is wrong. Submissions before the ICTY reveal that there is nowhere near any sort of unanimity amongst different jurisdictions around the world.[59] The battlelines are likely to be drawn, yet again, between those who want a more restrictive doctrine of constructive liability, for

54 *McAuliffe*, above n. 42 (High Court of Australia); *Powell and English*, above n. 46 (House of Lords); *Karadžić*, above n. 50 (ICTY).

55 *Lee Chez Kee*, above n. 7, at paras. [248]–[249].

56 *Ibid.*, at paras. [238]–[247].

57 *Ibid.*, at para. [253(d)] (emphasis in the original).

58 *Clayton v. R* [2006] HCA 58, at paras. [121]–[126], where Judge Kirby adopted a suggestion by J.C. Smith ('Criminal Liability of Accessories: Law and Law Reform' (1997) 113 *Law Quarterly Review* 453) that the standard should be one of virtual certainty.

59 Filed 25 May 2009, something the Appeals Chamber conveniently ignored, concentrating instead on its own pronouncements.

whom only knowledge to a likelihood will suffice, and those who desire a more expansive reach, for whom foreseeability of a possibility will do.

Death versus Serious Injury versus Any Injury

Despite the general applicability of JCE liability to any offence whatsoever, experience over almost all jurisdictions shows that almost all such prosecutions concern only murder. Murder, both at common law and under the IPC, is not just killing with an intention to kill or knowledge that death was likely. There is a constructive counterpart – at common law, an intention to cause grievous bodily harm (GBH) is sufficient,[60] and under the IPC, the intention to cause just any harm will do, as long as the injury was (objectively) 'sufficient in the ordinary course of nature to cause death'.[61] In other words, this variety of murder requires no contemplation of the possibility or probability of death at all. The question is whether this should be carried over into JCE liability for murder.

The common law decisions reveal that there is, to a degree, some sort of importation of the *mens rea* for regular murder into common purpose liability for murder. What is clear is that the confederate need only have foreseen the intentional infliction of GBH, and not necessarily the causation of death. What is not so clear is whether the confederate must also have foreseen death. Lord Hutton's formulation in *Powell and English* is this:

> … it is sufficient to found a conviction for murder for a secondary party *to have realised* that in the course of the joint enterprise the primary party *might kill* with intent to do so or with intent to cause grievous bodily harm.[62]

This seems to say that the confederate must have realised that the intended GBH 'might kill'. On the other hand, there are pronouncements like that of Lord Brown of Eaton-under-Heywood in *R. v. Rahman* which sound like this:

> By the *same token* that if someone intentionally inflicts [GBH] he takes the risk that his actions may kill, whereby he will be held liable for murder, so too if he participates in a venture foreseeing that another may act so as to commit murder, *he takes the risk that in that way also* he may himself become guilty of murder.[63]

If this is so, then just as the actual doer need only have intended GBH and need not have any inkling of death whatsoever, so the confederate need only have foreseen GBH and not necessarily death.

Interestingly, this very modern problem was, if we remember, anticipated in the old Straits Settlements decision of *Chhui Yi,*[64] where the court in Singapore seems to have held that, just as the primary offender need only have intended to cause injury (which objectively was sufficient in the ordinary course of nature to cause death), so too is the common intender liable for murder if he intended the joint enterprise to cause such an injury. No contemplation of death was necessary.

---

60 The opportunity to abolish the GBH rule for the common law was lost in *Hyam v. DPP* [1975] 1 AC 55, albeit by a narrow 3:2 majority.

61 The infamous third limb of IPC, s. 300. See above n. 23.

62 Above n. 46, at 27 (emphasis added).

63 [2009] 1 AC 129, para. [54] (emphasis added).

64 Above n. 32.

There is language in the recent decision of *Lee Chez Kee* which might have imported this into the modern rendition of common intention:

> ... it is sufficient, in the case of murder, that the secondary offender knew that one in his party might inflict a bodily injury which was sufficient in the ordinary course of nature to cause death.[65]

Again, this was not an issue squarely before the Singapore Court of Appeal, concentrating as it was on the matter of objective or subjective foreseeability or otherwise. Fortunately (or unfortunately, depending on where one stands on this issue), the problem is not so easily resolved under the Penal Code. The reason is that s. 113 contains an illustration which appears to be directly on point:

> A instigates B to cause grievous hurt to Z. B, in consequence of the instigation, causes grievous hurt to Z. Z dies in consequence. Here, *if A knew that the grievous hurt abetted was likely to cause death*, A is liable to be punished with the punishment provided for murder.[66]

Here is a JCE not just to cause any injury but grievous hurt, a rough Penal Code equivalent of the common law GBH. The confederate is to be liable for murder only if he knew that death was a likely consequence. Mere foreseeabilty, or even the intent to cause grievous hurt, is not enough. There is to be no importation of constructive murder into joint liability and this patently contradicts the suggestion to the contrary in both *Chhui Yi* and *Lee Chez Kee*. If indeed the project of the Singapore Court of Appeal was to harmonise common intention with s. 113, then it would not do to prescribe a lesser requirement for common intention under s. 34.

Again, we address the underlying question of who is right and who is wrong. The apparent common law position has the appeal of simplicity – sauce for the goose is sauce for the gander. But are the goose and the gander of the same species at all? The person who intentionally injures another (seriously, in the context of the common law) with intent 'takes the risk' of being guilty of murder if the victim dies. However, the confederate does not cause the injury, but merely foresees it to happen – there is no compelling reason why he too must 'take the risk' of being guilty of murder. More strikingly, the illustration to s. 113 also absolves the confederate where the common intention is to cause grievous hurt. This must flow from the realisation that constructive murder is in essence an aberration, a departure from principle which must be confined strictly to its core application to the actual doer. A similar philosophy underlies s. 301 of the Penal Code, which provides for the transfer of malice to an unintended victim, but not in the case of constructive murder.[67] Just because one is willing to *independently* construct group liability and liability for murder, it does not necessarily follow that one is also willing to allow them to operate in combination to impose constructive group liability for constructive murder. All this means that we have a choice of whether or not to do it – a choice which the Penal Code seems to have clearly made not to. This reflects an underlying decision to

65 Above n. 7, at para. [236].

66 Emphasis added.

67 IPC, s. 301 reads:

> If a person, by doing anything which he *intends or knows to be likely to cause death*, commits culpable homicide by causing the death of any person, whose death he neither intends nor knows himself to be likely to cause, the culpable homicide committed by the offender is of the description of which it would have been if he had caused the death of the person, whose death he intended or knew himself to be likely to cause. (Emphasis added)

Murder under the third limb of s. 300 is pointedly left out of its operation. For a discussion of s. 300, see Chapter 3 of this volume, above n. 16, at 66–8.

exalt the normal principles of criminal liability with the resulting parsimony in construing exceptions to them. Perhaps there are those who think otherwise, and they would be proceeding according to the 'logic' of the two exceptions, at the expense of the normal principles of criminal liability. Once an unprincipled exception is made, it is not easy to find principled limits to it.

Enigmatic Variations

The central operational problem with the common purpose doctrine in the common law in recent years has been how to deal with a deviation between the collateral offence contemplated and the offence actually committed. On the two occasions on which the House of Lords has had to confront common purpose, it has been with respect to the degree of deviation, which takes the collateral offence out of the reach of the doctrine, or conversely, which does not. While the verbal formula adopted to resolve this was apparently unexceptionable – there must be a 'fundamental' or 'radical' difference – there appears to be little unanimity with respect to when this point is reached.

Lord Hutton's attempts to provide some guidance in *Powell and English* are instructive of the difficulties involved.[68] When the contemplated collateral offence is injury with wooden posts, but the actual injury is caused by knives, that amounts to a fundamental difference and the common purpose doctrine is powerless. Lord Hutton appears to have assumed that wooden posts are not as 'dangerous' as knives, for he also says that if guns had been contemplated but knives were used instead, the picture would have been different. But how is dangerousness to be assessed – in the particular factual context or in isolation? It is not immediately obvious why wooden posts (in general) are less dangerous than knives (in general). Lord Hutton approved of a Northern Irish decision[69] which had exonerated confederates who had contemplated 'knee-capping' with a gun, but the victim was slit in the throat in the event. But he also said that if the actual cause of death was the firing of a gun into the head or body, the matter would have been 'more debatable'. Surely, there is no difference in dangerousness between slitting the throat and firing a gun into the head or body, so is there another criterion? The only possible difference is the kind of weapon used – but why is the identity of the weapon so important?

When the doctrine of common purpose emerged in the House of Lords again in *Rahman*,[70] the confederates had apparently contemplated the infliction of serious injuries with a knife (though not death), but the victim had been killed by a knife thrust that was intended not only to seriously injure but to kill. The House of Lords would have none of this subtlety. There was to be no 'fundamental difference' just because the fatal intent of the actual doer was not contemplated. No apparent regard was had to 'dangerousness', for one might have thought that an injury inflicted with an intention to kill is more likely to kill when compared with one which was inflicted merely to injure and not to kill. Indeed, one detects more than a hint of implicit distaste for, if not disapproval of, the earlier decision to let off the wooden post aggressor.[71] A number of their Lordships in *Rahman* had problems with the Northern Irish decision (approved by Lord Hutton in *Powell and English*) and one could not see why the situation of the use of a gun to shoot at the head or body as opposed

68 Above n. 46, at 28–30.

69 *R. v. Gamble* [1989] NI 268.

70 Above n. 63.

71 Lord Scott of Foscote, *ibid.*, put it most succinctly, at para. [31]:

> … but if parties embark on a punishment exercise that carries with it the foreseeable possibility of death of the victim, the instruments used for that purpose seem to me of much less importance than the purpose itself.

to the contemplated knee-cap was even debatable.[72] The assessment of 'fundamental difference' seemed to have taken place at a very high level of abstraction – to put it bluntly, serious injury was foreseen and serious injury was inflicted. All this would of course have meant that Mr English in the earlier case would not have escaped common purpose liability if the *Rahman* bench had been hearing it.

We simply cannot predict with any degree of conviction what succeeding courts will consider to be a 'fundamental difference'.[73] The English common law seems reluctant to use perhaps the only sensible criterion – that of dangerousness – or, in the case of murder, the degree of risk of death. The confederate 'takes the risk' of what he foresees and factual variations which are at least as dangerous as the scenario he foresaw. Why? One reason seems to be that such refinements would make jury directions too confusing,[74] but I must confess that I have scant sympathy for judges who create a doctrine which requires confusing distinctions to make it work sensibly and then, in order to avoid confusion, reject those distinctions. A more serious objection is the difficulty of the task of assessing the relative dangerousness of the foreseen scenario and what actually occurred. One can imagine situations where it will not be possible to tell, but that does not mean that we discard the test altogether. Where it is insufficiently clear that the factual variation is at least as dangerous as the contemplated one, the result is simply that the common purpose doctrine ought not to operate.

A few months after *Rahman* was decided, the High Court of Australia was faced with a very similar problem in *The Queen v. Keenan*,[75] a decision concerning the probable consequences doctrine of Griffith's Queensland Criminal Code. Here the confederate seems to have known that his party of assailants had brought along a baseball bat to exact revenge. In the course of the attack, one of them took out a gun, the existence of which was apparently unknown to the others, and shot the victim in the spine. The court was split. All the judges, save one, were in favour of a *Rahman*-esque analysis, namely that serious injury was intended and serious injury was suffered. Kirkby J. dissented alone, protesting that the probable consequences doctrine must be more limited than that and:

72 For example, Lord Brown of Eaton-under-Heywood, *ibid.*, at paras. [67]–[68]; Lord Neuberger of Abbotsbury, *ibid.*, at paras. [91]–[93].

73 It is difficult to share the optimism of Lord Bingham of Cornhill when he said in *Rahman*, *ibid.*, at para. [26]:

> I would also reject a subsidiary submission that the judge should have explained to the jury what was meant by 'fundamentally different'. This is not a term of art. It may, or may not, be regarded as a helpful turn of phrase, but its meaning is plain and cannot be misunderstood by a jury [otherwise properly directed].

Obviously, his Lordship thought that a jury would fare much better than some of his brethren on the House of Lords, who seem to have understood what is 'fundamentally different' differently.

74 For example, Lord Bingham of Cornhill, *ibid.*, at para. [24], expressed it in this fashion:

> [T]he law of joint enterprise in a situation such as this is already very complex … the appellants' submission, if accepted, would introduce a new and highly undesirable level of complexity. Given the fluid, fast-moving course of events in incidents such as that which culminated in the killing of the deceased, incidents which are unhappily not rare, it must often be very hard for jurors to make a reliable assessment of what a particular defendant foresaw as likely or possible acts on the part of his associates. It would be even harder, and would border on speculation, to judge what a particular defendant foresaw as the intention with which his associates might perform such acts. It is safer to focus on the defendant's foresight of what an associate might do …

75 [2009] HCA 1.

> … the limit will be reached where the principal offender introduces a gun or a knife where this seriously *escalates the level of risk of violence, the potential of serious injury and the nature of the peril inherent* in the joint enterprise as initially conceived.[76]

Perhaps this was the limiting principle Lord Hutton had sensed in *Powell and English*. It is probably not a coincidence that Kirkby J. alone appears to have been in favour of such a limitation, for he alone had protested against the equivalent common law doctrine of common purpose itself.[77] So it boils down, yet again, to whether or not we like or dislike the doctrine. If we like it, then we have little reason to look for limitations; if we do not, but have to accept that it exists, we will want as little of it as possible.

What does the Penal Code have to say about all this? The Singapore court in *Lee Chez Kee* did not address the issue, saying only that it did 'not think it is necessary for the actual method of execution (in murder) to have been known by the secondary offender'.[78] It reveals nothing about what the court would have done in the wooden post versus knife, or baseball bat versus gun, or intended wounding versus intended death kind of situation. Does 'method of execution' include the sort of weapon or the kind of intent? If and when the court is confronted with this, the provisions of the Penal Code provide some interesting clues about how it is to be resolved. There are several indications that quite a high level of specificity is required. This illustration to s. 111 is telling:

> (a) *A* instigates a child to put poison into the food of *Z*, and gives him poison for that purpose. The child, in consequence of the instigation, by mistake puts the poison into the food of *Y*, which is by the side of that of *Z*. Here, if the child was acting under the influence of *A*'s instigation, *and the act done was under the circumstances a probable consequence of the abetment*, *A* is liable in the same manner, and to the same extent, as if he had instigated the child to put the poison into the food of *Y*.

Here is a deviation we have not yet explored, namely a variation in the identity of the victim. A *Rahman*-esque approach would probably not have produced this illustration. Since A had contemplated (nay, intended) that death be caused, and death was indeed caused, why should it matter who died? Yet the illustration says that A is liable only if the child's mistake and the resulting death of Y (the person killed by mistake) was a probable consequence, that is, it was contemplated as a likely consequence. Foresight of the risk of death in general is not enough. Nor does it seem to matter whether the unforeseen turn of events increased or reduced the risk of death (in general). Is there any reason why the same principle of high specificity should not also apply to a variation in the weapon used or in the intent of the person who used the weapon? If, instead of putting the poison in Z's food, the child takes out a knife and stabs Z in the neck, would A not have to foresee this if he is to be liable?

There is also a similar indication in this illustration to s. 113:

> *A* instigates *B* to cause grievous hurt to *Z*. *B*, *in consequence of the instigation, causes grievous hurt* to *Z*. *Z* dies in consequence. Here, if *A* knew that the grievous hurt abetted was likely to cause death, *A* is liable to be punished with the punishment provided for murder.

76 *Ibid.*, at paras. [59]–[60] (emphasis added).

77 *Clayton v. R.*, above n. 58.

78 Above n. 7, at para. [236].

The grievous hurt caused must be the grievous hurt abetted. So, where the injury abetted is one which is effected by, say, a baseball bat, an injury caused by a gun is not that which was abetted. Similarly, where one abets grievous hurt in the form of knife wounds intended not to kill but to teach the victim a lesson, then a knife wound inflicted in such a manner and with such force that only one with an intent to kill would inflict, it is not 'grievous hurt' which is abetted. *Rahman* and *Keenan* would have probably turned out differently under the Penal Code. There are two other considerations that appear to have impressed the court in *Rahman* which are significantly different for IPC jurisdictions like Singapore. In Singapore, there has not been a jury to confuse for over four decades, and presumably judges would have no problems conceiving of such distinctions. Perhaps more importantly, the option of leaving the relative culpabilities to be determined by the sentencing regime is not available in Singapore because the punishment for murder is mandatory death.[79]

Yet, instinctively, even the clear preference for high specificity and low tolerance of factual variation in the IPC ought to give way (in principle) at some point. There must surely be insignificant variations – the confederate foresees stabbing in the chest, but the actual doer chooses to stab in the neck, or in our illustration to s. 111, the confederate foresees the use of a particular kind of poison, but a different one was used instead. We can craft a criterion along the lines of Kirkby J.'s assessment of dangerousness. But surely the variation in dangerousness is but one factor, albeit perhaps the most important one, in asking this crucial hypothetical question: if the confederate had foreseen the variation, would he still have embarked on the JCE? Where the variation increases the dangerousness of the enterprise, then we are no longer confident that the confederate would have gone ahead anyway.

This was perhaps the implicit basis of Lord Hutton's view that wooden posts are fundamentally different from knives. It would also mean that His Lordship ought not to have hesitated over the kneecapping versus shooting in the head situation – clearly there would be reason to doubt if the confederate would have gone ahead anyway. *Rahman* and *Keenan* would have been decided differently – if Rahman had foreseen that someone might stab with intent to kill, he may well have abandoned the criminal enterprise; if Keenan had been aware that one of his party had a gun with him, there is at least reasonable doubt that he would have persisted in the enterprise. Similarly, quite apart from dangerousness, in our illustration to s. 111, if the confederate had foreseen that the child might harm someone other than the intended victim, he may well have desisted.

This way of dealing with variations might just work if the courts are sufficiently cognisant of two things. First, that the task of trying to work out whether the confederate would have gone ahead if he had known of the variation can be a highly speculative exercise. Quite often we simply do not know. This brings us to the second thing that courts must bear closely in mind: that where we are left in reasonable doubt as to whether or not the confederate would have proceeded notwithstanding foresight of the variation, there is to be no liability for the variation. JCE liability attaches only

---

79 This very significant background difference is best expressed by Lord Scott of Foscote, above n. 63, at para. [32]:

> The circumstances attending upon a murder may cover a very broad spectrum, and, since the abolition of the death penalty and the introduction of specified minimum terms of imprisonment to be served by those on whom the mandatory sentence of life imprisonment is passed, *the degree of culpability and responsibility of those convicted of an unlawful killing can be reflected by the length of that specified minimum term.* This constitutes, in my opinion, a far more satisfactory means of dealing with those whose liability for the unlawful killing is secondary than a rule which would exonerate them from criminal liability on the ground that they did not know or suspect that the primary party was carrying the particular weapon that delivered the fatal blow. (Emphasis added)

when it is beyond reasonable doubt that the confederate would have made nothing of the variation if he had thought about it.

MOVING ON

I am reluctant to prescribe a 'one-size-fits-all' solution for all jurisdictions since the criminal law is, for better or for worse, all too often blown about by the shifting winds of public sentiment and governmental or official calculation of political imperatives.[80] What I will conclude with is my thoughts about what ought to be done with the Singaporean Penal Code, the jurisdiction I know best. No doubt quite a bit of the reasoning might also apply outside of Singapore, but I shall leave the connection to be made by those who might find my reasoning attractive.

I have explained why I remain sceptical about whether there is really a need for an extraordinary head of liability triggered by a JCE.[81] The person who commits the crime is guilty of it, and the person who abets someone else to commit it is guilty of abetment of that crime. Why we need to create something else in order to make the confederate liable for a crime he did not commit or abet is still a mystery to me. If it is group crime and criminal gangs we need to deal with, then they have to be dealt with whether or not a collateral crime is committed in a particular case. We need to deter group crimes and we need to deter more strongly group crimes which bear the risk of collateral injury, whether or not anything actually happens apart from the criminal plan. The one who kills, when the plan is either only to rob or only to cause injury, stands potentially guilty of murder. Those who in some way abetted murder will suffer the consequences thereof. Those who are part of the criminal gang, but who neither killed nor abetted the killing, do not escape liability. The planned crime is, in almost all situations for which the collateral crime may be murder, a very serious one carrying substantial penalties. For example, being part of a criminal plan to cause grievous hurt attracts a maximum penalty of 10 years' imprisonment plus fine and caning,[82] and aggravated forms go even higher: for causing grievous hurt by means of a dangerous weapon, it goes up to 15 years' imprisonment plus fine and caning.[83] The punishment for robbery is even more impressive: daytime robbery is punishable with a mandatory minimum of two years' imprisonment (up to a maximum of 10) and a mandatory minimum of six strokes of the cane (to a maximum of 20), and for similar nocturnal activities it goes up to between three and 14 years' imprisonment and a mandatory minimum of 12 strokes of the cane.[84] Do we have any reason to doubt that even if JCE liability does not exist, there is already considerable deterrence of criminal gangs intent on robbing or hurting others? The normal sentencing regime can deal very well with criminal enterprises resulting in or risking collateral crimes. Thus, one who ought to have foreseen them is punished more than one who cannot, while one who actually foresees it is punished even more; similarly, one who foresees a possibility receives more, and one who foresees a likelihood receives even more.

---

80 It is one thing to fight for a principle and to try to keep the scoring of political points out of criminal justice, but quite another to choose one's battles so that the achievement of what is practically possible is optimised.

81 A term taken from *Tadić*, above n. 47. It has been half-jokingly observed that JCE liability actually means 'Just Convict Everyone'.

82 Singaporean Penal Code, s. 325.

83 *Ibid*., s. 326.

84 *Ibid*., s. 392. There are a host of other aggravated forms of robbery for which the penalties are even higher – for example, s. 395 provides that gang robbery (five or more robbers) is punishable with between five and 20 years' imprisonment plus a mandatory minimum of not less than 12 strokes of the cane.

Ethical or retributive arguments in support of JCE liability are characteristically, more difficult to attack, simply because they are inherently vague. The principal one is this: the confederate who foresees and therefore risks a possibility of murder coming to fruition deserves to be convicted and punished for murder because he consciously took the risk of that eventuality. Yes, there is a sort of culpability with respect to the killing, but why the compulsion to hold him liable for murder as well? Murder is not about simply taking the risk that someone may die; it also involves (even if one ascribes to that other anachronism – constructive murder with intent to cause any (or grievous) bodily injury) the actual causation of death, something which the confederate who merely foresees cannot be said to have done. The problem with JCE liability (or at least its present form) is that it erases the difference in legal consequences between the actual murderer who does the killing and the abettor who intentionally helps him to kill (on the one hand) and the confederate who merely foresaw that that may happen (on the other). Blameworthy, yes, but not in the same league, I would think, as the murderer and his abettors. And the proportionate way to reflect that extra blameworthiness is to consider it an aggravating factor in the course of sentencing him for the crime which he did commit or abet.

My suspicion is that Macaulay had very similar sentiments and if he had thought that he could have pulled it off, he would have simply done away with the whole idea of constructive group liability in the same way that he exorcised the IPC of felony-murder and in the (eventually unsuccessful) attempt in his draft not to introduce the (grievous) bodily harm rule for murder. If we are willing to wipe the slate clean, then this is the best thing we can do with common purpose, common intention, probable consequences and the like – simply abolish them. If we never had it, I doubt if anyone would seriously suggest that we introduce it now.[85]

But Macaulay apparently did not think he could effect so radical a change, hence he did the next best thing by drafting a very tight and rigorous version of the doctrine in his draft Code. Subsequent tinkering brought into play, arguably, no less than three different formulations of the doctrine, but in a very courageous and correct judgment, the Singapore Court of Appeal swept the confusion aside and restored essentially what was Macaulay's original solution. At every point, Macaulay's formulation exhibited his underlying aversion to the whole enterprise of constructive liability. While the then-prevailing common law of England was going the way of objective foreseeability, Macaulay chose subjective knowledge, which was a position that the common law came around to many years later. While the common law and, it seems, 'international criminal law' is still intent on recklessness (foreseeability of a possibility), Macaulay struck out for foreseeability of a likelihood. On the matter of variations between what was foreseen and what actually happened, jurisdictions around the world are still trying to fathom what would amount to a 'fundamental difference' (which would absolve the confederate from liability), with a definite reluctance to let the confederate off for most variations; however, there is every indication in the Penal Code that only a very high level of coincidence between what was foreseen and what actually happened would suffice.

If we have to live with some kind of JCE liability, then Singapore has certainly been set on the right path by the Court of Appeal's restoration of Macaulay's original formula. But a lasting resolution can only lie in rewording the Penal Code so that the language represents the law that the court declared. The four major sources of JCE liability – common intention, common object, ss.

85 I am of course aware that extraordinarily emotional situations tend to drive legal systems to a state of 'insanity' – witness the aggressively tumourous growth of JCE in the ICTY and the almost uncharacteristic acceptance of common purpose in the English legal world in recent years (perhaps as knee-jerk or politically convenient reactions to perceived rising gang violence).

111 and 113[86] – ought to be repealed and replaced with a single regime – and one cannot improve on Macaulay's original and, in my view, timeless draft which we saw at the beginning of this discussion. Perhaps we need to add a provision which more explicitly says what is to happen for factual variations, to the effect that the court is to ask itself whether it was nonetheless beyond a reasonable doubt that the confederate would have gone ahead if he had known of the variation.

There is one other matter which is probably more relevant for Singapore, where mandatory penalties and, in particular, the mandatory death penalty for murder are not uncommon. Macaulay did not favour a mandatory death penalty for murder, and the IPC preserves the option between death and life imprisonment. But in the passage from India, it became a mandatory death penalty for British Malaya, and so it has remained.[87] This has made it impossible for the courts, once liability is established, to differentiate between the relative culpabilities of different confederates. One gets the distinct impression that the new-found favour with JCE in the international criminal tribunals is fueled by a desire to get the masterminds for whom evidence of (normal) complicity is insufficient. But, unfortunately, the doctrine does not distinguish between mastermind and minion, and if there is no discretion in sentencing, all die.[88] We have just such a precedent for conferring sentencing discretion for constructive group crime in s. 396 of the Singaporean Penal Code: where gang robbery results in murder, all members of the gang are constructively liable, but the court has the discretion to choose between death and life imprisonment.[89] Interestingly, a relatively recent amendment to the Penal Code of Israel, which formerly had a provision very similar to s. 34, has the general effect of relieving the court of any mandatory penalty (and allowing it to give any

86 One ought perhaps to add Singaporean Penal Code, s. 396 to the list:

> If any one of 5 or more persons who are conjointly committing gang-robbery, commits murder in so committing gang-robbery, every one of those persons shall be punished with death or imprisonment for life, and if he is not sentenced to death, shall also be punished with caning with not less than 12 strokes.

The time for being hysterical about gang robbery (or 'dacoity') is surely over.

87 No one has since been able to come up with a convincing account of why this change was made. 'British Malaya' was eventually to become the independent countries of Malaysia, Singapore and Brunei.

88 I have been alerted by Mark Findlay to a Chinese attempt to codify different criteria of liability for the mastermind on the one hand and the minion on the other, Criminal Law of the People's Republic of China, adopted 1 July 1979, amended 14 March 1997 (available online at http://www.colaw.cn/findlaw/crime/criminallaw1.html (last accessed 17 February 2011)):

> Article 26. A principal offender is one who organizes and leads a criminal group in conducting criminal activities or plays a principal role in a joint crime.
>
> A crime syndicate is a more or less permanent crime organization composed of three or more persons for the purpose of jointly committing crimes.
>
> The head who organizes or leads a crime syndicate shall bear criminal responsibility for all the crimes committed by the syndicate.
>
> A principal offender other that the one stipulated in the third paragraph shall bear criminal responsibility for all the crimes he participated in, organized, or directed.

The idea is attractive – constructive or vicarious liability operates only for the 'head' of a 'criminal syndicate' and not apparently otherwise. It would certainly be worthwhile to study how this provision has worked out in practice, for one can imagine the potentially serious interpretational problems associated with phrases like 'more or less permanent crime organization', 'organizes or leads' and 'all crimes committed by the syndicate'.

89 Above n. 86.

lesser sentence) if liability was by way of JCE.[90] Curiously, this solution might allow us to have our cake and eat it too. The confederate is found guilty of murder and that goes some way towards achieving what is felt in some quarters to be the necessary symbolic or cathartic functions of the criminal law;[91] but in the actual sentencing, the court is allowed to calibrate it according to relative blameworthiness.

I am of the view that these legislative reforms are necessary, both in order to bridge the gulf that has opened up between the language of the Code and the law as recently interpreted by the Singapore Court of Appeal, and to anticipate potential problems with mandatory penalties. If we do not do that, one can indeed foresee the possibility of a differently constituted Court of Appeal, perhaps in more unsettled times, taking the words of the existing Penal Code literally and undoing the good work the court has done. Now that we are all put on notice of that possibility, we must presumably bear responsibility for it if it comes to pass. I end with a very rough draft of a provision (based, obviously, on Macaulay) which could be enacted in replacement of all others seeking to impose constructive or vicarious liability, if indeed the need for such liability is felt to be an immovable:

> Wherever in the commission of an offence, a different offence is committed in furtherance of the first-mentioned offence, then whoever abetted the first-mentioned offence shall be liable to the punishment for the last-mentioned offence, if the last-mentioned offence were such as the said abettor knew to be likely to be committed in furtherance of the commission of the first-mentioned offence; and if both offences be actually committed, and the person who has committed them be liable to cumulative punishment, the abettor shall also be liable to cumulative punishment.

---

90 Penal Law of Israel (626/1996), s. 34A (unofficial English translation, available online at http://wings.buffalo.edu/law/bclc/israeli.htm (last accessed 17 February 2011)) is a fascinating piece of legislation which perhaps deserves much greater treatment than it is getting here:

(a) Where incidentally to the commission of an offence, another or additional offence is committed by the author, which according to the circumstances of the case, a reasonable person could have been aware of the possibility of its commission:
 (1) liability for it shall be borne also by the other authors. However, had the other or additional offence been committed with intent, the other authors shall bear liability for such as for an offence of indifference only;
 (2) the instigator or the abettor shall bear criminal liability for it, as an offence of negligence, if there is such an offence with the same factual elements.

(b) A court convicting an accused per subsection (a)(1) for an offence for which a mandatory penalty is prescribed, may impose a lighter penalty.

This is a conceptually attractive alternative to JCE liability – the confederate is liable not for the foreseeable or foreseen collateral offence, but for the negligent or reckless version of it, as the case may be. This appears to be something like what Sanford Kadish (S.H. Kadish, 'Reckless Complicity' (1996–7) 87 *Journal of Criminal Law and Criminology* 369) proposed – although grudgingly, like Macaulay before him – some time ago. But for a jurisdiction like Singapore where homicide offences do not neatly fall into the three (Model Penal Code-inspired) boxes of intention/knowledge, recklessness and negligence, an overhaul of the homicide offences must first be undertaken. I do not see that happening anytime soon.

91 Matthew Goode has suggested that a separate offence of 'being party to a joint criminal enterprise resulting in death' could be created with the attendant mitigated penalties, along the lines of proposals to introduce an independent offence of committing crimes under voluntary intoxication (see generally Chapter 11 of this volume: G. Ferguson, 'Intoxication'). It is an attractive idea, but such a solution has not yet, to my knowledge, been adopted anywhere – and it remains to be seen if proponents of constructive liability will consider this a sufficient response in terms of both retribution and deterrence.

Provided that where the punishment prescribed for the last-mentioned offence is either mandatory or contains a mandatory minimum penalty, the court shall have full discretion to sentence the abettor to anything less than the mandatory or mandatory minimum penalty.

Explanation 1 – An offence is committed in furtherance of the first-mentioned offence only if it is done with the intention of advancing the commission of the first-mentioned offence, and not if it is only committed in the course of or in consequence of the first-mentioned offence.

Explanation 2 – The abettor is said to know that the last-mentioned offence would be likely to be committed only if he or she was actually aware that the last-mentioned offence would be more likely than not to happen, and not if either he or she merely ought to have known, or that he or she knew of a mere possibility that the last-mentioned offence might occur.[92]

Explanation 3 – Where the last-mentioned offence is one which can be committed without knowledge of the relevant result or harm occurring, the abettor shall not be liable under this provision unless he or she had such knowledge. In particular, where the last-mentioned offence is murder or culpable homicide not amounting to murder, the abettor must have been aware of the likelihood of death being caused with the intention of causing death or knowledge that death was likely.

Explanation 4 – Where the abettor foresees the last-mentioned offence to be different from the offence that was actually committed, the abettor shall be liable under this section only if the difference is such that it would have been immaterial to the abettor's decision to abet the first-mentioned offence if the abettor had been aware of that eventuality.

POSTSCRIPT

On 3 September 2010, when the production of this work was already in a very advanced state, the Singapore Court of Appeal in *Daniel Vijay s/o Katherasan v. PP*[93] somewhat surprisingly overruled *Lee Chez Kee*,[94] holding that the true position was, after all, that which was thought to have been heresy since *Wong Mimi*[95] – that of *Vincent Banka*.[96] The doctrine of common intention can henceforth no longer be used to impose constructive or vicarious liability at all – common intenders are liable for collateral crimes only when they are commonly intended, and not otherwise, even if they are foreseen to be likely.

The Court of Appeal went on to decide that where common intention is coupled with murder under s. 300(c) of the Singaporean Penal Code, although the actual murderer might be judged on a constructive basis – that is, all that is required is an intention to cause the injury which objectively leads to death – the common intender must possess a graver *mens rea*. It is not entirely clear, at least to this reader, precisely what the additional ingredient for common intender liability is, but it seems to be actual foresight that the intended injury is likely to cause death.

---

92 I do not have the luxury of space to discuss the incorporation of a defence of withdrawal. A sensible formulation could be modelled after Arms Offences Act (Singapore), s. 5, above n. 12 ('unless he proves that he had taken all reasonable steps to prevent [the use of the firearm]'). A decision will have to be taken as to whether the effect should be complete exculpation or merely mitigation. The alleviation of mandatory penalties would already allow mitigation in the discretion of the sentencing court.

93 [2010] SGCA 33. For comment, see W. Chan, 'Criminal Law' in (2010) 11 *SAL Annual Review of Singapore Cases 2010* (forthcoming).

94 Above n. 7.

95 Above n. 33.

96 Above n. 31.

Some wishes do come true. Common intention in Singapore can no longer be the basis of constructive or vicarious liability. The operation of the anomalous s. 300(c) for murder extends no further than the actual killer. It is rather heartening to see the Singapore judiciary leading the way in stemming the rising tide of vicarious criminal liability in jurisdictions around the world where one might have expected a more enlightened position.

Unfortunately, the court did not find it fit to discuss the parallel abetment provisions in ss. 111 and 113, or the concept of common object in unlawful assemblies, which might be thought to impose vicarious responsibility. It is unclear if these provisions go beyond common intention (as presently conceived) – as the court found s. 396 (robbery/murder) to be – or if they will be interpreted to extend liability no further than common intention. In particular, if a common intender does not intend but merely foresees death to be likely, does he escape the s. 34 frying pan only to fall into the s. 111/s. 113 fire?

PART III
Principles of Exculpation

This part of the book comprises a study of several of the major defences contained in the Indian Penal Code (IPC).

Private defence, which includes self-defence, defence of property and others, is considered by Cheah Wui Ling in Chapter 8. She examines the right to private defence in the IPC using a historical lens and argues for its legislative reconsideration in the light of post-colonial developments. By situating this defence against British India's colonial landscape, it is argued that private defence was primarily viewed by Macaulay as a 'law and order' tool of governance. For him, private defence was to contribute to colonial law-enforcement efforts and build a 'manly' character in the natives. Today, while the text of these provisions has remained remarkably stable, its content has been significantly reshaped by judicial interpretation. Unfortunately, these judicial developments do not advance a coherent, alternative approach to Macaulay's 'law and order' conceptualisation of private defence. However, in some instances, they do reflect inconsistencies with that conceptualisation. The chapter concludes by suggesting how private defence can be reformulated in the IPC to reflect a more modern rights-based approach to private defence.

In Chapter 9, Stanley Yeo commences by observing that although Macaulay was against recognising the defences of duress and necessity in his draft Code, the IPC provides for these defences. Yeo goes on to argue for their retention as two separate defences, which should be made available to murder. An evaluation of the IPC provision on duress leads to the conclusion that, with some revisions made for added clarity, it has the makings of a conceptually sound and workable defence. By contrast, the IPC provision on necessity is poorly constructed and ambiguous in many respects, to the extent that a total redrafting of the provision is required. Drawing on modern common law and statutory formulations of both defences, two freshly worded provisions for the IPC are proposed which attempt to reconcile principle with pragmatism. In particular, they seek to meet Macaulay's core objectives when drafting a code of being as precise as practically possible and of minimising judicial discretion in interpreting and applying the conditions of the defences.

In Chapter 10, 'Insanity', Gerry Ferguson begins with an analysis of the manner in which Macaulay dealt with mental disorder as a defence in his draft Code. This was a contentious matter in nineteenth-century criminal law and Macaulay's provision on mental disorder as a defence was typically clear and succinct. It provided that 'nothing is an offence which a person does in consequence of being mad'. However, that simple provision was drafted six years before the House of Lords issued the much more detailed M'Naghten Rules on insanity, which became the main point of reference for all subsequent insanity defences in the common law world. The remainder of this chapter analyses the development of the insanity defence in the final 1860 version of the IPC and in other common law countries. The discussion concludes with a proposal for a new criminal code provision on mental impairment as a defence, including the difficult distinction between non-insane and insane automatism.

Ferguson then turns his attention in Chapter 11 to the defence of intoxication. In it, he analyses the manner in which Macaulay dealt with voluntary and involuntary intoxication in his draft

Code, the manner in which his provisions were dealt with in the IPC and the influence of these provisions in other common law countries. In short, Macaulay drafted a clear and progressive provision recognising involuntary intoxication as a defence on the basis of a lessened inhibitions standard. Regrettably, that provision was not followed in the IPC or in other common law jurisdictions until it was replicated in the Australian Commonwealth Criminal Code, which came into force in 1995. With regard to voluntary intoxication, Macaulay followed the common law view of the time, which held that voluntary intoxication was not a defence. This view was adopted in the IPC, but it gradually changed over the next 150 years, with some jurisdictions developing a specific-basic intent rule and other jurisdictions developing a 'negation of any subjective fault' rule. More recently, a few jurisdictions such as Montana and Scotland have returned to the strict common law rule adopted by Macaulay. After analysing various options, Ferguson proposes new and reformed code provisions for both voluntary and involuntary intoxication.

The final chapter of this part, Chapter 12, is on provocation, one of the partial defences in the IPC that reduces murder to the lesser offence of culpable homicide not amounting to murder. Ian Leader-Elliott notes that in its original form prepared by Macaulay in 1837, the partial defence required proof that the offender responded to grave and sudden provocation that would move a person of ordinary temper to violent passion. Macaulay's formulation was substantially modified when the IPC was enacted in 1860. The legislature added the requirement that the offender lose the power of self-control as a consequence of the provocation and eliminated the person of ordinary temper as a criterion of the gravity of the provocation. Once enacted, the partial defence accumulated an encrustation of English common law precedents on provocation. Leader-Elliott proposes a reformulation of the defence in the spirit of Macaulay's original proposal. He finds support for that formulation in the reports of the Law Commission for England and Wales on murder and the partial defences to murder of 2004 and 2006. In this proposed reformulation of the partial defence, extenuation of homicide on the grounds of provocation requires proof that the offender acted in response to a reasonable perception of serious wrongdoing by the victim. The requirement of loss of self-control is eliminated on the ground that it is logically incoherent. In its place, there is a requirement of extreme emotional disturbance resulting from the provocation.

Chapter 8
Private Defence

Cheah Wui Ling

INTRODUCTION

One-hundred-and-fifty years ago in colonial India, an enthusiastic Macaulay proposed a right of private defence in his draft Code with the ambitious project of encouraging a 'manly spirit' among the 'natives'.[1] The ideal Indian would stand his ground in the face of danger and would not hesitate to defend his own body or property, or that of another. He would respond with defensive force to prevent certain crimes, even to the extent of causing death.

This chapter analyses and contrasts the right of private defence as originally conceptualised by Macaulay and its contemporary interpretation in jurisdictions which have adopted the Indian Penal Code (IPC),[2] and will suggest that there is a need for legislative reconsideration of this right. Macaulay's proposed private defence provisions were generally maintained when his draft Code of 1837 was finally adopted by the British colonial authorities in 1860. Given this fact, this chapter will be referring to the current provisions in the IPC, but it will also point out the few differences between Macaulay's draft and these provisions where they exist. Macaulay's definition of the right of private defence has been remarkably stable over time, having remained intact and unamended since the inception of the IPC.

As a general idea, the right of private defence permits individuals to use defensive force that would otherwise be illegal to fend off illegal attacks threatening certain important interests. Like the defence of necessity,[3] the right of private defence authorises individuals to take the law into their own hands. This chapter focuses on this 'pure' form of private defence and will not deal with mistaken or 'putative' private defence, which authorises the use of defensive force against harms that are not strictly illegal in nature.[4]

Courts and commentators in IPC jurisdictions have suggested that the Code's provisions on private defence are based on the individual's right to life or bodily integrity.[5] This rights-based

---

1 T.B. Macaulay, J.M. Macleod, G.W. Anderson and F. Millett, *A Penal Code Prepared by the Indian Law Commissioners* (London: Pelham Richardson, 1838) (reprinted by the Lawbook Exchange, Ltd, 2002) Note B (On the Chapter of General Exceptions) 82. This chapter refers to the private defence provisions in Macaulay's draft Code as 'Macaulay's private defence' for convenience.

2 References to the IPC apply equally to the Malaysian and Singaporean Penal Codes, which have adopted the IPC almost in its entirety. India, Malaysia and Singapore are collectively referred to as 'IPC jurisdictions' in this chapter.

3 See Chapter 9 of this volume (S. Yeo, 'Duress and Necessity').

4 For a brief discussion of this issue, see Chapter 5 of this volume (K. Amirthalingam, 'Mistake and Strict Liability').

5 For Penal Code commentaries addressing the rationale of private defence, see generally H.S. Gour, *The Penal Law of India: An Analytical, Critical & Expository Commentary on the Indian Penal Code* (11th edn, Allahabad: Law Publishers (India) Pvt. Ltd., 2000) 796–968; R. Ratanlal and K.T. Dhirajlal, *Ratanlal & Dhirajlal's The Indian Penal Code* (32nd edn, New Delhi: LexisNexis Butterworths Wadhwa Nagpur, 2010)

conception of private defence reflects the position taken by courts and commentators in other common law countries.[6] However, a close analysis of the Code's private defence provisions reveals significant inconsistencies between them and a rights-based rationale. I shall evaluate the Code's private defence provisions within their historical context with the aim of ascertaining their original rationale. In essence, my contention is that, instead of a rights-based rationale, the Code's private defence provisions were shaped by nineteenth-century British ruling interests, reflecting paternalistic and transformative 'law and order' objectives.[7] As conceptualised by Macaulay, the right of private defence was to facilitate the British authorities' colonial project of crime prevention, security maintenance and character development in India.

My discussion then goes on to examine recent judicial pronouncements on the right of private defence from India and also from Malaysia and Singapore, which have adopted the IPC. While the legislative text of Macaulay's private defence remains unamended in these countries, judicial interpretations of the right have evolved over time. I examine the extent to which these judicial developments depart from Macaulay's 'law and order' conception of private defence and inquire whether they advance a different conception of private defence. While these judicial pronouncements (which have unevenly referred to common law developments) may be read as rejecting Macaulay's 'law and order' conception of private defence, they do not replace it with a consistent or coherent alternative. Given this, and in light of the post-independence political and constitutional landscape of IPC jurisdictions, I suggest the need for a comprehensive legislative reconsideration of the right of private defence and propose certain revisions to the IPC provisions on that right.

SITUATING MACAULAY'S PRIVATE DEFENCE PROVISIONS IN THEIR HISTORICAL CONTEXT

In organised societies, the state and its officials are given exclusive law-enforcement responsibilities. Private acts of retribution and violence are prohibited, with individuals having to depend on and defer to the state's monopoly over law enforcement. Like the defence of necessity, the right of private defence functions as an exception to this rule, authorising individuals to take the law into their own hands. However, being an exception, the scope of private defence is carefully circumscribed and influenced by the nature of state–individual relations.[8] Also, like the use of private force by one

---

427–543; S. Yeo, N. Morgan and W. Chan, *Criminal Law in Malaysia and Singapore* (Singapore: LexisNexis, 2007) Chapter 20.

6 For common law authors advocating a rights-based approach to self-defence, see generally F. Leverick, *Killing in Self-Defence* (Oxford: Oxford University Press, 2006); A.J. Ashworth, 'Self-Defence and the Right to Life' (1975) 34 *Cambridge Law Journal* 282.

7 In modern states subscribing to democratic and non-authoritarian rule, the relationship between politics and the criminal law is less transparent and is shaped by a more complex array of political, social, cultural and moral factors. It also responds to the demands of various actors beyond political actors. On the top-down processes of law reform and British moral assumptions and political objectives in connection with the IPC, see Chapter 2 of this volume (B. Wright, 'Macaulay's Indian Penal Code: Historical Context and Originating Principles').

8 The political dimension of criminal law has been emphasised by a number of scholars such as George Fletcher. For example, Fletcher explains how different 'ideal types of political theory' influence a state's use of coercive force through the criminal law. A state subscribing to libertarian theory treats the criminal law as a last resort because the individual's autonomy is treated as having sacrosanct value. A communitarian state employs punishment with the aim of reintegrating the offender into society and repairing the relationship damaged by the crime. A perfectionist state's use of the criminal law aims to improve the offender's 'character'

individual against another, the limits of private defence would be influenced by the nature of societal relationships and expectations of how individuals are to behave vis-à-vis one another.[9] Private defence thus impacts the political, moral and social dimensions of organised societies.

As a general idea, private defence authorises individuals to use coercive force to protect themselves from another's attack. A specific conception of this general idea contends that private defence will be influenced by particular political and moral ideas in society.[10] A society subscribing to a rights-based conception of private defence roots the exercise of defensive force in the individual's right to life and bodily integrity.[11] Such a rights-based approach will require the aggressor's rights to be given adequate consideration rather than ignored. Alternatively, a conception of private defence aimed at the protection of individual autonomy authorises an individual to use any defensive force necessary to preserve his or her autonomy, even force that is disproportionate to the harm posed.[12] Private defence may also be conceptualised as aimed at protecting the socio-legal order, with the individual exercising defensive force regarded as a 'representative or protector of society, public order and the legal system'.[13] Each of these conceptualisations provide different answers to the political question as to the extent to which individuals may be demanded by the state to defer to its monopoly over force, and to the social and moral question concerning the appropriate standard of interaction and behaviour among individuals within society.

Courts and commentators in India, Malaysia and Singapore have suggested various rationales for private defence. For example, the right to defend oneself has been justified on the basis of the individual's instinct of self-preservation.[14] The right to defend others, which is authorised by the right of private defence, has been argued to stem from the individual's duty to protect others in

---

and educate him or her on the error of his or her ways. Fletcher also notes that these approaches have seldom been deployed consistently or separately, some having more influence in certain areas of criminal law than others. See G.P. Fletcher, *The Grammar of Criminal Law* (Oxford: Oxford University Press, 2007) 156–88.

9 As observed by Kimberly Kessler Ferzan, a purely political approach to self-defence is insufficient to address many contentious questions. Addressing Fletcher's arguments, she notes the insufficiency of a purely political account in addressing self-defence. For example, she notes that even a perfectionist state will need to draw on particular moral theories to explain the kind of character it seeks to inculcate. In addition, the political does not structure every aspect of our relationship with others in society, which is implicated in the use of private force and may be given recognition by the criminal law. Moral accounts beyond the political are necessary to address certain aspects of self-defence, such as the use of force against an innocent aggressor. She argues that both moral and political theorising is necessary for a complete account of self-defence. See K.K. Ferzan, 'Self-Defence and the State' (2007–8) 5 *Ohio State Journal of Criminal Law* 449, at 468–70.

10 For an overview of the different possible rationales and frameworks that have been proposed to govern self-defence or private defence, see generally B. Sangero, *Self-Defence in Criminal Law* (Oxford: Hart Publishing, 2006) 60–90. Sangero himself proposes a framework that involves balancing a number of factors. These factors are: the legitimate interest of the person attacked; the autonomy of the person attacked; the guilt of the aggressor; the social-legal order; and the legitimate interest of the aggressor. For a critique of Sangero's framework, see F. Leverick, 'Defending Self-Defence' (2007) 27 *Oxford Journal of Legal Studies* 563.

11 See, generally, Ashworth, above n. 6; Leverick, above n. 6.

12 Sangero, above n. 10.

13 *Ibid.*, at 68.

14 Ratanlal and Dhirajlal, above n. 5, at 428 have stated that the right of private defence 'is based on the instinct of self-preservation. The instinct of self-preservation is indomitable in a human being and this instinct has been recognised as a lawful defence in the laws of all civilised countries.' It has also been recognised that 'the right to protect one's own person and property against the unlawful aggressions of others is a right inherent in man': Gour, above n. 5, at 826.

society. Private defence has also been viewed as furthering the social goal of crime deterrence.[15] I shall seek to ascertain Macaulay's original rationale for, and conception of, private defence with the aim of assessing its continuing relevance today. To do so, the IPC's legislative text should not be approached literally or through the lenses of contemporary theories; rather, it should be interpreted in the light of the existing political, moral and social contexts of the time.

Macaulay's drafting of the Code occurred when there was a move towards a more centralised and effective government by the British colonial authorities.[16] Codification was viewed, in part, as a means of more effective governance that would facilitate Britain's colonial rule of India.[17] While Macaulay was an undoubted liberal for his time, he also subscribed to a utilitarian 'enlightened despotism' and justified Britain's colonial rule of India in paternalistic and transformative terms.[18] Macaulay believed that British rule provided India with a good government, superior to any form of government that could be achieved through self-rule. British rule also brought 'civilisation' to Indian society, which was generally viewed by the British as primordial and depraved. Macaulay believed that Indian society would ultimately be transformed through British education and guidance into an image of its rulers. These political and moral visions of the day influenced Macaulay's codification projects and shaped his conceptualisation of private defence.[19] Macaulay saw his Code provisions on private defence as advancing the paternalistic and transformative 'law and order' objectives of crime prevention, security maintenance and character development.

Paternalistic and Transformative Objectives Motivating Macaulay's Conception of Private Defence

The right of private defence is the most detailed of the defences in the IPC. Macaulay and his fellow law commissioners noted in their introductory report that, apart from private defence, '[n]o portion of our work has cost us more anxious thought or has been more frequently re-written'.[20] The amount of work put into the formulation and drafting of private defence is reflected in the detailed and lengthy nature of its provisions. Despite their endeavours, the Indian Law Commission anticipated being criticised for the overly broad nature of its private defence provisions, particularly when considered against parallel English criminal law codification efforts on private defence at the time. The Indian Law Commission would later deny any substantive difference between these two codification efforts.[21] However, this was not correct. For example, the English Royal Commission's

15 'The duty of protecting the person and property of others is a duty which man owes to society of which he is a member and the preservation of which is both his interest and duty': Gour, *ibid.*, at 826.

16 For a comprehensive description of colonial attitudes towards codification and Macaulay's own political views, see Chapter 2 of this volume, above n. 7.

17 *Ibid.*

18 *Ibid.*

19 Elizabeth Kolsky also notes how the British authorities intended, through adopting a uniform code, to bring non-Europeans and Europeans under the same governing law. This was particularly important given the influx of Europeans into India and the high incidence of crimes committed by Europeans against the local population. The British authorities were concerned that a failure to address such crimes would undermine their legitimacy in the eyes of the local population. E. Kolsky, 'Codification and the Rule of Colonial Difference: Criminal Procedure in British India' (2005) 23 *Law and History Review* 631, at 646–51.

20 Above n. 1.

21 Indian Law Commissioners, *First Report on the Indian Penal Code* (1846) (reprinted in the British Parliamentary Papers 1847–8, vol. XXVIII) paras. [137]–[143].

codification of self-defence authorised deadly defensive force against 'any felony, that is to say ... any offence punishable with death or transportation' or when defending 'one's own person against violence, under reasonable apprehension of immediate death'.[22] In contrast, Macaulay's right of private defence authorised the use of deadly defensive force in a broader range of circumstances, which will be further discussed below.

Macaulay defended his broader conceptualisation of private defence on two grounds. First, reference was made to the problem of prevalent violent crimes in Indian society, such as 'the cruel depredations of gang-robbers' and 'trespass and mischief committed in the most outrageous manner by bands of ruffians'.[23] Secondly, he criticised the local population's tendency of being 'too little disposed to help themselves', a trait that was 'one of the most discouraging symptoms which the state of society in India presents'.[24] Given this, Macaulay was 'desirous rather to rouse and encourage a manly spirit' by providing for a generous right of private defence.[25] He was aware of the possibility that such a broad right of private defence might be abused, but nevertheless maintained that 'the evil which is likely to arise from the abuse of that right is far less serious than the evil which would arise from the execution of one person for overstepping what might appear to the Courts to be the exact line of moderation'.[26] Hence, in his view, the disadvantages stemming from the abuse of a broadly defined right of private defence were far less than the disadvantages of penalising an individual who exceeded a narrowly defined right of private defence.

Despite envisaging a broad right of private defence, Macaulay sought to regulate its exercise by establishing a relatively detailed and comprehensive framework in the IPC. The Code identifies the kinds of offences or harms giving rise to the right of private defence, as well as the maximum kind of defensive force which may be used in response. It also defines the duration of the right, specifically when it arises and when it comes to an end, and establishes certain conditions that need to be observed when exercising the right to use defensive force.

Upper Limits to the Exercise of Private Defence

The IPC's private defence framework begins by declaring that '[n]othing is an offence which is done in the exercise of the right of private defence'.[27] It then articulates upper limits to the right of private defence, restricting its exercise to certain kinds of threats and defining the maximum possible amount of defensive force to be used. When seeking to defend one's body, private defence

---

22 This narrower approach was affirmed in Stephen's *Digest,* which recognised that defensive killing was permissible if the individual faces 'immediate and obvious danger of instant death or grievous bodily harm': J.F. Stephen, *A Digest of the Criminal Law* (9th edn, London: Sweet & Maxwell, 1950) 251–3 (Art. 305).

23 Above n. 1.

24 *Ibid.*

25 *Ibid.*

26 The balancing approach taken by Macaulay reflects Jeremy Bentham's own approach to self-defence. Bentham observed that 'the death of an unjust aggressor is a lesser evil for society than the suffering of an innocent person. This right of defence is absolutely necessary. The vigilance of magistrates can never make up for the vigilance of each individual in his own behalf. The fear of the law can never restrain bad men so effectually as the fear of the sum total of individual resistance. Take away this right, and you become, in so doing, the accomplice of all bad men': J. Bentham, *The Theory of Legislation* (Bombay: N.M Tripathi, 1986) 165.

27 IPC, s. 96.

may only be exercised against 'any offence affecting the human body'.[28] When seeking to defend one's property, the right of private defence may only be exercised against 'theft, robbery, mischief or criminal trespass' or 'an attempt to commit theft, robbery, mischief or criminal trespass'.[29] Other threats to body or property do not give rise to the right of private defence. The right may also be exercised in defence of another's person or property.[30]

The IPC draws limits on when deadly defensive force may be used. When defending one's body against 'any offence affecting the human body', deadly defensive force may be applied if the offence defended against is 'an assault as may reasonably cause the apprehension that death will otherwise be the consequence of such assault', 'an assault as may reasonably cause the apprehension that grievous hurt will otherwise be the consequence of such assault', 'an assault with the intention of committing rape', 'an assault with the intention of committing non-consensual penile penetration of the anus', 'an assault with the intention of kidnapping or abducting' or 'an assault with the intention of wrongfully confining a person, under circumstances which may reasonably cause him to apprehend that he will be unable to have recourse to the public authorities for his release'.[31] When defending one's property, deadly defensive force may be used in response to a 'robbery', 'house-breaking by night', 'mischief by fire committed on any building, tent or vessel ... used as a human dwelling, or as a place for the custody of property' or 'theft, mischief or house-trespass, under such circumstances as may reasonably cause apprehension that death or grievous hurt will be the consequence' if private defence is not exercised.[32]

The IPC's list of situations attracting the possibility of deadly defensive force raises a number of concerns. Most of these situations are defined in terms of offences, as opposed to the kind of harm threatened or experienced by the accused defender. These offences, while serious in nature, do not necessarily always invoke a fear of death or grievous harm in the defender. It seems disproportionate, from the aggressor's perspective, to authorise the defender to use deadly defensive force when he or she does not apprehend death or grievous bodily harm. This is particularly so if one adopts a rights-based conception of private defence which places equal value on the rights of the aggressor and the rights of the defender. Permitting the use of deadly defensive force against an aggressor who does not pose a threat of death or grievous harm ignores his or her right to life and bodily integrity. The IPC's crime-centred approach reflects 'law and order' objectives. Macaulay intended to conclusively authorise the use of private defensive force to prevent certain crimes. Under his scheme, the more serious a threat an offence poses to law and order, in light of its prevalence (for example, property crimes, robbery and crimes associated with group criminality)[33] or social impact (for example, sexual crimes),[34] the more the degree of defensive force is permitted.

---

28 *Ibid.*, s. 97(a).

29 *Ibid.*, s. 97(b).

30 *Ibid.*, s. 97(a) and (b).

31 *Ibid.*, s. 100.

32 *Ibid.*, s. 103.

33 On particular measures against robberies and crimes committed by groups, which gave rise to special concerns over 'dacoits' and 'thuggees', see R. Singha, *A Despotism of Law: Crime and Justice in Early Colonial India* (Delhi: Oxford University Press, 1998).

34 See Chapter 2 of this volume, above n. 7. While Macaulay admired Bentham's universal approach to legislation, which aimed for provisions that transcended time and place, he took a pragmatic approach and found it necessary to draft provisions that made some concessions to local cultures. However in India, British authorities had generally taken a strict approach to regulating sexual behaviour which was not far off from the then-prevailing attitudes in Britain.

For other situations identified by the IPC as giving rise to a general right of private defence, a defender may use defensive force that does not extend to the 'voluntary causing of death'. In responding to these offences, the use of deadly defensive force is prohibited even if such force is necessary to prevent the aforementioned offence from occurring. Macaulay's scheme thus places non-negotiable limits on the exercise of private defence, prohibiting the use of deadly force unless defending oneself against a limited number of offences.

Duration of the Right

In addition to establishing non-negotiable upper limits on the exercise of private defence, the IPC regulates the right's crystallisation and demise. When defending one's body, the right to use defensive force only arises when one experiences a 'reasonable apprehension of danger to the body' from any 'attempt or threat' to commit an offence.[35] Macaulay, in his original draft, did not require any 'reasonable apprehension' of danger.[36] The standard of 'reasonableness' subsequently adopted may be argued to reflect an intention to encourage and recognise only 'reasonable' standards of behaviour, which is in line with the modern-day view of private defence as a justificatory plea as well as the then-existing colonial aspirations to shape human character through the law. When defending one's property, the preventive right begins once 'a reasonable apprehension of danger to the property' arises.[37] When these apprehensions no longer exist, the right of private defence comes to an end.

The IPC draws a distinction between the general right's crystallisation and the kind of defensive force which may be used. In order for the right to crystallise, there needs to be a reasonable apprehension of threat to the body or property. For example, an Indian case noted that with respect to bodily threats, the right of private defence arises when 'a reasonable apprehension of danger to the body arises … the right lasts so long as the reasonable apprehension of the danger to the body continues'.[38] However, upon crystallisation of the right, the *kind* or *degree* of defensive force permissible depends on the situation confronting the defender. Deadly defensive force may be used only if the situation concerned falls within ss. 100 or 103 of the IPC.

A mere 'attempt or threat' to commit a bodily offence could give rise to the right to defend one's body if the individual reasonably apprehends danger to the body.[39] In contrast, the right to defend property only arises when there is an 'attempt', and not just a 'threat', to commit the relevant property offences. This privileging of bodily harms may be explained by both a rights-based and a 'law and order' conceptualisation of private defence. A rights-based conceptualisation aims to protect the defender's rights and calibrates the permitted defensive force based on the danger experienced by the defender. Bodily harms generally result in more serious consequences to a defender than property harms, justifying a defensive response which is earlier in time. A 'law and order' conceptualisation of private defence, which focuses on maintaining a sense of security, would also support this distinction between bodily and property harms. Due to their serious and irreparable nature, bodily offences may be viewed as greater threats to 'law and order', justifying a more anticipatory response.

---

35 IPC, s. 102.

36 Macaulay's draft Code, cls. 78 and 81.

37 IPC, s. 105(1).

38 *Bishna @ Bhiswadeb Mahato v. State of West Bengal* AIR 2006 SC 302.

39 IPC, s. 102.

Conditions Governing the Exercise of the Right

Besides specifying upper limits for the exercise of private defence and specifying the right's duration, the IPC regulates the process of exercising defensive force through conditions set out in s. 99. Section 99(1) and (2) specifically prohibits the exercise of the right of private defence against acts done by public servants or at the 'direction' of public servants 'in good faith' and 'under the colour' of office. Defensive force is prohibited against public servants in these circumstances even if their acts 'may not be strictly justified by law'.[40] The only exception to this immunity is when the act done by, or at the direction of, the public servant 'reasonably cause(s) the apprehension of death or grievous hurt'.[41] Macaulay's original draft envisaged an even wider immunity, recognising conclusively that there would be no right of private defence against such acts when done or directed by public servants who are 'legally competent' to do so.[42] This immunity privileges and protects public officials associated with the state.[43] However, recognising an unmitigated right of private defence against public officials, especially in the light of Macaulay's generous definition of this right, could potentially undermine the colonial state's claim of ensuring good government.

Section 99(3) denies the right of private defence to an accused if there had been 'time to have recourse to the protection of the public authorities'.[44] If help could have been sought from professionally trained state agents, an individual's decision to use coercive force would seem unnecessary or, worse, as motivated by an intention to harm rather than an intention to defend. Instead of formulating this as a factor to be considered among others in deciding whether the force used was necessary or defensive in nature, Macaulay chose to draft this as an independent and separate condition. By requiring threatened individuals to seek recourse from state-sanctioned agents, this condition affirms the state's role as the keeper of law and order. The British authorities not only justified their colonial rule based on their ability to maintain security but sought to inculcate a genuine acceptance and appreciation of this state of affairs within Indian society.

The fourth and final condition of s. 99 is that the exercise of private defence 'in no case extends to the inflicting of more harm than it is necessary to inflict for the purpose of defence'.[45] The amount of defensive force used should only be that which is necessary to prevent harm to body or property. Necessary defensive force does not serve to punish the aggressor and it is not retributive in nature. Beyond this, the definition of what defensive force is 'necessary' would depend on the objectives and rationale furthered by the particular conception of private defence. For example, if private defence aims at the protection of individual autonomy, the amount of 'necessary' force would refer to any amount of force required to effectively protect the defender's interests.[46] However, a conceptualisation of private defence rooted in individual rights would consider the rights of the defender and the aggressor, requiring the defensive force used to 'bear a reasonable proportion' to

40 *Ibid.*, s. 99(1) and (2).

41 *Ibid.*

42 Macaulay's draft Code, cl. 75.

43 Gour, above n. 5, at 874, notes that this privilege is justified for a number of reasons: first, the acts of public servants are probably lawful; secondly, 'the law will set right what has been done in its name'; and, thirdly, it is 'good for society that public servants should be protected in the execution of their duty even where they are in error'.

44 IPC, s. 99(3).

45 *Ibid.*, s. 99(4). Macaulay's original draft noted that such recourse should be done 'in the manner indicated in the Code of Criminal Procedure': Macualay's draft Code, cl. 75.

46 Sangero, above n. 10, at 65–6. Legal systems subscribing to this view have sought to limit this right by prohibiting its abusive exercise.

the injury avoided.[47] Strictly speaking, while the concepts of proportionality and necessity may at times overlap, they are two different and distinct concepts. Necessity refers to the completion of a particular objective, such as the prevention of a crime by whatever means, while proportionality evaluates the relationship between the means used and objective pursued. Macaulay most likely did not intend 'necessary' force to include a proportionality requirement, in light of his 'law and order' conception of private defence as a supplementary means of crime prevention. He probably meant to address concerns over the use of disproportionate force through the non-negotiable upper limits placed by ss. 100 and 103 on the use of deadly defensive force.

JUDICIAL DEVELOPMENTS IN INDIA, MALAYSIA AND SINGAPORE

Though Macaulay's legislative text remains unchanged since its adoption, courts in countries which have embraced the IPC appear to have developed more restrictive interpretations of private defence over time. They have read a number of additional requirements into the right of private defence, thereby making the defence more restrictive.[48] Commentators have criticised these judicial restrictions by referring to Macaulay's original intention for a generous right of private defence. In this regard, it is recalled that Macaulay's vision of such a broad defensive right stemmed from his 'law and order' conception of private defence, which was itself shaped by the then-prevailing political and ideological philosophies of the British ruling groups.

Given post-colonial developments in India, Malaysia and Singapore, more critical reflection is appropriate, and modern reconsideration and possible reconceptualisation of private defence should be put on the law reform agenda. In the ensuing discussion, I analyse the extent to which courts in these jurisdictions have departed from, or adhered to, Macaulay's 'law and order' conception of private defence.

Disqualifying Aggressors

The IPC's private defence provisions do not make a distinction between individuals who have contributed to the situation giving rise to the need for defensive force and individuals who do not. On a plain reading of the provisions, both categories of individuals are entitled to claim the right of private defence. However, Indian courts have consistently denied the right to aggressors, even when they receive actual injuries from the objects of their aggression.[49] In *Ravikumar, Meganathan, Subramani and Ranganathan v. The State by the Inspector of Police*,[50] the Madras High Court defined aggression as referring to any 'unprovoked attacking or hostility shown by a person', adding that an individual is an aggressor if he 'attacks first, without being provoked'.[51] To decide whether an individual is to be deemed an aggressor, the courts have insisted on the need to evaluate

---

47 Ratanlal and Dhirajlal, above n. 5, at 489.

48 In doing so, the courts have occasionally referred to common law jurisprudence – particularly English case law. Such reliance on the common law runs counter to Macaulay's aim that the Code should replace, as far as possible, the need for judicial interpretation and discretion. See Chapter 2 of this volume, above n. 7.

49 For a recent case elaborating various guidelines for private defence, see *Darshan Singh v. State of Punjab* AIR 2010 SC 1212. Case law specifically dealing with the aggressor requirement includes *Bishna @ Bhiswadeb Mahato v. State of West Bengal*, above n. 38.

50 CA No. 5 of 1996, decided on 24 December 2003 (unreported), MANU/TN/1820/2003.

51 *Ibid.*, at para. [35].

the entire factual context. Thus, the presence of injuries or non-injuries does not conclusively prove or disprove that an individual was an aggressor.

This disqualification of aggressors is not provided for under the IPC but is a rule of English common law. Leverick notes that this rule was historically necessary because the English common law drew a distinction between justifiable and excusable self-defence.[52] If the individual had not contributed to the circumstances giving rise to the need for defensive force, he or she could claim justifiable self-defence and would then be fully acquitted.[53] However, if the individual had partially contributed to the circumstances giving rise to the need for defensive force, he or she could only claim excusable self-defence. In this case, a royal pardon would be granted, but the individual's property would be forfeited.[54]

Indian courts have defended their adoption of the disqualification rule on the assumption that these aggressors are not motivated by the intention of 'defending themselves by any stretch of the imagination'.[55] By way of criticism, this assumption does not necessarily apply to all aggressors or throughout the entire encounter. The Indian courts' justification does, however, support using aggression as an indicator of whether an individual intended to exercise private defence. The individual's aggressive behaviour may be a convincing indicator that he or she had not meant to exercise defensive force but had instead intended to punish the defender. For example, in the Singapore Magistrates' Court case of *Lwee Kwi Ling Mary v. Quek Chin Huat*,[56] given the fact that any struggle had ceased and that the victim was unarmed and smaller in size, the accused's conduct of rushing at the victim with a chopper was determined to be 'more an act of aggression and anger rather than an act of defence'.[57]

The Indian judicial approach of automatically disqualifying aggressors from claiming the right of private defence goes beyond using the status of aggressor as an indicator.[58] Such an automatic disqualification may be prompted by the view that aggressors are the cause of their circumstances.[59]

52 Leverick, above n. 6, at 114.

53 *Ibid.*

54 *Ibid.* Modern English case law does not preclude self-defence from an accused who contributed or initiated the circumstances leading to defensive force: *R. v. Rashford* [2005] EWCA Crim 3377. Cf. The US Model Penal Code which states that the use of 'deadly force' is not justifiable if 'the actor, with the purpose of causing death or serious bodily injury, provoked the use of force against himself in the same encounter': s.3.04(2)(b)(i).

55 *Bhanwar Singh v. State of Madhya Pradesh* AIR 2009 SC 768, at para. [44].

56 [2002] SGMC 21.

57 *Ibid.*, at para. [143]. The Singapore Magistrates' Court found that the accused had exceeded her right to defend her husband against the offence of voluntarily causing hurt by the victim and to defend her property against an act of criminal trespass. This right 'did not extend to making a death threat while wielding a chopper knife and charging' at the victim. The court noted that if she was really exercising her right of private defence, she could have 'shouted "Leave now", "Get out" or "'Stop" while holding the knife'.

58 This contrasts with the theory of 'forfeiture' put forth by some commentators as the basis for the right of private defence. According to the theory of 'forfeiture', an aggressor 'forfeits' his or her right to life or bodily integrity when he or she transgresses the rights of a victim who exercises his or her right of private defence. However, this 'forfeiture' is only temporary in nature. The aggressor regains his or her rights when the aggression halts or when the victim exceeds the right of private defence. In contrast, by absolutely disqualifying aggressors from exercising the right of private defence, the Indian courts permanently forfeit the aggressor's right of private defence.

59 This idea is reflected in other defences such as duress. A person may only claim duress if he 'did not of his own accord ... place himself in the situation by which he became subject to such a constraint': IPC, s. 94. See Chapter 9 of this volume (S. Yeo 'Duress and Necessity'), at 207–8. Duress is morally distinguishable

As aggressors have only themselves to blame, the state should not exempt them from the law by allowing them to use defensive force which would otherwise be criminal. This view also appears to have been endorsed by the Malaysian High Court in *PP v. Lim Yew Sen*, where it noted that, after a prior confrontation with the victim, the accused had gone 'to the scene ... knowing that there would be a fight since the accused himself carried with him a similar iron pipe'.[60] The accused had been disarmed by the victim, who was about to hit the accused with an iron pipe, whereupon the accused stabbed the victim with a screwdriver. The court held that the accused did not have a right of private defence because he had 'asked for this fight by going to the scene'.[61]

The courts in Singapore have recently considered this disqualification rule. In *PP v. Tan Chor Jin*, the Singapore High Court held that aggressors should always be disqualified from claiming private defence, explaining that 'it is inconceivable for an assailant to have a right of private defence against someone legitimately exercising his right of private defence ... If it were otherwise, the right of private defence would swing back and forth infinitely between victim and assailant like a perplexed pendulum'.[62] However, the Singapore Court of Appeal disagreed with the lower court, saying that it 'would not go so far as to say that this right will *never* be available to a defender where he is also the initial aggressor; much will depend on the facts of the particular case at hand'.[63] The court went on to say that if an individual was the aggressor, 'it is *prima facie* less likely' that he or she will be found to have the right of private defence.[64] In other words, aggressors will generally not have the right of private defence; whether they do will depend on the particular facts of the case.

By not automatically disqualifying an aggressor, the state gives equal consideration to the aggressor's rights to life and bodily integrity. This reflects a rights-based approach to private defence rather than a 'law and order' approach. On this approach, the aggressor should have the right to defend himself or herself if the defender's response to his or her initial aggression was disproportionate and unreasonable. An automatic disqualification of aggressors more closely approximates Macaulay's 'law and order' conception of private defence. This approach views individuals performing acts of aggression as being threats to law and order and who thus should not be legally authorised to use coercive force.

A halfway house approach that considers both the aggressor's rights as well as his or her blameworthiness could be considered. This appears in s. 35 of the Canadian Criminal Code, which permits an aggressor to claim the right of private defence so long as he or she had not, prior to the need arising, sought 'to cause serious bodily harm'. In addition, the aggressor must have 'declined further conflict and quitted or retreated from it as far as it was feasible to do before the necessity of preserving himself from death or grievous bodily harm arose'.[65] By imposing stricter requirements

---

from self-defence. In exercising self-defence, the accused responds to the source of the threat. In duress, the accused does not respond to the source of the duress, but rather harms an innocent third party who has no control or knowledge of the circumstances leading to the duress. It is the accused who could have avoided the situation.

60 [2004] 2 MLJ 97, at para. [35].

61 *Ibid.*, at para. [36].

62 *PP v. Tan Chor Jin* [2007] SGHC 77, at para. [99].

63 *Tan Chor Jin v. PP* [2008] 4 SLR(R) 306, at para. [45] (emphasis in the original).

64 *Ibid.*, at para. [46(c)].

65 Canadian Criminal Code, s. 35(b). Note, however, that due to inconsistencies between this provision, which deals specifically with defensive force resulting in death or grievous bodily harm, and s. 34, which deals generally with defensive force, judicial interpretation has been inconsistent and confusing: D. Stuart, *Canadian Criminal Law* (5th edn, Scarborough: Thomson Carswell Ltd., 2007) 504.

on an aggressor, this halfway house solution gives due consideration to the aggressor's failure to behave as a responsible member of society who refrains from aggressive acts. However, it continues to treat the aggressor as a holder of rights within society by giving him or her a qualified right of private defence.

Requiring Imminence

In order for one's right of private defence to crystallise, the IPC only requires an individual to experience 'reasonable apprehension' of danger to body or property.[66] However, there are Indian judicial decisions which have also required, as a separate and independent condition, that the threat faced has to be 'imminent'. For example, in defining when the right of private defence arises, the Indian Supreme Court in *Dharshan Singh v. State of Punjab* noted: 'A person who is in imminent *and* reasonable danger of losing his life or limb may in the exercise of the right of self-defence inflict any harm, even extending to death ...'[67] This condition was also emphasised by the High Court of Punjab and Haryana in the case of *Harbhagwant Singh v. State of Punjab* when it noted that in assessing an individual's 'apprehension of danger to life and property', there is a need for such apprehension to be 'imminent'. The court went on to say that '[i]t is the imminence of the danger and the urgency of the situation that is material'.[68]

A number of common law jurisdictions similarly require threats to be 'imminent'.[69] Adopting a strict 'imminence' rule limits the situations in which an individual would be permitted to exercise defensive force. The individual may experience a 'reasonable apprehension' of danger to body or property, but the danger may not be temporally 'imminent'. This 'imminence' rule has been severely criticised for denying the right of private defence to individuals confronted with threats which place them in serious and inevitable, but not imminent, danger.[70] Such a strict 'imminence' rule runs counter to Macaulay's 'law and order' conception of private defence. In some situations, by the time a threat becomes temporally 'imminent', the exercise of defensive force may be unable to prevent the harmful effects of the aggression.

Gour argues that the 'imminence' requirement is sensible because '[t]here are many threats which are only used as a form of abuse, but which are never intended to be taken seriously'.[71] On this basis, the value of a threat's 'imminence' lies in its indication that the threat was sufficiently serious to result in a 'reasonable apprehension' of danger to body or property. The 'imminence' of a threat could also assist in the determination of other private defence requirements. For example,

66 IPC, s. 102.

67 Above n. 49, at para. [36] (emphasis added).

68 2009 Cri LJ 1659, at para. [26].

69 US case law and some US states expressly permit defensive force to be used only against harm that is 'imminent': see, for example, *State v. Norman* 378 S.E.2d 8 (1989). In that case, the accused was in an abusive relationship, as a result of which she shot her sleeping husband. Mitchell J. held that the accused was not exercising self-defence as she was not under reasonable apprehension that she was faced with 'a threat of imminent death or great bodily harm'. She 'had ample time and opportunity to resort to other means of preventing further abuse by her husband'. The US Model Penal Code captures this imminence requirement using slightly different language, stating that defensive force may only be used when the actor believes that such force is 'immediately necessary' to protect himself or herself against unlawful force. s. 3.04(1).

70 Feminist scholars have criticised the 'imminence' requirement as favouring male concepts of violence and disadvantaging victims of domestic abuse.

71 Above n. 5, at 939.

the imminence could be relevant to determining whether the individual had time to 'have recourse to the protection of the public authorities' or whether the defensive force used by the individual was 'necessary'.[72] The more distant the threat is in the future, the harder it will be to predict with certainty if the threat will actually take place. Theoretically, an individual faced with such a future threat will have more time to take alternative protective measures.[73] Treating 'imminence' as an indicator does not require the automatic exclusion of threats which are not imminent, so long as these threats give rise to a 'reasonable apprehension' of danger to body or property. Treating 'imminence' as an indicator does, however, limit the amount of defensive force permitted in favour of the aggressor. It also ensures that the threat giving rise to defensive force is assessed from the perspective of the threatened individual, as opposed to focusing on the threat's temporal nature. Finally, 'imminence' as an indicator considers the interests and rights of the aggressor as well as the defender, approximating a rights-based conception of private defence.

Interpreting the Requirement to Have Recourse to Public Authorities

As noted earlier, the seeking of recourse from the public authorities is phrased in the IPC as an independent and separate condition of private defence. If the accused had time to seek such recourse but failed to do so, the IPC unequivocally denies him or her the right of private defence. However, Indian courts have interpreted this condition in ways that avoid it from being overly onerous on threatened individuals. They have held that an individual is required to seek the protection of the public authorities only if and when he or she has sufficiently detailed information about the pending attack. Such information should enable the public authorities to effectively respond to the threat reported by the individual. As Gour aptly observes, an individual is not required 'to carry idle gossip' to the authorities.[74]

In addition, the Indian courts have emphasised that recourse to the public authorities is only required if there was time for such recourse to be sought without any immediate and irreparable damage to an individual's bodily or property interests. If there was such time, it should be sought even when the crime was in the process of being committed. In the Andhra Pradesh High Court case of *In re Gangavaram Sankaraiah*,[75] the victims were in the process of committing criminal trespass on the defenders' land. The defenders argued that they had the right to use defensive force against the victims without first seeking recourse from the public authorities. The court rejected this argument, holding that 'there is no right to private defence unless the circumstances are such and the situation is so urgent that there is no time to have recourse to the protection of the public authorities'.[76] Since the victims had brought their bulls onto the trespassed land for the purpose of grazing, this trespass posed no immediate threat to the accuseds' property interests, and they were not entitled to use defensive force against the victims. Instead, the accused had a duty to seek recourse from the public authorities.

Some commentators have suggested that an individual does not automatically lose his or her right of private defence simply because he or she failed to seek recourse from public authorities

72 This approach has been taken by the Canadian Supreme Court. 'Imminence' is treated as a factor to be considered when determining if the accused had a reasonable apprehension of danger: *R. v. Pétel* [1994] 1 SCR 3.

73 Leverick, above n. 6, at 101.

74 Above n. 5, at 892.

75 1970 Cri LJ 1029.

76 *Ibid.*, at para. [13].

who are within easy reach or are present at the scene of the crime. If an individual continues to experience 'reasonable apprehension' of danger – despite the presence of the public authorities – he or she may still claim the right of private defence.[77] In contrast, other commentators have suggested that this requirement should be evaluated based on a purely objective 'reasonable' basis of whether there was sufficient 'time' and 'opportunity', as opposed to incorporating the individual's reasonable apprehension or perception.[78] They contend that the introduction of 'subjectivity' may cast doubt on the public authorities' effectiveness in affording protection to the individual. However, it is submitted that taking the individual's perception into account in determining 'time' and 'opportunity' does not necessarily involve questioning the public authorities' effectiveness. A purely objective standard assumes that all individuals have a common assessment standard regarding the authorities' protective capacity. Introducing a measured[79] subjectivity of assessing the recourse requirement from the perspective of the accused takes a more individual-centred and rights-based approach to private defence.

Assessing Necessary Force: Proportionality and Reasonableness

Section 99(4) provides that the force used in the exercise of private defence should not extend 'to the inflicting of more harm than it is necessary'. How should 'necessary' force be interpreted? Should it include a proportionality requirement? Does it refer to a reasonable or minimal level of force? Many common law jurisdictions impose a proportionality requirement on the exercise of private defence. However, as noted previously, Macaulay probably did not intend the concept of 'necessary' harm to include an assessment of proportionality.[80] So long as the illegal act defended against falls within the situations listed in s. 100 or 103, a defender is permitted to use any amount of defensive force 'necessary' to deflect the aforementioned illegal act, including deadly defensive force. The crimes listed in ss. 100 and 103 are deemed to be so serious that any amount of defensive force used is proportionate to the listed crime. Where the crime defended against does not fall within s. 100 or 103, deadly defensive force is never to be used. Such generous margins of proportionality are in line with Macaulay's 'law and order' conception of private defence, according to which the defence functions as a form of crime prevention.

Interestingly, courts and commentators in IPC jurisdictions have consistently interpreted the Code's reference to 'necessary' force as including a proportionality requirement. For example, in the recent case of *Dharshan Singh*, the Indian Supreme Court noted that in exercising private defence, 'the violence which the citizen defending himself or his property is entitled to use must not be unduly disproportionate to the injury which is sought to be averted or which is reasonably apprehended and should not exceed its legitimate purpose'.[81] Similarly, the editors of *Ratanlal & Dhirajlal's The Indian Penal Code* state that any defensive force used must be 'no more than is legitimately necessary' and 'must always be proportionate to the quantum of force used by the attacker'.[82] The basis for requiring the defensive force used to be proportionate to the harm defended against is that it protects the aggressor from retributive or vindictive force by the defender.

77 Gour, above n. 5, at 831, citing *Dhoora v. State* 1963 Raj.L.W. 436, at 441–2.
78 Yeo, Morgan and Chan, above, n. 5, at paras. [20.13]–[20.17].
79 'Measured' because the accused's perception must be based on reasonable grounds.
80 See above at 193.
81 *Darshan Singh v. State of Punjab*, above n. 49, at para. [33].
82 Above n. 5, at 461.

While reading proportionality into the concept of 'necessary' force limits the amount of defensive force which may be used, courts in IPC jurisdictions have consistently held that the 'necessity' of such force is to be generously assessed on the basis of a standard of reasonableness. Individuals exercising the right of private defence are usually under significant pressure and are therefore unable to judge the amount of defensive force necessary with exact certainty.[83] If private defence is intended to protect the rights of individuals, as opposed to furthering the state's 'law and order' objectives, consideration should be given to the pressures faced by individuals in such circumstances. Case law underscores that '[i]n adjudging the question as to whether more force than was necessary was used ... it would be inappropriate ... to adopt tests by detached objectivity which would be so natural in a Court room, or that which would seem absolutely necessary to a perfectly cool bystander'.[84] The individual is not expected 'to modulate his defence step by step' or to respond 'in the thinking of a man in ordinary times or under normal circumstances'.[85]

Unlike some common law countries, the IPC does not impose the duty to retreat in the face of danger on individuals.[86] In a classic exposition, the Lahore High Court in *Mahandi v. Emperor* noted that:

> ... the law does not require a citizen, however law-abiding he may be to behave like a rank coward on any occasion ... if a man is attacked he need not run away and he would be perfectly justified in the eye of law if he holds his ground and deliver, a counter attack to his assailants provided always, that the injury which he inflicts in self defence is not out of proportion to the injury with which he was threatened.[87]

The reasonableness standard, which argues against weighing an individual's defensive response on 'golden scales', has been consistently cited with approval by courts in IPC jurisdictions. However, judicial application of this standard to the facts has been more exacting at times. This is well illustrated in the Bombay High Court case of *Samir Nijam Landge v. The State of Maharashtra*,[88] where the accused had, in private defence, given the victim two blows. The court held that the accused should have stopped at the first blow because that was sufficient to immobilise the victim and it 'was not necessary for him to give the second blow'.[89] A similarly strict assessment of the facts was made by the Singapore Court of Appeal in the case of *Roshdi v. PP*.[90] The accused, who was being strangled by the victim, had struck the victim two or three times with a mortar, resulting in the latter's death. The court noted that the accused 'did exceed his right of private defence when he struck the deceased on the head with the mortar, which, after all, is a solid and weighty object, more than once'.[91] In these two cases, the courts seem to have in effect required the accused, in undertaking private defence, to exercise 'minimally' necessary force instead of 'reasonably' necessary force. In their view, anything beyond minimum force will not exonerate an accused.

---

83 Common law courts have also generally taken this approach. For example, Holmes J. stated in the US case of *Brown v. United States* that 'Detached reflection cannot be demanded in the presence of an uplifted knife': 256 US 335 (1921), at 343.

84 *Ranveer Singh v. State of Madhya Pradesh* AIR 2009 SC 1658, at para. [13].

85 *Ibid.*, at para. [13].

86 Yeo, Morgan and Chan, above n. 5, at para. [20.39].

87 *Mahandi v. Emperor* AIR 1930 Lah 93, at para. [7].

88 2006 Cri LJ 3429.

89 *Ibid.*, at para. [30].

90 [1994] 3 SLR(R) 1.

91 *Ibid.*, at para. [42].

Not all cases have applied the law so strictly. The Malaysian case of *PP v. Dato' Balwant Singh (No. 2)* is a good example.[92] The accused was held to be exercising his right of private defence when he shot the victim, who was in the process of attacking him with a stick. The Malaysian High Court does appear to have taken a more generous approach in this case by highlighting the numerous non-coercive steps taken by the accused prior to resorting to defensive force. In particular, the court observed that the accused had done 'everything possible to pacify the aggression of the deceased',[93] including trying to calm the victim with explanations, showing his gun to the victim and firing a warning shot.

All told, it is submitted that, while an individual is not required to retreat in the face of danger, he or she is required to genuinely take or consider non-coercive steps before resorting to force. The right of private defence should be exercised in a responsible manner which respects rather than undermines fundamental societal values. In a society based on democratic equality and constitutional rights, an aggressor should be treated as a subject with recognised rights and interests, despite his or her aggression. To claim the benefit of private defence, an individual should demonstrate that he or she is conscious and respectful of the aggressor's status as an equal subject.

REFORMULATING THE IPC PROVISIONS ON PRIVATE DEFENCE

As illustrated above, courts in IPC jurisdictions have departed in substantial ways from Macaulay's 'law and order' conception of private defence. However, these cases do not reflect a consistent alternative approach to private defence. On the one hand, judicial developments such as the imminence rule and the proportionality requirement indicate a rights-based approach to private defence by insisting on consideration being given to the aggressor's rights. On the other hand, the automatic disqualification of aggressors goes against a rights-based conception of private defence.

I shall conclude my discussion with proposals for reforming the law of private defence under the IPC. My proposals will be limited by the scope of my chapter, which has focused on examining Macaulay's conception of private defence and analysing subsequent judicial developments. In doing so, my analysis has concentrated on how the right of private defence, by which the state authorises individuals to take the law into their own hands, is necessarily influenced by the state's approach to law enforcement and underlying state–individual relations. As noted earlier, the colonial administrators viewed the maintenance of law and order as important for the effectiveness and legitimacy of British rule, and this influenced Macaulay's 'law and order' conceptualisation of private defence.

This 'law and order' approach needs to be reconsidered in the light of modern socio-legal developments in IPC jurisdictions. Legislative reconsideration is all the more necessary given inconsistencies in judicial approaches that have developed over time. Though the post-independence developments about to be described do not provide definitive answers for all aspects of private defence, they do argue for a number of re-orientations.[94]

92 [2003] 3 MLJ 395.

93 *Ibid.*

94 Ashworth advocates a human rights approach, but notes that other specific, contextual factors will need to be considered when addressing the various situations involving the use of private defensive force, such as 'the structure of society, the disposition of its members and its problems of law and order': above n. 6, at 291–2. Ferzan, above n. 9, at 457, argues that a moral, as opposed to a purely political, theory of self-defence is necessary to answer contested questions such as whether one has the right to kill an innocent aggressor. For example, even social contract theories presume the pre-political existence of the right to use

Post-independence, the IPC jurisdictions base their legitimacy on democratic consent and constitutional rule. Consequently, the state's law and order concerns should not completely trump the rights or interests of individuals, particularly their rights to life and bodily integrity. It follows that the contours of private defence should be defined according to threats to the rights of individuals instead of the state's 'law and order' concerns. Individuals exercising defensive force should be permitted a margin of reasonable action and should not be required to respond with the circumspection or minimal force expected of professional law-enforcement officers. Also, the rights of all individuals should be given equal attention. This applies even when an individual was the aggressor, though this fact could be considered as an indicator of whether the defensive force used was genuine or necessary. Furthermore, the defensive harm used should not only be necessary to avoid the harm, but also proportionate to the harm sought to be avoided. In light of this, the defence of property interests should not give rise to the right to inflict death.

To reflect these modern sentiments, the IPC should be amended by adopting the following provisions, with the revised portions italicised:

> Conditions for the exercise of the right of private defence
>
> 99. (4) *A person carries out conduct in private defence if and only if the defensive force used was reasonably necessary and proportionate to defend against the offence concerned.*
>
> *Explanation – In determining whether such force was necessary and proportionate, the following factors shall be taken into account:*
>
> (a) Imminence of harm;
>
> (b) If there were other alternative steps which could be taken without compromising his or her safety, such as retreat or having recourse to the protection of the public authorities.
>
> Commencement and continuance of the right of private defence
>
> 102. The right of private defence of the body commences as soon as *there is reasonable apprehension that there is* danger to the body arising from an attempt or a threat to commit the offence, though the offence may not have been committed; and it continues as long as such apprehension of danger to the body continues.
>
> Commencement and continuance of the right of private defence of property
>
> 105. (1) The right of private defence of property commences when *there is reasonable apprehension that there is* danger to the property.
>
> (2) The right of private defence of property against theft continues till the offender has effected his retreat with the property, or till the assistance of the public authorities is obtained, or till the property has been recovered.
>
> (3) The right of private defence of property against robbery continues as long as the offender causes or attempts to cause to any person death or hurt or wrongful restraint, or as long as the fear of instant death or of instant hurt or of instant personal restraint continues.
>
> (4) The right of private defence of property against criminal trespass or mischief, continues as long as the offender continues in the commission of criminal trespass or mischief.
>
> (5) The right of private defence of property against house-breaking by night continues as long as house-trespass which has been begun by such house-breaking continues.
>
> (6) *The right of private defence of property does not extend to the causing of death.*

---

defensive force, explaining why this right is not extinguished by the state, but do not go further to explain the pre-political existence of this right.

Chapter 9
Duress and Necessity

Stanley Yeo

There may be circumstances where people are compelled by threats to commit a crime which they would not otherwise do. Should the law exculpate them of criminal liability altogether or convict them but reduce their punishment? If the law should exculpate, what conditions must be met? These questions have troubled judges, legislators, law reformers and academics for centuries and continue to do so to this day, producing a host of views and approaches. One of the principal policy tensions involves the need for the law to recognise the immense pressure experienced by the defendant and to be steadfast in protecting society from the harm inflicted. Should the former be given prominence, the concern then shifts to ensuring that the defence is not so wide as to weaken the criminal law by permitting defendants to claim that they thought breaking the law was reasonable. At the same time, the conditions for the defence must not be so strict that it would be unjust to the defendant and out of step with what can realistically be expected of ordinary people when threatened.

In this chapter, two defences that are contained in the Indian Penal Code (IPC) will be examined which have, as their cardinal feature, this element of compulsion. They are the pleas of duress[1] and necessity[2] under ss. 94 and 81 of the IPC respectively, which operate as complete defences.[3] A person invoking the defence of duress claims that he or she had been threatened by another and ordered to commit the crime charged. Duress is a special form of necessity. Both duress and necessity involve situations where the threat presented the defendant with a choice of harms. In duress, the choice is between committing the crime demanded by the threatener or having the threat carried out. In necessity, the defendant has to choose between committing a crime which will avoid the peril or allowing the peril to occur. In each case, the ability to choose between the two harms is constrained by the threat confronting the defendant.

The discussion commences with Macaulay's views on duress and necessity when drafting his original Code of 1837. This is followed by a presentation of the provisions on duress and necessity in the IPC. Some modern formulations of duress and necessity will then be considered, after which the stage will be set for reformulating the existing IPC provisions on these defences for a modern IPC.

---

1 This term is used here to describe what has come to be known at common law as 'duress by threats'.

2 Unless the context shows otherwise, this term is used here to describe what has been called 'duress of circumstances'. For objections to this usage, see D. Ormerod, *Smith and Hogan's Criminal Law* (12th edn) (Oxford: Oxford University Press, 2008) 354.

3 The plea of private defence also shares this feature of compulsion by threat: see Chapter 8 of this volume (Cheah Lui Wing, 'Private Defence').

MACAULAY'S POSITION ON DURESS AND NECESSITY

In his Explanatory *Note B* accompanying the chapter on general exceptions, Macaulay gave his views as to why he had left out duress and necessity in his draft Code.[4] He began by explaining why he thought it was 'useless cruelty'[5] to convict and punish people who had committed crimes in certain circumstances out of fear or self-preservation. His example of duress was of a smith who had been tortured and threatened with death by a gang of dacoits into forcing a door open for them. With regard to necessity, he referred to a man who had caused the death of others by voluntarily jumping from a sinking ship into an overloaded boat. Macaulay's strong subscription to utilitarianism is evident when he remarked that, for these types of cases, it was 'vain to rely on the dread of a remote and contingent evil as sufficient to overcome the dread of instant death, or the sense of actual torture'.[6] More generally, he said:

> [A]s the Penal Code itself appeals solely to the fears of men, it never can furnish them with motives for braving dangers greater than the dangers with which it threatens them. Its utmost severity will be inefficacious for the purpose of preventing the mass of mankind from yielding to a certain amount of temptation. It can, indeed, make those who have yielded to the temptation miserable afterwards. But misery which has no tendency to prevent crime is so much clear evil.[7]

However, Macaulay went on to consider other cases which circumstances were such that society would be loath to exempt from punishment people who acted out of fear or self-preservation. They included cases where the defendant was at fault in creating the situation where he or she became subjected to the threat. As an example involving duress, Macaulay referred to a person who had voluntarily joined a gang of dacoits for the sole purpose of robbing and whose leader had threatened him with instant death if he refused to commit murder. As for necessity, he gave the example of a captain who had run his ship aground in order to cheat his insurers and who then sacrificed the lives of his crew in order to save himself. Macaulay applied this same rationale of prior fault[8] to explain why he thought a person who had stolen food as a result of intense hunger should nonetheless be punished for theft. While accepting that the threat of punishment was unlikely to deter such a thief from satiating his hunger, Macaulay opined that such a threat could effectively 'counteract the motives to that idleness … which end in bringing a man into a condition in which no law will keep him from committing theft'.[9]

Macaulay concluded his explanation for not including duress and necessity among the general exceptions in his draft Code in the following terms:

> There are, as we have said, cases in which it would be useless cruelty to punish acts done under the fear of death, or even of evils less than death. But it appears to us impossible precisely to define

4 T.B. Macaulay, J.M. Macleod, G.W. Anderson and F. Millett, *A Penal Code Prepared by the Indian Law Commissioners* (London: Pelham Richardson, 1838) (reprinted by the Lawbook Exchange, Ltd, 2002) Note B (On the Chapter of General Exceptions).

5 *Ibid.*, at 82.

6 *Ibid.*

7 *Ibid.*

8 See below at 207–8.

9 Macaulay, Macleod, Anderson and Millett, above n. 4, at 84.

> these cases. We have, therefore, left them to the Government which, in the exercise of its clemency, will doubtless be guided in a great measure by the advice of the Courts.[10]

Accordingly, Macaulay's preference was for cases involving duress or necessity to be dealt with through the exercise of executive clemency, which he hoped would be influenced by judicial recommendations concerning the particular circumstances. It may be observed that this stance runs directly counter to Macaulay's general principles, inspired by Jeremy Bentham, of rendering the criminal law clear and certain, thus curbing discretionary authority.[11]

Subsequently, in their first report on Macaulay's draft Code, the Commissioners agreed with him that a distinction should be made between cases of duress and necessity, and also that it was impossible to define precisely those cases where a defence of necessity would operate, so that such cases were best left to be dealt with through executive clemency.[12] However, the Commissioners thought that it was possible to formulate a defence of duress and did so in the following terms:

> Nothing is an offence except under clause 294 ['voluntary culpable homicide'], which is done by a person who is compelled to do it by threats, which may reasonably cause the apprehension that instant death to that person will otherwise be the consequence, the act being done in the presence of the person using the threat, and the threat being continued to the time of doing it, providing the party doing the act did not voluntarily place himself in the situation by which he became subject to such constraint.[13]

When eventually enacted, the IPC included a provision on duress in its chapter on general exceptions which was closely similar to the above formulation. Additionally, that chapter had a provision on necessity.

THE IPC PROVISIONS ON DURESS AND NECESSITY

The preceding discussion suggests that the state would be prepared only under certain limiting conditions to exculpate a defendant of a crime on the ground of duress or necessity. The presentation and evaluation of these conditions can be conveniently classified according to whether they involved: (i) the nature of the threat; (ii) the response to the threat; and (iii) the prior fault of the defendant.

Duress

The defence of duress is provided for under s. 94 of the IPC, which reads:

---

10 *Ibid.*

11 See Chapter 2 of this volume (B. Wright, 'Macaulay's Indian Penal Code: Historical Context and Originating Principles') at 53.

12 C.H. Cameron and D. Elliott, *The Indian Penal Code as Originally Framed in 1837 and the First and Second Reports Thereon* (Madras: Higginbotham, 1888) paras. [167]–[168].

13 *Ibid.*, at para. [169]. The provision is accompanied by three explanations (or, more accurately, illustrations) of its operation, two of which are identical to the 'explanations' accompanying the current IPC, s. 94.

> Except for murder, and offences against the State punishable with death, nothing is an offence which is done by a person who is compelled to do it by threats, which, at the time of doing it, reasonably cause the apprehension that instant death to that person will otherwise be the consequence:
> Provided that the person doing the act did not of his own accord, or from a reasonable apprehension of harm to himself short of instant death, place himself in the situation by which he became subject to such constraint.
> *Explanation 1.*[14] A person who, of his own accord, or by reason of a threat of being beaten, joins a gang of dacoits, knowing their character, is not entitled to the benefit of this exception on the ground of his having been compelled by his associates to do anything that is an offence by law.
> *Explanation 2.* A person seized by gang of dacoits, and forced, by threat of instant death to do a thing which is an offence by law; for example, a smith compelled to take his tools and to force the door of a house for the dacoits to enter and plunder it, is entitled to the benefit of this exception.

The Nature of the Threat

Section 94 unequivocally specifies that nothing short of a threat of death will suffice for the defence to apply.[15] Reviewing the IPC in 1971, the Indian Law Commission was attracted to the English common law position, which recognises threats of serious bodily harm as capable of being as compelling as the threat of death.[16] The Commission accordingly proposed that s. 94 be amended to include threats of 'grievous bodily harm', by which it meant 'permanent privation or impairment of the sight of either eye or the hearing of either ear, or privation or impairment of any organ, member or joint of the body'. However, this proposal was not enacted.

Section 94 requires the threat to be of *instant* death, by which it is meant that the coercer would kill the defendant within an extremely short time after the latter's refusal to carry out the crime he or she was ordered to commit.[17] 'Instant' is synonymous with 'immediate' and to be contrasted with 'imminent' or 'impending', which would permit a longer time interval.

A further requirement of s. 94 is that the threat must have been directed at the defendant and not some other person. Reviewing the IPC, the Indian Law Commission likewise saw the need to extend this aspect of s. 94 and did so by recommending that the defence be available to cases where the threats were directed at 'any near relative of [the defendant] who was present when the threats were made', with the term 'near relative' defined to mean 'parents, spouse, son or daughter'.[18] As with the Commission's other proposal concerning the type of threatened harm, this proposal was not implemented.

Unlike the draft provision of the Commissioners in their First Report,[19] there is nothing in the wording of s. 94 requiring the coercer to be physically proximate to the defendant at the time of the crime. Although, in practice, the coercer's presence will often be necessary to convince the trier of fact that the defendant did indeed commit the crime under compulsion, such presence is not a

---

14 This and the next 'explanation' are, more accurately, illustrations.

15 The courts have strictly applied this condition: see, for example, *Pandita Gangaram v. The Crown* AIR 1950 Nag 1.

16 Law Commission of India, *Indian Penal Code* (42nd Report) (New Delhi: Government of India, 1971) para. [4.45].

17 See *Bachchan Lal v. State* AIR 1957 All 184.

18 Above n. 16.

19 Reproduced above at 205.

strict legal condition.[20] Section 94 is concerned with the psychological impact of the threat on the defendant's mind, which will exist so long as the defendant reasonably believes that the coercer has the means to carry out the threat, whether from near or afar.

The phrase 'reasonably cause the apprehension' appearing in s. 94 injects an objective element into an assessment of the defendant's belief as to the existence and nature of the threat confronting him or her. It is not simply what the defendant himself or herself believed (in which case the test would be purely subjective) but what the defendant reasonably believed. This requires the trier of fact to consider what the defendant's belief as to the threat was, and to then decide whether such a belief was reasonably held. Unfortunately, s. 94 does not make it clear which personal characteristics or circumstances of a defendant, if any, can affect the reasonableness of his or her apprehension.

The Response to the Threat

Section 94 does not clearly deal with this aspect of the defence, apart from stating that a defendant who murders or commits crimes against the state punishable with death will be denied the defence. On first reading, the section does not appear to require a defendant to escape from his or her coercer if a reasonable opportunity presents itself. Indeed, it may be thought that the requirement of instant death dispenses with the issue of escape because the extremely brief time connoted by the word 'instant' inevitably renders absent any opportunity to escape. While this may be so, the circumstances when duress is pleaded nearly always involve a considerably longer time period between when the threat was made and when the crime was to be committed. It is during this period that a reasonable opportunity to escape from the coercer may arise. Since the main part of s. 94 is concerned only with 'the time of doing [a crime]', one would not expect to find any reference in this part to a requirement that the defendant must have taken evasive action. Instead, such a reference to the need to escape may be implied from the wording of the proviso to s. 94, which contemplates a longer time period prior to the commission of the crime. True, the statement in the proviso that 'the person doing the act did not of his own accord … place himself in the situation by which he became the subject to such constraint' has conventionally been regarded as being concerned with cases where a defendant had voluntarily joined a criminal gang and subsequently wished to withdraw from it. However, the wording of the proviso is sufficiently wide to encompass circumstances when a defendant had failed to take a reasonable opportunity to escape from his or her coercer, in which case, the defence will fail.[21]

Prior Fault

The proviso to s. 94 requires that the defendant 'did not of his own accord … place himself in the situation by which he became the subject' of threats. The first explanation (which is more of an illustration) of s. 94 describes a person who had voluntarily joined a gang of dacoits knowing of their character.[22] He is not entitled to the benefit of the defence should he subsequently be compelled by his associates to do anything which is a crime. Thus, *any* crime will suffice and not only those which the defendant knew or ought to have known he or she might be ordered

20 But see the Malaysian case of *Chu Tak Fai v. PP* [1998] 4 MLJ 246, which made physical presence a condition of the defence. The Malaysian Penal Code is virtually identical to the IPC.

21 For a case which interpreted the proviso in this way, see the Singaporean case of *Teo Hee Heng v. PP* [2000] 2 SLR(R) 351. The Singaporean Penal Code is virtually identical to the IPC.

22 For an actual case, see *Sanlaydo v. Emperor* AIR 1933 Rang 204.

to commit. It is unclear whether the proviso extends to exclude cases where the defendant had voluntarily associated with a gang (as opposed to joining it) and thereby exposed himself or herself to the risk of compulsion to commit a crime on the gang's behalf.

The above evaluation of s. 94 shows it to have described some conditions of the defence clearly, but to have been unclear on others. Furthermore, the drafters of the section had incorporated many of the ideas and views of Macaulay, such as the description of the threat being of 'instant death', the exclusion of the defence on account of the defendant's prior fault and the illustration of the smith succumbing to the threats of a gang of dacoits. Overall, with some revisions made to s. 94 for added clarity, it has the makings of a sound and workable formulation of a defence of duress.

Necessity

The IPC formulation of necessity is found in s. 81, which comprises a main provision, assisted by an explanation and by two illustrations. They read as follows:

> Nothing is an offence merely by reason of its being done with the knowledge that it is likely to cause harm, if it be done without any criminal intention to cause harm, and in good faith for the purpose of preventing or avoiding other harm to person or property.
>
> *Explanation* – It is a question of fact in such a case whether the harm to be prevented or avoided was of such a nature and so imminent as to justify or excuse the risk of doing the act with the knowledge that it was likely to cause harm.
>
> *Illustrations*
>
> (a) *A*, the captain of a steam vessel, suddenly and without any fault or negligence on his part, finds himself in such a position that, before he can stop his ship, he must inevitably run down a boat *B*, with 20 or 30 passengers on board, unless he changes the course of his vessel, and that, by changing his course he must incur risk of running down a boat *C*, with only two passengers on board, which he may possibly clear. Here, if *A* alters his course without any intention to run down the boat *C*, and in good faith for the purposes of avoiding the danger to the passengers in the boat *B*, he is not guilty of an offence, though he may run down the boat *C*, by doing an act which he knew was likely to cause that effect, if it be found as a matter of fact that the danger which he intended to avoid was such as to excuse him in incurring the risk of running down the boat *C*.
>
> (b) *A* in a great fire, pulls down houses in order to prevent the conflagration from spreading. He does this with the intention in good faith of saving human life or property. Here, if it be found that the harm to be prevented was of such a nature and so imminent as to excuse *A*'s act, *A* is not guilty of the offence.

The Nature of the Threat

Section 81 does not restrict its operation to specific types of threats, with the main provision simply referring to 'harm to person or property'.[23] This renders the potential for pleading the defence very large and stands in stark contrast to the closely related defences of duress and private defence. For duress under s. 94, only a threat of death will suffice and, for private defence, certain types of

23 'Harm' in this context has been judicially defined as meaning physical injury: see *Veeda Menezes v. Yusuf Khan* AIR 1966 SC 1773.

serious threats are specified where the defendant has applied fatal force.[24] The wide ambit given to the operation of s. 81 reflects its residual nature in that it serves to cover only those cases which cannot fit the description of duress or private defence. In other words, since duress and private defence are species of which the defence of necessity is the genus, the law is much more particular in spelling out the conditions when they will apply, such as the types and severity of threatened harm.

The explanation accompanying s. 81 describes the harm to be avoided as 'so imminent' as to justify or excuse the defendant's conduct. The illustrations bear out this requirement, with the captain in illustration (a) not having the time to stop his vessel and the great fire in illustration (b) so imminent as to warrant the need for A to form a firebreak by pulling down houses. It may be observed that s. 81 does not impose the more demanding test of the harm having to be instant or immediate, as is required by the defence of duress under s. 94. The illustrations also confirm that s. 81 does not require the threat to have been directed at the defendant. In illustration (a), it was the two passengers on boat C who were threatened, and illustration (b) described the fire as threatening human life or property without specifying that it was the defendant or his property that was endangered.

Section 81 is less clear on the issue of who assesses the nature of the threat. Is it the defendant or the trier of fact? If it is the defendant, is it his or her purely subjective belief or must that belief be based on reasonable grounds? A careful examination of s. 81, coupled with reliance on the provision on mistake of fact under s. 79 of the IPC, suggests the position to be that the nature of the threat is to be assessed according to the defendant's reasonable belief. That it is the defendant rather than the trier of fact who appraises the threat is due to the part of the main provision which states that the defendant has not committed any crime if his or her conduct was done 'for the purpose of preventing or avoiding other harm to person or property'. The emphasis placed on the defendant's reason for acting supports the contention that s. 81 is available to a person who had acted under a belief in the existence of the threat occasion.

As for the need for the defendant's belief to have been reasonable, reliance is placed on the explanation accompanying s. 81. Under the explanation, the trier of fact will initially have to determine what the defendant's perception of the threat was before proceeding to consider whether the danger as perceived by the defendant was of such a nature as to 'justify or excuse' him or her. The reasonableness of the defendant's perception is a prerequisite for the trier of fact concluding that the defendant's conduct was justifiable or excusable.[25] Where a defence of necessity based on justification is concerned, the state will encourage the performance of conduct intended to prevent a greater harm provided the actor had reasonable grounds to substantiate the existence of the threatened harm. Likewise, society will be prepared to excuse the actor for taking action to avoid a non-existent harm provided the actor's belief in the existence of such harm was based on reasonable grounds.

The mistake of fact provision under s. 79 of the IPC may also be relied upon to support the position that the defence of necessity under s. 81 requires the threat to be assessed according to the defendant's reasonable belief.[26] The relevant part of s. 79 states that '[n]othing is an offence which is done by any person who … by reason of a mistake of fact … in good faith believes himself to be justified by law, in doing it'.[27] The code defines 'good faith' under s. 52 as having to be made with

24 See IPC, ss. 101 and 103, and discussion in Chapter 8 of this volume, above n. 3, at 190.

25 See further S. Yeo, *Compulsion in the Criminal Law* (Sydney: Lawbook Company, 1990) 18–20, 234–7.

26 *Chirangi v. State* AIR 1952 Nag 282.

27 See further Chapter 5 of this volume (K. Amirthalingam, 'Mistake and Strict Liability').

'due care and attention', which can be readily translated to mean 'on reasonable grounds'. When read together, ss. 79 and 81 require the defendant to have reasonably believed the nature of the threat in order to be justified by law in doing the act.

The Response to the Threat

Section 81 is only applicable where the defendant was induced by the threat to perform the conduct complained of. This is borne out by the main provision, which requires the conduct to have been 'for the purpose of' preventing or avoiding the threat. Rather than describing the defendant's response using conventional concepts such as 'necessary' and 'reasonable' conduct, the main provision takes the unusual course of relying on the mental states of the defendant. The first of these is the defendant's 'knowledge that [his or her conduct] was likely to cause harm' and the second is that the defendant must have performed the conduct 'without any criminal intention to cause harm'. In relation to 'knowledge', a strict and literal reading of the part of s. 81 dealing with it will confine the application of the provision to those cases where defendants knowingly risked the causing of harm, such as the captain in illustration (a). The defence would be inapplicable to cases where the defendant had deliberately set out to cause the harm as part of his or her necessary response to the threat. Such a narrow reading of s. 81 would exclude from its operation many cases where the defence of necessity should be allowed to succeed, for example, illustration (b), where A had deliberately pulled down houses to create a firebreak.

Regarding the mental state of 'without criminal intention', this phrase implies that there are two types of intention – intention and criminal intention – and that s. 81 does not apply if the defendant had performed the harm-producing conduct with criminal intention.[28] Conversely, s. 81 will apply only if the defendant had the first type of intention but not criminal intention. The difference between these two types of intention is not evident. Conceivably, intention is not criminal so as to involve s. 81 if the primary purpose of the defendant's conduct was to prevent or avoid other harm to person or property. Embellishing illustration (b), A may have pulled down houses to achieve two purposes – to create a firebreak and to demolish houses which he considered ugly. He would successfully rely on s. 81 if he could show that his primary purpose was to prevent the fire from destroying human life or property.

Section 81 does not expressly specify that the defendant's response had to be necessary to avoid the threatened harm. However, this is implicit in the illustrations which are concerned with actors who were limited in their choice of means to avoid the harm. Likewise, while no mention is made of proportionality between the defendant's response and the threatened harm, the illustrations involve actors who had to perform a 'balancing of harms' exercise.

Unlike the defence of duress, s. 81 is available as a defence to murder with the operative words being that '*nothing* is an offence'[29] if it were done under the conditions described by the provision. That murder comes within the ambit of s. 81 is also supported by illustration (a), which envisages the two passengers on boat C being killed as a result of the captain's change of course.[30]

---

28 *Jai Prakesh v. Delhi Administration* (1991) 2 SCC 32.

29 Emphasis added.

30 Relying on the knowledge-based element for murder under the fourth limb of IPC, s. 300. See further Chapter 3 of this volume (N. Morgan, 'The Fault Elements of Offences') at 66–8. For an actual case, see the Pakistani High Court decision in *Muhammad Sarwar v State* PLD (1979) Lahore 711(2). The Pakistani Penal Code is virtually identical to the IPC.

Prior Fault

Section 81 makes only a passing reference to the relevance of the defendant's fault in creating the threatening circumstances. It is found not in the main provision or the explanation but in illustration (a), where the emergency confronting the captain is described as having arisen 'without any fault or negligence on his part'. The implication is that the defence would not have succeeded had the captain been blameworthy in creating the emergency. It is likely that the drafters of s. 81 had in mind Macaulay's example of the captain who had endangered the lives of himself and his crew by deliberately running his ship aground in order to claim from his insurers.

The above examination of s. 81 shows it to be a poorly constructed formulation of the defence of necessity, with several key conditions embedded in the explanation or illustrations rather than in the main provision. There is also uncertainty over some of the expressed conditions of s. 81, such as whether the defence is confined to cases where the defendant knew of (as opposed to intended) the likelihood of causing harm, and the meaning of 'without criminal intention'. Other criticisms of s. 81 are that it fails to clearly describe how the nature of the threat is to be assessed and that it is inadequate in its pronouncement on the type of response that is permitted to counter the threat.

MODERN FORMULATIONS OF DURESS

The various conditions of duress and necessity examined in the preceding discussion have been the subject of much comment. Space dictates that only a select number of recent views about these conditions can be considered here. The period from the 1970s to the present day will be studied because this was when many of the most significant ideas and developments occurred.[31] Jurisdictionally, English law and law reform has been chosen on account of the fact that English law was a primary source from which Macaulay and his Code-drafting successors drew upon.[32] Australia has been selected for its mix of common law and code jurisdictions,[33] and a recent national effort to draft a model criminal code.[34] The provision in the Rome Statute of the International Criminal Court[35] (ICC) dealing with duress and necessity will also be studied as it represents an emerging source of international criminal law which has been ratified by a large number of nations.[36] When read together, these sources of recent thinking about the law of duress and necessity comprise a sizable body of knowledge from which to assist with the formulation of new and improved provisions on duress and necessity for a modern IPC.

31 It is acknowledged that the English common law on necessity also developed considerably in the late nineteenth and early twentieth centuries. See A.W.B. Simpson, *Cannibalism and the Common Law* (Chicago: University of Chicago Press, 1984) for an engaging and informative study of necessity and Victorian moral sensibilities.

32 Chapter 2 of this volume, above n. 11, at 39–40.

33 Australia comprises a number of states whose criminal law is based on the common law, and other states which have criminal codes. For example, New South Wales, South Australia and Victoria are common law jurisdictions, whereas Queensland, Western Australia and Tasmania have codes. Interestingly, while Queensland and Western Australia codified the defence of necessity, Tasmania (as well as Canada and New Zealand) left it to the common law, which was heavily influenced by J.F. Stephen's formulation of the defence in his *A Digest of the Criminal Law* (9th edn, London: Sweet & Maxwell, 1950). See below at 220.

34 See M.R. Goode, 'Constructing Criminal Law Reform and the Model Criminal Code' (2002) 26 *Criminal Law Journal* 152 for a discussion of the background and development of such a code.

35 UN Doc. 2187 UNTS 90.

36 As of 12 October 2010, 114 nations had ratified the Statute.

For ease of reference, set out below are recent formulations of the defence of duress proposed by English and Australian law reform bodies and also the provision in the ICC Statute. The English Law Commission published a report in 1989 which recommended the enactment of a Criminal Code for England and Wales (English code). The English code includes separate provisions on duress, which is described as 'duress by threats', and necessity, which is called 'duress of circumstances'. The Law Commission fine-tuned these provisions in 1993 and its formulation of duress appears as cl. 25 of its proposed bill.[37] The relevant parts[38] of that clause read as follows:

> (1) No act of a person constitutes an offence if the act is done under duress by threats.
> (2) A person does an act under duress by threats if he does it because he knows or believes –
> (a) that a threat has been made to cause death or serious injury to himself or another if the act is not done; and
> (b) that the threat will be carried out immediately if he does not do the act or, if not immediately before he or that other can obtain effective official protection; and
> (c) that there is no other way of preventing the threat being carried out,
> and the threat is one which in all the circumstances (including any of his personal circumstances that affect its gravity) he cannot reasonably be expected to resist.
> ...
> (3) This section applies in relation to omissions as it applies in relation to acts.
> (4) This section does not apply to a person who has knowingly and without reasonable excuse exposed himself to the risk of the threat made or believed to have been made.

The Australian equivalent of the above-mentioned English codification exercise was the model criminal code proposed by a sub-committee of Australian Attorneys-General. The general principles of this code were published by the sub-committee in 1992[39] and were subsequently adopted by the Australian Commonwealth (that is, Federal) government to form part of the Commonwealth's Criminal Code 1995 (Australian Code).[40] Like the English Code, the defences of duress and necessity each have separate provisions under the Australian Code. Duress is defined in s 10.2 of the Code as follows:

> (1) A person is not criminally responsible for an offence if he or she carries out the conduct constituting the offence under duress.
> (2) A person carries out conduct under duress if and only if he or she reasonably believes that:
> (a) a threat has been made that will be carried out unless an offence is committed; and
> (b) there is no reasonable way that the threat can be rendered ineffective; and

37 Law Commission for England and Wales, *Legislating the Criminal Code. Offences Against the Person and General Principles* (Law Com. No. 218) (London: HMSO, 1993).

38 The parts that have been left out state that the defendant bears the legal burden of proving certain conditions of the defence. This is also the position in India, Malaysia and Singapore: see Chapter 3 of this volume, above n. 30, at 71. It is acknowledged that placing the legal burden on the accused could be significant to the outcome of the case with respect to proving the subjective and objective conditions of the defence.

39 Criminal Law Officers Committee of the Standing Committee of Attorneys-General, *Model Criminal Code, Report, Chapters 1 and 2, General Principles of Criminal Responsibility* (1992) (available online at http://www.scag.gov.au/lawlink/SCAG/ll_scag.nsf/vwFiles/MCLOC_MCC_Chapter_1_and_2_Report.pdf/$file/MCLOC_MCC_Chapter_1_and_2_Report.pdf, last accessed 11 April 2011).

40 The code applies to Federal offences. See further Chapter 13 of this volume (M. Goode, 'An Evaluation of Judicial Interpretations of the Australian Model Criminal Code').

(c) the conduct is a reasonable response to the threat.

(3) This section does not apply if the threat is made by or on behalf of a person with whom the person under duress is voluntarily associating for the purpose of carrying out conduct of the kind actually carried out.

The ICC Statute combines the defences of duress and necessity under the one provision. This was the result of the Rome Conference regarding the two defences as substantially similar.[41] Article 31(1)(d) reads as follows:

> [A] person shall not be criminally responsible if, at the time of that person's conduct … [t]he conduct which is alleged to constitute a crime within the jurisdiction of the Court has been caused by duress resulting from a threat of imminent death or of continuing or imminent serious bodily harm against that person or another person, and the person acts necessarily and reasonably to avoid this threat, provided that the person does not intend to cause a greater harm than the one sought to be avoided. Such a threat may either be:
> (i) made by other persons; or
> (ii) constituted by other circumstances beyond that person's control.

Cases involving threats 'made by other persons' are the equivalent of the defence of duress, and those involving threats 'constituted by other circumstances' are equated with the defence of necessity.

We are now in a position to consider recent thinking about those conditions of the defence of duress which were previously examined in respect of the IPC. The discussion will, in the main, commence with the common law of England and Australia. This will be followed by the position in the Australian code jurisdictions of Queensland, Western Australia and Tasmania, and the stance taken by the English and Australian codes and the ICC Statute.

The Nature of the Threat

English and Australian common law specifies that the threat required for the defence of duress is of death or serious bodily harm.[42] Threats to property will not suffice.[43] The Tasmanian Code,[44] the English Code[45] and the ICC Statute[46] take a similar approach. The Queensland Code recognises threats of serious harm to the person or to the detriment of property.[47] In contrast, the Western Australian[48] and Australian[49] Codes do not specify the types of harm, preferring to leave it to the trier of fact to decide the issue when considering whether the defendant's conduct was a necessary

41 P. Saland, 'International Criminal Law Principles' in R.S. Lee (ed.), *The International Criminal Court: The Making of the Rome Statute – Issues, Negotiations, Results* (The Hague: Kluwer, 1999) 208.

42 *R. v. Z* [2005] 2 AC 467; *R. v. Radford* [2004] EWCA Crim 2878; *R. v. Williamson* [1972] 2 NSWLR 281.

43 *DPP for Northern Ireland v. Lynch* [1975] AC 653, at 686.

44 Criminal Code (Tas), s. 20(1).

45 Above n. 37, cl. 25(2)(a).

46 Above n. 35, Art. 31(1)(d).

47 Criminal Code (Qld), s. 31(d)(i).

48 Criminal Code (WA), s. 32(2)(a)(iii) and (2)(b).

49 Criminal Code (Cth), s. 10.2(2)(a).

and reasonable response to the threat. This view is attractive for enabling a person to plead duress even when the threat was not one of death or serious bodily harm if the evil that he or she caused by submitting to the threat was clearly less than that which was thereby avoided. However, the difficulty with this view is that it may be practically impossible to balance one evil against the other, especially when they are entirely different in nature. It is therefore submitted that the specification of types of threats is to be preferred. Besides the preponderance of supporting authority, this stance complies with Macaulay's core objective of making the law clear, unequivocal and concise.[50] That said, while the proposal here is to require, as the minimum, a threat of serious bodily harm to support a defence of duress to any crime, a higher type of threatened harm (such as of death or life-threatening injury) will be required for crimes of great gravity. This point is especially relevant if duress were to be recognised as a defence to murder.

Another feature of the threat for duress pertains to the time interval between non-compliance with the coercer's orders and the carrying out of the threat. Most agree that the interval must be short, with the debate being over whether it should have been 'immediate' or the less restrictive 'imminent'. There are English case authorities supporting both tests,[51] with the most recent preferring the former. Australian common law favours the test of imminence.[52] The English and Australian courts have held that a closely related factor is whether the defendant had time to neutralise the threat by seeking the protection of the public authorities.[53] The Queensland and Western Australian Codes do not expressly lay down any time factor, leaving the matter to be taken into account when determining whether the defendant's response was proportionate[54] or reasonable[55] in the circumstances. In contrast, the Tasmanian Code provides that the threat must be immediate.[56] The English Code likewise stipulates that 'the threat will be carried out immediately if [the defendant] does not do the act' but goes on to add that 'if not immediately, before he or that other [person] can obtain effective official protection'.[57] The Australian Code, like its Queensland and Western Australian counterparts, is silent on this issue of time when the threat will be discharged, whereas the ICC Statute specifies that it must have been imminent. Macaulay's invocation for the law to be laid down as clearly and concisely as possible and to minimise judicial discretion[58] calls for an express specification of the time when the threat will be carried out. As to the choice between 'immediate' and 'imminent', the latter is more attractive for enabling the defence to succeed where, although there might be a short interval between the making of the threat and its carrying out, the psychological pressure on the defendant would still have been immense.

The issue of whether the threat can be directed at a third party has elicited several views. Under English common law, the threat may be directed at the defendant, a member of his or her

50 See Chapter 1 of this volume (S. Yeo and B. Wright, 'Revitalising Macaulay's Indian Penal Code'), at 4–5.

51 For examples of cases favouring 'immediate', see *R. v. Hurst* [1995] 1 Cr App R 82; and *R. v. Z*, above n. 42. For examples of cases supporting 'imminent', see *R. v. Hudson; R. v. Taylor* [1971] 2 QB 202; and *R. v. Abdul-Hussain* [1999] Crim LR 570.

52 *R. v. Williamson*, above n. 42, at 284; *R. v. Dawson* [1978] VR 536 at 538; *R. v. Brown* (1986) 43 SASR 33, at 39.

53 *R. v. Hudson; R. v. Taylor*, above n. 51; *R. v. Hurst*, above n. 51; *R. v. Brown, ibid.*

54 Criminal Code (Qld), s. 31(1)(d)(iii).

55 Criminal Code (WA), s. 32(2)(b).

56 Criminal Code (Tas), s. 20(1).

57 Above n. 37, cl. 25(2)(b).

58 Chapter 1 of this volume, above n. 50, at 4–5; Chapter 2 of this volume, above n. 11, at 28, 34, 41, and 53.

immediate family or someone for whose safety the defendant reasonably regarded himself or herself as responsible.[59] There is Australian common law authority that the threat may be directed at any person,[60] and this is also the position in the Queensland[61] and Western Australian[62] Codes. Turning to the views of recent law reform bodies, both the English[63] and Australian[64] Codes recommend that the threat may be directed at anyone, and this is also the position in the ICC Statute.[65] This position is attractive for recognising that there may be circumstances involving threats of bodily harm to people, including strangers, which can move ordinary people to commit a crime to prevent the harm occurring.

Regarding whether the law requires the coercer to have been physically present at the scene of the crime, English common law does not explicitly require it, which can be taken to mean that such presence is not a legal requirement.[66] Likewise, Australian common law only requires the threat to have been 'present and continuing'.[67] Clearly, this effect of the threat on the defendant might still operate despite the coercer not being physically present at the scene of the crime. This position is also subscribed to by the Queensland[68] and Western Australian[69] Codes. In contrast, actual presence of the coercer is a necessary condition under the Tasmanian code.[70] It is noteworthy that other recent code formulations also do not require the coercer's physical presence. They include the English and Australian codes as well as the ICC Statute.[71] The strong endorsement of this position is especially pertinent in this modern age of highly sophisticated and technological weapons which can cause harm from a great distance.

While the law of duress does not generally require the threat to have been real,[72] the defendant must, at a minimum, have genuinely believed (subjectively) the threat to be of the relevant gravity. The predominant view is that such belief must, in addition, have been based on reasonable grounds. Both the English[73] and Australian[74] common law subscribes to this hybrid subjective/objective position, as do the Queensland criminal Code[75] and the Australian Code.[76] In contrast, the Western Australian,[77] Tasmanian[78] and English[79] Codes require only a subjective belief by the defendant. It is submitted that the absence of any objective appraisal whatsoever of the defendant's belief works too much in his or her favour and to the detriment of the unfortunate (and very often

59 *R. v. Z*, above n. 42; *R. v. Shayler* [2001] EWCA Crim 1977.
60 *R. v. Abusafiah* (1991) 24 NSWLR 531; *R. v. Hurley and Murray* [1967] VR 526.
61 Criminal Code (Qld), s. 31(1)(d)(i).
62 Criminal Code (WA), s. 32(2)(i), which states simply that 'a threat has been made'.
63 Above n. 37, cl. 25(2)(a).
64 Criminal Code (Cth), s. 10.2(2)(a).
65 Above n. 35, Art. 31(1)(d).
66 See *R. v. Valderrama-Vega* [1985] Crim LR 220.
67 *Hurley and Murray*, above n. 60, at 543.
68 Criminal Code (Qld), s. 31(1)(d).
69 Criminal Code (WA), s. 32(2).
70 Criminal Code (Tas), s. 20(1).
71 Since these provisions are silent about the condition, one can infer that they do not require it.
72 Among the legal sources studied here, only the ICC Statute requires this.
73 *R. v. Graham* [1982] 1 All ER 801; *R. v. Howe* [1987] AC 417; *R. v. Z*, above n. 42.
74 *R. v. Abusafiah*, above n. 60.
75 Criminal Code (Qld), s. 31(d)(ii).
76 Criminal Code (Cth), s. 10.2(2)(a).
77 Criminal Code (WA), s. 32(2)(a)(i).
78 Criminal Code (Tas), s. 20(1).
79 Above n. 37, cl. 25(2).

innocent) victim. However, a balance has to be struck between societal protection and recognising the human reality that certain personal characteristics of the defendant could well affect his or her belief as to the nature of the threat. The English common law approach achieves this balance by infusing these personal characteristics into the concept of reasonableness of the belief. Under this approach, personal characteristics such as the defendant's age, vulnerability or a recognised psychiatric condition which makes him or her more likely than others to regard things said or done as threatening and to believe that they will be carried out will be taken into account when assessing the reasonableness of his or her belief concerning the threat.[80]

The Response to the Threat

Both the English and Australian common law restrict the permissible response of the defendant to the threat in a number of ways. First, certain types of serious crimes, notably murder and certain serious forms of treason, are excluded from the scope of the defence.[81] Secondly, an objective test has to be met as to whether a 'sober person of reasonable firmness', faced with the same circumstances as the defendant, could likewise have responded to the threat in the way the defendant did.[82] Thirdly, the defendant must have taken a reasonable opportunity to escape if one presented itself.[83] Some of the code formulations include these restrictions in closely similar terms. For example, the Queensland[84] and Tasmanian[85] Codes exclude a list of crimes, including murder, from the operation of the defence. The Queensland provision further requires the defendant to have reasonably believed that he or she was 'unable otherwise to escape the carrying out of the threat'.[86]

The most recent statutory formulations of duress permit it to be a defence to murder. They include the provisions in the Western Australian,[87] English and Australian Codes, and the ICC Statute. The primary reason for this stance is that it would be highly unjust to convict and punish a person for murder who, on the basis of a genuine and reasonable belief, had killed in fear of death or some other life-threatening injury in circumstances concerning which a trier of fact would have been satisfied that a person of reasonable firmness might have acted in the same way.[88] To withhold the defence of duress in these circumstances would support the view that 'people ought to act in an exceptionally moral and courageous way ... [and that] [t]hey are being punished for giving way to what will often be enormous fear and wholly understandable human frailty'.[89]

---

80 *R. v. Martin* [2000] 2 Cr App R 42. Cf. Ormerod, above n. 2, at 331, who doubts that this decision will stand in the light of *R. v. Z*, above n. 42, which had emphasised the objective nature of the defence.

81 *R. v. Howe*, above n. 73; *R. v. Japaljarri* (2002) 134 A Crim R 261.

82 See *R. v. Graham*, above n. 73, at 806; *R. v. Lawrence* [1980] 1 NSWLR 122.

83 For example, see *R. v. Hudson; R. v. Taylor*, above n. 51; *R. v. Brown*, above n. 52. Cf. *R. v. Z*, above n. 42, at para. [27].7

84 Criminal Code (Qld), s. 31(2).

85 Criminal Code (Tas), s. 20(1).

86 Criminal Code (Qld), s. 31(1)(d)(ii).

87 Although enacted in 1913, its provisions on duress and necessity underwent major revision in 2008.

88 For a fuller discussion of this and other reasons for recognising duress as a defence to murder, see Law Commission for England and Wales, above n. 37, at paras. [30.9]–[30.16]; Law Commission for England and Wales, *Murder, Manslaughter and Infanticide* (Law Com. No. 304) (London: The Stationery Office, 2006) Part 6; and Victorian Law Reform Commission, *Defences to Homicide: Final Report* (Melbourne: Victorian Law Reform Commission, 2004) paras. [3.150]–[3.151].

89 Law Commission for England and Wales, *Murder, Manslaughter and Infanticide*, *ibid.*, at para. [6.51].

More recent statutory formulations have replaced the tests of 'a person of reasonable firmness' and the 'duty to escape' with restrictions articulated in terms of necessity and reasonableness of the defendant's response. An example of the necessity of the defendant's response is the clause in the English code stating that there must have been 'no other way of preventing the threat being carried out'.[90] Similarly, the Australian Code provides that 'there is no reasonable way that the threat can be rendered ineffective'.[91] As for the reasonableness of the defendant's response, there is the part of the English Code formulation stating that 'the threat is one which in all the circumstances ... he cannot reasonably be expected to resist'.[92] The equivalent clause in the Australian Code states that 'the conduct is a reasonable response to the threat'.[93] The ICC Statute also succinctly imposes these two conditions by requiring the defendant to have acted 'necessarily and reasonably to avoid' the threat.[94] On account of their more encompassing and comprehensible nature, these descriptors of the type of response are preferable to the common law ones involving the person of reasonable firmness and the duty to escape.

As to the determination of whether the defendant's conduct was necessary and reasonable, all are agreed that the inquiry should be objective and not what the defendant genuinely believed to be necessary and reasonable. However, a degree of subjectivity is permissible, with the debate being over which of the defendant's personal characteristics the law should allow to be taken into account. The most subjective among the approaches studied in this chapter is that subscribed to by English common law, where the defendant's age, sex, serious physical disability and, most controversially, recognised psychiatric condition have been regarded as relevant.[95] Recognition of this last characteristic comes very close to the recommendation of the English Code for the threat to be 'one which in all the circumstances (including any of his personal circumstances that affect its gravity) he cannot reasonably be expected to resist'.[96]

Less subjectivity is afforded by the Australian common law, which holds that the person of reasonable firmness against whom the defendant is to be judged is 'a person of the same age and sex and background, and [having] other personal characteristics (except perhaps strength of mind)' as the defendant.[97] Accordingly, recognised psychiatric disorders which reduce the capacity to withstand the psychological pressure posed by threats are irrelevant. This was also the position recommended by the Law Commission reporting on murder, manslaughter and infanticide in relation to its proposed defence of duress to murder.[98] The Commission proposed that, when deciding whether a person of reasonable firmness might have acted as the defendant did, account may be taken of 'all the circumstances of the defendant, including his or her age, but not any other characteristic which bears upon his or her capacity to withstand duress'.[99] This latter approach has much to commend itself for recognising many of the defendant's personal characteristics and circumstances which may have affected his or her response to the threat, without unduly reducing societal protection.

90 Above n. 37, cl. 25(2)(c).
91 Criminal Code (Cth), s. 10.2(2)(b).
92 Above n. 37, cl. 25(2).
93 Criminal Code (Cth), s. 10.2(2)(c).
94 Above n. 35, Art. 31(1)(d).
95 *R. v. Bowen* [1996] 2 Cr App R 157.
96 Above n. 37, cl. 25(2).
97 *R. v. Palazoff* (1986) 43 SASR 99, at 109.
98 Law Commission for England and Wales, *Murder, Manslaughter and Infanticide*, above n. 88.
99 *Ibid.*, at paras. [6.84], [6.86].

Prior Fault

This condition of the defence does not involve the nature of the threat or the response to it. It prevents people from relying on the defence if they were culpable in exposing themselves to the circumstances which led to their being threatened. The term 'prior fault' aptly describes this form of culpability.[100] In relation to duress, it lies in a defendant voluntarily joining a criminal organisation which subsequently compelled him or her to commit the crime charged. With one exception, all the sources of law studied in this chapter include the defendant's prior fault as a condition of the defence of duress. Only the provision in the ICC Statute is silent on the matter. This omission is very likely to have been a drafting oversight as there is a body of international case law supporting the condition of prior fault for duress.[101] Several of the legal authorities which provide for the condition of prior fault stipulate further that it could be made out where the defendant associates with members of a criminal organisation, knowing of its violent character, who then compel him or her by threats to join the organisation.[102] The exclusion of these people from the scope of the defence is warranted in order to deter them from placing themselves at risk of being intimidated into joining the criminal organisation.

Different positions have been taken over two matters pertaining to this condition. The first is whether the defendant must have known that he or she risked being compelled to commit the type of crime alleged, or whether *any* crime would suffice. The former position, which is more generous to the defendant, is subscribed to by the Western Australian[103] and Australian[104] Codes. The latter position is supported by the English common law[105] and the Tasmanian Code.[106] It is submitted that the former stance is to be preferred for not denying the defence to people who may be compelled to commit a crime which fell completely outside their scope of contemplation. As one commentator has vividly stated, 'it is one thing to be aware that you are likely to be beaten up if you do not pay your debts, it is another that you may be aware that you may be required under threat of violence to commit other, though unspecified crimes, if you do not'.[107]

The second matter concerns whether the defendant must have known (subjectively) of the risk of being threatened into committing the crime alleged, or whether it will suffice that he or she ought to have known (objectively) of that risk. The former position has been adopted by the English[108] and Australian[109] Codes. The latter is supported by the English common law[110] and the Western

100 See Yeo, above n. 25, Chapter 5.

101 For a discussion of these authorities, see A. Cassese, *International Criminal Law* (Oxford: Oxford University Press, 2003) 245–6.

102 *R. v. Fitzpatrick* [1977] NI 20; *R. v. Ali* [2008] EWCA Crim 716; Criminal Code (Qld), s. 31(2); Criminal Code (WA), s. 32(3); Criminal Code (Cth), s. 10.2(3).

103 Criminal Code (WA), s. 32(3)(a).

104 Criminal Code (Cth), s. 10.2(3).

105 *R. v. Heath* [2000] Crim LR 109; *R. v. Harmer* [2002] Crim LR 401; *R. v. Z*, above n. 42. The Australian common law has not yet pronounced on this issue.

106 Criminal Code (Tas), s. 20(1). The position taken by the English Code and the Queensland Criminal Codes is uncertain, as their wording on the matter is far less explicit.

107 J.C. Smith, commenting on *R. v. Heath*, above n. 105, at 111.

108 Above n. 37, cl. 25(2).

109 Criminal Code (Cth), s. 10(3), which states that the defence is unavailable only if the defendant shared the *purpose* of the principal to engage in criminal conduct of that kind.

110 *R. v. Z*, above n. 42. The Australian common law has yet to rule on this matter.

Australian Code.[111] It is submitted that the more objective position is to be preferred for requiring a person who is considering joining or associating with a criminal organisation to take reasonable care to determine whether the organisation or its members have a propensity for violence. The objective standard is justified by the definite connection which exists between the person's prior fault in joining or associating with the organisation without taking due care to ascertain its character, and the reasonably anticipated consequence of being threatened into committing the alleged crime.

MODERN FORMULATIONS OF NECESSITY

Judicial and statutory pronouncements on the defence of necessity are scarce compared to those on duress.[112] Nevertheless, the past three decades have seen a small but growing number of authorities in England and Australia recognising necessity not merely as a general principle, but as a distinct defence which operates separately from duress. That said, the close similarity between these two defences demands that the conditions required for each of them should, as far as possible, be the same to achieve coherence, consistency and simplicity in the law. But it would be going too far to suggest that they are identical, save for the difference in the source of the threat. As will be seen in the ensuing discussion, there are a number of material differences between the defences to warrant keeping them separate. For this reason, the approach taken in the ICC Statute of combining both defences into the one provision should not be followed.

At this juncture, it would be helpful to reproduce two leading modern definitions of necessity under English and Australian common law, followed by two recent statutory formulations of the defence from these two jurisdictions. These will facilitate ease of reference in the ensuing discussion of the various conditions of the defence. The provision in the ICC Statute which was reproduced earlier[113] will also be referred to from time to time.

A leading recent pronouncement on necessity under the English common law appears in the Court of Appeal case of *Re A (Children)*[114] involving conjoined twins who had to be surgically separated in order to save the life of the stronger twin.[115] Brooke L.J. said that the defence comprised the following three conditions:

> 1. The act is needed to avoid inevitable and irreparable evil;
>
> 2. No more should be done than is reasonably necessary for the purpose to be achieved; and
> 3. The evil inflicted must not be disproportionate to the evil avoided.[116]

The leading pronouncement on necessity under the Australian common law was delivered by the Victorian Court of Criminal Appeal in *R. v. Loughnan*.[117] There, the defendant had claimed that his

---

111 Criminal Code (WA), s. 32(3)(b). The position taken by the Queensland and Tasmanian Codes is uncertain. If anything, they support an objective stance by denying the defence to a person who, by being a party to a criminal association or conspiracy, rendered himself or herself subject to compulsion.

112 Cf. See above n. 31.

113 See above at 213.

114 [2000] 4 All ER 961.

115 The same situation arose in *State of Queensland v. Nolan* [2002] 1 QR 454, where the Queensland Supreme Court authorised separation on the ground of necessity, applying the specific provisions on surgical operations (s. 282) and parental care (s. 286) of the Queensland Criminal Code.

116 Above n. 114, at 1051.

117 [1981] VR 443.

escape from prison was necessary to preserve himself from death threats issued against him by his fellow prisoners. In their joint judgment, Young C.J. and King J. described the defence as having three conditions:

> 1. The criminal act or acts must have been done only in order to avoid certain consequences which would have inflicted irreparable evil upon the accused or upon others he was bound to protect;
> 2. The accused must honestly believe on reasonable grounds that he was placed in a situation of imminent peril; and
> 3. The acts done to avoid the imminent peril must not be out of proportion to the peril to be avoided.[118]

The similarity in the use of terms and phrases in *Re A (Children)* and *Loughnan* may be explained by the heavy reliance both courts placed on the definition of necessity given by James Stephen in his *A Digest of the Criminal Law*.[119]

Turning now to modern statutory formulations, there is the 1993 version[120] by the English Law Commission of the defence of necessity contained in the English Code. Described as 'duress of circumstances', it appears as cl. 26 of the Commission's bill, the relevant parts[121] of which read as follows:

> (1) No act of a person constitutes an offence if the act is done under duress of circumstances.
> (2) A person does an act under duress of circumstances if –
> (a) he does it because he knows or believes that it is immediately necessary to avoid death or serious injury to himself or another, and
> (b) the danger that he knows or believes to exist is such that in all the circumstances (including any of his personal characteristics that affect its gravity) he could not reasonably be expected to act otherwise.
>
> ...
>
> (3) This section applies in relation to omissions as it applies in relation to acts.
> (4) This section does not apply to a person who knowingly and without reasonable excuse exposed himself to the danger known or believed to exist.
>
> ...
>
> (5) This section does not apply to –
> (a) an act done in the knowledge or belief that a threat has been made to cause death or serious injury to himself or another (see section 25),[122] or
> (b) the use of force within the meaning of section 27[123] or 28,[124] or an act immediately preparatory to the use of force, for the purposes mentioned in section 27(1) or 28(1).

118 *Ibid.*, at 448, and subsequently affirmed in *R. v. Rogers* (1996) 86 A Crim R 542; and *R. v. Lorenz* (1998) 146 FLR 369.

119 See above n. 33, Art. 11.

120 Law Commission for England and Wales, above n. 37.

121 Above n. 38.

122 The provision on duress by threats.

123 The provision on private defence and prevention of crime.

124 The provision on the use of force in effecting or assisting a lawful arrest.

The defence of necessity is described as 'sudden or extraordinary emergency' under the Australian Code. For the sake of brevity, it will be simply called 'necessity' here. It is defined in s. 10.3 as follows:

> (1) A person is not criminally responsible for an offence if he or she carries out the conduct constituting the offence in response to circumstances of sudden or extraordinary emergency;
> (2) This section applies if and only if the person carrying out the conduct reasonably believes that:
> (a) circumstances of sudden or extraordinary emergency exist; and
> (b) committing the offence is the only reasonable way to deal with the emergency; and
> (c) the conduct is a reasonable response to the emergency.

In addition to the above codes, reference will be made to the provisions on necessity appearing in the Queensland and Western Australian Codes.[125] These provisions, like the English Code, expressly exclude from their operation cases which are more appropriately dealt with under the provisions on duress and private defence.[126]

The Nature of the Emergency

Taking its cue from the Australian Code, the word 'emergency' more aptly describes the dire circumstances confronting the defendant than 'threat', which is better suited to cases of duress where the defendant had been threatened by another and ordered to commit the crime charged. In a similar vein, it is more appropriate to say that the defendant had been 'induced' by the emergency to commit the crime rather than 'compelled' to do so, the latter term being more suited to describe cases of duress. Take, for example, X who, having no legal duty to save Y from drowning, causes criminal damage to property as part of a rescue effort. X was not so much compelled to cause such damage since he had a choice not to be involved at all; rather, he was induced by a sense of social or moral responsibility to rescue Y.

Commencing with the types of danger or potential harm occasioned by the emergency, the English and Australian common law describe them as 'irreparable evil'. This non-specification is also evident in the Queensland, Western Australian and Australian Codes, which describe the danger in terms of 'circumstances of sudden or extraordinary emergency'. These common law and statutory descriptors are wide enough to cover any kind of harms including harm to property. In contrast, the English Code and the ICC Statute expressly require the danger to be of death or serious bodily harm. The restriction imposed by the ICC Statute is understandable given the very serious nature of the crimes falling within the jurisdiction of the International Criminal Court.[127] The stance taken by the English Code is much harder to justify and probably stems from a strong desire to keep the scope of the defence within very narrow limits. The non-specification of types of danger is much to be preferred for enabling the defence to be applied whenever the circumstances were such as to justify or excuse the defendant on the ground of necessity.

---

125 The Tasmanian Code does not have a specific provision on necessity. In that jurisdiction, the defence is preserved through s. 8.

126 Criminal Code (Qld), s. 25; Criminal Code (WA), s. 25(1); English Code, above n. 37, cl. 26(5)(b).

127 Namely, crimes against humanity, genocide, war crimes and aggression.

A similar debate over specificity has occurred over the time factor of the emergency for the defence of necessity. There are some authorities which require the emergency to have been 'immediate' or at least 'imminent'. They include the Australian common law,[128] the English Code[129] and the ICC Statute.[130] On the other hand, some authorities such as the Queensland,[131] Western Australian[132] and Australian[133] Codes have used the description of 'circumstances of sudden or extraordinary emergency'. While the adjective 'sudden' is concerned with time, it is about the unexpected onset of the emergency and not when the harmful consequences of the emergency will materialise. The essence of the description lies in the word 'emergency', which connotes circumstances causing immense psychological pressure on the defendant to choose whether or not to commit criminal conduct in order to avoid the danger posed by the emergency. While imminence of the danger may, in some cases, be a significant factor in this build-up of pressure, it is not a necessary condition of an emergency. One could readily imagine situations of emergency without this condition, for example, being trapped in a mine for days or the spread of a life-threatening and highly contagious disease which may take weeks to kill its victims. Given the multifarious circumstances when necessity may be justly invoked, the general descriptor of 'emergency' without more is to be preferred.[134]

All the sources of law studied here recognise that the defence of necessity is applicable to cases where the danger occasioned by the emergency was directed not only at the defendant but also at a third party. This properly encourages an altruistic spirit among members of society to take evasive action to protect the safety and welfare of others.

Concerning the issue of who assesses the nature of the emergency, three views have been expressed. The most subjective of these appears in the English Code, which refers to the defendant's knowledge or belief. At the opposite end is the ICC Statute, which requires the emergency to have been real as an objectively demonstrable fact.[135] The third and most popular view is the hybrid subjective/objective test of the emergency being believed by the defendant on reasonable grounds. This is subscribed to by the English[136] and Australian[137] common law, and the Queensland,[138] Western Australian[139] and Australian[140] Codes. The strong support for this view is on account of its accommodation of the defendant's subjective belief but is tempered with objectivity for the purpose of societal protection. As contended earlier, this is also the preferred position for the closely related defence of duress.[141] For the sake of clarity and consistency, this same approach should be adopted for the defence of necessity.

128 The second condition in the *Loughnan* definition of necessity, above n. 117.

129 Above n. 37, cl. 26(2)(b).

130 Above n. 35, Art. 31(1)(d).

131 Criminal Code (Qld), s. 25.

132 Criminal Code (WA), s. 25(2).

133 Criminal Code (Cth), s. 10,3(1) and (2)(a).

134 Cf. *Re A (Children)*, above n. 114, at 1051, which held that 'the existence of an emergency in the normal sense of the word is not an essential prerequisite for the application of the doctrine of necessity'.

135 Above n. 35, Art. 31(1)(d).

136 *R. v. Conway* [1988] 3 WLR 1238; *R. v. Martin* [1989] 1 All ER 652.

137 The second condition in the *Loughnan* definition of necessity, above n. 117.

138 Criminal Code (Qld), s. 25 read with s. 24 (mistake of fact).

139 Criminal Code (WA), s. 25(3)(a) and (c).

140 Criminal Code (Cth), s. 10.3(2).

141 See above at 216. There are no cases of necessity on this issue and the statutory formulations studied in this chapter are also silent on the matter.

The Response to the Emergency

All the sources of law studied here require the defendant's response to the emergency to have been necessary in the circumstances. In some, the term 'necessary' or a derivative is used,[142] while it is implied in others, an example of which is the provision in the Australian Code that 'committing the offence is the only reasonable way to deal with the emergency'.[143] An inquiry into the necessity for the response is required to ensure that there were no lawful means available to the defendant of avoiding the potential harm occasioned by the emergency besides committing the alleged crime.

Another requirement concerning the response to the emergency involves comparing the harm caused by the defendant in committing the alleged crime with the harm which the emergency would otherwise have produced. The English[144] and Australian[145] common law and the ICC Statute[146] express this in terms of the need for the defendant's response to have been proportionate to the potential harm. Another description is that the defendant's conduct must have been a 'reasonable' response to the potential harm. This is subscribed to by the Queensland,[147] Western Australian,[148] English[149] and Australian[150] Codes, and by the ICC Statute.[151] Casting the defendant's response in terms of reasonableness is attractive for avoiding undue weight to be given to proportionality. While a comparison of the harm caused by the defendant and the harm thereby avoided is often a significant consideration when assessing the reasonableness of his or her response to the emergency, it is not the single factor in deliberating over whether the defendant deserves to be exculpated.[152] Furthermore, making proportionality a strict legal condition of the defence of necessity would exacerbate the problem of having to compare the harm caused with the harm avoided when they are of an entirely different nature.

There is one qualifier to this proposed downplaying of proportionality, which concerns cases where necessity is pleaded as a defence to murder.[153] The arguments in favour of such a recognition

142 Condition 2 of the *Re A (Children)* definition, above n. 114; condition 1 of the *Loughnan* definition, above n. 117; Criminal Code (WA), s. 25(3)(a)(ii); English Code, above n. 37, cl. 26(2)(a); ICC Statute, above n. 35, Art. 31(1)(d).

143 Criminal Code (Cth), s. 10.3(2)(b).

144 Condition 3 of the *Re A (Children)* definition, above n. 114.

145 Condition 3 of the *Loughnan* definition, above n. 117.

146 See the part of Art. 31(1)(d), above n. 35, where it is stated that the defendant 'does not intend to cause greater harm than the one sought to be avoided'.

147 Criminal Code (Qld), s. 25, where it states that 'an ordinary person possessing ordinary power of self-control could not reasonably be expected to act otherwise'.

148 Criminal Code (WA), s. 25(3)(b).

149 Above n. 37, cl. 26(2)(b).

150 Criminal Code (Cth), s. 10.3(2)(c).

151 Above n. 35, Art. 31(1)(d), where it states that the defendant 'acts … reasonably to avoid this threat'.

152 In this regard, there is the Australian High Court's ruling in *Zecevic v. DPP (Vic)* (1987) 162 CLR 645, at 662 (concerning the law of private defence) that 'the whole of the circumstances should be considered, of which the degree of force used may be only part'.

153 Presently, the English common law does not recognise necessity as a defence to murder – see *R. v. Howe*, above n. 73; and *R. v. Selvaratnam* [2006] EWCA Crim 1321 – with the exception of the narrow circumstances delineated by the case of *Re A (Children)*, above n. 114. The Australian common law is unclear on the issue: see Yeo, above n. 25, at 154–5.

have been fully canvassed elsewhere and need not be repeated here.[154] What is well worth highlighting is the fact that every single one of the statutory formulations of necessity studied here permits the defence to apply to murder. Assuming that necessity is so available, there is good reason for making proportionality a separate legal condition over and above the reasonableness of the response. Since the defence of necessity has to be cast in broad terms to accommodate the infinite variety of circumstances where the defence should be made available, some reining in is needed where the defendant's response has been to kill another human being. In practical terms, this will require the trier of fact to compare the number of human lives lost with the number of lives consequently saved, an exercise which should pose few problems since exactly the same type of harm is involved.

Making proportionality a separate condition of the defence in murder cases forces a court to engage fully with the trade-off between one human life and another. However, the other condition of reasonableness prevents placing the sanctity of life principle at a premium and requires a court to take into account other important countervailing considerations, such as the fact that the victim's death was inevitable;[155] the defendant's conduct was done in the 'best interests' of the people involved; killing the victim was the 'lesser evil'; or there were conflicting duties facing the defendant.[156]

Regarding the assessment of whether the defendant's response was necessary and reasonable, it was earlier contended in respect of duress that this should be largely objective.[157] To achieve certainty and coherence in the law, this same approach should be taken by the defence of necessity. Accordingly, the defendant's response will be compared with that of a person of reasonable firmness, sharing the personal characteristics or circumstances of the defendant other than those which bear on his or her capacity to withstand the danger.

Prior Fault

The recognition of such a condition for the defence of necessity has been poor solely because the courts and law reformers have rarely applied their minds to it. Among the legal sources studied here, there are only two instances when this condition has been incorporated into the definition of necessity. One is the English Code, where the defence is unavailable 'to a person who has knowingly and without reasonable excuse exposed himself to the danger'.[158] The other and much

154 For example, see M. Bohlander, 'Of Shipwrecked Sailors, Unborn Children, Conjoined Twins and Hijacked Airplanes – Taking Human Life and the Defence of Necessity' (2006) 70 *Journal of Criminal Law* 147 and commentaries cited therein; and T. Stacy, 'Acts, Omissions and the Necessity of Killing Innocents' (2001–2) 29 *American Journal of Criminal Law* 481.

155 Sometimes described as persons who were 'designated for death', as occurred in the case of Mary in the English Court of Appeal case of *Re A (Children)*, above n. 114.

156 The English Court of Appeal in *Re A (Children)*, *ibid.*, relied on these various considerations to support its decision that necessity could successfully be pleaded in the case before it. For a critical evaluation of the judgments of the three members of the court, see S. Michalowski, 'Sanctity of Life – Are Some Lives More Sacred than Others?' (2002) 22 *Legal Studies* 377; R. Huxtable, 'Separation of Conjoined Twins: Where Next for English Law?' [2002] *Criminal Law Review* 459; I.H. Dennis, 'On Necessity as a Defence to Crime: Possibilities, Problems and the Limits of Justification and Excuse' (2009) 3 *Criminal Law and Philosophy* 2, at 42–3.

157 See above at 217–18.

158 See above n. 37, cl. 26(4).

less clear instance is the provision in the ICC Statute which states that the threat constituted circumstances which were 'beyond [the defendant's] control'.[159] This could be interpreted to mean that the defendant who had control of the circumstances before they turned into an emergency (and therefore were no longer within his or her control) would be denied the defence. Earlier on, the argument was made that the defence of duress should be unavailable to a defendant who knew or ought to have known that, by joining or associating with a criminal organisation, he or she risked being threatened by members of the organisation into committing a crime of the same type as the alleged crime.[160] Adopting this stance, the condition of prior fault for the defence of necessity could be framed in terms of denying the defence to people who were at fault in creating the situation in which they knew, or could have reasonably foreseen, could expose them to the danger which compelled them to commit a crime of the same type as that which was actually committed.

REFORMULATIONS OF DURESS AND NECESSITY FOR THE IPC

The preceding evaluation of the existing IPC provisions and modern formulations of the defences of duress and necessity provides a solid groundwork to revise the IPC provisions. In an endeavour to retain as much of the existing IPC provisions which have been assessed to be sound, the wording and structure of those provisions will be left unaltered wherever possible.

Duress

It is proposed that s. 94 of the IPC be reformulated to read as follows:

> Nothing is an offence which is done by a person who is compelled to do it by threats and who, at the time of doing it, reasonably believes that imminent death or grievous hurt to that person or another will otherwise be the consequence, provided:
>
> (1) the act was a necessary and reasonable response to the threat; and
>
> (2) the person doing the act did not of his own accord place himself in a situation in which he knows, or could have reasonably foreseen, that he would thereby expose himself to the risk of causing the type of harm complained of.
>
> *Explanation 1* – When assessing the reasonableness of the person's belief as to the threat, consideration will be given to any of his personal characteristics or circumstances that affects the gravity of the threat.
>
> *Explanation 2* – When assessing the necessity for and reasonableness of the person's response to the threat, consideration will be given to any of his personal characteristics or circumstances other than those which affect his capacity to withstand the threat.
>
> *Illustrations*
>
> (a) X, a smith, is seized by a gang of dacoits who threaten to kill Y, a stranger, within a short period of time if X does not force the door of a house some distance away for the dacoits to enter and plunder it. X does so while the gang holds the stranger hostage. X is entitled to the benefit of this exception provided he was not given a reasonable opportunity to escape from the gang or to seek the assistance of the public authorities without jeopardising Y's life.

159 See above n. 35, Art. 31(1)(d).

160 See above at 219.

(b) Y believes, as a result of his schizophrenia, that Z, his carer, has threatened to slice off his arm if he does not carry out Z's order to forge a document so as to benefit Z. In fact, Z has only threatened to feed Y a lesser amount of food. When deciding whether Y has reasonably believed that the threat was to cause the loss of his arm, the effect of his schizophrenia on that belief will be relevant. However, the schizophrenia will not be relevant for the purpose of determining whether Y's criminal conduct was a necessary and reasonable response to the threat if Y's schizophrenia had affected his capacity to resist the threat.

(c) A person who, of his own accord, joins or associates with a gang of dacoits, knowing their character, is not entitled to the benefit of this exception on the ground of his knowing or reasonably foreseeing that he may be compelled by his associates to commit the offence of extortion.

Following Macaulay's footsteps, brief explanatory notes are offered here to highlight some of the salient features of the proposed defence and to shed further light on the thinking behind them. The defence of duress has been given recognition as a concession to human frailty in the face of serious threats. Regarding the nature of the threat required, only threats of bodily harm in the form of death or grievous hurt will suffice. The present definition of 'grievous hurt' is outmoded and will require revision.[161] The reason for specifying these serious types of threats is in order to keep the scope of the defence within narrow limits. People are expected not to breach the law by yielding to threats of lesser types of harm – a view held by many legal systems.

The threatened harm must be 'imminent', which permits a short time interval between the defendant's non-compliance with the coercer's orders and the carrying out of the threat. The threat may be directed at anyone, including a total stranger. This serves to recognise that people may be so affected by the threat of death or grievous hurt to another human being as to comply with the coercer's orders. The coercer need not be physically present when the alleged crime was committed, it being sufficient that the defendant reasonably believed that the coercer had the means to carry out the threat wherever he or she might be situated. Illustration (a) is a case in point.

The defendant's response to the threat must have been both necessary and reasonable in the circumstances. The commission of the alleged crime would be regarded as an unnecessary response if there was any other reasonable way that the threat could have been rendered ineffective, such as by taking a reasonable opportunity to escape or seeking the protection of the public authorities. When considering whether the response was reasonable, the proportionality of the harm caused by the defendant and the harm consequently avoided will be one of several factors to be taken into account. The totality of the circumstances should be considered, including the degree of imminence of the threat, who the defendant and coercer were, and who was the subject of the threat. Illustration (a) provides a case example. The proposed defence permits duress to be pleaded in answer to a murder charge, in which case, the defendant will be claiming that it was a necessary and reasonable response to kill a person. For such a claim to succeed, the threat confronting the defendant must invariably be of death to a person; grievous hurt will not suffice.

The nature of the threat is to be assessed according to the defendant's belief based on reasonable grounds. Any of the defendant's personal characteristics and circumstances which have a bearing on the gravity of the threat will be relevant, including his or her age, vulnerability and recognised

161 For a discussion of this definition and proposals for reform, see S. Yeo, N. Morgan and W. Chan, *Criminal Law in Malaysia and Singapore* (Singapore: LexisNexis, 2007) paras. [11.33]–[11.42], [12.22]. There is also the definition proposed by the Law Commission of India in its 1971 report on the IPC, above n. 16, and reproduced at 206.

psychiatric condition. The evaluation of the need for and reasonableness of the defendant's response to the threat is on a more objective footing. It is for the trier of fact to make this evaluation, who will take into account any of the defendant's personal characteristics and circumstances which have a bearing on the matter, other than those which affect mental strength. Illustration (b) is a case example.

For the defence to succeed, the defendant must not have exposed himself or herself to the risk of being threatened by joining a criminal organisation or otherwise associating with members of the organisation, knowing of their violent nature. The defence will fail even if the defendant did not actually know of the risk, provided that it could have been reasonably foreseen by him or her. However, the defence remains available where the alleged crime was not of the same type as that which the defendant knew or could reasonably have foreseen he or she may be compelled to commit. Illustration (c) provides a case example.[162]

Necessity

The current provision on necessity in the IPC leaves much to be desired and will require radical transformation to make its conditions clear, comprehensible and workable. Since the defences of duress and necessity are very similar, it would be both appropriate and beneficial for the formulation of duress proposed above to serve as a template for the more general defence of necessity. With these considerations in mind, s. 81 of the IPC could read as follows:

> Nothing is an offence which is done by a person who is induced to do it in response to circumstances of emergency which, at the time of doing it, reasonably believes that harm will otherwise be the consequence, provided:
>
> (1) the act was a necessary and reasonable response to the emergency;
>
> (2) the person doing the act was not at fault in creating a situation in which he knows, or could have reasonably foreseen, that he would thereby expose himself to the risk of causing the type of harm complained of; and
>
> (3) as an answer to a murder charge, the act of killing was reasonably proportionate to the harm which was thereby avoided.
>
> (4) This section does not apply to –
>
> (a) an act done under a threat by a person of harming the defendant or some other person, or the property of the defendant or of some other person, if the defendant refused to do it,
>
> or
>
> (b) an act done in private defence of the person or of property.
>
> *Explanation 1* – When assessing the reasonableness of the person's belief as to the circumstances of emergency, consideration will be given to any of his personal characteristics or circumstances that affects the gravity of the danger posed by the emergency.
>
> *Explanation 2* – When assessing the necessity for and reasonableness of the person's response to the emergency, consideration will be given to any of his personal characteristics or circumstances other than those which affect his capacity to withstand the pressure created by the emergency.
>
> *Illustrations*
>
> (a) X, reasonably believing that a great fire is out of control, pulls down a row of houses in order to prevent the conflagration from spreading. He does this with the intention of saving more

162 Robbery is defined in IPC, s. 390 as involving either theft or extortion.

houses. If it is found that the emergency was such as to make it necessary and reasonable to do what X did, he is not guilty of an offence.

(b) Y, a teenage mother, steals food to feed her infant believing that it is on the verge of starving to death. When deciding the reasonableness of Y's belief that her infant was in danger of dying, Y's age will be relevant. However, Y cannot contend that her youth affected her capacity to resist the danger.

(c) Z, the captain of a steam vessel, suddenly and without any fault on his part, finds himself in a position where he reasonably believes that, before he can stop his vessel, he must inevitably run down a boat A, with 20 passengers on board, unless he changes the course of his vessel, and that, by changing his course, he will run down a boat B,[163] with only two passengers on board. Here, if Z alters his course for the purpose of avoiding the danger to the passengers in boat A, and there are no other reasonable means of avoiding running down boat B, he is not guilty of an offence though he may run down boat B and kill the two passengers.

The following explanatory note commences with the observation that any inconvenient overlap between the defence of necessity and those of duress and private defence is avoided by sub-section (4).

In order to accommodate the infinite variety of cases where the defence of necessity should be allowed, several of the conditions of this proposed formulation are far less restrictive than their equivalents in the reformulated s. 94 on duress. Thus, the types of potential harm occasioned by the emergency are left unspecified – they could certainly include damage to property belonging to anyone, as illustration (a) shows. Nor does the provision insist on the imminence of the emergency so as to cater for cases where the defence should be allowed to exculpate a defendant despite a considerable period of time lapsing before the harm occurs.

The remainder of the conditions are mostly identical to their counterparts in the provision on duress. One of these is the appraisal of the nature of the emergency according to the defendant's reasonable belief, taking into consideration any personal characteristic or circumstance of the defendant which has a bearing on the gravity of the danger created by the emergency. Another is the requirement for the defendant's response to have been necessary and reasonable to avoid the danger. Here, account will be taken of any of the defendant's personal characteristics and circumstances except those which have a bearing on the capacity to withstand the pressure created by the emergency. A case example is given in illustration (b). There is also the proviso relating to prior fault which denies the defence to persons who had created a situation in which they knew or ought to have known that they would thereby expose themselves to the risk of causing the type of harm for which they were charged. Illustration (c) uses the expression 'without fault on his part', which alludes to this proviso.

As with duress, necessity is recognised as a defence to murder. However, since the conditions pertaining to the nature of the danger are not as specific compared to duress, a requirement of proportionality has been added which has the effect of counting the number of lives saved with those lost. This aspect of the proportionality requirement is satisfied where only one life is taken in order to save another life, including the defendant's. However, the inquiry into proportionality is done in conjunction with the requirement that the killing was reasonable. This has the effect of requiring the court to take into consideration not only the sanctity of life principle but also other equally significant

163 Under the current IPC illustration, there is a chance that Z might be able to avoid running down boat B. This might be read as suggesting a restriction on the defence which is not warranted. To avoid this, the proposed illustration shows that the defence is available even where Z would inevitably run down boat B.

factors such as the 'best interest' principle, whether the victim's death was inevitable, whether there was a conflict of duties and whether killing the victim was the 'lesser evil'. In illustration (c), the captain's successful plea of necessity could be supported by his satisfying the requirement of proportionality combined with his duty to his passengers and the 'lesser evil' doctrine.

CONCLUSION

This chapter began with Macaulay's opinion that the defences of duress and necessity were too difficult to formulate for inclusion in his draft Penal Code and that cases where they were pleaded were best dealt with through the exercise of executive clemency. The framers of the IPC thought otherwise and included provisions on duress and necessity. Present-day legal opinion likewise strongly supports the recognition of these defences and their inclusion in modern criminal codes. Based on this, it is considered appropriate for duress and necessity to remain general exceptions in the IPC.

A critical evaluation of the existing IPC provision on duress found many of its conditions to be sound. Where they were not or where there was ambiguity, modern views on those conditions were relied upon to help devise improved and better articulated conditions. A similar exercise found the IPC provision on necessity to be much less satisfactory. The reconstructed provision proposed in this chapter constitutes a remodelling of the new provision on duress to suit the more general plea of necessity, coupled with modern views about the conditions for such a defence.

In this exercise of reformulating the IPC provisions on duress and necessity, several of Macaulay's core objectives when drafting his Code were borne in mind. They were that the law 'should cover all contingencies; ... it should suppress crime with least infliction of suffering and allow for the ascertaining of the truth at the smallest possible cost of time and money; ... its language should be clear, unequivocal and concise; ... and [u]niformity [is] to be the chief end'.[164] Consequently, the conditions of the defences were expressed with as much precision as practically possible, without making them so specific or restrictive as to cause deserving cases to fall outside the scope of the defences. While minimisation of judicial discretion in interpreting and applying the conditions was a dominant aim, some flexibility in the conditions was needed to accommodate the infinite variety of circumstances when duress or necessity could arise. This attempt to reconcile principle with pragmatism[165] is well represented in the concept of 'reasonableness' found in the reformulations of the two defences. Although the reformulated defences proposed in this chapter will never satisfy everyone, it is hoped that all will agree that they are definite improvements on the current provisions in the IPC.

164 T.B. Macaulay, *The Complete Works of Lord Macaulay* (vol. XI) (Albany edn) (London: Longham, Green & Co., 1898) Minute 4 June 1835; see also Chapter 2 of this volume, above n. 11, at 23 and 35.

165 Chapter 2 of this volume, above n. 11, at 41, 43 and 53.

Chapter 10
Insanity[1]

Gerry Ferguson

INTRODUCTION

It has long been recognised that persons who commit a criminal harm while insane should not be convicted or punished. If, due to insanity, they do not know what they are doing or that it is wrong, then they are not morally responsible for their conduct. Conviction and punishment in such circumstances would be unjust and unlikely to act as a deterrent. However, such persons may pose a continuing threat to society due to the risk of committing further offences. Thus, the law provides for a special, qualified verdict – not guilty on account of insanity. After such a verdict, the insane acquittee remains subject to state supervision and/or treatment, often in a mental hospital. The major legal challenge in respect to the insanity defence in a modern criminal code is to properly define its scope. How mentally impaired must a person be in order to successfully rely on the insanity defence?

While traditionally called the insanity defence in most countries, in the Indian Penal Code (IPC), for reasons that are not perfectly clear, the codifiers chose to use the expression 'unsoundness of mind'. More recently, some other countries have decided that the word 'insanity' is outdated or unduly pejorative, and have renamed the defence. In 1992, Canada dropped the word 'insanity' and substituted the words 'mental disorder'. Similarly, several Australian jurisdictions have exchanged the word 'insanity' for the words 'mental impairment'.[2] In the final section of this chapter on proposals for reform, I recommend that the words 'mental impairment' be used rather than 'unsoundness of mind' in a revised IPC. However, for convenience, I will continue to use the expression 'the insanity defence' in the text of this chapter.

Due to space limitations, I shall deal only with the substantive law issue of defining the scope of the insanity test (and its relationship to automatism) and not with other important, related procedural, evidentiary and dispositional issues.[3] This is, in a way, an unfortunate constraint since some of these other issues are critical to an understanding not only of the scope, but also

---

1 This chapter draws heavily from G. Ferguson, 'The Insanity Defence in Canada, Malaysia and Singapore: A Tale of Two Codes' (1990) 17 *Journal of Malaysian and Comparative Law* 1; S. Yeo, N. Morgan and W. Chan, *Criminal Law in Malaysia and Singapore* (Singapore: LexisNexis, 2007); and S. Yeo, 'The Insanity Defence in the Criminal Laws of the Commonwealth of Nations' [2008] *Singapore Journal of Legal Studies* 241.

2 See S. Bronitt and B. McSherry, *Principles of Criminal Law* (2nd edn, Pyrmont: Lawbook Co., 2005) 212–13.

3 Related issues include: (a) fitness to stand trial; (b) the precise name for the qualified verdict; (c) whether the accused or prosecutor bears the burden of proving insanity; (d) whether the prosecutor can raise the insanity defence at trial over the objection of the accused; (e) the use of expert psychiatric or psychological evidence; (f) whether the jury should be informed, before their deliberations, of the consequences of an insanity verdict (that is, continuing state supervision after such a verdict); and (g) what types of dispositions are available, or should be available, to the court after a verdict of not guilty by reason of insanity is rendered (for example, absolute or conditional discharge, or commitment to a treatment facility, and what type of

of the actual application and use of the insanity defence in various jurisdictions. I want to briefly mention three of these factors:

(1) The issue of disposition after a finding of not guilty by reason of insanity is the most important factor in its actual use. For the past 200 years, the tail has been wagging the dog. Apart from some relatively recent reforms in some jurisdictions, persons found not guilty by reason of insanity have been automatically committed to indefinite confinement in a mental institution at the pleasure of the state. In practice, this often meant lifetime commitment. Thus, the insanity defence was only relied upon by accused persons in the most serious of criminal cases, frequently murder, which was punishable by death or life imprisonment. The disposition after a verdict of not guilty due to insanity was too severe or draconian for the accused to choose to rely on the insanity defence for less serious offences, even if the defence would have succeeded. More recently, some jurisdictions, such as Canada, England and New South Wales to name just three, have authorised judges to use a full range of dispositions after a finding of not guilty by reason of insanity, including absolute discharges and discharges on conditions. Commitment to a mental institution is imposed only when necessary and is subject to frequent reviews and, in some jurisdictions, caps on the total length of confinement which can be no longer than the sentence for the offence which the accused would have been convicted if he or she was not found insane. Thus, regardless of whether the substantive definition of insanity is broad or narrow, the extent to which it is actually used will very much depend on the law and practices which govern dispositions after an insanity verdict is rendered.[4]

(2) Because the test for insanity has traditionally been quite high or strict, it very often fails even in cases where the accused was seriously mentally disordered at the time of the offence. This reality prompted a few jurisdictions to introduce a partial defence of diminished responsibility, where mental disorder short of insanity could reduce murder (in some cases punishable by death) to manslaughter (with flexible sentencing options). A defence of diminished responsibility has existed for some time in Scottish common law[5] and was legislatively enacted in England in 1957[6] and, following the English provision, in Singapore in 1961,[7] Queensland in 1961[8] and New South Wales in 1974 (as amended in 1997).[9] Most other jurisdictions, including India and Malaysia, have no diminished responsibility defence. In jurisdictions with a diminished responsibility defence, that defence is frequently relied upon instead of the insanity defence,

review procedures and safeguards should be in place for persons who are committed to a treatment facility following an insanity verdict).

4 For data on the increased use of the insanity defence in England after the enactment of changes which liberalised the disposition for those found unfit to plead or not guilty by reason of insanity, see R.D. Mackay, B.J. Mitchell and L. Howe, 'Yet More Facts about the Insanity Defence' [2006] *Criminal Law Review* 399.

5 In Scotland, the plea of diminished responsibility was significantly revised in *Galbraith v. HM Advocate (No. 2)* 2002 JC 1. See Scottish Law Commission, *Report on Insanity and Diminished Responsibility* (Edinburgh: The Stationery Office, 2004) 30–44; and J. Chalmers, 'Reforming the Pleas of Insanity and Diminished Responsibility: Some Aspects of the Scottish Law Commission's Discussion Paper' (2003) 8(2) *Scottish Law and Practice Quarterly* 79, at 86–94.

6 Homicide Act 1957 (Chapter 11) (UK), s. 2. This provision was significantly revised in 2009: see Chapter 14 of this volume (C. Clarkson, 'Recent Law Reform and Codification of the General Principles of Criminal Law in England and Wales: A Tale of Woe').

7 Singaporean Penal Code, s. 300, Exception 7.

8 Criminal Code (Qld), s. 304A.

9 Crimes Act (NSW), s. 23A.

and thus the need for a broader or more liberal definition of insanity is less pressing. Conversely, the broader the scope of the insanity defence, the less may be the need for the partial defence of diminished responsibility.[10] Thus, it can be seen that the existence, scope and actual use of a defence of diminished responsibility can in both theory and practice be highly relevant to how the insanity defence is or should be defined. The proposals for reform to the insanity defence in the IPC in this chapter are premised on the assumption that no defence of diminished responsibility exists.

(3) While the appropriate scope of the insanity defence and the words that should be chosen to properly describe its scope are important, there is some evidence (mainly from mock jury studies conducted in the US) that the precise wording of the insanity test is less relevant in deciding insanity cases than we might assume. In other words, there is some evidence that juries (and perhaps judges) often ignore the precise wording of the test and instead apply a more general, intuitive standard.[11] In practice, whether an accused's insanity defence succeeds in any given case may be affected more by a host of factors[12] other than the precise language of the test.[13] Cultural beliefs about mental disorder held by the public, the medical profession and the judiciary will also affect the use and application of the insanity defence, regardless of its specific wording.[14]

With the above constraints in mind, I will analyse the insanity/unsoundness of mind provisions in the IPC and then attempt to fashion the best test possible, a test which is based on, and consistent with, underlying legal and moral principles of responsibility.

---

10 Yeo, above n. 1, at 256–7, makes this point in the context of the diminished responsibility defence in Singapore.

11 Mock jury studies have shown that juries reach the same verdict in most cases regardless of which type of insanity test is used. See N.J. Finkel, R. Shaw, S. Bercaw and J. Koch, 'Insanity Defenses: From the Jurors' Perspective' (1985) 9 *Law and Psychology Review* 77; and J.R.P. Ogloff, 'A Comparison of Insanity Defense Standards on Juror Decision Making' (1991) 15 *Law and Human Behavior* 509.

12 Other factors that may influence the verdict more than the precise wording of the test include the nature of the offence (including the degree of violence and bizarreness of the offence), prior mental history (this increases the success rate), gender (females succeed in the insanity defence more than males), age (the older the offender, the greater the likelihood of success in pleading insanity), the nature and extent of medical evidence and the persuasiveness of expert witnesses, whether the accused's mental illness is treatable, the judge or jurors' prior experience with mental illness, and the judge or jurors' sometimes intuitive like or dislike of the accused. See, for example, K.E. Whittemore and J.R.P. Ogloff, 'Factors that Influence Jury Decision Making' (1995) 19 *Law and Human Behavior* 283; C. Cirincione, H.J. Steadman and M.A. McGreevy, 'Rates of Insanity Acquittals and the Factors Associated with Successful Insanity Pleas' (1995) 23 *Bulletin of the American Academy of Psychiatry and Law* 339; and C. Breheney, J. Groscup and M. Galietta, 'Gender Matters in the Insanity Defence' (2007) 31 *Law and Psychology Review* 93.

13 See G. Ferguson, 'A Critique of Proposals to Reform the Insanity Defence' (1989) 14 *Queen's Law Journal* 135, at 143.

14 See G. Ferguson, 'Legal Regulation of Mental Disorder: Looking East and West' in D.M. Johnson and G. Ferguson (eds), *Asia-Pacific Legal Development* (Vancouver: UBC Press, 1998).

BACKGROUND TO THE 1860 IPC PROVISION ON THE UNSOUNDNESS OF MIND DEFENCE

Macaulay's Draft Code (1837)

While Macaulay noted in the Introductory Letter attached to his proposed Penal Code for India[15] that his Code was not based on any one existing legal system, it was nonetheless to a large extent, with respect to substantive law, an improved version of the English law of the 1830s. However, in terms of style and form, his Code was light years ahead of the English statutes of the day.[16] Macaulay also indicated in the Introductory Letter that he derived valuable assistance in drafting his Code from examining the wording of similar concepts in the French Penal Code of 1810 and Edward Livingston's draft Penal Code for Louisiana of 1826.[17]

Macaulay's treatment of insanity as a defence reflects his reliance on English common law and the above two codes. For several centuries, the English common law recognised that certain persons were so lacking in reason that they could not be fairly convicted and punished for their actions.[18] As Blackstone noted, these persons included infants, idiots and lunatics (namely persons who were of previous sound mind but who had fallen into 'madness' at the time of the offence).[19] Consistent with that common law scheme, Macaulay drafted the following four provisions in Chapter III on 'General Exceptions':

> Clause 64. Nothing is an offence which is done by a child under seven years of age.
> Clause 65. Nothing is an offence which is done by a child above seven years of age and under twelve, who has not attained sufficient maturity of understanding to judge of the nature and consequences of his conduct on that occasion.
> Clause 66. Nothing is an offence which is done by a person in a state of idiotcy.
> Clause 67. Nothing is an offence which a person does in consequence of being mad or delirious at the time of doing it.

Clause 67 in Macaulay's draft Code is consistent with the straightforward provision on madness in Art. 64 of the French Penal Code of 1810 which, in its English translation, provides:

---

15 T.B. Macaulay, J.M. Macleod, G.W. Anderson and F. Millett, *A Penal Code Prepared by the Indian Law Commissioners* (London: Pelham Richardson, 1838) (reprinted by the Lawbook Exchange, Ltd, 2002).

16 Macaulay's draft Code was clear, concise, comprehensive, rationally organised and made use of unique legislative techniques such as Explanations and Illustrations to enhance clarity. See Chapter 2 of this volume (B. Wright, 'Macaulay's Indian Penal Code: Historical Context and Originating Principles') at 22–3 and 38–43; R. Cross 'The Making of English Criminal Law: (5) Macaulay' [1978] *Criminal Law Review* 519.

17 Edward Livingston's Introductory Report to the Code of Crimes and Punishments and his proposed Code of Crimes and Punishments, submitted to the Louisiana legislature in 1826, are reproduced in *The Complete Works of Edward Livingston on Criminal Jurisprudence* (Montclair: Patterson Smith, 1968 reprint).

18 See, for example, W. Blackstone, *Commentaries on the Laws of England* (Book IV) (New York: W.E. Dean, 1840) at 14, where he states:

> For where there is no discernment, there is no choice; and where there is no choice there can be no act of the will, which is nothing else but a determination of one's choice to do or to abstain from a particular action: he, therefore, that has no understanding, can have no will to guide his conduct.

And, at 16, Blackstone states: 'In criminal cases therefore idiots and lunatics are not chargeable for their own acts, if committed while under these incapacities …'

19 *Ibid.*, at 14.

> There is no crime or offence when the accused was in a state of madness [*démence*] at the time of the act …

Likewise, Art. 35 of Livingston's draft Penal Code for Louisiana is equally brief. It states:

> No act done by a person in a state of INSANITY can be punished as an offence.

However, Livingston also provided an interesting, though somewhat awkward, definition of insanity in the definition section of his Code.[20]

Macaulay provided no illustrations for cls. 64–7, nor did he discuss these provisions in the *Notes* attached to his Code. He was of the view that these, and most of the other defences or exceptions in Chapter III of his Code, 'require no explanation or defence'.[21] Notwithstanding Macaulay's silence on the point, the following comments are worth noting:

> (1) As we shall soon see, cl. 67 was not included in the enacted IPC; it was replaced by s. 84 which was significantly influenced by the 1843 M'Naghten Rules.[22]
> (2) Section 67 was a better drafted provision than the French or Louisiana provisions since it explicitly set out a requisite causal connection: the 'offence' must have been committed 'in consequence of being mad' and the madness must have existed 'at the time of doing it'.
> (3) Whether cl. 67 was broader than the English common law at that time is an open question; since it was never enacted, one can only speculate on how the judiciary would have interpreted the word 'mad', including the question of whether 'madness' required the accused to be totally bereft of the capacity to reason, or whether some lesser forms of 'madness' would suffice.[23]

The Common Law before the M'Naghten Rules

In the eighteenth century, the legal test for the defence of insanity or madness was quite stringent. It required total deprivation of understanding and it was sometimes described as requiring the accused to be in a state of mind akin to that of a wild beast.[24] The leading case was *R. v. Arnold* decided in

---

20 Livingston's style of drafting was to define words which were capitalised in his Code, above n. 17. In the definition section of his Code, he provided the following definition of insanity:

> INSANITY – a malady operating on the perceptive or on the reasoning faculties of the mind, which either prevents the person affected from receiving true impressions through his senses, or from drawing just conclusions from what is truly perceived; and existing in such a degree as to render him incapable of performing the usual duties or transacting the ordinary affairs of life.

21 Above n. 15, Note B (On the Chapter of General Exceptions) 79.

22 *Daniel M'Naghten's Case* (1843) 10 Cl & Fin 200, 8 ER 718.

23 J.D. Mayne, *The Criminal Law of India* (2nd edn, Madras: Higginbotham & Co., 1901), at 403–4, was of the view that the 1837 draft was more generous to the insane than the 1860 provision, that Macaulay appeared to believe he was laying down a plain statement of English law at that time and that his provision on insanity seemed to embody defence counsel Thomas Erskine's argument in *R. v. Hadfield* (1800) 27 St Tr 1281, discussed below, where Erskine told the jury: 'I must convince you, not only that the prisoner was a lunatic, but that the act in question was the immediate and unqualified offspring of the disease.'

24 See A.M. Platt and B.L. Diamond, 'The Origins and Development of the "Wild Beast" Concept of Mental Illness and its Relation to Theories of Criminal Responsibility' (1965) 1 *Journal of History of the Behavioral Sciences* 335; D.N. Robinson, *Wild Beasts and Idle Humours: The Insanity Defense from Antiquity to the Present* (Cambridge, MA: Harvard University Press, 1996).

1724, where the jury was told that the accused must be 'totally deprived of his understanding and memory'.[25] The accused attempted to kill the victim under the insane belief that the victim had sent devils and goblins to persecute him. The accused was convicted because he had sufficient reasoning powers to know that he was attempting to kill another human being even though his attempt to do so was entirely motivated by his insane delusions.[26] In 1760, in *R. v. Ferrers*,[27] Earl Ferrers was tried before the full House of Lords. All 117 Lords unanimously rejected his defence of insanity on a charge of murder on the grounds that he was not totally insane at the time of the murder. In spite of the stringent legal test, there were, nevertheless, approximately 50 successful insanity pleas in the Old Bailey for the 60-year period from 1740 to 1800.[28] No doubt some of these verdicts arose from a relaxed application of that test by sympathetic juries.

In 1800, a breakthrough of sorts occurred in the articulation of the insanity test in *R. v. Hadfield*.[29] The accused's famous counsel, Thomas Erskine, persuaded the trial judge, Lord Kenyon, that insanity need not be total, that the accused need not lack all understanding and that insanity could be established by showing that the accused suffered from an insane delusion that prompted his act. Hadfield was under the insane delusion that he had been commanded by God to sacrifice his life to save the world. He chose to sacrifice his life by firing a shot at the king in the hope that he would be tried, convicted and hanged for attempted treason. Obviously he knew what he was doing and that it was a crime. As such, he was not entirely bereft of reason. However, under those circumstances, the trial judge suggested to the jury that they should acquit Hadfield of treason by reason of insanity and they did.[30]

Forty years later, Daniel M'Naghten found himself in a similar situation. He appeared to have an insane delusion that the Prime Minister, Sir Robert Peel, and his Tories were persecuting him and wanted to kill him. Prompted by that delusion, he shot and killed Edward Drummond, whom he mistakenly thought was the Prime Minister. In essence, his counsel argued that although he knew what he was doing, he could not properly distinguish *and therefore choose* right from wrong due to his insane delusion.[31] The trial judge, Tindal C.J., instructed the jury that the test of insanity

25 (1724) 16 St Tri 695, at 765. Also discussed in N. Walker, *Crime and Insanity in England* (Edinburgh: Edinburgh University Press, 1968) 53–7; and F. McAuley and J.P. McCutcheon, *Criminal Liability* (Dublin: Round Hall Ltd., 2000) 645.

26 See McAuley and McCutcheon, *ibid.*, at 645.

27 (1760) 19 St Tr 885, discussed in Walker, above n. 25, at 55–8.

28 Walker, *ibid.*, at 67.

29 Above n. 23.

30 Walker, above n. 25, at 78. The *Hadfield* case promoted the hasty enactment in England of the Criminal Lunatics Act 1800 (Chapter 94) which mandated the special verdict 'not guilty on account of insanity' and the special disposition following such a verdict of being 'kept in strict custody … until His Majesty's pleasure shall be known'.

31 M'Naghten's defence, like Hadfield's, presented a real challenge to his able counsel, Alexander Cockburn. Based on the prosecution's evidence, Cockburn could not argue that M'Naghten was unaware of what he was doing or that he was totally unable to distinguish between right and wrong. In effect, he had to persuade the court, like Erskine did, to accept a test of insanity which was not really recognised by the authorities. He proceeded to supply a medical theory which would be of assistance to his case. He suggested that the mind was divided into two separate and distinct compartments; the intellect and the moral faculties (that is, sentiments, affections, propensities and passions). He further argued that insanity could be partial, operating upon one compartment but not the other. He then argued that M'Naghten's insanity involved an aberration of the latter compartment, namely his moral faculties, such that it took away his power of self-control and rendered him incapable of resisting his delusions. His reference to aberration of the 'moral faculties' was a clever attempt to smuggle the new notion (volitional impairment) into the insanity test under

was whether the accused, at the time of his act, 'had or had not the use of his understanding, so as to know that he was doing a wrong or wicked act'. The trial judge further stated that if M'Naghten 'was not sensible, at the time he committed [the act], [of the fact] that he was violating the laws both of God and man', then he was entitled to a verdict of not guilty on the ground of insanity. And finally he added that, 'if, on the contrary, [the jury] were of the opinion that when he committed the act he was in a sound state of mind, then their verdict must be [guilty]'.[32] Based on that instruction, the jury obviously felt he was not of sound mind and found him not guilty by reason of insanity, even though he knew what he was doing and knew that trying to kill the Prime Minister was against the law.

The M'Naghten Rules

The jury's verdict of not guilty by reason of insanity in *M'Naghten's Case* provoked public indignation and a debate in the House of Lords, after which the Lords referred a number of specific questions concerning the legal test for insanity to the judges of England. The judges' answers are commonly known as the M'Naghten Rules.[33] McAuley and McCutcheon[34] helpfully summarise the judges' answers as follows:

> *Rule 1.* Persons who labour under partial delusions only, and are not in other respects insane, and who act under the influence of an insane delusion of redressing or revenging some supposed grievance or injury, or producing some public benefit, are nevertheless punishable if they knew at the time of committing the crime that they were acting contrary to the law of the land.
> *Rule 2.* Every man is presumed to be sane and to possess a sufficient degree of reason to be responsible for his crimes until the contrary be proved.
> *Rule 3.* To establish a defence on the ground of insanity, it must be clearly proved that, at the time of the committing of the act, the party accused was laboring under such a defect of reason, from disease of the mind, as not to know the nature and quality of the act he was doing; or, if he did know it, that he did not know what he was doing was wrong. [With respect to the latter part of this Rule,] [i]f the accused was conscious that the act was one that he ought not to do, and if that act was at the same time contrary to the law of the land, he is punishable.
> *Rule 4.* A person labouring under a partial delusion only and not in other respects insane must be considered in the same situation with regard to responsibility as if the facts with respect to which the delusion exists were real. For example, if under the influence of his delusion he supposes another man to be in the act of attempting to take away his life and he kills that man as he supposes in self-defence, he would be exempt from punishment. If his delusion was that the deceased had inflicted a serious injury to his character and fortune, and he killed him in revenge for such supposed injury, he would be liable for punishment.

The M'Naghten Rules were fashioned with a clear intent to limit the scope and application of the insanity defence. The Rules did not recognise volitional impairment and narrowed the forms of cognitive impairment that constituted legal insanity. If the accused's criminal act was prompted by

---

the guise of 'inability to tell right from wrong'. Cockburn presented substantial medical evidence, which conveniently fit his theory of the defence. See Walker, above n. 25, at 94.

32 Above n. 22.

33 *Ibid.*

34 McAuley and McCutcheon, above n. 25, at 647.

an insane delusion, that insane delusion was no defence unless the circumstances of the delusion, had those circumstances actually been true, would in law justify the accused's acts. Had these rules been applied in Hadfield's or M'Naghten's trial, neither of them would have been entitled to a verdict of not guilty by reason of insanity.

Since their promulgation, the M'Naghten Rules have been very influential and, at the same time, controversial. They were adopted at one time or another, in whole or in part, throughout most of the common law world. The core of the M'Naghten test is found in the following words from Rule 3 above:

> [T]he party accused was labouring under such a defect of reason, from a disease of the mind, as not to know the nature and quality of the act he was doing; or, if he did know it, that he did not know he was doing what was wrong.

REPORTS OF THE ENGLISH CRIMINAL LAW COMMISSIONERS, 1843 AND 1846

It appears that the digest of criminal law prepared by the English Criminal Law Commissioners had some influence on the ultimate formulation of the unsoundness of mind defence in both Act IV of the Legislative Council of India in 1849 and the 1860 IPC. In their Seventh Report (1843), the English Commissioners on Criminal Law produced 'An Act of Crimes and Punishments', which contained all the Commissioners' digests of criminal law from their previous reports.[35] In the chapter on Preliminary Declarations, Article 1 stated:

> No person shall be criminally liable for any act who, at the time of such act, by reason of any disease, disorder, or delusion of mind, or of weakness or unripeness of understanding, is either unconscious of what he does, or unable to discern that what he does is wrong, and, therefore, knows not that he offends against the laws of God and man. The same rule shall apply to an omission.

Although published before the M'Naghten Rules were promulgated later that year, the Commissioners' proposed article incorporates the now-familiar two-prong insanity test – the accused must be either incapable of knowing what he or she is doing or incapable of knowing that it is wrong. And in respect to the meaning of 'wrong', the Commissioners' proposed article seems to include both legally and morally wrong since they specifically use the expression 'knows not that he offends against the laws of God and man'.[36] Article 1 also uses the word 'unconscious',

35 *Seventh Report of the Commissioners on Criminal Law, 1843*, British Parliamentary Papers (reproduced in the British Parliamentary Papers, *Legal Administration: Criminal Law* (vol. 4) (Shannon: Irish University Press, 1971)). For a helpful review of the English Commissioners' work, see R. Cross, 'The Reports of the Criminal Law Commissioners (1833–1849) and the Abortive Bills of 1853' in P.R. Glazebrook (ed.), *Reshaping the Criminal Law* (London: Stevens and Sons, 1978); and L. Farmer, 'Reconstructing the English Codification Debate: The Criminal Law Commissioners, 1833–1845' (2000) 18 *Law and History Review* 397. See also Chapter 2 of this volume, above n. 16, at 30.

36 See the English Commissioners' discussion of this article in their Seventh Report, *ibid.*, at 17–19, where the Commissioners explain that the rationale for the insanity defence is based on the fact that the just imposition of criminal liability and punishment presupposes that persons have the power to know what they are doing and to know that it is wrong, yet elect (choose) to do that which is forbidden. If, due to insanity, a person lacks such powers, then conviction and punishment is not warranted. The Commissioners argued that

but that word seems to mean 'unaware' of what he or she is doing, rather than 'unconscious' in the medical or physiological sense. In 1845, the Criminal Law Commissioners were reconstituted and in their Second Report in 1846 they produced a revised Act of Crimes and Punishments.[37] Article 1 stated:

> No person shall be criminally responsible for any act or omission, who at the time of such act or omission, is in a state of idiotcy.

Article 2 stated:

> No person shall be criminally responsible for any act or omission, who, at the time of such act or omission, by reason of unripeness or weakness of mind, or of any unsoundness, disease or delusion of mind, wants the capacity, which the law otherwise presumes every person to possess, of discerning that such act or omission is contrary to the law of the land.

While the majority of the Commissioners expressed the opinion that their proposed article was 'in consonance' with the M'Naghten Rules,[38] that conclusion is open to debate. First, their proposed article reduces the insanity test to one prong – discerning the act or omission is contrary to the law of the land.[39] Second, the Commissioners make it clear in both their proposed article and in their report that the defence does not include incapacity to know the act or omission is wrong in the sense of morally wrong.[40] One Commissioner dissented on this point.[41] However, the majority were of the view that inclusion of the word 'wrong' would create a dangerously vague and uncertain standard for the direction of juries.[42] It is also worth noting that the Commissioners used the expression 'unsoundness of mind' in their proposed article.

Act IV of the Legislative Council of India (1849)

In 1849, the Legislative Council of India enacted Act IV.[43] Section 1 of Act IV codified the defence of insanity in the following language:

---

the incapacity must be complete, not partial, on the grounds that it would be impossible to distinguish between degrees of partial insanity. The Commissioners also noted that the test for 'wrong' is not 'wrong' in general or in the abstract, but 'wrong' under the particular circumstances as the accused perceived them.

37 *Second Report of the Commissioners for Revising and Consolidating the Criminal Law*, 1846 (reproduced in the British Parliamentary Papers, *Legal Administration: Criminal Law* (vol. 5) (Shannon: Irish University Press, 1971)).

38 *Ibid.*, at 10.

39 Interestingly, in *Clark v. Arizona* (2006) 548 U.S. 735, a majority of the US Supreme Court upheld the constitutional validity of the revised Arizona insanity defence which had deleted 'the nature and quality' limb and only contained a 'wrong' limb. A majority of the Supreme Court held that the 'nature and quality' limb was effectively subsumed in the 'wrong' limb.

40 Above n. 37, at 10.

41 *Ibid.*, at 50, where Thomas Starkie, in a dissenting note, argued that the Commissioners' proposal should be amended 'to extend to incapability of discerning that the act or omission was wrong'. Starkie argued that this amendment was consistent with a great majority of the authorities, including the M'Naghten Rules.

42 *Ibid.*, at 10.

43 A similar provision was also enacted in the Straits Settlement: Ferguson, above n. 1, at n. 14.

No person can be acquitted for unsoundness of mind unless it can be proved that, by reason of unsoundness of mind, not willfully caused by himself, he was unconscious and incapable of knowing, in doing the act, that he was doing an act forbidden by the law of the land.

I have not found any original documents explaining the legislative background to this provision. However, the following observations can be made:

(1) The Indian Law Commissioners who examined and reported in detail on Macaulay's Code in 1846 and 1847 were apparently satisfied with his provision on the defence of madness and made no recommendations for change.[44]
(2) In 1848, Drinkwater Bethune was appointed as the new Law Member of the Indian Council. He profoundly disagreed with the style and content of Macaulay's draft Code and he drafted an entirely new code in 1852. Bethune died in 1854 and was succeeded by Barnes Peacock. Peacock chaired a Select Committee to examine and compare Bethune's and Macaulay's codes. Peacock's Select Committee rejected Bethune's code and in 1856 proposed the enactment of Macaulay's Code with some modifications.[45]
(3) As Law Member of the Indian Council from 1848 to 1852, presumably Bethune was responsible for the drafting of the 1849 Act. It is unclear to what extent Bethune relied on the M'Naghten Rules and/or the 1843 and 1846 English Commissioners' proposed insanity provisions in drafting s. 1. Section 1 appears to follow the English Commissioners' 1846 provision by using the expression 'unsoundness of mind' (but without other similar descriptors as used in the 1846 provision) and by reducing the insanity test to the single prong of being incapable of knowing it is legally wrong. It also confusingly adds the unmodified words 'he was unconscious', which are not used in the 1846 provision.[46]
(4) Peacock and his Select Committee rejected the language of the 1849 Act and proposed, in my view, a significantly improved provision on unsoundness of mind which became s. 84 of the IPC.[47]

---

44 The First Report in 1846, amongst other matters, dealt with the General Exceptions (Defences) in Chapter III of Macaulay's draft Code. In para. [652], the Indian Commissioners set out the test for insanity proposed by the English Commissioners in their Second Report in 1846. They then observe that the English Commissioners' proposal is 'quite new' and 'is strongly objected to by one of the [English] Commissioners, Mr. Starkie'. Then, in para. [654], the Indian Commissioners are content to observe that 'the simple enunciation in Clause 67 of the Indian Code … is in accordance with Mr. Livingstone's [*sic*] Code and with the Code Penal of France on the same point'. Earlier in their First Report (para. [118]), the Indian Commissioners also reject a suggestion that the word 'delirious' be deleted from cl. 67. It is interesting that there was no discussion of the M'Naghten Rules which had been decided on three years earlier. The Second Report did not deal with cl. 67. The First Report (1846) and the Second Report (1847) are reproduced in T.B. Macaulay, *The Indian Penal Code as Originally Framed in 1837* (Madras: Higginbotham & Co., 1888).

45 Cross, above n. 16, at 524.

46 The expression 'unconscious of what he does' appears in the Commissioners' 1843 proposal and is used as a synonym for 'does not know' or is 'unaware' of what he is doing. And in Rule 3 of the M'Naghten Rules, the Law Lords use the expression 'conscious that the act was one that he ought not to do' where again the word 'conscious' is used as a synonym for 'knows' or 'aware'.

47 Apparently there is no copy of the Select Committee Report in existence, so it is impossible to know whether they explicitly commented on why they rejected the language in Act IV in 1849 and chose instead the language found in IPC, s. 84.

THE IPC PROVISION AND ITS JUDICIAL INTERPRETATION

Section 84 of the IPC states:

> Nothing is an offence which is done by a person who, at the time of doing it, by reason of unsoundness of mind, is incapable of knowing the nature of the act, or that he is doing what is either wrong or contrary to law.

Some Preliminary Observations

(1) Section 84 has remained unchanged since its enactment in 1860, although in 1961, Singapore, but not India and Malaysia, enacted a defence of diminished responsibility which is a partial defence to murder, reducing it to the lesser offence of culpable homicide not amounting to murder.[48]
(2) While s. 84 does not use the word 'insanity' and instead uses the words 'unsoundness of mind', it is not uncommon for judges and commentators in India, Malaysia and Singapore to refer to s. 84 as the insanity defence.[49]
(3) One can only speculate as to why the drafters of the IPC chose to use the words 'unsoundness of mind' rather than insanity. The fact that 'unsoundness of mind' was used in the 1849 Act was perhaps an influencing factor but likely not a decisive one since the IPC codifiers departed from the language and content of the 1849 Act in most other respects. Certainly, the expression 'unsound mind' was not an entirely uncommon one in describing insanity. The common law Latin expression 'non compos mentis' was in common use and it literally meant 'not of sound mind'. In M'Naghten's Case, Tindal C.J. used the expression 'sound mind' in charging the jury. And the expression was also employed in the English Commissioners' 1846 proposed draft. Perhaps the IPC codifiers felt the expression 'unsoundness of mind' was simpler and clearer than the M'Naghten language of 'insanity' and 'defect of reason, from disease of the mind'.
(4) Unlike the 1849 Act, and the 1846 English Commissioners' proposal, s. 84 adopts the two-prong insanity test and appears to incorporate both morally wrong and legally wrong. In those respects, it is very similar to the M'Naghten Rules. However, s. 84 is not identical to the M'Naghten Rules. Nevertheless, courts in India, Malaysia and Singapore have sometimes, wrongly in my view, applied English decisions on the M'Naghten Rules as if s. 84 and the M'Naghten Rules were identical.[50] As

---

48 Namely Singaporean Penal Code, s. 300, Exception 7, whose wording is almost identical to the provision under the UK Homicide Act 1957 (Chapter 11). The UK provision was significantly revised in 2009. See Chapter 14 of this volume, above n. 6.

49 Ferguson, above n. 1, at 2.

50 See Ferguson, above n. 1, at 5. Yeo, Morgan and Chan, above n. 1, at para. [24.4], state:

> On the basis that s. 84 was borrowed directly from the *M'Naghten* Rules, there [have] been occasions when the local courts have applied the Rules instead of s. 84. This practice has been rightly criticised since s. 84 uses different expressions from the Rules in certain material respects. Specifically, the provision uses 'unsoundness of mind' instead of 'disease of the mind' under the Rules; 'incapable' instead of 'did not know'; 'nature of the act' instead of 'nature and quality of the act'; and 'either wrong or contrary to law' instead of 'wrong'. While our courts are certainly entitled to consider English judicial pronouncements on the *M'Naghten* Rules, they should not adopt them without first contemplating whether the expressions used in s. 84 require a different position from that taken by the Rules.

Barry Wright has observed,[51] this persistent deference to the English common law seems to be at odds with Macaulay's original intent to make a clean break from many arcane common law doctrines.
(5) Section 84, and other defences in the IPC, follow Macaulay's phraseology that 'Nothing is an offence' which is done, for example, while insane or in self-defence. This phraseology does not distinguish between justifications such as self-defence, which render the accused's act 'lawful', and excuses such as insanity, which exclude the accused from conviction and punishment but do not render the accused's act lawful. Thus, it is necessary to enact special provisions such as ss. 98 and 108 of the IPC, which in effect deem that the insane person's act is an offence for the purposes of anybody who abets the insane person to commit that 'offence', or for the purposes of a person who claims self-defence against the otherwise unlawful attack of an insane person.
(6) The essential elements of the defence of unsoundness of mind are listed in s. 84, but those elements are not further defined in the Code. Thus, there is a degree of uncertainty, and room for judicial debate, as to the proper scope and meaning of these elements. I will now turn to a brief analysis of those elements, as well as other elements that are not present in s. 84 but should be.

Unsoundness of Mind

Proof that the accused was suffering from 'unsoundness of mind' is the first prerequisite for establishing the defence under s. 84 of the IPC. However, the expression 'unsoundness of mind' is not defined in the Code, nor has it been extensively and authoritatively defined in the case law in India, Malaysia or Singapore.[52] It should be defined in a revised IPC. First, it should be given a legal, not a medical definition. Second, that definition should be broad; it should only exclude from its definition mental impairments which, for policy reasons, the law chooses to treat other than as insanity. These two definitional characteristics are consistent with the way that 'disease of the mind' and other similar expressions, under the M'Naghten Rules, are interpreted in other jurisdictions.

Deciding what circumstances should exempt a person from criminal liability on the basis of insanity is a legal and moral question, not a medical question. For many years, courts would not allow an accused to raise the insanity defence if that person's mental disorder was not classified by the medical profession as 'a disease of the mind'. But that approach has now been soundly rejected.[53] That does not mean that expert medical evidence is now irrelevant – quite the contrary. Expert medical evidence is indispensable in assisting the judge or jury to understand how the accused's entire mental faculties and functions were affected at the time of the offence. But the question of whether that degree of impairment of the accused's mental faculties and functions entitles the accused to be excused from criminal liability by reason of the insanity defence is and should be a legal and moral judgment, not a medical one.

---

51 See Chapter 2 of this volume, above n. 16, at 39 and 43.

52 See Ferguson, above n. 1, at 7; Yeo, Morgan and Chan, above n. 1, at para. [24.7]; and C.K. Thakker and M.C. Thakker, *Ratanlal & Dhirajlal's Law of Crimes* (26th edn, New Delhi: Bharat Law House, 2007) 310–11.

53 See the English cases of *R. v. Kemp* [1957] 1 QB 399; *Bratty v. AG for Northern Ireland* [1963] AC 386; and *R. v. Sullivan* [1983] 2 All ER 673; and the Canadian case of *R. v. Cooper* (1980) 51 CCC (2d) 129, discussed in Ferguson, above n. 1, at 7–8. See also the Australian cases of *The Queen v. Radford* (1985) 42 SASR 266 and *The Queen v. Falconer* (1990) 171 CLR 30. For example, in *Sullivan*, the House of Lords held that psychomotor epilepsy was a 'disease of the mind', even though the medical evidence was that the disruption of a person's brain functioning during an epileptic seizure was too brief to classify that person's condition as 'a disease of the mind'.

It is appropriate to give the definition of 'unsoundness of mind', or similar expressions, a broad meaning (subject to any policy exceptions discussed below) because unsoundness of mind by itself does not constitute the defence of insanity. It is simply a precondition to a consideration of the other, more important elements of the defence, namely the effect which an accused's mental impairment or abnormality had on his or her ability to know what he or she is doing or to know that it is wrong. The broad definition of 'disease of the mind' articulated by the Supreme Court of Canada in *R. v. Cooper*[54] is useful and instructive in this respect. The Supreme Court stated that 'disease of the mind' includes:

> ... any illness, disorder or abnormal condition which impairs the human mind and its functioning, excluding however, self-induced states caused by alcohol or drugs, as well as transitory mental states such as hysteria or concussion.

This broad definition ensures that a wide range of mental impairments (including personality disorders, psychopathy and neurosis) are not automatically excluded from consideration under the insanity defence. With a broad definition of disease of the mind, attention can be properly focused on the real issue: what effect did the disease of the mind have on the accused's mental functioning?[55]

A similar approach was adopted in *R. v. Sullivan*,[56] where the House of Lords held that the word 'mind' is used 'in the ordinary sense of the mental faculties of reason, memory and understanding' and that disease of the mind is an impairment of these faculties, whether organic or functional and whether permanent, transient or intermittent. However, the House of Lords made it clear that disease of the mind for the purposes of the insanity defence does not include temporary malfunctioning of the mind caused by alcohol or drugs, or by 'some external physical factor such as a blow on the head causing concussion or the administration of an anaesthetic for therapeutic purposes'. The above mental impairments are dealt with by the separate defences of intoxication and non-insane automatism.

Both *Cooper* and *Sullivan* make it clear that in some cases the impairment of a person's mental functioning should not be considered under the defence of insanity. For policy reasons, the law chooses to deal with these conditions in ways other than by the insanity defence. For example, some forms of mental impairment will be classified in law as non-insane automatism, a topic dealt with in the next section of this chapter. Likewise, temporary impairment of the mind that arises from voluntary and involuntary consumption of alcohol or drugs is excluded from the insanity defence and instead is dealt with by a separate set of rules for voluntary and involuntary intoxication. However, if intoxication produces an underlying and internalised condition with a degree of permanency beyond a mere transient state, such as brain damage, *delirium tremens* or alcohol dementia, then the accused's condition will be treated as a disease of the mind for the purposes of the insanity defence.[57]

---

54 *Ibid.*

55 Yeo, Morgan and Chan, above n. 1, at para. [24.10], properly assert that the Singapore Court of Appeal in *PP v. Rozman bin Jusoh* [1995] 2 SLR(R) 879 should not have rejected outright the diagnostic category of 'subnormal intellect' as a form of unsound mind, although the Court was correct in concluding in that case that the accused's subnormal intellect did not reach the level of depriving him of the cognitive requirements for a s. 84 defence.

56 Above n. 53.

57 See Chapter 11 of this volume (G. Ferguson, 'Intoxication') at 263. See also Ferguson, above n. 1, at 9–10; and Yeo, Morgan and Chan, above n. 1, at para. [24.11].

Insane and Non-Insane Automatism

It is a fundamental principle of criminal liability that no conduct can be criminal unless it was done voluntarily, that is, through a willed physical act or omission. Automatism describes a condition in which the accused is capable of action but does not have conscious control over what he or she is doing. The absence of conscious control renders the accused's conduct involuntary and therefore not deserving of conviction and punishment. Perhaps the biggest challenge is to formulate a definition of 'disease of the mind' or 'unsoundness of mind' which makes it clear which cases of automatism should be considered under the insanity defence (insane automatism) and which cases should be classified as non-insane automatism, thereby resulting in an unqualified acquittal.

If a person is acting in a state of altered consciousness (for example, sleepwalking, concussion or a severe dissociative state), that person will not normally know the nature and quality of his or her act or that it is wrong. In such cases, it is the definition of 'disease of the mind' or 'unsoundness of mind' which will determine whether that form of automatism will be classified as insane or non-insane. In most jurisdictions, the legal distinction between non-insane and insane automatism has been based on pragmatic policy grounds – fair or appropriate labelling and protection of the public from future harm. Although concerns with labelling epileptic, diabetic or sleepwalking accused persons as insane[58] have had some impact in some cases on the way those conditions are classified, perceived concerns for public protection normally trump fair labelling concerns.

At this juncture the question becomes: how, if at all, should the law distinguish between non-insane and insane automatism? Broadly speaking, there are three options:

(1) treat all forms of automatism as insanity;
(2) treat automatism as a special verdict, followed by special disposition provisions;
(3) draft a code provision which classifies some forms of automatism as non-insane and other forms as insane.

Option (1): Label All Forms of Automatism as Insanity

The only justification for classifying *all* forms of automatism as insane under existing law is to give the state the option of imposing supervision or custody, where needed, over a person who is acquitted on the basis of automatism. In some, and perhaps most, instances of automatism, there is little or no risk of reoccurrence of the automatistic state, or of the commission of an offence even if such a state were to reoccur. The classic example of this is a person who commits an offence while in a state of automatism due to a concussion from a physical blow to the head. Since there is no need to exercise continued state supervision over such a person, labelling such a person as insane is entirely unnecessary for public protection purposes and highly inappropriate on the basis of fair or accurate labelling. Indeed, it is these two factors which have prompted most jurisdictions to try to distinguish between non-insane and insane automatism. For the above reason, I suggest that option (1) is not appropriate and should not be adopted.

58 Deleting the word 'insanity' and substituting the words 'mental impairment' may marginally reduce the concern about adverse labelling.

Option (2): Special Verdict and Special Disposition Provisions for Automatism

The fact that the law currently treats non-insane automatism as an ordinary acquittal, with no special provisions for state intervention after the acquittal, has resulted in a strong judicial tendency to classify most forms of automatism as insane automatism, since the latter verdict does allow for the possibility of continued state supervision and custody. One way to avoid this inappropriate labelling of automatism as insanity is to treat automatism as a special verdict with special disposition provisions to deal with continuing public safety concerns. Under this option, *all* forms of automatism (that is, unconscious conduct) regardless of their cause would be dealt with by the special automatism verdict – not guilty on account of automatism. That option has the advantage of being relatively straightforward in its application. Alternatively, some supporters of the option of a special verdict for automatism in general may still prefer to continue to use the insanity defence for those limited forms of automatism which are caused by a condition that is generally recognised as a 'mental illness or disorder'. This latter option would necessitate a definition of 'mental illness or disorder' for this purpose, but that definition would be more narrowly defined than it is under current insanity/automatism jurisprudence.

While option (2) makes good sense to me, I am not aware of any jurisdiction which currently uses it. When a proposal of this sort was considered in Canada in the early 1990s, it was rejected by most groups.[59] It should also be noted that in Chapter 4 of this volume, Bob Sullivan has raised similar concerns where he states:

> First, the public safety concerns that drive this process can be much exaggerated. Secondly, if it should be the case that coercive procedures over a particular person following his or her involuntary conduct are in the public interest, they should be done by way of mental health processes and not through the criminal law.[60]

I am not in full agreement with the latter point. When the ongoing public safety concerns arise out of the accused having committed a 'criminal harm' while in a state of automatism, it is not inappropriate for the criminal law courts to consider whether ongoing control or supervision of the automatistic acquittee is required for public protection in the same way that the criminal law does with regard to insane acquittees. In addition, the current civil law processes in many jurisdictions do not effectively allow for intervention in such cases since they are narrowly constructed to protect against overzealous state intervention and control of persons who have not committed crimes or otherwise broken the law. Nonetheless, due to the apparently widespread opposition to option (2), I have not attempted in this chapter to develop it further. As a result, I have proceeded to draft this part of the chapter on the assumption that option (3) will be adopted.

---

59 In a submission to the Canadian Parliamentary Subcommittee on Recodification of the Criminal Law in October 1992, I proposed that the Criminal Code should define automatism and also treat it as a special verdict with special dispositions similar to dispositions following an insanity verdict. While this proposal was adopted in a government White Paper entitled 'Proposals to Amend the Criminal Code (General Principles)' (June 1993), the proposal was rejected by the Parliamentary Subcommittee, the Canadian Bar Association Criminal Code Task Force and the Canadian Association of Law Teachers Submission.

60 See Chapter 4 of this volume (B. Sullivan, 'The Conduct Element of Offences') at 96.

Option (3): Distinguishing Insane and Non-Insane Automatism

If an accused's lack of conscious control over his or her conduct arises out of an internal condition or weakness in the accused's psychological, emotional or physical make-up and is likely to recur, then a special verdict of insanity, rather than an outright acquittal on the basis of automatism, is generally considered appropriate since an insanity verdict, but not an automatism verdict, allows for ongoing supervision of the insane acquittee, thereby providing society with protection from the risk that this person's condition may reoccur and result in the commission of further offences. Thus, an internal weakness or disorder which may reoccur and result in the commission of another offence is a two-part standard which is frequently used in drawing a line between insane and non-insane automatism.

While there is some judicial disagreement, the following conditions have been viewed as internal disorders or diseases of the mind and therefore classified in most jurisdictions as insane automatism:[61]

(1) epilepsy;
(2) cerebral arteriosclerosis;
(3) diabetic and hypoglycaemic attacks;
(4) sleepwalking/somnambulism; and
(5) dissociative state caused by ordinary stresses and disappointments of life (for example, loss of job, break-up or rejection in relationships with others).

On the other hand, if the automatistic behaviour is caused by an external event or source, is temporary in nature and is unlikely to recur, the accused is not a continuing danger and an outright acquittal on the basis of non-insane automatism is generally considered appropriate. While there is some judicial disagreement, the following conditions have been classified as non-insane automatism in many jurisdictions:

(1) a concussion caused by a physical blow to the head;
(2) a psychological blow from an extraordinary external event which could cause an average, normal person to go into a dissociative state;
(3) sudden stroke;
(4) delirium from illness or infection;
(5) sleepwalking, if the risk of reoccurrence is low;[62] and

---

61 But note that conditions (1) to (4) have sometimes been classified as non-insane automatism where the risk of reoccurrence, or the risk of reoffending from such reoccurrence, is low. For a discussion of case law on classifying various conditions as non-insane or insane automatism, see D. Stuart, *Canadian Criminal Law* (5th edn, Scarborough: Thomson Canada Ltd., 2007) at 115–30; Yeo, Morgan and Chan, above n. 1, at paras. [26.1]–[26.33]; Bronitt and McSherry, above n. 2, at 228–38; D. Ormerod, *Smith and Hogan, Criminal Law* (12th edn, Oxford: Oxford University Press, 2008) 280–4; A.P. Simester and W.J. Brookbanks, *Principles of Criminal Law* (3rd edn, Wellington: Brookers Ltd., 2007) 301–13; McAuley and McCutcheon, above n. 25, at 680–8; and F. Leverick and J. Chalmers, *Criminal Defences and Pleas in Bar of Trial* (Edinburgh: W. Green & Son Ltd., 2006) 158–67.

62 The treatment of sleepwalking in Canadian case law is instructive. In *R. v. Parks* (1992) 75 CCC (3d) 287, the Supreme Court upheld the accused's acquittal of murder and attempted murder committed while sleepwalking on the basis of non-insane automatism. The Supreme Court held that sleepwalking was not a disease or abnormality of the mind and, based on the medical evidence presented at the trial, there was little or no risk of the accused engaging in another act of violence while sleepwalking. Thus, the Court held that

(6) involuntary intoxication.

In reforming s. 84 of the IPC, the concept of 'unsoundness of mind' (or 'mental impairment', which I will recommend as a preferable expression) needs to be defined with sufficient detail and clarity to indicate the types of conditions or circumstances which constitute insane automatism and the types of conditions or circumstances which constitute non-insane automatism. While many commentators have properly criticised the use of the internal/external test, when that distinction is combined with a consideration of 'likelihood of reoccurrence', the two factors combined seem to me to provide the best functional test that anyone has proposed to date. Thus, in my proposed cls. 83A(4) and 84(2)(b) at the end of this chapter, I adopt this approach and propose that involuntary behaviour involving 'temporary impairment of the mind caused by external factors which are unlikely to recur and do not demonstrate an internal weakness of the mind' should be classified as non-insane automatism.

Incapable of Knowing

Section 84 of the IPC uses the expression 'incapable of knowing' the nature of the act or that it is either wrong or contrary to law. The M'Naghten Rules do not use the word 'incapable' and instead simply refer to whether the accused, due to disease of the mind, 'did not know' the nature and quality of the act or that it was wrong. While some jurisdictions follow the M'Naghten words on this point, the majority use the language of incapacity.[63]

---

there was no basis for classifying the sleepwalking in this case as insanity. The Court acknowledged that if in another case there was medical evidence that violence while sleepwalking was likely to reoccur, then a verdict of insanity would be appropriate. However, in *R. v. Stone* (1999) 134 CCC (3d) 353, a majority of the Supreme Court strongly suggested that sleepwalking should always be classified as insane automatism on the grounds that there is no way of accurately predicting whether the sleepwalking will reoccur and result in an act of violence again. In the three or four sleepwalking cases which arose after *Stone*, the courts classified sleepwalking as insane automatism, but in *R. v. Luedecke* (2005) 35 CR (6th) 205, the trial judge acquitted the accused of sexual assault on the basis of non-insane automatism ('sexsomnia'). The judge noted that the expert evidence showed that the accused's sleep disorder was triggered by a series of external factors (including sleep deprivation, significant alcohol consumption and stress). The judge further noted that the accused had now voluntarily embarked on a plan of sleep hygiene, modest alcohol consumption and stress-reducing medication, and did not constitute a continuing danger; therefore, a verdict of insanity was inappropriate. On appeal, the Ontario Court of Appeal (2008) 236 CCC (3d) 317 disagreed with the trial judge's risk assessment and indicated that on the evidence in this case, a finding of insanity, not non-insane automatism, was warranted. The Court held that 'the trial judge failed to appreciate the significance of the hereditary nature of the respondent's condition, failed to give effect to the respondent's well established history of sexsomnia, and failed to appreciate the significance of the strong likelihood of the recurrence of the events that triggered his sexsomnia'. Ironically, after the accused was found not guilty on account of insanity, he was referred to the Ontario Psychiatric Review Board for disposition. After a 'full and complete risk assessment', the Board concluded that he did not constitute 'a significant threat to the safety of the public' and the Board therefore ordered that he be discharged absolutely under Canadian Criminal Code, s. 672.54(a). An absolute discharge means that the 'insane acquittee' is no longer subject to any form of supervision or conditions. The Board noted that he had not experienced any further episodes of 'involuntary sexual activity' during the four years since the original incident.

63 See Yeo, above n. 1, at 247–8, where he indicates that Ghana and the Australian Commonwealth use the expression 'did not know' (as do New South Wales, the Northern Territory, South Australia and Victoria),

While there is a distinction between incapacity and actual knowledge, and that distinction has been commented on in one Indian case,[64] courts have in general ignored that distinction, and wisely so. If incapacity were strictly applied to the requirement of incapable of knowing the nature of his or her act, then insanity would virtually never exist under that first branch, except perhaps in the classic examples such as a mother throwing her child into a fire in the insane belief that her child is actually a piece of wood. The relevant moral question is whether the accused knew the nature of his or her act and, if not, whether that lack of knowledge arose from a disease of the mind (or unsoundness of mind). In reforming s. 84, the words 'did not know' rather than 'incapable of knowing' should be used.

Know versus Appreciate or Understand

Section 84 of the IPC uses the word 'know' in respect to both branches of the defence: knowing the nature of the act or that it is wrong or contrary to law. The M'Naghten Rules also use the word 'know' for both branches of the insanity test. However, the English Royal Commission's draft Criminal Code (1879) used the word 'appreciating' instead of 'knowing' for both branches of the insanity test – 'incapable of appreciating the nature and quality of the act or that the act was wrong'.[65] The Commissioners did not comment in their report on the significance, if any, of that change.[66] Canada modelled its Code in 1892 after the English Commissioners' draft Criminal Code, but on this point the Canadian insanity provision used the word 'appreciate' only for the first branch and the word 'know' for the second branch.[67] The New Zealand Criminal Code of 1893 was also modelled on the English draft Criminal Code. In this regard, the New Zealand Criminal Code Commissioners noted that the English Commissioners had used the word 'appreciate', but the New Zealand Commissioners were mildly critical of that word[68] and recommended instead the use of the word 'understand' or 'know'. As a result, s. 23 of the New Zealand Criminal Code used the latter two expressions as follows: 'incapable of *understanding* the nature and quality of the act, [or] of *knowing* that such act or omission was wrong' (emphasis added). In Australia, in the Code states of Queensland (1899), Western Australia (1902) and Tasmania (1924), the codifiers

but Singapore, Malaysia, Canada, New Zealand, Queensland, Tasmania, Western Australia, Northern and Southern Nigeria and South Africa use the word 'capacity' or 'incapacity'.

64 *Lakshmi v. State* 1959 60 Cri LJ 1033, at 1034.

65 See s. 22 of the draft Criminal Code attached as an Appendix to the Report of the *Royal Commission Appointed to Consider the Law Related to Indictable Offences* (1879), reproduced in the British Parliamentary Papers, *Legal Administration: Criminal Law* (vol. 6) (Shannon: Irish University Press, 1971) 435.

66 See Report of the *Royal Commission Appointed to Consider the Law Related to Indictable Offences* (1879) at 17–18, reproduced in the British Parliamentary Papers, *Legal Administration: Criminal Law* (vol. 6) (Shannon: Irish University Press, 1971) at 385–6. In Bill 178, 1878 (available from House of Commons Parliamentary Papers Online: ProQuest Information and Learning Co., 2005), which the Commissioners were reviewing, James Fitzjames Stephen used the word 'knowing' in the first two branches of his insanity test in s. 20.

67 On this point, Canadian Criminal Code, s. 16, stated, then and now, 'incapable of appreciating the nature and quality of the act or omission, [or] of knowing that such act or omission was wrong'.

68 The Statute Revision Commission responsible for producing the draft Bill which became the 1893 New Zealand Criminal Code, in Report 8 (June, 1883), at 11, stated: '[Although the word "appreciate" is used in the English draft Code] it seems to us that "understand" or "know" would be preferable. "Appreciation" seems to imply an act of reasoning, or comparing the matter with some relative matter or standard, instead of a mere knowledge or understanding.'

also used 'understand' for the first branch and 'know' for the second branch.[69] While the words 'appreciate' and 'understand' are potentially broader than 'know', courts in various countries, including Canada[70] and Australia,[71] have shown that they are quite capable of interpreting all three words in either a broad or narrow fashion, as seems best suited to them at the time. Thus, I do not put much weight or relevance on which of the three words is used, although I think that the use of the word 'appreciate' for the first limb and 'know' for the second limb makes the most sense.

Nature and Quality of the Act

The M'Naghten Rules use the expression 'did not know the *nature and quality* of the act'. Section 84 of the IPC uses the expression 'incapable of knowing *the nature* of the act'. Some of the Australian Code states (for example, Queensland and Western Australia) have avoided either expression by using instead the words 'capacity to understand what he or she was doing'. Section 84 of the IPC does not define or clarify the expression 'nature of the act'. Nor is it clear whether the expression 'nature of the act' applies just to the act (or omission) or also extends to the consequences of the act (or omission). On this issue, I agree with Yeo's conclusion:

> ... the best stance would be for a formulation of the insanity defence to refer to the accused's 'appreciation of the nature or consequences' of his or her conduct. This would prevent the issue being left to judicial interpretation and would be a decided improvement of the *M'Naghten Case's* expression of 'knowing the nature or quality' of the conduct.[72]

Knowing that it is Wrong

The M'Naghten Rules express the second limb of the insanity test as follows: 'did not know he was doing what was wrong'. Several other jurisdictions follow the M'Naghten Rules on this point.[73] The meaning of the word 'wrong' has been a source of long-standing debate. Does it mean legally wrong, or morally wrong, or both?[74] For example, in England, the courts have held that wrong means contrary to law. In *R. v. Windle*,[75] the English Court of Criminal Appeal held that the test was whether the accused knew his or her conduct was contrary to law, not whether he or she knew it was morally right or wrong. If he or she knew it was contrary to law but nonetheless thought it was

---

69 See Bronitt and McSherry, above n. 2, at 212–13.

70 See Ferguson, above n. 1, at 13–14.

71 See Bronitt and McSherry above n. 2, at 217–18.

72 Yeo, above n. 1, at 250.

73 See *ibid.*, at 250–51.

74 The confusion can be traced in part to the use of different expressions in various parts of the M'Naghten Rules. See Ferguson, above n. 1, at 15. See also A. Platt and B.L. Diamond, 'The Origins of the "Right and Wrong" Test of Criminal Responsibility and its Subsequent Development in the United States: An Historical Survey' (1966) 54 *California Law Review* 1227. For a recent and perceptive analysis of the 'wrong' limb, see R.D. Mackay, 'Righting the Wrong? Some Observations on the Second Limb of the M'Naghten Rules' [2009] *Criminal Law Review* 80.

75 [1952] 2 QB 826.

morally right, he or she cannot rely on the insanity defence. That position was recently confirmed by the English Court of Appeal in *R. v. Johnson*.[76]

On the other hand, in *Stapleton v. The Queen*,[77] the High Court of Australia refused to follow *Windle* and held that even if the accused knew that his act was legally wrong, he could rely on the insanity defence if he believed his act was morally right in the sense of believing his act was right according to the ordinary moral standards of reasonable men. And in Canada, in 1976, in *R. v. Schwartz*,[78] the Supreme Court held that 'wrong' in s. 16 of the Canadian Criminal Code only meant 'legally wrong'; however, in 1990, the Supreme Court reversed itself in *R. v. Chaulk*,[79] holding that the word 'wrong' also includes 'morally wrong'. In *Chaulk*, the Supreme Court went on to define 'morally wrong' as follows:

> '[M]oral wrong' is not to be judged by the personal standards of the offender but by his awareness that society regards the act as wrong ... The accused will not benefit from substituting his own moral code for that of society. Instead, he will be protected by s. 16(2) [the Canadian insanity provision] if he is incapable of understanding that the act is wrong according to the ordinary moral standards of reasonable members of society.[80]

While there has been some criticism of this type of 'reasonable person' formulation of morally wrong, it has found favour in several jurisdictions.[81]

Section 84 of the IPC requires that a person of unsound mind be incapable of knowing that he or she is doing what is 'either wrong or contrary to law'. Since the expression 'either ... or' is used, it would be logical, and in accordance with the ordinary principles of statutory interpretation, to assume that 'wrong' means one thing and 'contrary to law' means something else. On that assumption, since the expression 'contrary to law' clearly means 'legally wrong', it is appropriate to infer that the alternative word 'wrong' is a reference to 'morally wrong' in the sense that the accused knows or has the capacity to know that his or her act would be considered wrong in the eyes of reasonable persons. In *Geron Ali v. Emperor*,[82] the Calcutta High Court applied what has been called a 'conjunctive approach', holding that an accused cannot rely on the insanity defence if he knew that what he or she was doing was contrary to law even though he or she did not know that it was morally wrong, or vice versa. The Court's decision might be explained on the basis that the Court assumed that 'morally wrong' referred to the accused's private ethics, rather than the standards of a reasonable person. On the other hand, the later case of *Ashiruddin Ahmed v. The King*,[83] without referring to *Geron Ali*, held that an accused was insane if he was capable of knowing that his act was contrary to law but not capable of knowing that it was morally wrong.

76 [2007] EWCA Crim 1978.

77 (1952) 86 CLR 358.

78 (1976) 29 CCC (2d) 1.

79 (1990) 62 CCC (3d) 193.

80 *Ibid.*, at 232–3.

81 In some Australian jurisdictions (for example, the Australian Capital Territory, Victoria and the Northern Territory), the following statutory expression has been used for the morally wrong test: 'he or she could not reason with a moderate degree of sense and composure about whether the conduct, as perceived by reasonable people, was wrong'. See Bronitt and McSherry, above n. 2, at 219.

82 AIR 1941 Cal 129. The High Court held that the accused was not guilty by reason of insanity on the basis that he did not know that what he was doing was wrong and did not know that it was contrary to law.

83 AIR 1949 Cal 182.

Yeo, Morgan and Chan argue that the correct and appropriate interpretation of s. 84 on this issue is to treat s. 84 as setting out a disjunctive test which can be satisfied by proof of the accused's incapacity to know that his or her conduct is either morally wrong or legally wrong. They provide several reasons for this conclusion.[84] I agree with their conclusion on this point.

Absence of a Volitional Component

The M'Naghten Rules do not recognise volitional (conative) incapacity arising from a disease of the mind as a separate basis for insanity. It is at least arguable that the notion of irresistible impulse (or volitional impairment) was a recognised basis for establishing the defence of insanity under English law prior to M'Naghten. However, to the extent that it may have been so, it did not survive after the M'Naghten Rules. Like the M'Naghten Rules, s. 84 of the IPC does not include irresistible impulse or volitional impairment as a separate limb of the unsoundness of mind test. While there is no existing record of the Code drafters' discussions of s. 84, there is no reason to think that they even considered including irresistible impulse or volitional impairment in s. 84.

Other jurisdictions have also followed the M'Naghten Rules in not including volitional impairment as a separate limb of the insanity defence. On the other hand, James Fitzjames Stephen argued that the insanity defence should include an irresistible impulse provision and he included such a provision in his Criminal Code Bill of 1878.[85] However, the English Royal Commissioners expressly excluded Stephen's recommendation in their draft Criminal Code of 1879.[86] In their Report on the draft Code, the Commissioners opposed inclusion of an irresistible impulse provision on the grounds that it was not 'practical or safe', in the sense that it would be nearly impossible to distinguish between an impulse which was irresistible because of insanity and one which was not resisted because of ordinary motives of 'revenge, hatred or ungoverned passion'.[87] Canada and New Zealand followed the English Commissioners' draft Criminal Code and therefore excluded an irresistible impulse component in the insanity provisions of their first criminal codes in 1892 and 1893, respectively.[88]

---

84 Yeo, Morgan and Chan, above n. 1, at para. [24.22], set out five reasons for this conclusion. The last two reasons are as follows:

> Fourthly, recognising an incapacity to know that an act was morally wrong accommodates particular kinds of cases not infrequently found in societies like Malaysia, Singapore and India. These are instances where the accused, owing to unsoundness of mind, believed that he or she was acting under divine instruction or as a result of spirit possession. In these cases, the accused is likely to know that the act was contrary to law but believed that he or she was morally right to have done it. The final and perhaps strongest reason in favour of the disjunctive view is that, from the standpoint of criminal responsibility, the deterrent effect of punishment would be useless on persons whose mental disorder was such as to enable them to know that their act was contrary to law but who nevertheless persisted in the firm belief that their act was morally justified. In such a case, clinical intervention rather than punishment is the proper recourse.

85 See House of Commons, Bill 178, 1878, above n. 66, s. 20. See also J.F. Stephen, *A History of the Criminal Law of England* (vol. 2) (London: MacMillan & Co., 1883) 167–80.

86 See English draft Criminal Code 1879, s. 22. The *Report of the Royal Commission Appointed to Consider the Law Related to Indictable Offences* (1879) and the draft Code are reproduced in the British Parliamentary Papers, *Legal Administration: Criminal Law* (vol. 6) (Shannon: Irish University Press, 1971) at 386.

87 *Ibid.*, at 17–18.

88 Canadian Criminal Code 1892, s. 11; New Zealand Criminal Code 1893, s. 23.

While it may be difficult in some instances to determine whether a person was unable to control their behaviour due to mental disorder or whether they were able, but simply chose not to control their behaviour due to other considerations, these distinctions are not impossible to make. Such distinctions can be inferred from all the surrounding circumstances and they are perhaps no more difficult to make than decisions about whether other states of mind such as intent, foresight or knowledge exist, or whether an accused had a temporary loss of control in the context of the provocation defence. And in this regard, it should not be forgotten that the accused bears the burden of proving insanity in most jurisdictions.

Distinguishing between volitional and non-volitional conduct in the context of the insanity defence has proven itself to be workable in the many jurisdictions that have included a volitional limb in their insanity defence. As Yeo notes, 'the majority of Commonwealth jurisdictions studied here have taken this position [to include volitional defects as one limb of the insanity defence], with several of them having done so quite recently'.[89] This inclusion of volitional impairment as a limb of the insanity defence has occurred not only through legislative amendments but also by judicial development in some common law jurisdictions where the insanity defence has not been codified. For example, the Irish Supreme Court recognised a defence of 'volitional insanity' in 1974 in *Doyle v. Wicklow County Council*.[90]

A strong claim can be made that the basic principles of criminal liability require the inclusion of a volitional limb in the insanity defence. Put simply, the criminal law and the imposition of criminal sanctions are based on an assumption about human nature – the assumption that human beings are both rational and autonomous. The criminal law assumes that ordinary persons have the capacity to reason right from wrong and the capacity to choose right or wrong. These assumptions may be incorrect, or at least not in perfect accord with modern, social-scientific insights into human behaviour, but they are, and are likely to remain, the theoretical basis of our criminal law. It is these dual capacities – reason and choice – which give moral justification to imposing criminal responsibility and punishment on offenders. If a person can reason right from wrong and has the ability to choose right or wrong, then attribution of responsibility and punishment is morally justified or deserved when that person consciously chooses wrong. Thus, to the extent that criminal law theory is based on a conception of human beings as rational and autonomous individuals, both conditions – reason and will – are relevant to attributing criminal responsibility to an individual. If there is no ability to reason, or no ability to choose, due to mental impairment, then conviction and punishment for conduct committed under such circumstances would be immoral. It is for this reason that a morally defensible insanity test must include some consideration of both cognitive and volitional impairment. As further noted in the next few pages, the precise language that needs to be used in a revised insanity test to ensure that an accused is not held criminally liable for an offence if the requisite cognitive and volitional components of that offence are absent due to mental impairment will vary, depending upon the manner in which the general conduct and mental fault elements for offences, discussed in Chapters 3 and 4 of this volume, are defined in a revised IPC.

An influential formulation of the volitional limb of the insanity test can be found in the 1962 US Model Penal Code provision on insanity, s. 4.01(1), where the drafters used the expression 'lacks substantial capacity … to conform his conduct to the requirements of the law'. Goldstein favourably comments on the inclusion of this volitional component in the insanity test, further noting that the word 'conform' is preferable to 'control' and that the proposal is a vast improvement

89 Yeo, above n. 1, at 254.

90 [1974] IR 55, discussed and critiqued fully in McAuley and McCutcheon, above n. 25, at 662–80. See now Irish Criminal Law (Insanity) Act 2006 (No. 11 of 2006), s. 5(1).

over the misleading words 'irresistible impulse'.[91] In Australia, most jurisdictions have adopted a volitional limb as part of their insanity test and have adopted the words 'capacity to control his or her actions' or 'unable to control his or her actions'.[92] The latter expression seems preferable to me.

Balancing the theoretical justification for including a volitional component against any practical concerns in its application, I favour the adoption of a volitional component in a revised IPC.

Involuntary Conduct and Non-Insane Automatism

The IPC does not contain an express provision declaring that voluntary conduct is a fundamental prerequisite of criminal liability. Nor does the IPC deal with automatism (sane or insane) as a subset of involuntariness. As Yeo, Morgan and Chan argue, provisions dealing with voluntariness and automatism should be covered in the IPC. They state:

> The preceding examination of the Penal Code has revealed a virtual non-recognition of the concept of voluntariness and its subset of automatism. While various suggestions have been made to read voluntariness and automatism into the Code provisions where one would most expect to find them, these suggestions involve a fair measure of ingenuity by a judge who acknowledges the importance of the issue and is keen to resolve this defect in the Code. A far better solution would be for Parliament to introduce legislative amendments to the Penal Code which expressly incorporate the basic principle of the criminal law that a person is not guilty of a crime unless his or her conduct was voluntary. Based on our discussion, the legislation would need to define an 'act' as meaning willed conduct. It would also need to add volitional incapacity to the cognitive ones presently mentioned in the defence of unsoundness of mind under s. 84, and of intoxication under s. 85. Finally, the provision on diminished responsibility should be amended to expressly articulate the volitional and cognitive defects of an 'abnormality of mind' rather than resorting to judicial pronouncements, as is presently the case.[93]

A full analysis of the voluntariness principle is beyond the scope of this chapter and the voluntariness principle is more fully considered in Chapter 4 of this volume by Sullivan. I have here opted for the inclusion of a provision setting out the general requirement that acts or omissions be voluntary (see cl. 83A in the next section of this chapter). On the other hand, rather than providing an all-embracing provision on the voluntariness requirement such as the one I have suggested, Sullivan in his chapter has incorporated the general principle that acts and omissions must be voluntary by excluding from his definition of acts and omissions a number of situations where those 'acts and

---

91 A.S. Goldstein, *The Insanity Defense* (New Haven: Yale University Press, 1967) 87. By 1980, 28 states and 10 out of 11 federal circuit courts had adopted the Model Penal Code provision on insanity as the best and most functional insanity test. See B.A. Weiner, 'Not Guilty By Reason of Insanity' (1980) 56 *Chicago-Kent Law Review* 1057, at 1063 and 1084 (Appendix A). However, the hugely unpopular not guilty by reason of insanity verdict in the attempted assassination of President Reagan by John Hinckley in 1982 has led to a huge retrenchment of the insanity test in many US jurisdictions, including the abolition of the insanity defence in some states. See, for example, S.D. Rozelle, 'Fear and Loathing in Insanity Law: Explaining the Otherwise Inexplicable *Clark v. Arizona*' (2007–8) 58 *Case Western Reserve Law Review* 19; and S.J. Morse and M.B. Hoffman, 'The Uneasy Entente Between Legal Insanity and Mens Rea: Beyond *Clark v. Arizona*' (2006–7) 97 *Journal of Criminal Law and Criminology* 1071.

92 See Bronitt and McSherry, above n. 2, at 212–13, for a list of such jurisdictions.

93 Yeo, Morgan and Chan, above n. 1, at para. [26.46].

omissions' are, in effect, involuntary and therefore, in law, do not constitute an act or omission for the purposes of criminal liability.[94]

Is There a Need for a Defence of Diminished Responsibility?

As noted in the Introduction, a partial defence of diminished responsibility has been introduced in England, New South Wales, Queensland, Scotland and Singapore as a supplement to the insanity defence. Apart from Singapore, countries which have based their criminal codes on the IPC do not contain a diminished responsibility defence. Should a diminished responsibility defence be included in a revised IPC? Yeo argues that with a broadened insanity defence which includes both a cognitive and volitional impairment limb along the lines proposed in this chapter, a defence of diminished responsibility could be dispensed with in Singapore.[95] However, that is an issue which is worthy of further examination and is beyond the scope of this chapter. The proposals for reform of the insanity defence in a revised IPC, which are set out in the next section of this chapter, are based on the assumption that a diminished responsibility defence does not exist in the current IPC.

PROPOSALS FOR REFORM

Based on the preceding discussion, I recommend deletion of the unsoundness of mind defence in s. 84 of the IPC and its replacement with a new cl. 84 set out below. The new provision is called the mental impairment defence. It clarifies and improves the first two limbs of the former defence and adds a new limb for volitional impairment. In addition, the proposed cl. 84 sets out criteria for determining what forms of automatism should be classed within the mental impairment defence. Whether a separate defence of diminished responsibility is desirable and necessary is beyond the scope of this chapter. A separate provision on the requirement of voluntariness (and the inclusion of non-insane automatism as a subset of involuntariness) is also provided. In drafting the new provisions, I have followed, at least for now, the existing IPC format of 'Nothing is an offence' rather than the alternative language of 'A person is not criminally responsible for an offence if …'. I have provisionally numbered the voluntary conduct provision as cl. 83A. The proposed new provisions read as follows:

> 83A. Conduct Must Be Voluntary
> (1) Nothing is an offence if it is done involuntarily.
> (2) Conduct is involuntary if it is not a willed act or omission or, in other words, if it is not a conscious choice to act or refrain from acting.
> (3) Sub-section (1) does not apply if the person's involuntary condition arose from fault on that person's part which is equivalent to the fault level for the offence charged.
> (4) Involuntary conduct arising out of mental impairment shall be dealt with under the mental impairment defence in section 84.
> *Explanation* – Involuntary conduct may be either conscious or unconscious. Conscious but involuntary conduct includes conduct such as a spasm, twitch or reflex action, lack of ability to control a vehicle or other equipment due to unexpected mechanical failure or other similar causes, a trip and fall, an act or movement caused by the physical compulsion of another, or omission of

94 Chapter 4 of this volume, above n. 60, cls. 1 to 4 at 99–101.
95 Yeo, above n. 1, at 256–7.

a legal duty due to physical inability to fulfil that duty. Unconscious involuntary behaviour which is not caused by mental impairment is non-mental impairment automatism and, when it exists, the accused is entitled to an unqualified acquittal under section 83A(1). Examples of non-mental impairment automatism are provided in the *Explanation* following section 84(2).

84. Defence of Mental Impairment

(1) Nothing is an offence which is done by a person who, at the time of carrying out the conduct, was suffering from mental impairment to the extent that the person:

(a) did not appreciate the nature or consequences of the conduct; or

(b) did not know that the conduct was contrary to law, or did not understand that the conduct would be regarded as morally wrong in the eyes of ordinary persons; or

(c) was unable to control the conduct.

(2) For the purposes of sections 83A and 84, mental impairment includes senility, intellectual disability, or any illness, disorder or abnormal condition that impairs the mind and its functioning excluding:

(a) impairment of the mind from the temporary intoxicating effects of alcohol or other drugs; and

(b) temporary impairment of the mind caused by external factors which are unlikely to recur and do not demonstrate an internal weakness of the mind.

Explanation – Mental impairment caused by temporary intoxication under paragraph (2)(a) above is dealt with in sections 85 and 86. Conduct that is not consciously controlled and is caused by external non-recurring factors does not constitute mental impairment for the purposes of section 84. Instead it is classified as non-mental impairment automatism and entitles the person to an unqualified acquittal under section 83A(1). Without restricting the generality of sub-section 2(b) above, conditions qualifying as non-mental impairment automatism would include concussions, sudden stroke, delirium from illness or infection, sleepwalking (if there is little risk of reoccurrence) and a psychological blow from an extraordinary external event which could cause an average normal person to go into a dissociative state.

Chapter 11
Intoxication

Gerry Ferguson

INTRODUCTION

Intoxication as a criminal law defence is normally classified as either voluntary or involuntary.[1] Macaulay's 1837 draft Code for India contained a clear and progressive provision which recognised *involuntary* intoxication as a defence. That provision was altered, in my opinion for the worse, in the final version of the Indian Penal Code (IPC). On the other hand, Macaulay's draft Code contained no provision on *voluntary* intoxication. In that respect, his Code reflected the prevailing view at the time that voluntary intoxication is never a defence to the commission of a crime. The IPC adopted the same view and inserted a provision that expressly recognised that voluntary intoxication is not a defence even though it negates the knowledge or intent required for an offence. That IPC provision was significantly altered in 1935 in Malaysia and Singapore,[2] but not in India, to allow intoxication to be a defence if it negates the intent required for the offence charged. For the past 150 years, many jurisdictions have struggled to find some compromise rule between never recognising voluntary intoxication as a defence and always recognising it as a defence when it negates the subjective fault element of an offence.

INVOLUNTARY INTOXICATION

Macaulay's Draft Code

> 68. Nothing is an offence which a person does in consequence of being, at the time of doing it, in a state of intoxication, provided that either the substance which intoxicated him was administered to him without his knowledge, or against his will, or that he was ignorant that it possessed any intoxicating quality.

Macaulay provided no explanations or illustrations to this clause. Likewise, there was no discussion of the defence of involuntary intoxication in Macaulay's *Notes* accompanying his draft Code. As he observed in *Note B*,[3] most of the defences or general exceptions included in Chapter III of his draft Code required no explanation or justification. Obviously, in Macaulay's view, cl. 68 fell into this category. In spite of this, the following observations on his draft provision are worth noting.

---

1 This distinction is important for analytic purposes even if the boundary line between voluntary and involuntary intoxication is not clear in all situations.

2 The IPC was introduced into these countries when they were under British colonial rule.

3 T.B. Macaulay, J.M. Macleod, G.W. Anderson and F. Millett, *A Penal Code Prepared by the Indian Law Commissioners* (London: Pelham Richardson, 1838) (reprinted by the Lawbook Exchange, Ltd, 2002) Note B (On the Chapter of General Exceptions) 79.

Clause 68 applies if two requirements are met. First, the act or omission which otherwise constitutes an offence must be committed by a person while intoxicated and 'in consequence of being intoxicated'. This causal requirement appears to be no higher than that the person would not have committed the offence but for the intoxicating effects of the substance consumed. There is no requirement that the person be so intoxicated that they did not intend or were not aware of what they were doing, or that it was wrong. It normally requires a fairly high level of intoxication to negate intent or to render a person unaware of what they are doing. But lower levels of intoxication will often loosen a person's inhibitions and cause that person to do things they would not otherwise do if sober. These lower levels of involuntary intoxication would be a defence under Macaulay's draft Code, and I would argue rightly so, in situations where the person's state of lessened inhibition occurred through no fault of their own. Interestingly, as discussed later, this defence of reduced inhibitions due to involuntary intoxication has been expressly accepted in several Australian criminal codes but rejected by the House of Lords in *R. v. Kingston*.[4] As we will see, Macaulay's lessened inhibitions test for involuntary intoxication was not adopted in the IPC.

The second requirement for the application of cl. 68 is that the intoxicating substance was administered under one of the following three circumstances:

(1) without the person's knowledge;
(2) against the person's will; or
(3) in ignorance of the fact that the substance possessed any intoxicating quality.

Circumstances (1) and (2) are classic examples of where the person is in no way at fault for becoming intoxicated. Imposing penal liability for offences committed because of intoxication caused through no fault of the accused seems contrary to the principles of fundamental justice. Circumstance (3) – ignorance of the intoxicating quality of a substance which a person voluntarily consumes – can arise either without fault, in which case it is analogous to circumstances (1) and (2), or with fault (negligence or subjective recklessness), in which case some penal liability may be warranted. This raises the vexing question of whether any degree of fault on a person's part deprives them of the claim that their conduct was involuntary.[5] Since ignorance of the intoxicating quality of a substance is one illustration of a mistake of fact, the Code's response to that question should be consistent with the Code's general treatment of mistake of fact as a defence.[6]

Macaulay's choice of language in circumstance (3), that a person must be ignorant of 'any' intoxicating effect of the substance, would seem to rule out claims of involuntary intoxication where the person claims that he or she knew that the substance consumed had 'some' intoxicating effect but did not know or appreciate the magnitude of the intoxicating effect, for example, when combining alcohol with certain medications or other drugs.

4 *R. v. Kingston* [1995] 2 AC 355.

5 See, for example, the discussion in D. Stuart, *Canadian Criminal Law* (5th edn, Scarborough: Thomson Canada Ltd., 2007) 132–4. With regard to fault in becoming involuntarily intoxicated, see my proposed draft of cl. 85(2) and a brief description of the issue below at 263–4. See also the discussion below at 265–7.

6 See Chapter 5 of this volume (K. Amirthalingam, 'Mistake and Strict Liability').

The IPC Provisions

> Involuntary intoxication[7]
> 85. Nothing is an offence which is done by a person who, at the time of doing it, is, by reason of intoxication, incapable of knowing the nature of the act, or that he is doing what is either wrong or contrary to law: provided that the thing which intoxicated him was administered to him without his knowledge or against his will.

Section 85 of the IPC creates a much narrower defence of involuntary intoxication than cl. 68 of the draft Code. Section 85 requires that the effects of involuntary intoxication on the accused's mind must meet the same high standard of cognitive impairment that is used in the insanity/unsoundness of mind defence under s. 84 of the IPC.[8] The accused's 'unsoundness of mind' under s. 84 and the accused's 'involuntary intoxication' under s. 85 must render the accused 'incapable of knowing the nature of the act or that he is doing what is either wrong or contrary to law'. This is an inappropriately high test for an involuntary intoxication defence. First, it still uses the discredited language of 'incapable of knowing' rather than expressing the test in terms of whether the accused 'actually knew'. Secondly, if applied literally, a person who lacks the requisite fault for a particular offence due to involuntary intoxication can still be convicted of that offence. For example, assume A stabs B with a knife and B dies. Due to involuntary intoxication, A does not appreciate, foresee or intend that the stab may cause death or grievous bodily harm. In those circumstances, the requisite fault for murder does not exist (at least in most jurisdictions). Nonetheless, the accused still 'knew the nature of his act' (that is, stabbing with a knife) and knew that stabbing was wrong. Thus, the requirements for reliance on the defence of involuntary intoxication under s. 85 are not met, even though that involuntary intoxication has negated the requisite fault for murder. An accused in such circumstances might arguably be able to rely on involuntary intoxication as a defence under s. 86 of the IPC if it negates fault. However, that interpretation has apparently been rejected, at least in India.[9] Thirdly, s. 85 clearly does not accept Macaulay's broader claim that involuntary intoxication should be a defence (even if fault exists) in circumstances where the involuntary intoxication lessened a person's inhibitions and caused that person to commit an offence that they would not otherwise have committed.

---

7 The headings preceding ss. 85 and 86 (denoting s. 85 as involuntary intoxication and s. 86 as voluntary intoxication) are found in W. Stokes (ed.), *The Anglo-Indian Codes* (Oxford: Clarendon Press, 1887). However, most other published versions of the IPC do not use the words voluntary and involuntary in the headings.

8 See Chapter 10 of this volume (G. Ferguson 'Insanity') at 247–51. It appears that the common law recognised involuntary intoxication as a defence if it produced the same effects as insanity on an accused's mind. See M. Hale, *Pleas of the Crown* (vol. 1) (Philadelphia: Robert H. Small, 1847) 32.

9 Section 86 of the IPC states:

> In cases where an act done is not an offence unless done with a particular knowledge or intent, a person who does the act in a state of intoxication shall be liable to be dealt with as if he had the same knowledge as he would have had if he had not been intoxicated, unless the thing which intoxicated him was administered to him without his knowledge or against his will.

This section seems to me to set out a rule that indicates that absence of the 'particular knowledge or intent' required for a crime is no defence where that absence is due to voluntary intoxication, but then goes on to state that this rule does not apply where such absence is due to involuntary intoxication (that is, involuntary intoxication is a defence if it negates the requisite knowledge or intent). That does not appear to be the interpretation given to s. 86 in India. See C.K. Thakker and M.C. Thakker, *Ratanlal and Dhirajlal's Law of Crimes* (New Delhi: Bharat Law House, 2007) 339. See also further discussion of s. 86 below at 270.

Section 85 of the IPC is narrower than Macaulay's draft Code in another respect. Section 85 excludes the third circumstance in the draft Code, which provides that 'ignorance of the fact that the substance possessed any intoxicating quality' is a form of involuntary intoxication. Perhaps this third circumstance was deleted on the assumption that it was unnecessary because it was viewed as part and parcel of the first circumstance – that is, 'without the person's knowledge'. While that assumption is arguably correct, I think the two circumstances refer to slightly different situations and therefore I favour Macaulay's approach of articulating them as separate circumstances.

Why was Macaulay's draft on involuntary intoxication changed and narrowed in the IPC? The exact reason may no longer be discoverable. No changes to Macaulay's draft provision were recommended in either the First Report (1846) or the Second Report (1847) of the Indian Law Commissioners on the draft Code.[10] Most of the changes to the draft Code were made by one of his successors, Sir Barnes Peacock, between 1854 and 1856. However, there does not appear to be any surviving copy of Peacock's final report in 1856 on the detailed revisions which he made and the rationale for them.[11] Undoubtedly part of the change came from the questionable decision to incorporate into Macaulay's involuntary intoxication provision some of the new language and criteria in the insanity/unsound mind defence. As I have noted in another chapter in this volume,[12] Macaulay's provision on insanity/madness (cl. 67) was significantly changed in the IPC (s. 84). The M'Naghten Rules[13] were not promulgated until 1843, six years after Macaulay completed his draft Code. Not surprisingly, the IPC used some of the language of the M'Naghten Rules in formulating the insanity/unsoundness of mind provision. In particular, s. 84 of the IPC provision used the two-pronged cognitive test from M'Naghten – 'incapable of knowing the nature of the act, or that he is doing what is either wrong or contrary to law'. Those same words were incorporated into the IPC involuntary intoxication provision (s. 85).

In my view, Macaulay's draft Code is preferable to the IPC version on both points discussed above. I will however suggest a few modest changes to Macaulay's draft later.

James Fitzjames Stephen and the English Royal Commission Draft Criminal Code (1879)

James Fitzjames Stephen was a great admirer of Macaulay and his draft Code for India.[14] Indeed, Stephen worked closely with the IPC when he was the law member of the Governor General's

---

10 The First Report (1846) and the Second Report (1847) are reproduced in T.B. Macaulay, *The Indian Penal Code as Originally Framed in 1837* (Madras: Higginbotham & Co., 1888). The 1846 and 1847 Commissioners carefully summarised criticisms of Macaulay's draft Code collected over the previous ten years from judges in India and other experts, but recommended the enactment of Macaulay's draft Code with only minor changes. Aspects of intoxication and insanity were touched upon at paras. [111], [112], [118], [119], [160] and [652]–[655] of the First Report and not at all in the Second Report. No amendments to Macaulay's provisions on intoxication or insanity were recommended in either Report. Another of Macaulay's successors, Drinkwater Bethune, profoundly disagreed with Macaulay's draft Code and proposed his own. In 1854, a commission chaired by Barnes Peacock rejected Bethune's draft in favour of Macaulay's. Peacock then spent the next two years making his own detailed revisions to Macaulay's draft before issuing his Report in 1856. See Chapter 2 of this volume (B. Wright, 'Macaulay's Indian Penal Code: Historical Context and Originating Principles') at 37; and R. Cross, 'The Making of English Criminal Law: (5) Macaulay' [1978] *Criminal Law Review* 519, at 524.

11 See Cross, *ibid.*, at 524.

12 Chapter 10 of this volume, above n. 8, at 234–5.

13 *Daniel M'Naghten's Case* (1843) 10 Cl & F 200, 8 ER 718.

14 Cross, above n. 10; Chapter 2 of this volume, above n. 10, at 23.

Council in India between 1869 and 1872.[15] In 1878, at the request of the Attorney-General, Stephen drafted a Criminal Code (Indictable Offences) Bill for England which was introduced into the House of Commons and, after its second reading, referred to a Royal Commission for further consideration and amendment. Clause 21 of Stephen's Bill provided that the provisions defining insanity in cl. 19 of his Bill also 'apply to involuntary drunkenness'.[16] That is the same approach to involuntary intoxication which was adopted in the IPC. There is no evidence that Stephen even considered Macaulay's lessened inhibitions provision for involuntary intoxication.[17] In my opinion, that is a pity. In any event, Stephen's failure to consider Macaulay's involuntary intoxication provision became moot when the Royal Commission in its draft Criminal Code (1879) deleted Stephen's provision on intoxication entirely and expressly chose instead to leave the matter of voluntary and involuntary intoxication to the common law.[18] England never enacted the English Commissioners' draft Criminal Code of 1879, but that draft Code did become the model for many British colonies, including Canada and New Zealand, both of which followed the English Commissioners' timid approach on this point. Thus, the Canadian Criminal Code of 1892 and the New Zealand Criminal Code of 1893 were silent on the issue of both voluntary and involuntary intoxication, and were content to leave both matters as uncodified, common law defences.

1935 Amendments in Malaysia and Singapore

In 1935, ss. 85 and 86 of the IPC were replaced in Malaysia and Singapore, but not in India, with the following provisions:

> 85. Intoxication when a defence
> (1) Save as provided in this section and in section 86, intoxication shall not constitute a defence to any criminal charge.
> (2) Intoxication shall be a defence to any criminal charge if by reason thereof the person charged at the time of the act or omission complained of did not know that such act or omission was wrong or did not know what he was doing and –
> (a) the state of intoxication was caused without his consent by the malicious or negligent act of another person; or
> (b) the person charged was by reason of intoxication insane, temporarily or otherwise, at the time of such act or omission.

15 R. Cross, 'The Making of English Criminal Law: (6) Sir James Fitzjames Stephen' [1978] *Criminal Law Review* 652.

16 Stephen's Criminal Code (Indictable Offences) Bill (Bill 178) is available through the English House of Commons Parliamentary Papers Online. Clause 21 also provided that an accused, charged with a specific intent offence, may introduce evidence of voluntary intoxication as a defence if that intoxication negated the specific intent.

17 There is no discussion of this issue in J.F. Stephen, *A Digest of the Criminal Law* (London: Macmillan and Co., 1883), nor in any of the three volumes of J.F. Stephen, *A History of the Criminal Law* (London: Macmillan and Co., 1883).

18 See Report of the *Royal Commission Appointed to Consider the Law Related to Indictable Offences* (1879) at 18, reproduced in the British Parliamentary Papers, *Legal Administration: Criminal Law* (vol. 6) (Shannon: Irish University Press, 1971) at 386.

86. Effect of defence of intoxication when established

(1) Where the defence under sub-section 85(2) is established, then in a case falling under paragraph (a) thereof the accused shall be acquitted, and in a case falling under paragraph (b), the provisions of section 84 of this Code, sections 347 and 348 of the Criminal Procedure Code shall apply.[19]

(2) Intoxication shall be taken into account for the purpose of determining whether the person charged had formed an intention, specific or otherwise, in the absence of which he would not be guilty of the offence.

(3) For the purposes of this and the preceding section 'intoxication' shall be deemed to include a state produced by narcotics or drugs.

The above version is from the Malaysian Penal Code. The same version is found in the Singaporean Penal Code with only minor inconsequential differences. As Yeo, Morgan and Chan note, 'while the motivation for introducing new provisions on intoxication in 1935 may have come from *Beard*, there are material differences between those provisions and that decision'.[20] One very telling difference is the fact that the House of Lords in *DPP v. Beard*[21] was only dealing with *voluntary* intoxication, but the 1935 Malaysian and Singaporean amendments reformulated the law for *both* voluntary and involuntary intoxication.

The 1935 amendments on involuntary intoxication are dealt with in ss. 85(2) and 86(1), and differ in several significant ways from the rule for involuntary intoxication in s. 85 of the IPC. First, the 1935 version of s. 85(2)(a) does not adopt Macaulay's lessened inhibitions standard as a defence in respect to involuntary intoxication. Instead, like s. 85 of the IPC, it is based on the same standards of cognitive impairment that are used for the insanity/unsoundness of mind test. But s. 86(2) also provides that 'intoxication shall be taken into account for the purpose of determining whether the person charged had formed an intention, specific or otherwise, in the absence of which he would not be guilty of the offence'. Since s. 86(2) uses the word 'intoxication' without any modifiers, presumably s. 86(2) applies to both voluntary or involuntary intoxication.[22]

Secondly, the 1935 version of s. 85 properly deletes the words 'incapable of knowing' and substitutes instead a reference to what the accused 'actually knew'. That change was subsequently adopted in other jurisdictions by case law.[23]

Thirdly, the words 'without his knowledge or against his will' in s. 85 of the IPC were changed in s. 85(2)(a) of the 1935 amendment to 'caused without his consent by the malicious or negligent act of another person'. As Yeo, Morgan and Chan point out, this change is undesirable:

> It is highly questionable why this defence is predicated on a third party's malice or negligence when the inquiry is concerned with the accused's blameworthiness. The injustice created is instanced by

19 Section 84 is the 'unsoundness of mind' defence, which is the IPC rendition of the insanity defence. Sections 347 and 348 of the Criminal Procedure Code deal with the verdict and disposition of persons who are found to have committed the offence charged by reason of insanity.

20 S. Yeo, N. Morgan and W. Chan, *Criminal Law in Malaysia and Singapore* (Singapore: LexisNexis, 2007) para. [25.5].

21 [1920] AC 479.

22 Yeo, Morgan and Chan, above n. 20, at para. [25.13], are also of the opinion that s. 86(2) is sufficiently wide to cover cases of involuntary intoxication.

23 See, for example, *Broadhurst v. The Queen* [1964] AC 441; *R. v. Kamipeli* [1975] 2 NZLR 610; *R. v. Clarke* [1992] 1 NZLR 147; *R. v. Pordage* [1975] Crim LR 575; *Viro v. The Queen* (1978) 141 CLR 88; *R. v. Robinson* (1996) 105 CCC (3d) 97; and *R. v. Daley* 2007 SCC 53.

> the denial of s. 85(2)(a) defence to an accused whose friend had spiked her drink as a practical joke. The defence would likewise be unavailable to an accused who had become intoxicated on account of being mistakenly prescribed a much higher dosage of a drug, unless the prescribing physician was proven to have been negligent.[24]

Finally, the addition of s. 85(2)(b) in the 1935 amendment is puzzling and unnecessary. It should instead clearly state that a person who, due to the temporary intoxicating effects of alcohol or drugs, does not know what he or she is doing, or that it is wrong, should not be classified in law as insane unless the intoxication has induced some other disease of the mind, such as *delirium tremens* or a psychotic abnormality which goes beyond the ordinary and temporary intoxicating effects of alcohol or drugs.[25]

Proposal for a Modernised IPC Involuntary Intoxication Provision

In my opinion, with respect to involuntary intoxication, Macaulay's provision is generally preferable to the IPC version and the 1935 amendment which is in force in Malaysia and Singapore. The proposed revision set out below adopts Macaulay's language with some modification. To be consistent with the drafting of the other defences in Macaulay's draft Code (and the IPC), I have used his opening words for describing defences, that is, 'Nothing is an offence …'. An alternative (and preferable) form for describing defences, which is used in the 1935 amendments to the Malaysian and Singaporean Penal Codes, is to state 'Intoxication is a defence to any criminal charge if …'.

In addition to Macaulay's objectives of drafting penal code provisions which are rational, clear and reasonably comprehensive,[26] I suggest, for reasons discussed below, that the substantive principle that should govern the defence of involuntary intoxication is that persons who are involuntarily intoxicated should not be held liable for an offence committed *as a consequence thereof* unless their intoxicated state arose from fault on their part equivalent to the level of fault required for the offence charged. With that principle in mind, I recommend the following provisions:

> Involuntary Intoxication
>
> 85.(1) Nothing is an offence which a person does in consequence of being, at the time of doing it, in a state of involuntary intoxication.
>
> *Explanation* – A person's acts or omissions shall be considered to have occurred 'in consequence of being involuntarily intoxicated' if that person would not have committed those acts or omissions but for their involuntary intoxication.
>
> (2) For the purpose of this section, a person is in a state of involuntary intoxication in circumstances where the substance which intoxicated that person was consumed by him or

24 Yeo, Morgan and Chan, above n. 20, at para. [25.10].

25 But see the contrary view expressed by the Singapore Court of Appeal in *Tan Chor Jin v. PP* [2008] 4 SLR(R) 306, which held that s. 85(2)(b) could be based on temporary effects of intoxication. Yeo, Morgan and Chan, above n. 20, at paras. [25.22]–[25.31], discuss the potential meaning of s. 85(2)(b).

26 See Chapter 2 of this volume, above n. 10, at 22–3 and 35.

administered to him:
(a) against his will; or
(b) without his knowledge; or
(c) in ignorance of its intoxicating quality;
and provided that the compulsion, lack of knowledge or ignorance in paragraphs (a) to (c) did not arise from subjective recklessness on his part in the case of subjective fault offences, or negligence (objective recklessness) in the case of objective fault offences.[27]

Explanation – If A commits a subjective fault offence (for example, assault, theft, mischief) while intoxicated by reason of circumstance (a), (b) or (c) in sub-section (2), A is involuntarily intoxicated and is not guilty of that subjective fault offence even if A acted with the requisite subjective fault for that offence, provided (1) A would not have committed that offence if A was not so intoxicated and (2) A was not subjectively reckless in becoming intoxicated by reason of circumstances (a) to (c). If A was subjectively reckless in regard to his intoxication under circumstance (a) to (c), A is not involuntarily intoxicated and cannot therefore rely on the defence of involuntary intoxication. In this latter circumstance, A may rely on voluntary intoxication as a defence if the requirements for voluntary intoxication have been met. On the other hand, if A was objectively reckless in becoming intoxicated under circumstances (a) to (c), A can rely on his involuntary intoxication as a defence to any subjective fault offence, but not to an objective fault offence such as causing death or grievous hurt by negligence.

Comments on Involuntary Intoxication Proposal

Definition of Involuntary Intoxication

My proposed cl. 85(2) sets out a definition of involuntary intoxication. It adopts the same three circumstances that Macaulay used in defining what constitutes involuntary intoxication. As argued earlier, in my view, Macaulay's three circumstances are preferable to the two circumstances in the IPC provision and to the 1935 amended provision in Malaysia and Singapore. While s. 8.1 of the Australian Commonwealth Criminal Code lists a number of circumstances that constitute self-induced intoxication,[28] I think Macaulay's three circumstances are broad enough to incorporate the other circumstances listed in the Commonwealth Code.

Section 85(2) of my proposal also prevents an accused from relying on involuntary intoxication as a defence to a subjective fault offence if the accused was subjectively reckless with regard to any of the three circumstances which otherwise constitute involuntary intoxication. Likewise, objective recklessness (negligence) with regard to any of the same three circumstances will preclude a person from claiming involuntary intoxication as a defence to an objective fault offence.

---

27 The language used to refer to subjective and objective mental fault elements in this provision should be modified to match the mental fault elements in a revised IPC once those fault elements have been decided upon. See Chapter 3 of this volume (N. Morgan, 'The Fault Elements of Offences').

28 Criminal Code (Cth), s. 8.1 states:
Definition – self-induced intoxication
For the purposes of this Division, intoxication is self-induced unless it came about:
(a) involuntarily; or
(b) as a result of fraud, sudden or extraordinary emergency, accident, reasonable mistake, duress or force.

Most jurisdictions preclude reliance on involuntary intoxication if it arose through some degree of fault on the part of the accused.[29]

Scope of the Involuntary Intoxication Rule

There are four main options in defining the scope of an involuntary intoxication rule. The first and narrowest option is to allow involuntary intoxication as a defence only if it produces the same sort of cognitive impairment as required for the insanity/unsoundness of mind defence. This option was adopted in the IPC (and to a lesser extent in the 1935 Malaysia and Singapore amended provisions). Likewise s. 28(1) of the Western Australia and Queensland Codes adopts this option. Section 28(1) provides that the provisions of s. 27 (which sets out the insanity defence) apply to unintentional (that is, involuntary) intoxication.[30] For the reasons I have already mentioned in discussing the IPC provision, I believe that this option is an inappropriately narrow rule.

The second option is to allow involuntary intoxication as a defence if it negates a subjective fault element required for an offence, regardless of whether that subjective fault element is specific or basic intent. Many jurisdictions have adopted this option. In Canada, England and Tasmania, the defence of *voluntary* intoxication is restricted to specific intent offences, but the courts in those jurisdictions are prepared to extend the defence of intoxication to basic intent offences when the intoxication is *involuntary*. This extension clearly reflects a sentiment that *involuntarily* intoxicated persons are deserving of a wider defence than *voluntarily* intoxicated persons.[31] In jurisdictions

29 In England, it has been held that ignorance of the strength of an alcoholic drink that is voluntarily consumed does not make that person's subsequent intoxication involuntary: *R. v. Allen* [1988] Crim LR 698. This decision may be premised on the assumption that knowingly and voluntarily consuming any quantity of alcohol constitutes subjective or objective recklessness as to the risk of impairment and the risk of commission of an offence while so impaired. On the other hand, English courts have recognised that where self-induced intoxication by medical drugs is 'faultless', that is, where the person has not been subjectively (or perhaps objectively) reckless as to the risks of aggression or impairment, that person's intoxication will be treated as involuntary intoxication. See *R. v. Hardie* [1985] 1 WLR 64 and the discussion of this issue in Law Commission for England and Wales, *Intoxication and Criminal Liability* (Law Com. No. 314) (London: HMSO, 2009) 39–42. In Canada, an objective-subjective test is used. If the person knew, or ought reasonably to have known, that the substance voluntarily consumed was an intoxicant, then a claim of involuntary intoxication will fail: *R. v. Chaulk* (2007) 223 CCC (3d) 174; *R. v. Saxon* (1975) 22 CCC (2d) 370, at 375–6; *R. v. Abel* (1999) 134 CCC (3d) 155. In Australia, see S. Bronitt and B. McSherry, *Principles of Criminal Law* (2nd edn, Pyrmont: Lawbook Co., 2005), at 257, where the authors note that the legislative provisions in some Australian jurisdictions indicate that intoxication which results from a 'reasonable' mistake will be considered involuntary: see Crimes Act 1900 (NSW), s. 428G; Criminal Code (NT), s. 1; Criminal Code (ACT), s. 34; and Criminal Code (Cth), s. 8.1.

30 The scope of the defence of involuntary intoxication is wider in the Western Australia and Queensland Codes than in the IPC. All three codes recognise involuntary intoxication as a defence when it produces the type of mental impairment necessary to establish the insanity defence, but since the scope of the insanity defence is broader under the Western Australia and Queensland Codes than under the IPC, that necessarily means that the scope of the involuntary intoxication defence is also broader under these Australian Codes than under the IPC. In particular, the insanity defence under the IPC is restricted to incapacity to know the nature of the act, or that it is wrong, while the Australian Codes include these two incapacities, plus the incapacity to control his or her conduct. This third incapacity is particularly relevant to intoxication, which normally diminishes a person's capacity to control his or her conduct.

31 In England, see M.J. Allen, *Textbook on Criminal Law* (10th edn, Oxford: Oxford University Press, 2009), at 168–9, discussing *R. v. Hardie*, above n. 29, and *R. v. Kingston*, above n. 4, which recognise that involuntary intoxication (unlike voluntary intoxication) is a defence if it negates basic intent. For a similar

where an *O'Connor*-type rule applies (that is, allowing *voluntary* intoxication to negate any subjective fault element), it logically follows that *involuntary* intoxication is also a defence when it negates any subjective fault element.[32]

The third option is to extend the second option to allow involuntary intoxication to negate both subjective and objective fault elements. This option recognises that an involuntarily intoxicated person has gotten into that state without fault and therefore is entitled to a broader defence than a voluntarily intoxicated person who has acted unreasonably by allowing himself or herself to become seriously intoxicated and thereby run the risk of committing an offence while intoxicated.

The fourth option is the broadest test for involuntary intoxication. It is based on a lessened inhibitions standard. Under this option, if a person is involuntarily intoxicated through no relevant fault of his or her own and, due to lessened inhibitions, commits an offence which he or she would not have committed otherwise, that person will be acquitted of that offence even if he or she committed it with the requisite mental fault element. At first glance, it may seem contrary to the ordinary principles of responsibility to acquit a person of an offence if the person has committed that offence with the requisite mental fault element. However, that is precisely what the law does in the context of lawful justifications and excuses, such as self-defence, necessity or duress. In each of those instances, the mental fault element for the offence committed exists, but the accused is excused or justified for committing that offence for sound policy reasons. In the case of involuntary intoxication, the accused should be entitled to an acquittal because his or her ordinary volitional control mechanisms are impaired, through no relevant fault of his or her own, to the extent that he or she has committed an offence which he or she would not have committed if sober. Under those circumstances, it is unfair to hold that person to blame for something which was in effect caused through no fault of his or her own.

As noted earlier, Macaulay's provision on involuntary intoxication incorporates this lessened inhibitions option. More recently, the lessened inhibitions standard for involuntary intoxication was adopted in s. 8.5 of the Australian Commonwealth Criminal Code.[33] That same provision was adopted in the Australian Capital Territory Criminal Code 2002 and was subsequently adopted in the Northern Territory Criminal Code 2005 (in force 20 December 2006). A lessened inhibitions standard for involuntary intoxication was also adopted by the English Court of Appeal in *R. v. Kingston*[34] under the rubric of a defence of 'innocent intent'. However, the House of Lords overruled that decision and held that there is no defence of innocent intent or lessened inhibitions by reason of involuntary intoxication.[35] Subsequently, the English Law Commission[36] and the

---

result in Canada, see *R. v. King* [1962] SCR 746 and *R. v. Chaulk*, above n. 29. The same rule seems to apply in Tasmania – see Tasmania Law Reform Institute, *Intoxication and Criminal Responsibility* (Final Report No. 7) (Hobart: Tasmania Law Reform Institute, 2006) 34–5.

32 For example, in New Zealand, where an *O'Connor*-type rule applies, A.P. Simester and W.J. Brookbanks, *Principles of Criminal Law* (3rd edn, Wellington: Brookers, 2007), at 352, state: 'The distinction between voluntary and involuntary intoxication is, of course, irrelevant in New Zealand – where the law simply asks, whatever the reason, *did* D have *mens rea*?' In Australia, see Tasmania Law Reform Institute, *ibid.*, at 94–102; see also Bronitt and McSherry, above n. 29, at 257.

33 See I. Leader-Elliott, *The Commonwealth Criminal Code: A Guide for Practitioners* (Canberra: Commonwealth Attorney-General's Department, 2002) 139–40 and 167–9.

34 [1994] 1 QB 81, at 87.

35 Above n. 4.

36 Law Commission for England and Wales, above n. 29, at 86–91.

Tasmania Law Reform Institute[37] have also rejected the idea of an intoxication defence based on lessened inhibitions.

Critics of the lessened inhibitions test argue that it is an unworkable test on the grounds that it would be virtually impossible to determine whether the accused would not have committed the offence had he or she not been involuntarily intoxicated. While this is a legitimate concern, it is not insurmountable. Like many other legal tests, it will be easy to infer in some cases and difficult to infer in other cases, just as inferences about the accused's fault or state of mind are easy to draw in some cases and difficult to draw in other cases. Judges and juries rely on their own experience and common sense in drawing such inferences.

A more substantial argument against the lessened inhibitions test is the claim that the accused is still morally blameworthy if he or she intentionally or recklessly commits an offence which he or she would not otherwise have committed if he or she were not involuntarily intoxicated.[38] This claim is often premised on the assumption that the involuntarily intoxicated person will become aware of his or her intoxication and at that stage has an obligation or responsibility to monitor his or her behaviour from that point on. In fact, in many cases, the involuntarily intoxicated person may not know they are intoxicated.[39] In addition, even if that person does become aware of his or her intoxication, it may be unfair to impose a duty or responsibility on that person to 'make special efforts to see and avoid risks' when their blameless state of intoxication has impaired the very qualities – intellectual and moral judgment and ordinary behaviour control mechanisms – that are relevant to taking special precautions to avoid commission of a crime.

A further concern with a lessened inhibitions test for involuntary intoxication is that it could be a complete defence to the intentional commission of the most serious of offences by persons whose inhibitions are only modestly impaired. For example, suppose A, while in a state of involuntary intoxication, intentionally kills V. An acquittal for murder in such circumstances would indeed be a cause for concern in most circumstances. But this sort of unlikely hypothetical must be put in context. The lessened inhibition defence for involuntary intoxication only applies in circumstances where the accused would not have committed the offence *but for* the involuntary intoxication. Involuntary intoxication is rare. Intentionally killing of another person while in such a state would be even rarer. If such a claim ever arose, a judge or jury would be very slow indeed to accept that an intentional killing was committed as a consequence of the accused's involuntary intoxication and would not have occurred but for the involuntary intoxication. In addition, under my proposal, the accused is not entitled to rely on involuntary intoxication to a subjective fault offence like murder if the accused was subjectively reckless in becoming intoxicated.

If the reduced inhibitions option which I have proposed above is rejected, I would recommend that option three be adopted. That option allows involuntary intoxication as a defence if it negates the fault element for the offence, whether that fault element is subjective or objective. Option three is set out below in an alternative draft of s. 85(1). Clause 85(2) of my original proposal, defining involuntary intoxication and excluding it if it is caused by recklessness, would continue to apply if alternative draft s. 85(1) is adopted:

---

37 Tasmania Law Reform Institute, above n. 31, at 94–102.

38 *Ibid.*, at 97.

39 Some commentators have suggested that the law should treat involuntarily intoxicated persons who are unaware that they are intoxicated more leniently than involuntarily intoxicated persons who become aware that they are intoxicated. While there may be some merit in that claim, I have not adopted it in my proposed draft.

Alternative Draft of Section 85(1): Option 3

(1) Nothing is an offence which is done by a person in a state of involuntary intoxication provided that person's act or omission is done without the requisite fault requirement for that offence.

Explanation – Sub-section (1) applies to all offences regardless of whether the requisite fault element is subjective or objective.

VOLUNTARY INTOXICATION

Introduction

As already noted, accepting voluntary intoxication as a defence to any crime is a controversial matter. This controversy is heightened by the indisputable fact that a very large percentage of crimes, and especially crimes of violence, are committed by persons who have voluntarily consumed alcohol or drugs.[40] However, it should not be forgotten that, while alcohol and drugs loosen an offender's inhibitions and render the commission of crime more likely, loss of inhibition induced by voluntary consumption of such intoxicating substances is no defence.[41] There are only a small percentage of intoxication cases where the intoxication is so extreme that the offender lacks the subjective state of mind required for the offence committed.[42] It is in this latter category of cases that the law struggles to craft an appropriate response. Clearly, a person who has committed a criminal harm while voluntarily intoxicated is deserving of both condemnation and some degree of punishment. The difficulty which arises as a matter of logic is the apparent inconsistency in convicting a person of an offence requiring a subjective state of mind when it is apparent that the person did not have that state of mind because of their high level of voluntary intoxication. Over the past two centuries, the common law and criminal codes have adopted various positions with respect to liability for offences committed while in a state of voluntary intoxication. These positions can be divided roughly into one of three options:

(1) voluntary intoxication is no defence even if it negates the subjective fault elements for the offence committed;[43]

(2) voluntary intoxication is a defence for crimes of specific intent, but not basic intent, provided the intoxication negates the specific intent (and if intoxication does negate the specific intent, the offender may be convicted instead, in some or all cases, of a lesser included basic intent or objective fault offence, or perhaps a new separate offence of criminal intoxication);

40 See, for example, Law Commission for England and Wales, above n. 29, at 1–2, where the Commission summarises data indicating that in 46 per cent of violent incidents, victims believe their offender(s) to be under the influence of alcohol and, 20 per cent of the time, under the influence of other drugs. See also G. Dingwall, *Alcohol and Crime* (Cullompton: Willan Publishing, 2006), especially Chapter 2.

41 See, for example, *DPP v. Beard*, above n. 21, at 501–2.

42 See, for example, C.N. Mitchell, 'The Intoxicated Offender – Refuting the Legal and Medical Myths' (1988) 11 *International Journal of Law and Psychiatry* 77, at 91, where the author cites studies indicating that intoxicated accused persons are rarely unaware of their actions and rarely act without intent. While intoxication may make people less concerned about the consequences of their actions, it seldom renders them unable to perceive those consequences.

43 Intoxication is not normally a defence to crimes of objective fault because the reasonable person is not a voluntarily intoxicated person.

and

(3) voluntary intoxication is a defence for any subjective fault crime (whether specific or general), provided the intoxication negates that subjective state of mind (and if the intoxication does negate the requisite subjective fault, the offender may be convicted instead, in some or all cases, of a lesser included objective fault offence, or perhaps a new separate offence of criminal intoxication).

There are weaknesses and disadvantages to each of these options. I will argue in the remainder of this chapter that options (1) and (2) are too narrow and that option (3), combined with conviction for a separate, lesser included intoxication offence, constitutes the most principled and fairest approach to the issue of voluntary intoxication.

Historical Development of Voluntary Intoxication Rules[44]

Prior to 1800, drunkenness was never considered a defence to crime;[45] in fact, it was sometimes considered an aggravation.[46] The first signs that voluntary drunkenness would be given some consideration appeared in the early nineteenth century.[47] In a series of cases starting with *R. v. Meakin* (1836),[48] *R. v. Cruse* (1838)[49] and *R. v. Monkhouse* (1849),[50] the courts held that if intoxication negated the specific or particular intent required for the offence charged, there could be no conviction for that offence. Although the expression 'specific intent' was used in these cases, there was no legal rule at this stage which divided intent into specific and basic intent crimes. In *R. v. Doherty* (1887)[51] and *R. v. Meade* (1909),[52] the English Court of Appeal held that drunkenness as a defence was not restricted to specific intent crimes and was available as a defence to any crime requiring proof of intent. However, in *Beard*,[53] the House of Lords articulated the intoxication rule in terms of specific intent, although, later in their judgment, they held that intoxication was not restricted to specific intent offences and could also be used to negate basic intent.[54] However, that wider rule was not followed in subsequent cases. Instead, the intoxication defence in England and other countries such as Canada and some Australian jurisdictions became a rigid rule that intoxication is admissible to negate specific intent but not basic intent.

---

44 For a more detailed historical account, see G.A. Ferguson, '*Mens Rea* Evaluated in Terms of the Essential Elements of a Crime, Specific Intent, and Drunkenness' (1970–1) 4 *Ottawa Law Review* 356, at 373–8, which relies in part on R.U. Singh, 'History of the Defence of Drunkenness in English Criminal Law' (1933) 49 *Law Quarterly Review* 528.

45 Singh, *ibid.*, at 536. See also *Reniger v. Fogossa* (1551) 1 Plowdon 2, 75 ER 1.

46 See *Beverley's Case* (1603) 4 Co Rep 123b at 125a, 76 ER 1118, at 1123.

47 See *William Rennie's Case* (1825) 1 Lewin 76, 168 ER 965; *Marshall's Case* (1830) 1 Lewin 76, 168 ER 965; *Pearson's Case* (1835) 2 Lewin 144, 168 ER 1108; *R. v. John Thomas* (1837) 7 C & P 817, 173 ER 356; cf. *R. v. Patrick Carroll* (1835) 7 C & P 145, 173 ER 64.

48 (1836) 7 C & P 297, 173 ER 131.

49 (1838) 8 C & P 541, 173 ER 610.

50 (1849) 4 Cox CC 55. See also the discussion in Simester and Brookbanks, above n. 32, at 336–7.

51 (1887) 16 Cox CC 306.

52 [1909] 1 KB 895.

53 Above n. 21.

54 *Ibid.*, at 504.

Macaulay's Draft Code

Macaulay's draft Code contained no provision recognising voluntary intoxication as a defence to intentional crimes, whether specific or general. And there was no discussion in his *Notes* which accompanied his draft Code on the issue of whether such a defence should be included. This is hardly surprising, since the notion that voluntary intoxication may negate intent had only been clearly adopted for the first time in England in *Meakin*, just one year before Macaulay completed his draft Code. Likewise, there was no English legislation recognising voluntary intoxication as a defence, nor had the subject matter been considered by the English Commissioners on Criminal Law in their first three reports published between 1834 and 1837.[55] Moreover, Macaulay also referred to the French Penal Code (1810) and Livingston's draft Code of Crimes and Punishments for Louisiana (1826)[56] when drafting the IPC. Consistent with the times, neither of these codes included a defence of voluntary intoxication.

The IPC and its Judicial Interpretation

The IPC expressly includes a provision on voluntary intoxication which appears to reject voluntary intoxication as a defence even if it negates specific intent or knowledge. Section 86 provides as follows:

> Offence Requiring Particular Intent or Knowledge Committed During Voluntary Intoxication
> 86. In cases where an act done is not an offence unless done with a particular knowledge or intent, a person who does the act in a state of intoxication shall be liable to be dealt with as if he had the same knowledge as he would have had if he had not been intoxicated, unless the thing which intoxicated him was administered to him without his knowledge or against his will.

This section was drafted at a time when the courts in *Meakin*, *Cruse* and *Monkhouse* had only hesitantly recognised that drunkenness negating the particular intent required for an offence prevented the accused's conviction for that offence. Notwithstanding this, the IPC drafters appear to have specifically rejected voluntary intoxication as a defence. There is no record of the drafters' deliberations on this point.

It seems clear that s. 86 was designed to adhere to the earlier common law position (also adopted by Macaulay) that voluntary intoxication was not a defence to subjective fault crimes (that is, crimes requiring knowledge or intent). However, strangely, Indian courts have found a way to limit s. 86 to offences requiring a particular knowledge and to adopt *Beard* as an applicable common law rule that applies to offences requiring specific intent.[57]

---

55 First Report of Commissioners on Criminal Law, Parliamentary Papers, 1834; Second Report of Commissioners on Criminal Law, Parliamentary Papers, 1836; and Third Report of Commissioners on Criminal Law, Parliamentary Papers, 1837, reproduced in British Parliamentary Papers, *Legal Administration: Criminal Law* (vol. 3) (Shannon: Irish University Press, 1971).

56 Edward Livingston's Introductory Report to the Code of Crimes and Punishments and his proposed Code of Crimes and Punishments were submitted to the Louisiana legislature in 1826 and are reproduced in *The Complete Works of Edward Livingston on Criminal Jurisprudence* (Montclair: Patterson Smith, 1968 reprint). There is no discussion of intoxication in the Introductory Report on the Code of Crime and Punishment, which appears in vol. 1. See also Chapter 2 of this volume, above n. 10, at 38–9 and 41.

57 Thakker and Thakker, above n. 9, at 337–8.

1935 Amendments in Malaysia and Singapore

In 1935, Malaysia and Singapore, but not India, amended ss. 85 and 86 of the IPC (reproduced above). With regard to voluntary intoxication, s. 86(2) of the 1935 amendment recognised voluntary intoxication as a defence when that intoxication resulted in the accused not forming the requisite intent, specific or otherwise, required for the crime charged. Section 86(2) provides as follows:

> Intoxication shall be taken into account for the purpose of determining whether the person charged had formed an intention, specific or otherwise, in the absence of which he would not be guilty of the offence.

While the motivation for the 1935 amendments may have been the House of Lords' decision in *Beard*, there are material differences between those amendments and *Beard*. Interestingly, the 1935 amendments are not restricted to the narrow 'specific intent' language in *Beard* and instead are consistent with the wider rule in *Beard* that voluntary intoxication is applicable to all intentional crimes, whether those crimes require specific or basic intent. As Yeo, Morgan and Chan state:

> The Penal Code provisions on intoxication do not adopt this extreme position under English common law. The Code's view is that the accused's moral turpitude in becoming intoxicated is only remotely connected to the offence charged. In particular, the Code does not regard a person as criminally liable for being reckless in some general sense when consuming alcohol or drugs. Closely following the general principle of criminal law that an accused's liability should be judged at the time of the commission of the alleged offence, the Code requires the accused to be acquitted should it be found that he or she lacked the fault or physical element of the crime charged at that time. And it would be immaterial that what rendered absent either of these offence elements was the accused's voluntary intoxication.[58]

However, the judicial interpretation of s. 86(2) in Malaysia and Singapore has been too strictly and narrowly interpreted in one significant way. As Yeo, Morgan and Chan explain:

> While s. 86(2) is wider in scope than the English common law as pronounced in *Beard*, the provision is nevertheless confined to intention-based crimes. Consequently, crimes based on other forms of fault elements such as knowledge, rashness, recklessness, wantonness or negligence fall outside the ambit of s. 86(2).[59]

COMPARATIVE PERSPECTIVES AND OPTIONS ON VOLUNTARY INTOXICATION

Option (1): No Defence of Voluntary Intoxication

As previously noted, the common law position for many centuries was that voluntary intoxication was no defence. In other words, voluntary intoxication could not be used by an accused to claim that he or she lacked the requisite fault element for a crime. That is the position that was adopted in Macaulay's draft Code and it appears to be the rule that was adopted in the IPC, although courts in

58 Yeo, Morgan and Chan, above n. 20, at para. [25.7].

59 *Ibid.*, at para. [25.15].

India have not interpreted the IPC provisions in that way. The position that voluntary intoxication is no defence even to specific intent offences has re-emerged in some jurisdictions. Since the decision of *Brennan v. H.M. Advocate*[60] in 1977, Scottish criminal law has not accepted voluntary intoxication as a defence, even if that intoxication prevented the accused from forming the requisite intent for the offence charged.[61] And in the US, strong public sentiment against voluntary intoxication as a defence has resulted in some states abolishing that defence. For example, the Montana Penal Code makes it clear that voluntary intoxication 'may not be taken into consideration in determining the existence of a mental state'. In *Montana v. Egelhoff*,[62] the accused argued that this rule prejudiced his right to a fair trial and denied him the presumption of innocence. That constitutional challenge was rejected by the US Supreme Court.

While a complete ban on voluntary intoxication as a defence may be consistent with widespread public sentiment, it is inconsistent with the fundamental principle of criminal liability that a person should not be convicted of a particular criminal offence unless that person had the fault level required for that offence (or at least a substituted or transferred fault level of the same degree).

Option (2): A Specific-Basic Intent Rule

The specific-basic intent rule continues to be used in many jurisdictions, but it is not interpreted and applied in the same way in all jurisdictions. For example, the articulation of the rule in terms of 'incapacity' in *Beard* rather than 'actual intent' has been expressly rejected in several countries such as Canada,[63] New Zealand[64] and some Australian jurisdictions,[65] and is no longer applied in England.[66] Likewise, it was not used in the 1935 amendment to the Malaysian and Singaporean Penal Codes. However 'incapacity' is still used in some codes, such as s. 17(2) and (3) of the Tasmanian Criminal Code, although there is no serious disagreement in Tasmania that the incapacity language should be abolished.[67]

The exclusion of voluntary intoxication as a defence to basic intent crimes is often justified on the same public perception/public policy grounds that support a complete ban on intoxication as a defence. For example, in *R. v. Majewski*, Lord Elwyn-Jones justified the rule that intoxication is no defence to basic intent offences on the grounds that a person who voluntarily:

> … takes a substance which causes him to cast off the restraints of reason and conscience … in my view supplies the evidence of *mens rea*, of guilty mind certainly sufficient for crimes of basic intent. It is a reckless course of conduct and recklessness is enough to constitute the necessary *mens rea* in assault cases …[68]

60 1977 JC 38.

61 For a thorough analysis and critique of *Brennan*, see F. Stark, 'Breaking Down Brennan' (2009) *Juridical Review* 155; and F. Leverick and J. Chalmers, *Criminal Defences and Pleas in Bar of Trial* (Edinburgh: W. Green & Son Ltd., 2006) Chapter 8.

62 518 U.S. 37 (1996).

63 *Robinson*, above n. 23.

64 *Kamipeli*, above n. 23; and *R. v. Hart* [1986] 2 NZLR 408.

65 *Viro*, above n. 23; see Crimes Act (NSW), s. 428C, as amended in 1996.

66 *R. v. Pordage*, above n. 23.

67 See, for example, Tasmania Law Reform Institute, above n. 31, at 48 and 72.

68 *R. v. Majewski* [1977] AC 443, at 474–5. For a similar rationale, see Lord Simon in *Majewski*, at 479. For another explanation of the moral and legal justifications of the specific-basic intent rule, see Mason J.'s

Notwithstanding the above moral and legal rationale, the specific-basic intent rule has been frequently criticised by courts, academics and law reform bodies as unprincipled, illogical and arbitrary, and has been expressly abolished by courts or legislatures in several jurisdictions. In brief, the primary criticisms[69] include the following:

(1) The specific-basic intent rule is considered unprincipled by many judges and commentators. For example, in *R. v. Daviault*,[70] Cory J., for the majority of the Supreme Court of Canada, held that preventing the admission of evidence of extreme intoxication to negate basic intent offences is unprincipled because it substitutes the intent or recklessness to get drunk for the intent or recklessness required to commit sexual assault in circumstances where the former is in no way equivalent to the latter.[71]
(2) The distinction between specific and basic intent offences is premised on linguistic manipulation of the definition or description of an offence, not on any morally significant differences between specific and basic intent offences.[72]
(3) It is difficult to articulate and apply the distinction between specific and basic intent offences.[73] This difficulty leads to arbitrary and inconsistent results from court to court, offence to offence and jurisdiction to jurisdiction.[74]
(4) The specific-basic intent rule is an inadequate compromise rule. Where a specific intent offence contains a lesser included basic intent (or even objective fault) offence, the intoxicated offender may be acquitted of the specific intent offence, but he or she is at least convicted and punished for the lesser included offence. However, some specific intent offences do not contain lesser included basic intent offences and therefore the intoxicated offender will escape conviction for any offence. For example, a thief who lacks the necessary specific intent for theft will be acquitted entirely, with no alternative conviction available.[75]

Despite these criticisms, the specific-basic intent rule continues to be the law in England,[76] Tasmania[77] and, in a modified way, under the Australian Commonwealth Criminal Code 1995,[78]

---

minority reasons in *The Queen v. O'Connor* (1980) 146 CLR 64, at 110–11.

69 For a more detailed critique of the specific-basic intent rule, see T. Quigley, 'Specific and General Nonsense?' (1987–8) 11 *Dalhousie Law Journal* 75. Likewise, Dickson J., dissenting in *R. v. Leary* (1977) 33 CCC (2d) 473, gives a cogent and convincing critique of the specific-basic intent rule.

70 [1994] 3 SCR 63.

71 *Ibid.*, at paras. [39]–[42].

72 See, for example, *O'Connor*, above n. 68, at 104.

73 The definition of specific-basic intent in *R. v. George* [1960] SCR 871 (*per* Fautaux J.) was adopted in *Majewski*, above n. 68. In *R. v. Heard* [2008] QB 43, the court interpreted the *Majewski* specific-basic distinction, which it acknowledged was elusive, as indicating that a specific intent offence requires 'proof of a state of mind addressing something beyond the prohibited act itself, namely its consequences'.

74 The commonly repeated distinction that specific intent offences require a *mens rea* which goes beyond the immediate *actus reus* – that is, an ulterior intent – fails to explain why murder is consistently classified as specific intent although it requires no ulterior intent. The offence of rape has also been difficult to classify.

75 Theft has been classified as a specific intent crime: see, for example, *Ruse v. Read* [1949] 1 KB 377, approved in *Majewski*, above n. 68; *George*, above n. 73.

76 See *Majewski*, *ibid.*; and *Heard*, above n. 73.

77 Criminal Code Act, 1924 (Tas), s. 17.

78 Criminal Code Act, 1995 (Cth), ss. 8.1–8.4, which provide that self-induced intoxication cannot be used to negate basic intent and restricts basic intent to intention to commit the prescribed act or omission, but

the Australian Capital Territory Criminal Code 2002[79] and the New South Wales Crimes Act, as amended in 1996.[80] Likewise, South Australia abolished the broad common law *O'Connor* rules in 2004[81] and reverted to a narrower specific-basic intent rule whereby a presumption is created that an accused possesses the necessary mental element in the act requirement of basic intent offences. However, where offences require proof that the accused foresaw particular consequences or was aware of particular circumstances, voluntary intoxication is admissible to rebut the existence of that foresight or awareness. The specific-basic intent rule still applies in Canada, although it was significantly modified by the Supreme Court in 1994 and by Parliament in 1995. The Canadian rule now provides that *extreme* intoxication *akin to automatism or insanity* is admissible to rebut, on a balance of probabilities, the requisite intent in basic intent offences, provided those basic intent offences do not involve assault or interference with the bodily integrity of a person.[82] No degree of voluntary intoxication is a defence for basic intent offences involving assault or interference with another's bodily integrity.

Option (3): Replace the Specific-Basic Intent Rule with a No Subjective Fault Rule

Serious deficiencies in respect to the specific-basic intent rule led the majority of the High Court of Australia in *O'Connor*[83] to abolish the Australian common law rule of specific-basic intent and replace it with a rule that evidence of intoxication may be used to negate any subjective mental element, including that found in the concept of voluntariness (namely choice or control over conduct), intention, knowledge or subjective recklessness. A similar approach was taken by the New Zealand Court of Appeal in *Kamipeli*[84] five years earlier. The rule in *Kamipeli* was examined and endorsed as the most appropriate rule by the New Zealand Criminal Law Reform Committee in its 1984 *Report on Intoxication as a Defence to a Criminal Charge*.[85]

One of the major concerns about the *Kamipeli* and *O'Connor* rules was the fear that these broad rules would result in a flood of acquittals and/or an increase in crime. Indeed, the *O'Connor* rule has been referred to as the 'drunk's defence'. However, studies have indicated that this fear has not materialised.[86] It takes a very high level of intoxication to negate a basic intent and

not intention with respect to requisite circumstances or results.

79 Criminal Code, 2002 (ACT), ss. 30–31 and 33. See Law Commission for England and Wales, above n. 29, at 126–7, where the relevant provisions in the Commonwealth and ACT Codes are summarised.

80 Crimes Legislation Amendment Act 1996, Part 11A, which is summarised in Tasmania Law Reform Institute, above n. 31, at 57.

81 Criminal Law Consolidation (Intoxication) Amendment Act, 2004, s. 268. The new sections are summarised in Tasmania Law Reform Institute, above n. 31, at 58–60.

82 Canadian Criminal Code, s. 33.1 was enacted in 1995 and partially overruled *Daviault*, above n. 70. See also the discussion of *Daviault* in n. 87 below.

83 Above n. 68. A similar attempt to abolish the specific-basic intent rule in favour of a negation of subjective fault rule was rejected by a majority of the Supreme Court of Canada in *Leary*, above n. 69, and was rejected again by a majority of the Supreme Court in *R. v. Bernard* (1988) 45 CCC (3d) 1.

84 Above n. 23, at 614. See the discussion of *Kamipeli* in Simester and Brookbanks, above n. 32, at 341–51.

85 New Zealand Criminal Law Reform Committee, *Report on Intoxication as a Defence to a Criminal Charge* (Wellington: Government Printer, 1984).

86 See the Tasmania Law Reform Institute, above n. 31, at 81, where the Report refers to some of these studies.

therefore it is not surprising that it seldom occurs, although it can still be argued that even one such acquittal may be one too many.[87]

The purported advantages of the *O'Connor* rule may be briefly summarised as follows:[88]

(1) It adheres to fundamental principles of responsibility by preventing conviction of a person for a crime in circumstances where the requisite volition or subjective fault element for *that crime* are not present.
(2) It is logical and straightforward in its application of the principles of responsibility.
(3) It does not result in a spate of acquittals or an increase in intoxicated crime.

The purported disadvantages and the arguments against adopting the *O'Connor* rule may be briefly summarised as follows:[89]

(1) Outright acquittal of a person who has voluntarily become intoxicated and thereby taken a risk of committing some offence in that state is unwarranted. Furthermore, such acquittals lead to public disillusionment in the criminal justice system.[90]
(2) Some have argued that the *O'Connor* rule will dramatically increase the number of cases in which intoxication is raised (and successfully relied upon) as a defence. But, as indicated above, experience indicates that this concern has not materialised, since the absence of basic intent due to intoxication is rare.
(3) Some argue that involuntariness caused by self-induced intoxication is a more blameworthy state of mind than involuntariness caused by somnambulism or post-traumatic stress disorder and should not be treated the same.

In spite of the above criticisms, the Tasmania Law Reform Institute has recommended the adoption of the *O'Connor* rule as the best intoxication option and has rejected adding to it a new lesser included offence of criminal intoxication for persons who are acquitted of the crime charged due to intoxication.[91]

---

87 The Supreme Court of Canada's decision in *Daviault*, above n. 70, that evidence of self-induced extreme intoxication akin to automatism was admissible to negate on a balance of probabilities the basic intent for assault and sexual assault was met with a barrage of public outrage and resulted in the Canadian Parliament quickly reversing that part of *Daviault* and enacting Canadian Criminal Code, s. 33.1, which prohibits the use of evidence of self-induced intoxication to negate the basic intent or voluntariness required for offences of assault and sexual assault. A similar outrage occurred in South Australia in regard to the acquittal of a Mr Nadruku, which sparked legislative reform in South Australia: see Tasmania Law Reform Institute, above n. 31, at 82. The 1995 Law Commission of England and Wales' Report rejected the *O'Connor* rule based on the same concern about acquittals of drunken accused persons leading to public outrage and loss of faith in the criminal justice system: Tasmania Law Reform Institute, above n. 31, at 83.

88 Tasmania Law Reform Institute, above n. 31, at 80–2.

89 *Ibid.*, at 82–4.

90 See discussion of this point in n. 87 above.

91 Tasmania Law Reform Institute, above n. 31, at 80–91.

Option (4): An Alternative Offence for Intoxicated Offenders

Various suggestions have been proposed, and in some circumstances enacted, to create an alternative offence for offenders who are acquitted of the offence charged due to voluntary intoxication. The following is a brief account of some of these proposals.

England

The Butler Committee on Mentally Abnormal Offenders[92] recommended the abolition of the specific-basic intent rule, in favour of a rule which allowed intoxication to negate requisite subjective fault elements. The Committee further recommended that a person acquitted of the offence charged due to self-induced intoxication would be held liable for a new 'fallback' offence called 'dangerous intoxication' which would apply if the offence for which the accused was acquitted due to intoxication was one of the serious or dangerous offences listed in the proposal. Strangely, the Committee only recommended a maximum of one year's imprisonment for first offenders, and a maximum of three years' imprisonment for subsequent offenders, who committed one of these serious or dangerous offences and who were acquitted of that offence due to voluntary intoxication.

The English Criminal Law Revision Committee in its Fourteenth Report[93] criticised that recommendation on two major grounds: (1) the offence of dangerous intoxication does not indicate the nature of the act committed, for example, whether it was an assault or a killing, and it would be unfair for both the offender and the public if that fact was hidden under the general label 'dangerous intoxication'; (2) the suggested penalty was too low for serious offences such as murder or rape. In response to the weaknesses in the Butler Committee's proposal, Professors Smith and Williams suggested a new offence of 'doing the act while in a state of voluntary intoxication'. However, the Criminal Law Revision Committee in its Fourteenth Report also rejected that proposal on the grounds that it would:

> (1) add to the already considerable number of matters which a jury often has to consider when deciding whether the offences charged have been proved;
> (2) give rise to difficulties in cases where one group of jurors concludes that the accused was drunk, but was nevertheless subjectively reckless for the purposes of the offence charged, whereas the other group concludes that the accused was so drunk that he or she can be liable only for the alternative offence of 'doing the act';
> (3) possibly result in accused persons raising intoxication in many more trials and seeking to plead guilty to the new offence to avoid being tried for and convicted of the offence charged, which may be regarded as the more serious offence, thereby placing the judge and prosecution in a difficult position; and
> (4) give rise to confusion amongst the general public.[94]

These four concerns are not at all convincing. They already arise for prosecutors, judges and juries when, for example, an accused is charged with a specific intent offence such as murder and there

92 *Report of the Committee on Mentally Abnormal Offenders* (Cmnd 6244) (London: HMSO, 1975).

93 Criminal Law Revision Committee, *Offences Against the Person* (Fourteenth Report) (Cmnd 7844) (London: HMSO, 1980) para. [261].

94 For the Smith and Williams proposal and its rejection, see Criminal Law Revision Committee, *ibid.*, at para. [263].

is some evidence of intoxication which may or may not warrant conviction for the lesser included offence of manslaughter. Leaving a lesser alternative intoxication offence for accused persons acquitted of subjective fault crimes due to intoxication is no different from leaving the prosecutor, judge or jury with the possibility of a conviction for the lesser included offence of manslaughter instead of murder.

In 1993, the Law Commission of England and Wales in its Consultation Paper on Intoxication and Responsibility recommended the creation of a new offence for persons who caused the harm set out in a number of 'listed' offences while in a state of self-induced intoxication which negated the intent or voluntariness for the listed offence. The listed offences involved harm to persons (except minor assaults), sexual assault, damage to property and serious public disorder offences. However, that recommendation was rejected in the Law Commission's Final Report in 1995 for reasons similar to the four concerns listed above.[95]

South Australia

Recent legislative changes in South Australia have included the enactment of a 'fallback offence' of criminal negligence where the accused's conduct resulted in serious harm but the accused was found not guilty of a subjective fault offence such as murder or assault by reason of self-induced intoxication. Where self-induced intoxication negates the requisite *mens rea* for murder, and the intoxicated accused's conduct falls so short of the standard appropriate to a reasonable and sober person in the accused's position that it amounts to criminal negligence, s. 268(4) of the South Australian Criminal Code provides that the accused may be convicted of manslaughter, which is punishable by a maximum of life imprisonment. Likewise, where self-induced intoxication negates the requisite *mens rea* for subjective fault offences causing serious mental or physical harm (or loss or damage to property exceeding $10,000), the accused may be convicted of the new offence, under s. 268(5), of 'causing serious harm by criminal negligence', which is punishable by imprisonment for up to four years, if the accused's conduct, judged by the standard appropriate to a reasonable and sober person in the accused's position, falls so short of that standard that it amounts to criminal negligence.[96]

Northern Territory

Under s. 318 of the Criminal Code of the Northern Territory, a person found not guilty of murder, manslaughter or any other offence against the person because of intoxication may be convicted of an alternative offence under s. 154 of the Code with respect to dangerous acts or omissions. In 2005, new legislation was enacted which replaced the existing offences of manslaughter and dangerous act with the new offences of manslaughter, endangerment and negligence relating to harm/serious harm and causing death or serious harm by dangerous driving.[97]

---

95 The Law Commission of England and Wales' 1993 Consultation Paper and 1995 Final Report on the creation of a separate offence are summarised in the Tasmania Law Reform Institute, above n. 31, at 90. A good summary of the reasons for the rejection of a new intoxication offence proposal by the Law Commission in its 1995 Final Report can be found in the 2009 Law Commission for England and Wales' Report, above n. 29, at 49–50.

96 See Tasmania Law Reform Institute, above n. 31, at 59–60.

97 See the Criminal Code Amendment (Criminal Responsibility Reform) Act 2005 (No. 37/2005).

South Africa

In 1981, the South African Appeal Court in *R. v. Chretien*[98] followed the lead in *Kamipeli* and *O'Connor* and rejected the *Majewski* rule which recognises voluntary intoxication as a defence for specific intent offences but not for basic intent offences. Subsequently, the South African Parliament enacted a separate offence of dangerous intoxication under s. 1 of the South African Criminal Law Amendment Act 1 of 1988 as follows:

> Any person who consumes or uses any substance which impairs his faculties to appreciate the wrongfulness of his acts or to act in accordance with that appreciation, while knowing that such substance has that effect, and who while such faculties are thus impaired commits any act prohibited by law under any penalty, but is not criminally liable because his faculties were impaired as aforesaid, shall be guilty of an offence and shall be liable on conviction to the penalty … which may be imposed in respect of the commission of that act.

Germany

The German Penal Code provides for an alternative offence of intoxication when the elements of the offence charged cannot be proven due to intentional or negligent intoxication. Bohlander[99] provides the following English translation of s. 323a of the German Penal Code:

> s. 323a Committing offences in a senselessly drunken state
> (1) Whosoever intentionally or negligently puts himself into a drunken state by consuming alcoholic beverages or other intoxicants shall be liable to imprisonment of not more than five years or a fine if he commits an unlawful act while in this state and may not be punished because of it because he was insane due to the intoxication or if this cannot be excluded.
> The penalty must not be more severe than the penalty provided for the offence which was committed while he was in the drunken state.

Perceived Advantages and Disadvantages of a Separate Criminal Intoxication Offence

Although separate intoxication offences have been enacted in jurisdictions such as South Australia and the Northern Territory, the Tasmania Law Institute Report in 2006 examined the option of creating a specific offence of dangerous or criminal intoxication for Tasmania and rejected that option.[100] The 2006 Report summarises the perceived advantages and disadvantages of a separate criminal intoxication offence. It suggests that the major advantage of a special criminal intoxication offence is that it meets the legitimate public concern that persons who commit offences as a result of self-induced intoxication deserve to be punished. The rationale for some measure of punishment is premised on the fact that it is common knowledge that consuming excessive amounts of alcohol or drugs can lead to the commission of crimes. Outright acquittals under either the specific-basic intent rule or the *O'Connor* rule are not justified for persons who knowingly take that risk and subsequently commit an offence while intoxicated.

---

98 (1981) 1 SA 1097.

99 M. Bohlander, *Principles of German Criminal Law* (Oxford: Hart Publishing, 2009) 134.

100 Tasmania Law Reform Institute, above n. 31, at 89–94.

The Report then briefly summarises the criticisms which have been directed against a special offence of criminal intoxication.[101] These criticisms include the following:

(1) The ethical basis of a special offence of dangerous intoxication is based on an assumption of recklessness that is questionable since most people do not commit dangerous acts even when extremely intoxicated.[102]
(2) A special offence will encourage plea bargaining and potentially increase jury compromise verdicts.
(3) A special offence will increase the complexity of the trial process and the number of issues that a jury is required to consider.
(4) Setting an appropriate sentence for an offence of criminal intoxication is difficult since the fault involved in self-induced intoxication is not specifically calibrated to the harm caused while in that state.
(5) A better approach is to apply the general offences of negligently causing death or bodily harm.

With regard to the first concern, I do not think it is inappropriate or questionable to characterise a person's conduct as reckless or negligent when that person gets extremely intoxicated and thereby runs the risk (even if slight) that he or she may commit an offence in that state. Punishment of that sort of risk-taking which actually results in the commission of an offence is deserved and is not in any way unethical. The same cannot be said for the alternative *O'Connor* rule, which grants an outright acquittal to an accused who has caused a serious criminal harm in circumstances where there is not a lesser included offence for which the intoxicated accused will be convicted. And, as previously noted, concerns (2) and (3) already exist in our trial process. The addition of a new offence will not significantly alter that situation. Finally, while setting an appropriate sentence is admittedly a difficult task, it is one which exists for all offences where the court must come up with a sentence which balances the degree of blameworthiness of the offender and the harm caused.

As discussed below, I recommend that the best and most principled manner to deal with cases where self-induced intoxication negates the requisite subjective fault element of the offence charged is to convict the accused of a new, lesser included, intoxication-based offence.

Option (5): Intoxication and the Fault Elements of Defences

There is disagreement and uncertainty in many jurisdictions on the question of whether an accused is entitled to rely on certain defences if, due to voluntary intoxication, that person has a mistaken belief with regard to an essential element of that defence.[103] The disagreement and controversy should only arise in respect to defences which contain some subjective fault elements. Where the essential elements of a defence are defined on a purely objective, reasonable person standard, there is no question that the accused's self-induced intoxication should not be relevant in determining whether those objective, reasonable standards have been met. A reasonable person is a sober person. While intoxication, by itself, is not an absolute bar to an accused relying on a defence such

101 *Ibid.*, at 91.

102 Law Reform Commission of Victoria, *Criminal Responsibility: Intention and Gross Intoxication* (Report No. 6) (Melbourne: Law Reform Commission of Victoria, 1986) para. [78]; Victorian Law Reform Committee, *Criminal Liability for Self-Induced Intoxication Report* (Melbourne: Victorian Law Reform Committee, 1999) para. [6.62].

103 See, for example, the discussion in Tasmania Law Reform Institute, above n. 31, at 104–12.

as self-defence, the intoxicated accused must nonetheless meet the objective standards required for that defence in spite of his or her intoxication. The issue of the relevance of intoxication with regard to defences has most frequently arisen in the context of self-defence, but the same issue can also arise with other defences such as provocation, duress and necessity. The analysis of a mistake of fact caused by voluntary intoxication with respect to an essential element of a defence needs to be analysed in a slightly different way than mistake of fact caused by voluntary intoxication which negates the fault element of an offence.

If intoxication causes a mistake of fact as to an essential conduct element of an offence, and the fault element of the offence requires intent or knowledge of that conduct element, then the intoxicated mistake negates that requisite intent. In a 'specific-basic intent' jurisdiction like England, an intoxicated mistake of fact as to a specific intent offence is a defence, but an intoxicated mistake of fact to a basic intent offence is not. For example, in a specific-basic intent jurisdiction, an intoxicated mistake of fact with respect to an essential conduct element of theft (a specific intent offence) is a defence, but it is not a defence with respect to the conduct elements of assault or sexual assault (which are basic intent offences). To decide otherwise would be to subvert the essence of the rule that intoxication is no defence to basic intent offences. On the other hand, in a jurisdiction where intoxication is a defence if it negates the requisite subjective fault, whether specific or basic, an intoxicated mistake of fact as to an essential element of the offence will be a defence to any subjective fault offence, including theft or assault. Jurisdictions such as Malaysia and Singapore,[104] and jurisdictions which follow an *O'Connor*-type rule, fall into this latter category.

For defences like self-defence, the key question is whether the law in the jurisdiction in question is defined solely in terms of objective elements or whether the defence contains a combination of subjective and objective elements. For example, the key elements of self-defence in s. 34(2) of the Canadian Criminal Code are defined in objective terms. Thus, the Supreme Court of Canada in *Reilly v. The Queen*[105] held that intoxication is not relevant in determining whether the accused had a 'reasonable' apprehension of death or bodily harm and whether the accused 'reasonably' believed he or she could not otherwise preserve himself or herself from death or bodily harm. Likewise, the key elements of the defence of private defence (ss. 102 and 105) in the Penal Codes of Malaysia and Singapore appear to be objective (that is, 'reasonable' apprehension of danger to one's body or property) and therefore intoxication should not be relevant.[106]

On the other hand, New Zealand and some Australian jurisdictions (including the Commonwealth, the Australian Capital Territory, New South Wales and Tasmania) have a combination of objective and subjective self-defence elements (that is, 'reasonable force/response in the circumstances as he or she perceives them').[107] Courts in New Zealand[108] and New South

104 The Malaysian and Singaporean Penal Codes have provisions on mistake of fact (ss. 76 and 79) which require the mistake to have been committed 'in good faith', which is defined in s. 52 as 'with due care and attention' (that is, reasonably believed). See further Chapter 5 of this volume, above n. 6, at 115–16. However, s. 86(2) governs cases of intoxicated mistake of fact, denying s. 79 a role in such circumstances. See Yeo, Morgan and Chan, above n. 20, at paras. [17.30]–[17.32].

105 [1984] 2 SCR 396. This also appears to have been the view of Cox C.J. in *Attorney-General's Reference No. 1 of 1996* (1998) 7 Tas R 293.

106 The nature and extent of objective elements must be analysed carefully in respect to each separate defence under the IPC. With regard to defences, see Chapters 8, 9 and 12 of this volume (Cheah Wui Ling 'Private Defence'; S. Yeo, 'Duress and Necessity'; and I. Leader-Elliott, 'Provocation', respectively).

107 Tasmania Law Reform Institute, above n. 31, at 104–10.

108 *R. v. Thomas* [1991] 3 NZLR 141.

Wales[109] have held that intoxication can be taken into account when determining the accused's perception of the circumstances in regard to the need for self-defence. The accused's perception of the circumstances is relevant to both the perceived but mistaken need for self-defence and the degree of force that is reasonable (an objective test) under the accused's mistaken perception of the circumstances (a subjective test). For example, if an accused, due to intoxication, wrongly thinks he or she is being unlawfully assaulted by another person with a gun, the accused's claim of self-defence would be judged upon his or her mistaken perception of the facts with regard to both the need for self-defence and the type of response that would be warranted if the mistaken facts actually existed. The Tasmania Law Reform Institute in its 2006 Report supports this latter approach and recommends that intoxication should be relevant to determining whether subjective, or partially subjective, elements of a defence exist.[110] I agree with this approach, subject to an important corollary principle. The position in the above jurisdictions seems to ignore the fact that the accused has caused a serious harm due to self-induced intoxication and is deserving of condemnation and some degree of punishment in the same way that the intoxicated offender who lacks the requisite subjective intent for an offence is deserving of punishment. Thus, I recommend that an accused who is acquitted of the offence charged on the basis of a defence which is only applicable due to a mistaken perception of the circumstances, where the mistake is caused by the accused's self-induced intoxication, should be convicted of the intoxication-based offence described below.

PROPOSAL FOR A MODERNISED IPC VOLUNTARY INTOXICATION PROVISION

In this chapter, I have argued: (1) that recognition of voluntary intoxication as a full or partial defence to some crimes is contentious and controversial; (2) that s. 86 of the IPC, which appears to reject voluntary intoxication as a defence to any fault-based offence, is inconsistent with the fundamental principles of fault; (3) that the common law specific-basic intent rule is arbitrary and inconsistent with the fundamental principles of fault; and (4) that the 1935 Malaysian and Singapore amendment to the IPC is confusing in part, too narrowly construed in part and does not provide for a 'fallback' offence in certain cases where voluntary intoxication negates the requisite intent for the crime charged. I have also examined the rejection of the specific-basic intent rule in favour of an *O'Connor*-type rule which allows intoxication to negate any subjective fault requirement including voluntariness. Finally, I have analysed various options for an alternative, back-up offence for offenders who successfully rely on a defence of voluntary intoxication. Based on the above analysis, I recommend that the best and most principled way to deal with voluntary intoxication is to create a set of rules which: (1) allow evidence of voluntary intoxication to negate the subjective fault elements and the voluntariness requirement[111] of offences and defences; (2)

109 *R. v. Katarzynski* [2002] NSWSC 613.

110 Indeed, the 2006 Report by the Tasmania Law Reform Institute, above n. 31, goes one step further and recommends that intoxication should also be relevant in assessing the accused's physical abilities (for example, slow reactions, poor co-ordination) and therefore the increased degree of force that might be necessary to defend oneself while intoxicated.

111 See Chapter 4 of this volume (B. Sullivan, 'The Conduct Element of Offences') at 100, where the author proposes in cl. 2(1)(c) that 'any bodily movement that otherwise is not a product of any effort or determination on the part of D, either conscious or habitual' is not 'an act'. In other words, a bodily movement which is not a willed movement is not an act and therefore does not constitute a basis for criminal liability. But cl. 2(2)(a) then creates an exception to that general principle by indicating that any bodily movement which occurs when D is voluntarily intoxicated is 'to be regarded as an act'. Under Sullivan's proposal, it appears that voluntary intoxication could not be used to negate the general requirement that acts or omissions

permit the conviction of persons who are acquitted of an offence by reason of voluntary intoxication to be convicted of a lesser included offence; (3) create a new lesser included offence which will be an unintentional form of the full offence and will be called 'unintentional (for example, rape, assault, theft) due to extreme intoxication'; and (4) make the new unintentional offence due to intoxication punishable by a specified portion of the punishment that exists for the full offence. Accordingly, I propose the following provision to replace the current one under the IPC, subject to the following two qualifications. First, the mental fault language used in the following provision may eventually need to be modified to match whatever mental fault language is ultimately chosen in a revised IPC. For detailed recommendations in that respect, see Chapter 3 of this volume by Neil Morgan entitled 'The Fault Elements of Offences'. Secondly, s. 86(1) and (2) of my proposed revision refers to situations where self-induced intoxication negates the 'voluntariness required for that offence'. This expression is drafted on the assumption that a revised IPC will include a general, all-embracing provision setting out the voluntariness requirement for the conduct elements of offences, perhaps along the lines of cl. 83A which I have suggested at the end of Chapter 10 of this volume. On the other hand, Bob Sullivan in Chapter 4 of this volume rejects the inclusion of a general, all-embracing provision on the voluntariness requirement for conduct and instead proposes definitions of acts and omissions which have a built-in voluntariness component. His definitions exclude voluntary intoxication as a defence even though it negates the voluntariness components of his definitions of acts and omissions. In a revised IPC, the inconsistency between his proposals and mine with regard to the nature and scope of the voluntariness requirement would need to be resolved. My proposed provision reads as follows:

Voluntary Intoxication

86 (1) Voluntary intoxication shall not constitute a defence to any criminal charge unless the conduct constituting the offence was done, as a consequence of that intoxication, without the subjective fault element or voluntariness required for that offence.

(2) Where the conduct constituting a criminal offence was done without the subjective fault element or voluntariness required for that offence due to voluntary intoxication, the accused shall be acquitted of that offence and convicted of a lesser included offence of unintentionally causing that offence due to extreme intoxication.[112]

Illustration

If A takes B's property without permission, but due to voluntary intoxication does not intend to do so, A will be acquitted of theft and convicted of the offence of unintentional theft due to extreme intoxication.

(3) The punishment for unintentionally causing an offence due to extreme intoxication in sub-section (2) shall be:

---

which constitute an offence must be voluntary, although it would still be a defence in those circumstances if the intoxication also negated the requisite intent. Under my proposed s. 86(2), persons so acquitted would be convicted of a lesser included offence of unintentionally causing that offence due to voluntary intoxication.

112 If it was considered desirable or expedient, a provision could be added to create an exception for the naming of the lesser included offence in cases in which the fault for murder is negated by voluntary intoxication. Under s. 86(2), the offence would be called 'unintentional murder due to extreme intoxication'. It could instead be deemed to be one of the lesser forms of homicide under the Indian, Malaysian or Singaporean Penal Codes: culpable homicide not amounting to murder, causing death by rashness or causing death by negligence. For a discussion of proposed reforms to the homicide provisions under a revised IPC, see Chapter 3 of this volume, above n. 27, at 81–4.

(a) not more than 15 [or some other nominated number] years where the offence he would have been convicted of but for the intoxication is punishable by life imprisonment, or

(b) in all other cases, not more than one-half of the maximum term of imprisonment for the offence that he would have been convicted of but for the intoxication.[113]

(4) Voluntary intoxication is not relevant in determining whether an accused has met objectively defined elements of a defence. However, where any element of a defence is based on a subjective belief or knowledge of a fact, an accused may rely upon his belief of that fact even though that belief is mistaken due to voluntary intoxication.

(5) Where an accused meets the requirements of a defence based on a mistaken belief, caused by voluntary intoxication, in respect to an essential subjective element of that defence, the accused shall be acquitted of the offence which he would have committed but for the intoxicated defence and shall be convicted of a lesser included offence of unintentionally causing that offence due to extreme intoxication, in accordance with sub-sections (2) and (3) above.

113 The reduced levels of punishment for offences where the requisite subjective fault has been negated by extreme intoxication are based on the same reduced levels of punishment for attempted offences (IPC, s. 511). The punishment levels, if thought appropriate, could be set higher or lower.

Chapter 12
Provocation

Ian Leader-Elliott

INTRODUCTION

Thomas Babington Macaulay remains the most radical of codifiers in the Anglo-American tradition. He brought to the task a matchless capacity for lucid, direct and forceful expression of his ideas. Among nineteenth-century codifiers, he was remarkable for his limited exposure to the practice of law.[1] He approached the task of drafting his Code as a legislator rather than a practitioner; his draft Code is distinguished by its succinct clarity no less than its moral rigour.[2] Though 20 years of intermittent debate elapsed between the completion of Macaulay's draft Code and enactment of the Indian Penal Code (IPC), his draft survived with comparatively few changes. That was not true, however, of the definitions of murder and its partial defences. The original provisions were altered, diluted and distorted by the Legislative Council, which was less willing than Macaulay to renovate the common law of murder. The meaning and effect of the provisions on provocation that were eventually enacted were further obscured by the accretions of English appellate case law, which continues to enjoy unwarranted influence in Indian courts and textbooks. English case law on provocation was a peculiarly inappropriate contribution to the exegesis of a code that was meant to fulfil the Benthamite dream of displacing the vagaries of judge-made law by legislation.[3]

The discussion and proposals for reform of the partial defence of provocation that follow take Macaulay's draft Code and his *Notes* on that Code as their guide.[4] This is no exercise in nostalgia. Macaulay anticipated, in essential respects, the Law Commission for England and Wales' proposals for reform of the law of murder and provocation in 2004 and 2006.[5] For the most part, the recommendations for reform that will be advanced in this chapter are a synthesis of Macaulay's original codification of murder and provocation and the Law Commission recommendations. From

---

1 See the survey by S.H. Kadish, 'Codifiers of the Criminal Law: Wechsler's Predecessors' (1978) 78 *Columbia Law Review* 1098. Of Macaulay and his Code, Kadish remarks (at 1107): '[O]ne of the great codes of law', drafted by 'an historian and man of letters with a mere smattering of legal training'.

2 On Macaulay's legislative orientation, see the discussion in Chapter 2 of this volume (B. Wright, 'Macaulay's Indian Penal Code: Historical Context and Originating Principles').

3 See, in particular, the discussion of the relationship between the legislature and the judiciary in T.B. Macaulay, J.M. Macleod, G.W. Anderson and F. Millett, *A Penal Code Prepared by the Indian Law Commissioners* (London: Pelham Richardson, 1838) (reprinted by the Lawbook Exchange, Ltd, 2002) iv–vii (Introductory Report on the Indian Penal Code).

4 *Ibid.* See also the *Special Reports of the Indian Law Commissioners: Report on the Indian Penal Code* (First Report) and *Second Report on the Indian Penal Code* (Second Report) (reprinted in the British Parliamentary Papers 1847–8, vol. XXVIII).

5 Law Commission for England and Wales, *Partial Defences to Murder* (Law Com. No. 290) (London: The Stationery Office, 2004). The recommendations of that Report for the reform of provocation were adopted by the Law Commission in *Murder, Manslaughter and Infanticide* (Law Com. No. 304) (London: The Stationery Office, 2006) para. [5.11].

the present vantage point it is apparent that the common law doctrine of provocation which so influenced the Indian Legislative Council in 1860 and which continues to influence the course of Indian criminal jurisprudence is beyond redemption. This harsh verdict on its defects is reinforced by the proposals for substantial doctrinal change or outright abolition of the provocation defence in England, Australia and New Zealand. It is a particularly appropriate moment to return to Macaulay's rejected draft of the law of murder: like a time capsule that has followed an extended parabolic trajectory, it has at last found a point of intersection with current proposals for reform.

THE MEANING OF MURDER

The definition of murder is contentious and varies from jurisdiction to jurisdiction.[6] For James Fitzjames Stephen, the meaning of murder could not be separated from the mandatory severity of its penalty. In Stephen's memorable aphorism, 'The fact that men are hung for murder is one great reason why murder is considered so dreadful a crime'.[7] The fact that murderers are no longer liable to hang for their crime in many anglophone jurisdictions, coupled with the variability of penalties for the offence, has had profound implications for the definition of murder and its various justifications, excuses and extenuations.[8] Execution is possible but unlikely in India, where the death penalty is reserved for offenders of exceptional depravity.[9] Life imprisonment is mandatory, however, for those who are not executed. In Singapore, murderers are regularly hanged. In jurisdictions that have abolished capital punishment for murder, the penalty varies. Life imprisonment is mandatory in the UK. In New Zealand, courts can impose a lesser sentence if life imprisonment would be manifestly unjust.[10] In Australia, where capital punishment for murder has been abolished, some jurisdictions make life imprisonment mandatory, though there is provision for courts to set a period after which the offender can be released on parole. In others, life imprisonment is a maximum rather than a mandatory penalty.

It is possible that some of the jurisdictions with which I will be concerned are moving, at glacial speed, to merge murder with the lesser homicides. A merger would be the most radical solution to the intractable problem of devising a morally acceptable definition of murder – a problem which has been a subject of serious concern from the mid-twentieth century at least.[11]

6 See J. Horder (ed.), *Homicide Law in Comparative Perspective* (Oxford: Hart Publishing, 2007); and Chapter 3 of this volume (N. Morgan, 'The Fault Elements of Offences') at 66 and 74.

7 J.F. Stephen, 'Capital Punishment' (1864) 69 *Fraser's Magazine* 753, at 761.

8 Space precludes any attempt to discuss the US law of murder and partial defences to murder. See, however, the essential paper by V. Nourse, 'Passion's Progress: Modern Law Reform and the Provocation Defense' (1996–7) 106 *Yale Law Journal* 1331 and the comparative study of US and Australian provocation law reform by C. Ramsey, 'Provoking Change: Comparative Insights on Feminist Homicide Reform' (2010) 100 *Journal of Criminal Law and Criminology* 33.

9 *Bachan Singh v. State of Punjab* AIR 1980 SC 898; *Macchi Singh v. State of Punjab* AIR 1983 SC 957. For a comprehensive survey of case law, see Amnesty International-India and the People's Union for Civil Liberties (Tamil Nadu and Puducherry), *Lethal Lottery: The Death Penalty in India, A Study of Supreme Court Judgments in Death Penalty Cases 1950–2006* (New Delhi, May 2008), AI Index: ASA 20/007/2008 (available online at http://www.amnesty.org/en/library/info/ASA20/007/2008; the summary report is available online at http://www.amnesty.org/en/report/info/ASA20/006/2008; last accessed 20 February 2011).

10 Crimes Act 1961 (NZ), s. 172; Sentencing Act 2002 (NZ), s. 102(1).

11 See, in particular, the various English engagements with the problem: *Royal Commission on Capital Punishment 1949–1953: Report* (Cmnd. 8932) (London: HMSO, 1973); A. Ashworth and B. Mitchell (eds), *Rethinking English Homicide Law* (Oxford: Oxford University Press, 2000); Law Commission for England and Wales, *Murder, Manslaughter and Infanticide,* above n. 5; Horder, above n. 6.

Variable sentencing for murder is similar in its effect to a merger. If murder is not merged with manslaughter, variable sentencing would allow their ancient façade to be retained, as a piece of cultural heritage, while the real work of discrimination among unlawful homicides would be done, behind the façade, by sentencing courts and correctional authorities.[12] In those circumstances, the question of whether provocation or other partial defences should continue to be available to reduce murder to manslaughter would have more aesthetic or political than moral significance. Rather than engage with that question in an enquiry that is already sufficiently complex, I will assume that murder will be retained as an offence that labels a distinctive and clearly delineated variety of human wickedness and also that murder will be punished with an invariant penalty of life imprisonment, or worse. Understood in that way, as a crime defined by its particular degree, kind of moral turpitude and an invariant penalty of maximum severity, murder requires the ameliorative moderation of the partial defence of provocation and the related partial defence of 'sudden fight'.[13]

Reform of the law of provocation would require reconsideration of the relationship with sudden fight as part of a fuller review of this area. With that caveat, consideration of the partial defence of sudden fight is unfortunately beyond the scope of this chapter.[14]

Whatever may be thought of the other partial defences, the state of the law of provocation is a cause for serious concern in most jurisdictions where it survives. Reform, if not abolition, is necessary. Considered as legal doctrine, the provocation defence must be counted among the least distinguished products of the common law tradition. Over the course of the latter half of the nineteenth century and the twentieth century, doctrinal formulations of provocation were increasingly vitiated by an accumulation of logical contradictions, confusing or incomprehensible jury directions,[15] morally indefensible restrictions on the defence when women killed men, and by the morally indefensible indulgence that the common law extended to men who kill women. This accumulation of moral failure and doctrinal confusion is the detritus left behind by more fundamental tides of change as applications of the partial defence expanded, contracted and expanded again[16] before reaching, in most jurisdictions, their current phase of contraction.

---

12 In reality, the mandatory life sentence is symbolic rather than real in many jurisdictions. See the Law Commission for England and Wales, *Murder Manslaughter and Infanticide*, above n. 5, at paras. [2.131], [5.9]–[5.10], for a discussion of 'release on licence'– 'a feature of "life" sentences that the public finds difficult to understand'.

13 The partial defence of 'sudden fight' in the IPC corresponds to the common law category of 'mutual combat'. See W.O. Russell, *A Treatise on Crimes and Misdemeanors* (C.S. Greaves, ed.) (vol. 1) (3rd edn, London: Saunders and Benning, 1843) 585–92.

14 See I. Leader-Elliott, 'Sudden Fight, Consent and the Principle of Comparative Responsibility under the Indian Penal Code' [2010] *Singapore Journal of Legal Studies* 282.

15 J.W. Cecil Turner, the last editor of *Russell on Crime*, dates the decline into nonsense from the judgment of Keating J. in *R. v. Welsh* (1869) 11 Cox CC 336, which launched the 'the ordinary and reasonable man' on his doctrinal career. See J.W.C. Turner, *Russell on Crime* (12th edn, London: Sweet & Maxwell) 522–3, 537. For modern criticism, see Law Commission for England and Wales, *Partial Defences to Murder* (Consultation Paper No. 173) (London: The Stationery Office, 2003) para. [1.23]: '[T]here has never been a time when the doctrine was truly coherent, logical or consistent. In more recent times the fault lines have widened', and para. [4.162]: 'The defence is inherently contradictory'; Victorian Law Reform Commission, *Defences to Homicide: Final Report*, (Melbourne: Victorian Law Reform Commission, 2004) 34–5, 58: 'conceptually confused, complex and difficult'; Model Criminal Code Officers Committee, *Model Criminal Code*, (Canberra: Commonwealth Attorney-General's Department, 1998), Chapter 5, *Fatal Offences Against the Person*, Discussion Paper, 103: 'internally incoherent and unacceptably complex'.

16 Indicative references must suffice here: M.J. Wiener, *Men of Blood: Violence, Manliness and Criminal Justice in Victorian England* (Cambridge: Cambridge University Press, 2004) provides a detailed

Before considering proposals for reform, it is necessary to distinguish two different ways in which 'provocation' may have a bearing on the defendant's trial for murder.

CODIFICATION AND THE BIFURCATION OF 'PROVOCATION'

For most of its history, provocation has had two distinguishable exculpatory functions. With the benefit of hindsight, one can isolate a limited 'doctrinal' function, when provocation is a partial defence to murder, from a more extended function that I will call, for want of a better term, an 'evidential' function – when evidence of provocation supports a denial of intention to kill or cause serious injury or of knowledge that either of those consequences is likely.

The *doctrinal* function of provocation is the familiar partial defence that reduces murder to manslaughter[17] despite proof that the defendant intended to kill the victim or cause serious injury. The doctrinal function was always restricted by legal rules, principles and criteria. Originally, the most common instances of its application involved sudden quarrels or mutual combat between men.[18] Reliance on the partial defence was limited by the rule that mere words were no provocation and by a requirement of proportionate response.[19] In domestic homicides, when the defendant killed a spouse or child in anger, the partial defence had few applications until the latter part of the nineteenth century, when the first signs of a relaxation of doctrinal constraints became apparent.[20] However, it was not until the latter half of the twentieth century that infidelity and hurtful words were recognised as generalised grounds for a partial defence of provocation in jurisdictions such as England, Australia and New Zealand.[21] Acceptance of infidelity and hurtful words as grounds for the defence occurred far earlier in India, where the IPC recognised that insult, indignity or dishonour might ground a provocation defence.[22]

In its broader *evidential* function, anger provoked by the victim can be relevant to the question of whether the defendant acted voluntarily and intended to kill or intended to cause serious injury. Evidence that a defendant was provoked to rage by the conduct of the victim can affect charge selection, trial, sentencing and the exercise of executive clemency. Though the distinction between evidential and doctrinal functions was often obscured by references to common law 'malice

---

history of the contraction of provocation in England during the course of the nineteenth century. The expansionary twentieth-century phase is acknowledged in the canonic article by A.J. Ashworth, 'The Doctrine of Provocation' (1976) 35 *Cambridge Law Journal* 292. Ashworth's article was a defence of 'objective' limits on provocation against what was then a strongly running academic tide in favour of a 'subjective' formulation of the partial defence. US studies provide more extreme accounts of the pathologies of provocation doctrine: see Nourse, above n. 8.

17 The equivalent offence under the IPC is 'culpable homicide not amounting to murder' under s. 299.

18 Provocation and mutual combat were distinct, though closely related, partial defences in early English common law. They began to merge in the early nineteenth century and are now indistinguishable in common law jurisdictions.

19 See J.M. Beattie, *Crime and the Courts in England 1660–1800* (Princeton: Princeton University Press, 1986) 91–6; and, for an extended study of nineteenth-century homicides, Wiener, above n. 16, in particular, Chapter 2 ('When Men Killed Men'). For a rare instance of violence by a wife providing the basis for a plea of provocation, see *R. v. Hopkins* (1866) 10 Cox CC 229.

20 Progressive relaxation of doctrinal limits in England, accelerated by the enactment of the Homicide Act 1957 (Chapter 11), s. 3, led to the extraordinary Court of Criminal Appeal decision in *R. v. Doughty* (1986) 84 Cr App R 319 that the crying of a 17-day-old baby might provide the basis for a plea of provocation.

21 See Wiener, above n. 16, at 289–91.

22 See the cases discussed in H.S. Gour, *The Penal Law of India* (vol. 3) (11th edn., Allahabad: Law Publishers (India) Pvt. Ltd, 2000) 2493–510.

aforethought', most of the cases of 'provocation' recounted in nineteenth-century legal texts, digests and in Martin Weiner's survey of nineteenth-century English homicides do not engage with provocation in the doctrinal sense at all. They are concerned with proof of intention in murder,[23] sentencing for manslaughter and decisions as to whether a person convicted of murder should be hanged for their crime.[24] In this extended sense of 'provocation', evidence that the defendant had been 'provoked' by the drunkenness, infidelity or scolding of a 'bad wife' gave sympathetic juries a licence to return a verdict of manslaughter on the ground that intention to kill or cause grievous bodily harm had not been proved or, in cases where his intention to kill or cause grievous bodily harm was undeniable, a verdict of murder with a recommendation for mercy.

The distinction between the doctrinal and evidential functions of provocation continues to be contentious when voluntariness or the fault elements for murder are in issue.[25] It is contentious because the doctrinal constraints on the partial defence have little or no purchase when fault is in issue. As a consequence, limits on the availability of the partial defence can be avoided, on occasion, by presenting evidence that the defendant was provoked in support of a denial of voluntariness or intention. There are persuasive arguments that some principled restraints on the evidential function of provocation are necessary when voluntariness is in issue and, perhaps, when intention is in issue.[26] Those arguments will not be pursued in this chapter. The discussion that follows is limited to consideration of provocation in its doctrinal function as a partial defence.

MURDER AND PROVOCATION IN MACAULAY'S CODE

In my opening remarks I referred to the similarity between the Law Commission recommendations for reform of the partial defence of provocation and Macaulay's formulation in the draft Code. The Law Commission recommendations have now been enacted with modifications.[27] The central point of resemblance between the Law Commission recommendations and Macaulay's conception of provocation is that both accept the premise that provocation requires evidence of serious wrongdoing by the victim. That central resemblance, and much else that follows from it, will be explored in more detail shortly. There is a preliminary point to be made about punishment. Though Macaulay and the Law Commission share similar views of the grounds for extenuation,

---

23 See Wiener, above n. 16, at 175–8, on the variable applications of evidence of provocative conduct in cases of domestic homicide.

24 Evidence of 'provocation' might provide grounds for: (1) a jury to make a recommendation for mercy when convicting an offender of murder; (2) for a judge to endorse that recommendation; (3) for mass petitions for a reprieve; or (4) for the Home Secretary to advise the granting of a reprieve to the condemned prisoner. For examples, see Wiener, above n. 16, at 126–7, 160, 166, n. 151. For an Indian parallel, where the death penalty was in issue, see *Francis Alias Ponnan v. State of Kerala* AIR 1974 SC 2281.

25 For a recent recognition of the distinction, see Law Commission for England and Wales, *Murder Manslaughter and Infanticide*, above n. 5, at para. [5.71].

26 For a recent Australian example, in which a jury gave an outright acquittal to a husband who shot his estranged wife during a quarrel over custody of their daughter, see *R. v. Singh* (2003) 86 SASR 473. See B. McSherry, 'It's A Man's World: Claims of Provocation and Automatism in "Intimate" Homicides' (2005) 29 *Melbourne University Law Review* 905. For Canadian examples, see J. Klineberg, 'Anger and Intent for Murder: The Supreme Court Decision in *R. v. Parent*' (2003) 41 *Osgoode Hall Law Journal* 37; and *R. v. Walle* (2007) 230 CCC (3d) 181. See also the decision of the South African Court of Criminal Appeal in *R. v. Tenganyika* (1958) 3 SA 7 and the reconsideration and rejection of that decision by the Lesotho Court of Appeal in *R. v. Marabe* (CRI/T/43/2000) [2000] LSCA 103.

27 Coroners and Justice Act 2009 (Chapter 25) (UK), ss. 54–56 (partial defence to murder: loss of self-control).

they part company on the rationale for the provocation defence. The Law Commission based its recommendations on sentencing considerations. If the UK government had been willing to consider the possibility of variable sentencing for murder, it is likely that the Commission would have recommended abolition.[28] Macaulay also accepted the practical necessity for a mandatory penalty of maximum severity for murder. Unlike the Law Commission, however, he perceived an important moral distinction between provoked and unprovoked violence that should be reflected in the structure of offences in the Code. Provocation is not restricted to murder in the IPC. It is available as a partial defence to lesser offences of causing injury and for assault.[29] In terms of the modern debate over provocation, that is consistent with the characterisation of the defence, by some theorists, as a 'partial justification'.[30] The offender's guilt is reduced in degree because the infliction of injury or death occurred in response to wrongdoing by the victim. The provisions on provocation go beyond a mere grant of a sentencing discretion to discount the penalty for a provoked attack. Formal recognition that provocation is a partial defence that reduces a serious to a less serious offence gives the offender the benefit of a less stigmatising 'label' for their wrongdoing.[31] The second and correlative effect is that the verdict, convicting the offender of a less serious offence, implicitly labels the victim as well, whose provocative conduct amounts to a form of complicity in their own injury.

Four Macaulayan Themes

Four themes that I take to be central to Macaulay's conception of the relationship between murder and provocation will be discussed here. They provide the premises for the reform proposals that will follow.

The 'Displacement Function' of Criminal Legislation

The reference to the 'displacement function' is taken from John Gardner's argument that the control of vengeance by the victims of wrongdoing is a central justification for the existence of criminal law.[32] State punishment for wrongdoing displaces private vengeance. So far as provocation is concerned, there are two complementary aspects of the displacement function to be considered. The first is meant to prevent resorting to vengeance rather than punishing it. Macaulay's draft

---

28 Law Commission for England and Wales, *Murder Manslaughter and Infanticide*, above n. 5, at para. [2.130]: 'While the mandatory sentence of life imprisonment for murder remains, the partial defences should remain.' See, too, J. Horder, 'Reshaping the Subjective Element in the Provocation Defence' (2005) *Oxford Journal of Legal Studies* 123.

29 Macaulay's draft Code, cls. 325 (voluntarily causing hurt on grave and sudden provocation); 326 (voluntarily causing hurt on grave and sudden provocation); and 342 (assault). The definition of 'grave and sudden provocation' in cl. 297 remains constant throughout.

30 See Ashworth, above n. 16, at 297–8. For a recent spectrum of US legal theorists' opinions on the partial justification/excuse issue, see P.H. Robinson, S.P. Garvey and K.K. Ferzan (eds), *Criminal Law Conversations* (New York: Oxford University Press, 2009) Chapter 15 ('Provocation: Explaining and Justifying the Defense in Partial Excuse, Loss of Self-Control Terms').

31 There is a brief history of labelling theory in J. Chalmers and F. Leverick, 'Fair Labelling in Criminal Law' (2008) 71 *Modern Law Review* 217, at 218–20.

32 J. Gardner, 'Crime: In Proportion and in Perspective' in A. Ashworth and M. Wasik (eds), *Fundamentals of Sentencing Theory* (Oxford: Clarendon Press, 1998) 31–52.

Code included an extended range of offences that one might describe as offences of 'giving provocation'.[33] There are offences of defamation[34] and offences of engaging in conduct intended to insult, annoy or outrage the modesty of women.[35] Chapter 15, 'Offences Relating to Religion and Caste', penalises conduct intended to insult another's religion or cause them to lose caste.[36] These offences of giving provocation, which were preserved and in some respects extended in the IPC, are striking in their anticipation of modern legislation against the promotion of hate and cultural denigration. Macaulay recognised a range of intersecting topographies of harm that go well beyond physical harms to the person to include intangible harms to honour, dignity, status, feelings and reputation. He justified this radical departure from the prevailing pattern of English criminal law on the pragmatic ground that legal condemnation and punishment would displace private revenge and vigilantism.[37] It is significant that Macaulay's draft Code substitutes the traditional and inaccurately titled category 'Offences Against the Person', which deals with *physical* harms to the person, with the far more accurate title of 'Offences Affecting the Human Body'.

The displacement function has its more familiar expression when deterrent punishment is inflicted on individuals who have taken revenge for perceived wrongs. Recognition of the partial defence of provocation arguably weakens that deterrent. In his critical evaluation of English proposals for reform of the law of murder, Jeremy Horder invokes the displacement principle and asks whether there is any good reason for permitting the partial defence of provocation as an exception to the 'monopoly claimed by the state over retributive punishment'.[38] If retention of the partial defence is justified against that objection, it can only be on the ground that V's provocation reduces D's moral culpability. So long as the moral distinction between murder and manslaughter is considered to be worth retaining, the partial defence and consequential weakening of the deterrent force of the law is the price that must be paid to maintain that distinction. The displacement function is served, with some loss of deterrent effectiveness, by convicting the offender of a lesser homicide.[39]

Macaulay on the Meaning of Murder

Like so much else in his Code, Macaulay's definition of the elements of murder is remarkable for his anticipation of the modern English law of homicide and current proposals for its reform. Murder is distinguished from the lesser homicides,[40] which have variable penalties, by mandatory penalties

33 The expression is adapted from Macaulay's draft Code, cl. 136, of 'giving provocation' by conduct intended or known to be likely to cause a riot.

34 Macaulay's draft Code, Chapter 25 (Of Defamation).

35 *Ibid.*, Chapter 26 (Of Criminal Intimidation, Insult, and Annoyance).

36 See, in addition, *ibid.*, Chapter 7 (Of Offences Against the Public Tranquillity) and the offence in cl. 136 of giving provocation by conduct intended or known to be likely to cause a riot.

37 For example, defiling holy places. Macaulay, Macleod, Anderson and Millett, above n. 3, Note J (On the Chapter of Offences Relating to Religion and Caste), at 102: 'No offence in the whole code is so likely to lead to tumult, to sanguinary outrage, and even to armed insurrection.'

38 Horder, above n. 28, at 124.

39 On the possibility of an expanded range of partial defences, see N. Lacey, 'Partial Defences to Homicide: Questions of Power and Principle in Imperfect and Less Imperfect Worlds' in Ashworth and Mitchell, above n. 11, at 125.

40 Macaulay distinguished four lesser homicides: (1) manslaughter, which was murder reduced by provocation; (2) 'voluntary culpable homicide in defence', which was murder reduced by excessive force in defence of a person or property; (3) 'voluntary culpable homicide by consent', each of which was punishable with a maximum penalty of 14 years' imprisonment; and (4) causing death by rash or negligent conduct,

of maximum severity. Murderers were to be punished by death, life imprisonment or permanent exile by transportation – a separation from community that, in Macaulay's view, resembled the separation 'which takes place at the moment of death'.[41] The severity of the penalty for murder is in stark contrast with the penalties exacted for the lesser homicides, which might be quite lenient.

It can be assumed that it was the invariant severity of the penalty that induced Macaulay to depart so markedly from nineteenth-century common law in his reformulation of the elements of murder. Like the other serious offences of violence in his Code, murder was to be restricted in its applications by the 'correspondence principle'.[42] Liability for murder or other serious offences of causing physical hurt was to be limited to a death or a hurt that the offender intended to inflict or knew to be a likely outcome of his or her conduct. Offences were differentiated and graded in seriousness by reference to fault. Provision was made for lesser offences of negligently causing death or injury. Macaulay's emphasis on fault requirements was a radical departure from the common law and it is radical even now, when many jurisdictions continue to accept the common law felony-murder rule or its statutory equivalents and most accept constructive liability for manslaughter.[43]

In the event, the correspondence principle was compromised in the IPC, which extends the fault elements of murder to include cases of fatality resulting from an intentional injury, though the defendant may have had no realisation of any risk that the injury would kill or cause grievous bodily harm.[44] Stephen described the IPC provisions on the fault element in murder as the 'weakest part of the Code', clumsy in expression and obscure in meaning.[45] The partial abandonment of the correspondence principle, which governed Macaulay's formulation of the offences of homicide and lesser bodily harms, was a step backwards into incoherence. English common law, assisted by the statutory elimination of the felony-murder rule by the Homicide Act 1957, has taken 150 years to approach the definition of the fault elements in murder proposed by Macaulay. The Law Commission has recommended a definition of murder consistent with the correspondence principle: murder would require proof of an intention to kill or inflict serious injury in the knowledge that

---

which was punishable with a maximum penalty of two years' imprisonment. See further Chapter 3 of this volume, above n. 6, at 63 and 66.

41 Macaulay, Macleod, Anderson and Millett, above n. 3, Note A (On the Chapter of Punishments), at 70. Macaulay restricted the death penalty to treason and murder, arguing that the peculiar atrocity of murder distinguished the offence from other atrocious offences, instancing 'gang robbery'; mutilation and rape: *ibid.*, at 330.

42 On the 'correspondence principle', see A.P. Simester and G.R. Sullivan, *Criminal Law: Theory and Doctrine* (3rd edn, Oxford: Hart Publishing, 2007) 186–91. Macaulay stated the principle in the introductory report to his Code, above n. 3, at iii–iv: 'If there be any distinction which more than any other it behoves the legislator to bear constantly in mind, it is the distinction between harm voluntarily caused and harm involuntarily caused. Negligence, indeed, often causes mischief, and often deserves punishment. But to punish a man whose negligence has produced some evil which he never contemplated as if he had produced the same evil knowingly, and with deliberate malice, is a course which, so far as we are aware, no jurist has ever recommended in theory, and which we are confident that no society would tolerate in practice.' See also Chapter 3 of this volume, above n. 6.

43 Though Stephen praised the IPC, he was critical of the omission of constructive manslaughter, describing the omission as 'remarkable': see J.F. Stephen, *A History of the Criminal Law of England* (vol. 3) (London: Macmillan and Co., 1883) 316.

44 IPC, ss. 209–304A.

45 Stephen, above n. 43, at 313. They do, however, have a notable apologist in S. Yeo, *Fault in Homicide* (Annandale: Federation Press, 1997). See also Chapter 3 of this volume, above n. 6.

there is a serious risk of death.[46] It remains to be seen whether the UK Parliament will enact the Law Commission's recommendations.

The moral coherence that Macaulay would have imposed on murder by his adherence to the correspondence principle was reinforced by an extended range of defences and partial defences that extenuate, excuse or justify the offence. The defences include the various General Exceptions in Chapter III of his draft Code that excuse or justify conduct that causes death and the partial defences of provocation, sudden fight, excessive force in defence of self or another and consent to death.

Injuries to Honour, Violent Passions and Communities of Feeling

Macaulay's conception of provocation was normative.[47] Provocation reduces liability for murder and lesser crimes of violence when retaliatory violence is prompted by a transgression that gave the offender cause for justifiable resentment. Exploration of the idea that V's fault can reduce D's guilt would require extended consideration.[48] For present purposes, the important thing is that Macaulay conceived the partial defence as a response to transgression rather than an indulgence extended to offenders who kill or injure others because they are unable to exercise self-control.[49] The transgression had to be grave before it could extenuate an offence of violence. His criterion of gravity – whether the provocation would put a 'person of ordinary temper' into a 'violent passion' – will be discussed later in the reformulation of the partial defence. For the moment, it is sufficient to note that it is the gravity of the transgression that provoked the defendant's fatal retaliation that does the exculpatory work. There is no reference to loss of 'the power of self-control' in Macaulay's draft Code or in his *Notes*. That was a later innovation by the authors of the IPC.

The same broad conception of harm that was apparent in his formulation of offences against caste or religion is evident again in Macaulay's formulation of the provocation defence, which extends beyond physical harms to include retaliation for intangible harms. Provocation merges seamlessly with excessive private defence against a physical threat and extends to retaliation against conduct that hurts the feelings rather than the body. In his account of provocation in the *Notes* on the Code, Macaulay concentrates on provocation as a harm to 'honour', which may be affronted, slighted, stained, traduced, diminished or lost as a consequence of the conduct or words of another. Macaulay departed radically from the common law in his acceptance that insults or other conduct that traduced honour might amount to grave provocation that would extenuate

46 Law Commission for England and Wales, *Murder Manslaughter and Infanticide*, above n. 5, at paras. [2.50]–[2.69], [9.5]. The Law Commission's recommendation is even narrower than Macaulay's draft Code. Proof that D was 'aware that his or her conduct involved a serious risk of causing death' can only lead to conviction for murder if D intended to cause serious injury to V. In Macaulay's draft Code, cl. 294 permits conviction for murder on proof that D knew that the conduct, whether or not intended to injure, was likely to cause death.

47 Compare the illuminating analysis of 'early modern honour theorists' in J. Horder, *Provocation and Responsibility* (Oxford: Clarendon Press, 1992) Chapters 3 and 4.

48 For the current debate on the issue of comparative fault, see V. Bergelson, *Victims' Rights and Victims' Wrongs* (Stanford: Stanford University Press, 2009) and the symposium on V. Bergelson's paper, 'Victims and Perpetrators: An Argument for Comparative Liability in Criminal Law' (2004–5) 8 *Buffalo Criminal Law Review* 385 and comments by symposiasts in that issue of the *Review*.

49 It is relevant to note, in relation to the absence of any reference to loss of self-control in the definition of provocation, that Macaulay made no allowance in his Code for defects of will falling short of madness and no allowance for coercion of the will when harm is threatened, whether by natural or human agency: Macaulay, Macleod, Anderson and Millett, above n. 3, Note B (On the Chapter of General Exceptions), at 82–84. See also Chapter 9 of this volume (S. Yeo, 'Duress and Necessity').

murder. Though the IPC modifies his formulation of the provocation defence, it did not restore the common law restrictions on its applications.

Though harm to honour may result in violent and unjustifiable retaliation from a 'blameable excess of feeling', it is important to make the point that Macaulay considered this to be a blameable excess of an *appropriate* feeling:

> It would be a fortunate thing for mankind if every person felt an outrage which left a stain upon his honour more acutely than an outrage which had fractured one of his limbs ... [W]hy should we treat an offence produced by the blameable excess of a feeling which all wise legislators desire to encourage, more severely than we treat the blameable excess of feelings certainly not more respectable?[50]

It is not the fact that honour is harmed that is the gist of provocation: it is the fact that a harm to honour may be a wrong against the offender that justifies resentment, though not, of course, a violent response intended to cause injury. The moral dimensions of honour and its cognate, shame, have been the subject of profound reflection by Bernard Williams, who emphasises the communal nature of these concepts in a culture where they provide a dominant theme in the structure of morality:

> People have at once a sense of their own honour and a respect for other people's honour; they can feel indignation or other forms of anger when honour is violated, in their own case or someone else's. These are shared sentiments with similar objects, and they serve to bind people together in a community of feeling.[51]

That idea of a wrong done within a community of feeling is the argumentative spine of Macaulay's explanation of provocation as a partial defence that extenuates a resort to violence.[52] It also provides him with a memorable hypothetical with which to advance a multicultural argument that provocation should extend to include insults and denigration relating to the offender's religion or caste. In his *Notes* on the draft Code, Macaulay asks his English readers to imagine the gravity of the provocation offered if the individual causing the provocation had taken 'indecent liberties with a modest female, in the presence of her father, her brother, her husband or her lover' and to consider whether a conviction for murder would be appropriate in such a case. That example, familiar to a nineteenth-century English audience,[53] provided the fulcrum for his argument that the same sympathetic understanding should be extended to a 'zealous Mohammedan' outraged by a

50 Macaulay, Macleod, Anderson and Millett, above n. 3, Note M (On Offences Against the Body), at 108.

51 B. Williams, *Shame and Necessity* (Berkeley: University of California Press, 1993) at 80.

52 Adam Smith provides a closely congruent account of honour, provocation and resentment and communities of feeling in *The Theory of Moral Sentiments* (edited by D.D. Raphael and A.L. Macfie) (Indianapolis: Liberty Fund, 1974). See, in particular, Smith's discussion of the 'noble and generous' quality of the 'irascible passion' of (justifiable) resentment at wrongs to honour or dignity (at 34–8) and the extended note on resentment (at 76–7).

53 A quotation from the much-anthologised eighteenth-century novel by Henry Mackenzie, *The Man of Feeling* (Oxford: Oxford University Press, 2001), at 50, provides a stereotypical original for Macaulay's example of a father's outrage. Harley, the hero of the book, is wrongly suspected by a father of debauching his daughter. The father responds to his suspicions with articulate outrage: 'Villain ... thou seest a father who had once a daughter's honour to preserve; blasted as it now is, behold him ready to avenge its loss!'

gross insult to his religion or 'some high-born Rajput' deprived of his caste and similarly outraged, who then kills or injures the provocateur.[54]

The irony of Macaulay's resort to an instance of English honour killing to encourage cultural sensitivity in matters relating to caste and religion requires no comment. His motive for making the comparison was impeccable. He was concerned to foster multicultural understanding, in part at least, to ensure that the laws imposed by the colonial power matched the expectations of its subjects.[55] Such a pragmatic stance enabled him to avoid the problem of determining the limits to cultural tolerance for differences among communities of feeling.

Honour and shame are elusive elements in what Williams, obviously addressing a Western readership, calls the 'modern moral consciousness'.[56] One can gain a clearer appreciation of the place of honour in Macaulay's moral cosmology if one infuses the concept with the related concept of 'dignity', which has a more assured place in the liberal democratic vocabulary.[57] However, there is nothing elusive about appeals to honour and the felt necessity for a violent extirpation of shame in cultures that condone the killing of women for transgressions against a recognised order of community feeling.[58]

An exploration of the relationship between guilt-based moralities and moralities based on honour and shame is well beyond the scope of this chapter. For present purposes, there are two things that I will take from Macaulay's account of the moral basis of the provocation defence. The first is that extenuation for intentionally taking another's life requires proof of a transgression by the victim within a community of feeling. The second is the question that Macaulay skirted – uneasily I suspect, for all his habitual assurance – in his comparison of the outraged English father with the 'high born Rajput' and 'zealous Mohammedan'. What is to count as a 'transgression' in a polity that includes diverse communities of feeling? It is a subsidiary function of the law of provocation to declare that some transgressions will not count as a basis for extenuation when liability for murder is in issue, whatever the mores of the community in which the killing occurs. It may be considered peculiarly appropriate that the penalty for some offenders who kill for honour should be conviction of murder followed by imprisonment for life and permanent exile from the community of feeling within which honour killings enjoy a measure of acceptance.[59]

---

54 Macaulay, Macleod, Anderson and Millett, above n. 3, Note M (On Offences Against the Body), at 108.

55 See, for example, Macaulay's scathing account of the offensiveness of English law and legal practice to local sensitivities, and the consequential threat to the governance of Bengal in the late eighteenth century: T.B. Macaulay, *Critical and Historical Essays* (London: Longman, Brown, Green and Longmans, 1851) 615–6: 'To these outrages the most distinguished families of Bengal, Bahara, and Orissa, were now exposed. Imagine what the state of our own country would be, if a jurisprudence were on a sudden introduced to among us, which should be to us what our jurisprudence was to our Asiatic subjects.'

56 Williams, above n. 51, at 94.

57 On wrongs to dignity as an essential ground for criminal liability, see M. Dan-Cohen, *Harmful Thoughts: Essays on Law, Self, and Morality* (Princeton: Princeton University Press, 2002) Chapter 5 ('Defending Dignity').

58 The literature on honour killings is extensive. For a recent and important collection of papers, see L. Welchman and S. Hossain, *'Honour': Crimes, Paradigms, and Violence Against Women* (London: Spinifex Press, 2005).

59 The problem arises in all jurisdictions when provocation is in issue. On unacceptable moralities, see Law Commission for England and Wales, *Partial Defences to Murder*, above n. 5, at para. [3.70] and Horder, above n. 47, at 144, on Terreblanche, his hypothetical racist who kills for a slight to honour.

Provocation Has No Paradigms – the Problematic Case of Adultery[60]

Macaulay's Code provides no illustrations of conduct that will amount to provocation. This was to remain the case when the IPC was enacted. Adultery, so often cited as a paradigm case of provocation in judicial decisions and legal texts, is conspicuous by its absence. The illustrative examples that do appear are all negative instances of conduct that cannot amount to provocation. Yet adultery has a central place in the lore of provocation. In Macaulay's time and thereafter, a common law rule declared that 'ocular inspection' of adultery was a provocation that would reduce murder to manslaughter.[61] There are several things to be said, however, about the origins of that common law rule that have been obscured by more recent developments. The first is that the requirement was originally stated as an exclusion – it was a conclusive ground for *rejecting* the husband's plea that he was provoked to kill by his wife's infidelity. Since nothing short of ocular inspection would do,[62] few cases in which a jealous husband killed could meet the requirements for extenuation.[63] The second is that Macaulay, like most of his contemporaries, did not allow for the possibility that adultery might extenuate murder when a husband killed his wife instead of her lover, even if he saw them in the act.[64] The extension of the defence to the case where the husband killed his wife was a common law development of which Macaulay was probably unaware. It occurred after his departure for India. That development, though of considerable theoretical interest, was unlikely to have had any immediate, practical effect; cases of ocular discovery followed by fatal attack were rare.

In reality, the evidential function of provocation in domestic homicides appears to have been of far more significance than the technical rules about ocular discovery of adultery. If the sympathies of jurors were sufficiently engaged, they would decline to convict on the ground that malice aforethought had not been proved and would convict the accused of manslaughter rather than murder. In practice, nineteenth-century English juries, courts and Home Office authorities continued to distinguish between men who killed their rivals, who were often treated with considerable lenience, and men who killed their wives for infidelity, who received scant tolerance and were often hanged.

Macaulay was probably idiosyncratic in expressing the view that the killing of an adulterous rival caught in the act was not even a presumptive ground for a plea of provocation. He thought that there could be no presumption in such cases because the fatal attack might be just as likely to

60 Though adultery has a central place in the lore of provocation, honour killings have a far broader range of victims. See L. Abu-Odeh, 'Comparatively Speaking: The "Honour" of the "East" and the "Passion" of the "West"' [1997] *Utah Law Review* 287, 291: '[T]he killing of "wives" is more of a cultural projection by [Western] feminists on other parts of the world. In the Arab world, unlike the United States, it is mostly "daughters" and "sisters" that are getting killed.'

61 See the early cases on the 'ocular inspection' rule: *Pearson's Case* (1835) 2 Lewin 216, 168 ER 1133; and *R. v. Kelly* (1848) 2 Car & K 814, 175 ER 342. In neither case did the facts support the *dictum*. Pearson was hanged.

62 Wiener, above n. 16, at 212.

63 Reported English examples satisfying the requirement of actual discovery are rare. See Beattie, above n. 19, at 95, listing an instance in 1756 and Wiener, *ibid.*, at 216, listing another in 1887. Indian examples are more common: see the cases noted in Gour, above n. 22, at 2474–520.

64 Macaulay, Macleod, Anderson and Millett, above n. 3, Note M (On Offences Against the Body), at 108. See, too, E. Livingston, *Code of Crimes and Punishments*, quoted in Macaulay, Macleod, Anderson and Millett, *ibid.* The third edition of Russell, published in 1843, departs from earlier editions and cites *Pearson*, above n. 61, for the proposition that the sight of adultery might extenuate the murder of a wife: Russell, above n. 13, at 581–2.

be prompted by 'mere brutality of nature, or … disappointed cupidity' as by feelings of 'wounded honour or affection'.[65] Macaulay's restraint was not shared by his successors. Once the 'ocular inspection' rule was abandoned, a confession of infidelity or a jealous husband's observation of some sign or symptom of infidelity was accepted as a basis for a partial defence. No one appears to have taken the point that Macaulay made no provision for provocation based on a misapprehension. Discussions of provocation in textbooks on the IPC are dominated by interminable and dismal catalogues of cases of women killed by their husbands, lovers, fathers and brothers for real or suspected sexual improprieties.[66] The most recent of these texts advances the extraordinary suggestion that the 'developing notion of equality of sex' and 'spread of education' might provide grounds for an *extension* of the partial defence of provocation by loosening the requirement that the husband's violent response to a confession of adultery be immediate rather than delayed.[67]

PROVOCATION REFORM – COMPARATIVE PERSPECTIVES

Any attempt to reconstruct a Macaulayan doctrine of provocation requires a comparison of reforms accomplished or awaiting legislative implementation in selected anglophone jurisdictions. The table that follows provides a summary account of the most recent of these.[68] It should be said at the outset, not to put too fine a point on it, that it is a primary objective of these proposals to ensure an increase in the rate of convictions for murder and an increase in the length of time in prison for jealous or possessive men who kill women.[69] That has been achieved in a number of jurisdictions by the abolition of the partial defence. In jurisdictions which have retained provocation, attempts have been made, with variable success, to extend its benefit to victims of domestic abuse and deny that benefit to perpetrators.

It will be immediately apparent from the table that the abolition of the partial defence has only occurred in jurisdictions which do not impose a mandatory sentence of life imprisonment or worse for murder. In jurisdictions where the punishment for murder is a mandatory life sentence at the least, the provocation defence has been retained, though limits have been placed on its applications.

---

65 Macaulay, Macleod, Anderson and Millett, above n. 3, Note M (On Offences Against the Body), at 108. See, too, Note Q (On the Chapter of Offences Relating to Marriage), at 458–9, on the variety of motives that may move a husband to kill for infidelity. See also his recommendation that adultery should not be a criminal offence. This was discussed by the Indian Law Commissioners in their First Report, above n. 4, at paras. [344]–[358], who rejected the recommendation. IPC, s. 497 makes adultery a criminal offence on the part of a man who has sexual intercourse with a woman who is married to another person.

66 Gour, above n. 22, at 2474–520; T. Bhattacharya, *Indian Penal Code* (Allahabad: Central Law Agency, 1997) 350–8.

67 C.K. Thakker and M.C. Thakker, *Ratanlal and Dhirajlal's Law of Crimes: A Commentary on the Indian Penal Code* (vol. 1) (New Delhi: Bharat Law House, 2007) 1430.

68 I have omitted reference to the recommendations of the New South Wales Law Reform Commission, *Partial Defences to Murder: Provocation and Infanticide* (Report No. 83) (Sydney: New South Wales Law Reform Commission, 1997). These recommendations run counter to the current tides of reform and seem unlikely ever to be adopted. Earlier legislation, passed in 1982, extended the timeframe during which retaliatory conduct by D might count as provocation: see Crimes (Homicide) Amendment Act 1982 (NSW), which provided a new definition of provocation in Crimes Act 1900 (NSW), s. 23.

69 See, for example, Law Commission for England and Wales, *Murder Manslaughter and Infanticide*, above n. 5, at para. [5.5]; and F. Stewart and A. Freiberg, *Provocation in Sentencing: Research Report* (2nd edn, Melbourne: Sentencing Advisory Council (Victoria), 2009) 79–86. The modern reform movement has also sought to exclude reliance on the partial defence when based on evidence of a non-violent homosexual advance. See, for example, Stewart and Freiberg, *ibid.*, at 50, 68–71.

Table 12.1 Comparative table of provocation law reform recommendations

Jurisdiction	Mandatory life	Abolish, restrict or extend the partial defence?	Enacted
Australia – Federal Law	No	Abolish	Yes[a]
Victoria	No	Abolish: partial defence of excessive defence introduced with particular application to family violence. Verdict of 'defensive homicide'	Yes[b]
Tasmania	No	Abolish	Yes[c]
Western Australia	No	Abolish	Yes[d]
Queensland	No[e]	Retain and restrict: requirement of violence or circumstances of 'extreme and exceptional' nature	No[f]
New Zealand	No	Abolish	Yes[g]
England, Wales and Northern Ireland	Yes	Retain and restrict: grave circumstances and justifiable sense of being seriously wronged or fear of serious violence	Yes[h]

Notes:

[a] The Commonwealth Criminal Code offences of murder make no provision for a partial defence of provocation: s. 71.2 (murder of a UN or associated person); s. 115.1 (murder of an Australian citizen or resident of Australia). The Code contains all the principles of criminal responsibility; it cannot be supplemented by common law defences: s. 2.1 (purpose).

[b] Crimes (Homicide) Act 2005 (Vic), s. 3.

[c] Criminal Code Amendment (Abolition of Defence of Provocation) Act 2003 (Tas).

[d] Law Reform Commission of Western Australia, *Final Report: Review of the Law of Homicide* (Project 97) (Perth: Law Reform Commission of Western Australia, 2007). The Law Reform Commission recommended the abolition of the partial defence, conditional on removal of the mandatory life penalty for murder. These recommendations were implemented in the Criminal Law Amendment (Homicide) Act 2008 (No. 29 of 2008), s. 13.

[e] See Criminal Code (Qld), s. 305, which permits courts to impose an indefinite sentence, subject to periodic review, in lieu of a life sentence.

[f] Recommendations by the Queensland Law Reform Commission, *A Review of the Excuse of Accident and the Defence of Provocation* (Report 64) (Brisbane: Queensland Law Reform Commission, 2008) 500–1 have not been implemented.

[g] Abolition of the partial defence was recommended by the New Zealand Law Commission, *The Partial Defence of Provocation* (Report 98) (Wellington: New Zealand Law Commission, 2007) 77. The partial defence was abolished by the Crimes (Provocation Repeal) Amendment Act 2009 (No. 64) (NZ), s. 5.

[h] Retention and restriction of the provocation defence was recommended by the Law Commission for England and Wales, *Murder Manslaughter and Infanticide*, above n. 5. See also Northern Ireland Law Commission, *Homicide: Murder and Involuntary Manslaughter* (Report 87) (Belfast: Northern Ireland Law Commission, 2008). Legislation effectively implementing the Law Commission's recommendations on provocation was passed in 2009. See Coroners and Justice Act 2009 (Chapter 25), ss. 54–56 (partial defence to murder: loss of self-control), applying to England, Wales and Northern Ireland.

Table 12.1 suggests that the distinction between murder and manslaughter is presumptive at best, insofar as moral blameworthiness is concerned, in jurisdictions that have abolished the provocation defence. A process of continuing slow erosion of the distinction in moral seriousness between the offences appears to be underway. There is ambivalence towards the idea that an extended range of partial defences would enable a more discriminating delineation of the moral gravity of murder.[70] With respect to provocation, abolitionist jurisdictions have accepted that consideration of the moral difference that provocation might make will be deferred until sentencing,[71] when a substantial overlap between the terms of imprisonment imposed for murder and manslaughter is possible. The Victorian Law Reform Commission went so far as to suggest that there might be rare cases in which a murder conviction might be followed by a non-custodial sentence.[72]

I mentioned earlier that the Law Commission for England and Wales recommended a redefinition of the fault elements in murder that would limit the offence to death inflicted intentionally or death resulting from conduct that was intended to cause a serious injury that the offender knew to be likely to kill. The reformulated offence would be known as murder in the 'first degree'. Provocation and diminished responsibility would reduce murder in the first degree to murder in the second degree, which would be punishable with a maximum penalty of life imprisonment. Murder in the second degree is distinguished in turn from manslaughter – the structural distinctions among the lesser homicides need not concern us here except to note, once again, the affinity with Macaulay's draft Code, which also distinguished among several varieties of unlawful homicide.

The fate of the Law Commission proposals for a comprehensive reform of the law of murder is uncertain.[73] The UK government adopted a 'staged' approach to the Law Commission recommendations. Consideration of proposed reform of the fault elements in murder and the introduction of a threefold division of homicide has been deferred.[74] I will not discuss this disappointingly partial response to the Law Commission Report. The discussion that follows will be restricted to consideration of the Commission's reformulation of the provocation defence.

So far as provocation is concerned, the resemblances between the Law Commission proposals and the provisions of Macaulay's draft Code can be drawn together and synthesised into five salient points which will provide the framework for the recommendations that follows:

(1) The provocation defence requires evidence of a serious wrong by the victim that particularly affects the interests of the defendant.
(2) The provocation defence is limited in its application by an objective test of wrongdoing, geared to the moral standards of an ordinary law-abiding citizen.

---

70 Compare Lacey, above n. 39, at 129–31. Lacey argues that the existing partial defences should be retained and extended, as an amelioration of the defects of the law of murder and manslaughter.

71 See Horder, above n. 28, at 139: 'In the modern era, the partial defences of provocation and diminished responsibility look like little more than half-hearted concessions to the need, in murder cases, to provide flexibility in point of sentence normally denied to judges by the mandatory life sentence.'

72 Victorian Law Reform Commission, above n. 15, at 276–9.

73 See Chapter 14 of this volume (C. Clarkson, 'Recent Law Reform and Codification of the General Principles of Criminal Law in England and Wales: A Tale of Woe').

74 Ministry of Justice, *Murder, Manslaughter and Infanticide: Proposals for Reform of the Law* (Response to Consultation, CP(R) 19/08) (London: Ministry of Justice, 2009) (available online at http://www.justice.gov.uk/consultations/docs/murder-review-response.pdf, last accessed 20 February 2011) paras. [3], [120].

(3) The serious wrong must cause the offender to suffer extreme emotional disturbance whether of anger, fear, loathing or despair.

(4) Provocation does not require proof of loss of self-control.

(5) As in the existing IPC, there will be specific rules of exclusion, designating conduct that cannot provide grounds for a partial defence. These exclusions are unstated but implicit in the Law Commission recommendations.[75]

Before discussing these proposals for reform, I will anticipate an obvious objection. I will follow Macaulay and the Law Commission and propose that there should be an 'objective' test which invokes the 'ordinary person' but eliminates any requirement that this ordinary person lose 'the power of self-control' and kill the provocateur. This proposal contradicts a common law doctrine that has a pedigree extending back to the mid-nineteenth century. It has been twice rejected by legislatures. The IPC departed from Macaulay's draft Code and required proof of loss of self-control in provocation.[76] The UK Parliament went even further in its partial implementation of the Law Commission recommendations and renamed the partial defence 'loss of self-control'.[77] The case for abolition of the requirement loss of self-control is nevertheless compelling.

The conjunction of a requirement of loss of self-control with an objective test that relies on the reasonable or ordinary person has been a source of continuing confusion. The common law of provocation yoked them together to produce an obvious absurdity. The reasonable or ordinary person of the common law does not simply get into a violent passion or 'lose self-control'. The partial defence is not available unless this supposedly reasonable or ordinary person would have lost self-control and killed the provocateur.[78] Lord Diplock explained the constitution of the ordinary person in a much-quoted passage in *DPP v. Camplin*:

> an ordinary person … not exceptionally excitable or pugnacious, but possessed of such powers of self control as everyone is entitled to expect that his fellow citizens will exercise in society as it is today.[79]

Though the statement has canonical status, its absurdity is obvious. We are all entitled to expect a good deal more in the way of self-control than Lord Diplock requires. To kill in response to provocation is to fail utterly to reach the minimal standards of self-control required of the ordinary person. To take an obvious example, an adulterer was always 'entitled to expect' that he would

---

75 There are, however, explicit exclusions in the Coroners and Justices Act 2009 (Chapter 25), s. 55(6). The partial defence is not available if the defendant was provoked by sexual infidelity or in circumstances where the conduct of the victim was incited by the defendant for the purpose of providing an excuse for retaliatory violence.

76 IPC, s. 300, Exception 1.

77 Coroners and Justice Act 2009 (Chapter 25), ss. 54–56 (partial defence to murder: loss of self-control).

78 *DPP v. Camplin* [1978] AC 705, at 718, *per* Lord Diplock: '[T]he question is not merely whether such a person would in like circumstances be provoked to lose his self-control but also whether he would react to the provocation as the accused did.'

79 *DPP v. Camplin ibid.*, at 717. Cf. the even more uncompromising formulation in *Holmes v. DPP* [1946] AC 588, 597, *per* Lord Simon: provocation, if it is to extenuate murder, must be capable of provoking an ordinary person to the same 'degree and method and continuance of violence which produces the death'. This is discussed in I. Leader-Elliott, 'Sex, Race and Provocation: In Defence of Stingel' (1996) 20 *Criminal Law Journal* 72, 93–4.

not be put to death by an enraged spouse, even if caught in the act. Any successful defence of provocation followed by conviction for manslaughter is *necessarily* a case of what Macaulay described as 'blameable excess'. The English test is morally incoherent. It is also empirically false. When subjected to grave provocation, the overwhelming majority of ordinary people, of whatever culture, do not kill the provocateur. The Law Commission has recognised the absurdity of the *Camplin* test and has recommended a substantial modification without, however, removing all traces of irrationality.[80]

In this respect, English common law presented a logical trap, entrenched by precedent, which Indian courts should have been able to avoid. Nothing in Macaulay's draft Code and nothing in the IPC, as enacted, required proof that a reasonable or ordinary person would have killed the provocateur. The original version of the provocation defence drafted by Macaulay reduces murder to manslaughter if a person of ordinary temper would have been moved to 'violent passion'. The IPC, which makes no mention of the ordinary or reasonable person, merely requires the defendant to have been 'deprived of the power of self-control' by 'grave and sudden provocation'.

If the *Camplin* absurdity is eliminated, there remains the question of whether 'loss of the power of self-control' is an intelligible or useful requirement in the law of provocation. Loss of the power of self-control could be understood as no more than a conventional description of a state of mind, a description not to be taken literally and akin to 'violent passion' in Macaulay's draft Code. A reformed law of provocation might simply ask the question of whether a reasonable or ordinary person would have lost the power of self-control if provoked in the same way as the defendant.[81] It might be suggested that there is no real difference in meaning or practical effect between a requirement of loss of the power of self-control and Macaulay's requirement that the provocation would have put a 'person of ordinary temper' in a 'violent passion'. Though an argument can be made along these lines for the retention of the traditional reference to loss of the power of self-control, there are substantial objections to this course. They will be considered in more detail presently. For the moment, it is sufficient to say that metaphors and fictions are insecure foundations for legal doctrine. If provocation really did involve loss of a 'power' of self-control, the plea would be one of involuntariness, leading to a complete acquittal. That is indeed a possibility, discussed earlier in relation to the 'evidentiary role' of provocation when voluntariness or other elements of the offence are in issue. But that has nothing to do with the defence of provocation. An offender whose provocation defence succeeds will be punished for his or her failure to exercise self-control, not for his or her incapacity to do so.

---

80 On absurdity, see Law Commission for England and Wales, *Partial Defences to Murder*, above n. 5, at paras. [3.113], [3.127]–[3.128]. The Commission subsequently resolved the problem, not entirely to its own satisfaction, by posing the test as whether an 'ordinary' as distinct from a 'reasonable' person 'might' kill the provocateur. When the jury considers this question, it is expected to exercise common sense and ignore logical niceties. See Law Commission for England and Wales, above n. 5, at paras. [3.127]–[3.128]. The recommendation was implemented in the Coroners and Justice Act 2009 (Chapter 25), s. 54(1)(c): the partial defence applies if a normal person of D's sex and age '*might* have reacted in the same or in a similar way to D' (emphasis added).

81 Stanley Yeo has presented the argument persuasively on a number of occasions. See, for example: S. Yeo, 'Lessons on Provocation from the Indian Penal Code' (1992) 41 *International and Comparative Law Quarterly* 615; S. Yeo, *Unrestrained Killings and the Law* (Delhi: Oxford University Press, 1998) 94–101. However, see S. Yeo, *Criminal Defences in Malaysia & Singapore* (Selangor: Malayan Law Journal, 2005) 283–6.

PROVOCATION RECONSTRUCTED: A MACAULAYAN REFORMULATION

Two elements of Indian criminal procedure have a significant bearing on the recommendations that will follow. First, trial by jury was abolished in India in 1960, as a consequence of the furore that followed the jury trial and acquittal of murder of Commander Kawas Nanavati, a naval officer who killed his wife's lover.[82] The problem of containing the prejudice of juries in favour of men who kill for honour, so evident in the Law Commission's consideration of provocation, does not arise in Indian criminal law. Secondly, though provocation is now an issue for the trial judge, it is still characterised as an issue of fact that must be decided with reference to the particular circumstances of the case. The court must be persuaded on the balance of probabilities that provocation extenuates the crime.[83]

Recommendations

The existing provisions of s. 300, Exception 1 of the IPC which define the partial defence of provocation should be replaced with the following provisions, shown in italics. Illustrations (a)–(f) in the existing provisions have been omitted in the interests of brevity:

> *Culpable homicide is not murder when it is committed:*
> *(a) by a person who acts on grave and sudden provocation; or*
> *(b) by a person who acts in good faith and on reasonable grounds in the belief that there are factual circumstances amounting to grave and sudden provocation; and*
> *the person killed is the person who is believed to have given that provocation or another whose death results by accident or mistake from conduct directed against the person who is believed to have given the provocation.*
> *Explanation – Provocation is 'grave and sudden' when:*
> *(a) an ordinary law-abiding citizen would consider that the person who gave the provocation had done a serious wrong to the offender; and*
> *(b) a law-abiding citizen of ordinary temperament would be likely to suffer an extreme emotional disturbance of temporary duration as a consequence of their perception of that serious wrong.*
> The above exception is subject to the following provisos:
> First – That the provocation is not sought or voluntarily provoked by the offender as an excuse for killing or doing harm to any person.
> Secondly – That the provocation is not given by anything done in obedience to the law, or by a public servant in the lawful exercise of the powers of such public servant.
> Thirdly – That the provocation is not given by anything done in the lawful exercise of the right of private defence.
> *Fourthly – That the provocation is not given by anything done in the exercise of one or more of the fundamental rights included in the Universal Declaration of Human Rights.*
> *Explanation* – Whether the provocation was grave and sudden enough to prevent the offence from amounting to murder is a question of fact.
> Illustrations

82 See *Nanavati v. State of Maharashtra* AIR 1962 SC 605.

83 The IPC does not extend the *Woolmington v. DPP* [1935] AC 462 presumption of innocence to defences.

(a) …

(g) Z, who is A's adult daughter, tells him that she intends to marry B, who is an adherent of a different religion from A and Z. A forbids the marriage but Z refuses to accept his prohibition. A is excited to violent rage by Z's disobedience and kills her. This is murder, for Z's refusal to comply with her father's command was an exercise of a fundamental human right.[84]

Discussion of the Recommendations

Provocation as a 'Serious Wrong' – an 'Ordinary Law-Abiding Citizen' Standard

The partial defence should not be available unless the defendant's fatal act was done in response to a serious wrong by the victim. This requires a court to be convinced that an ordinary law-abiding person would consider the victim's conduct to be a serious wrong. The mere fact that D was enraged by V's conduct is no mitigation of an attack on the victim: D's rage may be utterly unjustified and a ground for condemnation. The provisos in the existing version of the Code declaring that certain conduct *cannot* amount to provocation make it quite clear that loss of self-control and idiosyncratic judgments of wrongfulness are not grounds for extenuation. So, for example, an offender who kills in violent passion provoked by officials in the exercise of their lawful powers has no defence to murder. An offender who is enraged by the victim's exercise of a right of private defence – as in a case where the victim resists a sexual assault by the offender – cannot rely on provocation. In these instances, the defendant's violent passion, far from mitigating the crime, calls for punishment of the 'utmost rigour' reserved for murderers.[85]

Macaulay required provocation to be 'grave' before it could extenuate. Gravity was to be gauged by reference to the question of whether the conduct that induced the defendant to kill would be likely to move a 'person of ordinary temper' to 'violent passion'.[86] The person of ordinary temper was not Macaulay's invention. The probable source is the formulation in Livingston's Code, where Livingston refers to 'men of ordinary tempers' in his definition of manslaughter arising from sudden passion.[87] The ordinary person was meant to provide a criterion, independent of the defendant's judgment, that would determine whether the provocation was of sufficient gravity to amount to provocation. But Macaulay's formulation, like Livingston's, confuses two quite different things. A violent and passionate reaction, even when it is the violent and passionate reaction of an ordinary person, is not a criterion for determining whether a wrong has been done or a measure of the seriousness of wrongdoing. This confusion between the victim's wrongdoing and the offender's reaction to that wrongdoing was a precursor of the worse confusion that was to follow when loss of self-control was introduced as a defining element of provocation. The distinction that Macaulay

---

84 Universal Declaration of Human Rights, G.A. Res 217A(III), UN Doc A/810 at 71 (1948), Article 16.

85 Macaulay, Macleod, Anderson and Millett, above n. 3, Note M (On Offences Against the Body), at 108. It is apparent, however, that D may rely on provocation when officials *exceed* their lawful powers. See First Report of the Indian Law Commissioners, above n. 4, at paras. [277]–[279]. There is, it should be noted, neither a right of private defence nor a plea of excessive defence when D responds to an *un*lawful exercise of official powers by an official: Macaulay's draft Code, cl. 75; IPC, s. 99. For common law authority on the question, see the discussion in *R. v. Fry* (1992) 58 SASR 424, 436–9. At common law, provocation was presumed when D caused the death of a police officer who attempted to make an unlawful arrest.

86 Macaulay's draft Code, cl. 297.

87 E. Livingston, *A System of Penal Law for the State of Louisiana* (Philadelphia: James Kay Jun. and Brother, 1833) Chapter 5 ('Of Criminal Voluntary Homicide'), Article 534(4).

failed to make can be illustrated by Adam Smith's familiar distinction in his *Theory of Moral Sentiments*[88] between the responses of an 'impartial spectator' and the responses of the victim of wrongdoing – who is the subject of the impartial spectator's gaze.[89] Consider, for example, conduct that would always amount to a serious wrong. Tarquin has just raped Lucrece, who may or may not retaliate with fatal force. It is possible that the reaction of Lucrece will be one of violent passion. The anger of the victim is not, however, the criterion that measures the seriousness of the wrong that has been done. The wrong would be no less if the rape had reduced Lucrece to a state of suicidal despair and it would be no less if Lucrece survived the rape unscathed by psychic trauma and simply went and made a complaint to the police. Rape is a serious wrong because it involves a fundamental violation of the person and that is a judgment made from the standpoint of the impartial spectator.[90] It is a merely contingent fact that rape might induce violent passion in an ordinary person who had been raped. Failure to distinguish the question of whether the victim has *wronged* the offender from consideration of the reactions of the offender to some perception of hurtful conduct by the victim is one of the main reasons for the state of confusion of contemporary provocation doctrine.

The first step of any enquiry into the question whether D has a partial defence of provocation is to determine whether D has been the victim of a serious wrong. In other areas of law where judgments of wrongdoing must be made, modern legislation sets standards for criminal responsibility by reference to a familiar cast of exemplars – 'ordinary', 'reasonable' and 'decent' people – varieties of Adam Smith's impartial spectator – when defining offences of dishonesty, offensiveness and indecency. These imaginary exemplars set the standards of acceptable conduct or judgment in many criminal prohibitions. The 'ordinary law-abiding citizen' can serve the same function when provocation is in issue.[91] In a jurisdiction that includes diverse communities of feeling, an objective formulation of the standard is necessary. Nothing done by the victim should amount to provocation sufficient to extenuate murder unless an ordinary law-abiding citizen of the polity would characterise that conduct as a serious wrong to the defendant.[92] This criterion of wrongdoing is reinforced by the exclusionary provisos to the defence, declaring that certain kinds of conduct cannot amount to provocation by the victim of a homicide or lesser offence of bodily hurt.

---

88 Smith, above n. 52.

89 The impartial spectator most often plays the role of a standard of judgment internalised by the agent in Smith, *ibid.* But Smith also uses the impartial spectator as an external standard in his jurisprudence. See D.D. Raphael, *The Impartial Spectator* (Oxford: Clarendon Press, 2007) 113–14.

90 I choose the rape example because the wrongfulness of the offence has been the subject of extended and recent consideration by a number of criminal law theorists: see, in particular, J. Gardner, 'The Wrongness of Rape' and 'Reply to Critics' in J. Gardner, *Offences and Defences* (Oxford: Oxford University Press, 2007) 1–32, 242–5; K. Huigens, 'Is Strict Liability Rape Defensible?' in R.A. Duff and S.P. Green (eds), *Defining Crimes: Essays on the Special Part of the Criminal Law* (Oxford: Oxford University Press, 2005) 196–217.

91 Compare the 'ethically well disposed agent' in Horder, above n. 47, at 167. But see Law Commission of England and Wales, *Murder Manslaughter and Infanticide*, above n. 5, at para. [9.17]. The Law Commission's recommendations make no reference to the ordinary or reasonable person when the question of serious wrongdoing is in issue. All that the Commission requires is 'conduct that would cause the defendant to have a justifiable sense of being seriously wronged'. There is room for equivocation here on the question of whose standards of justification are to determine wrongdoing or its seriousness.

92 Formulated in this way, the criterion clarifies the distinction between the 'gravity' of provocation and 'proportionality' of response proposed by Ashworth, above n. 16, at 307. One does not have to attribute special characteristics to the ordinary or reasonable person to determine whether provocation was 'grave'. The question, asked from the position of the impartial spectator, is whether D has been seriously wronged.

The trial judge will be required to articulate the judgment that would be made by a law-abiding citizen as an impartial observer of the conduct of the victim and offender. This criterion readily extends to permit the condemnation of conduct that is a wrong to the offender by virtue of his or her membership of a particular minority. A Muslim judge, for example, can determine whether desecration or destruction of a Christian place of worship might amount to a serious wrong to one who worships there.[93] That desecration or destruction might, in appropriate circumstances, provide grounds for a provocation defence. The same criterion will require the court to deny reliance on provocation on occasion, even if the defendant killed in response to conduct that amounts to a serious wrong within a particular community of feeling. So, for example, reference to the standard of the ordinary law-abiding citizen will prevent reliance on provocation by a father who killed his daughter or a brother his sister for disobedience in her choice of a marital partner. Whatever the strength of feeling within a particular community, her disobedience cannot amount to a serious wrong against her father or brother in a liberal democratic society.

It is possible that Macaulay was of the view that provocation should be confined to the case where the serious wrong by the victim was real, rather than merely perceived. His formulation of the partial defence of provocation makes no provision for mistaken beliefs. The recommendation departs from Macaulay's draft Code in this respect. Modern common law theory draws no distinction between veridical perceptions and reasonable mistakes about exculpatory circumstances.

A Serious Wrong Resulting in 'Extreme Emotional Disturbance of Temporary Duration'

Responses to provocation are variable. The defendant's attack in response to a serious wrong may be an act of cool and calculated revenge that justifies a conviction for murder. The requirement of extreme emotional disturbance corresponds to and displaces the existing requirement that the defendant's attack occur as a consequence of loss of the power of self-control. The additional requirement that it be of temporary duration, taken together with the objective test that follows, is meant to exclude reliance on mental or psychological illness or disability, even though the illness or disability has been induced by a serious wrong to the defendant. Provocation is a partial defence 'for those who are in a broad sense mentally normal'.[94]

The reference to 'extreme emotional disturbance' is taken from the US Model Penal Code.[95] The expression is intended to extend the emotional range of provocation beyond common law limits. For Macaulay, provocation required proof that the victim's conduct moved the defendant to 'violent passion'. That expression probably had a broader range of reference in the early nineteenth century than it does in current usage, where it connotes anger. Until comparatively recently, English common law authorities on provocation accepted no emotion other than anger as a basis for the defence. Fear, resentment, despair, loathing and disgust went unrecognised.[96] The growing

---

93 Cf. T.B. Macaulay, *Speeches and Poems* (New York: Hurd & Houghton, 1867): 'Speech– [Against] Jewish Disabilities', at 151: a Jewish judge could be expected to enforce the law of blasphemy 'as well as a Christian ... if I were a judge in India, I should have no scruple about punishing a Christian who should pollute a mosque'.

94 Ashworth, above n. 16, at 312.

95 US Model Penal Code, s. 210.3. The Code refers to extreme 'mental or emotional' disturbance. The reference to mental disturbance, omitted in the proposal, extends the US defence beyond provocation to include diminished responsibility.

96 So acute a theorist as Ashworth once doubted that fear might provide a basis for the defence, above n. 16, at 297: 'A loss of self control caused by fear, panic or mental instability cannot be brought within the defence of provocation.'

realisation that this restriction involved systematic discrimination against women who plead provocation after killing abusive men has begun to broaden the emotional range of provocation to include fear and despair.[97] Loathing may be equally significant in those rare cases in which women kill men who have defiled their marriage, their home or their children by marital rape or incest.[98]

Extreme Emotional Disturbance and the Person of Ordinary Temperament

Circumstances in which D might respond to a serious wrong with the intention of killing the wrongdoer are infinitely variable. Some serious wrongs are sudden and shocking. Others are protracted, allowing time for the recovery of emotional resilience. The provocation defence should not succeed unless it is probable or likely that a person of ordinary temperament would have suffered from extreme emotional disturbance as a consequence of the serious wrong done by the victim.

The proposed requirement of extreme emotional disturbance is an adaptation of Macaulay's definition of grave provocation as conduct that 'would move a person of ordinary temper to violent passion'. Invocation of the ordinary person as a measure of the *offender's response* is to be distinguished from invocation of the ordinary law-abiding person who provides an impartial and objective measure of the *victim's wrongdoing.* At this point in the enquiry, after the victim's wrongdoing has been characterised as grave and sudden provocation, it is the offender's response to that wrongdoing that is in issue. Few ordinary people can be expected to be impartial spectators of their own suffering or victimisation. Let us suppose that the wrong is established, that the offender was reduced to a state of extreme emotional disturbance as a consequence and that a person of ordinary temperament would have been likely to suffer the same extremity of anger, fear, despair, loathing or disgust in consequence of the victim's wrongful conduct. An offender who is reduced to such a state of emotional turmoil as the victim of a serious wrong and kills the provocateur is certainly punishable, but the prevalence of the tendency to a blameable excess of feeling, among people of ordinary temper, extenuates the defendant's crime.

The two parts of the ordinary person criterion can now be put together. This ordinary person is a *law-abiding* citizen of *ordinary* tolerance and mental resilience.[99] When the question is whether the victim's conduct was a serious wrong to the defendant, the moral and cultural standards of the ordinary law-abiding citizen provide the framework for enquiry; there is no need to agonise over the characteristics of the ordinary person. They are determined by the necessity for proof that the offender was seriously wronged. The judgment of wrongdoing is made from the position of Adam Smith's impartial spectator who needs no particular characteristics other than an appreciation of the moral and cultural standards of their polity. Men and women who are appointed to the judiciary, whatever their age, sexual preference, religious persuasion or other personal characteristics, are expected to fill that role; it is one of the essential qualifications of their office. If they are ignorant of particular cultural mores, they can be informed by expert evidence. A decision as to whether the homicide victim had done a serious wrong to the defendant will certainly require consideration of any

97 Horder, above n. 47, at 31: 'The defence of provocation (focused on anger) is thus poorly equipped to deal with those who are driven to act as they do out of despair.' See also Law Commission of England and Wales, *Murder Manslaughter and Infanticide*, above n. 5, at para. [5.18].

98 See *R. v. Jeffrey* [1967] VR 467, in which Mrs Jeffrey killed her husband after enduring what would now be recognised as oral rape and accusations of incest with her sons. She was convicted of murder. Compare the compassionate acquittal by the jury in *R. v. R.* (1981) 28 SASR 321.

99 Cf. Law Commission of England and Wales, *Murder Manslaughter and Infanticide*, above n. 5, at para. [9.17].

of the defendant's characteristics that are relevant. What is excluded, however, is any consideration of factors that provided the basis for a defendant's idiosyncratic or unacceptable judgment that he or she had been seriously wronged. That is the first stage of the enquiry. When the court comes to consider the question whether a person of ordinary emotional resilience would have suffered extreme emotional disturbance, if they had suffered the same serious wrong as the defendant, those factors that have a rational bearing on emotional response, such as youth or other more particular characteristics, can be taken into account. A court might draw at this point on the law of duress in English and Australian law where ordinary resilience of character defines the limits of that defence.[100] Excluded, however, is any idiosyncratic susceptibility to extreme emotional responses. Idiosyncratic responses, if they indicate mental disability, require consideration in relation to the possibility of permitting a partial defence of diminished responsibility.

Provisos and Illustrations

Provisos, or limiting cases, where the defence of provocation will not run, are crystallised applications of the ordinary citizen test or standard.[101] They displace that standard with a rule or guiding principle. In its present form, the Code limits the availability of provocation by three provisos and their accompanying illustrations. The provisos which are concerned with the exercise of powers conferred by law and rights of private defence require no special comment. The recommendations for reform propose an additional, fourth, principle of limitation and an accompanying illustration. Conduct cannot amount to provocation if it is an exercise of a fundamental human right. The new proviso is supported by an illustration in which a woman's exercise of her right of choice of a marital partner so enrages her father that he kills her.

A proviso so fundamental in its nature requires nothing in the way of supporting argument. This is an implicit element of the ordinary law-abiding person standard, an element so obvious that it might be overlooked unless made explicit.

Cases of uncertainty at the margins of the exclusionary principle are quite possible. An exercise of a right, even an exercise of a universal right, may be coupled with other conduct that is so hurtful or abusive as to amount to the serious wrong required for provocation. But that is a familiar feature of the other provisos and requires a distinction to be drawn between those elements of the victim's conduct that can and that cannot amount to provocation.[102]

---

100 A caveat may be appropriate at this point. Duress can be a complete defence, either because D's offence was the lesser harm or because it would be unjust to expect an ordinary person to resist the threat. Provocation is never a complete defence, for the response is always excessive and inexcusable when the defendant resorts to serious violence. When provocation is in issue, it is *not* unjust to expect the defendant to refrain from violence. However, there is no paradox or inconsistency in using the same standard of emotional resilience for both duress and provocation. In each case, the central purpose of the test is to exclude reliance on the defence by individuals who suffer from an abnormal pathology of will, intellect or emotional balance.

101 On exceptions, see V.F. Nourse, 'Upending Status: A Comment on Switching, Inequality and the Idea of the Reasonable Person' (2004–5) 2 *Ohio State Journal of Criminal Law* 361; and C. Lee, '"Murder and the Reasonable Man" Revisited: A Response to Victoria Nourse' (2005–6) 3 *Ohio State Journal of Criminal Law* 301, which notes that the US state of Maryland legislated, in 1988, to deny the defence of provocation based on observation of a spouse in the act of adultery.

102 Compare the discussion in W. Morgan and A.C. McPherson, *The Indian Penal Code with Notes* (Calcutta: G.C. Hay and Co, 1861) 251–3, on provocation by conduct in excess of a legal right or duty by a public official.

Table 12.2 Proposal for a Macaulayan reconstruction of the partial defence of grave provocation: proposed defence and comparisons

Proposed provocation defence	Macaulay's version	Law Commission's version
Necessary factors for extenuation		
1. Grave provocation (by words or conduct or a combination thereof) that caused the defendant to have a sense of being seriously wronged	1. 'Grave' provocation	1. Gross provocation (by words or conduct or a combination thereof) that caused the defendant to have a justifiable sense of being seriously wronged; or fear of serious violence
2. An ordinary law-abiding person would have had a sense of being seriously wronged	2. Implied	2. The defendant has a 'justifiable' sense of being seriously wronged
3. Extreme mental or emotional disturbance that is an immediate response to the apprehension of a serious wrong	3. 'Sudden' provocation and 'violent passion'	3. No equivalent. However, the defence is barred if D responded to provocation with a 'considered desire for revenge'
4. Conduct that causes death 'is committed under the influence of extreme mental or emotional disturbance'	4. 'Violent passion'	4. No equivalent
5. The sense of being seriously wronged would have induced a state of extreme mental or emotional disturbance in an ordinary person	5. Provocation 'likely to move a person of ordinary temper to violent passion'	5. 'A person of the defendant's age and of ordinary temperament ... might have reacted in the same or a similar way'
6. An ordinary person has the qualities of temperament, tolerance, moral character and capacity for self-control that fall within the range expected of ordinary, law-abiding citizens	6. Implied	6. An ordinary person is of the 'defendant's age and of ordinary temperament, i.e., ordinary tolerance and self-restraint, in the circumstances of the defendant ...'
Exceptions and bars to extenuation: acts that cannot amount to provocation		
1. V's act was sought or provoked by D to provide an excuse for the attack	1. Implied[a]	1. Provocation incited to provide an excuse for violence
2. V's act was 'done in obedience to law'	2. V's act was 'done in obedience to the law'	2. No equivalent
3. V's act was authorised by law	3. V's act was authorised by law	3. No equivalent
4. V's act was that of a public servant done in the exercise of lawful power	4. V's act was that of a public servant done in the exercise of lawful power	4. No equivalent
5. V's act was done in the exercise of a right of private defence against D	5. V's act was done in the exercise of a right of private defence against D	5. No equivalent
6. V's act was an exercise of a fundamental human right, recognised in the Universal Declaration of Human Rights	6. No equivalent	6. No equivalent

Note:

[a] *See* IPC, s. 300. Macaulay made no provision for the exception, presumably on the ground that it went without saying: the defendant's violence, in such a case, is not a *response* to grave and sudden provocation.

Table 12.2 provides a summary comparison of the proposed reconstruction of provocation with the original provisions of Macaulay's draft Code and the recommendations of the Law Commission for England and Wales which were later enacted in the Coroners and Justice Act 2009.[103]

CONCLUSION

I began and I will end with the question of punishment. If murder continues to be punishable with death or its equivalent in the civil death that follows a sentence of imprisonment for life, that penalty must be taken to be intrinsic to the offence. The enormity of the crime and the mandatory severity of its penalty require a suite of defences and partial defences that will ensure, so far as possible, that conviction for murder is restricted to those who deserve to suffer the punishment reserved for murderers. The introduction of variable penalties for the offence might be sufficient reason to eliminate some and perhaps all of the partial defences. If that were to happen, circumstances that extenuate the offence would be considered after conviction, when the offender is sentenced for murder.

However, the case for abolition of partial defences in the IPC is significantly weaker than it is in other jurisdictions where that has occurred. Offences are tried without jury in Indian courts. The problem of containing jury prejudices favourable to the offender, so evident in other jurisdictions, does not arise. Nor does the problem of formulating doctrinal tests in language that cannot be misunderstood by a jury arise. Moreover, the burden of proof is cast on the defendant, who must persuade the court on the balance of probabilities. Evidence that vilifies the victim will be tested by the court rather than remaining suspended in the realm of reasonable doubt. The sentence for culpable homicide, in cases where the provocation defence succeeds, will be based on a finding of fact rather than on a bare possibility that must be assumed to be true. These are all reasons for retaining the provocation defence in these jurisdictions, even if the penalty were to be variable rather than mandatory.

It may be helpful to reiterate some of the limits of the argument that has been presented. The partial defence of sudden fight, which supplements provocation and reduces murder to culpable homicide, would require reconsideration in a more comprehensive consideration of the law of murder. Though the partial defences of provocation and sudden fight merged long ago in common law jurisdictions, the IPC distinguishes between them. Reform of the law of provocation would count for little if principled limitations on that defence were regularly subverted by defendants who chose to rely instead on sudden fight.

The reconstruction of the partial defence of provocation that I have proposed is based on a principle of comparative fault, which is implicit in Macaulay's draft Code and his *Notes* on the Code. In provocation, it is the fact that the victim has seriously wronged the defendant that extenuates murder. Overwhelming anger or 'loss of self-control' is no excuse. If, indeed, the offender's overwhelming anger and attack was a response to an exercise of autonomy rights by the victim, it aggravates rather than extenuates the crime.

Macaulay's draft Code and the Law Commission proposals provided the basis for my argument that the existing requirement of proof of loss of the 'power of self-control' should be eliminated in a reconstructed provocation defence. This particular legacy of the common law has been an

103 Law Commission of England and Wales, *Murder Manslaughter and Infanticide*, above n. 5, Part 9, List of Recommendations, at paras. [9.16], [9.17]. The recommendations were implemented with some variations in Coroners and Justice Act 2009 (Chapter 25), ss. 54–56. The most significant difference between the Law Commission recommendations and the parliamentary response was the retention of the common law requirement of 'loss of self-control' in the renovated provocation defence.

unnecessary source of confusion regarding the grounds for extenuation when a defendant pleads provocation. However, it is arguable that there is an exculpatory gap in the IPC, as there was in Macaulay's draft Code, in cases where the defendant's capacity to exercise self-control was impaired. A defence of diminished responsibility might supplement the other partial defences.[104] Duress, whether by threats or circumstances, might provide grounds for a complete or partial defence. Of these possibilities it is only necessary to say that the grounds for accepting diminished responsibility or duress as partial defences should not be confused with the grounds for extenuation when an attack was provoked by the wrongful conduct by the victim.[105]

104 Cf. Chapter 10 of this volume (G. Ferguson, 'Insanity') at 254.

105 For English debate on the relationship between provocation and diminished responsibility, see R. Mackay and B. Mitchell, 'Provoking Diminished Responsibility: Two Pleas Merging into One?' [2003] *Criminal Law Review* 745; and J. Gardner and T. Macklem, 'Compassion Without Respect? Nine Fallacies in *R. v. Smith*' [2001] *Criminal Law Review* 623.

PART IV
Challenges of Codification and Criminal Law Reform

The final part of this book examines the continuing issues and current challenges of codification and criminal law reform.

Chapter 13 comprises an evaluation by Matthew Goode of judicial interpretations of the Australian Model Criminal Code, which is one of the most successful manifestations of criminal law codification in recent times. The general principles of the Model Criminal Code have been implemented by the Commonwealth of Australia, the Australian Capital Territory (ACT) and the Northern Territory. Implementation of the Code's general principles by the Commonwealth was a major step, for it has generated prosecutions at a far greater rate than the ACT or the Northern Territory. The critical question for the attempt at national harmonisation of the Model Criminal Code, in particular its general principles, was (and remains) how well it has worked in practice for the courts applying it. Does the Code work? Goode seeks to answer this question by surveying and commenting on the resulting jurisprudence.

In Chapter 14, Chris Clarkson turns our attention to recent efforts at codification and criminal law reform in England and Wales. With regard to codification, progress in these jurisdictions is best summed up by the title to an editorial in the *Criminal Law Review*: 'R.I.P.: The Criminal Code (1968–2008)' [2009] *Criminal Law Review* 1. To put it bluntly, Clarkson says that the project is dead. In relation to law reform, the kindest phrases that spring to mind are 'piecemeal' and 'incoherent'. In short, it is a sad story. This chapter attempts first to address the question of how and why it has all gone so wrong. The second section of the chapter then considers those (few) areas of the General Part of the criminal law where law reform has actually been effected.

Chapter 15, the final chapter in this book, reflects on the impediments to criminal law codification and law reform occasioned by the modern trend of 'governing through crime'. In response to the detailed discussion of histories and characteristics of codification described in the preceding chapters, Mark Findlay pens thoughts which are designed to identify essential challenges to principled law reform. He contends that the political imperatives and pragmatic control agendas driving contemporary criminal law and procedure are more influential in constructing future directions for liability and sanction determinations than the integrity of a principled approach to criminal law, codified or otherwise.

Chapter 13
An Evaluation of Judicial Interpretations of the Australian Model Criminal Code

Matthew Goode[1]

INTRODUCTION

As a general proposition, Australian criminal jurisdictions generally fall into one of four kinds. The first are the 'common law' jurisdictions. In New South Wales, Victoria and South Australia, the criminal law is based on English common law as supplemented, extensively, by local and Imperial statutes.[2] By contrast, Queensland and Western Australia are what might be termed 'Griffith Code' jurisdictions, as their criminal law is codified, based on the code developed by Sir Samuel Griffith for Queensland at the turn of the twentieth century and supplemented extensively by local statutes. For present purposes, this study will not go beyond that general distinction. Tasmania, like New Zealand and Canada, combined local consolidations with Stephen's draft English Code 1878–80 as the primary model for codification.

The Commonwealth of Australia, that is to say, the federal Australian entity, the Australian Capital Territory (ACT) and the Northern Territory have adopted the Model Criminal Code. I will not explore the early history of codification of the criminal law in Australia and will not deal, except in passing, with the Griffith Codes.[3] While these Codes were an advance in their day as codifications, they have now long outlived their usefulness and are antiquated. The Griffith Code was based on the law as it was then thought to be (and certainly was, more or less).[4] But the common law has moved on and the Griffith Code has not. Comprehensive codes, such as the Griffith Code and the Indian Penal Code (IPC), despite being characterised by consistent principles of criminal responsibility, require comprehensive updating on a regular basis, which is seldom a legislative priority. The major problem with the existing Griffith Code is that it crystallised the development of the idea of criminal fault in 1900 or thereabouts. The Griffith Code jurisdictions have shown a consistent unwillingness to review their general principles of criminal responsibility from first

---

1 Nothing in this chapter reflects in any way the views or policy of the Attorney-General's Department of South Australia.

2 Those latter statutes may be very old inheritances.

3 On the Griffith Code and other nineteenth-century self-governing British jurisdiction codes, see Chapter 2 of this volume (B. Wright, 'Macaulay's Indian Penal Code: Historical Context and Originating Principles'). See also R.S. O'Regan, 'The Migration of the Griffith Code' in R.S. O'Regan, *New Essays on the Australian Criminal Codes* (Sydney: The Law Book Company, 1988); and B. Wright, 'Criminal Law Codification and Imperial Projects: The Self-Governing Jurisdiction Codes of the 1890s' (2008) 12 *Legal History* 19. I have also left out the interesting but not enacted efforts, notoriously the failed Pennefather Code, for which see G. Taylor, 'Dr Pennefather's Criminal Code for South Australia' (2002) 31 *Common Law World Review* 62.

4 Sir Samuel Griffith and other codifiers at the time would have been substantially influenced by such decisions as *R. v. Tolson* (1889) 23 QBD 168.

principles since then. Much has changed for the better in modern renditions of the criminal law. In particular, the concept of voluntariness has appeared and taken shape, and the ideas of fault and mistake have been rationalised and developed to a significant degree, both under Australian common law and code, and common law systems overseas.

The practice of the High Court of Australia (the highest Australian court) is to pull the general principles of the Griffith Code as far as it can in the direction of the recent developments in the general principles of the (common) criminal law,[5] but the Griffith Code states themselves stoutly and parochially resist the obvious policy shift that demands wholesale revision of the general principles.[6] I will have more to say on the general topic of flexibility in codifications later.

THE AUSTRALIAN MODEL CRIMINAL CODE[7]

Like the US (and unlike Canada, where criminal law comes under central federal government authority), criminal law in Australia is largely decentralised, falling under state jurisdiction. The formal role of the federal government in such matters is limited and must be enacted through a specified head of constitutional power such as customs (e.g. drug importation), telecommunications (e.g. child pornography) and referred power (e.g. terrorism). There have been long-standing attempts in the US to encourage greater conformity between state criminal laws, beginning with Herbert Wechsler's Model Penal Code.[8] A similar initiative was more recently undertaken in Australia.

On 28 June 1990, the Standing Committee of Attorneys-General (SCAG) placed the question of the development of a national model criminal code for Australian jurisdictions on its agenda. In order to advance the concept, the SCAG established a Committee consisting of an officer from each Australian jurisdiction with expertise in criminal law and criminal justice matters. This Committee was originally known as the Criminal Law Officers Committee but, in November 1993, the name was changed to the Model Criminal Code Officers Committee (MCCOC) in order to

5 When the High Court is given a choice between a subjective fault-based regime and a Griffith Code regime, it has adopted the former. An outstanding example is *Chew v. The Queen* (1992) 173 CLR 626, which concerned the interpretation of the fault elements of an offence in the Companies Code (WA). A recent High Court enunciation of the fact that the Griffith Code has to be reinterpreted against its literal words to take into account the development of later fundamental principles, can be found in *Murray v. The Queen* (2002) 131 A Crim R 215, especially at 225.

6 For example, in 1992, the Queensland Criminal Justice Commission advanced the quite ludicrous proposition that the Model Criminal Code draft general principles of criminal responsibility 'introduces many concepts and terminology which are foreign to most States'. That is simply not true. Murray J., of the Western Australian Supreme Court, who conducted the most thorough modern review of the Griffith Code to that time, said to the Senate Legal and Constitutional Legislation Committee: 'Time moves on and one's ideas change, but I have become involved in the process of the organisation of this bill and it is lovely to see it come forward ... I think it is a fine document ... There are a number of significant areas which seem to me to embody distinct improvements on the law, both the common law and, in some respects, the Griffith codes': Senate Legal and Constitutional Legislation Committee, *Hansard*, 22 November 1994, at 271.

7 Some of this material is taken from a far more detailed paper published as M.R. Goode, 'Constructing Criminal Law Reform and the Model Criminal Code' (2002) 26 *Criminal Law Journal* 152.

8 There is an immense American literature on this: see http://wings.buffalo.edu/law/bclc/Biblio.htm (last accessed 20 February 2011). See in particular H. Wechsler, 'The Challenge of a Model Penal Code' (1951–2) 65 *Harvard Law Review* 1097; S.H. Kadish, 'Codifiers of the Criminal Law: Wechsler's Predecessors' (1978) 78 *Columbia Law Review* 1098; and the papers published in (1987–8) 19 *Rutgers Law Journal* (Issue No. 3).

reflect the principal remit of the Committee directly.[9] When the Code project expired in 2001, the Committee's name was changed to reflect its altered status as a sub-committee of the SCAG to the Model Criminal Law Officers Committee. I will discuss this Committee more in due course.

The first formal meeting of the Committee took place in May 1991. In July 1992, the Committee released its first paper, a Discussion Draft on the general principles of criminal responsibility and, after a great deal of public consultation, including 52 written submissions and a lengthy seminar at the Fourth International Criminal Law Congress in Auckland in 1992, delivered a Final Report to the SCAG which was released in December 1992. With the exception of the general principles relating to intoxicated defendants,[10] the recommendations in that Final Report formed the basis for the Commonwealth Criminal Code Bill 1994, which was passed by the Commonwealth Parliament in March 1995. In 1994, both the Commonwealth Government and the State and Territory Premiers' Leaders Forum endorsed the Model Criminal Code project as one of national significance.

The ACT essentially enacted the general principles of the Model Criminal Code in 2002[11] and the Northern Territory followed suit in 2006.[12]

On 5 April 2002, the Commonwealth, States and Territories concluded an 'Agreement on Terrorism and Multi-jurisdictional Crime'. This agreement of the Council of Australian Governments Leaders included a decision to modernise the criminal law by legislating in the priority areas of:

- model forensic procedures;
- model computer offences; and
- model serious drug offences.[13]

IMPLEMENTATION

The political, constitutional, legal and cultural obstacles to the wide adoption of the Model Criminal Code are considerable and the General Part serves as a telling illustration. The general principles of criminal responsibility are the building blocks of the Model Criminal Code. It may be contended that a jurisdiction has not 'adopted' the Model Criminal Code unless it has adopted the general principles (commonly referred to as 'Chapter 2'). On this basis, only the Commonwealth, its small territories and the two major territories have 'adopted' the Code.

The Chapter 2 argument is a controversial contention. There is truth to both sides of it. On the one hand, it can properly be argued that the Chapter 2 principles are so fundamental to the Model Criminal Code that non-acceptance of them amounts to a rejection of the Code. On the other hand,

9 For general background, see M. Goode, 'Codification of the Australian Criminal Law' (1992) 16 *Criminal Law Journal* 5.

10 The Committee recommended that the law be based on the decision of the High Court in *The Queen v. O'Connor* (1980) 146 CLR 64, but the Standing Committee decided that it preferred the position taken in *R. v. Majewski* [1977] AC 443. That decision is not a principal focus of the discussion which follows. The very interesting debate is well-rehearsed in other places. However, the MCCOC's proposed solution to the SCAG decision is an unusual one which has not been well debated. There is a legislated model that can be found in South Australian Criminal Law Consolidation Act 1935, ss. 267A–269.

11 Criminal Code 2002 (ACT); Criminal Code Harmonisation Act 2005 (ACT).

12 Criminal Code (2006) (NT).

13 See http://www.coag.gov.au/coag_meeting_outcomes/2002-04-05/docs/terrorism.cfm (last accessed 20 February 2011).

it can be argued that a great deal of the other chapters of the Model Criminal Code which have been accepted are highly significant.

There is an intermediate position which, in my opinion, describes the true position. It is that non-acceptance of Chapter 2 is due to a lack of political will. Although Queensland withdrew from the project in opposition to twenty-first-century sexual offences proposals (apparently on the ground that consensual adult incest is too appalling for words and deserves condign punishment), this was just an excuse to back the mulish attitude of the then Queensland Supreme Court to the general principles.[14] For example, this court was resistant to recognising the consequences of the distinction between liability for acts and omissions. That distinction can be traced back to the championship of Macaulay in his work on the Indian Penal Code (IPC)[15] and early common law development.[16] In contrast, little attention has been paid to that distinction in the Griffith Code. The then Chief Justice of the Western Australian Supreme Court was sympathetic but, as with Tasmania, the key operative was most probably inertia. It was all too hard. Also, why move from something that had been in place for a century and which, although leaking oil, still covers the ground?

Noting that among the local jurisdictions that have adopted the Chapter 2 principles, one was Griffith Code (Northern Territory) and another was common law (ACT), it may be said with some confidence that there are really two main problems facing the state jurisdictions aside from plain parochialism. The first is that the task of adopting Chapter 2 principles is resource-intensive since one has to go through the entire penal legislation and consider each penal provision. The second is that, even if there is some doomed creature dedicated enough to do that, the task of finding the political and parliamentary priorities to devote to the task is daunting. We all know that in Western democracies at least, the priorities given to quick-fix action-oriented ‘law and order’ policies take precedence in political platforms, Cabinet considerations and parliamentary time.

Recent experience over the past 20 years has not been good for projects of this kind. The Canadian government abolished the Law Reform Commission of Canada, which had done an enormous amount of work on a new Criminal Code to replace their current one, first implemented in 1892 and based on Stephen’s draft English Code 1878–80. The English Law Commission still exists, but as Chapter 14 of this volume by Chris Clarkson notes, its reports notoriously languish unimplemented,[17] despite repeated calls for action by the legal profession and the judiciary.[18] A similarly dismal history characterises criminal law reform in the US, despite concerted attempts to promote a uniform Model Penal Code.[19]

The lesson here is straightforward. Reform of the criminal law, including codification or re-codification of the criminal law, is a political exercise. If the aspiring law reformer does not own or control a significant part of the politics of the exercise, the project is doomed to failure. So-called ‘new era’ law reform agencies set up as expensive, independent and expert *apolitical* bodies to generate ideas for law reform are, to be blunt, largely a waste of time in relation to criminal law

14 The pathetic history of this is detailed in Goode, above n. 7.

15 See Chapter 4 of this volume (B. Sullivan, ‘The Conduct Element of Offences) at 88.

16 An example is *R. v. Smith* (1826) 2 C & P 449, 172 ER 203.

17 A notable example is the Law Commission for England and Wales, *Legislating the Criminal Code: Offences Against the Person and General Principles* (Law Com No. 218, Cmnd 2370) (London: HMSO, 1993). See Chapter 14 of this volume (C. Clarkson, ‘Recent Law Reform and Codification of the General Principles of Criminal Law in England and Wales: A Tale of Woe’).

18 See, for example, the strong remarks of Lord Ackner in *R. v. Savage* [1992] 1 AC 699, at 752.

19 See discussion above and P.H. Robinson, ‘Are Criminal Codes Irrelevant?’ (1994–5) 68 *Southern California Law Review* 159.

reform for that reason.[20] The Australian Law Reform Commission regularly produces reports of one or two volumes the size or *War and Peace* – and *no-one reads them*. Not only do these agencies not own the politics, they seem to have absolutely no idea of, or wish to, participate in, let alone drive the political process.

But things have moved on. Implementation of Chapter 2 principles by the Commonwealth was the major step, for it generates prosecutions at a far greater rate than the ACT or the Northern Territory. The critical question for the attempt at national harmonisation of the Model Criminal Code, in particular the general principles of the Model Criminal Code, was (and remains) how well it has worked in practice with respect to the courts applying it, and it is to this that we now turn.

JUDICIAL CONSIDERATIONS OF THE GENERAL PRINCIPLES OF THE MODEL CRIMINAL CODE

There has not been a great deal of judicial consideration of the Model Criminal Code in any detail, despite the passage of time since its implementation by some jurisdictions. As the principal author of the general principles of the Model Criminal Code and of various parts of it, and also as an active member of the Model Criminal Code Officers Committee, I have followed the consequences of enactment with interest – and with some knowledge of what was intended. The ensuing discussion comprises a critical account of what the courts have done with those parts of the Model Criminal Code that have been litigated.

The first reported decision in time was straightforward. In *Hann v. DPP (Cth)*,[21] the appellant was charged with importation of prohibited goods, being reckless as to their forbidden character.[22] Gray J. simply and correctly applied the Code definition of recklessness. What he said is worth quoting in full:

> … risk of harm or illegality must be established and that risk must be 'substantial'. The requirement that the risk be substantial gives rise to conceptual problems and may vary depending on the context and gravity of the criminal activity. For example, a finding of recklessness with respect to conduct resulting in death is sufficient to establish the *mens rea* for murder. But recklessness is also an essential element of many trivial offences under federal law. This 'irreducible indeterminacy of meaning' appears to be a deliberate attempt by the legislature to provide flexibility having regard to the vast range of offences covered by the Code.
>
> The phrase 'substantial risk' raises the same issues of indeterminacy as the terms 'likely' and 'probable' in the common law. Academic and judicial commentary on the meaning of these terms is diverse. Criminal law commentators have suggested that the requirement of substantial risk varies in stringency with the gravity of the conduct that gave rise to the risk. Many agree that 'substantial risk' can include 'possible risk' in offences other than murder.

---

20 See, generally, my sometimes derided analysis in 'Complaints Against the Police in Australia: Where We Are Now and What We Might Learn About the Process of Law Reform, with some Comments About the Process of Legal Change' in A. Goldsmith (ed.), *Complaints Against The Police* (Oxford: Clarendon Press, 1991). A general expression of the idea in a favourable light can be found in A.C. Castles, 'The New Principle of Law Reform in Australia' (1977–8) 4 *Dalhousie Law Journal* 3.

21 (2004) 144 A Crim R 534.

22 Under Customs Act 1901 (Cth), s. 233BAB(5).

> There appears to be no case law directly discussing the meaning of 'awareness of substantial risk' in s. 5.4 of the Criminal Code. The term 'substantial risk' does not appear to be defined in Australian legal dictionaries. However, *Carswell's Words and Phrases*, an American legal dictionary, describes the phrase as meaning 'real and apparent on the evidence presented ... not a risk that is without substance or which is fanciful or speculative'. The word 'substantial' has been described in Australian legal dictionaries as 'real or of substance as distinct from ephemeral or nominal'. 'Risk' has been described as 'a possibility, chance or likelihood'.
>
> In order to establish recklessness under the Criminal Code it must also be shown that the defendant was *aware* of the substantial risk. Conscious awareness of risk is required; it is not enough to show that the risk was obvious or well known.
>
> In light of these descriptions, it can be said that 'aware of a substantial risk' in the context of this case conveys the meaning that the appellant was actually aware of the real or substantial possibility that that video disc was within the category of 'tier 2 goods'.[23]

That is precisely what the drafters of the Code intended for the fault element of 'recklessness' to mean.

In *R. v. Saengsai-Or*,[24] the accused was convicted of importing not less than a trafficable quantity of heroin under s. 233(B) of the Customs Act 1901 (Cth). The court neatly defined the Model Criminal Code issue before it as follows:

> The appellant's first ground of appeal raises the question of whether the offence created by s. 233B(1)(b) comprises a physical element of conduct alone (the act of importing the prohibited imports to which the section applies into Australia – in which case the default fault element is intention); or a physical element of conduct (importing the Remy Martin bottles into Australia) and a physical element of circumstance (that the bottles contained prohibited imports to which the section applies). In the latter case, the offence has two fault elements: intention with respect to the act of importing the bottles; and recklessness with respect to the circumstance that the bottles contained prohibited imports to which the section applies.[25]

The distinction between conduct and circumstance or results matters in the Model Criminal Code because it determines whether the prosecution must prove intention or recklessness with respect to a particular physical element of an offence. Bell J. said:

> I consider that the physical element of the offence created by s. 233B(1)(b) is one of conduct: the act of importing into Australia any prohibited import to which the section applies. In respect of this physical element, which consists only of conduct, the provisions of s. 5.6(1) of the *Criminal Code* apply. Intention is the fault element.[26]

Unfortunately, Bell J. misread the Code. The correct position is that recklessness is the fault element. Certainly, the conduct is the importing and that requires intention. However, the fact

23 Above n. 21, at paras. [23]–[27] (footnote references omitted; emphasis in the original).
24 (2004) 147 A Crim R 172.
25 *Ibid.*, at para. [45].
26 *Ibid.*, at para. [72].

that heroin is imported (or, more properly, a prohibited import) is a circumstance and that requires recklessness. This view was affirmed when the offence was moved over to the Commonwealth Criminal Code 1995, during the course of which it was expressly stated that the applicable fault element for this physical element was recklessness.[27]

Bell J. was faced with a problem of legal analysis with which she was not familiar and which she found difficult to comprehend. She solved the problem by extensive reference to the pre-existing common law – notably the Australian High Court decisions in *He Kaw Teh v. R.*[28] and *Kural v. R.*,[29] plus the notion that if the legislature had intended to make proof of the offence less burdensome for the prosecution, it might be expected to have done so in clear terms.[30]

The problem with Bell J.'s reasoning is very apparent to Code lawyers. The High Court has made the general principles clear for quite some time:

> [The provision under consideration] forms part of a code intended to replace the common law, and its language should be construed according to its natural meaning and without any presumption that it was intended to do no more than restate the existing law. It is not the proper course to begin by finding how the law stood before the Code, and then to see if the Code will bear an interpretation which will leave the law unaltered ...[31]

Ian Leader-Elliott said of these two decisions:

> The framers of the *General Principles* could not have wished for a more auspicious launch of their craft on the tides of judicial interpretation. The provisions worked as they were meant to work; there are no surprises in these decisions.[32]

Leader-Elliott differs from me over the nature of the distinction between conduct and circumstance. He takes a more expansive view of the former. In particular, he says:

> The 'intractable difficulties' to which Brennan J. referred have long been apparent in case law on the American *Model Penal Code*. Paul Robinson, with markedly less sympathy than Brennan J. for judges faced with the characterisation problem, refers to their 'improper manipulation' of the fault requirements of offences by 'altering the content of the categories "conduct", "result" and "circumstance"'. Robinson would require courts and legislatures alike to restrict the conduct element of offences to something approaching a muscular contraction. A law against insulting another, for example, would distinguish the act of speaking from the circumstance that the utterance was insulting. The *Guide to Framing Commonwealth Offences* is less doctrinaire. A criminal code that deals with complex human behaviour cannot restrict the vocabulary of prohibition in this way. So, for example, the layered complexities of the verb 'to appropriate' that defines the conduct element in theft cannot be reduced to muscular contractions accompanied by incriminating circumstances and results.[33]

27 Criminal Code Act 1995, s. 307.1 and following provisions.

28 (1985) 157 CLR 523.

29 (1987) 162 CLR 502.

30 *Krakouer v. The Queen* (1998) 194 CLR 202.

31 *Brennan v. The King* (1936) 55 CLR 253, at 263.

32 Case Comment (2005) 29 *Criminal Law Journal* 55.

33 *Ibid.*, at 58, referring to P.H. Robinson, *Structure and Function in Criminal Law* (Oxford: Clarendon Press, 1997).

I will not debate that here, but I do wish to make the point that critics of the Model Criminal Code assert that it has introduced these intransigent difficulties into the criminal law. I disagree. The effect of the Code is to make what has always existed open and transparent. In fact, the Griffith Code has grappled with versions of these issues over the years. Apart from the 'mystical' Western Australian provision that 'An act or omission which renders the person doing the act or making the omission liable to punishment is called an offence',[34] the notable Griffith Code sections are those dealing with mistake and accident. The judicial gloss on those sections of the Code shows, conclusively, that they heavily involve what critic Thomas J. of the Queensland Supreme Court believes to be 'the metaphysics of action'.[35]

In *R. v. JS*,[36] the New South Wales Court of Criminal Appeal was required to decide whether the qualifier 'federal judicial proceedings' appearing in the offence of 'knowing that any book, document, or other thing of any kind, is or may be required in evidence in a judicial proceeding, intentionally destroying it or rendering it illegible or undecipherable or incapable of identification, with intent thereby to prevent it from being used in evidence'[37] was one circumstance or two. This was quite a sterile debate. It made no whit of difference, for the real question was the fault element that attached to that concept. In the course of this complicated case, Spigelman C.J. said:

> Fundamental aspects of the law have been altered by the *Criminal Code* in substantial and indeed critical matters, by the replacement of a body of nuanced case law, which never purported to be comprehensive, with the comparative rigidity of a set of interconnecting verbal formulae which do purport to be comprehensive and which involve the application of a series of cascading provisions, including definitional provisions, expressed in language intended to be capable of only one meaning, which meaning does not necessarily reflect ordinary usage.
>
> Reference to prior case law concerning the element of intent for particular criminal offences is, in my opinion, almost always likely to be a distraction. The changes in the fault requirements implemented by the *Criminal Code*, compared with the former requirements of *mens rea* at common law, are of so fundamental a character that, where one is concerned with fault, it is almost certainly futile to seek to determine what the position was at common law.[38]

Spigelman C.J. was correct on the matter of interpretation[39] and I agree with his result on the question of fault. However, I do take issue with his criticism of the Code. It is arguably the anguished cry of

---

34 Criminal Code Act 1913 (WA), s. 2.

35 *Murray v. The Queen*, above n. 5, is a good example of this with respect to the Griffith Code.

36 (2007) 175 A Crim R 108.

37 Crimes Act 1914 (Cth), s. 39.

38 Above n. 36, at paras. [145]–[146].

39 Later on, he provides a neat summary of the principle (*ibid.*, at para. [149]):

> The general approach to interpretation of the Code is well established. (See *Bank of England v. Vagliano Brothers* [1891] AC 107 esp at 144–145; *Brennan v. The King* (1936) 55 CLR 253 esp at 263; *Robinson v. Canadian Pacific Railway Co* [1892] AC 481 at 481–487; *Vallance v. The Queen* (1961) 108 CLR 56 at 74–76; *R. v. Barlow* (1997) 188 CLR 1 esp at 18–19 and 31–32; 93 A Crim R 113 esp at 125–126 and 136–137.) There may be occasions on which it is appropriate to refer to the common law, e.g. where the Code employs a technical legal term or where an interpretation is well established or in the case of patent ambiguity. (See e.g. *Sungravure Pty Ltd v. Middle East Airlines Airliban SAL* (1975) 134 CLR 1, at 22; *Stuart v. The Queen* (1974) 134 CLR 426 at 437; *Lee v. The Queen* (2007) 170 A Crim R 287, at [19]–[26]).

a devotee of the common law – nuanced indeed – who sees the arid acres of judicial prose confined by statutory words which fence him in. The broader arguments for those who favour codification and regard the common law as a dying art form are beyond the scope of this chapter.

As a matter for the record, it should be said that the criminal law has observed distinctions between acts, circumstances and results for over 100 years. The distinction can be traced back to the championship of Macaulay in his work on the IPC[40] and common law developments from the nineteenth century.[41] While discussing the use of intoxication as a defence in the UK, John Child recently wrote about theft:

> Depending upon the commentator, the 'act' could defensibly be described as the 'body movement of D', the 'appropriation' or even the 'appropriation of another person's property'. Indeed, identical problems arise when trying to identify what the circumstance and result elements are (if there are any). Yet this separation could be essential in order to discover whether D's intoxication is relevant to his or her fault: the more widely the act element is defined, the less likely intoxication will be relevant. Therefore, unless the courts are given an objective technique to distinguish between external elements, policies relying upon the distinction will remain uncertain.[42]

Or maybe no such 'objective technique' exists? Strict certainty may not be possible, with the point being that the distinction is unavoidable.

The Model Criminal Code defence of duress was evaluated in *Oblach v. The Queen*.[43] Section 10.2(2) of the Code states:

> (2) A person carries out conduct under duress if and only if he or she *reasonably believes* that:
> (a) a threat has been made that will be carried out unless an offence is committed; and
> (b) there is no reasonable way that the threat can be rendered ineffective; and
> (c) the conduct is a reasonable response to the threat.[44]

The question was the meaning to be given to 'reasonably believes'. The appellant argued that the phrase meant what the accused himself might reasonably believe in all the circumstances in which he found himself, including consideration of all those personal characteristics of the accused which might have affected his appreciation of those circumstances. In line with this argument, the appellant contended that the phrase did not mean what a reasonable person would have believed.

Spigelman C.J. gave the matter a thorough analysis and concluded:

> The formulation of Mason J. in *Viro*, i.e. 'what the accused himself might reasonably believe in all the circumstances in which he found himself' is helpful. However, in my opinion, at least for [the] purposes of s. 10.2(2) this formulation must be applied to the accused's *objective* circumstances. To introduce a focus on the 'personal characteristics of (the) particular accused' (*Conlon*) or 'the

---

40 Above n. 15.

41 See, for example, *Smith*, above n. 16. A minor example can be found in *Fagan v. Commissioner of Metropolitan Police* [1969] 1 QB 439 and a very serious example can be found in *Airedale National Health Service Trust v. Bland* [1993] AC 789.

42 J. Child, 'Drink, Drugs and Law Reform: A Review of Law Commission Report No. 314' [2009] *Criminal Law Review* 488, at 493.

43 (2005) 158 A Crim R 586.

44 Emphasis added.

circumstances as the accused perceived them to be' (*Hawes*) is to reintroduce a subjective element which is inconsistent with the text of s. 10.2.

Assistance can also be obtained from the formulation in *Zecevic* at 661; 173–174:

> [W]hether the accused believed upon reasonable grounds that it was necessary in self-defence to do what he did.
>
> The two formulations from *Conlon* and *Hawes* divert attention from the objective reasonableness of the grounds into an inquiry about the mind of the accused, encompassing both his or her knowledge and perceptions.
>
> The Code requires that the relevant belief should be objectively justifiable. What is objectively reasonable must remain the primary focus. This focus is, at the least, blurred and perhaps overwhelmed if idiosyncrasy or even perversity in the knowledge or perception of an individual accused is a permissible subject of inquiry. Whatever the authority of *Conlon* or *Hawes* at common law, the approach should not be adopted when interpreting the Code.[45]

There can be little doubt that the thorough and perfectly code-oriented analysis adopted by Spigelman C.J. in this case was correctly done and led to the right result.

Lee v. The Queen[46] is a fascinating case. It concerned the default fault elements applicable to an offence under s. 31(1) of the Financial Transaction Reports Act 1988 (Cth) (FTRA). The offence, which is unfortunately extremely convoluted in style, reads as follows:

> (1) A person commits an offence against this section if:
> (a) the person is a party to 2 or more non-reportable cash transactions; and
> (b) having regard to:
> (i) the manner and form in which the transactions were conducted, including, without limiting the generality of this, all or any of the following:
> (A) the value of the currency involved in each transaction;
> (B) the aggregated value of the transactions;
> (C) the period of time over which the transactions took place;
> (D) the interval of time between any of the transactions;
> (E) the locations at which the transactions took place; and
> (ii) any explanation made by the person as to the manner or form in which the transactions were conducted;
> it would be reasonable to conclude that the person conducted the transactions in that manner or form for the sole or dominant purpose of ensuring, or attempting to ensure, that the currency involved in the transactions was transferred in a manner and form that:
> (iii) would not give rise to a significant cash transaction; or
> (iv) would give rise to exempt cash transactions.

45 Above n. 43, at paras. [57]–[59] (emphasis in the original), citing *Viro v. The Queen* (1978) 141 CLR 88; *Zecevic v. Director of Public Prosecutions (Vic)* (1987) 162 CLR 645, 25 A Crim R 163; *R. v. Conlon* (1993) 69 A Crim R 92; and *R. v. Hawes* (1994) 35 NSWLR 294.

46 (2007) 170 A Crim R 287.

It is necessary to reduce this offence to its essentials. Properly drafted, it would begin by saying:

> Any person who is a party to two or more non-reportable cash transactions and it is reasonable to conclude that the person did so for the sole or dominant purpose of ensuring that the process would (a) not give rise to a significant cash transaction or (b) would give rise to exempt cash transactions is guilty of an offence.

This is a smurfing[47] offence. The essence of the offence is to catch those who try to avoid the cash transactions reports scheme by dealing in amounts of money just under the reporting limit of $10,000.

Ms Lee, on appeal from conviction, raised essentially two issues. The first concerned the burden of proof. The court decided, logically enough, that the legislation meant what it said and that the 'standard of proof' was as stated, namely whether it was 'reasonable to conclude' that the transactions were done for an illicit purpose. The second issue concerned the fault elements of the offence. This led the court to embark on an elements analysis of the offence.

All three members of the court agreed that the offence consisted of two physical elements. The first was conduct which was 'being party to two or more non-reportable cash transactions'. That being conduct, the Code principles assign a default fault element of intention. So much is clear and unarguable. The second physical element is that 'the transactions do not give rise to a significant cash transaction'. All the judges agreed that that was a result. However, Sully J., dissenting, thought that the applicable fault element for this was intention. He said:

> The fault element for the physical element 1.2 is intention: that is to say, a meaning to bring about that result or an awareness that the result will occur in the ordinary course of events.[48]

It is far from clear how Sully J. came to that conclusion.

Spigelman C.J., with whom the other judges concurred, disagreed, saying:

> In my opinion, the element of the offence encompassed by the words 'sole or dominant purpose' is quite distinct from the 'result', identified above as the second physical element, and is not itself properly characterised as a 'physical element' at all.
>
> The word 'circumstance', referring to an aspect of either 'conduct' or the 'result of conduct', within the meaning of s. 4.1(1)(c) of the Code, is capable of extending to virtually any word of the English language in which an offence is expressed. Nevertheless, the structure of the Code distinguishes between 'physical elements' and 'fault elements'. Where a matter clearly involves an aspect of conduct which, in normal parlance, would be understood to involve fault on the part of the alleged perpetrator of an offence then, in my opinion, the matter should be classified as a 'fault element', rather than be swept up within the breadth of the word 'circumstance', as a physical element.

47 See B. Fisse and D. Fraser, 'Smurfing: Rethinking the Structured Transaction Provisions of the Cash Transaction Reports Act' in B. Fisse, D. Fraser and G. Coss (eds), *The Money Trail* (Sydney: Law Book Company, 1992).

48 Above n. 46, at para. [66].

> The words 'sole or dominant purpose' in s. 31(1)(b) of the FTRA refer, in my opinion, to the actuating purpose of the conduct, rather than to the 'result' of the conduct. An actuating purpose would, in ordinary discourse, be regarded as indicating 'fault' of itself.[49]

Hence, in the Chief Justice's view, 'sole or dominant purpose' is the fault element itself. Accordingly, there is no need to resort to the default fault elements.

Spigelman C.J. was quite right to read the statute in this way. The default fault elements were never intended to operate as a straitjacket. The legislature has specified what has to be proved to the jury. The Model Criminal Code default fault elements apply only if something has been left unsaid – and nothing had. The Code worked as intended by its drafters.

In *Crowther v. Sala*,[50] Crowther was charged with the Commonwealth offence of making offensive telephone calls under s. 474.17(1)(b) of the Criminal Code (Cth). The offence reads:

> (1) A person is guilty of an offence if:
> (a) the person uses a carriage service; and
> (b) the person does so in a way (whether by the method of use or the content of a communication, or both) that reasonable persons would regard as being, in all the circumstances, menacing, harassing or offensive.
> Penalty: Imprisonment for 3 years.

The defence argued that the words uttered were not intended to be menacing. Again, the court hearing the appeal was divided. McMurdo J., with whom Muir J. agreed, held that the fact that reasonable people would regard the way in which the telephone was used as menacing was a fact which was a physical element of the offence. He held that it was a circumstance. That is correct, as it describes the kind of communication involved. That being so, he went on to hold that there must be a fault element which is not provided and, accordingly, resort had to be made to the default fault element for circumstances under the Model Criminal Code, which is recklessness. Therefore:

> … what had to be proved in this case was that the applicant was at least aware of a substantial risk that a reasonable person would regard her conduct as menacing and that it was unjustifiable to take that risk.[51]

McMurdo J.'s reasoning is correct and the result is right.

Williams J.A. dissented, saying:

> The only rational conclusion is that, by providing that the test is whether or not reasonable persons would regard the conduct as menacing, the legislature has impliedly provided that the only fault elements for the offence in the present context are with respect to the use of the carriage service and the uttering of the words. If the relevant physical and fault elements are established, and reasonable persons would in the circumstances regard the conduct in question as menacing, the offence is established.[52]

---

49 *Ibid.*, at paras. [8]–[10].
50 (2007) 170 A Crim R 389.
51 *Ibid.*, at para. [45].
52 *Ibid.*, at para. [26].

This reasoning is incorrect because it ignores the entire purpose of the Code scheme of default fault elements. I will not rehearse the matter in detail here. In brief, the common law is characterised on this issue of 'implied fault' by a maze of poorly reasoned, inconsistent and *ad hoc* decisions wildly attempting, on the one hand, to divine the intention of Parliament (which had obviously given no thought to the issue) and, on the other hand, to arrive at a just and fair result. This was all beautifully described by Jordan C.J. many years ago:

> A fertile field of litigation has been created; multitudes of reported cases have come into existence, many of them irreconcilable, in which the common law rule has been treated as excluded or not excluded upon judge-made indicia derived from cases in which there has been a difference of opinion as to so-called necessary implications; and no-one can now be reasonably sure of the effect of a penal statute until it has been tested by prosecutions.[53]

The aim of having the default fault elements in the Model Criminal Code was to eliminate this sorry branch of the criminal law with default rules that came into effect when Parliament did not speak on the subject or – to put it in the terms used by Williams J.A. – to eliminate the fiction of implied intention. Thus, Williams J.A. missed the point.

In *Ansari v. The Queen*,[54] the appellants had been convicted of two counts of conspiracy to deal with money where they were reckless as to the fact that the money would become an instrument of crime. The issue before the court was whether it was possible under the Criminal Code (Cth) to charge a person with conspiracy to commit an offence which had recklessness as one of its fault elements. The leading judgment was given by Howie J. Hislop J. and Simpson J. concurred with some additional remarks. In relation to the analysis of the (different) money-laundering offence itself, Howie J. said:

> The elements of the offence under s. 400.3(2) that it was alleged that the appellants conspired to commit are therefore: the appellants agreed (a) to deal with money (b) to the value of $1 million or more (c) where there was a risk that the money would become an instrument of crime and (d) where they were reckless as to that risk. Applying the provisions of Chapter 2 of the Code to these elements: (a) above is a physical element of conduct, and (b), and (c) are physical elements of circumstance. The fault element for physical element (a) is intention by reason of s. 5.6(1). Absolute liability applies to the circumstance in (b) by reason of s. 400.3(4). It was therefore not necessary for the Crown to prove that either of the appellants knew of the value of the money. The fault element for physical element (c) is contained in element (d). It should be noted that even had (d) not existed, the default element for a physical element of circumstance is recklessness under s. 5.6(2).[55]

Hence, the fault element in question for the substantive offence was recklessness that the money was or would become an instrument of crime. But what about the fault element for conspiracy to commit that offence? Howie J. dealt with this question as follows:

> Therefore s. 11.5(1) contains a single physical element of conduct being to enter into the proscribed agreement. There is no fault element stated in s. 11.5(1), therefore, applying s. 5.6(1), the default

53 *R. v. Turnbull* (1944) 44 SR (NSW) 108, at 110.
54 (2007) 173 A Crim R 112.
55 *Ibid.*, at para. [55].

fault element for a physical element of conduct is intention. Applying the definition of 'intention' in s. 5.2(1) of the Code, the person must mean to enter into such an agreement.

This is precisely what MCCOC intended …

In my opinion the conspiracy alleged in each of the charges was not bad at law. There is nothing in the Code that indicates that a person cannot conspire to commit an offence of which the mental element is recklessness and there is no reason otherwise to impose such a restriction on the offence. There are two reasons for reaching that conclusion. Firstly the agreement entered into may be that another person will carry out the conduct. Provided that the conspirators know of all the facts that would make the conduct of the third party criminal, it would not matter that the person carrying out the conduct was committing an offence by acting recklessly.

Secondly recklessness under the Code can be proved by both intention and knowledge. Section 5.4(4) provides:

(4) If recklessness is a fault element for a physical element of an offence, proof of intention, knowledge or recklessness will satisfy that fault element.

Therefore, if the conspirators intended that they would carry out the conduct knowing all the facts that made that conduct criminal it would not matter that the offence arising from that conduct was one for which the fault element was recklessness.

It is the second reason that applies in the present case. Provided that the Crown was intending to prove as against the appellants that they knew that there was a risk that the money they dealt with would become an instrument of crime, that is that they knew of all the facts that made their dealing with the money criminal conduct, there was no impediment to the prosecution proving the offences charged.[56]

This is exactly as the Model Criminal Code intended. It is the right result reached on impeccable Code reasoning. This is not surprising for, in a former incarnation, Howie J. had chaired the Model Criminal Code Officers Committee for a number of years, becoming, in the process, an expert in analysing the Code's provisions on fault.

The mightiest test for the Model Criminal Code principles came with the decision of the Australian High Court in *The Queen v. Tang*.[57] The case involved a prosecution for sex slavery. It was a variation on the common story of poor Asian women brought to Australia on the promise of employment but being forced by circumstances to work off the so-called cost of their passage by the provision of sexual services. The defendant was convicted of five offences of intentionally possessing a slave and five offences of intentionally exercising over a slave a power attaching to the right of ownership, namely the power to use, which was contrary to s. 270.3(1)(a) of the Criminal Code (Cth). The offence reads:

(1) A person who, whether within or outside Australia, intentionally:

(a) possesses a slave or exercises over a slave any of the other powers attaching to the right of ownership; or

56 *Ibid.*, at paras. [63]–[64], [87]–[89].

57 (2008) 187 A Crim R 252.

> (b) engages in slave trading; or
> (c) enters into any commercial transaction involving a slave; or
> (d) exercises control or direction over, or provides finance for:
> (i) any act of slave trading; or
> (ii) any commercial transaction involving a slave;
>
> is guilty of an offence.
> Penalty: Imprisonment for 25 years.

The problem involving Model Criminal Code analysis arose because Eames J.A. in the Court of Appeal held that the prosecution had to prove not only that the defendant intentionally possessed and used the victims as slaves but also that the defendant knew or believed that she was possessing and using the victims as mere property – that is, that the fault element extended to the *source of the power* to control the victims.

Gleeson C.J. gave the majority judgment on this issue, with Hayne J. concurring with separate reasons. Gummow, Heydon, Crennan and Kiefel JJ. agreed with both judgments, while Kirby J. dissented.

Element analysis requires that one begin by setting out the statutory elements of the offence. For the sake of the argument, let us take the possession offence. The elements provided were: (a) intentionally; (b) possessing; (c) a slave. Element (a) is a fault element, while element (b) is a physical element involving conduct that is a state of affairs. Element (c) is a circumstance. Had element (a) been left out, the construction of this offence would have been simple. Under s. 5.6(1) of the Code, the default fault element for conduct is intention and the default fault element for circumstance is recklessness. Therefore, the prosecution would have to prove that the defendant possessed a slave, intending to possess that person and being reckless as to whether or not she was a slave. However, given that the word 'intentionally' is present in the offence definition, does that mean that the prosecution had to prove that the defendant intended that the person be a slave? Slavery is defined in the legislation as 'the condition of a person over whom any or all of the powers attaching to the right of ownership are exercised'. But it was conceded by all parties that the prosecution did not have to prove that the defendant knew that the victim was *in law* a slave. The case raised the following two questions:

(1) what significance, if any, does the addition of the word 'intentionally' (element (a)) have?; and
(2) what exactly does it mean to say that the defendant intends (or is reckless) to the victim being a slave?

The answers to these questions do not lie in element analysis. That merely gets one to the point of asking the right questions. The answers to these right questions lie in the construction of the slavery offence(s) as statutory offences in the context of a codified system.

For Gleeson C.J. and the majority, the answer to question (1) was that it had no significance. It merely declared what s. 5.6(1) would otherwise say.[58] Intention qualifies the conduct, namely of possession. For Kirby J, dissenting, the answer was that it had to have some significance. In his view, the rules of statutory interpretation were that Parliament does not say something duplicatory.

58 *Ibid.*, at paras. [47]–[49]. Hayne J. agreed at paras. [133]–[134].

The conscious addition of the word 'intention' had to mean something. Therefore, it had to mean that the defendant must be shown to have intended the slavery circumstance.[59]

The majority do not mention recklessness as to the circumstance. For them, there was no fault element attaching to that circumstance at all. Gleeson C.J. said:

> It is agreed on all sides that it was unnecessary for the prosecution to prove that the respondent knew or believed that the complainant was a slave, or even that she knew what a slave was. ...
>
> Insofar as a state of knowledge or belief is factually relevant to intention as the fault element of the offence, it is knowledge or belief about the facts relevant to possession or using, and knowledge or belief about the facts which determine the existence of the condition described in s. 270.1. This is a condition that results from the exercise of certain powers. Whether the powers that are exercised over a person are 'any or all of the powers attaching to the right of ownership' is for a jury to decide in the light of a judge's directions as to the nature and extent of the powers that are capable of satisfying that description. This is not to ignore the word 'intentionally' in s. 270.3(1). Rather, it involves no more than the common exercise of relating the fault element to the physical elements of the offence.[60]

This ruling is astonishing for ignoring the whole point of default fault elements. While there need not have to be proof of an intention with respect to, or knowledge of, the legal status of slave, there could be an intention to exercise any or all of the powers attaching to the right of ownership. The fault element for that circumstance could be intention or recklessness, depending on the view one takes of question (1).

Kirby J. fared no better in terms of elements analysis on question (1). He missed the point that default fault elements are just that – defaults. They are to be used when Parliament does not specify a fault element. Parliament did specify for the offence under consideration, making the defaults irrelevant. It is a distinct question of interpretation of the offence itself as to the extent to which the added word 'intentionally' qualifies all or some of the physical elements of the offence.

In sum, both the majority and the dissenter mistakenly applied element analysis.

In *R. v. Campbell*,[61] the appellant was convicted of importing a commercial quantity of a border-controlled precursor. The chemical was hidden inside furniture imported by the appellant. The appellant denied that she intended to import the chemical and denied any knowledge that the chemical was in the furniture. A key question in the case was the meaning of the physical element of the offence as constituted by the word 'imports'. The court decided that this occurred when the chemicals arrived in Australia from abroad and were delivered to a location, which resulted in the goods remaining in Australia. Nothing turns on that decision from the point of view of the Model Criminal Code as it was a matter of interpreting the transition of the importing offences from the old Customs Act structure to the new Criminal Code structure.

The Model Criminal Code general principles question arose in this way. It was clear on all sides that the prosecution had to prove that the appellant intended to import the chemicals and, for that to happen, there had to be proof that the appellant knew that the containers contained the chemicals. The case for the appellant was that she did not know but, even if she did, she did not know until after the importation was complete. Accordingly, the appellant claimed that the fault element did

59 *Ibid.*, at paras. [93], [102]–[103].

60 *Ibid.*, at paras. [48]–[49]. Hayne J. agreed at paras. [133]–[134].

61 (2008) 73 NSWLR 272.

not coincide (or concur) with the physical element. This is commonly known and referred to as the *Thabo Meli* problem, after the case in which it first received attention.[62] The attending principle is that the defendant cannot be convicted of an offence unless the fault elements of the offence are present at the same time that the physical elements of the offence are present. A question the court in *Campbell* had to answer was whether this principle was a part of the general principles of the Code. Spigelman C.J. and Weinberg A.J.A., in separate judgments,[63] held that it was (although it appears that no party was willing to argue that it was not). The reasoning involved is best illustrated by this passage from the judgment of Spigelman C.J.:

> Pursuant to s. 3.2(b) of the Code, 'in respect of each ... physical element' the specified fault element 'for' each physical element must be proved. As Mr Game submitted, the fault element must exist at the time of the commission of, or existence of, the physical element to which it attaches.[64]

The Model Criminal Code may be criticised for not addressing this issue directly, but the correct result has been reached by necessary implication from the terms of the Code itself. However, it would not be possible, necessary or desirable for the Code to try to solve the more difficult problem that lies at the heart of every so-called *Thabo Meli* problem – that is, the scope of the physical elements of the offence and, in particular, whether the particular crime was committed in one or more than one transaction.[65] That depends not on general principles, but on the interpretation of the particular offence in question.[66]

The attempt provisions of the general principles were examined in *Onuorah v. The Queen*.[67] This case concerned what is commonly referred to as a 'controlled importation' of, in this instance, a marketable quantity of cocaine. The Australian Federal Police substituted another substance for the contents of the parcel and then tried to get the appellant to collect it. After some gyrations, this was done. The charge was attempting to possess a marketable quantity of a border-controlled drug which had been unlawfully imported.

The defence was that the offence (and hence the attempt to commit the offence) could not be made out because there had never been an importation of a drug, since the cocaine had been removed by the Venezuelan authorities in Venezuela.[68] Consequently, a legal element of the principal offence never existed. In conventional common law terms, this was the argument that an attempt charged could not succeed because of 'legal impossibility'.[69] The high-water mark of this

---

62 *Thabo Meli v. The Queen* [1954] 1 WLR 228; [1954] 1 All ER 373.

63 Simpson J. concurring.

64 Above n. 61, at para. [44].

65 The case most commonly cited for this is *R. v. Church* [1966] 1 QB 59. See also the Canadian jurisprudence on the subject: *R. v. Cooper* [1993] 1 SCR 146; *R. v. Frizzell* (1993) 81 CCC (3d) 463; *R. v. Talbot* (2007) 217 CCC (3d) 415; *R. v. Marriott* (2007) 215 Man R (2d) 143; *R. v. Stewart* (2005) 78 OR (3d) 744.

66 The judgment of Weinberg A.J.A. contains a critique of the Model Criminal Code general principles for confining its accomplice liability provisions to traditional accomplice liability and not including general liability for being 'knowingly involved' in the commission of an offence. This is not really fair. The device of 'knowingly involved' was only used in the Commonwealth Customs Act offences concerning serious drugs and was clearly used as an exceptional device to widen the net to capture anyone remotely associated with the evil drug trade.

67 [2009] NSWCCA 238.

68 Citing *R. v. Barbouttis* (1995) 37 NSWLR 256 and distinguishing *R. v. Mai* (1992) 26 NSWLR 371.

69 See further Chapter 6 of this volume (W. Chan, 'Abetment, Criminal Conspiracy and Attempt').

argument was the decision in *Haughton v. Smith*.[70] However, beginning with *Britten v. Alpogut*,[71] Australian courts have rejected the argument that legal impossibility prevented a charge of attempt (or, for that matter, conspiracy).

A specially-convened bench of the New South Wales Court of Criminal Appeal discussed the relevant Australian common law case law in *Onuorah*.[72] The only inconvenient decision was *R. v. Barbouttis*,[73] which was distinguished as being concerned with the procedural niceties of pleading particulars rather than the substance of the attempt offence. Although Hodgson J.A. (for the Court) spent most of the judgment discussing the common law, the central point should have been the Model Criminal Code, because this was a Code charge. Eventually, almost as an afterthought, Hodgson J.A. got to it by saying:

> In my opinion, the effect of s. 11.1(2), (3) and (4)(a) [of the Model Criminal Code] is no different from that of the general law, as expounded in the cases and judgments referred to above which I consider to be correct.[74]

That is correct. Section 11.1(4)(a) provides that 'a person may be found guilty even if: (a) committing the offence attempted is impossible'. The aim of that provision was to codify the Australian common law. Hodgson J.A. did not refer to the relevant report on the matter but, had he done so, he would have found this bald statement:

> The Committee took the view that impossibility arising by reason of matters of fact or law should no longer be a bar to conviction. The Committee agreed with the Gibbs Committee proposed s. 7C(2).[75]

Hodgson J.A. was sidetracked by s. 11.1(6), which states that:

> Any defences, procedures, limitations or qualifying provisions that apply to an offence apply also to the offence of attempting to commit that offence.

This was meant to be straightforward in its meaning and application. Suppose, for example, that a prosecution for an offence was contingent on the consent of the Attorney-General. Such a condition is not uncommon. If some such condition applies to the substantive offence, it should apply to a charge of an attempt to commit that offence. This much is obvious. But lawyers must test the limits of common sense. A publication of the Commonwealth Attorney-General's Department, entitled *The Commonwealth Criminal Code: A Guide for Practitioners*, states that:

---

70 [1975] AC 476. The companion decision is *Anderton v. Ryan* [1985] AC 560.

71 [1987] VR 929. There is an interminable literature and common law sequence on this issue. In my jurisdiction, the leading decision is *R. v. Irwin* (2006) 94 SASR 480 and it comes to the same conclusion.

72 Above n. 67.

73 Above n. 68.

74 Above n. 67, at para. [33]. The references are to the general attempt provisions of the Criminal Code 1995 (Cth) which, in turn, are (mostly) the provisions of the Model Criminal Code.

75 Criminal Law Officers Committee of the Standing Committee of Attorneys-General, *Model Criminal Code, Report, Chapters 1 and 2, General Principles of Criminal Responsibility* (1992) (available online at http://www.scag.gov.au/lawlink/SCAG/ll_scag.nsf/vwFiles/MCLOC_MCC_Chapter_1_and_2_Report.pdf/$file/MCLOC_MCC_Chapter_1_and_2_Report.pdf, last accessed 20 February 2011) 83.

> … conviction of the principal offence requires proof that the drug was 'imported into Australia in contravention of this Act'. That limitation or qualification on liability for the principal offence should equally apply to the attempt so as to bar the possibility of conviction. The legislative rationale for the exception is the same, whether the attempt or completed offence is in issue.[76]

This argument ignores the plain words and the intention of the Code provision. The Model Criminal Code commentary[77] (not referred to by either the court or the above-mentioned publication) says:

> The Code provides that special rules applicable to the completed offence should also apply to the attempt. The word 'defences' is added to take account of *Beckwith* (1976) 135 CLR 569.

The specially-convened bench of the New South Wales Court of Criminal Appeal reached the correct result by mere assertion. Hodgson J.A. said:

> In my opinion, generally it could not: those expressions in s. 11.1(6) are apt to refer to matters extrinsic to the elements of the offence, rather than to the requirement on the prosecution to prove all the elements of the offence.[78]

Interestingly, given the commentary of the Model Criminal Code and the failure of Hodgson J.A. to refer to it, he then discusses *Beckwith* at length. That was, indeed, the issue at hand.[79]

While the result reached was entirely correct, the reasoning style was less than optimal. A Code lawyer starts with the Code and then tries to determine what it means. Hodgson J.A. started with the common law (which no longer applied) and then proceeded to see if the Code used it. It is plain that that is an incorrect way of approaching a Code problem.

White v. Patterson[80] was concerned with the meaning of criminal negligence in the general principles (Chapter 2) part of the Model Criminal Code. The respondent was charged under s. 38CA(1) of the Great Barrier Reef Marine Park Act 1975 (Cth) with the summary offence of negligently using a Marine National Park Zone of the Great Barrier Reef Marine Park for the purpose of fishing. Because his GPS was unserviceable, the respondent had no way of knowing whether the effect of wind and/or current or some deviation from the plotted course, caused by human error, might have taken him across the boundary and into the zone. His belief that he had not entered the zone was based upon the fact that 'three boats were fishing there'. He was convicted at trial, but that conviction was overturned on appeal.

On further appeal, the Court of Appeal held that the judge below had made two errors. The first was to treat the qualification on the fault element of criminal negligence, namely that the

---

76 I. Leader-Elliott, *The Commonwealth Criminal Code: A Guide for Practitioners* (Canberra: Commonwealth Attorney-General's Department, 2002) 243.

77 Above n. 75, at 85.

78 Above n. 67, at para. [35].

79 Hodgson J.A. then spent considerable time on the provision in s. 307.6(5) which says that the offence 'does not apply' if 'the person proves he or she did not know that the border controlled drug … was unlawfully imported'. His Honour held that this was a 'defence' within the meaning of s. 11.1(6) and that it would therefore apply if there was a charge of attempting to commit an offence against s. 307.6. That is plainly right. But for reasons that His Honour gives, the point is irrelevant, mostly because that was not what the appellant in this case was asserting.

80 [2009] QCA 320.

conduct warranted criminal punishment, as if it were a separate element of the fault element. It is not. As Chesterman J.A. explained:

> The grammatical structure of the section opposes any tendency to read the concluding phrase as a separate element or aspect of the definition of negligence. The section defines a compendium: it does not describe two (and certainly not three) elements. Negligence, for the purposes of the Code, is compendiously a departure from the relevant norm of carefulness creating a risk of such magnitude that the physical element of an offence would exist so that the conduct merits punishment. An overall assessment is called for, not a separate analysis of distinct elements though, of course, regard must be had to the whole description of negligence.[81]

The second error was to treat the qualification as if it referred to the same degree of criminal negligence whatever the nature and seriousness of the offence to which it applies. It does not work that way. In the words of Chesterman J.A.:

> It is, I think, clear from the terms of the section that no universal norm of criminality was intended. The inquiry in each case is one of relativity: is the conduct in question such that it merits punishment for the offence charged? Just as there are degrees of seriousness of criminal offences so there are degrees of blameworthiness or culpability.
>
> The words, 'for the offence', set the reference for the inquiry whether the conduct merits punishment. The inquiry is not a general one whether, in the abstract, conduct merits criminal punishment or is such as to depict the person whose conduct is in question a criminal. The inquiry is whether the conduct is such as to merit punishment for the particular offence.[82]

Again, the appellate court had the correct interpretation.

REVIEW AND REFORM

What is now the Model Criminal Law Officers Committee has two specific matters under review. Both relate to the part of the Model Criminal Code dealing with the general principles of criminal responsibility. The first concerns the matter of ulterior intent and the second of common intention.

Ulterior Intent

It has been suggested that the Model Criminal Code deals inadequately with what is known as 'ulterior intent' and that, as a result, there are problems with the application of the Code. The issue arises in this way. The Code is clear that a fault element question must be asked for each physical element of an offence. But the reverse is not true. If the fault element question has to be asked for each physical element, it does not follow that for each fault element there must be a physical element. In other words, a fault element can exist by itself. Consider the following example:

81 *Ibid.*, at para. [31].

82 *Ibid.*, at paras. [38]–[39].

> 31. Possession of object with intent to kill or cause serious harm
> (1) A person who, without lawful excuse, has the custody or control of an object that the person intends to use, or to cause or permit another to use –
> (a) to kill, or to endanger the life of, another; or
> (b) to cause serious harm to another,
> shall be guilty of an indictable offence and liable to be imprisoned for a term not exceeding 10 years.

This is a very serious offence. In pared-down terms, the elements of the offence are (a) custody or control (possession)[83] of (b) an object,[84] (c) intending to use it, etc., to kill or cause serious harm. Custody and control (possession) is a physical element. So is the 'object'. But the third specified element is a fault element with no attached physical element. The 'with intention to' formula is concerned with a situation where it is not necessary to prove that (in this case) death or serious harm happened at all. It suffices if the defendant intended that it would. This formula is not uncommon in very serious offences, but is rare in lesser offences. It may specify recklessness (for example) as well, and often does.

This 'hanging' fault element is often called 'ulterior intent' (even though it is not restricted to intention at all) because it comprises a fault element with no physical element.[85] There is a problem with the Model Criminal Code's handling of this form of fault. While the Code definitions of intention and recklessness are expressed to be 'with respect to' physical elements, it is unclear whether or not an ulterior intention is an intention 'with respect to' any physical element at all. It is submitted that the Code should be amended so that the definition of all default fault elements encompasses the situation where the fault element does not attach directly to any physical element.

Common Intention

Some dispute has arisen over the scope of the doctrine of common intention as a form of complicity in the Model Criminal Code. It seems clear that the Commonwealth version is less generous to the prosecution than the common law,[86] but it is less than clear that that is also the case for the Code provisions.[87] The Commonwealth government has a bill to rectify this for its version of the Code.[88] Regrettably, there has been less than adequate consultation about whether this is the most desirable form the provision should take.

---

83 This comprises conduct.

84 This comprises circumstances.

85 So far as recent history is concerned, the label 'ulterior intent' appears to have been invented by Lord Simon of Glaisdale in *R. v. Morgan* [1976] AC 182.

86 See further Chapter 7 of this volume (M. Hor, 'Vicarious Liability').

87 See, in general, S. Gray '"I Didn't Know, I Wasn't There": Common Purpose and the Liability of Accessories to Crime' (1999) 23 *Criminal Law Journal* 201, 216–17.

88 Crimes Legislation Amendment (Serious and Organised Crime) Bill 2009.

Other Issues

Leader-Elliott has made a number of suggestions for reform of the general provisions of the Model Criminal Code.[89] The major ones include:

- a considerable normative widening of the defence of mistake of law;
- moving *Ghosh* dishonesty (used in offence against interests in property) to Chapter 2 (on general principles);
- extending the definition of 'fault elements' to include failure to meet a standard of conduct; and
- amending the provisions of corporate criminal responsibility to include a more varied range of fault elements.

Some of these suggestions relate to supposed errors and others are original suggestions for reform such as might arise in any criminal jurisdiction from time to time.

CONCLUSION

The general principles of the Australian Model Criminal Code have now attracted a body of case law. Mostly, the principles have worked as intended. Common law judges have struggled with abandoning their common law reasoning for Code reasoning.[90] There have been mistaken judicial analyses but no disasters, at least certainly not in result.

Leader-Elliott has made the following observation in a recent review of the operation of the Model Criminal Code:

> After warning of the danger of interpretative drift in the introductory remarks to its report, Sir John Smith's Committee concluded with the suggestion that the Law Commission establish a permanent supervisory body to keep the general principles in good repair. It is a suggestion that deserves serious consideration in Australia. For the moment, however, there is an immediate need for a reference for emerging problems in Chapter 2 jurisprudence to an expert committee for review.[91]

---

89 I. Leader-Elliott, 'The Australian Criminal Code: Time For Some Changes' (2009) 37 *Federal Law Review* 205.

90 An outstanding example of this is to be found in the magistrate's reasoning that was overturned in *DPP (Cth) v. Neamati* [2007] NSWSC 746. The appellate court at para. [16] said:

> With the greatest respect to the Magistrate I do not understand how a common law case concerned with the construction of a statutory offence could assist her in the task of considering the evidence adduced by the prosecution in respect of an element of an offence under the Code. This was not a case of having to construe a provision of the Code that was ambiguous or where some doubt was raised as to what were the elements of the offence. Nor did the definition of 'knowledge' in the Code present any difficulty. Even had the Magistrate interpreted the structure of the offence in a manner different to the way that I have done, it could not have made the slightest difference having regard to the simple issue that was before her.

91 Leader-Elliott, above n. 89, at 233, citing the Law Commission for England and Wales, *Criminal Law: Codification of the Criminal Law – A Report to the Law Commission* (Law Com No. 143) (London: HSMO, 1985).

It should be clear by now that I do not believe that it can be demonstrated that there are emerging problems in Chapter 2 jurisprudence. However, I do believe that it is essential for a code to be under continuing expert review. It is absolutely vital for a modern criminal code to be a living thing, which is subject to regular and frequent review and, if necessary, reform. The days are long gone, if they ever existed, when a criminal code could be set in stone and handed down from the mountain to last forever. The faults of the late nineteenth-century codes in this respect have been laid bare by the pace of change in the late twentieth century and the start of the twenty-first century. This is as true of the Model Criminal Code as it is of any other statutory instrument. If it is not reviewed, it will cease to have modern (and model) relevance. A review process of the Model Criminal Code is underway, but regular and systematic review is necessary, as some form of adjunct to legislative processes, that addresses new situations, gaps and the effects of judicial interpretation.[92]

The question then arises as to how more precisely this regular and systematic review process is to be done. All code systems that have arisen from the British common law have, without exception, failed in this. It is commonly said that this is a task for which law reform commissions are well suited to undertake. The first problem with this answer is that in those codified systems that have law reform commissions, the success rate of getting the commission's recommendations enacted has been dismal. The second problem is that, even if there were a law reform commission in a codified system that set out to do the task systematically and on an ongoing basis, there is no guarantee that governments would, systematically and on an ongoing basis, accept recommendations made by law reform commissions on this (or any other) topic. All experience suggests otherwise.[93]

I have suggested elsewhere that one of the principal benefits of a criminal code is that, in contrast to the common law, it is democratically made and amended.[94] I suggest now that this is also true of its review and reformulation. This leads me to question the idea that the appeal to a law reform commission is an appeal to the interpretative powers of judges and academics. Markus Dubber has said:

> The age of the common penal law is over. Penal law now is made in codes by legislators, not in court opinions by judges. To deserve a say in penal legislation, American penal law scholars must become experts in penal legislation. And to have the ear of legislators, American penal law scholars must address legislators, not judges.[95]

In agreement with this contention, I suggest that the remedy may well lie in the continual review and oversight of the code by a standing committee of the jurisdictional legislature devoted to the task. This body gives the legislators and the legislature a continuing stake in the venture – one which they do not have at present.

Something similar was contemplated by Macaulay. The general explanation to his 1838 draft says:

92 See also Chapter 1 of this volume (S. Yeo and B. Wright, 'Revitalising Macaulay's Indian Penal Code').

93 For a similar lack of success by the Law Commission for England and Wales, see Chapter 14 of this volume, above n. 17.

94 Goode, above n. 9, at 14–16.

95 M.D. Dubber, 'Reforming American Penal Law' (1999–2000) 90 *Journal of Criminal Law and Criminology* 49, 50.

> Every judge of every rank whose duty it is to administer the law as contained in the Code should be enjoined to report to his official superiors every doubt which he may entertain as to any question of construction which may have arisen in his Court. Of these doubts all which are not obviously unreasonable ought to be periodically reported by the highest judicial authorities to the legislature. All the questions thus reported to the Government might with advantage be referred for examination to the Law Commission, if that Commission be a permanent body.[96]

Or, as I would argue, dealt with by a parliamentary committee. Some such mechanism is worth trying.

96 T.B. Macaulay, J.M. Macleod, G.W. Anderson and F. Millett, *A Penal Code Prepared by the Indian Law Commissioners* (London: Pelham Richardson, 1838) (reprinted by the Lawbook Exchange Ltd, 2002).

Chapter 14

Recent Law Reform and Codification of the General Principles of Criminal Law in England and Wales: A Tale of Woe

Chris Clarkson

THE DEATH OF THE MODERN CODIFICATION PROJECT

The nineteenth-century efforts to codify the criminal law of England and Wales, culminating in James Fitzjames Stephen's draft English Code, 1878–80, are surveyed elsewhere in this volume.[1] Only the recent efforts to achieve English codification are examined here.

In 1965 the Law Commission was established and mandated to review the law of England and Wales 'with a view to its systematic development and reform, including in particular the codification of such law, the elimination of anomalies ... the reduction of the number of separate enactments and generally the simplification and modernisation of the law'.[2] In 1968 it announced its objective of a programme of comprehensive examination of the law that would lead to codification of the criminal law.[3] The main arguments in favour of codification were (and are): (i) accessibility of the law; (ii) comprehensibility; (iii) consistency; (iv) certainty; (v) constitutional arguments concerning due process and fair warning, making a symbolic statement about the constitutional relationship between Parliament and the courts, and synthesising the criminal law's often conflicting aims of social protection and crime prevention with concern for legality and due process.[4] To these arguments one can now add the need to ensure that the law is compatible with the European Convention on Human Rights (ECHR).[5]

Some of the Law Commission's earlier reports on specific offences did lead to modernising legislation.[6] The project for a comprehensive code, including the general principles of criminal law, commenced in the early 1980s when a team of academics, chaired by Professor Sir John Smith, submitted a report to the Law Commission which the Commission published, with its own

1 Chapter 2 of this volume (B. Wright, 'Macaulay's Indian Penal Code: Historical Context and Originating Principles') at 29–31.

2 Law Commissions Act 1965 (Chapter 22) (UK), s. 3(1).

3 Law Commission for England and Wales, *Second Programme of Law Reform* (Law Com. No. 14) (London: HMSO, 1968) Item XVIII.

4 Law Commission for England and Wales, *Criminal Law: A Criminal Code for England and Wales* (Law Com. No. 177) (London: HMSO, 1989) paras. [2.1]–[2.11]; A.T.H. Smith, 'Codification of the Criminal Law: (1) The Case for a Code' [1986] *Criminal Law Review* 285. See also Chapter 1 of this volume (S. Yeo and B. Wright, 'Revitalising Macaulay's Indian Penal Code') at 4–6.

5 See, generally, M. Arden, 'Criminal Law at the Crossroads: The Impact of Human Rights from the Law Commission's Perspective and the Need for a Code' [1999] *Criminal Law Review* 439.

6 For example, the Criminal Damage Act 1971 (Chapter 48), the Forgery and Counterfeiting Act 1981 (Chapter 45), the Criminal Attempts Act 1981 (Chapter 47) and the Public Order Act 1986 (Chapter 64).

introduction, in 1985.[7] This was followed in 1989 by a revised and expanded draft Criminal Code[8] which covered both the general principles of criminal liability and many (but not all) specific offences. Rather than engaging in extensive law reform, the Code was largely a restatement of the law except: (i) where there were inconsistencies in the law; (ii) where there were 'rules of an arbitrary nature fulfilling no rational purpose and explicable, if at all, only on historical grounds'; (iii) where the existing law was uncertain; and (iv) where there had been recent official reports recommending law reform.[9]

However, despite the draft Bill receiving an 'overwhelmingly enthusiastic welcome'[10] and being endorsed by successive governments,[11] it soon became apparent that such an ambitious project was doomed as successive governments had other political priorities. The draft Bill was huge, containing 220 clauses. Many of the provisions, particularly those relating to specific offences, were highly controversial. This was particularly true of murder,[12] which would have involved considering, *inter alia*, the political hot potato of whether the mandatory life sentence should be abolished. A project of this magnitude would take up a huge amount of parliamentary time and departmental time and resources.[13] Recognising that the 'political realities [were] against the possibility of having a whole code enacted as one measure',[14] in 1992 the Commission felt that the best way of achieving its goal was to concentrate its efforts on the less ambitious project of 'codification by degrees'.[15] The objective became one of focusing on specific areas with the aim of producing a series of bills:

> ... each of which will be complete in itself and will contain proposals for the immediate reform and rationalisation of a major, discrete area of the criminal law ... so that in the longer term it ought to be possible with comparative simplicity to combine all the different parts of the new, statutory, criminal law into the single, unified criminal code that the law of England and Wales so badly needs.[16]

---

7 Law Commission for England and Wales, *Criminal Law: Codification of the Criminal Law* (Law Com. No. 143) (London: HMSO, 1985).

8 Law Commission for England and Wales, above n. 4.

9 *Ibid.*, at paras. [3.31]–[3.34].

10 G. de Búrca and S. Gardner, 'The Codification of the Criminal Law' (1990) 10 *Oxford Journal of Legal Studies* 559, at 559.

11 Secretary of State for the Home Department, *Criminal Justice: The Way Ahead* (Cm. 5074) (London: The Stationery Office, 2001); Secretary of State for the Home Department, the Lord Chancellor and the Attorney General, *Justice for All* (Cm. 5563) (London: The Stationery Office, 2002).

12 Law Commission for England and Wales, *Legislating the Criminal Code: Offences Against the Person* (Law Commission Consultation Paper No. 122) (London: HMSO, 1992) paras. [2.10]–[2.14].

13 R. Toulson, 'Forty Years On: What Progress in Delivering Accessible and Principled Criminal law?' (2006) 27 *Statute Law Review* 61, at 66. Research has revealed that Law Commission Bills actually take very little time in the House of Commons and House of Lords (Arden, above n. 5, 442, note 16). But, as Arden, *ibid.*, concedes: 'There is, however, always a concern that they will do so.'

14 A.T.H. Smith, 'Legislating the Criminal Code: The Law Commission's Proposals' [1992] *Criminal Law Review* 396, at 397.

15 Editorial, 'Legislating the Criminal Code' [1992] *Criminal Law Review* 393, at 395.

16 Law Commission for England and Wales, *Legislating the Criminal Code: Offences Against the Person and General Principles* (Law Com. No. 218) (London: HMSO, 1993) para. [1.3].

Indeed, in the 1990s the successive titles of the Law Commission's Consultation Papers and Reports were prefaced by the words 'Legislating the Criminal Code'.[17] Its first more limited project was a report proposing reform of the antiquated non-fatal offences against the person together with proposals to codify some general principles (supervening fault, transferred fault) and a few general defences (self-defence, duress). Other general principles (fault terms, intoxication and omissions) were dealt with only for the purpose of non-fatal offences against the person.

However, with notable exceptions relating to specific offences (for example, the Fraud Act 2006),[18] few of the Law Commission's proposals have resulted in reforming legislation, with the result that in 2008 the Commission abandoned its codification mission. The codification project was 'removed' from its programme[19] because the 'complexity of the common law ... the increased pace of legislation, layers of legislation being placed one on another with bewildering speed, and the influence of European legislation continue to make codification more difficult'.[20] Accordingly, the main priority now is to reform and to simplify areas of criminal law 'to enable it to return and codify the law at a subsequent stage'.[21]

SPECIFIC LAW REFORMS: THE PROBLEM

So, what has been achieved in reforming specific areas of criminal law over the past decade or two? In relation to specific offences, the answer is a great deal. Many would say too much. Between 1997 and 2008, 3,605 criminal offences have been created.[22] These include major reforming statutes such as the Sexual Offences Act 2003[23] and the Fraud Act 2006, some statutes covering new ground such as causing or allowing the death of a child or vulnerable adult contrary to the Domestic Violence, Crime and Victims Act 2004,[24] a host of provisions aimed at countering terrorism[25] and countless provisions criminalising relatively trivial matters.[26]

There is much political mileage (in terms of being 'tough on crime, tough on the causes of crime') in matters relating to criminal justice and sentencing where, since 1997, there have been 57 Acts of Parliament altering the rules on criminal justice.[27] It is also easier to push reform of certain

---

17 *Ibid*; see, for example, Law Commission for England and Wales, *Legislating the Criminal Code: Intoxication and Criminal Liability* (Law Com. No. 229) (London: HMSO, 1995); and Law Commission for England and Wales, *Legislating the Criminal Code: Involuntary Manslaughter* (Law Com. No. 237) (London: HMSO, 1996).

18 Chapter 35.

19 Law Commission for England and Wales, *Tenth Programme of Law Reform* (Law Com. No. 311) (London: The Stationery Office, 2008) para. [1.6].

20 *Ibid.*, at para. [1.4].

21 *Ibid.*, at para. [1.5].

22 *The Independent*, 4 September 2008. While this is the figure that has hit the headlines, a reasonable number of these offences are reformulated offences, for example, those in the Sexual Offences Act 2003 (Chapter 42).

23 Chapter 42.

24 Chapter 28, s. 5.

25 For example, the Terrorism Act 2006 (Chapter 11).

26 For example, repairing vehicles on a road or failing to nominate a key-holder in respect of premises fitted with an audible burglar alarm in designated areas (Clean Neighbourhoods and Environment Act 2005 (Chapter 16), ss. 4 and 71).

27 J.R. Spencer, 'The Drafting of Criminal Legislation: Need It Be So Impenetrable?' (2008) 67 *Cambridge Law Journal* 585. Some of these statutes are huge: the Criminal Justice Act 2003 (Chapter 44) contains 339 sections and 38 schedules.

high-profile specific offences up the political agenda. For instance, rape and other sexual offences attract much publicity, making them appealing targets for parliamentary time. Other legislation is the result of intense lobbying by pressure groups. For example, the Centre for Corporate Accountability and other victims' relatives groups were crucial in leading to the enactment of the Corporate Manslaughter and Corporate Homicide Act 2007.[28]

But what of law reform of the general principles of criminal liability, for example, in relation to the conduct elements (acts, omissions and causation) and the fault elements (intention, recklessness and negligence) of crimes? Almost nothing has been achieved in this regard. The main reason is that 'these issues are not ones on which MPs are bombarded by their constituents or on which tabloid editorials are written'.[29] As Lord Gardiner has stated:

> ... for a long time the principle on which we have acted is that you do not do anything about law reform unless somebody has made a fuss. If there was a pressure group or if the Daily Express digs something up about it, then the Lord Chancellor says, 'oh dear! I suppose we must do something about this'. But otherwise you do nothing.[30]

There are, of course, a few areas of the General Part that do excite media and other public attention, putting pressure on parliamentarians to address the issue: for example, the self-defence rules on the degree of force that householders can use against burglars; and provocation, particularly in relation to the victims of domestic violence. These topics are discussed below. But the same is not true of most of the General Part. The general public, the media and MPs tend not to get excited or agitated about, for example, rules on causation. That does not mean law reform is impossible but, within the broad criminal law and justice field, these matters feature low down on the list of political priorities dominated by criminal justice and sentencing matters.

In an attempt to increase the momentum of law reform, a protocol was agreed in 2010 between the government and the Law Commission.[31] This protocol covers the various stages of a project: before the Commission takes the project on; at the outset of the project; during the currency of the project; and after the project.[32] It is now agreed that the minister with relevant policy responsibility must respond to the Commission, setting out which recommendations the minister accepts, rejects or intends to implement in modified form and 'if applicable, the Minister will also provide the timescale for implementation'.[33] Whether this protocol will lead to improved rates of implementation of Law Commission reports or is mere rhetoric remains to be seen.

REFORMS OF ASPECTS OF THE GENERAL PART

Despite the gloom and despondency of the above, it is possible to point to a few reforms/partial 'codifications' on aspects of the general principles of criminal liability that have been effected.

---

28 Chapter 19.

29 Toulson, above n. 13, at 71.

30 Cited by Toulson, *ibid.*, at 72.

31 Law Commission for England and Wales, *Protocol between the Lord Chancellor (on behalf of the Government) and the Law Commission* (Law Com. No. 321) (London: The Stationery Office, 2010).

32 *Ibid.*, at para. [3].

33 *Ibid.*, at para. [19].

Self-Defence

The Law Commission's draft Criminal Code Bill in 1989 proposed a comprehensive codification of the law of self-defence covering all the issues traditionally associated with the defence. These proposals were largely carried forward into the Commission's draft Criminal Law Bill covering offences against the person and general principles in 1993.

While these proposals were gathering dust, there was growing public concern, fuelled by media reports, about the extent to which householders could or could not use force against burglars. Following on from the conviction of a Norfolk farmer for shooting a trespasser in the high-profile case of *R. v. Martin*,[34] pressure began mounting for legislation on the matter. This resulted in three Private Members' Bills (all of which failed)[35] being introduced in Parliament. These Bills would have allowed householders to use any degree of defensive force as long as it was not 'grossly disproportionate'. At the Labour Party Conference in 2007 (at a time when it was thought there might be a snap General Election soon afterwards), the Minister of Justice, Jack Straw, announced that there would be an urgent review of the law on self-defence and at a fairly late stage in the parliamentary progress of what is now the Criminal Justice and Immigration Act 2008,[36] s. 76 in that Act was introduced 'to amend and clarify for the better the law on self-defence ... Where people act reasonably, in good faith, the law should clearly be on their side'.[37] The aim was to clarify the law, not only for the courts, but to send a message to the police and the Crown Prosecution Service, who it was felt were, on occasion, conducting prolonged investigations which 'drag on for months, with all the anxiety that that involves'.[38]

Beyond this stated purpose of clarifying the law and forestalling further attempts to expand the protection given to householders (during the course of the Bill, there were several attempts, both in the Commons and the Lords, to introduce the 'grossly disproportionate' test that had been proposed in the above Private Members' Bills), one can only speculate as to why the government thought it appropriate to enact legislation that simply restates some parts of the common law. In introducing s. 76 in the House of Commons, Jack Straw referred to the fact that on four separate occasions he had personally been forced to act in self-defence to apprehend one burglar and three street robbers.[39] Whether this was a factor, along with an attempt to honour his commitment made at the Labour Party Conference, influencing the sudden and late introduction of s. 76 is a matter of conjecture.

Another possible factor prompting the introduction of the legislation (but, again, this is pure conjecture) was the hope of shielding the law on self-defence from attacks of incompatibility with the ECHR. Ever since *R. v. Williams (Gladstone)*,[40] the law has been clear that the defender must be judged according to his or her view of the facts. Any mistake as to the need for defensive force has only to be genuine; it does not need to be reasonable. However, increasingly, decisions from the European Court of Human Rights have questioned the compatibility of this approach with Article 2 of the ECHR.[41] The Court has stated that in determining whether the killing is 'absolutely

34 [2002] 2 WLR 1.

35 See House of Commons, *Parliamentary Debates* (9 January 2008), vol. 470, at col. 361.

36 Chapter 4.

37 Above n. 35, at col. 347.

38 *Ibid.*, at col. 348.

39 *Ibid.*, at col. 347.

40 (1984) 78 Cr App R 276.

41 ECHR, Art. 2(1) provides that 'Everyone's right to life shall be protected by law' and Art. 2(2) states that 'Deprivation of life shall not be regarded as inflicted in contravention of this Article when it results from

necessary', the honest beliefs of the defender must be based on 'good reasons'.[42] While the English courts have themselves ruled that the English rules on self-defence where someone is killed are not incompatible with the ECHR,[43] there was some nervousness that the *Williams (Gladstone)* rule could, when the point arose directly, be declared by the European Court of Human Rights to be incompatible with the ECHR. As we shall see, s. 76 has confirmed the *Williams (Gladstone)* test. Under s. 19 of the Human Rights Act 1998,[44] ministers introducing legislation into Parliament must state whether or not the Bill complies with the ECHR. With this provision having been checked for such compliance, it will now be more difficult for English judges to declare that this rule is incompatible with the ECHR. If this was one of the aims behind the legislation,[45] it is somewhat pointless and no more than a stalling tactic, as the European Court of Human Rights has the power to declare that a state is in violation of one or more of the provisions of the ECHR. Perhaps, though, having the rule enshrined in legislation will make it less likely that this will happen.

Section 76 is not a complete codification of the law: 'one is not seeking to provide an entire code for every area of the common law of self-defence but, rather, to put in place the principal message on how self-defence should be treated'.[46] The object of the section is 'to clarify the operation of the existing defences'[47] of common law self-defence and the statutory defence of acting in prevention of crime under s. 3 of the Criminal Law Act 1967.[48] This 'clarification' is aimed primarily at the two central blocks underpinning the defence: (i) the *Williams (Gladstone)* rule; and (ii) the interpretation of a 'reasonable' response.

With regard to the former, the subjectivist approach adopted in *Williams (Gladstone)* is now placed on a statutory footing. Section 76(3) provides that '[t]he question whether the degree of force used by D was reasonable in the circumstances is to be decided by reference to the circumstances as D believed them to be'[49] and specifies that D is entitled to rely on a mistaken belief 'whether or not ... the mistake was a reasonable one to have made'.[50]

Whether this provision is justifiable is a controversial matter. While such an approach is consistent with the English judiciary's strong commitment to subjectivism in relation to fault elements[51] and mistakes with regard to definitional elements,[52] a strong case can be made that only reasonable mistakes should be taken into account in self-defence.[53] For example, if a police

---

the use of force which is no more than absolutely necessary: (a) in defence of any person from unlawful violence'.

42 *McCann v. United Kingdom* (1996) 21 EHRR 97, at para. [200]; *Gul v. Turkey* (2002) 34 EHRR 28, at para. [78].

43 *R. (on the Application of Bennett) v. H.M. Coroner for Inner South London* [2006] EWHC 196 (Admin).

44 Chapter 42.

45 This issue was discussed in debate in the House of Lords, where Lord Davidson of Glen Clova concluded that the common law, as reflected in the Bill, was compliant with ECHR, Art. 2: House of Lords, *Parliamentary Debates* (23 April 2008), vol. 700, at col. 1514.

46 *Ibid.*, at col. 1528, *per* Lord Davidson of Glen Clova.

47 Criminal Justice and Immigration Act 2008 (Chapter 4), s. 76(9).

48 Chapter 58. See *ibid.*, s. 76(2).

49 *Ibid.*

50 *Ibid.*, s. 76(4)(b)(ii).

51 *R. v. G* [2004] 1 AC 1034.

52 *B (A Minor) v. DPP* [2000] 2 AC 428; *R. v. K* [2002] 1 AC 462.

53 Under the Indian Penal Code (IPC), s. 79, a mistake made 'in good faith' in self-defence exempts the defendant from liability. Section 52 of the IPC defines 'in good faith' as follows: 'Nothing is said to be done or believed "in good faith" which is done or believed without due care and attention.' K. Amirthalingam,

officer shoots a person whom he or she mistakenly thinks is a terrorist about to commit a suicide bombing, there should only be an exemption from liability if the officer has a *plausible* excuse for making such a mistake. If the mistake is unreasonable, it does not qualify as being plausible. As John Gardner puts it: 'The gist of an excuse ... is precisely that the person with the excuse lived up to our expectations.'[54] We excuse people if they acted for reasons that are understandable in the sense that we accept that socially responsible people could act in that way.[55] This approach means that actions should be measured against the standards of reasonable people (or reasonable police officers). Particularly with the police and the military, because of their training, there should be an insistence on their actions (including their beliefs and mistakes) being reasonable. This same reasoning can be extended to ordinary citizens – except that the standard of reasonableness would be adjusted to take account of their lack of training. Of course, there are alternative rationales of excuses: that an excuse is a 'concession to human frailty'[56] or that the defendant has not had a fair opportunity to make free choices. These alternative rationales allow for a subjective assessment of the defendant's predicament. It is unfortunate that the knee-jerk codification of aspects of self-defence in s. 76 was not preceded by careful debate of these controversial issues.

It should be noted that s. 76(5) contains a provision making it clear that a defendant cannot rely on 'any mistaken belief attributable to intoxication that was voluntarily induced'. This appears to confirm the common law rule established in *R. v. O'Grady*,[57] but does not address the dispute generated by *O'Grady* as to what the position is if the defendant, albeit intoxicated, makes a mistake that reasonable sober people would have made. The better view is that if the mistake was a reasonable one, the mistake would not be *attributable* to the intoxication; the intoxication would be coincidental. Whether this interpretation will be adopted remains to be seen. It is unfortunate that legislation aimed at clarifying the law does not address this issue.

The other major aspect of self-defence codified in s. 76 relates to the meaning of 'reasonable force'.[58] Section 76 applies when 'the question arises whether the degree of force used by D against a person ('V') was reasonable in the circumstances'.[59] The relevant test is then stated as follows:

> (6) The degree of force used by D is not to be regarded as having been reasonable in the circumstances as D believed them to be if it was disproportionate in those circumstances.
>
> (7) [In assessing this] the following considerations are to be taken into account ...
>
> (a) that a person acting for a legitimate purpose may not be able to weigh to a nicety the exact measure of any necessary action; and
>
> (b) that evidence of a person's having only done what the person honestly and instinctively thought was necessary for a legitimate purpose constitutes strong evidence that only reasonable action was taken by that person for that purpose.

---

in Chapter 5 of this volume ('Mistake and Strict Liability'), at 115–16, explains how Indian courts have applied this good faith test in a 'highly subjective manner', while Singapore courts have adopted an objective approach in interpreting 'good faith'.

54 J. Gardner, 'The Gist of Excuses' [1997–8] 1 *Buffalo Criminal Law Review* 575, at 578.

55 C.M.V. Clarkson, *Understanding Criminal Law* (4th edn, London: Sweet & Maxwell, 2005) 116.

56 *R. v. Howe* [1987] 1 AC 417.

57 [1987] 1 QB 995.

58 Under the IPC, only 'necessary' force may be inflicted. Cheah Wui Ling, in Chapter 8 of this volume ('Private Defence'), concludes that this has been judicially interpreted as requiring proportionality.

59 Above n. 36, s. 76(1)(b).

Accordingly, conduct is 'reasonable in the circumstances' if it is 'not ... disproportionate in those circumstances'. The standard is one of proportionality. *Prima facie*, this suggests an objective standard. But, then, drawing on the precise wording used in *Palmer v. The Queen*,[60] s. 76(7)(a) states that account should be taken of the fact that a defender may not be able to 'weigh to a nicety the exact measure of any defensive action'. In *Palmer* it was added that if a defendant had only done what he or she 'honestly and instinctively thought was necessary', this would be 'most potent evidence that only reasonable action had been taken'. This wording is followed slavishly in s. 76(7)(b), except that instead of this providing 'most potent evidence', such a belief now constitutes 'strong evidence'. Whether there is a difference between these two formulations is a moot point – although, literally, 'strong evidence' is weaker than 'most potent evidence'. If a householder shoots a burglar because he or she 'honestly and instinctively' thinks it is necessary for purposes of defending himself or herself, or his or her property and this is the 'most potent evidence' that the action is reasonable (the common law test), it will require overwhelming evidence to the contrary before the action will be declared unreasonable. But, now, under s. 76(7)(b), where such a belief is only 'strong evidence', less evidence to the contrary will suffice for the conduct to be regarded as unreasonable. Either way, this honest and instinctive belief seems to create some kind of presumption of reasonableness[61] and opens the door to householders escaping liability for killing or injuring burglars.

In this provision, s. 76, like the common law, makes it clear that, despite the insistence in s. 76 that the defendant's actions be 'reasonable in the circumstances', action need not actually be objectively reasonable and proportionate because what is 'reasonable' will be influenced by the defender's perception of the situation. The more one moves away from an objective standard of proportionality, the more self-defence ceases to have features of a justificatory defence and takes on attributes of an excusatory defence. This point is strengthened when one recalls that the defensive action need not actually be necessary at all, as long as the defender believes it is necessary.

What is the position if the defendant's perception of the danger he or she faces is distorted by a physical or mental characteristic that he or she possesses? In *Martin*,[62] the Court of Appeal rejected the reasoning employed in the earlier provocation cases[63] and stated that while physical characteristics could be taken into account, the fact that the defendant is suffering from 'some psychiatric condition' could not be taken into account 'except in exceptional circumstances'. So, if a defendant has, for example, a broken leg (making retreat more difficult), this can be taken into account but if, like the defendant in *Martin*, he or she is suffering from a paranoid personality disorder that makes him or her perceive a much greater danger to his or her physical safety than the 'normal' person, this cannot be taken into account.

Section 76 has, regrettably, chosen to remain silent on this issue. However, it stresses no less than three times that the defensive force must be reasonable *in the circumstances*. This has clearly opened the door to future interminable argument that both the defendant's physical and mental characteristics should be taken into account as part of the 'circumstances' of the case. It is unfortunate that s. 76 did not tackle this issue directly.

Even more regrettable is the fact that s. 76 represents only a partial codification of the common law on self-defence. Apart from the two issues covered and discussed above, the section is silent on the following important matters affecting the contours of the law on self-defence:

---

60 [1971] AC 814.

61 Editorial, 'A Pointless Exercise' [2008] *Criminal Law Review* 507.

62 Above n. 34.

63 *R. v. Smith* [2001] 1 AC 146.

(i) the purpose for which the force may be used: for example, whether defensive action to prevent trespass to property is permissible;

(ii) whether the attack must be unlawful: for example, a 'six-year-old boy indiscriminately shooting all and sundry in the school playground'[64] or a conjoined twin 'draining her [twin's] lifeblood'[65] or acting to prevent (lawful) drilling of genetically modified seeds;[66]

(iii) anticipatory self-defence: how imminent must the threat be? Under the common law, self-defence is only available in the face of 'imminent' threats. This issue is one of particular importance to victims of domestic violence who, in anticipation of further violence, take pre-emptive action and, as in *R. v. Ahluwalia*,[67] for example, kill their sleeping husband. A golden opportunity for addressing this thorny issue has been missed by s. 76;

(iv) opportunity to retreat: this is also a matter of immense importance to battered women who, for cultural and economic reasons, may not be in a position to retreat from their home. Again, it is unfortunate that this issue has not been addressed by a statute codifying the law on self-defence.

A final 'omission' from the list of issues that could have been addressed by the statute was probably deliberate. There have long been calls for the introduction of a partial defence of excessive self-defence which would reduce murder to manslaughter.[68] However, the government has rejected such calls[69] and instead has enacted s. 54 of the Coroners and Justice Act 2009,[70] allowing a killing in fear of serious violence to qualify as a trigger for a plea of loss of control which reduces murder to manslaughter. This new provision, which is discussed below, does not apply to those who use a disproportionate amount of defensive force if their fear of serious violence did not cause them to lose control.

Loss of Control/Diminished Responsibility

In English law, loss of control (formerly provocation) and diminished responsibility are partial defences only to murder, reducing liability to manslaughter. For all other crimes, they are only relevant at the sentencing stage. Nevertheless, these doctrines can be regarded as belonging to the General Part because the issue of whether a person should be afforded an exculpatory defence (whether full or partial) goes to the core of whether they are culpable (or fully culpable). Further, while these defences are only particular defences to murder under English law, there is no principled reason why they could not apply generally in a utopian criminal code. Indeed, in Macaulay's draft

64 *Re A (Conjoined Twins: Surgical Separation)* [2001] Fam 147.

65 *Ibid.*

66 In *DPP v. Bayer* [2004] 1 Cr App R 38, it was held that in acting to defend property, self-defence is only available against an unlawful act.

67 [1992] 4 All ER 889.

68 For example, N. Lacey, 'Partial Defences to Homicide: Questions of Power and Principle in Imperfect and Less Imperfect Worlds' in A. Ashworth and B. Mitchell (eds), *Rethinking English Homicide Law* (Oxford: Oxford University Press, 2000) 124, 129.

69 Home Office, *Report of the Inter-Departmental Review of the Law on the Use of Lethal Force in Self-Defence or the Prevention of Crime* (London: Home Office, 1996) para. [83].

70 Chapter 25.

Code, provocation was not restricted to murder but was also a partial defence to lesser offences of causing injury.[71]

Loss of Control

By the turn of the current century, judicial interpretations of the defence of provocation contained in s. 3 of the Homicide Act 1957[72] were coming under immense attack. The objections related to both limbs of the defence.

First, under the subjective limb, the defendant had to have been provoked to a 'sudden and temporary loss of control'.[73] While the strictness of this rule had been ameliorated somewhat,[74] the rule was still condemned as being based on a male typology of anger[75] and not taking into account the effects of slow-burn anger experienced by many women, particularly those who are the victims of domestic abuse.

Secondly, under the objective limb, the provocation had to be such that a 'reasonable man' would have responded similarly. The question of who this reasonable man was, and what attributes or characteristics of the defendant could be attributed to him, had become the subject of extensive judicial interpretations. In *R. v. Camplin*,[76] it was held that the age and sex of the defendant could be taken into account. Subsequent cases drew a distinction between characteristics affecting the gravity of the provocation (provocativeness) and characteristics affecting the power of self-control (provocability).[77] With regard to the former, any factor bearing on the gravity of the provocation could be taken into account. If a person had a particular characteristic (for example, being a glue-sniffer, as in *R. v. Morhall*)[78] and was taunted about it, the provocation would be more grave than it would be for other people and thus could be taken into account. With regard to the latter (characteristics affecting the power of self-control), two lines of authority emerged. On the one hand, some cases held that only the age and sex of the defendant could be permitted to vary the strict reasonable man standard.[79] On the other hand, several Court of Appeal decisions held that a wide array of characteristics of the defendant could be taken into account. For example, in *R. v. Humphries*,[80] it was held that the abnormal immaturity and attention-seeking characteristics of the defendant could be taken into account. The House of Lords in *Smith*[81] rejected this distinction between characteristics affecting the gravity of the provocation and those affecting self-control, and held that the jury could take into account 'everything' to determine the effect it would have on the reasonable man. The test was whether the defendant had exercised 'a reasonable level of self-control for someone with her history, her experience and her state of mind' (Lord Clyde).[82] This decision was widely condemned as leading to a complete obliteration of the objective reasonable man test specified in s. 3 of the Homicide Act 1957. As Lord Hobhouse (dissenting) put it: 'if one

71 Macaulay's draft Code, cl. 325. See also Chapter 12 of this volume (I. Leader-Elliott, 'Provocation').
72 Chapter 11.
73 *R. v. Duffy* [1949] 1 All ER 932.
74 Above n. 67.
75 K. O'Donovan, 'Defences for Battered Women Who Kill' (1991) 18 *Journal Law and Society* 219.
76 [1978] AC 705.
77 *R. v. Newell* (1980) 71 Cr App R 331; *R. v. Morhall* [1996] 1 AC 90.
78 *Ibid.*
79 *Luc Thiet Thuan v. The Queen* [1997] AC 131.
80 [1995] 4 All ER 1008.
81 Above n. 63.
82 *Ibid.* at 177.

adds all the characteristics of the defendant to the notional reasonable man, the reasonable man becomes "reincarnated" in the defendant'.[83] Accordingly, a specially-convened nine-member panel of the Privy Council in *AG for Jersey v. Holley*[84] effectively 'overruled'[85] *Smith* and adopted the view that while any factor affecting the gravity of the provocation could be taken into account, the only relevant factors affecting the power of self-control were age and sex.

After two Law Commission Reports[86] and a Ministry of Justice Consultation Paper,[87] the Coroners and Justice Act 2009 was enacted abolishing the defence of provocation[88] and replacing it with a new defence of loss of control.[89]

The Subjective Limb Under s. 54 of the Coroners and Justice Act 2009, there must be a loss of control.[90] The Law Commission had proposed dispensing with this, requiring simply that there be a 'gross provocation' causing the defendant to have a justifiable sense of being seriously wronged or to have a fear of serious violence. Such an approach would have allowed defendants such as the battered wife in *Ahluwalia* to have come within the ambit of the defence (she acted out of fear of violence but had not lost self-control). However, the underlying rationale of the new law is, like that of the old law, that the defence is a concession to human infirmity.[91] For partial exculpation, the defendant must have been deprived of his or her control and powers of reasoning. Section 54(4) underlines this: the partial defence will not apply if the defendant 'acted in a considered desire for revenge'.However, s. 54(2) introduces an important change: 'it does not matter whether or not the loss of self-control was sudden'. The government expressly recognised that this could allow for slow-burn anger to be taken into account.[92] This *could* make it easier for battered women and others suffering domestic abuse to come within the ambit of the defence – but, of course, the longer the time period between the taunt and the response, the more difficult it will be, evidentially, to establish an actual loss of control.

Under the old law of provocation, anything said or done could suffice as the provocation. For example, in *R. v. Doughty*,[93] a baby's crying was the relevant provocation. Under the new law, however, the loss of control must be attributable to one of two specified 'qualifying triggers':

---

83 *Ibid.* at 201.

84 [2005] 2 AC 580.

85 This was confirmed in *R. v. James; R. v. Karimi* [2006] 1 Cr App R 29.

86 Law Commission for England and Wales, *Partial Defences to Murder* (Law Com. No. 290) (London: The Stationery Office, 2004); Law Commission for England and Wales, *Murder, Manslaughter and Infanticide* (Law Com. No. 304) (London: The Stationery Office, 2006).

87 Ministry of Justice, *Murder, Manslaughter and Infanticide: Proposals for Reform of the Law* (CP 19/08) (London: Ministry of Justice, 2008).

88 Above n. 70, s. 56.

89 *Ibid.*, ss. 54, 55. While the Law Commission had proposed retaining the label 'provocation', the government felt that this term carried 'negative connotations' (above n. 87, para. [34]). See S. Yeo, 'English Reform of Provocation and Diminished Responsibility: Whither Singapore?' [2010] *Singapore Journal of Legal Studies* 177 for a critique of this new defence and a comparison with the defence of provocation under the IPC.

90 In Macaulay's draft Code, there was no requirement that the defendant lose self-control; this was a later innovation by the authors of the IPC. Leader-Elliott, in Chapter 12 of this volume, above n. 71, proposes that a revised IPC should dispense with this requirement and instead demand that the defendant be in 'a state of extreme mental or emotional disturbance'.

91 *R. v. Hayward* (1908) 21 Cox CC 692, at 694.

92 Above n. 87, at para. [37].

93 (1986) 83 Cr App R 319.

(i) If D's loss of self-control was attributable to D's fear of serious violence from V against D or another identified person.[94]

The old law of provocation was primarily concerned with angry responses. This new provision recognises that other emotions, namely fear and panic, can warrant partial exculpation. Both the Law Commission[95] and the government[96] cite the example of a victim of domestic violence who, fearful of further attack, kills her abuser as a case falling within the new provision. However, as already seen, this is only going to avail those who are so fearful that they lose self-control and act in a state of panic. The defence will still not be available to those, like Mrs Ahluwalia, who have not lost self-control. The test is a subjective one: the defendant must fear serious violence; the threat need not be real. So, a battered woman who has been subjected to frequent serious violence can bring herself within the ambit of the defence even though on the specific occasion her fear of serious violence was mistaken.

(ii) If D's loss of self-control was attributable to a thing or things done or said (or both) which:
(a) constituted circumstances of an extremely grave character;[97] and
(b) caused D to have a justifiable sense of being seriously wronged.[98]

Whether the circumstances are of an 'extremely grave character' is an objective test designed to exclude unmeritorious cases such as parents claiming they were provoked by the crying of a baby, as in *Doughty*, or honour killings.[99] This exclusion of trivial and 'morally or politically unacceptable grounds'[100] is reinforced by giving the judge more control over the defence than under the old law.[101] Further, seemingly not trusting judges (and juries) to exclude unacceptable 'triggers', it specifies that 'the fact that a thing done or said constituted sexual infidelity is to be disregarded'.[102] This exclusion is bound to be troublesome in cases where a taunt of infidelity is part of a range of taunts.[103]

A further mechanism for excluding unacceptable taunts comes from the requirement that the taunt must cause the defendant 'to have a justifiable sense of being seriously wronged'. While this looks like a subjective test (caused a *sense* of), the requirement that it be a *justifiable* sense 'imports an objective quality to the test, implying that if called upon to justify her sense of being seriously wronged to a group of her peers, the defendant would be capable of doing so'.[104]

94 Above n. 70, s. 55(3).

95 Law Commission for England and Wales, *Murder, Manslaughter and Infanticide*, above n. 86.

96 Above n. 87, para. [28].

97 This is similar to Macaulay's conception of provocation, which required evidence of a 'serious wrong' by the victim. See Chapter 12 of this volume, above n. 71.

98 Above n. 70, s. 55(4).

99 Such cases would also be excluded under s. 55(4)(b), as the defendant would not have a *justifiable* sense of being seriously wronged.

100 A. Norrie, 'The Coroners and Justice Act 2009 – Partial Defences to Murder: (1) Loss of Control' [2010] *Criminal Law Review* 275, at 279.

101 Above n. 70, s. 54(6). The evidence adduced must, in the opinion of the trial judge, be sufficient that 'a jury, properly directed, could reasonably conclude that the defence might apply'.

102 *Ibid.*, s. 55(6)(c). Also excluded are cases of self-induced loss of control (ss. 55(6)(a) and (b)).

103 Norrie, above n. 100, at 289.

104 C.M.V. Clarkson, H.M. Keating and S.R. Cunningham, *Clarkson and Keating, Criminal Law: Text and Materials* (7th edn, London: Sweet & Maxwell, 2010) 677.

The Objective Limb The new law attempts to enshrine the law as previously stated in *Holley*. To qualify for the defence, it must be established that 'a person of D's sex and age, with a normal degree of tolerance and self-restraint and in the circumstances of D, might have reacted in the same or in a similar way to D'.[105] Section 54(3) elaborates on the reference to 'the circumstances of D' that it is 'a reference to all of D's circumstances other than those whose only relevance to D's conduct is that they bear on D's general capacity for tolerance or self-restraint'.

Age and sex are the only specified characteristics that can be taken into account.[106] Characteristics affecting the defendant's general capacity to exercise self-control are to be ignored. The Law Commission gave examples of such characteristics: alcoholism, intoxication, irritability, being jealous or obsessive, mental deficiency or disorder. They also included some 'hard cases' to the list: taking prescribed medicine, having suffered a stroke, involuntary intoxication by an allergic reaction of some kind or by a bang on the head.[107] Such persons should instead plead diminished responsibility.

Nevertheless, it is clear from s. 54(3) that all the defendant's characteristics can be taken into account as part of 'the circumstances of D' provided their only relevance is not that they simply bear on the defendant's general capacity for tolerance or self-restraint. This confirms the *Holley* position that characteristics affecting provocativeness are part of the 'circumstances' because they have a relevance beyond the defendant's general capacity for tolerance or self-restraint.

However, it is possible to argue that a defendant's characteristics (for example, mental disorder) *can* be taken into account even if that was not the object of the taunt, provided their *only* relevance is not that they bear on the defendant's general capacity for tolerance and self-restraint. For example, suffering from 'battered women's syndrome' could be taken into account because its relevance is not limited to its effect on the power of self-control. The cumulative abuse a woman has suffered also affects the gravity of the provocation to her and can cause her to have a justifiable sense of being seriously wronged.[108]

The reference to the sex of the defendant in s. 54(1)(c) is likely to be mainly applicable to those who act out of fear of serious violence. So, if a woman is attacked by a man, her response will be measured against the yardstick of how women in general would respond. This is problematic. How do women in general (as opposed to men in general) respond when fearing serious violence? If this is meant to permit account to be taken of the physical characteristics of the woman (say, being smaller and weaker than the man), the reference to 'sex' is superfluous, as her physical characteristics would, in any event, be regarded as part of 'the circumstances of D', since such physical characteristics will (normally) not bear on her general capacity for tolerance and self-restraint.

As seen in the above discussion, the new provisions on self-control are likely to give rise to numerous interpretive problems, but this is inevitable with any statute, given the imprecision of language. What is to be welcomed is that these provisions, unlike those on self-defence, have attempted a complete 'codification' of this particular area of law.

---

105 Above n. 70, s. 54(1)(c).

106 The sex of the defendant is mainly relevant to the fear of serious violence trigger. See below at 352.

107 Law Commission for England and Wales, *Murder, Manslaughter and Infanticide*, above n. 86, at paras [5.40]–[5.41].

108 Cf. Norrie, above n. 100, who makes a similar point, albeit not in relation to s. 54(3).

Diminished Responsibility

Fundamental to the General Part is the issue of responsibility and what constitutes a lack of responsibility. The defence of insanity in English law is still governed by the antiquated M'Naghten Rules of 1843.[109] No concerted efforts at their reform have been attempted since the Butler Committee Report,[110] although the Law Commission is currently reviewing this area of the law.[111] The partial defence of diminished responsibility (reducing murder to manslaughter) is, in practice, used far more extensively. The original provision in s. 2 of the Homicide Act 1957 has long attracted criticism, particularly as that law was felt to be incapable of adjustment to modern developments in psychiatry and because it has resulted in confusion between the roles of the jury and psychiatric expert witnesses. For example, research revealed that expert psychiatrists were testifying about the defendant's 'responsibility' (a moral and not a medical concept) in almost 70 percent of cases.[112]

Accordingly, drawing on the work of the Law Commission,[113] s. 52 of the Coroners and Justice Act 2009 has introduced a new, reformed partial defence of diminished responsibility. Section 2 of the Homicide Act 1957 now reads:

> (1)A person ('D') who kills or is a party to the killing of another is not to be convicted of murder if D was suffering from an abnormality of mental functioning which —
> (a) arose from a recognised medical condition,
> (b) substantially impaired D's ability to do one or more of the things mentioned in subsection (1A), and
> (c) provides an explanation for D's acts and omissions in doing or being a party to the killing.
> (1A) Those things are —
> (a) to understand the nature of D's conduct;
> (b) to form a rational judgment;
> (c) to exercise self-control.
> (1B) For the purposes of subsection (1)(c), an abnormality of mental functioning provides an explanation for D's conduct if it causes, or is a significant contributory factor in causing, D to carry out that conduct.
> ...
> (3)... [he] shall be liable instead to be convicted of manslaughter.

Abnormality of Mental Functioning Under the pre-existing law, the defendant had to be suffering from an 'abnormality of mind'. This caused problems about what a 'mind' is and the difference between a mind and a brain – and it was not a psychiatric term. However, it is far from clear that the new term 'abnormality of mental functioning' is any clearer. It is also not a psychiatric term but, according to the Law Commission, was the term preferred by psychiatrists. One cannot rule

109 *Daniel M'Naghten's Case* (1843) 10 Cl & Fin 200, 8 ER 718.

110 Home Office and the Department of Health and Social Security, *Report of the Committee on Mentally Abnormal Offenders* (Cmnd 6244) (London: HMSO, 1975).

111 Above n. 19.

112 Law Commission for England and Wales, *Partial Defences to Murder*, above n. 86, at para [5.51].

113 Law Commission for England and Wales, *Partial Defences to Murder*, above n. 86; Law Commission for England and Wales, *Murder, Manslaughter and Infanticide*, above n. 86.

out the possibility that in interpreting 'abnormality', the courts might continue to make reference to the old leading case of *R. v. Byrne*.[114]

Recognised Medical Condition Under the old law, the abnormality of mind had to be caused by one of the 'bracketed causes', namely 'whether arising from a condition of arrested or retarded development of mind or any inherent causes or induced by disease or injury'.[115] Now, the abnormality of mental functioning must have arisen from a recognised medical condition. This is a significant reform designed to ensure that developments in diagnostic practice can be accommodated.[116] For a medical condition to be recognised, it would seem that it would have to be listed in one of the accepted classificatory systems such as the World Health Organization's *International Classification of Diseases* or the American Psychiatric Association's *Diagnostic and Statistical Manual of Mental Disorders*.[117] This provision has the advantage that expert medical witnesses will be asked to testify about matters within their medical expertise (which was not the case under the old s. 2 of the Homicide Act 1957). It is a moot point as to whether the new law is narrower than the bracketed causes under the old s. 2. Under the old s. 2, the vagueness of the language enabled psychiatrists, as expert witnesses (with the collusion of judges and juries), to stretch the interpretation of the bracketed causes to cover cases where a conviction of murder was thought to be inappropriate. Mackay suggests that the new requirement might exclude mercy-killers who came within the old s. 2 as a result of a 'benevolent conspiracy' between courts and experts.[118] However, the World Health Organization lists 'mood [affective] disorders', which covers a range of depressive illnesses, including reactive depression and depressive reaction.[119] It is likely that mercy-killers could still come within this and be regarded as having a recognised medical condition.

Substantially Impaired D's Ability The question of whether an impairment is 'substantial' is one for the jury.[120] The abnormality of mental functioning must substantially impair the defendant's ability to either: (a) understand the nature of his or her conduct; (b) to form a rational judgment; or (c) to exercise self-control. This is a marked improvement on the old law, under which medical experts were testifying about whether D's 'responsibility' had been substantially impaired, a process described by psychiatrists as 'an expensive farce' and a 'blot on psychiatric practice'.[121] Now, psychiatrists will be able to testify about matters within their medical expertise

---

114 [1960] 2 QB 396.

115 Homicide Act 1957 (Chapter 11), s. 2.

116 Gerry Ferguson, in Chapter 10 of this volume ('Insanity'), argues that a revised IPC should define 'unsoundness of mind' (for an insanity defence) in legal, and not medical, terms because 'the question of whether that degree of impairment of the accused's mental faculties and functions entitles the accused to be excused from criminal liability by reason of the insanity defence is and should be a legal and moral judgment, not a medical one' (at 242).

117 Above n. 87, para. [49].

118 R.D. Mackay, 'The Coroners and Justice Act 2009 – Partial Defences to Murder: (2) The New Diminished Responsibility Plea' [2010] *Criminal Law Review* 290, at 294.

119 *International Classification of Diseases* (10th Revision, 2007), Classifications F30–F39: see http://apps.who.int/classifications/apps/icd/icd10online/ (last accessed 20 February 2011).

120 Law Commission for England and Wales, *Murder, Manslaughter and Infanticide*, above n. 86, at para. [5.118].

121 Prison Reform Trust, *Report of the Committee on the Penalty for Homicide* (London: Prison Reform Trust, 1993), 33.

(for example, whether a defendant could form a rational judgment) rather than matters beyond their competence (issues of responsibility).

Mackay argues that this 'spelling out what abilities need to be impaired, inevitably means that "abnormality of mental functioning" is now narrower than "abnormality of mind" in that the only activities of the mind which are included are the three specified things'.[122] However, perhaps this fear is unfounded, as the three 'things' are based on the judgment in *Byrne*, where 'abnormality of mind' was stated to cover 'the perception of physical acts and matters' (which is similar to 'understand the nature of D's conduct'), 'the ability to form a rational judgment'[123] and 'the ability to exercise will power to control physical acts'.

Provides an Explanation for D's Acts Section 1(B) now states that an abnormality of mental functioning provides an explanation for D's conduct if it causes, or is a significant contributory factor in causing, D to carry out that conduct.[124] The Law Commission noted that it was never clear under the pre-existing law whether the abnormality of mind had to in some sense 'cause' the defendant to kill.[125] The law now makes it clear that there must be a connection between the abnormality of mental functioning and the killing. This means that where the jury thinks that the abnormality of mental functioning made no difference to the defendant's behaviour, he or she will not succeed in a plea of diminished responsibility.[126] Arguably, this new requirement will lead to a reduction in the number of successful diminished responsibility pleas. For example, Mrs Ahluwalia was suffering from Battered Woman's Syndrome (arguably a recognised medical condition). But it is far from clear that this condition was a significant contributory factor in her killing her husband. It was the final episode of abuse, combined with fear of further abuse, that led her to kill.

Conclusion As suggested above, the new provisions on diminished responsibility, particularly in relation to the role of medical experts, are to be welcomed. However, in an era where so little law reform has been achieved, it is odd that diminished responsibility should have been reformed when, while there were some criticisms, there were no pressing concerns about the actual operation of the old law[127] and the Law Commission had concluded it was operating successfully.[128] The real reason for these reforms was the intense dissatisfaction with the provocation defence, and diminished responsibility seems to have been swept within the wider reform of partial defences to murder.[129] The Law Commission is currently reviewing the insanity defence as part of its latest programme of law reform.[130] It would surely have been sensible for the reform of the two defences,

---

122 Mackay, above n. 118, at 297.

123 In *Byrne*, above n. 114, this was limited to rational judgments 'as to whether an act is right or wrong' (at 403).

124 The inclusion of 'causes' in this sub-section is superfluous as it suffices that the abnormality of mental functioning is a 'significantly contributory factor' in causing the conduct.

125 Law Commission for England and Wales, *Murder, Manslaughter and Infanticide*, above n. 86, at para. [5.122].

126 Ministry of Justice, *Murder, Manslaughter and Infanticide: Proposals for Reform of the Law* (Response to Consultation, CP(R) 19/08) (London: Ministry of Justice, 2009) (available online at http://www.justice.gov.uk/consultations/docs/murder-review-response.pdf, last accessed 20 February 2011) para. [95].

127 Mackay, above n. 118, at 302.

128 Law Commission for England and Wales, *Partial Defences to Murder*, above n. 86, at para. [5.86].

129 Mackay, above n. 118, at 302.

130 Law Commission of England and Wales, above n. 20.

which would have involved a consideration of the relationship between them,[131] to have been undertaken as a joint project.

Encouraging or Assisting Crime

In 1993 the Law Commission proposed abolishing the common law on derivative liability for participation in crime and recommended that two new inchoate offences be created: assisting crime and encouraging crime.[132] Subsequently, the Commission abandoned this proposal and produced three Reports[133] covering both assisting and encouraging an offence, and participating in a joint criminal venture. This was an attempt to introduce a coherent package of measures where the width of the new assisting and encouraging offences would be balanced by a narrowing of the law on complicity.

The government's response was to ignore the package and, instead, enact (with significant departures from the Law Commission's proposals) only certain aspects of one of the Law Commission's proposals in the Serious Crime Act 2007.[134] This was a knee-jerk response to growing concern about serious, organised and terrorist crime.[135] This has resulted in a distortion of the original package of reforms, with the result that the remaining parts of the package cannot be enacted without reconsideration.[136]

Part 2 of the Serious Crime Act 2007 abolishes the common law of incitement,[137] which was felt to be defective mainly because it was limited to encouraging crime and did not extend to facilitating or assisting crime.[138] In its place, the Act creates three new inchoate offences of encouraging or assisting crime, each carrying the same maximum penalty as the anticipated offence:[139]

> 44. Intentionally encouraging or assisting an offence
> (1) A person commits an offence if—
> (a) he does an act capable of encouraging or assisting the commission of an offence; and
> (b) he intends to encourage or assist its commission.
> (2) But he is not to be taken to have intended to encourage or assist the commission of an offence merely because such encouragement or assistance was a foreseeable consequence of his act.

---

131 Mackay, above n. 118, at 302. For example, understanding the 'nature of D's conduct' in sub-s. 1(A) is very similar to the M'Naghten requirement of not knowing the nature and quality of one's acts.

132 Law Commission for England and Wales, *Assisting and Encouraging Crime* (Consultation Paper No. 131) (London: HMSO, 1993).

133 Law Commission for England and Wales, *Inchoate Liability for Assisting and Encouraging Crime* (Law Com. No. 300) (London: The Stationery Office, 2006); Law Commission for England and Wales, *Murder, Manslaughter and Infanticide*, above n. 86; Law Commission for England and Wales, *Participating in Crime* (Law Com. No. 305) (London: The Stationery Office, 2007).

134 Chapter 27.

135 G.R. Sullivan, 'Inchoate Liability for Assisting and Encouraging Crime' [2006] *Criminal Law Review* 1047.

136 D. Ormerod and R. Fortson, 'Serious Crime Act 2007: The Part 2 Offences' [2009] *Criminal Law Review* 389, at 390.

137 Above n. 134, s. 59.

138 Law Commission for England and Wales, *Inchoate Liability for Assisting and Encouraging Crime*, above n. 133, at paras. [1.3]–[1.5].

139 Above n. 134, s. 58(2), (3).

This applies where D *intentionally* encourages or assists an offence: for example, where D supplies a gun, intending that P will kill X.

45. Encouraging or assisting an offence believing it will be committed
(1) A person commits an offence if —
(a)he does an act capable of encouraging or assisting the commission of an offence; and
(b) he believes —
(i) that the offence will be committed; and
(ii) that his act will encourage or assist its commission.

This applies where *D believes* his or her acts will encourage or assist a crime and that the offence *will* be committed: for example, where D sells a gun, being only interested in the profit, but believes that P will (not might) use it to kill someone; if he or she only thinks that P might kill someone, there will be no liability for this offence.

46 Encouraging or assisting offences believing one or more will be committed
(1) A person commits an offence if —
(a) he does an act capable of encouraging or assisting the commission of one or more of a number of offences; and
(b) he believes —
(i) that one or more of those offences will be committed (but has no belief as to which); and
(ii) that his act will encourage or assist the commission of one or more of them.
(2) It is immaterial for the purposes of subsection (1)(b)(ii) whether the person has any belief as to which offence will be encouraged or assisted.

This applies where D *believes* that his or her acts will encourage or assist the commission of one or more offences but is unsure as to which offence might be committed. Take, for example, a taxi-driver (D) who drives a group of armed men to a destination and believes they will commit either aggravated burglary or robbery, or a grievous bodily harm (GBH) offence or murder. In such a situation, even though P only commits robbery (or, indeed, commits no offence), D can be charged with assisting murder.

These new inchoate offences now sit alongside the existing common law rules on derivative liability, meaning that in cases where the principal offence has actually been committed, the prosecution has a wide discretion as to whether to charge the defendant with one of the new offences[140] or to charge him or her with aiding and abetting the offence (or another[141] offence). This is incoherent because the focus of the two schemes is quite different: with inchoate liability the emphasis is on protecting against *threatened harms*; with secondary participation the focus is on the defendant's liability in playing a *role in the resulting harm*.[142] Further, 'there are differences of *mens rea*, different defences that may apply, different rules of procedure and jurisdiction and, of course, different labels to attach to the offender: someone convicted as an accessory is labeled as if a principal; those convicted under Part 2 will be liable as assisters or encouragers'.[143]

140 *Ibid.*, s. 56.

141 For example, the defendant could be liable under s. 44 for encouraging murder but liable (under participation rules) for a GBH offence if that was all that was actually committed.

142 Ormerod and Fortson, above, n. 136, at 393.

143 *Ibid.*

Sections 44 and 45 are, broadly speaking, similar to provisions in Macaulay's draft Code, which were carried forward into s. 107 of the Indian Penal Code (IPC). Wing-Cheong Chan in Chapter 6 of this volume has suggested an amendment to the Code incorporating a provision along the lines of ss. 44–46.[144] However, the striking difference between s. 107 and ss. 44–46 is the simplicity of the former provision compared to the complexity of the new English law. Simplicity is an admirable quality – but there is the danger that too much then needs to be filled in by judicial interpretation.[145] In contrast, the new English offences are extraordinarily complex: they present 'an interpretive nightmare'[146] and are 'over-detailed, convoluted and unreadable'.[147] The main provisions, set out above, are given complex and technical extended definitions in ss. 47–67, and yet some of the core concepts such as 'encouraging', 'assisting' and 'capable of' are not defined. An exploration of the intricacies of all these provisions would require a lengthy paper in its own right. In the context of this more general chapter, only a few main points and interpretative problems will be highlighted.

Central to all three offences is the requirement that the defendant do an act[148] which is 'capable of' encouraging or assisting the commission of an offence.[149] Whilst these terms are undefined,[150] it is clear that it is unnecessary that the principal is in fact encouraged or assisted or is even aware of the defendant's actions. This is far wider than the common law offence of incitement (where the incitement had to be communicated) and the law of conspiracy (where there has to be a meeting of minds). There is no requirement that the defendant's acts need provide substantial or significant encouragement or assistance; an act of minimal facilitation will suffice. This is just one illustration of the wide reach of the new offences.

What *mens rea* is required for these offences? For s. 44, the defendant must *intend* to encourage or assist the commission of the offence. Intention is not defined, but s. 44(2)(b) excludes cases where the encouragement or assistance of the commission of the offence 'was a foreseeable consequence of his act'. Some commentators have concluded that this means the defendant must have a purposive intent.[151] Excluding foreseeable consequences should involve excluding foresight of all degrees of probability – including foresight of a virtual certainty. However, it is arguable that the *R. v. Woollin*[152] test of oblique intent could apply here. This test, involving foresight of a virtual certainty, could be applicable as this involves a far greater degree of foresight than merely of a

---

144 See 134.

145 In Chapter 6 of this volume, Chan suggests amendments to the IPC, s. 107 to provide more detail on the physical and fault elements for abetment.

146 Ormerod and Fortson, above, n. 136, at 414.

147 J. Spencer and G. Virgo, 'Encouraging and Assisting Crime: Legislate in Haste, Repent at Leisure' (2008) *Archbold News* 7, at 8.

148 This includes a course of conduct (s. 67).

149 This is extended by s. 65(2) – it is enough if the defendant: (a) takes steps to reduce the possibility of criminal proceedings being brought in respect of the offence, for example, supplying a disguise so that the principal can avoid detection (D. Ormerod, *Smith and Hogan Criminal Law* (12th edn, Oxford: Oxford University Press: 2008), at 451, suggests that this can cover acts done *after* the commission of the crime, such as providing a false passport to enable the principal to flee the country); or (b) fails to take reasonable steps to discharge a duty, for example, a security guard who deliberately fails to turn on a burglar alarm (Law Commission for England and Wales, *Inchoate Liability for Assisting and Encouraging Crime*, above n. 133, at para. [5.62]).

150 In relation to 'encouraging', s. 65(1) provides that this includes threatening or otherwise putting pressure on a person to commit an offence.

151 Ormerod, above n. 149, at 453.

152 [1999] 1 AC 82.

'foreseeable consequence'. Further, under the evidential interpretation[153] of *Woollin*, foresight of a virtual certainty cannot be excluded as evidence of intent.[154]

Sections 45 and 46 require a *belief* that the offence *will* (not 'might') be committed. The term 'believes' is not defined. Andrew Ashworth argues that it is much closer to knowledge than mere suspicion and, when coupled with the word *will*, 'indicates a high level of confidence in D's mind that P is going to commit the anticipated offence'.[155]

The *mens rea* required for the three offences involves recourse to the complex provisions of s. 47 and, in particular, s. 47(5), under which the defendant must have *mens rea* in relation to: (i) the principal's *mens rea*; and (ii) the circumstances and consequences of the principal's offence:

> In proving for the purposes of this section whether an act is one which, if done, would amount to the commission of an offence –
> (a) if the offence is one requiring proof of fault, it must be proved that –
> (i) D believed that, were the act to be done, it would be done with that fault;
> (ii) D was reckless as to whether or not it would be done with that fault; or
> (iii) D's state of mind was such that, were he to do it, it would be done with that fault; and
> (b) if the offence is one requiring proof of particular circumstances or consequences (or both), it must be proved that –
> (i) D believed that, were the act to be done, it would be done in those circumstances or with those consequences; or
> (ii) D was reckless as to whether or not it would be done in those circumstances or with those consequences.

Mens Rea as to P's *Mens Rea*

Section 47(5)(a)(i) and (ii) is consistent with the common law participation rule established in *R. v. Powell*[156] that the accessory to a joint unlawful enterprise must foresee that the principal will commit the offence with the requisite *mens rea*. Possibly the most important provision here is s. 47(5)(a)(iii), which will apply in other cases. It is primarily aimed at situations where D tricks P into doing something which would not be an offence (or would be a lesser offence)[157] for P to do. However, this provision will also apply to most of the cases covered by s. 47(5)(a)(i) and (ii). For example, D encourages P to beat up X seriously. If D had done the act, he would have had the appropriate *mens rea* for a GBH offence; it is unnecessary that he have *mens rea* as to P's *mens rea* under (i) or (ii). Indeed, it requires a feat of imagination to dream up scenarios when (i) and (ii) but not (iii) would apply. Consider a variation of the *R. v. Morgan*[158] and *R. v. Cogan*[159] cases. D regularly has consensual sexual intercourse with his wife. He encourages P to have sexual intercourse with her, telling him that she will consent. Here, (i) and (ii) are not satisfied. If P did

153 Clarkson, Keating and Cunningham, above n. 104, at 143–9.

154 Sullivan, above n. 133, at 1049.

155 A. Ashworth, *Principles of Criminal Law* (Oxford: Oxford University Press, 2009) 460.

156 [1999] 1 AC 1.

157 For example, D knows that X has an egg-shell skull. He encourages P to punch X in the face, believing this will cause death. D is liable for encouraging murder even though, if P were to do the act, he would only be liable for battery (if X does not die) or constructive manslaughter (if X does die).

158 [1976] AC 182.

159 [1976] QB 217.

have sexual intercourse with her, he would not have the *mens rea* of rape (assuming, for argument's sake, that P's belief would be regarded as reasonable). Would D be covered by (iii)? 'Were *he* (D) to do it', he would not have the requisite *mens rea* (because his wife always consents). But were he in P's position (that is, not the husband), he would have the necessary fault and so would be liable under (iii) but not under (i) or (ii).

Mens Rea as to Circumstances or Consequences

If the offence is one that requires proof of circumstances and/or consequences or both, s. 47(5)(b) requires that the defendant believed or was reckless as to whether P's conduct would have those consequences or be done in those circumstances. Suppose D provides P with an iron bar, intending that P use it to cause grievous bodily harm to the victim, but P uses it intentionally to kill the victim. Under s. 47(5)(a), D has the requisite *mens rea* for encouraging murder, but under s. 47(5)(b), D does not believe and is not reckless as to the consequence (death), and so cannot be liable for encouraging murder. Equally, if D only intended that P use it to cause some injury and X died, D cannot be liable for encouraging manslaughter. While P can be liable for constructive manslaughter (if he or she performs a dangerous unlawful act which causes death), D must foresee the consequence (death). There is no room for constructive liability here. The defendant would only be liable for encouraging an offence against the person – provided this offence was specified in the indictment. According to the Explanatory Notes to the Act, it would be unfair to hold the defendant liable for encouraging and assisting murder, unless he or she also believed or was reckless as to whether the victim was killed.[160] In such cases, the prosecution has a choice. It can charge D with encouraging GBH or can charge D with murder or constructive manslaughter under the common law participation rules.

Defence of Acting Reasonably

The Act provides for a defence of acting reasonably.[161] If D knows or believes (and this belief is reasonable) that certain circumstances exist, he or she is not liable if it was reasonable for him or her to act as he did in those circumstances.[162] Whether D believes the acts are reasonable is irrelevant. The burden of proof rests on the defence to prove this reasonableness.[163]

Conclusion

In proposing the reforms that led to the creation of the new offences, the Law Commission put forward the following arguments in favour of inchoate liability for assisting a crime: (i) it would assist intelligence-led policing in combating serious organised crime;[164] (ii) the benefits of avoiding

160 Home Office, *Explanatory Notes to the Serious Crime Act 2007* (available online at http://www.legislation.gov.uk, last accessed 20 February 2011) para. 157.

161 Serious Crime Act 2007, s. 51 contains another defence codifying the *R. v. Tyrrell* ([1894] 1 QB 710) principle that if a statute is aimed at protecting a particular category of persons, a person in that protective category cannot be liable for encouraging or assisting offences designed to protect him or her.

162 *Ibid.*, s. 50.

163 Placing the burden on the defence is likely to lead to challenges of incompatibility with the ECHR.

164 Law Commission for England and Wales, *Inchoate Liability for Assisting and Encouraging Crime*, above n. 133, at para. [4.4].

harm outweigh any concerns about premature interventions;[165] (iii) it would eliminate the element of chance (under the pre-existing law, D's liability was dependant on whether P actually committed the crime and this could be a matter of chance);[166] (iv) the act of assisting (or encouraging) a crime is in itself sufficiently culpable conduct to warrant the imposition of criminal liability;[167] (v) knowing that there would be liability for merely facilitating a crime could deter people from providing such assistance;[168] and (vi) it would label D's wrongdoing more accurately.[169]

However, apart from the interpretative nightmares involved in the over-complex provisions introduced, there must be deep concerns about the new offences which pose a 'stark risk of over-criminalisation'.[170] All inchoate offences involve a departure from the paradigm of a blameworthy actor causing a prohibited harm. With attempt, under English law, the actor must come very near to committing the full crime. With conspiracy there must be a meeting of minds which, arguably at least, raises 'dangerousness of collaboration' arguments. Conversely, the new offences criminalise conduct that can be very far removed from the ultimate harm. All that is required is a minimal act 'capable of' encouraging or assisting a crime.

Consider the following two examples of potential over-criminalisation:

> (i) D, a generous host, allows the 'wine to flow' at a dinner party, knowing that P is going to drive home. However, at the end of the evening P decides to sleep overnight at D's house.[171] If P were actually to drive over the statutory limit, there is a case (albeit controversial) for holding D liable for an offence.[172] However, criminalising the conduct of a person who pours several glasses of wine to his or her guest, based purely on his or her beliefs, rather smacks of thought-crime;
> D supplies a gun, believing that P will murder X. In fact, P merely intends to shoot rabbits.[173] While liability for a firearms offence might be appropriate in such a case, surely it is extending the criminal law too far to hold D liable for assisting *murder* and rendering him or her liable for a sentence up to a maximum of life imprisonment.

Because inchoate offences involve a departure from the paradigmatic crime (causing harm), most of them (for example, attempts) require maximum culpability in the form of intention. Sections 45 and 46, however, are satisfied by a lesser culpability than intent; belief is sufficient. It must be doubted whether liability for such serious offences (with such high maximum penalties) can be justified when such lesser forms of culpability suffice.

Another problem with these offences (although this is an issue with other inchoate offences as well) is that they are seriously increasing the potential for double inchoate liability. There can be liability for attempting or conspiring to commit a Part 2 offence. Conversely, under s. 44,[174] it is an offence to encourage or assist an attempt or a conspiracy to commit a crime. As if this

165 *Ibid.*, at para. [4.5].

166 *Ibid.*, at para. [4.6].

167 *Ibid.*, at para. [4.7].

168 *Ibid.*, at para. [4.8].

169 *Ibid.*, at para. [4.10].

170 Ormerod and Fortson, above n. 136, at 395.

171 K.J.M. Smith, 'The Law Commission Consultation Paper on Complicity: (1) A Blueprint for Rationalism' [1994] *Criminal Law Review* 239, at 241.

172 *Blakely v. DPP* [1991] RTR 405; *R. v. Webster* [2006] EWCA Crim 415.

173 Law Commission for England and Wales, *Inchoate Liability for Assisting and Encouraging Crime*, above n. 133, at para. [4.13], citing Sir John Smith's response to their Consultation Paper.

174 But not under ss. 45 and 46.

were not enough, there can also be liability for encouraging or assisting an act of encouraging or assisting. So, if D encourages P1 to encourage P2 to commit a crime, D is liable for possibly a very serious offence even if nothing is ever done pursuant to the initial encouragement. While some might think this is necessary, given the various layers of command in some terrorist or organised crime networks, this is surely criminalising conduct too far removed from the envisaged harm. As Ormerod plaintively asks, 'where will it all end?'.[175]

Finally, as already adverted to, these new offences sit uncomfortably with the existing rules on participation. The 'coherent package' of reforms put forward by the Law Commission has been shattered. Reform of the old participation rules now looks increasingly less likely. It is going to be very tempting for prosecutors to rely on the new offences rather than resorting to the complex law on aiding and abetting. That, in itself, could take the pressure off the need to reform the old law. A far simpler and more satisfactory solution would have been a codification of the existing law of incitement coupled with an offence of facilitation of crime.[176]

Strict Liability

Of critical importance to the General Part of the criminal law are the issues of responsibility and culpability. Criminal conviction results in stigmatic punishment and censure. It is widely thought that only the blameworthy deserve such treatment. This, of course, involves an account of what culpability means. But, equally, this raises the issue of whether criminal liability can be justified in the absence of culpability. The Draft Criminal Code Bill 1989 proposed a presumption that a fault element be required for all offences unless otherwise specifically provided for.[177] In Canada it has been held that strict liability is precluded for offences carrying the possibility of a custodial sentence.[178]

In England and Wales there is a presumption that *mens rea* (or fault) is an essential ingredient of all offences unless Parliament has indicated a contrary intention either expressly or by necessary implication. While the strength of this presumption has been repeatedly emphasised by the House of Lords,[179] the fact remains that it has been estimated that more than half of the roughly 8,000 criminal offences in England and Wales involve elements of strict liability[180] – and, in reported judicial decisions, the presumption of *mens rea* is seemingly displaced more often than it is upheld. Further, hopes that strict liability offences might be declared incompatible with the ECHR have been dashed with a series of decisions, both by the European Court of Human Rights[181] and English courts,[182] declaring that it is permissible for Parliament to enact offences dispensing with fault.

175 Ormerod, above n. 149, at 457.

176 Ashworth, above n. 155, at 462.

177 Law Commission for England and Wales, above n. 4, cl. 20(1).

178 *References re Section 94(2) of the Motor Vehicles Act* (1986) 48 CR (3d) 289. The US Model Penal Code proposed a similar rule in s. 1.04(5).

179 *Sweet v. Parsley* [1970] AC 132; *B (A Minor) v. DPP* [2000] 2 AC 428; *R. v. K*, above n. 52; *DPP v. Collins* [2006] UKHL 40.

180 A. Ashworth, 'Is the Criminal Law a Lost Cause?' (2000) 116 *Law Quarterly Review* 225.

181 *Salabiaku v. France* (1991) 13 EHRR 379.

182 *Muhamad v. R.* [2003] 2 WLR 1050; *Barnfather v. Islington Education Authority* [2003] 1 WLR 2318. In *R. v. G* [2009] 1 AC 92, it was held that the strict liability offence of rape of a child under 13 contrary to Sexual Offences Act 2003, s. 5 was not incompatible with ECHR, Art. 6.2 (presumption of innocence) or with Art. 8 (right to privacy and family life). See, generally, G.R. Sullivan, 'Strict Liability for Criminal

It was against this backdrop that in 2006 the government commissioned the Macrory Report to examine the use of civil sanctions instead of traditional criminal punishments.[183] This Report proposed that much regulatory non-compliance should be dealt with by administrative remedies outside the criminal justice system. These recommendations have been given effect by the Regulatory Enforcement and Sanctions Act 2008,[184] which allows ministers to introduce statutory instruments providing civil sanctions to a wide range of strict liability offences contained in a long list of statutes: for example, the Control of Pollution Act 1974,[185] the Dangerous Dogs Act 1991,[186] the Fireworks Act 2003,[187] the Food Safety Act 1990[188] and the Medicines Act 1968.[189] In all, 142 statutes are listed.[190] These civil sanctions can also be applied to a further 45 statutes under which ministers have the power by statutory instrument to create criminal offences.[191]

In these cases, where a regulator (for example, the Environment Agency, the Food Standards Agency, the Health and Safety Executive or the Office of Fair Trading)[192] is satisfied beyond reasonable doubt that a person has committed one of the specified offences, instead of a criminal prosecution, the regulator may impose one of the following civil sanctions:

(a) A fixed monetary penalty:[193] usually capped at £5,000.[194]

(b) Discretionary requirements.[195] The regulator may impose one or more of the following: (i) a variable monetary penalty; (ii) a compliance notice; (iii) a restoration notice.

(c) Stop notices[196] (preventing a person from carrying on an activity until specified steps have been taken).

(d) Enforcement undertakings[197] (an undertaking to take specified corrective action).

In all these cases there is a right of appeal to a tribunal, but not to a court of law.[198] Provision may be made for the regulator to recover monetary penalties either as a civil debt or, on the order of a court, as if payable under a court order.[199]

Offences in England and Wales Following Incorporation into English Law of the European Convention on Human Rights' in A.P. Simester (ed.), *Appraising Strict Liability* (Oxford: Oxford University Press, 2005).

183 R. Macrory, *Regulatory Justice: Making Sanctions Effective* (Final Report) (London: Cabinet Office, 2006).

184 Chapter 13.

185 Chapter 40.

186 Chapter 65.

187 Chapter 22.

188 Chapter 16.

189 Chapter 68.

190 Above n. 184, Sched. 6.

191 *Ibid.*, s. 62, Sched. 7.

192 *Ibid.*, Sched. 5 lists 27 designated regulators.

193 *Ibid.*, s. 39.

194 Ministry of Justice, *Guidance on Creating New Regulatory Penalties and Offences* (London: Ministry of Justice, 2009) (available online at https://www.justice.gov.uk/guidance/docs/guidance-regulatory-penalties-offences-jan09.pdf, last accessed 20 February 2011) para. [11].

195 Above n. 184, s. 42.

196 *Ibid.*, s. 46.

197 *Ibid.*, s. 50.

198 *Ibid.*, s. 54.

199 *Ibid.*, s. 52(2).

Under these provisions, the criminal process and the criminal courts will be bypassed, although a breach of any of the orders could ultimately result in judicial sanctions. These provisions do not involve any decriminalisation of existing offences. A criminal prosecution remains an option.

The advantage of these new provisions is that they can close the 'compliance gap, where some regulators lack the appropriate enforcement tools to address regulatory non-compliance'.[200] Also, through bypassing the criminal process, the civil sanctions will not carry the same stigma as a criminal conviction. This might lessen the objections to such strict liability offences.

However, there are potential problems with this 'semi-decriminalisation' of strict liability offences. In particular, this bypassing of the criminal process could result in a loss of the protection offered by the criminal justice system, for example, in relation to the burden of proof. It can be anticipated that as soon as these provisions become fully operational, there will be challenges of incompatibility with the ECHR.

Further, there is an irony here. Many, if not most, strict liability offences govern the operations not of individuals but of businesses. Most of the provisions in the Regulatory Enforcement and Sanctions Act 2008 are aimed at corporate non-compliance with regulatory laws (but are not limited to such cases). It is ironic that these provisions, which could be seen as being 'soft' on corporate wrongdoing, have been introduced at a time when there have been increasing calls for the criminal law to be 'tougher' on corporations and other organisations. Enormous pressure to hold organisations appropriately accountable when their negligence led to the death of workers and others resulted in the enactment of the Corporate Manslaughter and Corporate Homicide Act 2007. There have been calls for specific provisions to be enacted for cases when corporate negligence has caused injury or serious injury to such persons.[201] The Law Commission is currently examining the whole issue of when and how businesses should be held criminally responsible and how the criminal law can be used as a way of promoting regulatory objectives.[202] It is symptomatic of the law reform process over the past decade that knee-jerk specific reforms have been introduced without any overall view of how they relate to each other being taken. Had a full codification process been continued, one could have hoped for a coherent package to have emerged. This, however, has not been the case.

A final development, not dissimilar to the introduction of the above civil sanctions, deserves a brief mention. Over the past decade and more, the government has broadly adopted a policy of 'if there's a problem, let's criminalise it'. However, perhaps in response to libertarian claims about over-criminalisation, a new technique is being increasingly employed. Instead of employing strict liability criminal offences, the civil law and civil sanctions are being utilised.

In 2009 Baroness Scotland, the Attorney-General, was 'fined' (according to the press) £5,000 by the UK Border Agency for employing an illegal worker. Baroness Scotland is reported as saying: 'It's a civil penalty just as if you drive into the city and don't pay a congestion charge. It's not a criminal offence. I made an administrative technical error.'[203]

---

200 Ministry of Justice, above n. 194, at para. [3].

201 House of Commons, Home Affairs and Work and Pensions Committees, *Draft Corporate Manslaughter Bill: First Joint Report of Session 2005–06, Vol. 1: Report* (London: The Stationery Office, 2005) para. [81].

202 This replaces the earlier project on corporate criminal liability (see http://www.lawcom.gov.uk/regulation_liability.htm, last accessed 20 February 2011).

203 J. Beattie, 'Baroness Scotland Refuses to Resign after £5K Fine for Hiring an Illegal Worker' *The Mirror*, 23 September 2009.

It is notoriously difficult to define a crime.[204] Perhaps the most widely accepted definition is that of Glanville Williams that a crime is 'an act that is capable of being followed by criminal proceedings, having one of the types of outcome (punishment etc.) known to follow these proceedings'.[205] Applying this test to the Baroness Scotland case, this was indeed a civil penalty (and not a fine) that was imposed under s. 15 of the Immigration, Asylum and Nationality Act 2006.[206] Section 15 refers to a 'penalty' and uses the civil language that '[i]t is contrary to this section to employ ...'. This can be contrasted with s. 21 of the same Act, which states that '[a] person commits an *offence* if he employs another ... *knowing* that the employee is ... subject to immigration control'.[207] Of course, the nomenclature chosen by Parliament is not determinative, but what is important, in distinguishing this from a crime, is that this civil penalty 'may be recovered by the Secretary of State as a debt due to him'.[208]

Similarly, s. 155 of the Housing Act 2004[209] imposes a duty on a seller of a home to have in his or her possession or under his or her control a home information pack relating to the property to be sold. Failure to comply with this duty can result in a penalty charge not exceeding £500.[210] This penalty charge is recoverable 'as a debt owed to the authority'.[211]

These two examples raise profound questions that are beyond the scope of this chapter. What is a 'crime'? What is a 'punishment'? What are the criteria for determining whether conduct should be 'criminalised' or be made a 'civil offence'? What assurances are there that the loss of procedural safeguards involved in these 'civil offences' will not lead to administrative malpractice? Distinctions between 'criminal' and 'civil' offences have long been drawn in some other jurisdictions, such as Germany. No real debate on this matter has, however, occurred in England and Wales.

Nevertheless, one thing does seem sure as a result of the above two developments. While strict liability offences seem certain to remain a part of the English law landscape for the foreseeable future, it is likely that the way in which many of these offences are dealt with will increasingly be changed with greater recourse to administrative remedies being adopted.

CONCLUSION

From the above patchwork of scattered reforms, it appears that, *prima facie*, there have only been fairly minimalist reforms of aspects of the General Part of the criminal law of England and Wales over the past decade. This is, of course, to ignore the contribution of the judiciary who, in truth, are continually moving the law forwards (or backwards, depending on one's view). The following leading cases can be cited as examples: *R. v. Kennedy (No. 2)*[212] (causation); *R. v. Evans*[213] (omissions); *R. v. G*[214] (affirming a subjective test of recklessness); *R. v. Dica*[215] (consent); *R. v. Z*[216]

204 Ormerod, above n. 149, at 9–18.
205 G. Williams, 'The Definition of Crime' (1955) 8 *Current Legal Problems* 107, at 128.
206 Chapter 13.
207 Emphasis added.
208 Above n. 206, s. 18.
209 Chapter 34.
210 *Ibid.*, s. 168.
211 *Ibid.*, Sched. 8(8)(1).
212 [2008] 1 AC 269.
213 [2009] 1 WLR 1999.
214 Above n. 51.
215 [2004] QB 1257.
216 [2005] 2 AC 467.

(duress); *Re A (Conjoined Twins: Surgical Separation)*[217] (necessity); *R. v. Heard*[218] (intoxication); *R. v. JTB*[219] (lack of age); *R. v. Saik*[220] (conspiracy); and *R. v. Rahman*[221] (participation).

However, none of the developments in these decisions can truly count as 'law reform' (and thus have been excluded from this chapter) for two reasons. First, judicial decisions do not 'reform' the law; under an old (and somewhat absurd) fiction, they simply 'restate' the law as it always was. Secondly, such decisions are not preceded by any wider debate (outside the courtroom) as to what the law should be, what policy factors ought to influence its direction and so on. To take one example of this latter point: in *Kennedy (No. 2)*, the House of Lords endorsed the primacy of the rule that the free, deliberate and informed intervention of a party breaks the causal chain. This decision was decided in the context of whether the self-injection of drugs will break the chain of causation between the supply of drugs and an ensuing death. It is far from clear whether this rule now replaces the old 'reasonable foresight' rule established in cases such as *Roberts*[222] dealing with victims fleeing from attackers. The result is that, while causation rules in drug-supply and analogous cases are relatively clear, the law on causation in other situations is far less clear than it was.

Other developments in the Special Part have an enormous potential to impact on the General Part. For example, in relation to the culpability element required for crimes other than those of strict liability, it had become the accepted wisdom that the *mens rea* requirement involved either intention or recklessness (and, since *R. v. G*, recklessness involves subjective foresight of the possibility of a consequence occurring or a circumstance existing). Crimes of negligence were regarded as being exceptional and restricted to minor offences such as motoring (with the established exception of manslaughter, where gross negligence suffices). However, the Sexual Offences Act 2003 has raised the stakes on the debate as to whether negligence can be regarded as sufficient culpability for serious offences: virtually all sexual offences (including rape) can now be committed by negligence (as to consent). While it can be argued that sexual offences are a special case (because of the necessary proximity between the defendant and the victim making it simple for him to ensure there is consent), the fact is that negligence is being increasingly employed as the culpability element for numerous other new offences[223] and there has been a significant increase in the number of *prima facie* strict liability offences to which due diligence defences are being offered (effectively making them crimes of negligence).[224] The Sentencing Advisory Panel[225] classified negligence as one of the four levels of culpability (along with intention, recklessness and knowledge).[226] The upshot of all this is that the debate has grown considerably as to whether negligence should be more widely employed as the *mens rea* element in other crimes. If, and when,

217 Above n. 64.

218 [2007] EWCA Crim 125.

219 [2009] UKHL 20.

220 [2006] UKHL 18.

221 [2008] UKHL 45.

222 (1972) 56 Cr App R 95.

223 For example, causing or allowing the death of a child or vulnerable adult (Domestic Violence, Crime and Victims Act 2004 (Chapter 28), s. 5).

224 See generally, Clarkson, Keating and Cunningham, above, n. 104, at 223–5.

225 Sentencing Guidelines Council, *Overarching Principles: Seriousness* (London: Sentencing Guidelines Secretariat, 2004).

226 In its most recent Report, however, negligence is no longer regarded as demonstrating culpability: Sentencing Advisory Panel, *Advice to the Sentencing Guidelines Council: Overarching Principles of Sentencing* (London: Sentencing Advisory Panel, 2010) para. [83], recommendation 6.

the Law Commission were to return to examine culpability, the debate will have somewhat moved on from the position in 1989 when it was almost assumed as axiomatic that *mens rea* only involved intention or recklessness and that there should be a presumption that recklessness, at least, was required for all criminal offences.

Other proposals for law reform of the General Part have been put forward and are under active consideration. In addition to the proposals suggested by the Law Commission on participation in crime (mentioned earlier in this chapter), the Law Commission has published both a Consultation Paper[227] and a Report[228] on the inchoate offences of attempt and conspiracy and a Report on intoxication.[229] However, it is doubtful whether these proposals will ever lead to law reform. For example, in its Consultation Paper on attempts, the Commission suggested the radical idea (to English lawyers) of subdividing the existing offence into two separate crimes: attempt and criminal preparation. Strong opposition[230] to these proposals led to the abandonment of this idea. While certain reform proposals were retained in the final Report, these are hardly significant enough to warrant the parliamentary time involved in pushing through legislation.

In short, it is something of a tale of woe: patchy micro-reforms without any macro-consideration of the bigger picture. Whether the recent protocol between the Law Commission and the government will lead to more reforming legislation remains to be seen. But, in terms of law reform where all the bits of the jigsaw fit together into a coherent whole, the prospects look bleak and it is to be regretted that the codification process has, for the time being, been abandoned.

Whether the prospects of revising the IPC are any greater is a matter of speculation. However, were such a process to be embarked upon, the fact that there is already an established Code in existence would mean that any such revision would not be as radical a step as the introduction of a completely new code in England and Wales. Stanley Yeo and Barry Wright, in their introductory chapter to this volume, have called for a 'revitalising' of the IPC. In a similar vein, Neil Morgan, in Chapter 3 of this volume on the fault elements of offences, has suggested that the IPC should be 'renovated [and] not reconstructed'.[231] While many of the various reforms proposed in this volume would doubtless be controversial, revitalisation and renovation would clearly be a more achievable goal, and politically more manageable, than constructing *de novo* an entirely new and comprehensive code of the criminal law – an area of law that is often politically contentious and that many regard as fundamental to the social order.

227 Law Commission for England and Wales, *Conspiracy and Attempts* (Law Com. Consultation Paper No. 183) (London: The Stationery Office, 2007).

228 Law Commission for England and Wales, *Conspiracy and Attempts* (Law Com. No. 318) (London: The Stationery Office, 2009).

229 Law Commission for England and Wales, *Intoxication and Criminal Liability* (Law Com. No. 314) (London: The Stationery Office, 2009).

230 For example, C.M.V. Clarkson, 'Attempt: The Conduct Requirement' (2009) 29 *Oxford Journal of Legal Studies* 25.

231 Chapter 3 of this volume (N. Morgan, 'The Fault Elements of Offences') at 84.

Chapter 15

Principled Criminal Law Reform: Could Macaulay Survive the Age of Governing through Crime?[1] Reflections from the Floor

Mark Findlay

The intention of these reflections is to briefly and thematically examine the fate of principled law reform in modern criminal jurisdictions. In so doing, codification, using Macaulay's draft Code for India as an exemplar, is reflected against the inconsistent expediency of contemporary criminal law reform. The political utility of the penal sanction in an era of 'governing through crime' is suggested as the reason why criminal law as we know it may be a 'lost cause'.

Why is it that more than 150 years on, Macaulay's draft Code would, if presented today, be nothing less than a model of principled law reform despite its roots in early nineteenth-century legal theory and British imperial concerns? In his chapter, Chris Clarkson identifies the state of codification in the contemporary criminal law and process of England and Wales as a 'tale of woe'. Despite a brighter picture being painted by Matthew Goode as to the state of codification in Australian Commonwealth law, the take-up rate for the Model Criminal Code in vital state and territory legislation is, he admits, sporadic at best. How might we explain the radical aversion to criminal law codification in current common law law-making?

The anti-codification environment cannot be explained through any political reluctance to explore the utility of the penal sanction. Quite the contrary! We live in an age where, at least up until the cost-benefit critique on government in the wake of the global financial collapse, the industries of criminal justice such as surveillance and risk assessment are flourishing under an aggressive political sponsorship and a punitive popular wisdom. Parliaments and their bureaucracies spend more time legislating and institutionalising the penal sanction than any other regulatory form at their disposal. Bob Sullivan critiques the burgeoning of a prophylactic criminal law through a radical reliance on strict liability offences and civil sanctions that short-circuit even the most meagre remaining protections of criminal justice due process. Protective orders, preventive detention, confiscation of assets and the assertion of victim interests have been manifest through an explosion of patchy micro-reform which has left the criminal law even in code states devoid of consistency and predictable principle. Attacks on the principles which would underlie any codified General Part are a feature of present-day 'law and order' legislative activity. Strict and absolute liability rejections of subjective responsibility, omissions and duty founding criminal conduct and constructing causation, and reverse onus provisions for exculpation are just some of the legislative rush from foundational features of traditional criminal justice. And as Michael Hor notes regarding joint criminal enterprise, activist judicial interpretation has complimented moves away from subjective fault.

1 J. Simon, *Governing through Crime: How the War on Crime Transformed American Democracy and Created a Culture of Fear* (Oxford: Oxford University Press, 2007).

Additional impediments against a codification sentiment in contemporary politicised criminal law reform are the rejection of central considerations behind the code project, identified in Neil Morgan's chapter as the jewels in Macaulay's crown. Symmetry, simplicity and consistent subjective standards of liability cannot be found even in the conservative and protectionist atmosphere of criminal justice law-making. Defences have largely contracted in scope, coverage and application under the oppression of the reasonable person and even in the face of efforts to reinstate their scope through judicial activism. Stanley Yeo reviews the incompatible applications of necessity and duress. The *lawful use of force* through the private defence of excessive self-defence and the protection of householder property (Cheah Wui Ling), when looked at against the demise of provocation (Ian Leader-Elliot) and the other restrictive excuses (Gerry Ferguson), tend to confound the search for a consistent calcification of factors effecting liability. Macaulay achieved what centuries of legislative and judicial intervention have unravelled. Why is this so?

Perhaps the worry for codification advocates exists in the project itself. Macaulay's draft Code is adept, carefully theorised, consistent, liberal in the true sense and, above all else, inviolate. There is also irony here in that concerns about effective and legitimate criminal law helped to make Macaulay's Code a legislative priority, a pattern also seen in the enactment of other nineteenth-century British jurisdiction codes that stamped imperial outreach as much as trade or military interests. Its translation into the Indian Penal Code and its more recent colonial derivatives demonstrates the power of political expedience over the beauty of an artful code. Even if Macaulay's intent and construction had survived its first major legislative incarnation, it would have faced the challenges against change. Without systematic re-codification, particularly in a changing international rights environment (Cheah; Leader-Elliot), codes are barriers to reform in themselves. Integrity fights dynamism in the same way as it is poisoned by tortuous and ill-conceived political expediency.

What are these challenges to change (codified or otherwise) towards a rational criminal law? They include the following, to mention a few:

- The disconnection between what principle endorses and legislators do.
- The often irrational connection between community aspirations, political fear-mongering and legal limits.
- The tensions on the apparatus of the criminal law because of increasing preventive and prophylactic encroachments.
- The monopoly of the state over the penal sanction (through investigation, prosecution and punishment), alienating the parties perpetrating and suffering harm, and who would otherwise have a strong interest in real and predictable, rather than didactic and normative, outcomes resulting from this tether to the state.
- Arcane connections with institutional and process frameworks preceding even Macaulay.
- The unhealthy and dehistoricised modern alliance between the criminal law and Austinian sovereignty when in their earlier incarnations the principles on which the criminal law rests were a specific and operational break on state power.
- The contemporary use of the criminal law through a proliferation of regulatory offences and civil penalty options against the otherwise law-abiding community.
- The obsession with appellate case law rather than legislative activism as the scholarship of criminal law, thus proliferating the judicial rationalist rather than legislative pragmatist perspective.

The answer to institutional myopia, if not to political capture, lies in both a recognition of the value of codification and a routine and rigorous commitment to re-codification. Perhaps, however, as Sullivan suggests, with the regrettable developments in criminal conduct conceptualising, fundamental questions need to precede a codification commitment about the modern concept of crime and what theory, if any, informs the purpose of the criminal law.

It could be said about the current era of governing through crime that the normative informs the substantive and depends on (and directs) the procedural dimensions. In reality, the legislative purpose is in reverse. The necessity of translating political interest into regulatory form turns what Jeremy Bentham hoped to be a *legislative science* into a technology of short-term governance. To return to the conditions of his conception of a *science*, the codification project needs to be imagined against the contexts of:

- the nature and significance of harm, pre-determining and constraining fault;
- the manner in which the accused has 'wronged' the victim;
- the extent to which the accused acts with knowledge, intent or emotional disturbance to explain his or her responsibility for the 'wrong' (both from the perspective of culpability and excuse);
- appropriateness of the predictive and preventive functions of the law; and
- the need to break free from confusing and pre-existing legislative technologies (such as attempt, causation and common purpose).

It could be said that codification as a practical tool for justice relies as much on considerations of proof as it does on semantic debates about justice and form. Having the General Part settled around default offences and defences might assist in this recognition. Macaulay's Benthamite rejection of judicial reinterpretation of principle puts the challenge back to the codifiers to achieve a dynamic language for the law which is community-sensitive and flexible in facing the demands of modernity, while still being resilient to expedient modification of its core principles. Hence the need for contemporary codification projects to properly reflect rights and the rule of law when considering the harm and responsibility from serious wrong.

As the era of governing through crime demonstrates in legislative activity, the principles of criminal law are at their most vulnerable when determined as being at odds with the control function of governability. It is one thing for politicians to ignore essential historical reflection about the role of criminal justice in resisting the excesses of the state. However, legislative reformers and some criminal law scholars also seem more interested in making the governance application of the criminal law sharper and ignoring its essence in restricting rather than facilitating state power and authority.

This incapacity to see the criminal law as an active element in the 'separation of powers' and its critical importance to the rule of law and constitutional legality is evidenced in the flight from subjective responsibility. Criminal laws now commonly prefer probable consequences as opposed to actual knowledge, 'within contemplation' in place of foresight of certainty, and the strange construct of subjective foreseeabilty.

In order that the criminal law ensures its fragile commitment to individual liability, all sorts of legislative and judicial travesties have been done to the concept of 'responsibility' in practice. Community sentiment is translated through the overbearance of the mind of the ordinary person, whose ordinariness is anything but settled. Collective sentiment is not understood as organisational cultures or through contribution to the overall criminal enterprise, but is mystified through participation and complicity, and equated with the principal offender. Degrees of participation and distance from the offence are conflated for the artificial purpose of punitive severity. When the fault element for complicity and the substantive offence differ significantly in terms of knowledge and intention, the degree of compromise over the fault for complicity is at its most apparent in the face of the political will. The law is now so often satisfied with 'ought to have' as it is with 'known'. And, yet again, the protection of a consistent approach to fault and wrong comes back to proof. If the law's understandings of a consistent and comprehensive process of proof were trusted in popular culture and politics (and not distorted, as with the intoxication defence, to satisfy moral preference), then the deductive nature of knowledge may be enough to connect it with reason and rationality, without such legislative distortion.

In 2000 Andrew Ashworth published a critique intoning 'Is the Criminal Law a Lost Cause?'.[2] In addressing the explosion of criminal legislation in England and Wales in a climate of inconsistency,[3] Ashworth wondered whether criminal offences could any longer be distinguished from other wrongs by reference to content or by procedural and functional distinctions. In an effort to make that case, he relied on four interlinked principles which he believed formed the core of the criminal law:

1. Criminal law should only be used to censure persons for substantial wrongdoing.
2. Criminal laws should be enforced in a manner that is respectful of equal treatment and proportionality.
3. Persons accused of substantial wrongdoing ought to be afforded the protections of due process (in minimum form as declared in the European Convention on Human Rights).
4. Maximum sentences and effective sentence levels should be proportionate to the seriousness of the wrongdoing.

With these themes, Macaulay and all committed codifiers after him would no doubt have little with which to disagree. Principled law-making is not just about consistency, compatibility and comprehension. As Leader-Elliott suggests in his chapter, when examining wrongdoing sufficient for criminalisation, it is errant not to recognise human rights foundations, even in the face of cultural idiosyncrasy.

Yet, in recognising the difficulty of the principled approach to distinguishing modern criminal law-making, Ashworth admits that:

> Having demonstrated the difficulties in that approach, we move from the descriptive to the normative, in search of features for a model of criminal laws which is more principled, conceptually more coherent, and constitutionally and politically more appropriate …
>
> What emerges is nothing so concrete as a formula for determining whether or not certain conduct should be criminalised. Rather, arguments are presented in favour of a more principled development of the criminal law, recognising the essential links between procedure, enforcement and sentence. Without a principled approach of this kind, the criminal law is likely to remain something of a lost cause.[4]

These observations surrounding the challenges facing principled criminal law-making (codified or otherwise) distil down to the dangerous symbiosis of state interest and criminal law in the

2 A. Ashworth, 'Is the Criminal Law a Lost Cause?' (2000) 116 *Law Quarterly Review* 225.

3 A. Norrie, *Crime, Reason and History* (2nd edn, London: Butterworths, 2001).

4 Above n. 2, at 225–6.

'governing through crime' era. Macaulay was no infant when it came to appreciating the politicality of the legislative endeavour. In his letter to Lord Auckland, Governor General of India, covering his submission of the draft Penal Code, Macaulay observed:

> We are perfectly aware that law-givers ought not to disregard even the unreasonable prejudices of those for whom they legislate. So sensible are we of the importance of these considerations … The power of constructing the law in cases in which there is any real reason to doubt what the law is amounts to the power of making the law …[W]e are confident that your Lordship in Council will not grudge anything that may be necessary for the purpose of enabling the people who are placed under your care to know what the law is according to which they are required to live.[5]

Criminal law reform should be concerned with the integrity, durability and the effectiveness of the criminal law, enhancing a genuine rule of law rather than facilitating narrow and reactive policing impulses. The challenges of principled law reform would be minimised through a tight code and a routine and rigorous commitment to re-codification in a climate of continual critical reflection concerning the rights and responsibilities of those that the law serves.

5 T.B. Macaulay, J.M. Macleod, G.W. Anderson and F. Millett, *A Penal Code Prepared by the Indian Law Commissioners* (London: Pelham Richardson, 1838) (reprinted by the Lawbook Exchange, Ltd, 2002) i, v, viii.

Index

Page numbers in *italics* refer to tables. An *f* after a page number refers to a footnote on that page.

For Product Safety Concerns and Information please contact our EU representative GPSR@taylorandfrancis.com Taylor & Francis Verlag GmbH, Kaufingerstraße 24, 80331 München, Germany

Batch number: 10726294

Printed by Printforce, the Netherlands